PHILOSOPHY
A Modern Encounter

PHILOSOPHY
A Modern Encounter

ROBERT PAUL WOLFF

Department of Philosophy
University of Massachusetts

PRENTICE-HALL, INC., ENGLEWOOD CLIFFS, NEW JERSEY

13-663385-4

*Library of Congress Catalog Card Number: 71-137897.
Printed in the United States of America.*

Current printing (last number):

10 9 8 7 6 5 4 3 2

PRENTICE-HALL INTERNATIONAL, INC., LONDON

PRENTICE-HALL OF AUSTRALIA, PTY. LTD., SYDNEY

PRENTICE-HALL OF CANADA, LTD., TORONTO

PRENTICE-HALL OF INDIA PRIVATE LIMITED, NEW DELHI

PRENTICE-HALL OF JAPAN, INC., TOKYO

The author gratefully acknowledges the photographs in this
book as follows:

IRENE BAYER FOR MONKMEYER, p. 164
DENNIS BRACK FOR BLACK STAR, p. 534
DOLORES FLATLEY FOR MONKMEYER, p. 258
AARON FRYER FOR BLACK STAR, p. 548 (BOTTOM)
JUAN GUZMAN FOR BLACK STAR, p. 476
PETER LAKE FOR BLACK STAR, p. 404
STEFAN MOSES FOR BLACK STAR, p. 548 (TOP)
JACK PITKIN, pp. ii, 76 (TOP)
ANDREW TAYLOR FOR BLACK STAR, p. xii
WIDE WORLD, p. 76 (BOTTOM)

PREFACE

I began the preparation of this book with three convictions which had grown upon me during my fifteen years of teaching: **First,** the great philosophy of the past two thousand years is directly and importantly relevant to the major moral, social and political issues which confront us as citizens and responsible men and women; **second,** philosophy is presented to college students in a way which makes it difficult, if not impossible, for them to see its relation to their own concerns; and **third,** a method for introducing students to philosophy can be found which focuses on the contemporary relevance of the great philosophical texts **without in any way distorting those texts or watering down their intellectual content.**

This book is my attempt to demonstrate in actual practice the truth of these three convictions. Obviously, I have been able to touch on only a few of the many issues which confront young men and women today. Nothing has been said in these pages about sex, race, or environmental pollution, to mention only three issues of contemporary concern. But I hope this book will help you to develop the ability to see for yourself the philosophical questions hidden in such issues. When you think about social problems, or debate them with your friends, I would like to believe that your arguments will be deeper and more cogent because of your encounter with this book.

A number of people have helped me in the preparation of the book. My colleague, Professor Richard Kuhns, made a number of invaluable suggestions for readings in the section on Aesthetics. Miss Diane Almond did a good deal of the leg-work connected with assembling the selections, running down copyrights, and preparing the manuscript for publication. David Grady, under whose editorship the project was adopted by Prentice-Hall, proved himself to be one of those rare persons in the publishing world who simultaneously puts an author at ease and spurs him on to greater efforts. It is due in considerable measure to his fine direction that this book has come into being.

Many years ago, Plato wrote a dialogue in which one of the characters, named Callicles, ridiculed Socrates for devoting his life to philosophy. By all means study philosophy as a boy, Callicles says. It is a sign of good breeding. But when a grown man continues to talk about philosophical questions, then one wants to hit him! "Such a fellow," Callicles concludes, "must spend the rest of his life skulking in corners, whispering with two or three little lads, never producing any large, liberal, or meaningful utterance." (**Gorgias,** trans. by W. C. Helmbold, Liberal Arts Press, 1952.)

To Callicles we can reply: Those who do not reflect on the philosophical foundations of their beliefs and actions will be condemned repeatedly to making fools of themselves, for thoughtless speech is a mark of the child, and wise understanding a sign of maturity.

New York   ROBERT PAUL WOLFF

CONTENTS

III THEORY OF KNOWLEDGE

ESP: The Criteria of Empirical Knowledge   165

IV ETHICS ✓

Christ and Nietzsche: The Principles of Morals   259

V PHILOSOPHICAL ANTHROPOLOGY

Repression in America: Politics and
Human Nature   334

VI POLITICAL PHILOSOPHY

The Draft: Foundations of Political Obligation   405

VII

AESTHETICS
Pornography and Censorship: The Social Value of Art 477

VIII

PHILOSOPHY AND RELIGION

Drugs Again: The Nature of Religious Experience 549

INTRODUCTION

A friend of mine who taught at the University of Chicago in the early 1960s had the disconcerting habit of straying from the assigned reading in his classroom discussions. One day, after he had managed to wander so far from the **Republic** that it was all but lost from sight, a student asked him why he paid so little attention to the arguments in the text and so much to whatever issues he and the class happened to bring up. "Because," he replied with crushing logic, "Plato is dead and we are alive"!

Why should we struggle with the words and ideas of philosophers who have been dead one hundred, five hundred, even two thousand years? We live in a world they never knew—a world of poverty amidst affluence, of explorations reaching out to the moon and deep into the recesses of the human mind. How can the writings of the great philosophers possibly be relevant to our concerns today? Can Plato help us to decide whether to try the consciousness-expansion of LSD? Will Hobbes and Locke help us to choose between obeying an induction notice or fleeing to Canada? What is there in the philosophical classics to clarify our religious doubts or guide our political involvements? In short, why study philosophy at all these days?

This book has one simple purpose: To show you how the great philosophy of the past 2500 years relates directly to problems which thoughtful concerned men and women face in the world today. The authors whose writings have been selected for this volume come from many nations and historical eras. Some, like Plato and Aristotle, lived in small Greek towns two millennia ago; others, like Hobbes and Hume, belong to the early years of the modern era of nation-states and a capitalist economy. Still others, such as Jean-Paul Sartre, are men of our own time.

Now, an introductory course in philosophy can simply throw some readings at the students and leave it to them to discover points of relevance and connection with their own life. Some students may take to philosophy right away, just as some take to chemistry or history or mathematics. Others may plug away until finally a bit of daylight shines through the darkness. But all too many students are turned off by the strangeness, the difficulty, the technical look of philosophical writings, before they have had a chance to relate what they are reading to their own problems. As a result, they miss out on the excitement of philosophy, like language students who get fed up with grammar exercises and quit before they have ever had a chance to read a short story or carry on an interesting conversation in a foreign tongue.

In an attempt to help more students to enjoy philosophy, this text has been organized in a new and different way. Each section of the book is built around a contemporary issue of immediate interest and importance, in which is embedded a major philosophical problem. The contemporary issue is presented by means of selections from twentieth-century writers—not necessarily philosophers—who have taken strong and suggestive positions on the question. An editorial commentary then calls attention to a major philosophical problem raised by the controversy, and a number of texts discussing this problem are brought together from the philosophical literature. Finally, an editorial postscript draws the discussion together and indicates some of the concrete alternative solutions to the contemporary dispute which the philosophical readings have suggested.

To see how this actually works in practice, let us look at the first section of the book. We open with a very controversial topic indeed: whether or not to take LSD and other hallucinogenic or "consciousness-expanding" drugs. Timothy Leary, the nation's leading exponent of consciousness expansion, debates the issue with Dr. Jerome Lettvin, an MIT biophysicist.

Most arguments about drug use focus on two practical aspects of the issue, namely, possible harmful after-effects, and the fact that most drugs are illegal. Now physical health and violations of the law are important, of course. But anyone who is seriously debating whether to use drugs will immediately ask: Would it be wrong to take LSD if it were legal, as alcohol is, and had no dangerous after-effects? In other words, would a safe, legal psychedelic drug be perfectly all right?

When we put the question this way, a number of very deep philosophical problems begin to surface. To make up our mind on these problems, we must go beyond mere health warnings or rules of thumb about obeying the law, to some basic considerations of the sort that philosophers have been investigating for a very long time. Strange as it may seem, the debate over LSD can lead us into Ethics, the Philosophy of Religion, the Theory of Knowledge, and even into what philosophers call Metaphysics.

In Section I of this book, we focus on one of the basic problems raised by the LSD dispute, namely, whether we can meaningfully draw a distinction between the "appearance" that is perceived by us under the influence of LSD and the "reality" that we normally experience; whether, perhaps, the psychedelic experience isn't the true reality and our ordinary perception merely appearance; and, finally, whether there is any good reason for preferring reality to illusion or appearance, even though the reality may on occasion be less beautiful, less pleasant, or less emotionally satisfying than the appearance.

It turns out that these questions have been high up on philosophy's agenda for a long, long time. Our first philosophical text is by Plato, the great Athenian pupil of Socrates who lived and wrote in the fourth century before Christ. Plato advances the paradoxical claim that invisible Forms are more real than the physical objects we see and touch. He counsels us to turn our attention away from what we call the world, and focus our minds instead on a realm of pure, eternal Ideas.

We listen next to Descartes, writing at the dawn of the modern world, as he systematically casts doubt upon the scientific distinction between objective reality and subjective illusion. Then we turn to the great German philosopher Imanuel Kant and hear his answer to the scepticism of Descartes. In a dramatic shift of style and focus, Sören Kierkegaard transcends Kant's secular treatment of the problem and reinterprets it in terms of the extremely subjective Christianity of the Protestant Reformation. Finally, the twentieth-century American philosopher Clarence Irving Lewis offers a complex and rather technical analysis of the concepts of reality and appearance which draws on, but strives to go beyond, the thought of the previous four authors. Not one of our five philosophers ever tried LSD, although Plato and Kierkegaard knew something about the sort of religious ecstasy that psychedelic drugs are said to induce. But every one of them, in one way or another, struggled with the metaphysical problem of distinguishing the real from the illusory, and at least three of them (Plato, Kierkegaard, and Lewis) are prepared to argue for choosing one over the other. If you are personally uncertain about what place drugs should play in your life, then I think you will find the writings in this section helpful to you. Naturally, you will want to translate the arguments into your own terms. Five philosophers writing over a span of twenty-five centuries must obviously use a considerable assortment of technical terms, some of which may now be obsolete. Nevertheless, the underlying issues remain the same, and so the arguments even of Plato or Descartes are still relevant.

The primary aim of this book, then, is to lead you into the world of philosophical argument through a succession of controversies on vital issues, in the hope that your thinking will be clarified and strengthened by the experience. It is very definitely not the purpose of the book to get you to believe one way rather than any other. As a socially concerned philosopher and citizen, I have very strong convictions about every one of the contemporary issues raised in these pages. As editor and author of this Introduction, however, I care only that you should make up your own mind, on the basis of your own reasoning and experience, after a thoughtful consideration of the major alternatives which have been defended by the ablest philosophers in the Western tradition.

The eight sections of the text range over most of the major areas of philosophy. Sections I and II raise basic metaphysical problems. Section III explores some of the many questions which fall under the rubric Epistemology, or Theory of Knowledge. Section IV deals with a central problem of Ethics; Section V with the nature of man, a subject which philosophers call Philosophical Anthropology; and Section VI with a related dispute in Political Philosophy. Section VII explores a perennial controversy in the Philosophy of Art, and Section VIII brings us full circle, for although it is concerned with the nature of religious experience, it begins with the issue of drugs. We are thus reminded that in the real world of contemporary controversy, a single practical decision may involve many different philosophical problems.

One word of warning, before you turn to the text and begin your confrontation with the first issue. In putting this book together, I have drawn very heavily on what are usually called the "classics of philosophical literature." Somewhere in these pages, you will find selections from such immortal works as Plato's **Republic,** Aristotle's **Poetics,** St. Augustine's **City of God,** Descartes' **Meditations,** Kant's **Critique of Pure Reason,** and Kierkegaard's **Concluding Unscientific Postscript.** These are all great books, and they deserve your deepest respect. But as my Chicago colleague would say, their authors are dead, and you are alive. If you approach the great philosophers with too much awe, they will remain safely dead, like the ashes of honored ancestors resting upon an altar. The only way to bring them to life again is to challenge them, argue with them, poke them and prod them until they are forced to defend themselves against your objections. Socrates started philosophy, as we know it, by needling the authorities of his day with irreverent questions. The sincerest respect you can pay to Socrates and his descendants is to be just as irreverent to them!

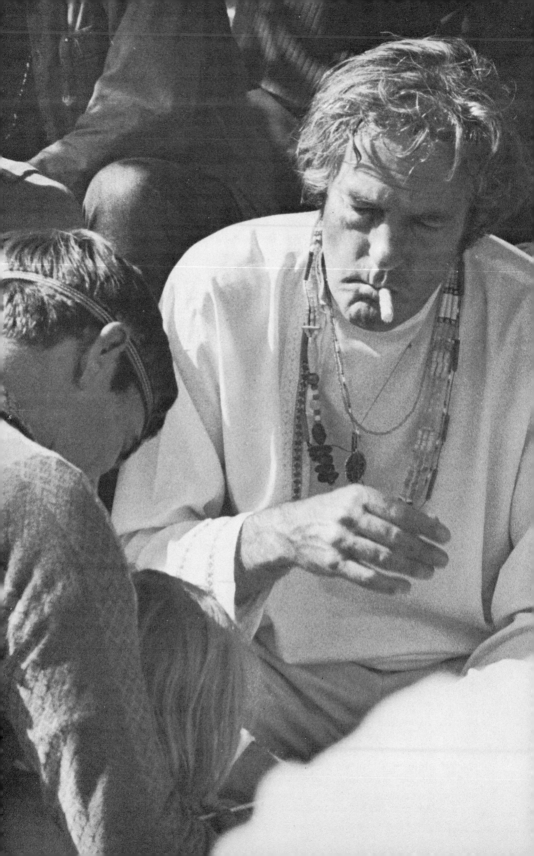

I
METAPHYSICS

LSD:
Appearance
and Reality

INTRODUCTION TO THE CONTEMPORARY ISSUE

We begin our philosophical journey with one of the hottest issues of contemporary college life: **drugs.** Many people are asking themselves, "Should I seek the expansion of consciousness promised by the defenders of LSD, or should I heed the warnings of parents, teachers, and some former users, and shun it like the plague? So many profound philosophical problems come together in this controversy that we could easily build an entire introduction to philosophy around the single issue of drugs.

The two opposed sides of the argument are vividly set forth here in the transcript of a debate between Dr. Timothy Leary, the leading exponent of consciousness expansion, and Dr. Jerome Lettvin, Professor of Communications Physiology at Massachusetts Institute of Technology. Try, if you can, to visualize the scene: a large, modern auditorium, filled to overflowing with MIT students, most of them concentrators in science or engineering. Leary, dressed entirely in white, has somewhat the air of an Indian mystic or religious leader. His voice has a mesmeric quality, and as he delivers his opening speech, a light-and-music show of psychedelic effects accompanies him. He sits cross-legged on the edge of the stage, as if conducting a service.

Lettvin, a big, corpulent man with flamboyant gestures and informal manner, strides energetically up and down, his hands describing arcs in the air as though he would like to reach out and buttonhole his audience. Both men give an impression of great intelligence and self-confidence, but Leary seems quiet, peaceful, while Lettvin is impatient, constantly in motion.

Viewed purely as an intellectual contest, the debate was a standoff. Neither speaker decisively defeated the other. You must decide for yourself which side more nearly captured the truth.

LSD: Lettvin vs. Leary

ANNOUNCER: One evening this spring, as part of a student-run lecture series, two men vied for the souls of students who packed MIT's Kresge Auditorium. They were Dr. Timothy Leary, founder of the League for Spiritual Discovery which advocates LSD as a religious sacrament, and MIT Professor Jerome Lettvin, who thinks Dr. Leary is an agent of the devil. Timothy Leary began experiments with LSD as a lecturer in Psychology at Harvard. Harvard dis-

A complete transcript of National Educational Television's NET Journal. First broadcast, Nov. 20, 1967. Produced for National Educational Television by WGBH-TV, Boston.

missed him in 1963. He is now out on bond for possession of marijuana. Dr. Leary spoke first, mainly in darkness, while psychedelic effects were projected on a screen behind him. We have recreated these effects in color.

DR. TIMOTHY LEARY: I am beginning tonight's ceremony by offering this chalice, which I am drinking to all of us. The chalice contains a powerful and dangerous chemical, given to me by the Boston Water Supply. It's odorless, colorless, tasteless. It's addictive! As a matter of fact, if you get hooked on it and they take it away from you, you crawl on your hands and knees, and your tongue gets black, and your eyes bulge. It's also a dangerous chemical. You have to know how to use it. Too much of it in the wrong place, like in your lungs, and it will kill you. Ten feet of it coming over your rowboat . . . maybe we should pass a law against it, because it's so dangerous, and so addictive. Maybe only scientists should be allowed to play with it. Or maybe we can learn how to teach our kids how to use it, in which case they'll discover that water has many uses and indeed has been used for thousands of years, for millions of years, for billions of years, as a way of life.

It's also been used for thousands of years as a sacrament. Now you know what a sacrament is. A sacrament is a psychedelic technique, is something that you use to get high—get high—yes. A sacrament is something that gets you high, gets you off the television stage set. Pretty solid here. Amazing how solid they make these sets these days. Ha! Gets you off the fake pop television stage set, MIT, Cambridge, United States of America, and reminds you that you're not just a college student, you're not just 22 or 23 or 24 years old. You're two billion years old. Had you forgotten that? Matter of fact, water can remind you where you came from. Remember, you spent nine months in a watery medium; first nine months, this trip, this planet? Remember all that sloshing?

Could we have the lights out now, please? I opened our ceremony . . . could I have all the lights out, please?

You're going to see on the screen home movies and slide projections of little travels, trips that we take. The slides give you the LSD experience from the inside, and the movies present the observer's view of an LSD trip from the outside. The movies are unedited film that's been shot minute after minute, hour after hour, during LSD sessions.

I lit a candle to open our ceremony tonight, again to remind us who we are, where we come from, and what it's all about, because that's what you're here at MIT to learn, isn't it? Fire has been used as a sacrament for thousands of years. It reminds us that we're all creatures of the sun, that we all have little fires burning inside of us from solar energy. Now a fire is dangerous. Fire can kill. Fire can burn, destroy. As a matter of fact, the first fellow who invented fire, Prometheus, got in a lot of trouble with the FDA down in Washington. Remember? They said, "Wait a minute, you're going too fast. Maybe we're not ready for fire." As a matter of fact that's a question that occurs to many of us these days. Maybe man isn't ready for powerful chemicals like LSD and the many new ones that are coming. Maybe man's little mind isn't ready at this moment in evolution to deal with too much, too fast in the way of reality. Fire is dangerous. Maybe we should pass a law against it. Maybe we should peck out the livers of everybody that uses it. Certainly can't let high school and college children have it. What are we going to do about it? How are we going to keep people from burning themselves up and hurting themselves, killing themselves with fire? Well, we gotta start training our kids from the time they can listen to us that fire is here, that water is here, that there are a lot of energies around that are here, that aren't going to go away and they better learn how to use them from the very earliest moments and know what they can and what they can't do, and how they destroy. Because sometimes when I see what fire is doing to the thin layer of topsoil on this planet, I wonder. Maybe they were right about Prometheus, and maybe the human race isn't ready even now to deal with powers like fire.

Now it may seem eccentric to you that I come to Massachusetts Institute of Technology and start talking about sacraments and earth and air and fire and water and ceremonies, but I don't really think it should be that odd. The uniform I'm wearing may be one out of date in this particular brief show you have going here, but people have been sitting barefoot as I am sitting now, in front of you, for thousands of years, in front of candlelight, talking about what I'm talking about; where are we going; what's it all about; what can we do about it; how can we figure it out; how can we tune it back in. Don't you know that the real, real goal of a scientist is to flip out? Don't you know that? Had you forgotten? Oh, you thought that the role of a scientist was to build bigger and bigger stage sets for the television show you got going here? Ya, we have to have a big road running from the cops and robbers game here to the cowboy and Indian show over there, and you engineers are supposed to build them so we can go faster and faster, and farther and farther. From television show to television show.

But if you take science seriously, and you take the history of science seriously, you'll realize that every great scientist wasn't in it for the TV show, commercial payoff. He was in it to find out what it's all about, what's the nature of energy, what are the many levels of energy, what are the levels of consciousness, how can we map them out, and how can we use them. And as he got to know more and more, and to penetrate deeper and deeper into the mysteries of energy around us, he began to flip out, he began to flip out. Look at Einstein, $E = MC_2$. Come on, you mean that . . . that's all energy? Wow! Einstein did it without LSD?

You have been led to believe, most of you, that religion is something that's serious; that's something that's mildly hypocritical, and it has really little to do with the basic questions of life, material or science. Well the facts of the matter are that religion is supposed to be fun; an ecstacy, because you know it's all a play that we're involved in, or energy. And you think that a religious person is one who goes around with a long face reciting the Boy Scout oath? Religion starts as science has always started: in the pursuit, the quest for the ultimate questions. . . . And it's fun. Science should be fun. Science should be pleasure. Science should be flipping out, going out of your mind—really stunned by the joy of this incredible energy situation.

Now the message I have is an old one. It's the simplest and most classic message ever passed on in the world's history. It's those six words: "Drop out, turn on; then come back and tune it in, and then drop out again and turn on and tune it back in." It's a rhythm, and most of us are brain-damaged by what Marshall McLuhan would call the Gutenberg Galaxy, and most of us think that God made this universe in the nature subject, object, predicate sentences. There's no level of energy and no process in biology or physics that operates with subject-predicate sentences. Turn on; tune in; drop out; period; end of paragraph, turn the page. It's all a rhythm, it's all a beat, Jackie . . . give us that beat. You turn on, you find it inside, you have to come back. You can't stay high all the time and you have to start building a better model, building a better building, building a better temple, building a better pawn, building a better language, building a better music. It's always been done that way, but don't get caught, don't get hooked, don't get attracted by the thing you're building, 'cause you gotta drop out, and it's a cycle. Turn on, tune in, drop out, keep it going, keep it going, 'cause the nervous system operates that way. Hundred thousand, million signals a second, right? I'm sorry, a thousand million signals a second coming in your nervous system. It's that same beat, gotta keep it flowing. I want to talk for a minute about the term "turn on." You have to have a key to get in touch with the neurological, sensory, and cellular information that you've got stored in that two-billion-year-old receptacle you call your body. Now how do you "turn on"? Well I'll tell you this, you can't turn on with words. You can't turn on with thinking. You can't think your way out of the sticky black-molasses chessboard of American education. I'm sorry. And good works won't do it for you either. You can be as virtuous and good as you want to but you're not going to "turn on" and get the key to the mystery that way. In order to "turn on" you've got to have what the religious metaphor calls a sacrament. What's a sacrament? A sacrament is something that changes your body, that changes your nervous system. And if the sacrament you use doesn't affect your body, doesn't bring about this internal change, then it's not a sacrament. It's a television show prop that they've given you to keep you nice and quiet in the corner of the studio.

It staggers the imagination to think of the means and the methods that men have used in the past to "turn on," to bring about a change in the sensory neural equipment that we carry around with us. There's hardly any activity, physical, sensory, or even television prop studio activity that men had to use at one time to get high, to go out of their minds, to come to their senses, to take a trip; flagellation, solitude, hiding together in large temples, silence, music, the tampura, the Indian beat, the drums in Africa, sexual abstinence, carefully worked out and systematic routines of sexuality in which you find the divine with a member of the opposite sex; fasting, or the ingestion of sacred foods. Now today, the sacrament is a chemical, or it's a series of chemicals. Now let's not get upset about LSD. In the first place, there are longer and stronger and more powerful chemicals that have the same effect as LSD that are in circulation right now in the United States. They'll be many more coming along. I make this flat prediction: as fast as the government passes a law against one of these molecules, a new one will come along, because for thousands of years Caesar has been trying to stop people from wandering off the stage set, off the studio game and getting outside under the stars and getting back inside to figure out what it's all about. So let's not get too upset about LSD, because even the era of vile chemistry for bringing about the same experience is almost over.

Within your lifetime, you will see the new sacrament or the new key to the internal process developed. As a matter of fact, most of you are going to have a terrible time with your kids in about 25 years, because you'll be sitting around home smoking marijuana and preparing for your next weekly LSD session like good, tidy, conventional people should, and your kids are going to come up and say, "Hey, Dad and Mom, down in the Village there's a new technique called electronic brain stimulation," and you're going to say, "No implanting electrodes in my children's head." And your kids will be growing pigtails, and you're going to get upset and say, "Why don't you use the old tried and true methods of finding out where it's at, like LSD?"

Now there's much confusion about the scientific status and the evidence about LSD. And I'll say this, quite flatly, there's no evidence that I know of, and I read the literature pretty carefully, can tell us much about what LSD does to the consciousness or to the nervous system or to the genetic material. Any time you hear any one talking to you about LSD, and pretending to give you scientific facts, whether they're pro or con LSD, I suggest you be very skeptical. I don't know whether LSD is good or bad. I don't know the effects of LSD on the nervous system, on the brain, or on the genetic material. It's a gamble, it's a risk. The sacrament is always a risk. Did you really think that it could be guaranteed for you? Hey, wake up, have you forgotten who you are or where you came from, that the whole thing is an adventure, and that you're from a whole line of adventurers who got into leaky boats and leaky crafts and put strange things in their mouths and put strange things in the ground, not quite knowing what they're doing? Yuh, taking a psychedelic chemical is a risk, taking LSD is a risk, it's a gamble, it's Russian roulette, but what isn't? Can you name anything that you breathe or put in your body, or let filter through the atmosphere into your nervous system, like television waves, that aren't an unknown gamble? And of all the Russian roulette games I see around me, including Vietnam and polluted air, I would say the Russian roulette of LSD is about the best gamble in the house.

To show you the difficult nature of the scientific study of LSD, I want to tell you a story on what happened with the scientific study of marijuana in the United States. You know marijuana has been around a long time. Everyone has their mind made up about marijuana. How many of you have ever read a scientific paper in a scientific journal following the customary checks and controls and language of science? How many of you have evidence about marijuana as sound as any such as you would expect that you'd have to have to base your opinions on any other aspect of the energy system around us? As a matter of fact, you know it's impossible in the United States for the last fifteen or twenty years to do scientific research on marijuana. There was a man named Ansinger, back in the thirties, who got Congress to pass a law saying that marijuana was bad. Now as Judeo-Christians, we just have to have something that's bad; has to be communist; there have to be witches; there have to be devils; there has to be possessions, or the infidel, or the pagan, or we have to have something that is bad, then we pass a law against it. Now, the facts of the matter are, there were some studies done on marijuana, mainly in England, suggesting that marijuana could be a useful psychiatric cure for depression 'cause it sure makes you feel good. But for the last fifteen years it has almost been impossible to do research on marijuana. If a full-fledged, kosher, bonafide scientist wanted to do research on marijuana, he had to apply for a government license. And you know what happens when you apply for a government license? Government inspectors come around and, "What do you want to do research on marijuana for?" You say, "Well, I want to find out what marijuana is about." "What do you mean, we know what it's all about. It's written in the *Lotus* all about it. Marijuana is a narcotic, is an addictive drug, and it causes rape, violence, aggression. You're not certainly gonna give MIT students in your lab marijuana, because only the Massachusetts State Legislature can think about that, huh?" Ha! It's impossible to do research on marijuana!

Now I'd like to tell you a little research that I've done on marijuana. Now I wanna tell you, lay my cards right on the table, that I came into the research biased, I was very much against LSD. I happen to be an Irish-American and I like to drink. As a middle-class teacher at Harvard, or at the University of California, I'd heard about marijuana but I'd had no occasion to use it, because beatniks used it, and I didn't know any beatniks. And people like Ginsberg and Jack Kerouac seemed to be having a lot of fun, perhaps more fun than I was having. There was no way I could get marijuana and be interested in it. Then we got involved up at Harvard doing research on LSD and I found out, to my surprise, that enormous numbers of people were using marijuana, even Harvard students and graduate students. I have to laugh when I hear about the problems of the dean of Harvard now, when the Crimson announces that 70 percent of the freshman class smoke marijuana and the dean has to announce that they'll throw people out of Harvard if they use marijuana because seven years ago I was saying the same things to the people in our research project, because I didn't think we should study marijuana, because in my contract with Harvard we were going to study LSD, which was legal in those days. It's amazing, you could just write away and get it. I didn't think it would be fair to mix LSD with marijuana in our research so I would go around just like the dean at Harvard, around our research projects in Newton or in Mexico, and I'd say, "Daddy don't allow no pot smokin' in here." It wasn't, as a matter of fact, 'til I left Harvard and left institutional commitments, that I decided that I would do some research on marijuana. But actually I didn't get around to doing it seriously until I went to India, and about the first week I was in India, I went to a place called the Ganga shop, licensed in the city of Calcutta, and I bought about four ounces of marijuana for a dime or so. And I was with a holy man, a guru named Asokvokir, and he took me down to the Ganges River and we sat there with a group of Sivites sitting around the burning gats, and I really began to learn something about marijuana. And I was in India for five months and I smoked marijuana every day, trying it out in different contexts and different activities. Now this is the thing about marijuana. You see, marijuana, I'm sorry to say, might be learned robots of "Menopausal Institute of Technology." [sic] There's no good or evil in this world. Marijuana is neither good nor bad, LSD is neither good nor bad. As a matter of fact, there's probably no activity that you engage in from day to day, week to week, that wouldn't be helped or hindered by the use of marijuana. And the scientific question is, which ones would be hindered? In which case you don't ban marijuana, you just don't use the energy that way, and find out which activities are helped by marijuana and go down to the licensed Ganga store in Cambridge and get it.

Now I want to conclude my sermon with some comments about dropping out. This at the moment tends to be the controversial part of the motto, "turn on, tune in, drop out." Everyone nowadays accepts the notion of turning on. Even Madison Avenue is telling you that Salem cigarettes will turn you on. Everyone wants to be tuned in. But drop out, well you can't say drop out. You can't tell husbands they should drop out of college. You can't tell middle-aged people who have mortgages to pay they should drop out of their jobs.

Now I'm sorry, I mean, I didn't invent this, I'm just reading the lines that were given to me. You've got to drop out. Now there's a lot said about education. "Well you've got to finish your education." When I hear that said, I shudder and my cells shrink because, and I'm sorry to say this, but I say this with great love and great affection because I'm part of this whole institution, the way I'm going. But the education system at the present time in the United States does neurological damage to the nervous system and functions as a narcotic, addictive drug. It rather shocks me to think about how we take our children, our children who are born with 13 billion nerve cells, our children who are Buddhist born, the final product, up-to-date, last-minute version of a two-billion-year-old assembly line back in some Detroit, checking the new models, consumer research—hey, how's the weather up there, ah yes, the Ice Age is going back, all right, take a little more air off the next model, yeh, what color eyes does she like this millennium, how blue, a little more blue in the next model.

We were all born perfect, right up-to-date models. But what happened at the age of four or five? Our parents with the best intentions turned us over to a bunch of strangers that they didn't know and probably that they wouldn't even have had to dinner at their house, to be trained in the only crucial issue of life, control of consciousness. The educational process is a real dangerous drug. Use it carefully 'cause you're likely to get hooked.

Now you, the youngest generation in particular, have got to drop out. By drop out I mean all the way. You can't vote, I urge you not to politic, don't picket, don't get involved in any of these menopausal mind games, because it doesn't make any difference. You remember 1962? We voted for a peace candidate, ha, ha, and you think it makes a difference? Now you face the problem. It's never been faced in this particular magnitude in human history. The speed-up, the acceleration of technology and knowledge and means of changing things. Your generation has grown up in a society that's a thousand or ten thousand years beyond the society of your grandfather and even of your parents. And I want to present one scientific hypothesis, and there's plenty of evidence to back it up. One hypothesis which is so shocking and so frightening to our sense of the way it should be, that I suspect that this finding and sim- plification have been really repressed in the Freudian sense, because it's a stag- gering set of data and it's this: after the age of twenty or twenty-five, neurological studies show us that the human nervous system begins to lose cells. That means you have less cells at thirty and at thirty-five and forty and forty- five than you had at twenty. You're losing brain cells every year of your life after you leave college. Which means that at my age, forty-five, I'm partly brain damaged. It means, ha, ha, you like that, you knew that anyway. Dr. Sydney Cohen in California said and made me promise that I'll turn my brain over to neurologists after I die. And he's going to do the same for me.

Now what does this mean? It means that you young people cannot buy the system of the menopausal mentality generation. You know the men who are running this world, the country, this state, have their minds made up about 1910, 1915, you remember rat-tat-tat-tat machine guns in the old World War, trenches and prohibition booze, ha! You can't just buy their system—you just buy this system. If you ever get around to running for office, which I hope none of you will; if you ever get around to making laws, I suggest the first law you pass be based upon this neurological fact about brain damage. No one over the age of fifty years old should be allowed to vote or hold power over young, seed-carrying people, should they?

Does that make neurological sense to yourselves? Doesn't to mine. Now in the next six months, a year, two years, there's going to be a lot of tension in this country about the control of consciousness. Because, like it or not, believe it or not, we have entered into a new age and I would call it the age of con- sciousness. And the implications of this revolution of consciousness are much greater than the technological or the atomic or the electronic age, because this age is focusing inside, and for the first time in human history, at least in Western history ('cause they knew all this for 4,000 years in India), for the first time in human Western history, man has finally caught on that it doesn't make as much difference what goes on out there as it does how much control and freedom you have in here. The internal trip can be observed, it can be labeled, it can be manipulated, it can be controlled, and it can be replicated just as easily as an experiment in external science. And you've got to "turn on" your parents. And I can't turn on LBJ, but he's got some young people around, and if they've been to good colleges, the statistics tell us that half of them, that means that either she or her roommate is turned on, so that's the way we've got to do it. We've got to say, "Daddy-bird, you've done enough. Daddy-bird, it was thirty years ago you ran for the president of a bank and you've got steel all over the world now, Daddy-bird. And you've done enough. Come on, drop out, and turn on and learn how to make love all over again and come to your senses." I think it's time to stop, drop out. Thank you.

NARRATOR: When Dr. Timothy Leary, the high priest of the League for Spiritual Discovery, finished speaking, Dr. Jerome Lettvin took the floor. Dr. Lettvin was senior psychologist at the Mantina State Hospital in Illinois. He is now Professor of Communications Physiology in the Departments of Biology and Electrical Engineering at MIT. He also lectures in the Humanities Department. Dr. Lettvin, who has three teenage children, is known at MIT as a man students can talk to.

DR. JEROME LETTVIN: Now, Tim, your argument is exceedingly seductive and in the main, I must admit that I find the press of middle age and the middle class enormously powerful here in Cambridge. Here in Cambridge it's all hell. The horror, in part, is that I, too, sit in front of TV sets, feel myself slumping, pay the taxes. But the problem is whether the navel really replaces TV. I mean, you, sitting in front of your navel, strike me as being, in a sense, being very little better off. First, let's put it this way: No surprises are likely to come about, and you aren't even beguiled by good commercials. Nevertheless, I think that we must take your thesis extremely seriously, and I will not do you the dishonor of either attacking you on scientific grounds, because the question, as is very obvious, is not scientific but moral. Therefore, for this reason, I would like to confine my remarks strictly to the—turn that damn thing off . . . confine my remarks strictly to the pathological questions involved. By that I mean simply questions which constitute good and evil. But I feel somehow or another that this man is in the hands of the devil—that is to say, he is in a private hell of a curious and somewhat sultrian devising. That is, having made his pact with the devil, that is what he asked for, and that is what he gets. For I suspect that in making these pacts, very much like monkey's paw pacts, that what we get, we get literally, and what we lose, we lose; rather mocks us.

To look at this man, sitting there with the smile, this supernal smile, this ecstatic smile, I feel sick. I don't feel that I want to trade. I feel sick for him. And I ask of you how many would trade? He assures you he is in the utmost ecstasy—when you can get to him. Otherwise he's in that ecstasy. Why would not any of you trade? Let us take another trade that has been offered in the past. You and I lived through the period of lobotomies. You walk into the office. "I don't like my mama." They lift your eyelid up, you know, flash, flash, and you go out. It doesn't matter. You see, you have traded for—it doesn't matter—a hunk of brain tissue. After all, brain tissue, as he tells it, you're losing so much, what's a little bit more? Does it really matter? No. Here, you traded. How many of you would take a lobotomy, given the guarantee that thereafter you don't care? You come in saying, "I don't want to care, everything is bothering the hell out of me. I wanna stop caring, I wanna be happy." And so he takes, you know, bang bang. Is this a trade you would make? Why not? . . . No, wait a minute, this is strictly a rhetorical question. . . .

I'm asking a question of myself for I found Tim's presentation extremely compelling, shorn, if you'll excuse me, of those adornments: I think you ought to change them; they're not beautiful; they're symmetrical, but not pretty. At any rate, I find Tim's thesis terribly compelling, and for this reason I feel that I have to answer it for myself, you see. You are selling off the noyetic functions. You're selling off exactly those functions which have set you aside critically, in every possible way, you're abrogating, you're dissolving these. Henceforth, suspended judgment for awhile. You take your martini at five o'clock. You come home, you don't want to remember what sort of a damn fool you were during the day. You don't want to remember being pushed down by this guy—the compromise you made that went against your grain. You see, all of these things, you've got to forget them. You cop out with the martini. But with the assurance that when the alcohol wears off, you are possibly back to a state where judgment miraculously has been restored. This is the same, incidentally, with marijuana, and as an aside, Tim, let me agree with you that I can conceive of no more immoral thing than has been done by the government than the wholesale banning of drugs, for I suspect that, since the time of Mellon, this is like the Hearst papers trying to abolish pornography. The more there is of it around the more they thrive. There is a fundamentally monstrous thing about forbidding rather than reasoning people out. If you have a thesis, you advance the thesis. There is a counter thesis, one argues. One does not argue with force of the kind the government has done, spurring the crime rate, as it has been done by the morphine addicts, etc. And I feel very violently about this because I used to take care of an addict ward when I was back in Mantino. As I say, I'm perfectly willing to admit with you that the government has done a monstrous thing in forbidding many of the drugs that are around. The forbidding of marijuana, I believe, is pure nonsense, in the light of the LaGuardia report. It is, however, the law of the land, and I therefore cannot advise people in conscience to break the law of the land for the very simple reason that I'm not permitted to.

But when it comes to LSD, to psylosybin, to all of these other drugs that you have been handing out, that you have been talking about, at this point, sir, I look upon you as a tool of the devil and I look upon you as a fundamentally vicious tool of the devil, and I will explain to you why.

In general, when one takes something like a drink, a martini or a drink of wine, or gets drunk with one's friends in the evening, and wakes up the next day with a hangover, there is a reassurance, the miraculous reassurance, somehow or another, of judgment to yourself. Question: with LSD, with psylosybin, with mescaline, do we have this reassurance? You have said, "Sure, it's Russian roulette. Sure, it's dangerous." But let us look specifically at the danger. And I'm not going to talk neurologically because it would only be gobbledygook. What is the fundamental danger? Let us say that one person out of fifty will have a reaction like this: he will take a dose, he will take a trip, and three days later he takes a return trip, and a week later takes a return trip, not having taken any more drugs. How is it possible for anybody on observing this to say to any person, "You take one chance in one hundred; the return trips, they're for free." What is a return trip? Let me ask you. If there is no cause, how come the return trip, the flipping in suddenly, and the flipping out suddenly? Suddenly the colors whirl about, suddenly smells have color, suddenly colors have sounds, and then you're back in the normal world. And what does this smell like clinically, Tim, what does this smell like to you? As a clinician, what is this? If you saw a patient who complained of this, what is it that he would have? What would you diagnose him as?

LEARY: A visionary mystic.

LETTVIN: Bullshit! You would diagnose him as a temporal lobe epileptic with an aura. And you know that Goddamn well! Where else . . . he looks this way at me . . . those of you who are well . . .

LEARY: Don't tell me what I know.

LETTVIN: If you read the description of the aura, either in Penfield and Erickson's book, called *Epilepsy and Cerebral Localization*, written many years ago, or if you'll get hold of an exceedingly charming book by McDonald Riechly called *The Bridal Lobe* where he discusses all of these things, or if you will simply read Dostoyevsky, which is far simpler for most of you, you'll get a notion of what this aura is. And you can become addicted to an aura. When a man comes to me and says, "I haven't had a shot, I haven't had any LSD for three months, but I still flip in and flip out," as a clinician what do I think about, what do I worry about? And what I worry about here, specifically, is that he has a functional lesion. This sounds a joke to you, functional lesion, 'cause I can't show it by cutting him open; but a functional lesion because, clinically, it goes along with other things that have turned out to be, like tumors, like scars, like hits on the head, and things of the sort. Very well, this is one thing, temporal lobe—very weird stuff about the temporal lobe, and I will not go into it, I will simply remark that this is that particular portion of the brain that is affected in half the axe murderers that we have in this country. Has it ever occurred to you, why is it you read about a guy coming home and he knocks off his wife, his three kids, you know, and at the station he stands there and says, "I don't remember"? Ha, you know, real amnesia. You know, well, let me assure you, half of these things are temporal lobe syndromes, what are called psychomotor seizures. What this fellow had, who shot in Texas at the campus, shot the various people, this is roughly the sort of seizure he had. In his case, they found the tumor.

What about LSD, psylosybin? I know a set of physicists who took a while ago, in a group, because they're curious people (all physicists are curious people, that is, they're not curious to look at), they took in a group of about five or six of them, they took some psylosybin on the recipe gotten from the telephone number here in Cambridge that you're supposed to call to get that recipe. And having taken it, they got violently sick the first day, and every one of them for three months thereafter was incapable of doing any theoretical work. On all behavioral counts, the same, but clearly apparent in their higher critical functions, as Tim said. But with a hangover of this, a hangover that lasts not an hour or two hours, but several days, several months. Let us give it only several days, let's be conservative. A hangover for a few days, something happens and your judgment, by which you weigh things, goes down. You're now in the position of regenerating this by taking, say, one trip every three days, one trip every four days, and you pay for the vision of yourself by the loss of judgment. You pay for getting out by the loss of judgment. You pay for whatever visions you get by this loss in judgment. And the loss of judgment that stays and stays.

Now, you might say, how do I know this? Have I ever taken it, huh? No! Now I haven't taken it for a rather simple reason: the price seems to be a little bit big, a little steep to pay. I'm giving the devil my judgment, my soul, my intellect, all of the things I've worked for. For this kick, like a nymphomaniac, not like a neurotic person, but like a nymphomaniac. After all, there she is, having orgasm after orgasm. Wonderful! All day long without a stop. Beautiful! Terrific! Can anybody envy her? Does anybody envy her? Why? Because you didn't envy that guy sitting in the state hospital either! The kick is cheap! The ecstasy is cheap! And you are settling for a permanently second-rate world by the complete abrogation of the intellect. In the old days, if it wasn't done by lobotomy, it was done by psychoanalysis. Now it's done by drugs. I can find in myself no joy in such an outlook.

LEARY: Now I share the basic concern that we listened to tonight. I don't know whether LSD's a devil's toy. As a matter of fact, I spend many hours a week, many, many hours in the last few years, thinking about: you know it's very possible that LSD is the worst thing that could ever come along . . . that, maybe, the insidious thing is that as I take this, as I have over 400 times, I've lost discriminating ability, and maybe I may feel better and better as I'm lying in the gutter with my nose running, but I'm too brain-damaged, too dazed to realize. Now, several years ago I began, myself, urging other people to take LSD, to keep a checklist as to where you are. Not in television-game terms about whether your grades are higher or lower and that sort of thing, but where you are basically in terms of your two-billion-year-old status on this planet. Now each and every one of you have a different checklist. Mine had to do with how many hours I'm spending with children opposed to game-playing with adults. Am I making more money or less? (I'm making less. I think that's good.) And so forth. But I still don't know, and I still have an open mind, as to whether I'm a spokesman for, I would say the devil, before a dangerous and diabolical situation.

However, I just want to underline one difference, and it's an ancient difference. We've heard a great deal of praise about the neurotic function of the mind. Do you want to keep your mind? Well, if you want to keep your mind and that judgmental function, stay away from LSD. Stay away from religious experience. Because when you take LSD, you realize that what you call your mind is about twenty years old, or at least two or three hundred years old, and the experience that I'm talking about is much more ancient, and much liberating experience. I want everyone to be warned. Don't take this trip unless you know you're playing around a blind roulette game with the most precious thing you have . . . a thirty billion cell nervous system. Read the labels. Read Duskin. Read the *New England Journal*. Read our journal. Read the ancient stories of mystics and visionaries. And when you've read the whole thing, then forget the books and talk to the people who have had the experience. And then look at yourself in the mirror and then decide yourself. Because the only control of LSD is self-control.

COMMENTARY ON THE CONTEMPORARY ISSUE

Now that you have read the Leary-Lettvin dispute, let us try to sort out the various issues raised by the disputants and see whether we can arrive at a deeper understanding of the basis of this disagreement.

First of all, they are obviously not concerned primarily with the legal problems associated with drugs. To be sure, Leary has had a number of encounters with the law since he began using drugs, and Lettvin strongly opposes the severe penalties which have been meted out to users of marijuana and other substances. Nevertheless, legality is not the issue. If the laws regulating drug use were all to be repealed, neither Lettvin nor Leary would alter his argument by so much as a word.

Nor do the speakers really disagree about the danger of harmful aftereffects of drug use. Lettvin emphasizes those dangers more, perhaps, but Leary does not dispute the warnings which Lettvin issues. Indeed, he insists upon them, cautioning us that consciousness-expansion is a risky business. If a "safe" form of LSD were discovered, one which produced no chromosome breaks or unwanted second trips, Lettvin would continue to argue against its use, for his objection is with the primary "hallucinatory" impact of the drug. As for Leary, we can be sure that he would willingly take even greater gambles with his health in order to achieve the consciousness-expansion he seeks.

The real dispute between Leary and Lettvin is over the very nature of reality itself, and over the right way for man to establish his relationship to it. Lettvin speaks for all those who believe that reality is what we can see and feel, what we can infer from experiments or discover through the investigations of science. For Lettvin, the public world of physical objects in space and time is the **real** world, and man's dignity as a rational being depends upon his willingness to live in that world and master its laws.

Leary expresses the ancient conviction that the visible world is merely a pale reflection of a truer reality which exists within the mind. For him, things unseen by the physical eye are greater by far than the mere objects of our five senses. The visions induced by psychedelic drugs lead us, he believes, to a reality with which the soul can truly commune.

Lettvin speaks as an apostle of reason, while Leary gives voice to the conviction that the soul has a power of insight higher than reason. For Lettvin, man's greatest gift is his power to judge, to weigh evidence, draw inferences, adjust desire to reality and act to expectation. Leary sees this glorification of the rational faculty as an anchor weighing man down, holding him to the earth so that he cannot soar to the heights of vision and transcendent insight.

It might seem that Leary represents the religious style of thought and life while Lettvin represents the secular, but that would be a misleadingly simple way of describing their disagreement. Many men have spoken like Leary without adhering to any coherent religious doctrine, while Lettvin's cool rationalism would have appealed to the great St. Thomas Aquinas himself.

There are really two separate disputes here, overlapping and inter-twining in complex ways. The first, which we may call metaphysical, con-cerns the nature of the distinction between appearance and reality. The second, which belongs more properly to the philosophy of religion, con-cerns the nature and significance of religious experience. In the present section, we shall deal only with the metaphysical problem of appearance and reality. The nature of religious experience is postponed to the con-cluding section of this book, at which point we shall return to the subject of drugs.

Lettvin thinks Leary's drug-induced visions are merely pathological hallucinations akin to those caused by brain damage. Leary thinks Lettvin never encounters true reality, limited as he is to the reports of his senses and reason. Can we find some way to determine what is truly real and what is mere appearance, mere illusion or reflection? And if we must choose between the two, which should we prefer, reality or appearance?

We all learn very early in life to distinguish between what is real and what merely appears to be real. However, when we try to formulate pre-cisely the difference between the real and the apparent, we discover how slippery the distinction is. We might say, as a first attempt, that the real is what we can actually see, hear, and feel, whereas the apparent is what we only imagine (wrongly) that we can see, hear, and feel. So, for example, the pen on my desk is real, for I can see it, reach out and pick it up, make a noise by rapping it on the desk, and so forth. On the other hand, the pens I **think** I see when I press the side of my eyeball (an easy way to make yourself "see double") are not real, for when I reach out my hand, I do not feel two slender, cylindrical objects. By an analogous line of reason-ing, we conclude that mirages, hallucinations, and after-images are "mere appearances," whereas rocks, trees, cars, and other people are real.

Of course, the matter is not closed. Many of you will already have said to yourselves, "But when a man sees a mirage, **he really sees it.** So isn't it therefore real?" When I press my eyeball, don't I really see double? Why call the two pens "mere appearances"? Some philosophers would answer that the crucial difference between reality and appearance lies in the public or **intersubjective** nature of the real as opposed to the private or subjective nature of appearance. Other people can see and feel the pen on my desk, but no one else can see those two "pens" that appear when I press my eyeball. How do we check on the reality of an object, after all? We ask someone else whether he sees it too.

There are still some problems with this answer, to be sure. What shall we say about an entire caravan of desert travelers, all of who claim to see an oasis in the distance? The fact that all of them are having the same hallucination won't make it any easier for them to get a drink of water. Nevertheless, with some subtle and complicated additions to the definition, we can formulate a distinction between appearance and reality which many philosophers would be prepared to endorse. The last selection in this sec-tion, by the twentieth-century American philosopher C. I. Lewis, presents one of the most sophisticated definitions in what philosophers call the Empiricist tradition.

America today. Shall they leave the university for the political arena, or shun the bustle of social action for a life of quiet contemplation? If one believes, with Plato, that eternal Ideas are the true reality, or with Timothy Leary that reality lies within the confines of subjective consciousness, then politics will appear a sham, a shadow play of half-real images. On the other hand, if one holds, as Thomas Hobbes and Karl Marx did many years later, that physical objects and social institutions are the true realities, then both the psychedelic turn-on of Leary and the philosophical quest of Plato will seem no better than excuses for fleeing the field of battle.

As you probably have already noted, Plato does not define the problem of appearance and reality in quite the same way as Leary and Lettvin. Each of our other four authors also puts his own interpretation on the problem, for one of the distinguishing marks of a first-rate philosophical mind is the ability to see an issue from a unique perspective.

At this point, we pick up the Dialogue. Socrates is speaking, and he asks, by what system of education are we to develop the class of philosophical rulers who will govern the just state?

Levels of Reality and the Allegory of the Cave

. . . And so with pain and toil we have reached the end of one subject, but more remains to be discussed;—how and by what studies and pursuits will the saviours of the constitution be created, and at what ages are they to apply themselves to their several studies?

. . . The . . . question of the rulers must be investigated from the very beginning. We were saying, as you will remember, that they were to be lovers of their country, tried by the test of pleasures and pains, and neither in hardships, nor in dangers, nor at any other critical moment were to lose their patriotism—he was to be rejected who failed, but he who always came forth pure, like gold tried in the refiner's fire, was to be made a ruler, and to receive honours and rewards in life and after death. This was the sort of thing which

From *Republic* of Plato, trans. by Benjamin Jowett.

was being said, and then the argument turned aside and veiled her face; not liking to stir the question which has now arisen.

I perfectly remember, he said.

Yes, my friend, I said, and I then shrank from hazarding the bold word; but now let me dare to say—that the perfect guardian must be a philosopher. . . .

And do not suppose that there will be many of them; for the gifts which were deemed by us to be essential rarely grow together; they are mostly found in shreds and patches.

What do you mean? he said.

You are aware, I replied, that quick intelligence, memory, sagacity, cleverness, and similar qualities, do not often grow together, and that persons who possess them and are at the same time high-spirited and magnanimous are not so constituted by nature as to live orderly and in a peaceful and settled manner; they are driven any way by their impulses and all solid principle goes out of them. . . .

On the other hand, those steadfast natures which can better be depended upon; which in a battle are impregnable to fear and immovable, are equally immovable when there is anything to be learned; they are always in a torpid state, and are apt to yawn and go to sleep over any intellectual toil. . . .

And yet we were saying that both qualities were necessary in those to whom the higher education is to be imparted, and who are to share in any office or command.

Certainly, he said.

And will they be a class which is rarely found?

Yes, indeed.

Then the aspirant must not only be tested in those labours and dangers and pleasures which we mentioned before, but there is another kind of probation which we did not mention—he must be exercised also in many kinds of knowledge, to see whether the soul will be able to endure the highest of all, or will faint under them, as in any other studies and exercises.

Yes, he said, you are quite right in testing him. But what do you mean by the highest of all knowledge?

You may remember, I said, that we divided the soul into three parts; and distinguished the several natures of justice, temperance, courage, and wisdom?

Indeed, he said, if I had forgotten, I should not deserve to hear more.

And do you remember the word of caution which preceded the discussion of them?

To what do you refer?

We were saying, if I am not mistaken, that he who wanted to see them in their perfect beauty must take a longer and more circuitous way, at the end of which they would appear; but that we could add on a popular exposition of them on a level with the discussion which had preceded. And you replied that

such an exposition would be enough for you, and so the inquiry was continued in what to me seemed to be a very inaccurate manner; whether you were satisfied or not, it is for you to say.

Yes, he said, I thought and the others thought that you gave us a fair measure of truth.

But, my friend, I said, a measure of such things which in any degree falls short of the whole truth is not fair measure; for nothing imperfect is the measure of anything, although persons are too apt to be contented and think that they need search no further.

Not an uncommon case when people are indolent.

Yes, I said; and there cannot be any worse fault in a guardian of the State and of the laws.

True.

The guardian, then, I said, must be required to take the longer circuit, and toil at learning as well as at gymnastics, or he will never reach the highest knowledge of all which, as we were just now saying, is his proper calling.

What, he said, is there a knowledge still higher than this—higher than justice and the other virtues?

Yes, I said, there is. And of the virtues too we must behold not the outline merely, as at present—nothing short of the most finished picture should satisfy us. When little things are elaborated with an infinity of pains, in order that they may appear in their full beauty and utmost clearness, how ridiculous that we should not think the highest truths worthy of attaining the highest accuracy!

A right noble thought; but do you suppose that we shall refrain from asking you what is this highest knowledge?

Nay, I said, ask if you will; but I am certain that you have heard the answer many times, and now you either do not understand me or, as I rather think, you are disposed to be troublesome; for you have often been told that the idea of good is the highest knowledge, and that all other things become useful and advantageous only by their use of this. You can hardly be ignorant that of this I was about to speak, concerning which, as you have often heard me say, we know so little; and, without which, any other knowledge or possession of any kind will profit us nothing. Do you think that the possession of all other things is of any value if we do not possess the good? or the knowledge of all other things if we have no knowledge of beauty and goodness?

Assuredly not.

You are further aware that most people affirm pleasure to be the good, but the finer sort of wits say it is knowledge? . . .

And you are aware too that the latter cannot explain what they mean by knowledge, but are obliged after all to say knowledge of the good?

How ridiculous!

Yes, I said, that they should begin by reproaching us with our ignorance of the good, and then presume our knowledge of it—for the good they define to be knowledge of the good, just as if we understood them when they use the term "good"—this is of course ridiculous.

Most true, he said.

And those who make pleasure their good are in equal perplexity; for they are compelled to admit that there are bad pleasures as well as good, . . . and therefore to acknowledge that bad and good are the same. . . .

Further, do we not see that many are willing to do or to have or to seem to be what is just and honourable without the reality; but no one is satisfied with the appearance of good—the reality is what they seek; in the case of the good, appearance is despised by every one.

Very true, he said.

Of this, then, which every soul of man pursues and makes the end of all his actions, having a presentiment that there is such an end, and yet hesitating because neither knowing the nature nor having the same assurance of this as of other things, and therefore losing whatever good there is in other things,—of a principle such and so great as this ought the best men in our State, to whom everything is entrusted, to be in the darkness of ignorance?

Certainly not, he said.

I am sure, I said, that he who does not know how the beautiful and the just are likewise good will be but a sorry guardian of them; and I suspect that no one who is ignorant of the good will have a true knowledge of them. . . . And if we only have a guardian who has this knowledge our State will be perfectly ordered.

Of course, he replied; but I wish that you would tell me whether you conceive this supreme principle of the good to be knowledge or pleasure, or different from either?

Aye, I said, I knew all along that a fastidious gentleman like you would not be contented with the thoughts of other people about these matters.

True, Socrates; but I must say that one who like you has passed a lifetime in the study of philosophy should not be always repeating the opinions of others, and never telling his own.

Well, but has any one a right to say positively what he does not know?

Not, he said, with the assurance of positive certainty; he has no right to do that: but he may say what he thinks, as a matter of opinion.

And do you not know, I said, that all mere opinions are bad, and the best of them blind? You would not deny that those who have any true notion without intelligence are only like blind men who feel their way along the road?

Very true.

And do you wish to behold what is blind and crooked and base, when others will tell you of brightness and beauty?

Still, I must implore you, Socrates, said Glaucon, not to turn away just as you are reaching the goal; if you will only give such an explanation of the good as you have already given of justice and temperance and the other virtues, we shall be satisfied. . . .

Yes, I said, but I must first come to an understanding with you, and remind you of what I have mentioned in the course of this discussion, and at many other times.

What?

The old story, that there is a many beautiful and a many good, and so of other things which we describe and define; to all of them the term "many" is applied.

True, he said.

And there is an absolute beauty and an absolute good, and of other things to which the term "many" is applied there is an absolute; for they may be brought under a single idea, which is called the essence of each. . . . The many, as we say, are seen but not known, and the ideas are known but not seen. . . . And what is the organ with which we see the visible things?

The sight, he said.

And with the hearing, I said, we hear, and with the other senses perceive the other objects of sense?

True.

But have you remarked that sight is by far the most costly and complex piece of workmanship which the artificer of the senses ever contrived?

No, I never have, he said.

Then reflect: has the ear or voice need of any third or additional nature in order that the one may be able to hear and the other to be heard?

Nothing of the sort.

No, indeed, I replied; and the same is true of most, if not all, the other senses—you would not say that any of them requires such an addition?

Certainly not.

But you see that without the addition of some other nature there is no seeing or being seen?

How do you mean?

Sight being, as I conceive, in the eyes, and he who has eyes wanting to see; colour being also present in them, still unless there be a third nature specially adapted to the purpose, the owner of the eyes will see nothing and the colours will be invisible.

Of what nature are you speaking?

Of that which you term light, I replied.

True, he said.

Noble, then, is the bond which links together sight and visibility, and great beyond other bonds by no small difference of nature; for light is their bond, and light is no ignoble thing?

Nay, he said, the reverse of ignoble.

And which, I said, of the gods in heaven would you say was the lord of this element? Whose is that light which makes the eye to see perfectly and the visible to appear?

You mean the sun, as you and all mankind say.

May not the relation of sight to this deity be described as follows? . . . Neither sight nor the eye in which sight resides is the sun. . . .

Yet of all the organs of sense the eye is the most like the sun. . . . And the power which the eye possesses is a sort of effluence which is dispensed from the sun. . . . Then the sun is not sight, but the author of sight who is recognized by sight?

True, he said.

And this is he whom I call the child of the good, whom the good begat in his own likeness, to be in the visible world, in relation to sight and the things of sight, what the good is in the intellectual world in relation to mind and the things of mind.

Will you be a little more explicit? he said.

Why, you know, I said, that the eyes, when a person directs them towards objects on which the light of day is no longer shining, but the moon and stars only, see dimly, and are nearly blind; they seem to have no clearness of vision in them. . . . But when they are directed towards objects on which the sun shines, they see clearly and there is sight in them. . . . And the soul is like the eye: when resting upon that on which truth and being shine, the soul perceives and understands, and is radiant with intelligence; but when turned towards the twilight of becoming and perishing, then she has opinion only, and goes blinking about, and is first of one opinion and then of another, and seems to have no intelligence. . . . Now, that which imparts truth to the known and the power of knowing to the knower is what I would have you term the idea of good, and this you will deem to be the cause of science, and of truth in so far as the latter becomes the subject of knowledge; beautiful too, as are both truth and knowledge, you will be right in esteeming this other nature as more beautiful than either; and, as in the previous instance, light and sight may be truly said to be like the sun, and yet not to be the sun, so in this other sphere, science and truth may be deemed to be like the good, but not the good; the good has a place of honour yet higher.

What a wonder of beauty that must be, he said, which is the author of science and truth, and yet surpasses them in beauty; for you surely cannot mean to say that pleasure is the good?

God forbid, I replied; but may I ask you to consider the image in another point of view? . . . You would say, would you not, that the sun is not only the author of visibility in all visible things, but of generation and nourishment and growth, though he himself is not generation?

Certainly.

In like manner the good may be said to be not only the author of knowledge to all things known, but of their being and essence, and yet the good is not essence, but far exceeds essence in dignity and power.

Glaucon said, with a ludicrous earnestness: By the light of heaven, how amazing! . . . Pray continue. . . . Let us hear if there is anything more to be said about the similitude of the sun. . . .

You have to imagine, then, that there are two ruling powers, and that one of them is set over the intellectual world, the other over the visible. . . . May I suppose that you have this distinction of the visible and intelligible fixed in your mind?

I have.

Now take a line which has been cut into two unequal parts, and divide each of them again in the same proportion, and suppose the two main divisions to answer, one to the visible and the other to the intelligible, and then compare the subdivisions in respect of their clearness and want of clearness, and you will find that the first section in the sphere of the visible consists of images. And by images I mean, in the first place, shadows, and in the second place, reflections in water and in solid, smooth, and polished bodies and the like: Do you understand?

Yes, I understand.

Imagine, now, the other section, of which this is only the resemblance, to include the animals which we see, and everything that grows or is made. . . . Would you not admit that both the sections of this division have different degrees of truth, and that the copy is to the original as the sphere of opinion is to the sphere of knowledge?

Most undoubtedly.

Next proceed to consider the manner in which the sphere of the intellectual is to be divided. . . . There are two subdivisions, in the lower of which the soul uses the figures given by the former division as images; the inquiry can only be hypothetical, and instead of going upwards to a principle descends to the other end; in the higher of the two, the soul passes out of hypotheses, and goes up to a principle which is above hypotheses, making no use of images as in the former case, but proceeding only in and through the ideas themselves.

I do not quite understand your meaning, he said.

Then I will try again; you will understand me better when I have made some preliminary remarks. You are aware that students of geometry, arithmetic, and the kindred sciences assume the odd and the even and the figures and three kinds of angles and the like in their several branches of science; these are their hypotheses, which they and everybody are supposed to know, and therefore they do not deign to give any account of them either to themselves or others; but they begin with them, and go on until they arrive at last, and in a consistent manner, at their conclusion?

Yes, he said, I know.

And do you not know also that although they make use of the visible forms and reason about them, they are thinking not of these, but of the ideals which they resemble; not of the figures which they draw, but of the absolute square and the absolute diameter, and so on—the forms which they draw or make, and which have shadows and reflections in water of their own, are converted by them into images, but they are really seeking to behold the things themselves, which can only be seen with the eye of the mind?

That is true.

And of this kind I spoke as the intelligible, although in the search after it the soul is compelled to use hypotheses; not ascending to a first principle, because she is unable to rise above the region of hypothesis, but employing the objects of which the shadows below are resemblances in their turn as images, they having in relation to the shadows and reflections of them a greater distinctness, and therefore a higher value.

I understand, he said, that you are speaking of the province of geometry and the sister arts.

And when I speak of the other division of the intelligible, you will understand me to speak of that other sort of knowledge which reason herself attains by the power of dialectic, using the hypotheses not as first principles, but only as hypotheses—that is to say, as steps and points of departure into a world which is above hypotheses, in order that she may soar beyond them to the first principle of the whole; and clinging to this and then to that which depends on this, by successive steps she descends again without the aid of any sensible object, from ideas, through ideas, and in ideas she ends.

I understand you, he replied; not perfectly, for you seem to me to be describing a task which is really tremendous; but, at any rate, I understand you to say that knowledge and being, which the science of dialectic contemplates, are clearer than the notions of the arts, as they are termed, which proceed from hypotheses only: these are also contemplated by the understanding, and not by the senses: yet, because they start from hypotheses and do not ascend to a principle, those who contemplate them appear to you not to exercise the higher reason upon them, although when a first principle is added to them they are cognizable by the higher reason. And the habit which is concerned with geometry and the cognate sciences I suppose that you would term understanding and not reason, as being intermediate between opinion and reason.

You have quite conceived my meaning, I said; and now, corresponding to these four divisions, let there be four faculties in the soul—reason answering to the highest, understanding to the second, faith (or conviction) to the third, and perception of shadows to the last—and let there be a scale of them, and let us suppose that the several faculties have clearness in the same degree that their objects have truth.

I understand, he replied, and give my assent, and accept your arrangement.

And now, I said, let me show in a figure how far our nature is enlightened or unenlightened:—Behold! human beings living in an underground den, which has a mouth open towards the light and reaching all along the den; here they have been from their childhood, and have their legs and necks chained so that they cannot move, and can only see before them, being prevented by the chains from turning their heads. Above and behind them a fire is blazing at a distance, and between the fire and the prisoners there is a raised way; and you will see, if you look, a low wall built along the way, like the screen which marionette players have in front of them, over which they show the puppets.

I see.

And do you see . . . men passing along the wall carrying all sorts of vessels and statues and figures of animals made of wood and stone and various materials, which appear over the wall? Some of them are talking, others silent.

You have shown me a strange image, and they are strange prisoners.

Like ourselves, I replied; and they see only their own shadows, or the shadows of one another, which the fire throws on the opposite wall of the cave?

True, he said; how could they see anything but the shadows if they were never allowed to move their heads?

. . . Of the objects which are being carried in like manner they would only see the shadows? . . .

And if they were able to converse with one another, would they not suppose that they were naming what was actually before them?

Very true.

And suppose further that the prison had an echo which came from the other side, would they not be sure to fancy when one of the passers-by spoke that the voice which they heard came from the passing shadow?

No question, he replied.

To them, I said, the truth would be literally nothing but the shadows of the images.

That is certain.

And now look again, and see what will naturally follow if the prisoners are released and disabused of their error. At first, when any of them is liberated and compelled suddenly to stand up and turn his neck round and walk and look towards the light, he will suffer sharp pains; the glare will distress him, and he will be unable to see the realities of which in his former state he had seen the shadows; and then conceive some one saying to him, that what he saw before was an illusion, but that now, when he is approaching nearer to being and his eye is turned towards more real existence, he has a clearer vision, —what will be his reply? And you may further imagine that his instructor is pointing to the objects as they pass and requiring him to name them,—will he not be perplexed? Will he not fancy that the shadows which he formerly saw are truer than the objects which are now shown to him?

And if he is compelled to look straight at the light, will he not have a pain in his eyes which will make him turn away to take refuge in the objects of vision which he can see, and which he will conceive to be in reality clearer than the things which are now being shown to him?

True, he said.

And suppose once more, that he is reluctantly dragged up a steep and rugged ascent, and held fast until he is forced into the presence of the sun himself, is he not likely to be pained and irritated? When he approaches the light his eyes will be dazzled, and he will not be able to see anything at all of what are now called realities.

Not all in a moment, he said.

He will require to grow accustomed to the sight of the upper world. And first he will see the shadows best, next the reflections of men and other objects in the water, and then the objects themselves; then he will gaze upon the light of the moon and the stars and the spangled heaven; and he will see the sky and the stars by night better than the sun or the light of the sun by day?

Certainly.

Last of all he will be able to see the sun, and not mere reflections of him in the water, but he will see him in his own proper place, and not in another; and he will contemplate him as he is. . . . He will then proceed to argue that this is he who gives the season and the years, and is the guardian of all that is in the visible world, and in a certain way the cause of all things which he and his fellows have been accustomed to behold. . . .

And when he remembered his old habitation, and the wisdom of the den and his fellow-prisoners, do you not suppose that he would felicitate himself on the change, and pity them?

Certainly, he would.

And if they were in the habit of conferring honours among themselves on those who were quickest to observe the passing shadows and to remark which of them went before, and which followed after, and which were together; and who were therefore best able to draw conclusions as to the future, do you think that he would care for such honours and glories, or envy the possessors of them? Would he not say with Homer,

Better to be the poor servant of a poor master,

and to endure anything, rather than think as they do and live after their manner?

Yes, he said, I think that he would rather suffer anything than entertain these false notions and live in this miserable manner.

Imagine once more, I said, such a one coming suddenly out of the sun to be replaced in his old situation; would he not be certain to have his eyes full of darkness?

To be sure, he said.

And if there were a contest, and he had to compete in measuring the shadows with the prisoners who had never moved out of the den, while his sight was still weak, and before his eyes had become steady (and the time which would be needed to acquire this new habit of sight might be very considerable), would he not be ridiculous? Men would say of him that he went up and down and he came without his eyes; and that it was better not even to think of ascending; and if any one tried to loose another and lead him up to the light, let them only catch the offender, and they would put him to death.

No question, he said.

This entire allegory, I said, you may now append, dear Glaucon, to the previous argument; the prison-house is the world of sight, the light of the fire is the sun, and you will not misapprehend me if you interpret the journey upwards to the ascent of the soul into the intellectual world according to my poor belief, which, at your desire, I have expressed—whether rightly or wrongly God knows. But, whether true or false, my opinion is that in the world of knowledge the idea of good appears last of all, and is seen only with an effort; and, when seen, is also inferred to be the universal author of all things beautiful and right, parent of light and of the lord of light in this visible world, and the immediate source of reason and truth in the intellectual; and that this is the power upon which he who would act rationally either in public or private life must have his eye fixed. . . . Moreover, I said, you must not wonder that those who attain to this beatific vision are unwilling to descend to human affairs; for their souls are ever hastening into the upper world where they desire to dwell; which desire of theirs is very natural, if our allegory may be trusted. . . . And is there anything surprising in one who passes from divine contemplations to the evil state of man, misbehaving himself in a ridiculous manner; if, while his eyes are blinking and before he has become accustomed to the surrounding darkness, he is compelled to fight in courts of law, or in other places, about the images or the shadows of images of justice, and is endeavouring to meet the conceptions of those who have never yet seen absolute justice?

Anything but surprising, he replied.

Any one who has common sense will remember that the bewilderments of the eyes are of two kinds, and arise from two causes, either from coming out of the light or from going into the light, which is true of the mind's eye, quite as much as of the bodily eye; and he who remembers this when he sees any one whose vision is perplexed and weak, will not be too ready to laugh; he will first ask whether that soul of man has come out of the brighter life, and is unable to see because unaccustomed to the dark, or having turned from darkness to the day is dazzled by excess of light. And he will count the one happy in his condition and state of being, and he will pity the other; or, if he have a mind to laugh at the soul which comes from below into the light, there will be more reason in this than in the laugh which greets him who returns from above out of the light into the den. . . .

But then, if I am right, certain professors of education must be wrong when they say that they can put a knowledge into the soul which was not there before, like sight into blind eyes. . . . Whereas, our argument shows that the power and capacity of learning exists in the soul already; and that just as the eye was unable to turn from darkness to light without the whole body, so too the instrument of knowledge can only by the movement of the whole soul be turned from the world of becoming into that of being, and learn by degrees to endure the sight of being, and of the brightest and best of being, or in other words, of the good. . . . And must there not be some art which will effect conversion in the easiest and quickest manner; not implanting the faculty of sight, for that exists already, but has been turned in the wrong direction, and is looking away from the truth?

Yes, he said, such an art may be presumed.

And whereas the other so-called virtues of the soul seem to be akin to bodily qualities, for even when they are not originally innate they can be implanted later by habit and exercise, the virtue of wisdom more than anything else contains a divine element which always remains, and by this conversion is rendered useful and profitable; or, on the other hand, hurtful and useless. Did you never observe the narrow intelligence flashing from the keen eye of a clever rogue—how eager he is, how clearly his paltry soul sees the way to his end; he is the reverse of blind, but his keen eyesight is forced into the service of evil, and he is mischievous in proportion to his cleverness.

Very true, he said.

But what if there had been a circumcision of such natures in the days of their youth; and they had been severed from those sensual pleasures, such as eating and drinking, which, like leaden weights, were attached to them at their birth, and which drag them down and turn the vision of their souls upon the things that are below—if, I say, they had been released from these impediments and turned in the opposite direction, the very same faculty in them would have seen the truth as keenly as they see what their eyes are turned to now. . . . And there is another thing which is likely, or rather a necessary inference from what has preceded, that neither the uneducated and uninformed of the truth, nor yet those who never make an end of their education, will be able masters of State; not the former, because they have no single aim of duty which is the rule of all their actions, private as well as public; nor the latter, because they will not act at all except upon compulsion, fancying that they are already dwelling apart in the islands of the blest.

Very true, he replied.

Then, I said, the business of us who are the founders of the State will be to compel the best minds to attain that knowledge which we have already shown to be the greatest of all—they must continue to ascend until they arrive at the good; but when they have ascended and seen enough we must not allow them to do as they do now.

What do you mean?

I mean that they remain in the upper world: but this must not be allowed; they must be made to descend again among the prisoners in the den, and partake of their labours and honours, whether they are worth having or not.

But is not this unjust? he said; ought we to give them a worse life, when they might have a better?

You have again forgotten, my friend, I said, the intention of the legislator, who did not aim at making any one class in the State happy above the rest; the happiness was to be in the whole State, and he held the citizens together by persuasion and necessity, making them benefactors of the State, and therefore benefactors of one another; to this end he created them, not to please themselves, but to be his instruments in binding up the State.

True, he said, I had forgotten.

Observe, Glaucon, that there will be no injustice in compelling our philosophers to have a care and providence of others; we shall explain to them that in other States, men of their class are not obliged to share in the toils of politics: and this is reasonable, for they grow up at their own sweet will, and the government would rather not have them. Being self-taught, they cannot be expected to show any gratitude for a culture which they have never received. But we have brought you into the world to be rulers of the hive, kings of yourselves and of the other citizens, and have educated you far better and more perfectly than they have been educated, and you are better able to share in the double duty. Wherefore each of you, when his turn comes, must go down to the general underground abode, and get the habit of seeing in the dark. When you have acquired the habit, you will see ten thousand times better than the inhabitants of the den, and you will know what the several images are, and what they represent, because you have seen the beautiful and just and good in their truth. And thus our State, which is also yours, will be a reality, and not a dream only, and will be administered in a spirit unlike that of other States, in which men fight with one another about shadows only and are distracted in the struggle for power, which in their eyes is a great good. Whereas the truth is that the State in which the rulers are most reluctant to govern is always the best and most quietly governed, and the State in which they are most eager, the worst. . . .

And will our pupils, when they hear this, refuse to take their turn at the toils of State, when they are allowed to spend the greater part of their time with one another in the heavenly light?

Impossible, he answered; for they are just men, and the commands which we impose upon them are just; there can be no doubt that every one of them will take office as a stern necessity, and not after the fashion of our present rulers of State.

Yes, my friend, I said; and there lies the point. You must contrive for your future rulers another and a better life than that of a ruler, and then you may have a well-ordered State; for only in the State which offers this, will they rule who are truly rich, not in silver and gold, but in virtue and wisdom, which are the true blessings of life. Whereas if they go to the administration of public affairs, poor and hungering after their own private advantage, thinking that hence they are to snatch the chief good, order there can never be; for they will be fighting about office, and the civil and domestic broils which thus arise will be the ruin of the rulers themselves and of the whole State.

Most true, he replied.

And the only life which looks down upon the life of political ambition is that of true philosophy. . . . And those who govern ought not to be lovers of the task. For, if they are, there will be rival lovers, and they will fight. . . .

Who then are those whom we shall compel to be guardians? Surely they will be the men who are wisest about affairs of State, and by whom the State is best administered, and who at the same time have other honours and another and a better life than that of politics. . . .

DESCARTES

René Descartes (1596–1650) is the father of modern philosophy. His Six Meditations, *first published in 1641, provoked so great a storm of controversy that a series of objections by many of Europe's most distinguished thinkers appeared subsequently, together with Descartes' replies. Descartes is known to modern students as the creator of cartesian, or analytic geometry, and his contributions to science and mathematics, as well as to philosophy, make him one of the truly seminal minds of the modern era.*

Descartes, writing at the beginning of the era of modern science, is more concerned with appearance and reality in relation to our knowledge of physics and mathematics than he is with the choice between social involvement and philosophical contemplation. In the first of his Six Meditations, *he throws out a challenge to the traditional authorities of the established universities: Is there anything in all your books and lectures of which I can be absolutely certain? Why should I believe the theories I read in physics books or historical narratives? Indeed, why should I believe that there is any world of planets and people and houses and horses at all? Can I trust the theorems of Euclid's geometry? Is there a God? Is there anything at all?*

For Descartes, the crucial problem is to show the existence of a real world corresponding to the appearances of my subjective experience. As Plato throws doubt upon the value and meaningfulness of politics, so Descartes raises serious questions about the enterprise of science. Men may go right on performing scientific experiments without being bothered by Descartes' doubts, just as many Athenians in Plato's day persisted in the ordinary pursuit of politics, despite his theories. Still, what keeps a scientist going when his experiments are negative and his theories don't work is the faith that he is adding to man's knowledge of what the universe really is. To a student about to set out on a career in science, therefore, Descartes' sceptical doubts should raise some important and fundamental questions.

The Method of Doubt

Meditation I

OF THE THINGS OF WHICH WE MAY DOUBT

Several years have now elapsed since I first became aware that I had accepted, even from my youth, many false opinions for true, and that consequently what I afterwards based on such principles was highly doubtful; and from that time I was convinced of the necessity of undertaking once in my life to rid myself of all the opinions I had adopted, and of commencing anew the work of building from the foundation, if I desired to establish a firm and abiding superstructure in the sciences. But as this enterprise appeared to me to be one of great magnitude, I waited until I had attained an age so mature as to leave me no hope that at any stage of life more advanced I should be better able to execute my design. On this account, I have delayed so long that I should henceforth consider I was doing wrong were I still to consume in deliberation any of the time that now remains for action. Today, then, since I have opportunely freed my mind from all cares [and am happily disturbed by no passions], and since I am in the secure possession of leisure in a peaceable retirement, I will at length apply myself earnestly and freely to the general overthrow of all my former opinions. But, to this end, it will not be necessary for me to show that the whole of these are false—a point, perhaps, which I shall never reach; but as even now my reason convinces me that I ought not the less carefully to withhold belief from what is not entirely certain and indubitable, than from what is manifestly false, it will be sufficient to justify the rejection of the whole if I shall find in each some ground for doubt. Nor for this purpose will it be necessary even to deal with each belief individually, which would be truly an endless labour; but, as the removal from below of the foundation necessarily involves the downfall of the whole edifice, I will at once approach the criticism of the principles on which all my former beliefs rested.

All that I have, up to this moment, accepted as possessed of the highest truth and certainty, I received either from or through the senses. I observed, however, that these sometimes misled us; and it is the part of prudence not to place absolute confidence in that by which we have even once been deceived.

But it may be said, perhaps, that, although the senses occasionally mislead us respecting minute objects, and such as are so far removed from us as to be beyond the reach of close observation, there are yet many other of their informations (presentations), of the truth of which it is manifestly impossible to doubt; as for example, that I am in this place, seated by the fire, clothed in a winter dressing-gown, that I hold in my hands this piece of paper, with other intimations of the same nature. But how could I deny that I possess these

From *Meditations on the First Philosophy* by René Descartes, trans. by John Veitch.

hands and this body, and withal escape being classed with persons in a state of insanity, whose brains are so disordered and clouded by dark bilious vapours as to cause them pertinaciously to assert that they are monarchs when they are in the greatest poverty; or clothed [in gold] and purple when destitute of any covering; or that their head is made of clay, their body of glass, or that they are gourds? I should certainly be not less insane than they, were I to regulate my procedure according to examples so extravagant.

Though this be true, I must nevertheless here consider that I am a man, and that, consequently, I am in the habit of sleeping, and representing to myself in dreams those same things, or even sometimes others less probable, which the insane think are presented to them in their waking moments. How often have I dreamt that I was in these familiar circumstances—that I was dressed, and occupied this place by the fire, when I was lying undressed in bed? At the present moment, however, I certainly look upon this paper with eyes wide awake; the head which I now move is not asleep; I extend this hand consciously and with express purpose, and I perceive it; the occurrences in sleep are not so distinct as all this. But I cannot forget that, at other times, I have been deceived in sleep by similar illusions; and, attentively considering those cases, I perceive so clearly that there exist no certain marks by which the state of waking can ever be distinguished from sleep, that I feel greatly astonished; and in amazement I almost persuade myself that I am now dreaming.

Let us suppose, then, that we are dreaming, and that all these particulars —namely, the opening of the eyes, the motion of the head, the forth-putting of the hands—are merely illusions; and even that we really possess neither an entire body nor hands such as we see. Nevertheless, it must be admitted at least that the objects which appear to us in sleep are, as it were, painted representations which could not have been formed unless in the likeness of realities; and, therefore, that those general objects, at all events—namely, eyes, a head, hands, and an entire body—are not simply imaginary, but really existent. For, in truth, painters themselves, even when they study to represent sirens and satyrs by forms the most fantastic and extraordinary, cannot bestow upon them natures absolutely new, but can only make a certain medley of the members of different animals; or if they chance to imagine something so novel that nothing at all similar has ever been seen before, and such as is, therefore, purely fictitious and absolutely false, it is at least certain that the colours of which this is composed are real.

And on the same principle, although these general objects, viz. [a body], eyes, a head, hands, and the like, be imaginary, we are nevertheless absolutely necessitated to admit the reality of at least some other objects still more simple and universal than these, of which, just as of certain real colours, all those images of things, whether true and real, or false and fantastic, that are found in our consciousness (*cogitatio*), are formed.

To this class of objects seem to belong corporeal nature in general and its extension; the figure of extended things, their quantity or magnitude, and their number, as also the place in, and the time during, which they exist, and other things of the same sort. We will not, therefore, perhaps reason illegitimately if we conclude from this that physics, astronomy, medicine, and all the other sciences of the same class, which regard merely the simplest and most general objects, and scarcely inquire whether or not these are really existent, contain somewhat that is certain and indubitable: for whether I am awake or dreaming, it remains true that two and three make five, and that a square has but four sides; nor does it seem possible that truths so apparent can ever fall under a suspicion of falsity [or incertitude].

Nevertheless, the belief that there is a God who is all-powerful, and who created me, such as I am, has for a long time obtained steady possession of my mind. How, then, do I know that he has not arranged that there should be neither earth, nor sky, nor any extended thing, nor figure, nor magnitude, nor place, providing at the same time, however, for [the rise in me of the perceptions of all these objects, and] the persuasion that these do not exist otherwise than as I perceive them? And further, as I sometimes think that others are in error respecting matters of which they believe themselves to possess a perfect knowledge, how do I know that I am not also deceived each time I add together two and three, or number the sides of a square, or form some judgment still more simple, if more simple indeed can be imagined? But perhaps Deity has not been willing that I should be thus deceived, for he is said to be supremely good. If, however, it were repugnant to the goodness of Deity to have created me subject to constant deception, it would seem likewise to be contrary to his goodness to allow me to be occasionally deceived; and yet it is clear that this is permitted. Some, indeed, might perhaps be found who would be disposed rather to deny the existence of a being so powerful than to believe that there is nothing certain. But let us for the present refrain from opposing this opinion, and grant that all which is here said of a Deity is fabulous: nevertheless, in whatever way it be supposed that I reached the state in which I exist, whether by fate, or chance, or by an endless series of antecedents and consequents, or by any other means, it is clear (since to be deceived and to err is a certain defect) that the probability of my being so imperfect as to be the constant victim of deception will be increased exactly in proportion as the power possessed by the cause, to which they assign my origin, is lessened. To these reasonings I have assuredly nothing to reply, but am constrained at last to avow that there is nothing at all that I formerly believed to be true of which it is impossible to doubt, and that not through thoughtlessness or levity, but from cogent and maturely considered reasons; so that henceforward, if I desire to discover anything certain, I ought not the less carefully to refrain from assenting to those same opinions than to what might be shown to be manifestly false.

But it is not sufficient to have made these observations; care must be taken likewise to keep them in remembrance. For those old and customary opinions perpetually recur—long and familiar usage giving them the right of occupying my mind, even almost against my will, and subduing my belief; nor will I lose the habit of deferring to them and confiding in them so long as I shall consider them to be what in truth they are, viz., opinions to some extent doubtful, as I have already shown, but still highly probable, and such as it is much more reasonable to believe than deny. It is for this reason I am persuaded that I shall not be doing wrong, if, taking an opposite judgment of deliberate design, I become my own deceiver, by supposing, for a time, that all those opinions are entirely false and imaginary, until at length, having thus balanced my old by my new prejudices, my judgment shall no longer be turned aside by perverted usage from the path that may conduct to the perception of truth. For I am assured that, meanwhile, there will arise neither peril nor error from this course, and that I cannot for the present yield too much to distrust, since the end I now seek is not action but knowledge.

I will suppose, then, not that Deity, who is sovereignly good and the fountain of truth, but that some malignant demon, who is at once exceedingly potent and deceitful, has employed all his artifice to deceive me; I will suppose that the sky, the air, the earth, colours, figures, sounds, and all external things, are nothing better than the illusions of dreams, by means of which this being has laid snares for my credulity; I will consider myself as without hands, eyes, flesh, blood, or any of the senses, and as falsely believing that I am possessed of these; I will continue resolutely fixed in this belief, and if indeed by this means it be not in my power to arrive at the knowledge of truth, I shall at least do what is in my power, viz. [suspend my judgment], and guard with settled purpose against giving my assent to what is false, and being imposed upon by this deceiver, whatever be his power and artifice.

But this undertaking is arduous, and a certain indolence insensibly leads me back to my ordinary course of life; and just as the captive, who, perchance, was enjoying in his dreams an imaginery liberty, when he begins to suspect that it is but a vision, dreads awakening, and conspires with the agreeable illusions that the deception may be prolonged; so I, of my own accord, fall back into the train of my former beliefs, and fear to arouse myself from my slumber, lest the time of laborious wakefulness that would succeed this quiet rest, in place of bringing any light of day, should prove inadequate to dispel the darkness that will arise from the difficulties that have now been raised.

KANT

For nearly two centuries after Descartes published the Meditations, *the greatest philosophical minds of Europe struggled to give a proof of the reality of the world of science. The search culminated in the systematic philosophical theories of the great German thinker Immanuel Kant (1724–1804). Kant's philosophy combines Plato's concern for moral spiritual questions with Descartes' interest in the foundation of modern science. One might say that Kant brought about a compromise between the two, for although he offered a proof that science and mathematics really are genuine knowledge, he agreed with Plato that the spatio-temporal world of the physicist is merely the appearance of a realm of things more real still. Nevertheless, Kant cannot agree with Plato's claim that reason can know the truly real. In the end, he insists that our science and mathematics concern only appearances. Such insight as we have into ultimate reality is made possible through moral action rather than through rational contemplation.*

Kant published his greatest work, the Critique of Pure Reason, *in 1781, after almost a lifetime of thought and preparation. Long and complex though it is, the* Critique *is only the first of a series of volumes in which Kant set forth his systematic critique of man's intellectual powers. Because of the difficulty of the work, Kant wrote a short, introductory exposition of the principal ideas in the* Critique, *which he called* Prolegomena to any Future Metaphysics. *In this section we have included one selection from the* Critique *and one from the* Prolegomena.

In these two selections Kant sets forth the doctrine which he calls the "transcendental ideality and empirical reality" of things in space and time. According to him, the physical universe is an appearance of ultimately real things-in-themselves whose nature we can never know. But though the spatio-temporal world is thus "transcendentally ideal," still it is empirically real, for physical objects are not mere illusions or hallucinations. This sounds like a flat contradiction, of course. Either the physical world is real or it is not, we want to insist. But Kant maintains that there is a middle ground between Cartesian scepticism and the naive realism of natural science.

Don't be surprised if Kant's theory still seems partially obscure to you after reading these two selections. Sometimes you must study a great deal of a philosopher's writings before his thought is completely clear.

Empirical Reality and Transcendental Ideality

. . . Space does not represent any property of things in themselves, nor does it represent them in their relation to one another. That is to say, space does not represent any determination that attaches to the objects themselves, and which remains even when abstraction has been made of all the subjective conditions of intuition. For no determinations, whether absolute or relative, can be intuited prior to the existence of the things to which they belong, and none, therefore, can be intuited *a priori*.

Space is nothing but the form of all appearances of outer sense. It is the subjective condition of sensibility, under which alone outer intuition is possible for us. Since, then, the receptivity of the subject, its capacity to be affected by objects, must necessarily precede all intuitions of these objects, it can readily be understood how the form of all appearances can be given prior to all actual perceptions, and so exist in the mind *a priori*, and how, as a pure intuition, in which all objects must be determined, it can contain, prior to all experience, principles which determine the relations of these objects.

It is, therefore, solely from the human standpoint that we can speak of space, of extended things, etc. If we depart from the subjective condition under which alone we can have outer intuition, namely, liability to be affected by objects, the representation of space stands for nothing whatsoever. This predicate can be ascribed to things only in so far as they appear to us, that is, only to objects of sensibility. The constant form of this receptivity, which we term sensibility, is a necessary condition of all the relations in which objects can be intuited as outside us; and if we abstract from these objects, it is a pure intuition, and bears the name of space. Since we cannot treat the special conditions of sensibility as conditions of the possibility of things, but only of their appearances, we can indeed say that space comprehends all things that appear to us as external, but not all things in themselves, by whatever subject they are intuited, or whether they be intuited or not. For we cannot judge in regard to the intuitions of other thinking beings, whether they are bound by the same conditions as those which limit their intuition and which for us are universally valid. If we add to the concept of the subject of a judgment the limitation under which the judgment is made, the judgment is then unconditionally valid. The proposition, that all things are side by side in space, is valid under the limitation that these things are viewed as objects of our sensible intuition. If, now, I add the condition to the concept, and say that all things, as outer appearances, are side by side in space, the rule is valid universally and without limitation. Our exposition therefore establishes the *reality*, that is, the

From *The Critique of Pure Reason* by Immanuel Kant, trans. by Norman Kemp Smith. New York: St. Martin's Press, Inc. Reprinted by permission of St. Martin's Press, Inc., Macmillan & Co., and The Macmillan Company of Canada Limited.

objective validity, of space in respect of whatever can be presented to us outwardly as object, but also at the same time the *ideality* of space in respect of
things when they are considered in themselves through reason, that is, without
regard to the constitution of our sensibility. We assert, then, the *empirical
reality* of space, as regards all possible outer experience; and yet at the same
time we assert its *transcendental ideality*—in other words, that it is nothing at
all, immediately we withdraw the above condition, namely, its limitation to
possible experience, and so look upon it as something that underlies things in
themselves.

With the sole exception of space there is no subjective representation, referring to something *outer*, which could be entitled [at once] objective [and]
a priori. For[1] there is no other subjective representation from which we can
derive *a priori* synthetic propositions, as we can from intuition in space.
Strictly speaking, therefore, these other representations have no ideality, although they agree with the representation of space in this respect, that they
belong merely to the subjective constitution of our manner of sensibility, for
instance, of sight, hearing, touch, as in the case of the sensations of colours,
sounds, and heat, which, since they are mere sensations and not intuitions, do
not of themselves yield knowledge of any object, least of all any *a priori*
knowledge.

The above remark is intended only to guard anyone from supposing that
the ideality of space as here asserted can be illustrated by examples so altogether insufficient as colours, taste, etc. For these cannot rightly be regarded
as properties of things, but only as changes in the subject, changes which may,
indeed, be different for different men. In such examples as these, that which
originally is itself only appearance, for instance, a rose, is being treated by the

---

[1] In the First Edition of 1781 Kant also drew the following distinction between appearance and reality within the world of sense experience:

This subjective condition of all outer appearances cannot, therefore, be compared
to any other. The taste of a wine does not belong to the objective determinations of wine,
not even if by the wine as an object we mean the wine as appearance, but to the special
constitution of sense in the subject that tastes it. Colours are not properties of the bodies to
the intuition of which they are attached, but only modifications of the sense of sight, which
is affected in a certain manner by light. Space, on the other hand, as condition of outer
objects, necessarily belongs to their appearance of intuition. Taste and colours are not
necessary conditions under which alone objects can be for us objects of the senses. They
are connected with the appearances only as effects accidentally added by the particular
constitution of the sense organs. Accordingly, they are not *a priori* representations, but are
grounded in sensation, and, indeed, in the case of taste, even upon feeling (pleasure and
pain), as an effect of sensation. Further, no one can have *a priori* a representation of a
colour or of any taste; whereas, since space concerns only the pure form of intuition, and
therefore involves no sensation whatsoever, and nothing empirical, all kinds and determinations of space can and must be represented *a priori*, if concepts of figures and of their
relations are to arise. Through space alone is it possible that things should be outer objects
to us.

empirical understanding as a thing in itself, which, nevertheless, in respect of its colour, can appear differently to every observer. The transcendental concept of appearances in space, on the other hand, is a critical reminder that nothing intuited in space is a thing in itself, that space is not a form inhering in things in themselves as their intrinsic property, that objects in themselves are quite unknown to us, and that what we call outer objects are nothing but mere representations of our sensibility, the form of which is space. The true correlate of sensibility, the thing in itself, is not known, and cannot be known, through these representations; and in experience no question is ever asked in regard to it. . . .

When I say that the intuition of outer objects and the self-intuition of the mind alike represent the objects and the mind, in space and in time, as they affect our senses, that is, as they appear, I do not mean to say that these objects are a mere *illusion*. For in an appearance the objects, nay even the properties that we ascribe to them, are always regarded as something actually given. Since, however, in the relation of the given object to the subject, such properties depend upon the mode of intuition of the subject, this object as *appearance* is to be distinguished from itself as object *in itself*. Thus when I maintain that the quality of space and of time, in conformity with which, as a condition of their existence, I posit both bodies and my own soul, lies in my mode of intuition and not in those objects in themselves, I am not saying that bodies merely *seem* to be outside me, or that my soul only *seems* to be given in my self-consciousness. It would be my own fault, if out of that which I ought to reckon as appearance, I made mere illusion.[2] That does not follow as a consequence of our principle of the ideality of all our sensible intuitions—quite the contrary. It is only if we ascribe *objective reality* to these forms of representation, that it becomes impossible for us to prevent everything being thereby transformed into mere *illusion*. For if we regard space and time as properties which, if they are to be possible at all, must be found in things in themselves, and if we reflect on the absurdities in which we are then involved, in that two infinite things, which are not substances, nor anything actually inhering in substances, must yet have existence, nay, must be the necessary condition of the existence of all things, and moreover must continue to exist, even although all existing things be removed,—we cannot blame the good

[2] The predicates of the appearance can be ascribed to the object itself, in relation to our sense, for instance, the red colour or the scent to the rose. That which, while inseparable from the representation of the object, is not to be met with in the object in itself, but always in its relation to the subject, is appearance. Accordingly the predicates of space and time are rightly ascribed to the objects of the senses, as such; and in this there is no illusion. On the other hand, if I ascribe redness to the rose *in itself* or extension to all outer objects *in themselves*, without paying regard to the determinate relation of these objects to the subject, and without limiting my judgment to that relation, illusion then first arises.

Berkeley for degrading bodies to mere illusion. Nay, even our own existence, in being made thus dependent upon the self-subsistent reality of non-entity, such as time, would necessarily be changed with it into sheer illusion—an absurdity of which no one has yet been guilty. . . .

The Bounds of Pure Reason

Having adduced the clearest arguments, it would be absurd for us to hope that we can know more of any object, than belongs to the possible experience of it, or lay claim to the least atom of knowledge about anything not assumed to be an object of possible experience, which would determine it according to the constitution it has in itself. For how could we determine anything in this way, since time, space, and the categories, and still more all the concepts formed by empirical experience or perception in the sensible world (*Anschauung*), have and can have no other use, than to make experience possible. And if this condition is omitted from the pure concepts of the understanding, they do not determine any object, and have no meaning whatever.

But it would be on the other hand a still greater absurdity if we conceded no things in themselves, or set up our experience for the only possible mode of knowing things, our way of beholding (*Anschauung*) them in space and in time for the only possible way, and our discursive understanding for the archetype of every possible understanding; in fact if we wished to have the principles of the possibility of experience considered universal conditions of things in themselves.

Our principles, which limit the use of reason to possible experience, might in this way become transcendent, and the limits of our reason be set up as limits of the possibility of things in themselves (as Hume's dialogues may illustrate), if a careful critique did not guard the bounds of our reason with respect to its empirical use, and set a limit to its pretensions. Scepticism originally arose from metaphysics and its licentious dialectics. At first it might, merely to favor the empirical use of reason, announce everything that transcends this use as worthless and deceitful; but by and by, when it was perceived that the very same principles that are used in experience, insensibly, and apparently with the same right, led still further than experience extends, then men began to doubt even the propositions of experience. But here there is no danger; for common sense will doubtless always assert its rights. A certain

From *Prolegomena to Any Future Metaphysics* by Immanuel Kant, trans. by Dr. Paul Carus.

confusion, however, arose in science which cannot determine how far reason is to be trusted, and why only so far and no further, and this confusion can only be cleared up and all future relapses obviated by a formal determination, on principle, of the boundary of the use of our reason.

We cannot indeed, beyond all possible experience, form a definite notion of what things in themselves may be. Yet we are not at liberty to abstain entirely from inquiring into them; for experience never satisfies reason fully, but in answering questions, refers us further and further back, and leaves us dissatisfied with regard to their complete solution. This any one may gather from the Dialectics of pure reason, which therefore has its good subjective grounds. Having acquired, as regards the nature of our soul, a clear conception of the subject, and having come to the conviction, that its manifestations cannot be explained materialistically, who can refrain from asking what the soul really is, and, if no concept of experience suffices for the purpose, from accounting for it by a concept of reason (that of a simple immaterial being), though we cannot by any means prove its objective reality? Who can satisfy himself with mere empirical knowledge in all the cosmological questions of the duration and of the quantity of the world, of freedom or of natural necessity, since every answer given on principles of experience begets a fresh question, which likewise requires its answer and thereby clearly shows the insufficiency of all physical modes of explanation to satisfy reason? Finally, who does not see in the thorough-going contingency and dependence of all his thoughts and assumptions on mere principles of experience, the impossibility of stopping there? And who does not feel himself compelled, notwithstanding all interdictions against losing himself in transcendent ideas, to seek rest and contentment beyond all the concepts of a Being, the possibility of which we cannot conceive, but at the same time cannot be refuted, because it relates to a mere being of the understanding, and without it reason must needs remain forever dissatisfied?

Bounds (in extended beings) always presuppose a space existing outside a certain definite place, and inclosing it; limits do not require this, but are mere negations, which affect a quantity, so far as it is not absolutely complete. But our reason, as it were, sees in its surroundings a space for the cognition of things in themselves, though we can never have definite notions of them, and are limited to appearances only.

As long as the cognition of reason is homogeneous, definite bounds to it are inconceivable. In mathematics and in natural philosophy human reason admits of limits, but not of bounds, viz., that something indeed lies without it, at which it can never arrive, but not that it will at any point find completion in its internal progress. The enlarging of our views in mathematics, and the possibility of new discoveries, are infinite; and the same is the case with the discovery of new properties of nature, of new powers and laws, by continued experience and its rational combination. But limits cannot be mistaken here, for mathematics refers to appearances only, and what cannot be an object of sensuous contemplation, such as the concepts of metaphysics and morals, lies entirely without its sphere, and it can never lead to them; neither does it require them. It is therefore not a continual progress and an approximation towards these sciences, and there is not, as it were, any point or line of contact. Natural science will never reveal to us the internal constitution of things, which though not appearance, yet can serve as the ultimate ground of explaining appearance. Nor does that science require this for its physical explanations. Nay, even if such grounds should be offered from other sources (for instance, the influence of immaterial beings), they must be rejected and not used in the progress of its explanations. For these explanations must only be grounded upon that which as an object of sense can belong to experience, and be brought into connexion with our actual perceptions and empirical laws.

But metaphysics leads us towards bounds in the dialectical attempts of pure reason (not undertaken arbitrarily or wantonly, but stimulated thereto by the nature of reason itself). And the transcendental Ideas, as they do not admit of evasion, and are never capable of realisation, serve to point out to us actually not only the bounds of the pure use of reason, but also the way to determine them. Such is the end and the use of this natural predisposition of our reason, which has brought forth metaphysics as its favorite child, whose generation, like every other in the world, is not to be ascribed to blind chance, but to an original germ, wisely organised for great ends. For metaphysics, in its fundamental features, perhaps more than any other science, is placed in us by nature itself, and cannot be considered in the production of an arbitrary choice or a casual enlargement in the progress of experience from which it is quite disparate.

Reason with all its concepts and laws of the understanding, which suffice for empirical use, i.e., within the sensible world, finds in itself no satisfaction because ever-recurring questions deprive us of all hope of their complete solution. The transcendental ideas, which have that completion in view, are such problems of reason. But it sees clearly, that the sensuous world cannot contain this completion, neither consequently can all the concepts, which serve merely for understanding the world of sense, such as space and time, and whatever we have adduced under the name of pure concepts of the understanding. The sensuous world is nothing but a chain of appearances connected according to the universal laws; it has therefore no subsistence by itself; it is not the thing in itself, and consequently must point to that which contains the basis of this experience, to beings which cannot be cognised merely as phenomena, but as things in themselves. In the cognition of them alone reason can hope to satisfy its desire of completeness in proceeding from the conditioned to its conditions. . . .

And thus there remains our original proposition, which is the *résumé* of the whole *Critique:* "that reason by all its *a priori* principles never teaches us anything more than objects of possible experience, and even of these nothing more than can be cognised in experience." But this limitation does not prevent reason leading us to the objective boundary of experience, viz., to the reference to something which is not in itself an object of experience, but is the ground of all experience. Reason does not however teach us anything concerning the thing in itself: it only instructs us as regards its own complete and highest use in the field of possible experience. But this is all that can be reasonably desired in the present case, and with which we have cause to be satisfied. . . .

KIERKEGAARD

Sören Kierkegaard (1813–1855) is one of the most provocative thinkers of the nineteenth century. In a number of witty and challenging books, many of them published under strange pseudonyms, the Danish writer attacked the religious complacency which, he believed, afflicted so many Christians in Europe. The Concluding Unscientific Postscript, *his major philosophical work, is a sober presentation of this analysis of the essential subjectivity of the individual conscious man. Despite its formidable tone, the book is full of sly digs at the pomposities of the system-building professors of philosophy whom Kierkegaard hated. Even the title is a joke, for the book is presented as a 600-page "postscript" to a brief, 80-page essay,* The Philosophical Fragments *by Kierkegaard.*

Kierkegaard goes against more than two thousand years of Western philosophy by denying the link between objectivity and reality. For Plato, Descartes, Kant, and many others, the real was the objective, the "out-there," the realm of things that could be known by many thinkers in common. Kierkegaard insists that the inward subjectivity of individual consciousness is, for each man, the true reality. My awareness of myself, my fear of eventual death, my anxious concern for the future of my soul, and my desparate faith in the redeeming promise of God—these are truly real to me. All else—the public world of business, politics, churches, universities—is a mere aesthetic possibility.

Kierkegaard reacts strongly against the extremely dry and academic philosophical systems elaborated by Hegel and his followers. He makes fun of serious professors who construct huge, multivolume theories of the entire universe and yet somehow manage to forget about their own reality as individual persons.

Shunning the political arena like Plato, Kierkegaard refuses to place his trust in reason, insisting rather on a leap of faith which will place the individual in a perilous, uncertain relationship to God. As the father of the school of philosophy known as Christian Existentialism, Kierkegaard has very powerfully influenced those modern Protestants who emphasize the subjective quality of religious faith rather than relying upon a body of rational theological doctrine.

The Reality of Inwardness

POSSIBILITY AS HIGHER THAN REALITY—REALITY AS HIGHER THAN POSSIBILITY
POETIC AND INTELLECTUAL IDEALITY—ETHICAL IDEALITY

Aristotle remarks in his *Poetics* that poetry is higher than history, because history merely tells us what has happened, while poetry tells us what might have happened and ought to have happened, i.e. poetry commands the possible. From the poetic and intellectual standpoint, possibility is higher than reality, the aesthetic and the intellectual being disinterested. There is only one interest, the interest in existence; disinterestedness is therefore an expression for indifference to reality. This indifference is forgotten in the Cartesian *cogito ergo sum*, which injects a disturbing element into the disinterestedness of the intellectual and affronts speculative thought, as if it were instrumental to something else. I think, *ergo* I think; but whether I exist or it exists in the sense of an actuality, so that "I" means an individually existing human being and "it" means a definite particular something, is a matter of infinite indifference. That the content of my thought exists in the conceptual sense needs no proof, or needs no argument to prove it, since it is proved by my thinking. But as soon as I proceed to impose a teleology upon my thought, and bring it into relation with something else, interest begins to play a rôle in the matter. The instant this happens the ethical is present, and absolves me from any further responsibility in proving my own existence. It forbids me to draw a conclusion that is ethically deceitful and metaphysically unclear, by imposing upon me the duty of existing.

In our own day the ethical tends more and more to be ignored. This has had among other things the harmful consequence that poetry and speculative thought have become unsettled, and have deserted the lofty disinterestedness of the possible in order to reach out for reality. Instead of assigning to each sphere its own proper scale of values, a double confusion has been introduced. Poetry makes one attempt after the other to play the rôle of reality, which is entirely unpoetical. Speculative thought repeatedly attempts to reach reality within its own domain, assuring us that whatever is thought is real, that thought is not only capable of thinking reality but of bestowing it, while the truth is the direct opposite; and simultaneously a forgetfulness of what it means to exist, extends itself more and more. The age becomes increasingly unreal, and the people in it; hence these substitutes to make up for what is lacking. The ethical tends more and more to be abandoned; the life of the individual not only becomes poetic, but is unsettled by an abnormal historical conscious-

From *Concluding Unscientific Postscript*, by Sören Kierkegaard, trans. by David F. Swenson and Walter Lowrie (Copyright 1941 by Princeton University Press. Princeton Paperback, 1968), pp. 282–291. Reprinted by permission of Princeton University Press and the American Scandinavian Foundation.

ness that prevents him from existing ethically. It follows that reality must be provided in other ways. But this spurious reality resembles what would happen if a generation and its members had become prematurely old, and sought to obtain an artificial youth. Instead of recognizing that ethical existence is reality, the age has grown overwhelmingly contemplative, so that not only is everyone engrossed in contemplation, but this has finally become falsified as if it were reality. We smile at the life of the cloister, and yet no hermit ever lived so unreal a life as is common nowadays. For the hermit abstracted from the entire world, but he did not abstract from himself. We know how to describe the fantastic situation of the cloister, far from the haunts of men, in the solitude of the forest, in the distant blue of the horizon; but we take no notice of the fantastic situation of pure thought. And yet, the pathetic unreality of the hermit is far preferable to the comic unreality of the pure thinker; and the passionate forgetfulness of the hermit, which takes from him the entire world, is much to be preferred to the comical distraction of the philosopher engrossed in the contemplation of universal history, which leads him to forget himself.

Ethically regarded, reality is higher than possibility. The ethical proposes to do away with the disinterestedness of the possible, by making existence the infinite interest. It therefore opposes every confusing attempt, like that of proposing ethically to *contemplate* humanity and the world. Such ethical contemplation is impossible, since there is only one kind of ethical contemplation, namely, self-contemplation. Ethics closes immediately about the individual, and demands that he exist ethically; it does not make a parade of millions, or of generations of men; it does not take humanity in the lump, any more than the police arrest humanity at large. The ethical is concerned with particular human beings, and with each and every one of them by himself. If God knows how many hairs there are on a man's head, the ethical knows how many human beings there are; and its enumeration is not in the interest of a total sum, but for the sake of each individual. The ethical requirement is imposed upon each individual, and when it judges, it judges each individual by himself; only a tyrant or an impotent man is content to decimate. The ethical lays hold of each individual and demands that he refrain from all contemplation, especially of humanity and the world; for the ethical, as being the internal, cannot be observed by an outsider. It can be realized only by the individual subject, who alone can know what it is that moves within him. This ethical reality is the only reality which does not become a mere possibility through being known, and which can be known only through being thought; for it is the individual's own reality. Before it became a reality it was known by him in the form of a conceived reality, and hence as a possibility. But in the case of another person's reality he could have no knowledge about it until he conceived it in coming to know it, which means that he transformed it from a reality into a possibility.

To other philosophers, however, this entire line of reasoning seems a mistake. The real, they say, is the enduring, the unchanging, that which remains as all else alters and passes away. Repelled by the ceaseless alteration of the visible world, by the transience of our perceptions, philosophers have sought another realm in which eternal, changeless, "truly real" objects can be found. Some philosophers identify this realm with God, others with the abstract entities of mathematics and logic.

Such a conception of reality, like the first, has its difficulties. Numbers and logical truth may be eternal, at least in the sense that they do not come into existence and change like physical objects. But philosophers from Plato's time to the present day have had trouble explaining just what sort of existence can be attributed to abstract entities. The nature of God is also mysterious, precisely because He is so often described as being totally **unlike** anything in our experience.

Yet a third view of the real construes it as whatever is most forcefully and immediately present to the self, whether that be intense sensation, as Timothy Leary would claim, or the inward awareness of one's own selfhood, as the existentialist Sören Kierkegaard maintains. There is a kind of philosophical underground which over the centuries has defended the claims of subjectivity against the dominant philosophical tendency to identify reality with the objective, the public, the impersonal. The radical scepticism expressed by René Descartes in our selection from his **Meditations** has contributed to that counterview, despite Descartes' own intentions. The more doubtful are my beliefs about God, the world, and other persons, the more I am thrown back on the immediate, undeniable reality of subjective consciousness.

PLATO

The Republic, *from which this selection is taken, is the greatest work of the Athenian philosopher Plato* (427?–347 B.C.), *whose Dialogues have preserved for us the thought and character of his teacher Socrates. The* Republic *is a discussion of the nature of justice, but in its pages virtually all the major questions of philosophy are raised and debated. After developing an elaborate analogy between the healthy personality and the healthy society, Socrates asks his two interlocutors, Glaucon and Adeimantus, how such a just and well-ordered society can be brought about? His answer is the famous Platonic paradox: Philosophers must become kings, or else kings must become philosophers! The least political men must be placed at the head of the state.*

Instead of defending his doctrine by factual and moral arguments alone, Plato attempts to strengthen his case by appeal to a metaphysical account of the nature of appearance and reality. The visible world of objects and persons, Plato claims, is mere appearance, not completely real and hence not worthy of our loyalty or concern. The real world, he says, is a realm of immaterial, eternal Forms, or Ideas, which find only a pale reflection in the objects of our senses.

Thus far, Plato might seem to agree with Leary rather than Lettvin. But Plato shuns the mystic's path of dreams and visions. Instead, he, like Lettvin, counsels us to perfect our rational powers through the abstract study of mathematics and philosophy. In that way, he thinks, the best of us may some day grasp the essence of the highest Form of all, the Idea of the Good. The just state will be ruled by an elite of those who have achieved this pinnacle of philosophical knowledge.

All this might seem a trifle "academic," and yet Plato himself was forced to make a crucial life choice on the basis of just such theoretical considerations. As a member of one of the wealthiest and most powerful families in Athens, he was expected to take an active part in the political life of his community. Nevertheless, all his deepest convictions pulled him toward a life of quiet contemplation and philosophical discussion with a circle of friends and disciples. In middle life, he faced the problem squarely and opted for philosophy rather than politics. Needless to say, his decision must have been strongly influenced by his personal tastes and preferences, but the metaphysical theory set forth in the selection here played an indispensable role.

A very similar choice faces many young men and women in

With respect to every reality external to myself, I can get hold of it only through thinking it. In order to get hold of it really, I should have to be able to make myself into the other, the acting individual, and make the foreign reality my own reality, which is impossible. For if I make the foreign reality my own, this does not mean that I become the other through knowing his reality, but it means that I acquire a new reality, which belongs to me as opposed to him.

When I think something which I propose to do but have not yet done, the content of this conception, no matter how exact it may be, if it be ever so much entitled to be called a conceived reality, is a possibility. Conversely, when I think about something that another has done, and so conceive a reality, I lift this given reality out of the real and set it into the possible; for a conceived reality is a possibility, and is higher than reality from the standpoint of thought, but not from the standpoint of reality. This implies that there is no immediate relationship, ethically, between subject and subject. When I understand another person, his reality is for me a possibility, and in its aspect of possibility this conceived reality is related to me precisely as the thought of something I have not done is related to the doing of it.

Frater Taciturnus, in *Stages on Life's Way*, says that one who cannot understand, with reference to the same matter, the conclusion *ab posse ad esse* as well as he can understand the conclusion *ab esse ad posse*, does not lay hold of the ideality involved; that is, he does not understand it, does not think it. (The question concerns, that is, the understanding of a foreign reality.) If the thinker with a resolving *posse* comes upon an *esse* that he cannot resolve, he must say: this is something I cannot think. He thus suspends his thinking with respect to it; and if he nevertheless persists in trying to establish a relationship to this reality as a reality, he does not do so by way of thought, but paradoxically. (The reader is asked to remember from the preceding the definition there given of faith in the Socratic sense, *sensu laxiori* and not *sensu strictissimo*: an objective uncertainty, uncertain because the resolving *posse* has come upon a refractory *esse*, held fast in passionate inwardness.)

In connection with the aesthetic and the intellectual, to ask whether this or that is real, whether it really has happened, is a misunderstanding. So to ask betrays a failure to conceive the aesthetic and the intellectual ideality as a possibility, and forgets that to determine a scale of values for the aesthetic and the intellectual in this manner, is like ranking sensation higher than thought. Ethically it is correct to put the question: "Is it real?" But it is important to note that this holds true only when the individual subject asks this question of himself, and concerning his own reality. He can apprehend the ethical reality of another only by thinking it, and hence as a possibility.

The Scriptures teach: "Judge not that ye be not judged." This is expressed in the form of a warning, an admonition, but it is at the same time an impossibility. One human being cannot judge another ethically, because he cannot understand him except as a possibility. When therefore anyone attempts to judge another, the expression for his impotence is that he merely judges himself.

In *Stages on Life's Way* occurs the following: "It is intelligent to ask two questions: (1) Is it possible? (2) Can I do it? But it is unintelligent to ask these two questions: (1) Is it real? (2) Has my neighbor Christopherson done it?" In this passage reality is accentuated ethically. It is fatuous from the aesthetic and the intellectual point of view to raise the question of reality; and the same holds true from the ethical point of view if the question is raised in the interest of contemplation. But when the ethical question is raised in connection with my own reality, I ask about possibility; only that this possibility is not an aesthetically and intellectually disinterested possibility, but as being a conceived reality it is related as a possibility to my own reality, so that I may be able to realize it.

The mode of apprehension of the truth is precisely the truth. It is therefore untrue to answer a question in a medium in which the question cannot arise. So for example, to explain reality within the medium of the possible, or to distinguish between possibility and reality within possibility. By refraining from raising the question of reality from the aesthetic or intellectual point of view, but asking this question only ethically, and here again only in the interest of one's own reality, each individual will be isolated and compelled to exist for himself. Irony and hypocrisy as opposite forms, but both expressing the contradiction that the internal is not the external, irony by seeming to be bad, hypocrisy by seeming to be good, emphasize the principle anent the contemplative inquiry concerning ethical inwardness, that reality and deceit are equally possible, and that deceit can clothe itself in the same appearance as reality. It is unethical even to ask at all about another person's ethical inwardness, in so far as such inquiry constitutes a diversion of attention. But if the question is asked nevertheless, the difficulty remains that I can lay hold of the other's reality only by conceiving it, and hence by translating it into a possibility; and in this sphere the possibility of a deception is equally conceivable. This is profitable preliminary training for an ethical mode of existence: to learn that the individual stands alone.

It is a misunderstanding to be concerned about reality from the aesthetic or intellectual point of view. And to be concerned ethically about another's reality is also a misunderstanding, since the only question of reality that is ethically pertinent, is the question of one's own reality. Here we may clearly note the difference that exists between faith *sensu strictissimo* on the one hand (referring as it does to the historical, and the realms of the aesthetic, the intellectual) and the ethical on the other. To ask with infinite interest about a reality which is not one's own, is faith, and this constitutes a paradoxical relationship to the paradoxical. Aesthetically it is impossible to raise such a question except in thoughtlessness, since possibility is aesthetically higher than reality. Nor is it possible to raise such a question ethically, since the sole ethical interest is the interest in one's own reality. The analogy between faith and the ethical is found in the infinite interest, which suffices to distinguish the believer absolutely from an aesthetician or a thinker. But the believer differs from the ethicist in being infinitely interested in the reality of another (in the fact, for example, that God has existed in time).

The aesthetic and intellectual principle is that no reality is thought or understood until its *esse* has been resolved into its *posse*. The ethical principle is that no possibility is understood until each *posse* has really become an *esse*. An aesthetic and intellectual scrutiny protests every *esse* which is not a *posse*; the ethical scrutiny results in the condemnation of every *posse* which is not an *esse*, but this refers only to a *posse* in the individual himself, since the ethical has nothing to do with the possibilities of other individuals. In our own age everything is mixed up together: the aesthetic is treated ethically, faith is dealt with intellectually, and so forth. Philosophy has answered every question; but no adequate consideration has been given the question concerning what sphere it is within which each question finds its answer. This creates a greater confusion in the world of the spirit than when in the civic life an ecclesiastical question, let us say, is handled by the bridge commission.

Is the real then the same as the external? By no means. Aesthetically and intellectually it is usual and proper to stress the principle that the external is merely a deception for one who does not grasp the ideality involved. Frater Taciturnus says: "Mere knowledge of the historical helps simply to produce an illusion, in which the mind is beguiled by the raw material of the externality. What is it that I can know historically? The external detail. The ideality I can know only by myself, and if I do not know it by myself I do not know it at all; mere historical knowledge avails nothing. Ideality is not a chattel which can be transported from one person to another, nor is it something to be had gratis when buying in large quantities. If I know that Caesar was a great man, I know what greatness is, and it is on this knowledge that I base my judgment of Caesar; otherwise I do not know that Caesar was great. The testimony of history, the assurances of responsible people that no risk is involved in accepting this opinion, the certainty of the conclusion that he was great because the results of his life demonstrate it—all this helps not a jot. To believe an ideality on the word of another is like laughing at a joke because someone has said that it was funny, not because one has understood it. In such case the witticism might as well be left unsaid; for anyone who laughs at it because of the respect he entertains for some guarantor, and on the ground

of his faith in him, could laugh with the same emphasis notwithstanding."
What then is the real? It is the ideality. But aesthetically and intellectually the
ideality is the possible (the translation from *esse ad posse*). Ethically the ideality is the real within the individual himself. The real is an inwardness that is
infinitely interested in existing; this is exemplified in the ethical individual.

Precisely in the degree to which I understand a thinker I become indifferent to his reality; that is, to his existence as a particular individual, to his having really understood this or that so and so, to his actually having realized his
teaching, and so forth. Aesthetic and speculative thought is quite justified in
insisting on this point, and it is important not to lose sight of it. But this does
not suffice for a defense of pure thought as a medium of communication between man and man. Because the reality of the teacher is properly indifferent
to me as his pupil, and my reality conversely to him, it does not by any means
follow that the teacher is justified in being indifferent to his own reality. His
communication should bear the stamp of this consciousness, but not directly,
since the ethical reality of an individual is not directly communicable (such a
direct relationship is exemplified in the paradoxical relation of a believer to the
object of his faith), and cannot be understood immediately, but must be
understood indirectly through indirect signs.

When the different spheres are not decisively distinguished from one
another, confusion reigns everywhere. When people are curious about a
thinker's reality and find it interesting to know something about it, and so
forth, this interest is intellectually reprehensible. The maximum of attainment
in the sphere of the intellectual is to become altogether indifferent to the
thinker's reality. But by being thus muddle-headed in the intellectual sphere,
one acquires a certain resemblance to a believer. A believer is one who is
infinitely interested in another's reality. This is a decisive criterion for faith,
and the interest in question is not just a little curiosity, but an absolute dependence upon faith's object.

The object of faith is the reality of another, and the relationship is one of
infinite interest. The object of faith is not a doctrine, for then the relationship
would be intellectual, and it would be of importance not to botch it, but to
realize the maximum intellectual relationship. The object of faith is not a
teacher with a doctrine; for when a teacher has a doctrine, the doctrine is *eo
ipso* more important than the teacher, and the relationship is again intellectual,
and it again becomes important not to botch it, but to realize the maximum
intellectual relationship. The object of faith is the reality of the teacher, that
the teacher really exists. The answer of faith is therefore unconditionally yes
or no. For it does not concern a doctrine, as to whether the doctrine is true or
not; it is the answer to a question concerning a fact: "Do you or do you not
suppose that he has really existed?" And the answer, it must be noted, is with
infinite passion. In the case of a human being, it is thoughtlessness to lay so
great and infinite a stress on the question whether he has existed or not. If the

object of faith is a human being, therefore, the whole proposal is the vagary of a stupid person, who has not even understood the spirit of the intellectual and the aesthetic. The object of faith is hence the reality of the God-man in the sense of his existence. But existence involves first and foremost particularity, and this is why thought must abstract from existence, because the particular cannot be thought, but only the universal. The object of faith is thus God's reality in existence as a particular individual, the fact that God has existed as an individual human being.

Christianity is no doctrine concerning the unity of the divine and the human, or concerning the identity of subject and object; nor is it any other of the logical transcriptions of Christianity. If Christianity were a doctrine, the relationship to it would not be one of faith, for only an intellectual type of relationship can correspond to a doctrine. Christianity is therefore not a doctrine, but the fact that God has existed.

The realm of faith is thus not a class for numskulls in the sphere of the intellectual, or an asylum for the feeble-minded. Faith constitutes a sphere all by itself, and every misunderstanding of Christianity may at once be recognized by its transforming it into a doctrine, transferring it to the sphere of the intellectual. The maximum of attainment within the sphere of the intellectual, namely, to realize an entire indifference as to the reality of the teacher, is in the sphere of faith at the opposite end of the scale. The maximum of attainment within the sphere of faith is to become infinitely interested in the reality of the teacher. . . .

LEWIS

Our discussion of appearance and reality concludes with the opening chapter of one of the classics of American philosophy, Clarence Irving Lewis's Mind and the World-Order. *Lewis (1883–1964) was, during his entire professional life, a teacher of philosophy at Harvard University. In his numerous books and articles he developed a form of the doctrine known as Pragmatism, which originated at Harvard at the turn of the century in the work of such men as Charles Sanders Pierce and William James. According to Lewis, our categories of thought derive from man's purposeful attempt to transform the world so that it can satisfy his bodily and intellectual needs.* Mind and the World-Order *was an early (1929) attempt by Lewis to combine the insights of Pragmatism with some of the doctrines developed by Kant in the* Critique of Pure Reason.*

As an exponent of the doctrine known as Pragmatism, Lewis argues that the line between reality and appearance is one which we draw to fit our collective social needs. Reality is what matters to us, what works in our dealings with the world. To the eighteenth-century scientist, physical reality is anything whose mass and spatial location we can measure. The modern physicist alters the definition of "real" to fit electrons, which turn out not to have a single, measurable location at all. In a way, Lewis is the most daring of our five philosophers, despite his rather dry manner, for he tells us that the very boundary between the real and the unreal can shift as our needs change and our interests develop.

The Categories of Reality

The general character of any philosophy is likely to be determined by its initial assumptions and its method. When Descartes proposed to sweep the boards clean by doubting everything which admitted of doubt and announced the initial criterion of certainty to be the inner light of human reason, the distinguishing characteristics of the philosophic movement which resulted were thereby fixed. In similar fashion, the development from Locke to Hume is, for the most part, the logical consequence of the doctrine that the mind is a blank

Chap. 1, "Introduction." From *Mind and the World-Order* by C. I. Lewis. New York: Dover Publications, Inc., 1929. Reprinted through the permission of the publisher.

tablet on which experience writes. And when Kant proposed to inquire, not whether science is possible, but how it is possible, and identified the possibility of science with the validity of synthetic judgments a priori, the successive attempts of the nineteenth century to deduce the major philosophic truths as presuppositions of experience was foreordained.

Because method has this peculiar importance in philosophy, I believe that the reader of any philosophic book is entitled to know in advance what are the underlying convictions of this sort with which the writer sets out. It is right and proper that one should begin with some statement of program and method.

It is—I take it—a distinguishing character of philosophy that it is every-body's business. The man who is his own lawyer or physician will be poorly served; but everyone both can and must be his own philosopher. He must be, because philosophy deals with ends, not means. It includes the questions, What is good? What is right? What is valid? Since finally the responsibility for his own life must rest squarely upon the shoulders of each, no one can delegate the business of answering such questions to another. Concerning the means whereby the valid ends of life may be attained, we seek expert advice. The natural sciences and the techniques to which they give rise, though they may serve some other interests also, are primarily directed to the discovery of such means. But the question of the ultimately valuable ends which shall be served, remains at once the most personal, and the most general of all questions.

And everyone *can* be his own philosopher, because in philosophy we in-vestigate what we already know. It is not the business of philosophy, as it is of the natural sciences, to add to the sum total of phenomena with which men are acquainted. Philosophy is concerned with what is already familiar. To know in the sense of familiarity and to comprehend in clear ideas are, of course, quite different matters. Action precedes reflection and even precision of behavior commonly outruns precision of thought—fortunately for us. If it were not for this, naïve commonsense and philosophy would coincide, and there would be no problem. Just this business of bringing to clear conscious-ness and expressing coherently the principles which are implicitly intended in our dealing with the familiar, is the distinctively philosophic enterprise.

For instance, everybody knows the difference between right and wrong; if we had no moral sense, philosophy would not give us one. But who can state, with complete satisfaction to himself, the adequate and consistent grounds of moral judgment? Likewise, everyone knows the distinction of cogent rea-soning from fallacy. The study of logic appeals to no criterion not already present in the learner's mind. That logical error is, in the last analysis, some sort of inadvertance, is an indispensable assumption of the study. Even if it should be in some part an unwarranted assumption, we could not escape it, for the very business of learning through reflection or discussion presumes our logical sense as a trustworthy guide.

That the knowledge sought in ethics and in logic is, thus, something already implicit in our commerce with the familiar, has usually been recognized. But that the same is true in metaphysics, has not been equally clear. Metaphysics studies the nature of reality in general. Reality is presumably independent of any principles of ours, in a sense in which the right and the valid may not be. At least initial presumption to the contrary might be hopelessly prejudicial. Moreover, reality forever runs beyond the restricted field of familiar experience. What hope that cosmic riddles can be solved by self-interrogation! The secret which we seek may be in some field which is not yet adequately explored or even opened to investigation. Or it may be forever beyond the reach of human senses.

But it is not the business of philosophy to go adventuring beyond space and time. And so far as a true knowledge of the nature of reality depends on determining questions of phenomenal fact which are not yet settled, the philosopher has no special insight which enables him to pose as a prophet. We can do nothing but wait upon the progress of the special sciences. Or if speculate we must, at least such speculation is in no special sense the philosopher's affair. It is true that metaphysics has always been the dumping ground for problems which are only partly philosophic. Questions of the nature of life and mind, for example, are of this mixed sort. In part such issues wait upon further data from the sciences, from biology and physical-chemistry and psychology; in part they are truly philosophic, since they turn upon questions of the fundamental criteria of classification and principles of interpretation. No amassing of scientific data can determine these.

If, for example, the extreme behaviorists in psychology deny the existence of consciousness on the ground that analysis of the "mental" must always be eventually in terms of bodily behavior, then it is the business of philosophy to correct their error, because it consists simply in a fallacy of logical analysis. The analysis of any immediately presented X must always interpret this X in terms of its constant relations to other things—to Y and Z. Such end-terms of analysis—the Y and Z—will not in general be temporal or spatial constituents of X, but may be anything which bears a constant correlation with it. It is as if one should deny the existence of colors because, for purposes of exact investigation, the colors must be defined as frequencies of vibratory motion. In general terms, if such analysis concludes by stating "X is a certain kind of Y-Z complex, hence X does not exist as a distinct reality," the error lies in overlooking a general characteristic of logical analysis—that it does not discover the "substance" or cosmic constituents of the phenomenon whose nature is analyzed but only the constant context of experience in which it will be found.

So far, then, as the divergence of psychological theories, from behaviorism which interprets mind in terms of physical behavior to theories of the subconscious which assimilate much of physiological activity to mind, represents no dispute about experimental fact but only disparity of definition and methodological criteria, psychology and metaphysics have a common ground. The delineation of the fundamental concepts "mind" and "mental" is a truly philosophic enterprise. A similar thing might be discovered in the case of other sciences.

Newly discovered scientific data might make such problems of fundamental concepts and classification easier—or more difficult—but of itself it cannot solve them because, in the nature of the case, they are antecedent to the investigation. Such concepts are not simply dictated by the findings of the laboratory, or by any sort of sense-experience. Their origin is social and historical and represents some enduring human interest. It is the human mind itself which brings them to experience, though the mind does not invent them in a vacuum or cut them from whole cloth. The tendency to forget that initial concepts are never merely dictated by empirical findings is precisely what accounts for the absurd prejudice—now happily obsolescent—that science is "just the report of facts." And this likewise helps to explain the common failure to distinguish between those cosmological speculations which are not philosophic at all, because they are merely guesses at what future observation or experiment may reveal, from the legitimate and necessary philosophic question of a coherent set of fundamental categories, such as "life" and "mind" and "matter," in terms of which experience may consistently and helpfully be interpreted.

It would, of course, be captious to reserve this problem of initial concepts to philosophers, even though we should remember that, since everybody is to be his own philosopher, this merely means reserving them as *general* problems. The expert in the scientific field will have his special competence with respect to them; but they are not his exclusive property, because they are to be resolved as much by criticism and reflection as by empirical investigation. Conversely, it would be pedantic if we should forbid the philosophic student to speculate concerning undetermined scientific fact. It is even questionable to deny the caption "metaphysics" to those cosmological and ontological problems which have this partly speculative and partly critical or reflective character. Historically their title to the name is fairly good. All I wish to point out is that there is a real distinction here between the speculative and the reflective elements; that this distinction coincides with a difference in the method by which resolution of the problem is to be sought; and that it is only the reflective element in such "metaphysical" problems which coincides in its nature and in the method of its solution with the problems of ethics and logic.

With this explanation, I hope I shall cause no confusion if I say that it is only so far as they are thus critical and reflective that the problems of ontology and cosmology are truly philosophic; and that metaphysics as a philosophic discipline is concerned with the nature of the real only so far as that problem is amenable to the reflective method and does not trench upon the field where only scientific investigation can achieve success. There are such reflective problems within any special science, and these may be said to constitute the philosophy of that science. There are also those problems of initial principle and criteria which are common to all the sciences and to the general business of life. These last are the problems of philosophy proper.

There is another sense in which metaphysics has often been speculative and departed from its proper philosophic business and method; that is, not by seeking to anticipate the science of the future, but through attempting by sheer force of rational reflection to transcend experience altogether. Dogmatism is out of fashion since Kant.[1] But that philosophic legerdemain which, with only experience for its datum, would condemn this experience to the status of appearance and disclose a reality more edifying, is still with us. The motives of this attitude are, indeed, ingrained in human nature, and I am reluctant to lay hands on that idealism which has played the rôle of Father Parmenides to all the present generation of philosophers. But at least we must observe that such metaphysics turn away from one type of problem which is real and soluble to another which may not be. Even if all experience be appearance, and all everyday thought and truth infected with contradiction, at least it must be admitted that some appearances are better than others. The mundane distinction of real and unreal *within* experience has its importance and calls for formulation of its criteria. It may be that Reality, with a capital *R*, the concrete-universal Reality which transcends all particular phenomena and underlies them, is a kind of philosophical *ignis fatuus*. Perhaps the idea of "whole" applies only *within* experience, and no whole can validly be conceived except such as stands in contrast with something else and has concrete bounds. Perhaps the whole of Reality is, as Kant thought, an inevitable idea but also a necessarily empty one, to remind us forever of the more which is to be learned and connected with our previous knowledge. But whether this be so or not, there is the less ambitious and more important problem of determining the criteria by which the adjective "real" is correctly applied—the problem of the *abstract* universal. And if any be inclined to think that this question is too simple or too meager for a philosophic discipline, I shall hope to indicate his error.

A metaphysics which takes this as its problem will remain strictly within the reflective method. It will seek to determine the nature of the real, as ethics seeks to determine the good, and logic, the valid, purely by critical consideration of what does not transcend ordinary experience. That is, it will seek to *define* "reality," not to triangulate the universe. It will be concerned with the formulation of principles, but of principles already immanent in intelligent practice. A person with no sense of reality (other-worldly philosophers, for example) will not acquire one by the study of metaphysics. And by no possibility can such investigation reveal reality as something esoteric and edifying and tran-

---

[1] Perhaps I should say, "*has been* out of fashion," since just now we are being treated to various new forms of dogmatism. But this, I take it, comes partly as a counsel of despair, and partly it represents a reaction against the often exaggerated claims of "idealism" and post-Kantian "criticism" to be able to proceed a priori without reference to particular results of the empirical sciences.

scendent of ordinary experience. Any metaphysics which portrays reality as something strangely unfamiliar or beyond the ordinary grasp, stamps itself as thaumaturgy, and is false upon the face of it.

The problem of a correctly conceived metaphysics, like the problem of ethics and of logic, is one to be resolved by attaining to clear and cogent self-consciousness. As it turns out, the problem of metaphysics is "the problem of the categories."[2] The reason for this lies in a curious complexity of the meaning of "reality." Logical validity is at bottom of one single type. And perhaps the good and the right are relatively simple in their ultimate nature. But the adjective "real" is systematically ambiguous and can have a single meaning only in a special sense. The ascription of reality to the content of any particular experience is always elliptical: some qualification—material reality, psychic reality, mathematical reality—is always understood. And whatever is real in one such sense will be unreal in others. Conversely, every given content of experience is a reality of some sort or other; so that the problem of distinguishing real from unreal, the principles of which metaphysics seeks to formulate, is always a problem of right understanding, of referring the given experience to its proper category. The mirage, for example, though not real trees and water, is a real state of atmosphere and light; to relegate it to the limbo of nothingness would be to obliterate a genuine item of the objective world. A dream is illusory because the dreamer takes its images for physical things; but to the psychologist, interested in the scientific study of the mental, just these experienced images, occurring in just this context of other circumstance, constitute a reality to be embraced under law and having its own indisputable place in the realm of fact. The content of every experience is real when it is correctly understood, and is that kind of reality which it is then interpreted to be. Metaphysics is concerned to reveal just that set of major classifications of phenomena, and just those precise criteria of valid understanding, by which the whole array of given experience may be set in order and each item (ideally) assigned its intelligible and unambiguous place.

So understood, the principles of the categories, which metaphysics seeks, stand, on the one side, in close relation to experience and cannot meaningfully transcend it. But on the other side—or in a different sense—they stand above or before experience, and are definitive or prescriptive, and hence a priori.

Whatever principles apply to experience must be phrased in terms of experience. The clues to the categorial[3] interpretation—the correct understanding—of any presentation of sense must be empirical clues. If they are not contained within that segment of experience which constitutes the phenomenon

---

[2] A more logical terminology would qualify this as the "categories of reality," and would distinguish these from the "categories of value."

[3] "Categorial" is used throughout with the meaning "pertaining to the categories." This avoids possible confusion with "categorical," meaning specifically "unconditional, not hypothetical."

itself, then they must be discoverable in its relation to other empirical fact. If the dream or illusion is not betrayed by internal evidence, then its true nature must be disclosed by the conjunction with what precedes or follows. But while the distinguishing marks of reality of any particular sort are thus experimental, the principles by which the interpretation or classification is made are prior to the experience in question. It is only because the mind is prepared to judge it real or unreal according as it bears or fails to bear certain marks, that interpretation of the given is possible at all, and that experience can be understood.

It is through reflective examination of experience (more particularly of our own part in it or attitude toward it) that we may correctly formulate these principles of the categories, since they are implicit in our practical dealings with the empirically given. But they are not empirical generalizations in the sense that some later experience may prove an exception and thus invalidate them. They formulate an attitude of interpretation or discrimination by which what would be exceptional is at once thrown out of court. For example, no experience of the physical can fail to bear those marks the absence of which would bar the given content of experience from interpretation as physical reality. The formulation of our deliberately taken, and consistently adhered to, attitude of interpretation constitutes a categorial *definition* of "the physical." Such a categorial definitive principle forbids nothing in the way of experience; it prohibits neither illusion nor senseless dream. Thus such principles are not material truths: they can be a priori—knowable with certainty in advance of experience—precisely because they impose no limitation upon the given but, as principles of interpretation, nevertheless condition it as a constituent of *reality*.

So conceived, the principles which formulate criteria of the real, in its various types, are a priori in precisely the same sense as are the canons of ethics and of logic. Experience does not itself determine what is good or bad, or the nature of goodness, nor does it determine what is valid or invalid, or the nature of logical validity. Equally it does not determine what is real or unreal (in any particular sense), or the nature of reality. Experience does not categorize itself. The criteria of interpretation are of the mind; they are imposed upon the given by our active attitude.

The main business of a sound metaphysics is, thus, with the problem of the categories; the formulation of the criteria of reality, in its various types. It is to the shame of philosophy that these problems, which by their nature must be capable of precise solution since they require only persistent regard for fact and self-conscious examination of our own grounds of judgment, have been so generally neglected. Just this common disregard of verifiable fact and mundane criteria of the real is largely responsible for that quagmire of incertitude and welter of the irrelevant and vague which at present bears the name of metaphysics. The problems of the categories admit of as much real progress as those of logic; in fact, they are problems of the same general type. We may congratulate ourselves, I think, that a growing interest in such study, in this reflective or phenomenalistic or critical spirit, is one of the characteristic of the present period in philosophy.[4]

The definition of the real in general, and the picturing of reality as a whole, are subordinate matters; and perhaps, as has been suggested, the second of these is not possible. The word "real" has a single meaning, of course, in the same sense that "useful" or any other such elliptical terms has a single meaning. Nothing is useful for every purpose, and perhaps everything is useful for some purpose. A definition of "useful" *in general* would not divide things into two classes, the useful and the useless. Nor could we arrive at such a definition by attempting to collect all useful things into a class and remark their common characters, since we should probably have everything in the class and nothing outside it to represent the useless. Instead, we should first have to consider the different types of usefulness or of useful things and then discover, if possible, what it is that characterizes the useful as contrasted with the useless in all these different cases. We should find, of course, that it was not some sense-quality but a relation to an end which was the universal mark of usefulness. Similarly, to arrive at a general definition of "the real" it would not do to lump together all sorts of realities in one class and seek directly for their common character. Everything in this class would be at once real, in some category, and unreal in others. And nothing would be left outside it. The subject of our generalization must be, instead, the distinction real-unreal in all the different categories. What definition of reality in general we might thus arrive at, we need not pause to inquire. Obviously it would be found to embrace some relation to empirical givenness in general or to our interpreting attitude, or to something involving both of these, rather than any particular and distinguishing empirical characteristics.

That in any case a successful definition of the real in general would not carry us far in any cosmological attempt to plumb the deeps of the universe, is evident from the fact that it would delimit reality in intension only, and would leave quite undetermined the particular content of reality *in extenso*. The total picture of reality can be drawn only when the last experience of the last man, and the final facts of science, are summed up. Why cosmology in this sense should be supposed to be the business of the philosopher—or of anyone else—I cannot see. In the nature of the case, it must be a coöperative enterprise, and presumably one that is always incomplete.

What we have here seen concerning the significance of "the real" will have its importance for certain topics discussed in later chapters. But our immediate interest in it lies in the fact that it brings metaphysics—which threatened to prove an exception—back into line with other branches of philosophy with respect to the method by which it should be pursued. It is only in and through the general course of human experience that we have a content for our philosophic thinking, and the significance of philosophic truth lies always

---

[4] I have in mind, as examples, Whitehead's "Concept of Nature" and "Principles of Natural Knowledge," Russell's "Analysis of Mind,'" and Broad's "Scientific Thought."

in its application to experience. But it is experience from a certain point of view, or a certain aspect of it, with which we are concerned. Ethics cannot tell us how much of life is good, what particular sins are committed, or what proportion of men are moral; nor does metaphysics describe the course of the universe or determine the extent and the particulars of the real. It is the logical essence of goodness, the canons of validity, the criteria of the beautiful, and likewise, the principles of the distinction of real from unreal, that philosophy may hope to formulate. These criteria and principles, the mind itself brings to experience in its interpretation, its discriminations, and its evaluation of what is given. Thus philosophy is, so to speak, the mind's own study of itself in action; and the method of it is simply reflective. It seeks to formulate explicitly what from the beginning is our own creation and possession.

However, I should not like to appear to defend the notion that such analysis is a simple matter or that it requires only to express in precise terms the principles of common-sense. As has often enough been emphasized, common-sense is itself a naïve metaphysics and one which frequently breaks down on examination. Just as naïve morality may become confused before the dialectical attack, so common-sense categories of reality fail in crucial cases to meet the tests of consistency and accord with intelligent practice. It is true in metaphysics, as it is in ethics and in logic, that while valid principles must be supposed somehow implicit in the ordinary intercourse of mind with reality, they are not present in the sense of being fatally adhered to. If they were, the philosophic enterprise would have no practical value. Self-consciousness may be an end in itself, but if it did not have eventual influence upon human action it would be a luxury which humanity could not afford. That we coincide in our logical sense, does not make logic a work of supererogation. No more does coincidence in our ultimate sense of reality and in our categories render metaphysical discussion nugatory. Just as the study of logic may conduce to cogency of thought, and ethics contribute to greater clarity and consistency in moral judgment, so too the elucidation of metaphysical problems may contribute to the precision and adequacy of our interpretation of the real; it may even serve, on occasion, to work improvement in the concepts of the special sciences. Philosophy cannot be merely a verbally more precise rendering of common-sense, nor a direct generalization from actual practice. Though it rises from what is implicit in experience, its procedure must be critical, not descriptive. So far as it is to be of use, it must assume the function of sharpening and correcting an interpretation which has already entered into the fabric of that experience which is its datum. Logical principles aim to replace the uncritical moral sense, ethics, our naïve morality, and metaphysics, our unreflective ontological judgments. Such an enterprise is no simple matter of formulating the obvious.

The reflective method must, of course, be dialectical—in the Socratic-Platonic, not the Hegelian, sense. It accords with the Socratic presumption that the truth which is sought is already implicit in the mind which seeks it, and needs only to be elicited and brought to clear expression. It accords, further, in the recognition that it is definitions or "essences" which are the philosophic goal. And it likewise recognizes that the hope of agreement between minds, to be reached by philosophic discussion, must rest upon the presumption that this accord somehow exists already.

Historically, however, the dialectical method has been overlaid with all sorts of addenda, and perverted by extraneous assumptions which are fallacious. So that I should choose the name "reflective" as less liable to unwarranted interpretation. It does not follow from the dialectical method that the basis of the accord between minds represents some universal pattern of human reason, apart from the world of sense in which we live; nor that the mind has access to some realm of transcendent concepts which it recovers, of its own powers, at the instigation of experience; nor that agreement of minds presumes initial principles which are self-evident. It does not even follow that the agreement which we seek is already implicitly complete in all respects. To all such notions there is an alternative, to account for this agreement between minds, which is simple and even obvious. The coincidence of our fundamental criteria and principles is the combined result of the similarity of human animals, and of their primal interests, and the similarities of the experience with which they have to deal. More explicitly, it represents one result of the interplay between these two; the coincidence of human modes of behavior, particularly when the interests which such behavior serves involve coöperation.

Our categories are guides to action. Those attitudes which survive the test of practice will reflect not only the nature of the active creature but the general character of the experience he confronts. Thus, indirectly, even what is a priori may not be an exclusive product of "reason," or made in Plato's heaven in utter independence of the world we live in. Moreover, the fact that man survives and prospers by his social habits serves to accentuate and perfect agreement in our basic attitudes. Our common understanding and our common world may be, in part, created in response to our need to act together and to comprehend one another. Critical discussion is but a prolongation of that effort which we make to extend the bounds of successful human coöperation. It is no more necessary to suppose that agreement in fundamental principles is completely ready-made than it is to suppose that infants must already have precisely those ideas which later they find words to express. Indeed our categories are almost as much a social product as is language, and in something like the same sense. It is only the *possibility* of agreement which must be antecedently presumed. The "human mind" is a coincidence of individual minds which partly, no doubt, must be native, but partly is itself created by the social process. Even the likeness which is native would seem to consist in capacities and tendencies to action, not in mental content or explicit modes of thought. That the categories are fundamental in such wise that the social process can neither create nor alter them, is a rationalistic prejudice without foundation. There is much which is profound and true in traditional conceptions of the a priori. But equally it should be clear that there is much in such conceptions which smacks of magic and superstitious nonsense. Particularly it is implausible that what is a priori can be rooted in a "rational nature of man" which is something miraculous and beyond the bounds of psychological analysis and genetic explanation.

It may be pointed out also that if we recognize critical reflection or dialectic as the only method which holds promise in philosophy, we do not thereby commit ourselves to the assumption that coherence or internal consistency is the only test, or a sufficient test, of philosophic truth. In philosophy, as elsewhere, consistency is only a negative test of truth; it is possible, however unlikely, to be consistently in error. Consistency would be a sufficient test only if we should suppose that there is nothing external to our logic which we must be true to. The reflective method does not take it for granted that all fact follows, Hegelian-fashion, from the logical structure of thought itself. As has been suggested, it does not even presuppose that what is a priori and of the mind—our categorial attitude of interpretation—is completely independent of the general character of experience.

It is of the essence of the dialectical or reflective method that we should recognize that proof, in philosophy, can be nothing more at bottom than persuasion. It makes no difference what the manner of presentation should be, whether deductive from initial assumptions, or inductive from example, or merely following the order dictated by clarity of exposition. If it be deductive, then the initial assumptions cannot coerce the mind. There are no propositions which are self-evident in isolation. So far as the deductive presentation hopes to convince of what was not previously believed, it must either seek out initial agreements from which it may proceed, or—as is more frequently the case—the deductively first propositions must be rendered significant and acceptable by exhibiting the cogency and general consonance with experience of their consequences. If the method be inductive from example, then the principles to be proved are implicit in the assumption that cited examples are veridical and typical and genuinely fall under the category to be investigated. There can be no Archimedean point for the philosopher. Proof, he can offer only in the sense of so connecting his theses as to exhibit their mutual support, and only through appeal to other minds to reflect upon their experience and their own attitudes and perceive that he correctly portrays them. If there be those minds which find no alternatives save certainty, apart from all appeal to prior fact, or skepticism, then to skepticism they are self-condemned. And much good may it do them! As philosophers, we have something we must be faithful to, even if that something be ourselves. If we are perverse, it is possible that our philosophy will consist of lies.

Already this introductory analysis of method is too long. But the conception of the a priori here suggested is a novel one: a little further discussion may have its value by way of anticipating briefly what is to follow.

If philosophy is the study of the a priori, and is thus the mind's formulation of its own active attitudes, still the attitude which is the object of such study is one taken toward the content of an experience in some sense independent of and bound to be reflected in the attitude itself. What is a priori —it will be maintained—is prior to experience in almost the same sense that purpose is. Purposes are not dictated by the content of the given; they are our own. Yet purposes must take their shape and have their realization in terms of experience; the content of the given is not irrelevant to them. And purposes which can find no application will disappear. In somewhat the same fashion what is a priori and of the mind is prior to the content of the given, yet in another sense not altogether independent of experience in general.

It is an error common to rationalism and to pure empiricism that both attempt an impossible separation of something called the mind from something else called experience. Likewise both treat of knowledge as if it were a relation of the individual mind to external object in such wise that the existence of other minds is irrelevant; they do not sufficiently recognize the sense in which our truth is social. Traditional rationalism,[5] observing that any principles which should serve as ultimate criterion or determine categorial interpretation must be prior to and independent of the experience to which it applies, has supposed that such principles must be innate and so discoverable by some sort of direct inspection. If a canon of their truth is requisite, this must be supplied by something of a higher order than experience, such as self-evidence or the natural light of reason. The mistakes of this point of view are two. In the first place, it assumes that mind is immediate to itself in a sense in which the object of experience is not. But what other means have we of discovering the mind save that same experience in which also external objects are presented? And if the object transcends the experience of it, is not this equally true of the mind? The single experience exhausts the reality of neither. Any particular experience is a whole within which that part or aspect which represents the legislative or categorial activity of mind and that which is given content, independent of the mind's interpretation, are separable only by analysis. We have no higher faculty or more esoteric experience through which the mind discovers itself. And second, rationalism fallaciously assumes that what is prior to, or legislative for, the particular experience must be likewise independent of experience in general. Though categorical principle must, in the nature of the case, be prior to the particular experience, it nevertheless represents an attitude which the mind has taken in the light of past experience as a whole, and one which would even be susceptible of change if confronted with some pervasive alteration in the general character of what is presented. An example here may be of service: It is an a priori principle that physical things must have mass. By this criterion, they are distinguished from mirror-images and illusion. Since this is so, no particular experience could upset this principle, because any experience in which it should be violated would be repudiated as

[5] The rationalism (if that term is justified) of post-Kantian idealism rests upon different assumptions and proceeds by different methods. It is not here in point.

non-veridical or "not correctly understood." That is, by the principle itself, the phenomenon must be referred to some other category than the physical. In that sense, the truth of the principle is independent of the particular phenomenon. But a world in which we should experience phenomena having a persistence and independence not characteristic of imagination, and a coherence not characteristic of our dreams, but things which would still not be amenable to any gravitational generalizations, is entirely conceivable. In such a world our a priori principle would not be rendered false—since it is definitive of the physical; but the category "physical" might well be useless. (Incidentally it may be pointed out that this criterion of the physical is a historical and social product. Aristotle and the ancients knew it not.)

Though we bring the a priori principle, as criterion, to any particular experience, yet this legislative attitude of mind is clearly one which is taken because, our experience on the whole being what it is, this principle helps to render it intelligible, and behavior in accord with it is normally successful. The mind must bring to experience whatever serve as the criteria of interpretation—of the real, as of the right, the beautiful, and the valid. The content of experience cannot evaluate or interpret itself. Nevertheless the validity of such interpretation must reflect the character of experience in general, and meet the pragmatic test of value as a guide to action.

The fallacy of pure empiricism is the converse of that which rationalism commits. In seeking to identify the real with what is given in experience, apart from construction or interpretation by the mind, and to elicit general principles directly from the content of experience, empiricism condemns itself to a vicious circle. Experience as it comes to us contains not only the real but all the content of illusion, dream, hallucination, and misapprehension. When the empiricist supposes that laws or principles can be derived simply by generalization from experience, he *means* to refer only to *veridical* experience, forgetting that without the criterion of legislative principle experience cannot first be sorted into veridical and illusory.

It is this vicious circle which makes inevitable the historical dénouement of empiricism in Hume's skepticism. Berkeley pointed out that the real cannot be distinguished from the unreal by any relation between the idea in the mind and an independent object, but only by some relation within experience itself. In this, of course, he is right, whether we agree with his idealism or not: mind cannot transcend itself and discover a relation of what is in experience to what is not. Berkeley then seeks to indicate our actual empirical criteria: the real in experience is distinguished (1) by that independence of the will which is exhibited in the content of perception as contrasted with imagination, (2) by the greater liveliness of perception, (3) by the interconnection of veridical perceptions according to the "laws of nature." Obviously only the last of these is sufficient in critical cases such as hallucination and errors of observation. Hume wrecks the empiricist structure when he points out that such "laws of nature" cannot be derived by generalization from experience. For this, the distinction of necessary from contingent would be requisite. The basis of this distinction is not to be found in the content of experience; it is of the mind. Generalization from experience always presumes that the categorial interpretation already has been made. Laws which characterize all experience, of real and unreal both, are non-existent, and would in any case be worthless.

It is obvious that similar considerations hold for the other problems of philosophy. The nature of the good can be learned from experience only if the content of experience be first classified into good and bad, or grades of better and worse. Such classification or grading already involves the legislative application of the same principle which is sought. In logic, principles can be elicited by generalization from examples only if cases of valid reasoning have first been segregated by some criterion. It is this criterion which the generalization is required to disclose. In esthetics, the laws of the beautiful may be derived from experience only if the criteria of beauty have first been correctly applied.

The world of experience is not given in experience: it is constructed by thought from the data of sense. This reality which everybody knows reflects the structure of human intelligence as much as it does the nature of the independently given sensory content. It is a whole in which mind and what is given to mind already meet and are interwoven. The datum of our philosophic study is not the "buzzing, blooming confusion" on which the infant first opens his eyes, not the thin experience of immediate sensation, but the thick experience of every-day life.

This experience of *reality* exists only because the mind of man takes attitudes and makes interpretations. The buzzing, blooming confusion could not become reality for an oyster. A purely passive consciousness, if such can be conceived, would find no use for the concept of reality, because it would find none for the idea of the *un*real; because it would take no attitude that could be balked, and make no interpretation which conceivably could be mistaken.

On the other hand, we can discover mind and its principles only by analysis in this experience which we have. We cannot, unless dogmatically, construct experience from a hypothetical and transcendent mind working upon a material which likewise is something beyond experience. We can only discover mind and what is independently given to it by an analysis within experience itself. And it is only because mind has entered into the structure of the real world which we know and the experience of everyday, that analysis, or *any* attempted knowledge, may discover it.

In finding thus that the principles and criteria which philosophy seeks to formulate must be significant at once of experience and of our active attitudes, the reflective method inevitably is pragmatic also. Concepts and principles reveal themselves as instruments of interpretation; their meaning lies in the empirical consequences of the active attitude. The categories are ways of dealing with what is given to the mind, and if they had no practical consequences, the mind would never use them. Since philosophy seeks to formulate what is implicit in mind's every-day interpretations, we may test the significance of any philosophic principle, and pave the way for determining its truth, if we ask: How would experience be different if this should be correct than if it should be false? or, How differently should we orient ourselves to experience and deal with it if this should be so than if it should be not so?

Metaphysical issues which would supposedly concern what is transcendent of experience altogether, must inevitably turn out to be issues wrongly taken. For example, if one say—as Mr. Broad has recently said[6]—that scientific reality of perduring electrons or what not, is something which at best is probable only, since it does not enter our direct experience of "sensa," then I think we may justly challenge him as Berkeley challenged Locke: Why not a world of sensa with *nothing* behind them? What makes "scientific reality" even probable if direct experience could be the same without its existence? Unless the modern physicist hopelessly deludes himself, does not the existence of electrons mean something verifiable in the laboratory? Otherwise, would he not be constrained to answer any question about electrons as Laplace is reputed to have answered Napoleon's question about God—that he had no need of this hypothesis? But if the existence or non-existence of "scientific reality" makes certain verifiable differences in experience, then these empirical criteria are the marks of the kind of reality which can be predicated of it. They are the "cash-value" of the category; they constitute what it means to be real in just the way that electrons can be real. "Scientific reality" is either an interpretation of certain parts and aspects of experience or it is a noise, signifying nothing.

The totality of the possible experiences in which any interpretation would be verified—the completest possible empirical verification which is conceivable—constitutes the entire meaning which that interpretation has. A predication of reality to what transcends experience completely and in every sense is not problematic; it is nonsense.

Perhaps another illustration may make the point more clear. Occasionally philosophers amuse themselves by suggesting that the existences of things are intermittent; that they go out when we cease to notice them and come into being again at the moment of rediscovery. The answer is not given by any question-begging reference to the independent object or to the conservation of matter. What we need to inquire is why this notion of permanent objects was ever invented. If nothing in experience would be different whether the existence of things should be intermittent or continuous, what character of experience is predicated by their "permanence"? When we have answered to such questions, we have discovered the whole meaning of "permanent existence" and nothing further, unless paradox of language, remains to be discussed. Reflection upon experience and our attitude to what is given cannot discover what is not implicitly already there—and there is nothing else which philosophic reflection can hope to disclose.

[6] "Scientific Thought," see esp. pp. 268 *ff*.

To sum up, then: The reflective method is empirical and analytic in that it recognizes experience in general as the datum of philosophy. But it is not empirical in the sense of taking this experience to coincide with data of sense which are merely given to the mind. Nor is it analytic in the sense of supposing that experience is complete and ready-made.

Rather, it finds that philosophy is particularly concerned with that part or aspect of experience which the mind contributes by its attitude of interpretation. In thus recognizing that the principles which are sought are in some sense a priori, it is rationalistic.

It is not rationalistic, however, in the sense of presuming the mind as a Procrustean bed into which experience is forced, or as an initial datum which can be assumed or its findings known apart from sense-experience. Nor does it presume the "rational human mind" as something completely identical in and native to all human beings, or as a transcendent entity which, even if it lived in some other world of sense, would still possess precisely the same categories and pattern of intelligence.

The reflective method is pragmatic in the same sense that it is empirical and analytic. It supposes that the categories and principles which it seeks must already be implicit in human experience and human attitude. The significance of such fundamental conceptions must always be practical because thought and action are continuous, and because no other origin of them can be plausible than an origin which reflects their bearing on experience. Further, it claims for philosophy itself the pragmatic sanction that reflection is but a further stretch of that critical examination of our own constructions and interpretations by which we free them from inconsistency and render them more useful. Since experience is not just given but is in part a product of the mind, philosophy itself may work some alteration of the active attitude by which the given in experience is met and moulded. But the reflective method is not, or need not be, pragmatic in the sense of supposing, as current pragmatism sometimes seems to do, that the categories of biology and psychophysics have some peculiar advantage for the interpretation of the practical attitudes of thought.

The reflective method necessarily leads to the repudiation of any reality supposed to be transcendent of experience altogether. A true philosophic interpretation must always follow the clues of the practical reasons for our predications. A philosophy which relegates any object of human thought to the transcendent is false to the human interests which have created that thought, and to the experience which gives it meaning. Philosophic truth, like knowledge in general, is about experience, and not about something strangely beyond the ken of man, open only to the seer and the prophet. We all know the nature of life and of the real, though only with an exquisite care can we tell the truth about them.

AFTERWORD

The controversy between Timothy Leary and Jerome Lettvin over the use of LSD led us into an exploration of the distinction between appearance and reality. In developing some of the ways in which that distinction can be drawn, we have moved very far from the original problem of drugs. The time has come to reflect upon the philosophical arguments of Plato, Descartes. Kant, Kierkegaard, and Lewis, in order to see whether they have anything to say to us about the LSD dispute. Needless to say, we cannot expect to find them, like an advice-to-the lovelorn column, full of up-to-the-minute suggestions. Great philosophy does not operate at that level. Still, if Plato and the others are really relevant to our contemporary concerns, then it ought to be possible to find some guidelines to action in what they have written.

There are three questions which we need to answer before we can make a reasoned decision about LSD.

1. Is the intersubjective world of physical things the ultimate reality, or is there another realm, either within or beyond, to which we should turn our eyes?
2. If there is such a realm, more real, more valuable than mundane reality, can we approach it by the use of our rational faculties, or must we develop nonrational ways of establishing our relationship to it?
3. Finally, if there **is** a higher reality, and if it can be approached only nonrationally, should we use artificial devices such as drugs in an attempt to facilitate our search?

What answers do our five philosophers offer to these three questions? So far as the reality of the visible world is concerned, Plato and Kierkegaard agree with Timothy Leary that there is some other, and more important, reality. Descartes' extreme scepticism about all our scientific beliefs leads him eventually to rely upon the absolute certainty of his own subjective consciousness. Despite his efforts, in other writings, to re-establish the reality of the public world of space and time, Descartes' lasting contribution to metaphysics was his discovery of the primacy of the private and subjective. In that sense, Descartes is the true forefather of Kierkegaard's subjectivism. Kant struggled against the antiobjective implications of Descartes' metaphysics, but he achieved only a partial victory. To be sure, he presents us with a proof of the "objective reality" of the space-time world of material objects, but that world possesses only a qualified or conditional reality. It is a world of things "as they appear to the mind." The Platonic realm of eternal, objective forms, according to Kant, is completely cut off from us and is unknowable.

Lewis would appear to side with the objectivists. Certainly his tone and style suggest the hardheaded scientist rather than the visionary mystic. But the matter is not quite so simple as that, for Lewis admits that our collective needs and experiences shape our conception of what is "real." In a society of mystics and drug-takers, therefore, Lewis would be very hard-pressed to deny that the visions were real. Indeed, Lewis's theory is potentially the most revolutionary of the five we have studied, for he refuses to rule out in advance any way of classifying reality and appearance, no matter how different from what we are accustomed to.

On the second question, Plato differs decisively from Kierkegaard. The dominant theme of Plato's entire philosophy is that men can gain knowledge of true reality, and thereby liberate themselves from the cave of illusion and false belief, only by the rigorous development of their rational faculties. Plato may sound a bit mystical, but his idea of good preparation for philosophical wisdom is a careful study of plane and solid geometry! Kierkegaard, on the other hand, denies that reason can grasp either the inwardness of subjectivity or the absurdity of man's relationship to God. Kierkegaard views with a mixture of amusement and despair the efforts of philosophers to reason themselves into religious faith. Like other Christian thinkers before him, he doubts the value of proofs for the existence of God, analysis of the concepts of immortality and eternity, and all the other paraphernalia of the rational theologian. In his mocking rejection of the beliefs, life-styles, and values of established bourgeois society, Kierkegaard is very close to the attitude of contemporary rebels. The difference, of course, is that Kierkegaard, like Leary, shuns political and social involvement as a diversion from higher and more important concerns.

Descartes, Kant, and Lewis all follow Plato in their reliance on reason to guide man toward the real. Indeed, so heavily is Western philosophy committed to rationality that one must search very hard indeed for expressions of the antirational counterculture that has maintained an outcast existence during the past 2,500 years.

It is difficult to say just where our five authors would stand on the third question—namely, whether we should use drugs to assist our exploration of reality. Kierkegaard did not directly face the problem, of course, but it is hard to see how he could seriously have objected to Leary's proposal. Of course, the visions themselves are not equivalent to religious faith, but if, through drugs, men were able to make the leap of faith; and if, after the drugs wore off, they continued to sustain the same religious commitment, then there could be no reason for shunning LSD. As for the health risks and legal dangers, Kierkegaard would surely agree with Leary that life is risky anyway, and any gamble is worth taking in order to have a chance for salvation.

The other authors would almost certainly have recoiled in horror from Leary's injunction to "Turn on, tune in, and drop out." The overwhelming preponderance of Western philosophical thought is against such nonrational paths to reality. However, since in philosophy, neither tradition nor consensus carries any authority, nothing is proved by the fact that Plato, Descartes, Kant, and Lewis outnumber Kierkegaard.

II
METAPHYSICS

The Insanity Defense:
Free Will
    and Determinism

INTRODUCTION TO THE CONTEMPORARY ISSUE

A succession of television dramas, news headlines, and public debates have familiarized us all with the courtroom plea, "not guilty by reason of insanity." We know that more and more frequently, in recent years, judges and juries have been willing to accept the argument that a man may not be responsible for a criminal action because, at the time of its commission, he was not fully sane. Very few of us, however, have really faced the host of complicated issues raised by the insanity defense. The future lawyers among you will of course wish to pay particular attention to the materials in this section, for you may some day find yourselves defending an accused man with some version of an insanity plea. But every citizen needs to understand this issue better, for its implications, as we shall see, reach out beyond the law to touch on politics, social welfare, education, and even the way we bring up our children.

We begin with a very famous legal case, **Durham v. United States.** The decision handed down by Judge Bazelon of the U.S. Appeals Court, known as the "Durham rule," has become the standard against which insanity pleas are judged throughout the American legal system. Despite the court's reliance on precedents—that is, decisions handed down by other courts in previous cases—Judge Bazelon confronts the moral and psychological issue directly, so that his opinion becomes an impressive piece of philosophical reasoning as well as a legal argument.

Against the Durham rule, we pit Dr. Thomas Szasz, one of the most controversial figures in modern American medicine. Dr. Szasz is a psychiatrist who denies that there is any such thing as "mental illness." To him, the notion is merely an excuse for denying men's responsibility, for treating them as objects rather than as persons. Once the courts have declared a man insane, Dr. Szasz warns, they can deprive him of his civil rights, put him behind bars for an indefinite period of time, and take away all the resources with which he might fight for his freedom.

After you have read the Durham decision and Szasz's attack on the notion of mental illness, we shall explore some of the philosophical implications of this controversy.

Durham v. United States

BEFORE EDGERTON, BAZELON AND WASHINGTON, CIRCUIT JUDGES

BAZELON, CIRCUIT JUDGE

Monte Durham was convicted of housebreaking by the District Court sitting without a jury. The only defense asserted at the trial was that Durham was of unsound mind at the time of the offense. We are now urged to reverse

Durham v. United States, 94 U.S. App. D.C. 228.

the conviction (1) because the trial court did not correctly apply existing rules governing the burden of proof on the defense of insanity, and (2) because existing tests of criminal responsibility are obsolete and should be superseded.

I

Durham has a long record of imprisonment and hospitalization. In 1945, at the age of 17, he was discharged from the Navy after a psychiatric examination had shown that he suffered "from a profound personality disorder which renders him unfit for Naval service." In 1947 he pleaded guilty to violating the National Motor Theft Act and was placed on probation for one to three years. He attempted suicide, was taken to Gallinger Hospital for observation, and was transferred to St. Elizabeths Hospital, from which he was discharged after two months. In January of 1948, as a result of a conviction in the District of Columbia Municipal Court for passing bad checks, the District Court revoked his probation and he commenced service of his Motor Theft sentence. His conduct within the first few days in jail led to a lunacy inquiry in the Municipal Court where a jury found him to be of unsound mind. Upon commitment to St. Elizabeths, he was diagnosed as suffering from "psychosis with psychopathic personality." After 15 months of treatment, he was discharged in July 1949 as "recovered" and was returned to jail to serve the balance of his sentence. In June 1950 he was conditionally released. He violated the conditions by leaving the District. When he learned of a warrant for his arrest as a parole violator, he fled to the "South and Midwest obtaining money by passing a number of bad checks." After he was found and returned to the District, the Parole Board referred him to the District Court for a lunacy inquisition, wherein a jury again found him to be of unsound mind. He was readmitted to St. Elizabeths in February 1951. This time the diagnosis was "without mental disorder, psychopathic personality." He was discharged for the third time in May 1951. The housebreaking which is the subject of the present appeal took place two months later, on July 13, 1951.

According to his mother and the psychiatrist who examined him in September 1951, he suffered from hallucinations immediately after his May 1951 discharge from St. Elizabeths. Following the present indictment, in October 1951, he was adjudged of unsound mind in proceedings under § 4244 of Title 18 U.S.C., upon the affidavits of two psychiatrists that he suffered from "psychosis with psychopathic personality." He was committed to St. Elizabeths for the fourth time and given subshock insulin therapy. This commitment lasted 16 months—until February 1953—when he was released to the custody of the District Jail on the certificate of Dr. Silk, Acting Superintendent of St. Elizabeths, that he was "mentally competent to stand trial and . . . able to consult with counsel to properly assist in his own defense."

He was thereupon brought before the court on the charge involved here. The prosecutor told the court:

> So I take this attitude, in view of the fact that he has been over there [St. Elizabeths] a couple of times and these cases that were charged against

him were dropped, I don't think I should take the responsibility of dropping these cases against him; then Saint Elizabeths would let him out on the street, and if that man committed a murder next week then it is my responsibility. So we decided to go to trial on one case, that is the case where we found him right in the house, and let him bring in the defense, if he wants to, of unsound mind at the time the crime was committed, and then Your Honor will find him on that, and in your decision send him back to Saint Elizabeths Hospital, and then if they let him out on the street it is their responsibility.

Shortly thereafter, when the question arose whether Durham could be considered competent to stand trial merely on the basis of Dr. Silk's ex parte statement, the court said to defense counsel:

I am going to ask you this, Mr. Ahern: I have taken the position that if once a person has been found of unsound mind after a lunacy hearing, an ex parte certificate of the superintendent of Saint Elizabeths is not sufficient to set aside that finding and I have held another lunacy hearing. That has been my custom. However, if you want to waive that you may do it, if you admit that he is now of sound mind.

The court accepted counsel's waiver on behalf of Durham, although it had been informed by the prosecutor that a letter from Durham claimed need of further hospitalization, and by defense counsel that ". . . the defendant does say that even today he thinks he does need hospitalization; he told me that this morning."[1] Upon being so informed, the court said, "Of course, if I hold he is not mentally competent to stand trial I send him back to Saint Elizabeths Hospital and they will send him back again in two or three months." In this atmosphere Durham's trial commenced.

His conviction followed the trial court's rejection of the defense of insanity in these words:

I don't think it has been established that the defendant was of unsound mind as of July 13, 1951, in the sense that he didn't know the difference between right and wrong or that even if he did, he was subject to an irresistible impulse by reason of the derangement of mind.

While, of course, the burden of proof on the issue of mental capacity to commit a crime is upon the Government, just as it is on every other issue, nevertheless, the Court finds that there is not sufficient to contradict the usual presumption of [sic] the usual inference of sanity.

[1] Durham showed confusion when he testified. These are but two examples:
"Q. Do you remember writing it? A. No. Don't you forget? People get all mixed up in machines.
"Q. What kind of a machine? A. I don't know, they just get mixed up.
"Q. Are you cured now? A. No, sir.
"Q. In your opinion? A. No, sir.
"Q. What is the matter with you? A. You hear people bother you.
"Q. What? You say you hear people bothering you? A. Yes.
"Q. What kind of people? What do they bother you about? A. (No response.)" . . .

There is no testimony concerning the mental state of the defendant as of July 13, 1951, and therefore the usual presumption of sanity governs.

While if there was some testimony as to his mental state as of that date to the effect that he was incompetent on that date, the burden of proof would be on the Government to overcome it. There has been no such testimony, and the usual presumption of sanity prevails.

. . . .

Mr. Ahern, I think you have done very well by your client and defended him very ably, but I think under the circumstances there is nothing that anybody could have done. [Emphasis supplied.]

We think this reflects error requiring reversal.

II

It has been ably argued by counsel for Durham that the existing tests in the District of Columbia for determining criminal responsibility, *i.e.*, the so-called right-wrong test supplemented by the irresistible impulse test, are not satisfactory criteria for determining criminal responsibility. We are urged to adopt a different test to be applied on the retrial of this case. This contention has behind it nearly a century of agitation for reform.

A. The right-wrong test, approved in this jurisdiction in 1882, was the exclusive test of criminal responsibility in the District of Columbia until 1929 when we approved the irresistible impulse test as a supplementary test in Smith v. United States. The right-wrong test has its roots in England. There, by the first quarter of the eighteenth century, an accused escaped punishment if he could not distinguish "good and evil," *i.e.*, if he "doth not know what he is doing, no more than . . . a wild beast." Later in the same century, the "wild beast" test was abandoned and "right and wrong" was substituted for "good and evil." And toward the middle of the nineteenth century, the House of Lords in the famous M'Naghten case restated what had become the accepted "right-wrong" test in a form which has since been followed, not only in England but in most American jurisdictions as an exclusive test of criminal responsibility:

> . . . the jurors ought to be told in all cases that every man is to be presumed to be sane, and to possess a sufficient degree of reason to be responsible for his crimes, until the contrary be proved to their satisfaction; and that, to establish a defence on the ground of insanity, it must be clearly proved that, at the time of the committing of the act, the party accused was labouring under such a defect of reason, from disease of the mind, as not to know the nature and quality of the act he was doing, or, if he did know it, that he did not know he was doing what was wrong.[2]

As early as 1838, Isaac Ray, one of the founders of the American Psychiatric Association, in his now classic Medical Jurisprudence of Insanity,

[2] 8 Eng.Rep. 718, 722 (1843).

called knowledge of right and wrong a "fallacious" test of criminal responsibility. This view has long since been substantiated by enormous developments in knowledge of mental life. In 1928 Mr. Justice Cardozo said to the New York Academy of Medicine: "Everyone concedes that the present [legal] definition of insanity has little relation to the truths of mental life."

Medico-legal writers in large number, The Report of the Royal Commission on Capital Punishment 1949–1953, and The Preliminary Report by the Committee on Forensic Psychiatry of the Group for the Advancement of Psychiatry present convincing evidence that the right-and-wrong test is "based on an entirely obsolete and misleading conception of the nature of insanity." The science of psychiatry now recognizes that a man is an integrated personality and that reason, which is only one element in that personality, is not the sole determinant of his conduct. The right-wrong test, which considers knowledge or reason alone, is therefore an inadequate guide to mental responsibility for criminal behavior. As Professor Sheldon Glueck of the Harvard Law School points out in discussing the right-wrong tests, which he calls the knowledge tests:

> It is evident that the knowledge tests unscientifically abstract out of the mental make-up but one phase or element of mental life, the cognitive, which, in this era of dynamic psychology, is beginning to be regarded as not the most important factor in conduct and its disorders. In brief, these tests proceed upon the following questionable assumptions of an outworn era in psychiatry: (1) that lack of knowledge of the "nature or quality" of an act (assuming the meaning of such terms to be clear), or incapacity to know right from wrong, is the sole or even the most important symptom of mental disorder; (2) that such knowledge is the sole instigator and guide of conduct, or at least the most important element therein, and consequently should be the sole criterion of responsibility when insanity is involved; and (3) that the capacity of knowing right from wrong can be completely intact and functioning perfectly even though a defendant is otherwise demonstrably of disordered mind.

Nine years ago we said:

> The modern science of psychology . . . does not conceive that there is a separate little man in the top of one's head called reason whose function it is to guide another unruly little man called instinct, emotion, or impulse in the way he should go.

By its misleading emphasis on the cognitive, the right-wrong test requires court and jury to rely upon what is, scientifically speaking, inadequate, and most often, invalid and irrelevant testimony in determining criminal responsibility.

The fundamental objection to the right-wrong test, however, is not that criminal irresponsibility is made to rest upon an inadequate, invalid or indeterminable symptom or manifestation, but that it is made to rest upon *any* particular symptom. In attempting to define insanity in terms of a symptom, the courts have assumed an impossible role, not merely one for which they have no special competence. As the Royal Commission emphasizes, it is dangerous "to abstract particular mental faculties, and to lay it down that unless these particular faculties are destroyed or gravely impaired, an accused person, whatever the nature of his mental disease, must be held to be criminally responsible. . . ." In this field of law as in others, the fact finder should be free to consider all information advanced by relevant scientific disciplines.

Despite demands in the name of scientific advances, this court refused to alter the right-wrong test at the turn of the century. But in 1929, we reconsidered in response to "the cry of scientific experts" and added the irresistible impulse test as a supplementary test for determining criminal responsibility. Without "hesitation" we declared, in Smith v. United States, "it to be the law of this District that, in cases where insanity is interposed as a defense, and the facts are sufficient to call for the application of the rule of irresistible impulse, the jury should be so charged." We said:

> . . . The modern doctrine is that the degree of insanity which will relieve the accused of the consequences of a criminal act must be such as to create in his mind an uncontrollable impulse to commit the offense charged. This impulse must be such as to override the reason and judgment and obliterate the sense of right and wrong to the extent that the accused is deprived of the power to choose between right and wrong. The mere ability to distinguish right from wrong is no longer the correct test either in civil or criminal cases, where the defense of insanity is interposed. The accepted rule in this day and age, with the great advancement in medical science as an enlightening influence on this subject, is that the accused must be capable, not only of distinguishing between right and wrong, but that he was not impelled to do the act by an irresistible impulse, which means before it will justify a verdict of acquittal that his reasoning powers were so far dethroned by his diseased mental condition as to deprive him of the will power to resist the insane impulse to perpetrate the deed, though knowing it to be wrong.

As we have already indicated, this has since been the test in the District. . . .

We find that as an exclusive criterion the right-wrong test is inadequate in that (a) it does not take sufficient account of psychic realities and scientific knowledge, and (b) it is based upon one symptom and so cannot validly be applied in all circumstances. We find that the "irresistible impulse" test is also inadequate in that it gives no recognition to mental illness characterized by brooding and reflection and so relegates acts caused by such illness to the application of the inadequate right-wrong test. We conclude that a broader test should be adopted. . . .

The rule we now hold must be applied on the retrial of this case and in future cases not unlike that followed by the New Hampshire court since

1870. It is simply that an accused is not criminally responsible if his unlawful act was the product of mental disease or mental defect.

We use "disease" in the sense of a condition which is considered capable of either improving or deteriorating. We use "defect" in the sense of a condition which is not considered capable of either improving or deteriorating and which may be either congenital, or the result of injury, or the residual effect of a physical or mental disease.

Whenever there is "some evidence" that the accused suffered from a diseased or defective mental condition at the time the unlawful act was committed, the trial court must provide the jury with guides for determining whether the accused can be held criminally responsible. We do not, and indeed could not, formulate an instruction which would be either appropriate or binding in all cases. But under the rule now announced, any instruction should in some way convey to the jury the sense and substance of the following: If you the jury believe beyond a reasonable doubt that the accused was not suffering from a diseased or defective mental condition at the time he committed the criminal act charged, you may find him guilty. If you believe he was suffering from a diseased or defective mental condition when he committed the act, but believe beyond a reasonable doubt that the act was not the product of such mental abnormality, you may find him guilty. Unless you believe beyond a reasonable doubt either that he was not suffering from a diseased or defective mental condition, or that the act was not the product of such abnormality, you must find the accused not guilty by reason of insanity. Thus your task would not be completed upon finding, if you did find, that the accused suffered from a mental disease or defect. He would still be responsible for his unlawful act if there was no causal connection between such mental abnormality and the act. These questions must be determined by you from the facts which you find to be fairly deducible from the testimony and the evidence in this case.

The questions of fact under the test we now lay down are as capable of determination by the jury as, for example, the questions juries must determine upon a claim of total disability under a policy of insurance where the state of medical knowledge concerning the disease involved, and its effects, is obscure or in conflict. In such cases, the jury is not required to depend on arbitrarily selected "symptoms, phases or manifestations" of the disease as criteria for determining the ultimate questions of fact upon which the claim depends. Similarly, upon a claim of criminal irresponsibility, the jury will not be*required to rely on such symptoms as criteria for determining the ultimate question of fact upon which such claim depends. Testimony as to such "symptoms, phases or manifestations," along with other relevant evidence, will go to the jury upon the ultimate questions of fact which it alone can finally determine. Whatever the state of psychiatry, the psychiatrist will be permitted to carry out his principal court function which, as we noted in Holloway v. United States, "is to inform the jury of the character of [the accused's] mental disease [or defect]." The jury's range of inquiry will not be limited to, but may include, for example, whether an accused, who suffered from a mental disease or defect, did not know the difference between right and wrong, acted under the compulsion of an irresistible impulse, or had "been deprived of or lost the power of his will. . . ."

Finally, in leaving the determination of the ultimate question of fact to the jury, we permit it to perform its traditional function which, as we said in Holloway, is to apply "our inherited ideas of moral responsibility to individuals prosecuted for crime. . . ." Juries will continue to make moral judgments, still operating under the fundamental precept that "Our collective conscience does not allow punishment where it cannot impose blame." But in making such judgments, they will be guided by wider horizons of knowledge concerning mental life. The question will be simply whether the accused acted because of a mental disorder, and not whether he displayed particular symptoms which medical science has long recognized do not necessarily, or even typically, accompany even the most serious mental disorder.

The legal and moral traditions of the western world require that those who, of their own free will and with evil intent (sometimes called *mens rea*), commit acts which violate the law, shall be criminally responsible for those acts. Our traditions also require that where such acts stem from and are the product of a mental disease or defect as those terms are used herein, moral blame shall not attach, and hence there will not be criminal responsibility. The rule we state in this opinion is designed to meet these requirements.

Reversed and remanded for a new trial.

THOMAS SZASZ   *What Is Mental Illness?*

At the core of virtually all contemporary psychiatric theories and practices lies the concept of mental illness. This is especially so in forensic psychiatry—that is, in those areas of life where psychiatrists seek to influence the legal process. For example, although anthropologists, political scientists, psychologists, social workers, and sociologists all address themselves to problems of human conduct, only psychiatrists are considered experts on mental illness. We shall begin, therefore, with a critical examination of this concept.[1]

From *Law, Liberty, and Psychiatry: An Inquiry into the Social Uses of Mental Health Practices* by Thomas S. Szasz. New York: The Macmillan Company. Reprinted with permission of The Macmillan Company. © by Thomas S. Szasz, 1963.

[1] In my book *The Myth of Mental Illness* (1961), I traced in detail the origin and evolution of the concept of mental illness. My present aim is to present certain less technical considerations which lead to the same conclusions as I have reached there.

Let us launch our inquiry by asking, somewhat rhetorically, whether there is such a thing as mental illness. My reply is that there is not. Of course, mental illness is not a thing or physical object. It can exist only in the same sort of way as do other theoretical concepts. Yet, to those who believe in them, familiar theories are likely to appear, sooner or later, as "objective truths" or "facts." During certain historical periods, explanatory conceptions such as deities, witches, and instincts appeared not only as theories but as *self-evident* causes of a vast number of events. Today mental illness is widely regarded in a somewhat similar fashion, that is, as the cause of innumerable diverse happenings.

As an antidote to the complacent use of the notion of mental illness—as self-evident phenomenon, theory, or cause—let us ask: What is meant by the assertion that a person is mentally ill? In this chapter I shall describe briefly the main uses of the concept of mental illness. I shall argue that this notion has outlived whatever usefulness it may have had and that it now functions as a myth.

Mental Illness as a Sign of Brain Disease

The notion of mental illness derives its main support from such phenomena as syphilis of the brain or delirious conditions—intoxications, for instance—in which persons may manifest certain disorders of thinking and behavior. Correctly speaking, however, these are diseases of the brain, not of the mind. According to one school of thought, *all* so-called mental illness is of this type. The assumption is made that some neurological defect, perhaps a very subtle one, will ultimately be found to explain all the disorders of thinking and behavior. Many contemporary psychiatrists, physicians, and other scientists hold this view, which implies that people's troubles cannot be caused by conflicting personal needs, opinions, social aspirations, values, and so forth. These difficulties—which I think we may simply call *problems in living*—are thus attributed to the physiochemical processes which in due time will be discovered (and no doubt corrected!) by medical research.

Mental illnesses are thus regarded as basically no different from other diseases. The only difference, in this view, between mental and bodily disease is that the former, affecting the brain, manifests itself by means of mental symptoms; whereas the latter, affecting other organ systems—for example, the skin, liver, and so on—manifests itself by means of symptoms referable to those parts of the body.

In my opinion, this view is based on two fundamental errors. In the first place, a disease of the brain, analogous to a disease of the skin or bone, is a neurological defect, not a problem in living. For example, a *defect* in a person's visual field may be explained by correlating it with certain definite lesions in the nervous system. On the other hand, a person's *belief*—whether it be in Christianity, in Communism, or in the idea that his internal organs are rotting and that his body is already dead—cannot be explained by a defect or disease of the nervous system. Explanations of this sort of occurrence—assuming that one is interested in the belief itself and does not regard it simply as a symptom or expression of something else that is more interesting—must be sought along different lines.

The second error is epistemological. It consists of interpreting communications about ourselves and the world around us as symptoms of neurological functioning. This is an error not in observation or reasoning, but rather in the organization of expression of knowledge. In the present case, the error lies in making a dualism between mental and physical symptoms, a dualism which is a habit of speech and not the result of known observations. Let us see if this is so.

In medical practice, when we speak of physical disturbances we mean either signs (for example, fever) or symptoms (for example, pain). We speak of mental symptoms, on the other hand, when we refer to a patient's communications about himself, others, and the world about him. He might state that he is Napoleon or that he is being persecuted by the Communists. These would be considered mental symptoms *only* if the observer believed that the patient was *not* Napoleon or that he was *not* being persecuted by the Communists. This makes it apparent that the statement "X is a mental symptom" involves rendering a judgment. The judgment entails, moreover, a covert comparison or matching of the patient's ideas, concepts, or beliefs with those of the observer and the society in which they live. The notion of mental symptom is therefore inextricably tied to the *social*, and particularly the *ethical*, context in which it is made, just as the notion of bodily symptom is tied to an *anatomical* and *genetic* context.

To sum up: For those who regard mental symptoms as signs of brain disease, the concept of mental illness is unnecessary and misleading. If they mean that people so labeled suffer from diseases of the brain, it would seem better, for the sake of clarity, to say that and not something else.

Mental Illness as a Name
for Problems in Living

The term "mental illness" is also widely used to describe something very different from a disease of the brain. Many people today take it for granted that living is an arduous process. Its hardship for modern man, moreover, derives not so much from a struggle for biological survival as from the stresses and strains inherent in the social intercourse of complex human personalities. In this context, the notion of mental illness is used to identify or describe some feature of an individual's so-called personality. Mental illness—as a deformity

of the personality, so to speak—is regarded as the cause of interpersonal or social disharmony. It is implicit in this view that social intercourse between
people is regarded as something inherently harmonious, its disturbance being
due solely to the presence of mental illness in many people. Clearly, this is faulty
reasoning, for it makes the abstraction "mental illness" into a *cause*, even
though this abstraction was originally created to serve as a shorthand expression for certain types of human behavior. It now becomes necessary to ask:
What kinds of behavior are regarded as indicative of mental illness, and by
whom?

The concept of illness, whether bodily or mental, implies deviation from
a clearly defined norm. In the case of physical illness, the norm is the struc-
tural and functional integrity of the human body. Although the desirability
of physical health, as such, is an ethical value, what health is can be stated in
anatomical and physiological terms. What is the norm deviation from which is
regarded as mental illness? This question cannot be easily answered. But whatever this norm may be, we can be certain of only one thing: namely, that it
must be stated in terms of psychosocial, ethical, and legal concepts. For example, notions such as "excessive repression" or "acting out an unconscious
impulse" illustrate the use of psychological concepts for judging so-called
mental health and illness. The idea that chronic hostility, vengefulness, or
divorce are indicative of mental illness is an illustration of the use of ethical
norms (that is, the desirability of love, kindness, and a stable marriage relationship). Finally, the widespread psychiatric opinion that only a mentally ill
person would commit homicide illustrates the use of a legal concept as a norm
of mental health. The norm from which deviation is measured, when one
speaks of a mental illness, is a *psychosocial and ethical* one. Yet, the remedy is
sought in terms of *medical* measures which—it is hoped and assumed—are free
from wide differences of ethical value. The definition of the disorder and the
terms in which its remedy is sought are therefore at odds with one another.
The practical significance of this covert conflict between the alleged nature of
the defect and the remedy can hardly be exaggerated.

Having identified the norms used for measuring deviations in cases of mental illness, we shall now turn to the question: Who defines the norms and hence
the deviation? Two basic answers may be offered. First, it may be the person
himself—that is, the patient—who decides that he deviates from a norm. For example, an artist may believe that he suffers from a work inhibition. He may
implement this conclusion by seeking help *for* himself from a psychotherapist.
Second, it may be someone other than the patient who decides that the latter
is deviant—for example, relatives, physicians, legal authorities, society generally.
A psychiatrist may then be hired by persons other than the patient to do something *to* the patient in order to correct the deviation.

These considerations underscore the importance of asking the question,
"Whose agent is the psychiatrist?" and of giving a candid answer to it. The
psychiatrist (or nonmedical psychotherapist) may be the agent of the patient,

the relatives, the school, the military services, a business organization, a court of law, and so forth. In speaking of the psychiatrist as the agent of these persons or organizations, it is not implied that his values concerning norms, or his ideas and aims concerning the proper nature of remedial action, must coincide with those of his employer. For example, a patient in individual psychotherapy may believe that his salvation lies in a new marriage; his psychotherapist need not share his hypothesis. As the patient's agent, however, he must not resort to social or legal force to prevent the patient from putting his beliefs into action. If his *contract* is with the patient, the psychiatrist (psychotherapist) may disagree with him to stop his treatment, but he cannot engage others to obstruct the patient's aspirations. Similarly, if a psychiatrist is retained by a court to determine the sanity of an offender, he need not fully share the legal authorities' values and intentions in regard to the criminal, nor the means deemed appropriate for dealing with him. The psychiatrist cannot testify, however, that the accused is not insane, but that the legislators are—for passing the law which decrees the offender's actions illegal. Such an opinion could be voiced, of course, but not in a courtroom, and not by a psychiatrist who is there to assist the court in performing its daily work.

Clearly, psychiatry is much more intimately related to problems of ethics than is medicine. I used the word "psychiatry" here to refer to the contemporary discipline concerned with problems in living, and not with diseases of the brain, which belong to neurology. Difficulties in human relations can be analyzed, interpreted, and given meaning only within specific social and ethical contexts. Accordingly, the psychiatrist's socio-ethical orientations will influence his ideas on what is wrong with the patient, on what deserves comment or interpretation, in what directions change might be desirable, and so forth. Even in medicine proper, these factors play a role, as illustrated by the divergent orientations which physicians, depending on their religious affiliations, have toward such things as birth control and therapeutic abortion. Can anyone really believe that a psychotherapist's ideas on religion, politics, and related issues play no role in his practical work? If, on the other hand, they do matter, what are we to infer from it? Does it not seem reasonable that perhaps we ought to have different psychiatric therapies—each recognized for the ethical positions which it embodies—for, say, Catholics and Jews, religious persons and atheists, democrats and Communists, white supremacists and Negroes, and so on? Indeed, if we look at the way psychiatry is actually practiced today, especially in the United States, we find that people seek psychiatric help in accordance with their social status and ethical beliefs. This should occasion no greater surprise than being told that practicing Catholics rarely frequent birth-control clinics.

To recapitulate: In contemporary social usage, the finding of mental illness is made by establishing a deviance in behavior from certain psychosocial, ethical, or legal norms. The judgment may be made, as in medicine, by the patient, the physician (psychiatrist), or others. Remedial action, finally, tends to be sought in a therapeutic—or covertly medical—framework. This creates a situation in which it is claimed that psychosocial ethical, and/or legal deviations can be corrected by medical action. But is this rational?

Choice, Responsibility, and Psychiatry

While I argue that mental illnesses do not exist, obviously I do not wish to imply that the social and psychological occurrences *so labeled* do not exist. Like the personal and social troubles people had in the Middle Ages, they are real enough. What concerns us is the labels we give them, and, having labeled them, what we do about them. The demonologic conception of problems in living gave rise to therapy along theological lines. Today, a belief in mental illness implies—nay, requires—therapy along medical or psychotherapeutic lines.

I do not here propose to offer a new conception of "psychiatric illness" or a new form of "therapy." My aim is more modest and yet also more ambitious. It is to suggest that the phenomena now called mental illnesses be looked at afresh and more simply, that they be removed from the category of illnesses, and that they be regarded as the expressions of man's struggle with the problem of *how* he should live. By problems in living I refer to that explosive chain reaction which began with man's fall from divine grace by partaking of the fruit of the tree of knowledge. Man's awareness of himself and of the world about him seems to be a steadily expanding one, bringing in its wake an ever larger *burden of understanding* (an expression borrowed from Susanne Langer). This burden is to be expected, and must not be misinterpreted. Our only rational means for easing it is more understanding, and appropriate action based on it. The main alternative is to behave as if the burden were not what we perceive it to be, and to take refuge in an essentially theological view of man, whether this parades in scientific guise or not. But today is not a propitious time in human history for obscuring the issue of man's responsibility for his actions, by hiding it behind the skirt of an all-expanding conception of mental illness.

Conclusions

I have tried to show that the notion of mental illness has outlived whatever usefulness it may have had and that it now functions as a convenient myth. As such, it is a true heir to religious myths in general, and to the belief in witchcraft in particular.

When I assert that mental illness is a myth, I am not saying that personal unhappiness and socially deviant behavior do not exist; but I am saying that we categorize them as diseases at our own peril.

The expression "mental illness" is a metaphor which we have come to mistake for a fact. We call people physically ill when their body-functioning violates certain anatomical and physiological norms; similarly, we call people mentally ill when their personal conduct violates certain ethical, political, and social norms. This explains why many historical figures, from Jesus to Castro, and from Job to Hitler, have been diagnosed as suffering from this or that psychiatric malady.

Another way of highlighting the distinction between physical and mental sickness is to emphasize that physical illness is usually something that *happens* to us, whereas mental illness is something we *do* (or feel or think). Brown [J. A. C. Brown, *Freud and the Post-Freudians*] expressed the same idea when he wrote that "Neurosis is not a disease in the medically accepted sense; . . . it is not something a person *has* but rather something that he *is*."

It may be objected that whether or not we choose to call certain events in the universe "mental illness" is chiefly a semantic issue. Yes and no. The point is that when a scientific judgment becomes the basis for social action, the consequences are far-reaching. For example, when equal protection of the laws is withdrawn because a person has been labeled "mentally ill," we are confronted with an act of discrimination. Surely, from the victim's point of view, it makes little difference whether his right to vote is denied because of his race, or whether his right to stand trial is denied because of his mental illness. In the past, discrimination has been based chiefly on nationality, race, religion, and economic status; today, there is a mounting tendency to base it on psychiatric considerations. Since these practices rest on allegedly scientific grounds, and are implemented by professional persons, the ethical issues they pose are especially delicate.

Finally, the myth of mental illness encourages us to believe in its logical corollary: that social intercourse would be harmonious, satisfying, and the secure basis of a "good life" were it not for the disrupting influences of mental illness or "psychopathology." However, universal human happiness, in this form at least, is but another example of a wishful fantasy. I believe that human happiness is possible—not just for a select few, but on a scale hitherto unimaginable. But this can be achieved only if many men, not just a few, are willing and able to confront frankly, and tackle courageously, their ethical, personal, and social conflicts.

COMMENTARY ON THE CONTEMPORARY ISSUE

The philosophical issues underlying the dispute over the "insanity defense" are so close to the surface that we need do no more than call attention to them. When, if ever, is it reasonable to hold men **responsible** for their actions? Can anyone truly be said to be **free** to choose how he shall act? Do we deny man's freedom, and hence his dignity, by pointing to the causes of his actions?

The traditional name for this tangle of questions is the "Free Will–Determinism issue." In the seven selections included in this section, you will encounter a wide range of views on the subject, including such opposed positions as St. Augustine's paradoxical assertion of **both** human freedom **and** divine foreknowledge and Jean-Paul Sartre's dramatic defense of the absolute unfettered freedom of the individual moral agents. Perhaps it would be interesting in these transitional remarks to explore the wider social and moral implication of the free will issue, so that you can see just how much hangs on your answer to this ancient question.

There is an old French saying: Tout comprendre, c'est tout pardonner. To understand all is to forgive all. We seem always to be caught on the horns of a dilemma: on the one hand, if we are to treat a man with dignity, then surely we must hold him responsible for his actions. We may excuse children or idiots with the explanation, "they don't know what they are doing," but it hardly seems a mark of respect to say the same thing of a mature, reasonable adult. On the other hand, the deeper we look into a man's heart, the more we tend to believe that he could not help the wicked deeds he may have performed.

When, for example, we describe crime as a "social problem" whose causal roots lie in poverty, ghetto housing, broken homes, and discrimination, we are saying essentially that the individual criminals are not entirely responsible for their actions. Since a child cannot help being born in a slum, it seems harsh indeed to blame him for the antisocial acts which flow from such a childhood. We see a steady movement in America toward a reliance on corrective social legislation rather than on a rigorous and punitive enforcement of the penal code.

But are we really willing to accept the implications of such a shift in our conception of crime? Do we wish to view men—rich or poor, advantaged or disadvantaged—as being determined by social forces over which they have no individual control? Can no case be made for the old-fashioned doctrine that a man is responsible for what he does, both for the good and the bad? Is all our praising of virtue and condemning of vice a mistake, on a par with the tendency of primitive people to impute motives to trees and stones and rain clouds?

We can imagine the way an argument might go between a lawyer for an accused murderer and our traditionalist, Dr. Szasz:

Dr. Szasz: Men are free and responsible agents and they must be held to account for their actions.

Lawyer: You will agree, I am sure, that a man cannot be blamed for firing a gun if his arms were held by a powerful assailant and his fingers forced to move the trigger.

Dr. Szasz: Of course.

Lawyer: And you will surely grant as well that he cannot be blamed if a tumor in his brain caused an involuntary squeezing of his finger muscles?

Dr. Szasz: That also I will grant.

Lawyer: But then, if I can produce scientific evidence establishing a causal link between his childhood experience and his adult behavior, **such that I can predict in advance with high probability that this same man will commit a crime of violence,** then by parity of reasoning you must grant that he cannot be blamed for that crime.

Now, what are we—and Dr. Szasz—to say? Our instinct is to insist that the cases are different, and some of the authors in this section develop elaborate proofs of that difference. But if we were privy to the intimate details of the life history of the accused; if we had seen his life warped and twisted by the conditions of his infancy; if, indeed, we had predicted that the little boy would grow up to be a criminal, **and then had seen our prediction tragically confirmed**—if all this had occurred—would we really be so ready to condemn? Or might we not wish to say: "Tout comprendre, c'est tout pardonner."

One of the most problematic aspects of the free will debate is that everyone—even the defender of determinism—has one view of himself and a quite different view of the rest of mankind. No matter how "understanding" I may be about the determining causes of **your** behavior, I find it impossible to take the same attitude toward the decision now facing **me!** I simply **cannot** believe that my own action, right now, is merely the last link in a causal chain reaching back to my youth or even beyond. As I now deliberate, I am certain that there is a real choice before me, and hence that I am responsible for what I finally decide to do.

Is this belief an illusion? Would I give it up if only I knew, in greater detail, the causes of my behavior? Or is there a fundamental difference between my **awareness** of myself as an agent and my **knowledge** of human behavior, including even my own? If there is such a difference, what does it imply about our relationships to others? Can I even relate to a person **as a person,** or must I always view even those closest to me as causally determined "things"? This is the problem Kierkegaard was trying to get at in the last section, when he wrote that "I can lay hold of the other's reality only by conceiving it, and hence by translating it into a possibility." Perhaps, contrary to what Kierkegaard himself says, we must have faith in one another, which is to say that we must "ask with infinite interest" about the reality of another person.

All of which leaves the judge, the social worker, the legislator completely in the dark. Judge Bazelon and his colleagues had to decide whether to send Monte Durham to jail or to send him back for a new trial in which a plea of "not guilty by reason of insanity" might be sustained. Society as a whole must decide whether to view individuals as responsible agents who can be made to pay for their transgressions, or as beings whose behavior is to be treated rather than rewarded or punished. And if some line of definition is to be drawn, society must determine where it is just and reasonable to draw the line.

As you read the arguments of our seven authors, you will develop a sense of the true complexity of the problem, for each philosopher interprets the issue in his own way. You will probably begin to suspect that many other philosophical issues are bound up with this one. Clearly, we must understand causation in order to make up our minds about free will. And we must decide what the grounds are for claiming that an action is right or wrong before we can determine who is to be praised and blamed. In this way, you will come to see why many philosophers have felt the need to work out a "system" in which different philosophical problems are dealt with at the same time.

ARISTOTLE

Aristotle (384–322 B.C.) is widely believed to be the greatest philosopher of all time. St. Thomas held him in such high regard that he referred to him merely as "the philosopher," as though there were no other. In the Nichomachean Ethics, *from which this selection is taken, Aristotle pulls together our most firmly held convictions concerning virtue, justice, happiness, responsibility, and the good life, and expounds them in a systematic, rationalized manner. Unlike Plato, who put forth controversial and unpopular moral opinions, Aristotle is very much a figure of the Establishment.*

The present selection is devoted to the complexities of choice, deliberation, and responsibility. Aristotle uses a series of brief hypothetical examples to show us the dimensions and limitations of our concept of responsibility. We would not blame a layman for failure to cure our illness, for we know that he is ignorant of the medical techniques required. So ignorance is, in some measure, a legitimate excuse. But we would blame a doctor whose ignorance resulted from his inattention to studies in medical school. So ignorance is sometimes not an excuse. The lawyer, like the moral philosopher, must figure out just exactly why ignorance is an excuse in some cases but not in others. What is more, both must try to generalize from such cases so that new situations can be decided in terms of established principles. The "insanity defense" is just such an attempt to extend a legally recognized plea into new areas on the basis of new psychological knowledge.

Strange as it may seem, Aristotle's style of analysis and argument is very similar to that of recent English and American philosophers in what is called the "ordinary language" school of philosophy. Indeed, with a few alterations to bring him up to date, this selection by Aristotle could quite easily appear as a paper in a modern journal of philosophy. Great philosophy, like great literature, has a timeless immediacy which makes even ancient writings relevant to our contemporary concerns.

Choice, Deliberation, and the Limits of Responsibility

I

Since virtue is concerned with passions and actions, and on voluntary passions and actions praise and blame are bestowed, on those that are involuntary pardon, and sometimes also pity, to distinguish the voluntary and the involuntary is presumably necessary for those who are studying the nature of virtue, and useful also for legislators with a view to the assigning both of honours and of punishments.

Those things, then, are thought involuntary, which take place under compulsion or owing to ignorance; and that is compulsory of which the moving principle is outside, being a principle in which nothing is contributed by the person who is acting or is feeling the passion, e.g. if he were to be carried somewhere by a wind, or by men who had him in their power.

But with regard to the things that are done from fear of greater evils or for some noble object (e.g. if a tyrant were to order one to do something base, having one's parents and children in his power, and if one did the action they were to be saved, but otherwise would be put to death), it may be debated whether such actions are involuntary or voluntary. Something of the sort happens also with regard to the throwing of goods overboard in a storm; for in the abstract no one throws goods away voluntarily, but on condition of its securing the safety of himself and his crew any sensible man does so. Such actions, then, are mixed, but are more like voluntary actions; for they are worthy of choice at the time when they are done, and the end of an action is relative to the occasion. Both the terms, then, "voluntary" and "involuntary," must be used with reference to the moment of action. Now the man acts voluntarily; for the principle that moves the instrumental parts of the body in such actions is in him, and the things of which the moving principle is in a man himself are in his power to do or not to do. Such actions, therefore, are voluntary, but in the abstract perhaps involuntary; for no one would choose any such act in itself.

For such actions men are sometimes even praised, when they endure something base or painful in return for great and noble objects gained; in the opposite case they are blamed, since to endure the greatest indignities for no noble end or for a trifling end is the mark of an inferior person. On some actions praise indeed is not bestowed, but pardon is, when one does what he ought not under pressure which overstrains human nature and which no one could withstand. But some acts, perhaps, we cannot be forced to do, but ought

Book III, chaps. 1–5 from "Nichomachean Ethics," trans. by W. D. Ross from *The Oxford Translation of Aristotle*, ed. W. D. Ross, Vol. IX, 1925. Reprinted by permission of the Clarendon Press, Oxford.

rather to face death after the most fearful sufferings; for the things that "forced" Euripides' Alcmaeon to slay his mother seem absurd. It is difficult sometimes to determine what should be chosen at what cost, and what should be endured in return for what gain, and yet more difficult to abide by our decisions; for as a rule what is expected is painful, and what we are forced to do is base, whence praise and blame are bestowed on those who have been compelled or have not.

What sort of acts, then, should be called compulsory? We answer that without qualification actions are so when the cause is in the external circumstances and the agent contributes nothing. But the things that in themselves are involuntary, but now and in return for these gains are worthy of choice, and whose moving principle is in the agent, are in themselves involuntary, but now and in return for these gains voluntary. They are more like voluntary acts; for actions are in the class of particulars, and the particular acts here are voluntary. What sort of things are to be chosen, and in return for what, it is not easy to state; for there are many differences in the particular cases.

But if some one were to say that pleasant and noble objects have a compelling power, forcing us from without, all acts would be for him compulsory; for it is for these objects that all men do everything they do. And those who act under compulsion and unwillingly act with pain, but those who do acts for their pleasantness and nobility do them with pleasure; it is absurd to make external circumstances responsible, and not oneself, as being easily caught by such attractions, and to make oneself responsible for noble acts but the pleasant objects responsible for base acts. The compulsory, then, seems to be that whose moving principle is outside, the person compelled contributing nothing.

Everything that is done by reason of ignorance is *not* voluntary; it is only what produces pain and repentance that is *in*voluntary. For the man who has done something owing to ignorance, and feels not the least vexation at his action, has not acted voluntarily, since he did not know what he was doing, nor yet involuntarily, since he is not pained. Of people, then, who act by reason of ignorance, he who repents is thought an involuntary agent, and the man who does not repent may, since he is different, be called a not voluntary agent; for, since he differs from the other, it is better that he should have a name of his own.

Acting by reason of ignorance seems also to be different from acting *in* ignorance; for the man who is drunk or in a rage is thought to act as a result not of ignorance but of one of the causes mentioned, yet not knowingly but in ignorance.

Now every wicked man is ignorant of what he ought to do and what he ought to abstain from, and it is by reason of error of this kind that men become unjust and in general bad; but the term "involuntary" tends to be used not if a man is ignorant of what is to his advantage—for it is not mistaken purpose that causes involuntary action (it leads rather to wickedness), nor ignorance of the universal (for *that* men are *blamed*), but ignorance of particulars, i.e. of the circumstances of the action and the objects with which it is concerned. For it is on these that both pity and pardon depend, since the person who is ignorant of any of these acts involuntarily.

Perhaps it is just as well, therefore, to determine their nature and number. A man may be ignorant, then, of who he is, what he is doing, what or whom he is acting on, and sometimes also what (e.g. what instrument) he is doing it with, and to what end (e.g. he may think his act will conduce to some one's safety), and how he is doing it (e.g. whether gently or violently). Now of all of these no one could be ignorant unless he were mad, and evidently also he could not be ignorant of the agent; for how could he not know himself? But of what he is doing a man might be ignorant, as for instance people say "it slipped out of their mouths as they were speaking," or "they did not know it was a secret," as Aeschylus said of the mysteries, or a man might say he "let it go off when he merely wanted to show its working," as the man did with the catapult. Again, one might think one's son was an enemy, as Merope did, or that a pointed spear had a button on it, or that a stone was pumice-stone; or one might give a man a draught to save him, and really kill him; or one might want to touch a man, as people do in sparring, and really wound him. The ignorance may relate, then, to any of these things, i.e. of the circumstances of the action, and the man who was ignorant of any of these is thought to have acted involuntarily, and especially if he was ignorant on the most important points; and these are thought to be the circumstances of the action and its end. Further, the doing of an act that is called involuntary in virtue of ignorance of this sort must be painful and involve repentance.

Since that which is done under compulsion or by reason of ignorance is involuntary, the voluntary would seem to be that of which the moving principle is in the agent himself, he being aware of the particular circumstances of the action. Presumably acts done by reason of anger or appetite are not rightly called involuntary. For in the first place, on that showing none of the other animals will act voluntarily, nor will children; and secondly, is it meant that we do not do voluntarily *any* of the acts that are due to appetite or anger, or that we do the noble acts voluntarily and the base acts involuntarily? Is not this absurd, when one and the same thing is the cause? But it would surely be odd to describe as involuntary the things one ought to desire; and we ought both to be angry at certain things and to have an appetite for certain things, e.g. for health and for learning. Also what is involuntary is thought to be painful, but what is in accordance with appetite is thought to be pleasant. Again, what is the difference in respect of involuntariness between errors committed upon calculation and those committed in anger? Both are to be avoided, but the irrational passions are thought not less human than reason is, and therefore also the actions which proceed from anger or appetite are the man's actions. It would be odd, then, to treat them as involuntary.

II

Both the voluntary and the involuntary having been delimited, we must next discuss choice; for it is thought to be most closely bound up with virtue and to discriminate characters better than actions do.

Choice, then, seems to be voluntary, but not the same thing as the voluntary; the latter extends more widely. For both children and the lower animals share in voluntary action, but not in choice, and acts done on the spur of the moment we describe as voluntary, but not as chosen.

Those who say it is appetite or anger or wish or a kind of opinion do not seem to be right. For choice is not common to irrational creatures as well, but appetite and anger are. Again, the incontinent man acts with appetite, but not with choice; while the continent man on the contrary acts with choice, but not with appetite. Again, appetite is contrary to choice, but not appetite to appetite. Again, appetite relates to the pleasant and the painful, choice neither to the painful nor to the pleasant.

Still less is it anger; for acts due to anger are thought to be less than any others objects of choice.

But neither is it wish, though it seems near to it; for choice cannot relate to impossibles, and if any one said he chose them he would be thought silly; but there may be a wish even for impossibles, e.g. for immortality. And wish may relate to things that could in no way be brought about by one's own efforts, e.g. that a particular actor or athlete should win in a competition; but no one chooses such things, but only the things that he thinks could be brought about by his own efforts. Again, wish relates rather to the end, choice to the means; for instance, we wish to be healthy, but we choose the acts which will make us healthy, and we wish to be happy and say we do, but we cannot well say we choose to be so; for, in general, choice seems to relate to the things that are in our own power.

For this reason, too, it cannot be opinion; for opinion is thought to relate to all kinds of things, no less to eternal things and impossible things than to things in our own power; and it is distinguished by its falsity or truth, not by its badness or goodness, while choice is distinguished rather by these.

Now with opinion in general perhaps no one even says it is identical. But it is not identical even with any kind of opinion; for by choosing what is good or bad we are men of a certain character, which we are not by holding certain opinions. And we choose to get or avoid something good or bad, but we have opinions about what a thing is or whom it is good for or how it is good for him; we can hardly be said to opine to get or avoid anything. And choice is praised for being related to the right object rather than for being rightly related to it, opinion for being truly related to its object. And we choose what we best know to be good, but we opine what we do not quite know; and it is not the same people that are thought to make the best choices and to have the best opinions, but some are thought to have fairly good opinions, but by reason of vice to choose what they should not. If opinion precedes choice or accompanies it, that makes no difference; for it is not this that we are considering, but whether it is *identical* with some kind of opinion.

What, then, or what kind of thing is it, since it is none of the things we have mentioned? It seems to be voluntary, but not all that is voluntary to be an object of choice. Is it, then, what has been decided on by previous deliberation? At any rate choice involves a rational principle and thought. Even the name seems to suggest that it is what is chosen before other things.

III

Do we deliberate about everything, and is everything a possible subject of deliberation, or is deliberation impossible about some things? We ought presumably to call not what a fool or a madman would deliberate about, but what a sensible man would deliberate about, a subject of deliberation. Now about eternal things no one deliberates, e.g. about the material universe or the incommensurability of the diagonal and the side of a square. But no more do we deliberate about the things that involve movement but always happen in the same way, whether of necessity or by nature or from any other cause, e.g. the solstices and the risings of the stars; nor about things that happen now in one way, now in another, e.g. droughts and rains; nor about chance events, like the finding of treasure. But we do not deliberate even about all human affairs; for instance, no Spartan deliberates about the best constitution for the Scythians. For none of these things can be brought about by our own efforts.

We deliberate about things that are in our power and can be done; and these are in fact what is left. For nature, necessity, and chance are thought to be causes, and also reason and everything that depends on man. Now every class of men deliberates about the things that can be done by their own efforts. And in the case of exact and self-contained sciences there is no deliberation, e.g. about the letters of the alphabet (for we have no doubt how they should be written); but the things that are brought about by our own efforts, but not always in the same way, are the things about which we deliberate, e.g. questions of medical treatment or of money-making. And we do so more in the case of the art of navigation than in that of gymnastics, inasmuch as it has been less exactly worked out, and again about other things in the same ratio, and more also in the case of the arts than in that of the sciences; for we have more doubt about the former. Deliberation is concerned with things that happen in a certain way for the most part, but in which the event is obscure, and with things in which it is indeterminate. We call in others to aid us in deliberation on important questions, distrusting ourselves as not being equal to deciding.

We deliberate not about ends but about means. For a doctor does not deliberate whether he shall heal, nor an orator whether he shall persuade, nor a statesman whether he shall produce law and order, nor does any one else deliberate about his end. They assume the end and consider how and by what means it is to be attained; and if it seems to be produced by several means they consider by which it is most easily and best produced, while if it is achieved by one only they consider how it will be achieved by this and by what means *this* will be achieved, till they come to the first cause, which in the order of discovery is last. For the person who deliberates seems to investigate and analyse in the way described as though he were analysing a geometrical construction[1] (not all investigation appears to be deliberation—for instance mathematical investigations—but all deliberation is investigation), and what is last in the order of analysis seems to be first in the order of becoming. And if we come on an impossibility, we give up the search, e.g. if we need money and this cannot be got; but if a thing appears possible we try to do it. By "possible" things I mean things that might be brought about by our own efforts; and these in a sense include things that can be brought about by the efforts of our friends, since the moving principle is in ourselves. The subject of investigation is sometimes the instruments, sometimes the use of them; and similarly in the other cases—sometimes the means, sometimes the mode of using it or the means of bringing it about. It seems, then, as has been said, that man is a moving principle of actions; now deliberation is about the things to be done by the agent himself, and actions are for the sake of things other than themselves. For the end cannot be a subject of deliberation, but only the means; nor indeed can the particular facts be a subject of it, as whether this is bread or has been baked as it should; for these are matters of perception. If we are to be always deliberating, we shall have to go on to infinity.

The same thing is deliberated upon and is chosen, except that the object of choice is already determinate, since it is that which has been decided upon as a result of deliberation that is the object of choice. For every one ceases to inquire how he is to act when he has brought the moving principle back to himself and to the ruling part of himself; for this is what chooses. This is plain also from the ancient constitutions, which Homer represented; for the kings announced their choices to the people. The object of choice being one of the things in our own power which is desired after deliberation, choice will be deliberate desire of things in our own power; for when we have decided as a result of deliberation, we desire in accordance with our deliberation.

We may take it, then, that we have described choice in outline, and stated the nature of its objects and the fact that it is concerned with means.

[1] Aristotle has in mind the method of discovering the solution of a geometrical problem. The problem being to construct a figure of a certain kind, we suppose it constructed and then analyse it to see if there is some figure by constructing which we can construct the required figure, and so on till we come to a figure which our existing knowledge enables us to construct.

IV

That *wish* is for the end has already been stated; some think it is for the good, others for the apparent good. Now those who say that the good is the object of wish must admit in consequence that that which the man who does not choose aright wishes for is not an object of wish (for if it is to be so, it must also be good; but it was, if it so happened, bad); while those who say the apparent good is the object of wish must admit that there is no natural object of wish, but only what seems good to each man. Now different things appear good to different people, and, if it so happens, even contrary things.

If these consequences are unpleasing, are we to say that absolutely and in truth the good is the object of wish, but for each person the apparent good; that that which is in truth an object of wish is an object of wish to the good man, while any chance thing may be so to the bad man, as in the case of bodies also the things that are in truth wholesome are wholesome for bodies which are in good condition, while for those that are diseased other things are wholesome—or bitter or sweet or hot or heavy, and so on; since the good man judges each class of things rightly, and in each the truth appears to him? For each state of character has its own ideas of the noble and the pleasant, and perhaps the good man differs from others most by seeing the truth in each class of things, being as it were the norm and measure of them. In most things the error seems to be due to pleasure; for it appears a good when it is not. We therefore choose the pleasant as a good, and avoid pain as an evil.

V

The end, then, being what we wish for, the means what we deliberate about and choose, actions concerning means must be according to choice and voluntary. Now the exercise of the virtues is concerned with means. Therefore virtue also is in our own power, and so too vice. For where it is in our power to act it is also in our power not to act, and *vice versa;* so that, if to act, where this is noble, it is our power, not to act, which will be base, will also be in our power, and if not to act, where this is noble, is in our power, to act, which will be base, will also be in our power. Now if it is in our power to do noble or base acts, and likewise in our power not to do them, and this was what being good or bad meant,[2] then it is in our power to be virtuous or vicious.

The saying that "no one is voluntarily wicked nor involuntarily happy" seems to be partly false and partly true; for no one is involuntarily happy, but wickedness *is* voluntary. Or else we shall have to dispute what has just been said, at any rate, and deny that man is a moving principle or begetter of his actions as of children. But if these facts are evident and we cannot refer actions

---

[2] See the seventh paragraph of Chapter II in this selection. [Ed.]

to moving principles other than those in ourselves, the acts whose moving principles are in us must themselves also be in our power and voluntary.

Witness seems to be borne to this both by individuals in their private capacity and by legislators themselves; for these punish and take vengeance on those who do wicked acts (unless they have acted under compulsion or as a result of ignorance for which they are not themselves responsible), while they honour those who do noble acts, as though they meant to encourage the latter and deter the former. But no one is encouraged to do the things that are neither in our power nor voluntary; it is assumed that there is no gain in being persuaded not to be hot or in pain or hungry or the like, since we shall experience these feelings none the less. Indeed,[3] we punish a man for his very ignorance, if he is thought responsible for the ignorance, as when penalties are doubled in the case of drunkenness; for the moving principle is in the man himself, since he had the power of not getting drunk and his getting drunk was the cause of his ignorance. And we punish those who are ignorant of anything in the laws that they ought to know and that is not difficult, and so too in the case of anything else that they are thought to be ignorant of through carelessness; we assume that it is in their power not to be ignorant, since they have the power of taking care.

But perhaps a man is the kind of man not to take care. Still they are themselves by their slack lives responsible for becoming men of that kind, and men make themselves responsible for being unjust or self-indulgent, in the one case by cheating and in the other by spending their time in drinking bouts and the like; for it is activities exercised on particular objects that make the corresponding character. This is plain from the case of people training for any contest or action; they practise the activity the whole time. Now not to know that it is from the exercise of activities on particular objects that states of character are produced is the mark of a thoroughly senseless person. Again, it is irrational to suppose that a man who acts unjustly does not wish to be unjust or a man who acts self-indulgently to be self-indulgent. But if *without* being ignorant a man does the things which will make him unjust, he will be unjust voluntarily. Yet it does not follow that if he wishes he will cease to be unjust and will be just. For neither does the man who is ill become well on those terms. We may suppose a case in which he is ill voluntarily, through living incontinently and disobeying his doctors. In that case it was *then* open to him not to be ill, but not now, when he has thrown away his chance, just as when you have let a stone go it is too late to recover it; but yet it was in your power to throw it, since the moving principle was in you. So, too, to the unjust and to the self-indulgent man it was open at the beginning not to become men of this kind, and so they are unjust and self-indulgent voluntarily; but now that they have become so it is not possible for them not to be so.

---

[3] This connects with the words earlier in this paragraph, "unless they have acted . . . as a result of ignorance for which they are not themselves responsible."

But not only are the vices of the soul voluntary, but those of the body also for some men, whom we accordingly blame; while no one blames those who are ugly by nature, we blame those who are so owing to want of exercise and care. So it is, too, with respect to weakness and infirmity; no one would reproach a man blind from birth or by disease or from a blow, but rather pity him, while every one would blame a man who was blind from drunkenness or some other form of self-indulgence. Of vices of the body, then, those in our own power are blamed, those not in our power are not. And if this be so, in the other cases also the vices that are blamed must be in our own power.

Now some one may say that all men desire the apparent good, but have no control over the appearance, but the end appears to each man in a form answering to his character. We reply that if each man is somehow responsible for his state of mind, he will also be himself somehow responsible for the appearance; but if not, no one is responsible for his own evildoing, but every one does evil acts through ignorance of the end, thinking that by these he will get what is best, and the aiming at the end is not self-chosen but one must be born with an eye, as it were, by which to judge rightly and choose what is truly good, and he is well endowed by nature who is well endowed with this. For it is what is greatest and most noble, and what we cannot get or learn from another, but must have just such as it was when given us at birth, and to be well and nobly endowed with this will be perfect and true excellence of natural endowment. If this is true, then, how will virtue be more voluntary than vice? To both men alike, the good and the bad, the end appears and is fixed by nature or however it may be, and it is by referring everything else to this that men do whatever they do.

Whether, then, it is not by nature that the end appears to each man such as it does appear, but something also depends on him, or the end is natural but because the good man adopts the means voluntarily virtue is voluntary, vice also will be none the less voluntary; for in the case of the bad man there is equally present that which depends on himself in his actions even if not in his end. If, then, as is asserted, the virtues are voluntary (for we are ourselves somehow partly responsible for our states of character, and it is by being persons of a certain kind that we assume the end to be so and so), the vices also will be voluntary; for the same is true of them.

With regard to the virtues in *general* we have stated their genus in outline, viz. that they are means and that they are states of character, and that they tend, and by their own nature, to the doing of the acts by which they are produced, and that they are in our power and voluntary, and act as the right rule prescribes. But actions and states of character are not voluntary in the same way; for we are masters of our actions from the beginning right to the end, if we know the particular facts, but though we control the beginning of our states of character the gradual progress is not obvious, any more than it is in illnesses; because it was in our power, however, to act in this way or not in this way, therefore the states are voluntary.

ST. AUGUSTINE

St. Augustine (354–430), a towering figure of the early Christian church, is one of the religious thinkers who fused the philosophical tradition of Greece and Rome with the religious teachings of the Old and New Testaments.

A major problem facing devout Christians was the apparent contradiction between the omnipotence and omniscience of God and the responsibility of the individual for his actions. On the one hand, it would seem that I cannot be held responsible for my actions, for if an all-knowing God can foresee my transgression long before it occurs, then it hardly makes sense to say that I am free to avoid committing it. On the other hand, the Bible clearly teaches that I am to be rewarded or punished according to my life on earth, which means that I am to be held responsible by God.

Augustine sets himself the task of resolving the contradiction by means of an analysis of the concepts of "will" and "free" and "necessity." When philosophers find that two strongly held, apparently reasonable beliefs conflict, they frequently try to remove the conflict by analyzing the key terms in the dispute, in order to see whether our words have led us astray. We shall find a number of authors in this section trying such a tactic in their attempts to deal with the vexing problems of free will.

Divine Foreknowledge and Free Will

IX

CONCERNING THE FOREKNOWLEDGE OF GOD
AND THE FREE WILL OF MAN,
IN OPPOSITION TO THE DEFINITION OF CICERO

The manner in which Cicero addresses himself to the task of refuting the Stoics, shows that he did not think he could effect anything against them in argument unless he had first demolished divination. And this he attempts to

From *The City of God* by Saint Augustine, Book V, Chaps. 9–10. In *The Basic Writings of Saint Augustine*, ed. by Whitney J. Oates. Vol. II. New York: Random House, Inc., 1948. Reprinted by permission of Random House, Inc., and T. & T. Clark, Edinburgh.

accomplish by denying that there is any knowledge of future things, and maintains with all his might that there is no such knowledge either in God or man, and that there is no prediction of events. Thus he both denies the fore-knowledge of God, and attempts by vain arguments, and by opposing to him-self certain oracles very easy to be refuted, to overthrow all prophecy, even such as is clearer than the light (though even these oracles are not refuted by him).

But, in refuting these conjectures of the mathematicians, his argument is triumphant, because truly these are such as destroy and refute themselves. Nevertheless, they are far more tolerable who assert the fatal influence of the stars than they who deny the foreknowledge of future events. For, to confess that God exists, and at the same time to deny that He has foreknowledge of future things, is the most manifest folly. This Cicero himself saw, and there-fore attempted to assert the doctrine embodied in the words of Scripture, "The fool hath said in his heart, There is no God." That, however, he did not do in his own person, for he saw how odious and offensive such an opinion would be; and therefore, in his book on the nature of the gods, he makes Cotta dis-pute concerning this against the Stoics, and preferred to give his own opinion in favor of Lucilius Balbus, to whom he assigned the defence of the Stoical position, rather than in favor of Cotta, who maintained that no divinity exists. However, in his book on divination, he in his own person most openly opposes the doctrine of the prescience of future things. But all this he seems to do in order that he may not grant the doctrine of fate, and by so doing destroy free will. For he thinks that, the knowledge of future things once conceded, fate follows as so necessary a consequence that it cannot be denied.

But, let these perplexing debatings and disputations of the philosophers go on as they may, we, in order that we may confess the most high and true God Himself, do confess His will, supreme power, and prescience. Neither let us be afraid lest, after all, we do not do by will that which we do by will, because He, whose foreknowledge is infallible, foreknew that we would do it. It was this which Cicero was afraid of, and therefore opposed foreknowledge. The Stoics also maintained that all things do not come to pass by necessity, although they contended that all things happen according to destiny. What is it, then, that Cicero feared in the prescience of future things? Doubtless it was this—that if all future things have been foreknown, they will happen in the order in which they have been foreknown; and if they come to pass in this order, there is a certain order of things foreknown by God; and if a certain order of things, then a certain order of causes, for nothing can happen which is not preceded by some efficient cause. But if there is a certain order of causes according to which everything happens which does happen, then by fate, says he, all things happen which do happen. But if this be so, then is there nothing in our own power, and there is no such thing as freedom of will; and if we grant that, says he, the whole economy of human life is subverted. In vain are laws enacted. In vain are reproaches, praises, chidings, exhortations had re-course to; and there is no justice whatever in the appointment of rewards for the good, and punishments for the wicked. And that consequences so disgraceful, and absurd, and pernicious to humanity may not follow. Cicero chooses to reject the foreknowledge of future things, and shuts up the religious mind to this alternative, to make choice between two things, either that something is in our own power, or that there is foreknowledge—both of which cannot be true; but if one is affirmed, the other is thereby denied. He therefore, like a truly great and wise man, and one who consulted very much and very skillfully for the good of humanity, of those two chose the freedom of the will, to confirm which he denied the foreknowledge of future things; and thus, wishing to make men free, he makes them sacrilegious. But the religious mind chooses both, confesses both, and maintains both by the faith of piety. But how so? says Cicero; for the knowledge of future things being granted, there follows a chain of consequences which ends in this, that there can be nothing depending on our own free wills. And further, if there is anything depending on our wills, we must go backwards by the same steps of reasoning till we arrive at the conclusion that there is no foreknowledge of future things. For we go backwards through all the steps in the following order:—If there is free will, all things do not happen according to fate; if all things do not happen according to fate, there is not a certain order of causes; and if there is not a certain order of causes, neither is there a certain order of things foreknown by God—for things cannot come to pass except they are preceded by efficient causes—but, if there is no fixed and certain order of causes foreknown by God, all things cannot be said to happen according as He foreknew that they would happen. And further, if it is not true that all things happen just as they have been foreknown by Him, there is not, says he, in God any foreknowledge of future events.

Now, against the sacrilegious and impious darings of reason, we assert both that God knows all things before they come to pass, and that we do by our free will whatsoever we know and feel to be done by us only because we will it. But that all things come to pass by fate, we do not say; nay we affirm that nothing comes to pass by fate; for we demonstrate that the name of fate, as it is wont to be used by those who speak of fate, meaning thereby the position of the stars at the time of each one's conception or birth, is an unmeaning word, for astrology itself is a delusion. But an order of causes in which the highest efficiency is attributed to the will of God, we neither deny nor do we designate it by the name of fate, unless, perhaps, we may understand fate to mean that which is spoken, deriving it from *fari*, to speak; for we cannot deny that it is written in the sacred Scriptures, "God hath spoken once; these two things have I heard, that power belongeth unto God. Also unto Thee, O God, belongeth mercy: for Thou wilt render unto every man according to his works." Now the expression, "Once hath He spoken," is to be understood as meaning *"immovably,"* that is, unchangeably hath He spoken, inasmuch as He knows unchangeably all things which shall be, and all things which He will do. We might, then, use the word fate in the sense it bears when derived from *fari*, to speak, had it not already come to be understood in

another sense, into which I am unwilling that the hearts of men should unconsciously slide. But it does not follow that, though there is for God
a certain order of all causes, there must therefore be nothing depending on the
free exercise of our own wills, for our wills themselves are included in that
order of causes which is certain to God, and is embraced by His foreknowledge, for human wills are also causes of human actions; and He who foreknew
all the causes of things would certainly among those causes not have been ignorant of our wills. For even that very concession which Cicero himself
makes is enough to refute him in this argument. For what does it help him to
say that nothing takes place without a cause, but that every cause is not fatal,
there being a fortuitous cause, a natural cause, and a voluntary cause? It is
sufficient that he confesses that whatever happens must be preceded by a cause.
For we say that those causes which are called fortuitous are not a mere name
for the absence of causes, but are only latent, and we attribute them either to
the will of the true God, or to that of spirits of some kind or other. And as to
natural causes, we by no means separate them from the will of Him who is
the author and framer of all nature. But now as to voluntary causes. They are
referable either to God, or to angels, or to men, or to animals of whatever
description, if indeed those instinctive movements of animals devoid of reason,
by which, in accordance with their own nature, they seek or shun various
things, are to be called wills. And when I speak of the wills of angels, I mean
either the wills of good angels, whom we call the angels of God, or of the
wicked angels, whom we call the angels of the devil, or demons. Also by the
wills of men I mean the wills either of the good or of the wicked. And from
this we conclude that there are no efficient causes of all things which come to
pass unless voluntary causes, that is, such as belong to that nature which is the
spirit of life. For the air or wind is called spirit, but inasmuch as it is a body,
it is not the spirit of life. The spirit of life, therefore, which quickens all
things, and is the creator of every body, and of every created spirit, is God
Himself, the uncreated spirit. In His supreme will resides the power which acts
on the wills of all created spirits, helping the good, judging the evil, controlling
all, granting power to some, not granting it to others. For, as He is the creator
of all natures, so also is He the bestower of all powers, not of all wills; for
wicked wills are not from Him, being contrary to nature, which is from Him.
As to bodies, they are more subject to wills: some to our wills, by which I
mean the wills of all living mortal creatures, but more to the wills of men than
of beasts. But all of them are most of all subject to the will of God, to whom
all wills also are subject, since they have no power except what He has bestowed upon them. The cause of things, therefore, which makes but is not
made, is God; but all other causes both make and are made. Such are all created
spirits, and especially the rational. Material causes, therefore, which may rather
be said to be made than to make, are not to be reckoned among efficient
causes, because they can only do what the wills of spirits do by them. How,
then, does an order of causes which is certain to the foreknowledge of God
necessitate that there should be nothing which is dependent on our wills, when

our wills themselves have a very important place in the order of causes? Cicero, then, contends with those who call this order of causes fatal, or rather designate this order itself by the name of fate; to which we have an abhorrence, especially on account of the word, which men have become accustomed to understand as meaning what is not true. But, whereas he denies that the order of all causes is most certain, and perfectly clear to the prescience of God, we detest his opinion more than the Stoics do. For he either denies that God exists —which, indeed, in an assumed parsonage, he has labored to do, in his book *De Natura Deorum*—or if he confesses that He exists, but denies that He is prescient of future things, what is that but just the fool saying in his heart there is no God? For one who is not prescient of all future things is not God. Wherefore our wills also have just so much power as God willed and foreknew that they should have; and therefore whatever power they have, they have it within most certain limits; and whatever they are to do, they are most assuredly to do, for He whose foreknowledge is infallible foreknew that they would have the power to do it. Wherefore, if I should choose to apply the name of fate to anything at all, I should rather say that fate belongs to the weaker of the two parties, will to the stronger, who has the other in his power, than that the freedom of our will is excluded by that order of causes, which, by an unusual application of the word peculiar to themselves, the Stoics call *Fate*.

X

WHETHER OUR WILLS ARE RULED BY NECESSITY

Wherefore, neither is that necessity to be feared, for dread of which the Stoics labored to make such distinctions among the causes of things as should enable them to rescue certain things from the dominion of necessity, and to subject others to it. Among those things which they wished not to be subject to necessity they placed our wills, knowing that they would not be free if subjected to necessity. For if that is to be called *our necessity* which is not in our power, but even though we be unwilling effects what it can effect—as, for instance, the necessity of death—it is manifest that our wills by which we live uprightly or wickedly are not under such a necessity; for we do many things which, if we were not willing, we should certainly not do. This is primarily true of the act of willing itself—for if we will, it *is*; if we will not, it *is* not—for we should not will if we were unwilling. But if we define necessity to be that according to which we say that it is necessary that anything be of such or such a nature, or be done in such and such a manner, I know not why we should have any dread of that necessity taking away the freedom of our will. For we do not put the life of God or the foreknowledge of God under necessity if we should say that it is necessary that God should live forever, and foreknow all things; as neither is His power diminished when we say that He cannot die or fall into error—for this is in such a way impossible to Him, that if it were possible for Him, He would be of less power. But assuredly He is rightly called omnipotent, though He can neither die nor fall into error. For He is called omnipotent on account of His doing what He wills, not on account of His suffering what He wills not; for if that should befall Him, He would by no means be omnipotent. Wherefore, He cannot do some things for the very reason that He is omnipotent. So also, when we say that it is necessary that, when we will, we will by free choice, in so saying we both affirm what is true beyond doubt, and do not still subject our wills thereby to a necessity which destroys liberty. Our wills, therefore, *exist* as *wills*, and do themselves whatever we do by willing, and which would not be done if we were unwilling. But when any one suffers anything, being unwilling, by the will of another, even in that case will retains its essential validity—we do not mean the will of the party who inflicts the suffering, for we resolve it into the power of God. For if a will should simply exist, but not be able to do what it wills, it would be overborne by a more powerful will. Nor would this be the case unless there had existed will, and that not the will of the other party, but the will of him who willed, but was not able to accomplish what he willed. Therefore, whatsoever a man suffers contrary to his own will, he ought not to attribute to the will of men, or of angels, or of any created spirit, but rather to His will who gives power to wills. It is not the case, therefore, that because God foreknew what would be in the power of our wills, there is for that reason nothing in the power of our wills. For He who foreknew this did not foreknow nothing. Moreover, if He who foreknew what would be in the power of our wills did not foreknow nothing, but something, assuredly, even though He did foreknow, there is something in the power of our wills. Therefore we are by no means compelled, either, retaining the prescience of God, to take away the freedom of the will, or retaining the freedom of the will, to deny that He is prescient of future things, which is impious. But we embrace both. We faithfully and sincerely confess both. The former, that we may believe well; the latter, that we may live well. For he lives ill who does not believe well concerning God. Wherefore, be it far from us, in order to maintain our freedom, to deny the prescience of Him by whose help we are or shall be free. Consequently, it is not in vain that laws are enacted, and that reproaches, exhortations, praises, and vituperations are had recourse to; for these also He foreknew, and they are of great avail, even as great as He foreknew that they would be of. Prayers, also, are of avail to procure those things which He foreknew that he would grant to those who offered them; and with justice have rewards been appointed for good deeds, and punishments for sins. For a man does not therefore sin because God foreknew that he would sin. Nay, it cannot be doubted but that it is the man himself who sins when he does sin, because He, whose foreknowledge is infallible, foreknew not that fate, or fortune, or something else would sin, but that the man himself would sin, who, if he wills not, sins not. But if he shall not will to sin, even this did God foreknow.

DESCARTES

You have already encountered the first of René Descartes' Six Meditations *in the first section of this book. Here we read the Fourth Meditation, which Descartes devotes to the subject of truth and error. For a scientist and mathematician like Descartes, there is a close connection between "error" in the sense of a wrong or immoral action, and "error" in the sense of a mistake in reasoning. In both cases, he claims, man's unlimited will unwisely carries him beyond the capacities of his limited reason. By identifying immoral action with errors in reasoning, Descartes seems to imply that men aren't really responsible for their wrongdoing. After all, we wouldn't condemn a mathematician for making a mistake in a proof, would we? But this raises a deeper and more troubling question: why do men* ever *do what they know to be wrong? Something like this puzzle lies behind the willingness of the courts to excuse a man who does not "know the quality" of the criminal act he has committed. In this area of philosophy there is never a very long distance between abstract theory and practical consequences.*

Perfect Will and Imperfect Intellect

Meditation IV

OF TRUTH AND ERROR

I have been habituated these bygone days to detach my mind from the senses, and I have accurately observed that there is exceedingly little which is known with certainty respecting corporeal objects,—that we know much more of the human mind, and still more of God himself. I am thus able now without difficulty to abstract my mind from the contemplation of [sensible or] imaginable objects, and apply it to those which, as disengaged from all matter, are purely intelligible. And certainly the idea I have of the human mind in so far as it is a thinking thing, and not extended in length, breadth, and depth, and participating in none of the properties of body, is incomparably more dis-

From *Meditations* by René Descartes, trans. by John Veitch.

tinct than the idea of any corporeal object; and when I consider that I doubt, in other words, that I am an incomplete and dependent being, the idea of a complete and independent being, that is to say of God, occurs to my mind with so much clearness and distinctness,—and from the fact alone that this idea is found in me, or that I who possess it exist, the conclusions that God exists, and that my own existence, each moment of its continuance, is absolutely dependent upon him, are so manifest,—as to lead me to believe it impossible that the human mind can know anything with more clearness and certitude. And now I seem to discover a path that will conduct us from the contemplation of the true God, in whom are contained all the treasures of science and wisdom, to the knowledge of the other things in the universe.

For, in the first place, I discover that it is impossible for him ever to deceive me, for in all fraud and deceit there is a certain imperfection: and although it may seem that the ability to deceive is a mark of subtlety or power, yet the will testifies without doubt or malice and weakness; and such, accordingly, cannot be found in God. In the next place, I am conscious that I possess a certain faculty of judging [or discerning truth from error], which I doubtless received from God, along with whatever else is mine; and since it is impossible that he should will to deceive me, it is likewise certain that he has not given me a faculty that will ever lead me into error, provided I use it aright.

And there would remain no doubt on this head, did it not seem to follow from this, that I can never therefore be deceived; for if all I possess be from God, and if he planted in me no faculty that is deceitful, it seems to follow that I can never fall into error. Accordingly, it is true that when I think only of God (when I look upon myself as coming from God), and turn wholly to him, I discover [in myself] no cause of error or falsity: but immediately thereafter, recurring to myself, experience assures me that I am nevertheless subject to innumerable errors. When I come to inquire into the cause of these, I observe that there is not only present to my consciousness a real and positive idea of God, or of a being supremely perfect, but also, so to speak, a certain negative idea of nothing,—in other words, of that which is at an infinite distance from every sort of perfection, and that I am, as it were, a mean between God and nothing, or placed in such a way between absolute existence and non-existence, that there is in truth nothing in me to lead me into error, in so far as an absolute being is my creator; but that, on the other hand, as I thus likewise participate in some degree of nothing or of non-being, in other words, as I am not myself the supreme Being, and as I am wanting in many perfections, it is not surprising I should fall into error. And I hence discern that error, so far as error is something real, which depends for its existence on God, but is simply defect; and therefore that, in order to fall into it, it is not necessary God should have given me a faculty expressly for this end, but that my being deceived arises from the circumstance that the power which God has given me of discerning truth from error is not infinite.

Nevertheless this is not yet quite satisfactory; for error is not a pure negation [in other words, it is not the simple deficiency or want of some knowledge which is not due], but the privation or want of some knowledge which it would seem I ought to possess. But, on considering the nature of God, it seems impossible that he should have planted in his creature any faculty not perfect in its kind, that is, wanting in some perfection due to it: for if it be true, that in proportion to the skill of the maker the perfection of his work is greater, what thing can have been produced by the supreme Creator of the universe that is not absolutely perfect in all its parts? And assuredly there is no doubt that God could have created me such as that I should never be deceived; it is certain, likewise, that he always wills what is best: it is better, then, that I should be capable of being deceived than that I should not?

Considering this more attentively, the first thing that occurs to me is the reflection that I must not be surprised if I am not always capable of comprehending the reasons why God acts as he does; nor must I doubt of his existence because I find, perhaps, that there are several other things, besides the present respecting which I understand neither why nor how they were created by him; for, knowing already that my nature is extremely weak and limited, and that the nature of God, on the other hand, is immense, incomprehensible, and infinite, I have no longer any difficulty in discerning that there is an infinity of things in his power whose causes transcend the grasp of my mind: and this consideration alone is sufficient to convince me, that the whole class of final causes is of no avail in physical [or natural] things; for it appears to me that I cannot, without exposing myself to the charge of termerity, seek to discover the [impenetrable] ends of Deity.

It further occurs to me that we must not consider only one creature apart from the others, if we wish to determine the perfection of the works of Deity, but generally all his creatures together; for the same object that might perhaps, with some show of reason, be deemed highly imperfect if it were alone in the world, may for all that be the most perfect possible, considered as forming part of the whole universe: and although, as it was my purpose to doubt of everything, I only as yet know with certainty my own existence and that of God, nevertheless, after having remarked the infinite power of Deity, I cannot deny that he may have produced many other objects, or at least that he is able to produce them, so that I may occupy a place in the relation of a part to the great whole of his creatures.

Whereupon, regarding myself more closely, and considering what my errors are (which alone testify to the existence of imperfection in me), I observe that these depend on the concurrence of two causes, viz., the faculty of cognition which I possess, and that of election or the power of free choice,—in other words, the understanding and the will. For by the understanding alone, I [neither affirm nor deny anything, but] merely apprehend (*percipio*) the ideas which I may form a judgment; nor is any error, properly so called, found in it thus accurately taken. And although there are perhaps innumerable objects in the world of which I have no idea in my understanding, it cannot, on that account, be said that I am deprived of those ideas [as of something that is due to my nature], but simply that I do not possess them, because, in truth, there is no ground to prove that Deity ought to have endowed me with a larger faculty of cognition than he has actually bestowed upon me; and however skilful a workman I suppose him to be, I have no reason, on that account, to think that it was obligatory on him to give to each of his works all the perfections he is able to bestow upon some. Nor, moreover, can I complain that God has not given me freedom of choice, or a will sufficiently ample and perfect, since, in truth, I am conscious of will so ample and extended as to be superior to all limits. And what appears to me here to be highly remarkable is that, of all the other properties I possess, there is none so great and perfect as that I do not clearly discern it could be still greater and more perfect. For, to take an example, if I consider the faculty of understanding which I possess, I find that it is of very small extent, and greatly limited, and at the same time I form the idea of another faculty of the same nature, much more ample and even infinite; and seeing that I can frame the idea of it, I discover, from this circumstance alone, that it pertains to the nature of God. In the same way, if I examine the faculty of memory or imagination, or any other faculty I possess, I find none that is not small and circumscribed, and in God immense [and infinite]. It is the faculty of will only, or freedom of choice, which I experience to be so great that I am unable to conceive the idea of another that shall be more ample and extended; so that it is chiefly my will which leads me to discern that I bear a certain image and similitude of Deity. For although the faculty of will is incomparably greater in God than in myself, as well in respect of the knowledge and power that are conjoined with it, and that render it stronger and more efficacious, as in respect of the object, since in him it extends to a greater number of things, it does not, nevertheless, appear to me greater, considered in itself formally and precisely: for the power of will consists only in this, that we are able to do or not to do the same thing (that is, to affirm or deny, to pursue or shun it), or rather in this alone, that in affirming or denying, pursuing or shunning, what is proposed to us by the understanding, we so act that we are not conscious of being determined to a particular action by any external force. For, to the possession of freedom, it is not necessary that I be alike indifferent towards each of the two contraries; but, on the contrary, the more I am inclined towards the one, whether because I clearly know that in it there is the reason of truth and goodness, or because God thus internally disposes my thought, the more freely do I choose and embrace it; and assuredly divine grace and natural knowledge, very far from diminishing liberty, rather augment and fortify it. But the indifference of which I am conscious when I am not impelled to one side rather than to another for want of a reason, is the lowest grade of liberty, and manifests defect or negation of knowledge rather than perfection, of will; for if I always clearly knew what was true and good, I should never have any difficulty in determining what judgment I ought to come to, and what choice I ought to make, and I should thus be entirely free without ever being indifferent.

From all this I discover, however, that neither the power of willing, which I have received from God, is of itself the source of my errors, for it is exceedingly ample and perfect in its kind; nor even the power of understanding, for as I conceive no object unless by means of the faculty that God bestowed upon me, all that I conceive is doubtless rightly conceived by me, and it is impossible for me to be deceived in it.

Whence, then, spring my errors? They arise from this cause alone, that I do not restrain the will, which is of much wider range than the understanding, within the same limits, but extend it even to things I do not understand, and as the will is of itself indifferent to such, it readily falls into error and sin by choosing the false in room of the true, and evil instead of good.

For example, when I lately considered whether aught really existed in the world, and found that because I considered this question, it very manifestly followed that I myself existed, I could not but judge that what I so clearly conceived was true, not that I was forced to this judgment by any external cause, but simply because great clearness of the understanding was succeeded by strong inclination in the will; and I believed this the more freely and spontaneously in proportion as I was less indifferent with respect to it. But now I not only know that I exist, in so far as I am a thinking human being, but there is likewise presented to my mind a certain idea of corporeal nature; hence I am in doubt as to whether the thinking nature which is in me, or rather which I myself am, is different from that corporeal nature, or whether both are merely one and the same thing, and I here suppose that I am as yet ignorant of any reason that would determine me to adopt the one belief in preference to the other: whence it happens that it is a matter of perfect indifference to me which of the two suppositions I affirm or deny, or whether I form any judgment at all in the matter.

This indifference, moreover, extends not only to things of which the understanding has no knowledge at all, but in general also to all those which it does not discover with perfect clearness at the moment the will is deliberating upon them; for, however probable the conjectures may be that dispose me to form a judgment in a particular matter, the simple knowledge that these are merely conjectures, and not certain and indubitable reasons, is sufficient to lead me to form one that is directly the opposite. Of this I lately had abundant experience, when I laid aside as false all that I had before held for true, on the single ground that I could in some degree doubt of it. But if I abstain from judging of a thing when I do not conceive it with sufficient clearness and distinctness, it is plain that I act rightly, and am not deceived; but if I resolve to deny or affirm, I then do not make a right use of my free will; and if I affirm what is false, it is evident that I am deceived: moreover, even although I judge according to truth, I stumble upon it by chance, and do not therefore escape the imputation of a wrong use of my freedom; for it is a dictate of the natural light, that the knowledge of the understanding ought always to precede the determination of the will.

And it is this wrong use of freedom of the will in which is found the privation that constitutes the form of error. Privation, I say, is found in the act, in so far as it proceeds from myself, but it does not exist in the faculty which I received from God, nor even in the act, in so far as it depends on him; for I have assuredly no reason to complain that God has not given me a greater power of intelligence or more perfect natural light than he has actually bestowed, since it is of the nature of a finite understanding not to comprehend many things, and of the nature of a created understanding to be finite; on the contrary, I have every reason to render thanks to God, who owed me nothing, for having given me all the perfections I possess, and I should be far from thinking that he has unjustly deprived me of, or kept back, the other perfections which he has not bestowed upon me.

I have no reason, moreover, to complain because he has given me a will more ample than my understanding, since, as the will consists only of a single element, and that indivisible, it would appear that this faculty is of such a nature that nothing could be taken from it [without destroying it]; and certainly, the more extensive it is, the more cause I have to thank the goodness of him who bestowed it upon me.

And, finally, I ought not also to complain that God concurs with me in forming the acts of this will, or the judgments in which I am deceived, because those acts are wholly true and good, in so far as they depend on God; and the ability to form them is a higher degree of perfection in my nature than the want of it would be. With regard to privation, in which alone consists the formal reason of error and sin, this does not require the concurrence of Deity, because it is not a thing [or existence], and if it be referred to God as to its cause, it ought not to be called privation, but negation [according to the signification of these words in the schools]. For in truth it is no imperfection in Deity that he has accorded to me the power of giving or withholding my assent from certain things of which he has not put a clear and distinct knowledge in my understanding; but it is doubtless an imperfection in me that I do not use my freedom aright, and readily give my judgment on matters which I only obscurely and confusedly conceive.

I perceive, nevertheless, that it was easy for Deity so to have constituted me as that I should never be deceived, although I still remained free and possessed of a limited knowledge, viz., by implanting in my understanding a clear and distinct knowledge of all the objects respecting which I should ever have to deliberate; or simply by so deeply engraving on my memory the resolution to judge of nothing without previously possessing a clear and distinct conception of it, that I should never forget it. And I easily understand that, in so far as I consider myself as a single whole, without reference to any other being in the universe, I should have been much more perfect than I now am, had Deity created me superior to error; but I cannot therefore deny that it is not somehow a greater perfection in the universe, that certain of its parts are not exempt from defect, as others are, than if they were all perfectly alike.

And I have no right to complain because God, who placed me in the world, was not willing that I should sustain that character which of all others is the chief and most perfect; I have even good reason to remain satisfied on the ground that, if he has not given me the perfection of being superior to error by the first means I have pointed out above, which depends on a clear and evident knowledge of all the matters regarding which I can deliberate, he has at least left in my power the other means, which is, firmly to retain the resolution never to judge where the truth is not clearly known to me: for, although I am conscious of the weakness of not being able to keep my mind continually fixed on the same thought, I can nevertheless, by attentive and oft-repeated meditation, impress it so strongly on my memory that I shall never fail to recollect it as often as I require it, and I can acquire in this way the habitude of not erring; and since it is in being superior to error that the highest and chief perfection of man consists, I deem that I have not gained little by this day's meditation, in having discovered the source of error and falsity.

And certainly this can be no other than what I have now explained: for as often as I so restrain my will within the limits of my knowledge, that it forms no judgment except regarding objects which are clearly and distinctly represented to it by the understanding, I can never be deceived; because every clear and distinct conception is doubtless something, and as such cannot owe its origin to nothing, but must of necessity have God for its author—God, I say, who, as supremely perfect, cannot, without a contradiction, be the cause of any error; and consequently it is necessary to conclude that every such conception [or judgment] is true. Nor have I merely learned to-day what I must avoid to escape error, but also what I must do to arrive at the knowledge of truth; for I will assuredly reach truth if I only fix my attention sufficiently on all the things I conceive perfectly, and separate these from others which I conceive more confusedly and obscurely: to which for the future I shall give diligent heed.

HUME

*David Hume (1711–1776) is far and away the most important phi-
losopher ever to write in the English language. Hume published his
three-volume* Treatise of Human Nature *while still in his twenties.
He intended it to be a complete system of "Moral Philosophy," as
the eighteenth century called the study of man, analogous to the
system of "Natural Philosophy," or physics, which Isaac Newton
had produced in the previous century. In the present selection,
which comes from the second book of the* Treatise, *Hume offers
an analysis of the notions of liberty and necessity as part of a
broader account of man's passions and emotions.*

*It is hard to say which side of the free will debate Hume is
on. To be sure, he affirms that our choices are causally determined,
and thus far he would seem to lend support to the view that men
cannot be held responsible for what they do. But he confounds our
expectations by claiming that men can be praised or blamed precisely* because *their actions flow in predictable ways from their
character and circumstances. This twist in the argument is very
perplexing, and two of our remaining three authors subject it to
further analysis.*

Of Liberty and Necessity

I

We come now to explain the *direct* passions, or the impressions, which
arise immediately from good or evil, from pain or pleasure. Of this kind are,
desire and aversion, grief and joy, hope and fear.

Of all the immediate effects of pain and pleasure, there is none more
remarkable than the WILL; and tho', properly speaking, it be not comprehended
among the passions, yet as the full understanding of its nature and properties, is
necessary to the explanation of them, we shall here make it the subject of our
enquiry. I desire it may be observ'd, that by the *will*, I mean nothing but *the
internal impression we feel and are conscious of, when we knowingly give rise
to any new motion of our body, or new perception of our mind.* This im-

From *The Philosophical Works*, Part III, "Of the Will and Direct Passions," by David
Hume.

pression, like the preceding ones of pride and humility, love and hatred, 'tis impossible to define, and needless to describe any farther; for which reason we shall cut off all those definitions and distinctions, with which philosophers are wont to perplex rather than clear up this question; and entering at first upon the subject, shall examine that long disputed question concerning *liberty and necessity;* which occurs so naturally in treating of the will.

'Tis universally acknowledg'd, that the operations of external bodies are necessary, and that in the communication of their motion, in their attraction, and mutual cohesion, there are not the least traces of indifference or liberty. Every object is determin'd by an absolute fate to a certain degree and direction of its motion, and can no more depart from that precise line, in which it moves, than it can convert itself into an angel, or spirit, or any superior substance. The actions, therefore, of matter are to be regarded as instances of necessary actions; and whatever is in this respect on the same footing with matter, must be acknowledg'd to be necessary. That we may know whether this be the case with the actions of the mind, we shall begin with examining matter, and considering on what the ideas of a necessity in its operations are founded, and why we conclude one body or action to be the infallible cause of another.

It has been observ'd already, that in no single instance the ultimate connexion of any objects is discoverable, either by our senses or reason, and that we can never penetrate so far into the essence and construction of bodies, as to perceive the principle, on which their mutual influence depends. 'Tis their constant union alone, with which we are acquainted; and 'tis from the constant union the necessity arises. If objects had not an uniform and regular conjunction with each other, we shou'd never arrive at any idea of cause and effect; and even after all, the necessity, which enters into that idea, is nothing but a determination of the mind to pass from one object to its usual attendant, and infer the existence of one from that of the other. Here then are two particulars, which we are to consider as essential to necessity, *viz.* the constant *union* and the *inference* of the mind; and wherever we discover these we must acknowledge a necessity. As the actions of matter have no necessity, but what is deriv'd from these circumstances, and it is not by any insight into the essence of bodies we discover their connexion, the absence of this insight, while the union and inference remain, will never, in any case, remove the necessity. 'Tis the observation of the union, which produces the inference; for which reason it might be thought sufficient, if we prove a constant union in the actions of the mind, in order to establish the inference, along with the necessity of these actions. But that I may bestow a greater force on my reasoning, I shall examine these particulars apart, and shall first prove from experience, that our actions have a constant union with our motives, tempers, and circumstances, before I consider the inferences we draw from it.

To this end a very slight and general view of the common course of human affairs will be sufficient. There is no light, in which we can take them, that does not confirm this principle. Whether we consider mankind according

to the difference of sexes, ages, governments, conditions, or methods of education; the same uniformity and regular operation of natural principles are dis-
cernible. Like causes still produce like effects; in the same manner as in the
mutual action of the elements and powers of nature.

There are different trees, which regularly produce fruit, whose relish is
different from each other; and this regularity will be admitted as an instance of
necessity and causes in external bodies. But are the products of *Guienne* and of
Champagne more regularly different than the sentiments, actions, and passions
of the two sexes, of which the one are distinguish'd by their force and maturity, the other by their delicacy and softness?

Are the changes of our body from infancy to old age more regular and
certain than those of our mind and conduct? And wou'd a man be more
ridiculous, who wou'd expect that an infant of four years old will raise a
weight of three hundred pound, than one, who from a person of the same
age, wou'd look for a philosophical reasoning, or a prudent and well-concerted
action?

We must certainly allow, that the cohesion of the parts of matter arises
from natural and necessary principles, whatever difficulty we may find in
explaining them: And for a like reason we must allow, that human society is
founded on like principles; and our reason in the latter case, is better than even
that in the former; because we not only observe, that men *always* seek society,
but can also explain the principles, on which this universal propensity is
founded. For is it more certain, that two flat pieces of marble will unite together, than that two young savages of different sexes will copulate? Do the
children arise from this copulation more uniformly, than does the parents' care
for their safety and preservation? And after they have arriv'd at years of discretion by the care of their parents, are the inconveniences attending their
separation more certain than their foresight of these inconveniencies, and their
care of avoiding them by a close union and confederacy?

The skin, pores, muscles, and nerves of a day-labourer are different from
those of a man of quality: So are his sentiments, actions and manners. The
different stations of life influence the whole fabric, external and internal; and
these different stations arise necessarily, because uniformly, from the necessary
and uniform principles of human nature. Men cannot live without society, and
cannot be associated without government. Government makes a distinction of
property, and establishes the different ranks of man. This produces industry,
traffic, manufactures, law-suits, war, leagues, alliances, voyages, travels, cities,
fleets, ports, and all those other actions and objects, which cause such a diversity, and at the same time maintain such an uniformity in human life.

Shou'd a traveller, returning from a far country, tell us, that he had seen
a climate in the fiftieth degree of northern latitude, where all the fruits ripen
and come to perfection in the winter, and decay in the summer, after the same
manner as in *England* they are produc'd and decay in the contrary seasons, he
wou'd find few so credulous as to believe him. I am apt to think a traveller
wou'd meet with as little credit, who shou'd inform us of people exactly of the

same character with those in *Plato's* republic on the one hand, or those in *Hobbes's Leviathan* on the other. There is a general course of nature in human actions, as well as in the operations of the sun and the climate. There are also characters peculiar to different nations and particular persons, as well as common to mankind. The knowledge of these characters is founded on the observation of an uniformity in the actions, that flow from them; and this uniformity forms the very essence of necessity.

I can imagine only one way of eluding this argument, which is by denying that uniformity of human actions, on which it is founded. As long as actions have a constant union and connexion with the situation and temper of the agent, however we may in words refuse to acknowledge the necessity, we really allow the thing. Now some may, perhaps, find a pretext to deny this regular union and connexion. For what is more capricious than human actions? What more inconstant than the desires of man? And what creature departs more widely, not only from right reason, but from his own character and disposition? An hour, a moment is sufficient to make him change from one extreme to another, and overturn what cost the greatest pain and labour to establish. Necessity is regular and certain. Human conduct is irregular and uncertain. The one, therefore, proceeds not from the other.

To this I reply, that in judging of the actions of men we must proceed upon the same maxims, as when we reason concerning external objects. When any phænomena are constantly and invariably conjoin'd together, they acquire such a connexion in the imagination, that it passes from one to the other, without any doubt or hesitation. But below this there are many inferior degrees of evidence and probability, nor does one single contrariety of experiment entirely destroy all our reasoning. The mind ballances the contrary experiments, and deducting the inferior from the superior, proceeds with that degree of assurance or evidence, which remains. Even when these contrary experiments are entirely equal, we remove not the notion of causes and necessity; but supposing that the usual contrariety proceeds from the operation of contrary and conceal'd causes, we conclude, that the chance or indifference lies only in our judgment on account of our imperfect knowledge, not in the things themselves, which are in every case equally necessary, tho' to appearance not equally constant or certain. No union can be more constant and certain, than that of some actions with some motives and characters; and if in other cases the union is uncertain, 'tis no more than what happens in the operations of body, nor can we conclude any thing from the one irregularity, which will not follow equally from the other.

'Tis commonly allow'd that mad-men have no liberty. But were we to judge by their actions, these have less regularity and constancy than the actions of wise-men, and consequently are farther remov'd from necessity. Our way of thinking in this particular is, therefore, absolutely inconsistent; but is a natural consequence of these confus'd ideas and undefin'd terms, which we so commonly make use of in our reasonings, especially on the present subject.

We must now shew, that as the *union* betwixt motives and actions has the same constancy, as that in any natural operations, so its influence on the understanding is also the same, in *determining* us to infer the existence of one from that of another. If this shall appear, there is no known circumstance, that enters into the connexion and production of the actions of matter, that is not to be found in all the operations of the mind; and consequently we cannot, without a manifest absurdity, attribute necessity to the one, and refuse it to the other.

There is no philosopher, whose judgment is so riveted to this fantastical system of liberty, as not to acknowledge the force of *moral evidence*, and both in speculation and practice proceed upon it, as upon a reasonable foundation. Now moral evidence is nothing but a conclusion concerning the actions of men, deriv'd from the consideration of their motives, temper and situation. Thus when we see certain characters or figures describ'd upon paper, we infer that the person, who produc'd them, wou'd affirm such facts, the death of *Cæsar*, the success of *Augustus*, the cruelty of *Nero;* and remembering many other concurrent testimonies we conclude, that those facts were once really existent, and that so many men, without any interest, wou'd never conspire to deceive us; especially since they must, in the attempt, expose themselves to the derision of all their contemporaries, when these facts were asserted to be recent and universally known. The same kind of reasoning runs thro' politics, war, commerce, oeconomy, and indeed mixes itself so entirely in human life, that 'tis impossible to act or subsist a moment without having recourse to it. A prince, who imposes a tax upon his subjects, expects their compliance. A general, who conducts an army, makes account of a certain degree of courage. A merchant looks for fidelity and skill in his factor or super-cargo. A man, who gives orders for his dinner, doubts not of the obedience of his servants. In short, as nothing more nearly interests us than our own actions and those of others, the greatest part of our reasonings is employ'd in judgments concerning them. Now I assert, that whoever reasons after this manner, does *ipso facto* believe the actions of the will to arise from necessity, and that he knows not what he means, when he denies it.

All those objects, of which we call the one *cause* and the other *effect*, consider'd in themselves, are as distinct and separate from each other, as any two things in nature, nor can we ever, by the most accurate survey of them, infer the existence of the one from that of the other. 'Tis only from experience and the observation of their constant union, that we are able to form this inference; and even after all, the inference is nothing but the effects of custom on the imagination. We must not here be content with saying, that the idea of cause and effect arises from objects constantly united; but must affirm, that 'tis the very same with the idea of these objects, and that the *necessary connexion* is not discover'd by a conclusion of the understanding, but is merely a perception of the mind. Wherever, therefore, we observe the same union, and wherever the union operates in the same manner upon the belief and opinion, we have the idea of causes and necessity, tho' perhaps we may avoid those expressions. Motion in one body in all past instances, that have fallen under our observation, is follow'd upon impulse by motion in another. 'Tis impossible for the mind to penetrate farther. From this constant union it *forms* the idea of cause and effect, and by its influence *feels* the necessity. As there is the same constancy, and the same influence in what we call moral evidence, I ask no more. What remains can only be a dispute of words.

And indeed, when we consider how aptly *natural* and *moral* evidence cement together, and form only one chain of argument betwixt them, we shall make no scruple to allow, that they are of the same nature, and deriv'd from the same principles. A prisoner, who has neither money nor interest, discovers the impossibility of his escape, as well from the obstinacy of the gaoler, as from the walls and bars with which he is surrounded; and in all attempts for his freedom chuses rather to work upon the stone and iron of the one, than upon the inflexible nature of the other. The same prisoner, when conducted to the scaffold, foresees his death as certainly from the constancy and fidelity of his guards as from the operation of the ax or wheel. His mind runs along a certain train of ideas: The refusal of the soldiers to consent to his escape, the action of the executioner; the separation of the head and body; bleeding, convulsive motions, and death. Here is a connected chain of natural causes and voluntary actions; but the mind feels no difference betwixt them in passing from one link to another; nor is less certain of the future event than if it were connected with the present impressions of the memory and senses by a train of causes cemented together by what we are pleas'd to call a *physical necessity*. The same experienc'd union has the same effect on the mind, whether the united objects be motives, volitions and actions; or figure and motion. We may change the names of things; but their nature and their operation of the understanding never change.

I dare be positive no one will ever endeavour to refute these reasonings otherwise than by altering my definitions, and assigning a different meaning to the terms of *cause, and effect, and necessity, and liberty, and chance*. According to my definitions, necessity makes an essential part of causation; and consequently liberty, by removing necessity, removes also causes, and is the very same thing with chance. As chance is commonly thought to imply a contradiction, and is at least directly contrary to experience, there are always the same arguments against liberty or free-will. If any one alters the definitions, I cannot pretend to argue with him, 'till I know the meaning he assigns to these terms.

✦ II

I believe we may assign the three following reasons for the prevalence of the doctrine of liberty, however absurd it may be in one sense, and unintelligible in any other. First, After we have perform'd any action; tho' we confess we were influenc'd by particular views and motives; 'tis difficult for us to perswade ourselves we were govern'd by necessity, and that 'twas utterly impossible for us to have acted otherwise; the idea of necessity seeming to imply something of force, and violence, and constraint, of which we are not sensible. Few are capable of distinguishing betwixt the liberty of *spontaneity*, as it is call'd in the schools, and the liberty of *indifference*; betwixt that which is oppos'd to violence, and that which means a negation of necessity and causes. The first is even the most common sense of the word; and as 'tis only that species of liberty, which it concerns us to preserve, our thoughts have been principally turn'd towards it, and have almost universally confounded it with the other.

Secondly, There is a *false sensation or experience* even of the liberty of indifference; which is regarded as an argument for its real existence. The necessity of any action, whether of matter or of the mind, is not properly a quality in the agent, but in any thinking or intelligent being, who may consider the action, and consists in the determination of his thought to infer its existence from some preceding objects: As liberty or chance, on the other hand, is nothing but the want of that determination, and a certain looseness, which we feel in passing or not passing from the idea of one to that of the other. Now we may observe, that tho' in reflecting on human actions we seldom feel such a looseness or indifference, yet it very commonly happens, that in performing the actions themselves we are sensible of something like it: And as all related or resembling objects are readily taken for each other, this has been employ'd as a demonstrative or even an intuitive proof of human liberty. We feel that our actions are subject to our will on most occasions, and imagine we feel that the will itself is subject to nothing; because when by a denial of it we are provok'd to try, we feel that it moves easily every way, and produces an image of itself even on that side, on which it did not settle. This image or faint motion, we perswade ourselves, cou'd have been compleated into the thing itself; because, shou'd that be deny'd, we find, upon a second trial, that it can. But these efforts are all in vain; and whatever capricious and irregular actions we may perform; as the desire of showing our liberty is the sole motive of our actions; we can never free ourselves from the bonds of necessity. We may imagine we feel a liberty within ourselves; but a spectator can commonly infer our actions from our motives and character; and even where he cannot, he concludes in general, that he might, were he perfectly acquainted with every circumstance of our situation and temper, and the most secret springs of our complexion and disposition. Now this is the very essence of necessity, according to the foregoing doctrine.

A third reason why the doctrine of liberty has generally been better receiv'd in the world, than its antagonist, proceeds from *religion*, which has been very unnecessarily interested in this question. There is no method of reasoning more common, and yet none more blameable, than in philosophical debates to endeavour to refute any hypothesis by a pretext of its dangerous consequences to religion and morality. When any opinion leads us into absurdities, 'tis certainly false; but 'tis not certain an opinion is false, because 'tis of dangerous consequence. Such topics, therefore, ought entirely to be fore-born, as serving nothing to the discovery of truth, but only to make the person of an antagonist odious. This I observe in general, without pretending to draw any advantage from it. I submit myself frankly to an examination of this kind, and dare venture to affirm, that the doctrine of necessity, according to my explication of it, is not only innocent, but even advantageous to religion and morality.

I define necessity two ways, conformable to the two definitions of *cause*, of which it makes an essential part. I place it either in the constant union and conjunction of like objects, or in the inference of the mind from the one to the other. Now necessity, in both these senses, has universally, tho' tacitely, in the schools, in the pulpit, and in common life, been allow'd to belong to the will of man, and no one has ever pretended to deny, that we can draw inferences concerning human actions, and that those inferences are founded on the experienc'd union of like actions with like motives and circumstances. The only particular in which any one can differ from me, is either, that perhaps he will refuse to call this necessity. But as long as the meaning is understood, I hope the word can do no harm. Or that he will maintain there is something else in the operations of matter. Now whether it be so or not is of no consequence to religion, whatever it may be to natural philosophy. I may be mistaken in asserting, that we have no idea of any other connexion in the actions of body, and shall be glad to be farther instructed on that head: But sure I am, I ascribe nothing to the actions of the mind, but what must readily be allow'd of. Let no one, therefore, put an invidious construction on my words, by saying simply, that I assert the necessity of human actions, and place them on the same footing with the operations of senseless matter. I do not ascribe to the will that unintelligible necessity, which is suppos'd to lie in matter. But I ascribe to matter, that intelligible quality, call it necessity or not, which the most rigorous orthodoxy does or must allow to belong to the will. I change, therefore, nothing in the receiv'd systems, with regard to the will, but only with regard to material objects.

Nay I shall go farther, and assert, that this kind of necessity is so essential to religion and morality, that without it there must ensue an absolute subversion of both, and that every other supposition is entirely destructive to all laws both *divine* and *human*. 'Tis indeed certain, that as all human laws are founded on rewards and punishments, 'tis suppos'd as a fundamental principle, that these motives have an influence on the mind, and both produce the good and prevent the evil actions. We may give to this influence what name we please; but as 'tis usually conjoin'd with the action, common sense requires it shou'd be esteem'd a cause, and be look'd upon as an instance of that necessity, which I wou'd establish.

This reasoning is equally solid, when apply'd to *divine* laws, so far as the deity is consider'd as a legislator, and is suppos'd to inflict punishment and bestow rewards with a design to produce obedience. But I also maintain, that even where he acts not in his magisterial capacity, but is regarded as the avenger of crimes merely on account of their odiousness and deformity, not only 'tis impossible, without the necessary connexion of cause and effect in human actions, that punishments cou'd be inflicted compatible with justice and moral equity; but also that it cou'd ever enter into the thoughts of any reasonable being to inflict them. The constant and universal object of hatred or anger is a person or creature endow'd with thought and consciousness; and when any criminal or injurious actions excite that passion, 'tis only by their relation to the person or connexion with him. But according to the doctrine of liberty or chance, this connexion is reduc'd to nothing, nor are men more accountable for those actions, which are design'd and premeditated, than for such as are the most casual and accidental. Actions are by their very nature temporary and perishing; and where they proceed not from some cause in the characters and disposition of the person, who perform'd them, they infix not themselves upon him, and can neither redound to his honour, if good, nor infamy, if evil. The action itself may be blameable; it may be contrary to all the rules of morality and religion: But the person is not responsible for it; and as it proceeded from nothing in him, that is durable or constant, and leaves nothing of that nature behind it, 'tis impossible he can, upon its account, become the object of punishment or vengeance. According to the hypothesis of liberty, therefore, a man is as pure and untainted, after having committed the most horrid crimes, as at the first moment of his birth, nor is his character any way concern'd in his actions; since they are not deriv'd from it, and the wickedness of the one can never be us'd as a proof of the depravity of the other. 'Tis only upon the principles of necessity, that a person acquires any merit or demerit from his actions, however the common opinion may incline to the contrary.

But so inconsistent are men with themselves, that tho' they often assert, that necessity utterly destroys all merit and demerit either towards mankind or superior powers, yet they continue still to reason upon these very principles of necessity in all their judgments concerning this matter. Men are not blam'd for such evil actions as they perform ignorantly and casually, whatever may be their consequences. Why? but because the cause of these actions are only momentary, and terminate in them alone. Men are less blam'd for such evil actions as they perform hastily and unpremeditatedly, than for such as proceed from thought and deliberation. For what reason? but because a hasty temper, tho' a constant cause in the mind, operates only by intervals, and infects not the whole character. Again, repentance wipes off every crime, especially if attended with an evident reformation of life and manners. How is this to be accounted for, but by asserting that actions render a person criminal, merely as they are proofs of criminal passions or principles in the mind; and when by any alteration of these principles they cease to be just proofs, they likewise cease to be criminal? But according to the doctrine of *liberty* or *chance* they never were just proofs, and consequently never were criminal.

Here then I turn to my adversary, and desire him to free his own system from these odious consequences before he charge them upon others. Or if he rather chuses, that this question should be decided by fair arguments before philosophers, than by declamations before the people, let him return to what I have advanc'd to prove that liberty and chance are synonimous; and concerning the nature of moral evidence and the regularity of human actions. Upon a review of these reasonings, I cannot doubt of an entire victory. . . .

BROAD

Charlie Dunbar Broad (1887–) is one of the best-known English philosophers of the past half-century. His writings range over a wide spectrum of philosophical problems, both technical and popular, including not only metaphysics, theory of knowledge, and ethics, but also such controversial topics as the validity of extrasensory perception.

In this paper, Broad carefully sorts out a number of arguments which have been used by one side or another in the free will debate. His primary aim is to clarify the issue so that we can figure out precisely what is being claimed by the proponents of the major competing positions. To this end, he formulates arguments with great care, labels them clearly so that we can keep track of them, and considers all possible variants or alternatives so that every reader will feel that his particular view has been considered.

But clarification and analysis are hardly Broad's only aims. By making the libertarian position unambiguously clear, Broad intends to show that it is untenable. Do not be misled by the dry and technical surface of the argument. Broad is telling us that morality and responsibility, as we ordinarily conceive them, are simply nonsense. According to him, it never makes sense to blame a man for his wrongdoing, or to praise him for his good acts either. Those of you who disagree will have to come up with some very strong arguments to refute Broad.

Determinism, Indeterminism, and Libertarianism

The Implications of Obligability

We often make retrospective judgments about the past actions of ourselves or other people which take the form: "You ought not to have done the action X, which you in fact did; you ought instead to have done the action Y,

From *Ethics and the History of Philosophy* by C. D. Broad. London: Routledge & Kegan Paul, 1952, pp. 195–217.

which in fact you did not." If I make such a judgment about a person, and he wants to refute it, he can take two different lines of argument. (1) He may say: "I could have done Y instead of X, but you are mistaken in thinking that Y was the action that I ought to have done. In point of fact, X, the action that I did, was the one that I ought to have done." If I had done Y, I should have done what I ought not to have done." (2) He may say: "I could not help doing X," or he may say: "Though I need not have done X, I could not possibly have done Y."

If the accused person makes an answer of the first kind, he is admitting that the alternatives "ought" and "ought not" apply to the actions X and Y, but he is objecting to my applying "ought" to Y and "ought not" to X. He is saying that "ought" applies to X, and "ought not" to Y. It is as if two people, who agree that X and Y are each black or white, should differ because one holds that X is black and Y white whilst the other holds that X is white and Y black. If the accused person makes an answer of the second kind, he is denying the applicability of the alternatives "ought" and "ought not." If he says: "I could not help doing X," he assumes that his critic will admit that neither "ought" nor "ought not" has any application to an action which the agent could not help doing. If he says: "Though I need not have done X, yet I could not possibly have done Y," he assumes that his critic will admit that neither "ought" nor "ought not" has any application to an action which the agent could not have done. It is as if one person should say that X is black and Y is white, and the other should answer that at least one of them is unextended and therefore incapable of being either black or white.

Obligability Entails Substitutability

Now we are concerned here only with the second kind of answer. The essential point to notice is that it is universally admitted to be a *relevant* answer. We all admit that there is some sense or other of "could" in which "ought" and "ought not" entail "could." We will now try to get clear about the connexion between these two notions.

Judgments of obligation about past actions may be divided into two classes, viz. (1) judgments about actions which were actually done, and (2) judgments about conceivable actions which were not done. Each divides into two sub-classes, and so we get the following fourfold division. (1·1) "You did X, and X was the action that you ought to have done." (1·2) "You did X, and X was an action that you ought not to have done." (2·1) "You did not do X, and X was the action that you ought to have done." And (2·2) "You did not do X, and X was an action that you ought not to have done." Now both judgments of the first class entail that you could have helped doing the action which you in fact did. If the action that you did can be said to be one that you ought to have done, or if it can be said to be one that you ought not to have done, it must be one that you *need not* have done. And, since you actually did it, it is obviously one that you *could have* done. Both judgments of the second class entail that you could have done an action which you did not in fact do. If a conceivable action which you did not do can be said to be one which you ought to have done, or if it can be said to be one that you ought not to have done, it must be one that you *could have* done. And, since you actually failed to do it, it is obviously one that you *need not* have done.

It is worth while to notice that the common phrases: "You ought to have done so and so" and "You ought not to have done so and so" are generally equivalent to our judgments (2 · 1) and (1 · 2) respectively. The former is generally used to mean: "You did not do so and so, and that was an action which you ought to have done." The latter is generally used to mean: "You did so and so, and that was an action which you ought not to have done." But we often need to express what is expressed by our judgments (1 · 1) and (2 · 2). We often want to say that a person did what he ought on a certain occasion, and we often want to say that a person avoided doing something which he ought not to have done on a certain occasion. For this is exactly the state of affairs which exists when a person has in fact done an unpleasant duty in face of a strong temptation to shirk it by lying.

Now the importance of this connexion between "ought" and "ought not," on the one hand, and "could," on the other, is very great. People constantly make judgments of obligation of the four kinds which we have distinguished, and such judgments have constantly been made throughout the whole course of human history. Every single one of these judgments has been false unless there have been cases in which actions which *were* done could have been left undone and actions which *were not* done could have been done. And these judgments would all have been false in principle, and not merely in detail. They would have been false, not in the sense that they asserted "ought" where they should have asserted "ought not," or *vice versa*. They would be false in the sense that nothing in the world has ever had that determinable characteristic of which "ought to be done" and "ought not to be done" are the determinate specifications. They would be false in the sense in which all judgments which predicated redness, blueness, etc., of any object would be false in a world which contained no objects except minds and noises.

It will be convenient to call an action "obligable" if and only if it is an action of which "ought to be done" or "ought not to be done" can be predicated. It will be convenient to call an action "substitutable" if, either it was done but could have been left undone, or it was left undone but could have been done. We may then sum up the situation by saying that an action is obligable if and only if it is, in a certain sense, substitutable; that, unless all judgments of obligations are false in principle, there are obligable actions; and therefore, unless all judgments of obligation are false in principle, there are actions which are, in this sense, substitutable.

Various Senses of "Substitutable"

This is one aspect of the case. The other aspect is the following. There are several senses of "could" in which nearly everyone would admit that some actions which were done could have been left undone, and some actions which were left undone could have been done. There are thus several senses of "substitutable" in which it would commonly be admitted that some actions are substitutable. But, although an action which was *not* substitutable in these senses would *not* be obligable, it seems doubtful whether an action which was substitutable *only* in these senses *would be* obligable. It seems doubtful whether an action would be obligable unless it were substitutable in some further sense.

At this stage two difficulties arise. (i) It is extremely difficult to grasp and to express clearly this further sense of "substitutable," i.e. this further sense of "could" in which an action that was done could have been left undone or an action which was not done could have been done. Many people would say that they can attach no meaning to "substitutable" except those meanings in which it is insufficient to make an action obligable. (ii) Even if this other meaning of "substitutable" can be grasped and clearly expressed, many people would say that no action is substitutable in this sense. They would claim to see that no action which has been done could have been left undone, and that no action which was not done could have been done, in that sense of "could" which is required if an action is to be obligable.

Now anyone who holds these views is in a very awkward position. On the one hand, it is not easy to believe that every judgment of obligation is false, in the sense in which every judgment ascribing colour to an object would be false in a world containing only minds and noises. On the other hand, it is highly depressing to have to admit that there is a sense of "could" which you can neither grasp nor clearly express. And it is equally unsatisfactory to have to believe that some actions *are* substitutable in a sense in which it seems to you self-evident that no action *could be* substitutable.

There are two problems to be tackled at this point. (i) To try to discover and state the sense of "substitutable" in which being substitutable is the necessary and sufficient condition of being obligable. And (ii), if we can do this, to consider whether any action could be substitutable in this sense.

Voluntary Substitutability

Let us begin by considering an action which has actually been performed. In some cases we should say that the agent "could not have helped" performing it. We should certainly say this if we had reason to believe that the very same act would have been performed by the agent in these circumstances even though he had willed that it should not take place. It is obvious that there are actions which are "inevitable," in this sense, since there are actions which take place although the agent is trying his hardest to prevent them. Compare, e.g., the case of a conspirator taken with an uncontrollable fit of sneezing.

Next consider a conceivable action which was not in fact performed. In some cases we should say that the agent "could not possibly" have performed it. We should certainly say this if the act would not have taken place in these circumstances no matter how strongly the agent had willed it. It is obvious that there are conceivable acts which are "impossible" in this sense, since there are cases where such an act fails to take place although the agent is trying his hardest to bring it about. Compare, e.g., the case of a man who is bound and gagged, and tries vainly to give warning to a friend.

We will call acts of these two kinds "not voluntarily substitutable." It is plain that an act which is not voluntarily substitutable is not obligable. No one would say that the conspirator ought not to have sneezed, or that the bound and gagged man ought to have warned his friend. At most we may be able to say that they ought or ought not to have done certain things in the past which are relevant to their present situation. Perhaps the conspirator ought to have sprayed his nose with cocaine before hiding behind the presumably dusty arras, and perhaps the victim ought not to have let himself be lured into the house in which he was gagged and bound. But these are previous questions.

We see then that to be voluntarily substitutable is a *necessary* condition for an action to be obligable. But is it a *sufficient* condition? Suppose I performed the action *A* on a certain occasion. Suppose that I should not have done *A* then if I had willed with a certain degree of force and persistence not to do it. Since I did *A*, it is certain that I *did not* will with this degree of force and persistence to avoid doing it. Now suppose that at the time I *could not* have willed with this degree of force and persistence to avoid doing *A*. Should we be prepared to say that I ought not to have done *A*?

Now take another case. Suppose that on a certain occasion I failed to do a certain conceivable action *B*. Suppose that I should have done *B* if I had willed with a certain degree of force and persistence to do it. Since I did not do *B*, it is certain that I *did not* will with this degree of force and persistence to do it. Now suppose that at the time I *could not* have willed with this degree of force and persistence to do *B*. Should we be prepared to say that I ought to have done *B*? It seems to me almost certain that, under the supposed conditions, we should not be prepared to say either that I ought not to have done *A* or that I ought to have done *B*.

Consider, e.g., the case of a man who gradually becomes addicted to some drug like morphine, and eventually becomes a slave to it. At the early stages we should probably hold that he could have willed with enough force and persistence to ensure that the temptation would be resisted. At the latest stages we should probably hold that he could not have done so. Now at every stage, from the earliest to the latest, the hypothetical proposition would be true: "If he had willed with a certain degree of force and persistence to avoid taking morphine, he would have avoided taking it." Yet we should say at the earlier stages that he ought to have resisted, whilst, at the final stages, we should be inclined to say that "ought" and "ought not" have ceased to apply.

Primary and Secondary Substitutability

An action which was in fact done, but would not have been done if there had been a strong and persistent enough desire in the agent not to do it, will be called "primarily avoidable." Suppose, in addition, that there could have been in the agent at the time a desire of sufficient strength and persistence to prevent the action being done. Then the action might be called "secondarily avoidable." If this latter condition is not fulfilled, we shall say that the action was "primarily avoidable, but secondarily inevitable." Similarly, an action which was not in fact done, but would have been done if there had been in the agent a strong and persistent enough desire to do it, will be called "primarily possible." Suppose, in addition, that there could have been in the agent at the time a desire of sufficient strength and persistence to ensure the action being done. Then the action may be called "secondarily possible." If this latter condition is not fulfilled, we shall say that the action is "primarily possible, but secondarily impossible." An action will be called "primarily substitutable" if it is either primarily avoidable or primarily possible. It will be secondarily substitutable if it is either secondarily avoidable or secondarily possible. In order that an action may be obligable it is not enough that it should be primarily substitutable, it must be at least secondarily substitutable.

We are thus led on from the notion of voluntarily substitutable *actions* to that of substitutable *volitions*. Suppose that, on a certain occasion and in a certain situation, a certain agent willed a certain alternative with a certain degree of force and persistence. We may say that the volition was substitutable if the same agent, on the same occasion and in the same circumstances, could instead have willed a different alternative or could have willed the same alternative with a different degree of force and persistence. Now there is one sense of "could" in which it might plausibly be suggested that many volitions are substitutable. It seems very likely that there are many occasions on which I *should* have willed otherwise than I did, *if* on previous occasions I had willed otherwise than I did. So it seems likely that many volitions have been voluntarily substitutable.

It is necessary to be careful at this point, or we may be inadvertently granting more than we are really prepared to admit. Obviously it is often true that, if I had willed otherwise than I did on certain earlier occasions, I should never have got into the position in which I afterwards made a certain decision. If, e.g., Julius Caesar had decided earlier in his career not to accept the command in Gaul, he would never have been in the situation in which he decided to cross the Rubicon. This, however, does not make his decision to cross the

Rubicon substitutable. For a volition is substitutable only if a different volition could have occurred in the agent in the *same* situation. Again, it is often true that, if I had willed otherwise than I did on certain occasions, my state of knowledge and belief would have been different on certain later occasions from what it in fact was. In that case I should have thought, on these later occasions, of certain alternatives which I did not and could not think of in my actual state of knowledge and belief. Suppose, e.g., that a lawyer has to decide what to do when a friend has met with an accident. If this man had decided years before to study medicine instead of law, it is quite likely that he would now think of, and perhaps choose, an alternative which his lack of medical knowledge prevents him from contemplating. This, however, does not make the lawyer's volition in the actual situation substitutable. For, although the external part of the total situation might have been the same whether he had previously decided to study medicine or to study law, the internal part of the total situation would have been different if he had decided to study medicine, instead of deciding, as he did, to study law. He would have become an agent with different cognitive powers and dispositions from those which he in fact has. No one would think of saying that the lawyer ought to have done a certain action, which he did not and could not contemplate, merely because he would have contemplated it and would have decided to do it if he had decided years before to become a doctor instead of becoming a lawyer.

Having cleared these irrelevances away, we can now come to the real point. A man's present conative-emotional dispositions, and what we may call his "power of intense and persistent willing," are in part dependent on his earlier volitions. If a person has repeatedly chosen the easier of the alternatives open to him, it becomes increasingly difficult for him to choose and to persist in pursuing the harder of two alternatives. If he has formed a habit of turning his attention away from certain kinds of fact, it will become increasingly difficult for him to attend fairly to alternatives which involve facts of these kinds. This is one aspect of the case. Another, and equally important, aspect is the following. If a man reflects on his own past decisions, he may see that he has a tendency to ignore or to dwell upon certain kinds of fact, and that this had led him to make unfair or unwise decisions on many occasions. He may decide that, in future, he will make a special effort to give due, and not more than due, weight to those considerations which he has a tendency to ignore or to dwell upon. And this decision may make a difference to his future decisions. On the other hand, he may see that certain alternatives have a specially strong attraction for him, and he may find that, if he pays more than a fleeting attention to them, he will be rushed into choosing them, and will afterwards regret it. He may decide that, in future, he will think as little as possible about such alternatives. And this decision may make a profound difference to his future decisions.

We can now state the position in general terms. Suppose that, if the agent had willed differently on earlier occasions, his conative-emotional dispositions and his knowledge of his own nature would have been so modified that he would now have willed differently in the actual external situation and in his actual state of knowledge and belief about the alternatives open to him. Then we can say that his actual volition in the present situation was "voluntarily avoidable," and that a volition of a different kind or of a different degree of force and persistence was "voluntarily possible." An action which took place was secondarily avoidable if the following two conditions are fulfilled. (i) That this action would not have been done if the agent had willed with a certain degree of force and persistence to avoid it. (ii) That, if he had willed differently in the past, his conative-emotional dispositions and his knowledge of his own nature would have been such, at the time when he did the action, that he would have willed to avoid it with enough force and persistence to prevent him doing it. In a precisely similar way we could define the statement that a certain conceivable action, which was not done, was secondarily possible. And we can thus define the statement that an action is secondarily substitutable.

Can we say that an action is obligable if it is secondarily substitutable, in the sense just defined, though it is not obligable if it is only primarily substitutable? It seems to me that the same difficulty which we noticed before reappears here. Suppose that the agent could not have willed otherwise than he did in the remoter past. It is surely irrelevant to say that, *if* he had done so, his conative dispositions *would* have been different at a later stage from what they in fact were then, and that he *would* have willed otherwise than he then did. One might, of course, try to deal with this situation by referring back to still earlier volitions. One might, of course, try to deal with this situation by referring back to still earlier volitions. One might talk of actions which are not only primarily, or only secondarily, but are tertiarily substitutable. But it is quite clear that this is useless. If neither primary nor secondary substitutability, in the sense defined, suffice to make an action obligable, no higher order of substitutability, in this sense, will suffice. The further moves are of exactly the same nature as the second move. And so, if the second move does not get us out of the difficulty, none of the further moves will do so.

Categorical Substitutability

The kind of substitutability which we have so far considered may be called "conditional substitutability." For at every stage we have defined "could" to mean "would have been, if certain conditions had been fulfilled which were not." Now I have concluded that merely conditional substitutability, of however high an order, is not a sufficient condition for obligability. If an action is to be obligable, it must be *categorically* substitutable. We must be able to say of an action, which was done, that it could have been avoided, in some sense of "could" which is not definable in terms of "would have, if." And we must be able to say of a conceivable action, which was not done, that it could have been done, in some sense of "could" which is not definable in terms of "would have, if." Unless there are some actions of which such things can truly be said, there are no actions which are obligable. We must therefore consider whether any clear meaning can be attached to the phrase "categorically substitutable," i.e. whether "could" has any clear meaning except "would have, if." And, if we can find such a meaning, we must enquire whether any actions are categorically substitutable.

Various Senses of "Obligable"

Before tackling these questions I must point out that the words "ought" and "ought not" are used in several different senses. In some of these senses obligability does not entail categorical substitutability.

(i) There is a sense of "ought" in which we apply it even to inanimate objects. It would be quite proper to say: "A car ought to be able to get from London to Cambridge in less than three hours" or: "A fountain-pen ought not to be constantly making blots." We mean by this simply that a car which did take more than three hours would be a poor specimen of car, or would be in a bad state of repair. And similar remarks apply to the statement about the fountain-pen. We are comparing the behaviour of a certain car or fountain-pen with the average standard of achievement of cars or fountain-pens. We are not suggesting that *this* car or *this* pen, in its present state of repair, unconditionally could go faster or avoid making blots. Sometimes when we make such judgments we are comparing an individual's achievements, not with those of the *average* member, but with those of an *ideally perfect* member, of a certain class to which it belongs. We will call "ought," in this sense, "the comparative ought." And we can then distinguish "the average-comparative ought" and "the ideal-comparative ought."

(ii) Plainly "ought" and "ought not" can be, and often are, used in this sense of human actions. But, in the case of human actions, there is a further development. Since a human being has the power of cognition, in general, and of reflexive cognition, in particular, he can have an idea of an average or an ideal man. He can compare his own achievements with those of the average, or the ideal, man, as conceived by him. And he will have a more or less strong and persistent desire to approximate to the ideal and not to fall below the average. Now it is part of the notion of an ideal man that he is a being who would have a high ideal of human nature and would desire strongly and persistently to approximate to his ideal. Obviously it is no part of the notion of an ideal horse or an ideal car that it is a being which would have a high ideal of horses or cars and a strong and persistent desire to live up to this. When we say that a man ought not to cheat at cards we often mean to assert two things. (*a*) That the average decent man does not do this, and that anyone who does falls in this respect below the average. And (*b*) that a man who does this either has a very low ideal of human nature or a very weak and unstable desire to approximate to the ideal which he has. So that, in this further respect, he falls below the average.

Now neither of these judgments implies that a particular person, who cheated on a particular occasion, categorically could have avoided cheating then; or that he categorically could have had a higher ideal of human nature; or that he categorically could have willed more strongly and persistently to live up to this ideal which he had. For an action to be obligable, in this sense, it is plain enough that it should be secondarily substitutable, in the sense already defined.

The Categorical Ought

Some philosophers of great eminence, e.g., Spinoza, have held that the sense of "ought" which I have just discussed is the only sense of it. Plainly it is a very important sense, and it is one in which "ought" and "ought not" can be applied only to the actions of intelligent beings with power of reflexive cognition, emotion, and conation. I think that a clear-headed Determinist should hold either that this is the only sense; or that, if there is another sense, in which obligability entails *categorical* substitutability, it has no application.

Most people, however, would say that, although we often do use "ought" and "ought not" in this sense, we quite often use them in another sense, and that in this other sense they entail categorical substitutability. I am inclined to think that this is true. When I judge that I ought not to have done something which I in fact did, I do not as a rule seem to be judging merely that a person with higher ideals, or with a stronger and more persistent desire to live up to his ideals, would not have done what I did. Even when this is part of what I mean, there seems to be something more implied in my judgment, viz. that I *could* have had higher ideals or *could* have willed more strongly and persistently to live up my ideals, where "could" does not mean just "would have, if." Let us call this sense of "ought" the "categorical ought." It seems to me then that when we must distinguish between an action being obligable in the categorical sense; and that, if any action were categorically obligable, it would have to be categorically substitutable.

Analysis of
Categorical Substitutability

We can now proceed to discuss the notion of categorical substitutability. It seems to me to involve a negative and a positive condition. I think that the negative condition can be clearly formulated, and that there is no insuperable difficulty in admitting that it may sometimes be fulfilled. The ultimate difficulty is to give any intelligible account of the positive condition. I will now explain and illustrate these statements.

Suppose that, on a certain occasion, I willed a certain alternative with a certain degree of force and persistence, and that, in consequence of this volition, I did a certain voluntary action which I should not have done unless I had willed this alternative with this degree of intensity and persistence. To say that I categorically could have avoided doing this action implies at least that the following negative condition is fulfilled. It implies that the process of my willing this alternative with this degree of force and persistence was not completely determined by the nomic, the occurrent, the dispositional, and the background conditions which existed immediately before and during this process of willing. In order to see exactly what this means it will be best to contrast it with a case in which we believe that a process is completely determined by such conditions.

Suppose that two billiard-balls are moving on a table, that they collide at a certain moment, and that they go on moving in modified directions with modified velocities in consequence of the impact. Let us take as universal premisses the general laws of motion and of elastic impact. We call these "nomic premisses." Let us take as singular premisses the following propositions. (i) That each ball was moving in such and such a direction and with such and such a velocity at the moment of impact. We call this an "occurrent premiss." (ii) That the masses and co-efficients of elasticity of the balls were such and such. We will call this a "dispositional premiss." (iii) That the table was smooth and level before, at, and after the moment of impact. We will call this a "background premiss." Lastly, let us take the proposition that the balls are moving, directly after the impact, in such and such directions with such and such velocities. Then this last proposition is a *logical consequence* of the conjunction of the nomic, the occurrent, the dispositional, and the background premisses. That is to say, the combination of these premisses with the denial of the last proposition would be *logically inconsistent*. It is so in exactly the sense in which the combination of the premisses of a valid syllogism with the denial of its conclusion would be so.

The Negative Condition

We can now work towards a definition of the statement that a certain event *e* was completely determined in respect of a certain characteristic. When we have defined this statement it will be easy to define the statement that a certain event was not completely determined in respect of a certain characteristic. I will begin with a concrete example, and will then generalize the result into a definition.

Suppose that a certain flash happened at a certain place and date. This will be a manifestation of a certain determinable characteristic, viz. colour, in a certain perfectly determinate form. It may, e.g., be a red flash of a certain perfectly determinate shade, intensity, and saturation. We may call shade, intensity, and saturation the three "dimensions" of colour, and we shall therefore symbolize the determinable characteristic colour by a three-suffix symbol C_{123}. When we want to symbolize a certain perfectly determinate value of this we shall use the symbol C_{123}^{abc}. This means that the shade has the determinate value a, that the intensity has the determinate value b, and that the saturation has the determinate value c. Each *index* indicates the determinate value which the dimension indicated by the corresponding *suffix* has in the given instance.

Now the statement that this flash was completely determined in respect of colour has the following meaning. It means that there is a set of true nomic, occurrent, dispositional, and background propositions which together entail the proposition that a manifestation of colour, of the precise shade, intensity, and saturation which this flash manifested, would happen at the place and time at which this flash happened. To say that this flash was *not* completely determined in respect of colour means that there is *no* set of nomic, occurrent, dispositional, and background propositions which together entail the proposition that a manifestation of colour, of the precise shade, intensity, and saturation which this flash manifested, would happen at the place and time at which this flash happened.

There are two remarks to be made at this point. (i) It seems to me that the second statement is perfectly *intelligible,* even if no such statement be ever true. (ii) It is a purely *ontological* statement, and not in any way a statement about the limitations of our knowledge. Either there is such a set of true propositions, or there is not. There may be such a set, even if no one knows that there is; and there may be no such set, even if everyone believes that there is.

We can now give a general definition. The statement that a certain event e was completely determined in respect of a certain determinable characteristic C_{123} is equivalent to the conjunction of the following two propositions. (i) The event e was a manifestation of C_{123} in a certain perfectly determinate form C_{123}^{abc} at a certain place and date. (ii) There is a set of true nomic, occurrent, dispositional, and background propositions which together entail that a manifestation of C_{123} in the form C_{123}^{abc} would happen at the place and date at which e happened. The statement that e was *not* completely determined in respect of C_{123} is equivalent to the conjoint assertion of (i) and denial of (ii).

The next point to notice is that an event might be partly determined and partly undetermined in respect of a certain characteristic. As before, I will begin with a concrete example. Our flash might be completely determined in respect of shade and saturation, but not in respect of intensity. This would be equivalent to the conjunction of the following two statements. (i) That there is a set of true propositions, of the kind already mentioned, which together entail that a flash, of precisely the shade and saturation which this flash had, would happen at the place and date at which this flash happened. (ii) There is no such set of true propositions which together entail that a flash, of precisely the intensity which this flash had, would happen at the time and place at which this flash happened. We thus get the notion of "orders of indetermination" in respect of a given characteristic. If an event is undetermined in respect of one and only one dimension of a certain determinable characteristic, we say that it has "indetermination of the first order" in respect of this characteristic. If it is undetermined in respect of two and only two dimensions of a certain determinable characteristic, we say that it has "indetermination of the second order" in respect of this characteristic. And so on.

It is obvious that there is another possibility to be considered, which I will call "range of indetermination in respect of a given dimension of a given characteristic." Suppose that our flash is undetermined in respect of the intensity of its colour. There may be a set of true propositions, of the kind mentioned, which together entail that a flash, whose intensity falls within certain limits, would happen at the time and place at which this flash happened. This range of indetermination may be wide or narrow. Complete determination in respect of a given characteristic is the limiting case where the range of indetermination shuts up to zero about the actual value of this dimension for this event. Thus the "extent of indetermination" of an event with respect to a given characteristic depends in general upon two factors, viz. (i) its order of indetermination with respect to the dimensions of this characteristic, and (ii) its range of indetermination with respect to those dimensions for which it is not completely determined.

We can now define the statement that a certain event e was completely determined. It means that e has zero range of indetermination for every dimension of every determinable characteristic of which it is a manifestation. The statement that a certain event e was *not* completely determined can now be defined. It means that e had a finite range of indetermination for at least one dimension of at least one of the characteristics of which it was a manifestation.

And now at last we can define "Determinism" and "Indeterminism." Determinism is the doctrine that *every* event is completely determined, in the sense just defined. Indeterminism is the doctrine that some, and it may be all, events are not completely determined, in the sense defined. Both doctrines are, *prima facie*, intelligible, when defined as I have defined them.

There is one other point to be noticed. An event might be completely determined, and yet it might have a "causal ancestor" which was not completely determined. If Y is the total cause of Z, and X is the total cause of Y, I call both Y and X "causal ancestors" of Z. Similarly, if W were the total cause of X, I should call Y, X, and W "causal ancestors" of Z. And so on. If at any stage in such a series there is a term, e.g. W, which contains a cause-factor that is not completely determined, the series will stop there, just as the series of human ancestors stops with Adam. Such a term may be called the "causal progenitor" of such a series. If Determinism be true, every event has causal ancestors, and therefore are no causal progenitors. If Indeterminism be true, there are causal progenitors in the history of the world.

We can now state the negative condition which must be fulfilled if an action is to be categorically substitutable. Suppose that, at a certain time, an agent deliberated between two alternatives, A and B, and that he actually did A and not B. Suppose that the following conditions are fulfilled. (i) The doing of A by this agent at this moment was completely determined. (ii) The total cause of A being done contained as cause-factors a desire of a certain strength and persistence for A and a desire of a certain strength and persistence for B. (iii) These two desires were not completely determined in respect of strength and persistence. (iv) The range of indetermination was wide enough to include in it, as possible values, so strong and persistent a desire for B or so weak and fleeting a desire for A as would have determined the doing of B instead of the doing for A. Conditions (iii) and (iv) are the negative conditions which must be fulfilled if B is to be categorically substitutable for A. They amount to the following statement. It is consistent with (a) the laws of nature, including those of psychology, (b) the facts about the agent's dispositions and the dispositions of any other agent in the world at the moment of acting, (c) the facts about what was happening within and without the agent at that moment, and (d) the facts about the general background conditions at that moment, that the strength and persistence of the desires mentioned in (ii) should have any value that falls within the range mentioned in (iv).

Before we go further there is one point to be mentioned. Strictly speaking, what I have just stated are the negative conditions for *primary* categorical substitutability. For I have supposed the incomplete determination to occur at the *first* stage backwards, viz. in one of the cause-factors in the total cause of the action A. It would be quite easy to define, in a similar way, the negative conditions for secondary, or tertiary, or any other order of categorical substitutability. All that is needed is that, at *some* stage in the causal ancestry of A, there shall be a total cause which contains as factors desires of the agent answering to the conditions which I have stated. That is to say, all that is necessary is that A shall have a causal ancestor which is a causal progenitor, containing as a factor an incompletely determined desire of the agent's.

We come now to the final question. Supposing that this negative condition were fulfilled, would this *suffice* to make an action categorically obligable? It seems to me plain that it would not. Unless some further and positive condition were fulfilled, all that one could say would be the following: "The desire to do A happened to be present in me with such strength and persistence, as compared with the desire to do B, that I did A and avoided B. The desire to do B might have happened to be present in me with such strength and persistence, as compared with the desire to do A, that I should have done B and avoided A." Now, if this is all, the fact that I did A and not B is, in the strictest sense, an *accident*, lucky or unlucky as the case may be. It may be welcomed or it may be deplored, but neither I nor anything else in the universe can properly be praised or blamed for it. It begins to look as if the categorical ought may be inapplicable, though for different reasons, both on the hypothesis that voluntary actions have causal progenitors and on the hypothesis that none of their causal ancestors are causal progenitors.

The Positive Condition

Let us now try to discover the positive conditions of categorical obligability. I think that we should naturally tend to answer the sort of objection which I have just raised in the following way. We should say: "I deliberately identified myself with my desire to do *A*, or I deliberately threw my weight on the side of that desire. I might instead have made no particular effort in one direction or the other; or I might have identified myself with, and thrown my weight on the side of, my desire to do *B*. So my desire to do *A* did not just happen to be present with the requisite strength and persistence, as compared with my desire to do *B*. It had this degree of strength and persistence because, and only because, I *reinforced* it by a deliberate effort, which I need not have made at all and which I could have made in favour of my desire to do *B*." Another way of expressing the same thing would be this: "I forced myself to do *A*; but I need not have done so, and, if I had not done so, I should have done *B*." Or again: "I might have forced myself to do *B*; but I did not, and so I did *A*."

It is quite plain that these phrases express a genuine positive experience with which we are all perfectly familiar. They are all, of course, metaphorical. It will be noticed that they all attempt to describe the generic fact by metaphors drawn from specific instances of it, e.g. deliberately pressing down one scale of a balance, deliberately joining one side in a tug-of-war, deliberately thrusting a body in a certain direction against obstacles, and so on. In this respect they may be compared with attempts to describe the generic facts about time and change by metaphors drawn from specific instances, such as flowing streams, moving spots of light, and so on. The only use of such metaphors is to direct attention to the sort of fact which one wants one's hearers to contemplate. They give no help towards analysing or comprehending this fact. A metaphor helps us to understand a fact only when it brings out an analogy with a fact of a *different* kind, which we already understand. When a generic fact can be described only by metaphors drawn from specific instances of itself it is a sign that the fact is unique and peculiar, like the fact of temporal succession and the change of events from futurity, through presentness, to pastness.

Granted that there is this unique and peculiar factor of deliberate effort or reinforcement, how far does the recognition of it help us in our present problem? So far as I can see, it merely takes the problem one step further back. My doing of *A* is completely determined by a total cause which contains as factors my desire to do *A* and my desire to do *B*, each of which has a certain determinate strength and persistence. The preponderance of my desire to do *A* over my desire to do *B*, in respect of strength and persistence, is completely determined by a total cause which contains as a factor my putting forth a certain amount of effort to reinforce my desire for *A*. This effort-factor is not completely determined. It is logically consistent with all the nomic, occurrent, dispositional, and background facts that no effort should have been made, or that it should have been directed towards reinforcing the desire for *B* instead of the desire for *A*, or that it should have put forth more or less strongly than it actually was in favour of the desire for *A*. Surely then we can say no more than that it just happened to occur with a certain degree of intensity in favour of the desire for *A*.

I think that the safest course at this stage for those who maintain that some actions are categorically obligable would be the following. They should admit quite frankly what I have just stated, and should then say: "However paradoxical it may seem, we do regard ourselves and other people as morally responsible for accidents of this unique kind, and we do not regard them as morally responsible, in the categorical sense, for anything but such accidents and those consequences of them which would have been different if the accidents had happened differently. Only such accidents, and their causal descendants in the way of volition and action, are categorically obligable." If anyone should take up this position, I should not know how to refute him, though I should be strongly inclined to think him mistaken.

This is not, however, the position which persons who hold that some actions are categorically obligable generally do take at this point. I do not find that they ever state quite clearly what they think they believe, and I suspect that is because, if it were clearly stated, it would be seen to be impossible. I shall therefore try to state clearly what I think such people want to believe, and shall try to show that it is impossible. I suspect that they would quarrel with my statement that, on their view, the fact that one puts forth such and such an effort in support of a certain desire is, in the strictest sense, an accident. They would like to say that the putting forth of a certain amount of effort in a certain direction at a certain time *is* completely determined, but is determined in a unique and peculiar way. It is literally determined *by the agent or self*, considered as a substance or continuant, and not by a total cause which contains as factors *events in* and *dispositions of* the agent. If this could be maintained, our puttings-forth of effort would be completely determined, but their causes would neither be events nor contain events as cause-factors. Certain series of events would then originate from causal progenitors which are continuants and not events. Since the first event in such a series would be completely determined, it would not be an accident. And, since the total cause of such an event would not be an event and would not contain an event as a cause-factor, the two alternatives "completely determined" and "partially undetermined" would both be inapplicable to it. For these alternatives apply only to events.

I am fairly sure that this is the kind of proposition which people who profess to believe in Free Will want to believe. I have, of course, stated it with a regrettable crudity, of which they would be incapable. Now it seems to me clear that such a view is impossible. The putting-forth of an effort of a certain intensity, in a certain direction, at a certain moment, for a certain duration, is quite clearly an event or process, however unique and peculiar it may be in other respects. It is therefore subject to any conditions which self-evidently apply to every event, as such. Now it is surely quite evident that, if the beginning of a certain process at a certain time is determined at all, its total cause *must* contain as an essential factor another event or process which *enters into* the moment from which the determined event or process *issues*. I see no *prima facie* objection to there being events that are not completely determined. But, in so far as an event *is* determined, an essential factor in its total cause must be other *events*. How could an event possibly be determined to happen at a certain date if its total cause contained no factor to which the notion of date has any application? And how can the notion of date have any application to anything that is not an event?

Of course I am well aware that we constantly use phrases, describing causal transactions, in which a continuant is named as the cause and no event in that continuant is mentioned. Thus we say: "The stone broke the window," "The cat killed the mouse," and so on. But it is quite evident that all such phrases are elliptical. The first, e.g., expresses what would be more fully expressed by the sentence: "The coming in contact of the moving stone with the window at a certain moment caused a process of disintegration to begin in the window at that moment." Thus the fact that we use and understand such phrases casts no doubt on the general principle which I have just enunciated.

Let us call the kind of causation which I have just described and rejected "non-occurrent causation of events." We will call the ordinary kind of causation, which I had in mind when I defined "Determinism," and "Indeterminism," "occurrent causation."

Now I think we can plausibly suggest what may have made some people think they believe that puttings-forth of effort are events which are determined by non-current causation. It is quite usual to say that a man's putting-forth of effort in a certain direction on a certain occasion was determined by "Reason" or "Principle" or "Conscience" or "The Moral Law." Now these impressive names and phrases certainly do not denote events or even substances. If they denote anything, they stand for propositions or systems of propositions, or for those peculiar universals or systems of universals which Plato called "Ideas." If it were literally true that puttings-forth of effort are determined by such entities, we should have causation of events in time by timeless causes. But, of course, statements like "Smith's putting-forth of effort in a certain direction on a certain occasion was determined by the Moral Law" cannot be taken literally. The Moral Law, as such, has no causal efficacy. What is meant is that Smith's *belief* that a certain alternative would be in accordance with the Moral Law, and his *desire* to do what is right, were cause-factors in the total cause which determined his putting-forth of effort on the side of that alternative. Now this belief was an event, which happened when he began to reflect on the alternatives and to consider them in the light of the moral principles which he accepts and regards as relevant. And this desire was an event, which happened when his conative-emotional moral dispositions were stirred by the process of reflecting on the alternatives. Thus the use of phrases about action being "determined by the Moral Law" may have made some people think they believe that some events are determined by non-occurrent causation. But our analysis of the meaning of such phrases shows that the facts which they express give no logical support to this belief.

Libertarianism

We are now in a position to define what I will call "Libertarianism." This doctrine may be summed up in two propositions. (i) Some (and it may be all) voluntary actions have a causal ancestor which contains as a cause-factor the putting-forth of an effort which is not completely determined in direction and intensity by occurrent causation. (ii) In such cases the direction and the intensity of the effort are completely determined by non-occurrent causation, in which the self or agent, taken as a substance or continuant, is the non-occurrent total cause. Thus, Libertarianism, as defined by me, entails Indeterminism, as defined by me; but the converse does not hold.

If I am right, Libertarianism is self-evidently impossible, whilst Indeterminism is *prima facie* possible. Hence, if categorical obligability entails Libertarianism, it is certain that no action can be categorically obligable. But if categorical obligability entails only Indeterminism it is *prima facie* possible that some actions are categorically obligable. Unfortunately, it seems almost certain that categorical obligability entails more than Indeterminism, and it seems very likely that it entails Libertarianism. It is therefore highly probable that the notion of categorical obligability is a delusive notion, which neither has nor can have any application.

FOOT

Philippa Foot is an Oxford philosopher whose writings on ethical subjects are strongly influenced by the so-called "Oxford linguistic philosophy" of the past quarter-century. In this paper, Miss Foot examines the attempt by David Hume and others to show that freedom of the will can be reconciled with some form of causal determinism. Her arguments against the Humean position sound very much like Aristotle's in their emphasis upon the character of choice, deliberation, and voluntary action.

If Broad is correct in rejecting the traditional libertarian doctrine, and Miss Foot is correct in refusing to accept a Humean substitute, then it is very hard to see how we can hope to preserve our strongly held belief that normal, reasonable, sane adult men and women are morally responsible for their actions.

Free Will as Involving Determinism

The idea that free will can be reconciled with the strictest determinism is now very widely accepted. To say that a man acted freely is, it is often suggested, to say that he was not constrained, or that he could have done otherwise if he had chosen, or something else of that kind; and since these things could be true even if his action was determined it seems that there could be room for free will even within a universe completely subject to causal laws. Hume put forward a view of this kind in contrasting the "liberty of spontaneity . . . which is oppos'd to violence" with the nonexistent "liberty of indifference . . . which means a negation of necessity and causes."[1] A. J. Ayer, in his essay "Freedom and Necessity"[2] was summing up such a position when he said, "from the fact that my action is causally determined . . . it does not necessarily follow that I am not free"[3] and "it is not when my action has any

"Free Will As Involving Determinism" by Philippa Foot. *The Philosophical Review*, LXVI, No. 4 (October 1957), 439–50. © 1957 by Philosophical Review. Reprinted by permission of Philosophical Review.

[1] *Treatise*, bk. II, pt. III, sec. 2.

[2] *Polemic*, no. 5 (1946); reprinted in his *Philosophical Essays* (London, 1954).

[3] *Philosophical Essays*, p. 278.

cause at all, but only when it has a special sort of cause, that it is reckoned not to be free."[4]

I am not here concerned with the merits of this view but only with a theory which appears more or less incidentally in the writings of those who defend it. This is the argument that so far from being incompatible with determinism, free will actually requires it. It appears briefly in Hume's *Treatise* and was set out in full in an article by R. E. Hobart.[5] P. H. Nowell Smith was expressing a similar view when he said of the idea that determinism is opposed to free will that "the clearest proof that it is mistaken or at least muddled lies in showing that I could not be free to choose what I do *unless* determinism is correct . . . Freedom, so far from being incompatible with causality, implies it."[6] Ayer has taken up a similar position, arguing that the absence of causal laws governing action "does not give the moralist what he wants. For he is anxious to show that men are capable of acting freely in order to infer that they can be morally responsible for what they do. But if it is a matter of pure chance that a man should act in one way rather than another, he may be free but he can hardly be responsible."[7]

This argument is not essential to the main thesis of those who use it; their own account of free will in such terms as the absence of *constraining* causes might be correct even though there were no inconsistencies in the suggestion put forward by their libertarian opponents. But if valid the argument would be a strong opponent, disposing of the position of anyone who argued both that free will required the absence of determining causes and that free will was a possibility. That the argument is not valid, and indeed that it is singularly implausible, I shall now try to show. It is, I think, surprising that it should have survived so long; this is perhaps because it has not had to bear much weight. In any case the weapons which can be used against it are ones which are in general use elsewhere.

In discussing determinism and free will it is important to be clear about the sense which is given in this context to words such as "determined" and "caused." Russell gave this account:

> The law of universal causation . . . may be enunciated as follows: There are such invariable relations between different events at the same or different times that, given the state of the whole universe throughout any finite time, however short, every previous and subsequent event can theoretically be determined as a function of the given events during that time.[8]

This seems to be the kind of determinism which worries the defender of free will, for if human action is subject to a universal law of causation of this type,

---

[4] *Ibid.*, p. 281.
[5] "Freewill as Involving Determinism," *Mind*, XLIII (1934), 1–27.
[6] "Freewill and Moral Responsibility," *Mind*, LVII (1948), 46.
[7] *Philosophical Essays*, p. 275.
[8] "On the Notion of Cause," in *Our Knowledge of the External World* (London, 1914), p. 221.

there will be for any action a set of sufficient conditions which can be traced back to factors outside the control of the agent.

We cannot of course take it for granted that whenever the word "determined" or the word "cause" is used this is what is implied, and what is intended may be in no way relevant to the question of free will. For instance, an action said to be determined by the desires of the man who does it is not necessarily an action for which there is supposed to be a sufficient condition. In saying that it is determined by his desires we may mean merely that he is doing something that he wants to do, or that he is doing it for the sake of something else that he wants. There is nothing in this to suggest determinism in Russell's sense. On the whole it is wise to be suspicious of expressions such as "determined by desire" unless these have been given a clear sense, and this is particularly true of the phrase "determined by the agent's character." Philosophers often talk about actions being determined by a man's character, but it is not certain that anyone else does, or that the words are given any definite sense. One might suppose that an action was so determined if it was *in* character, for instance the generous action of a generous man; but if this is so we will not have the kind of determinism traditionally supposed to raise difficulties for a doctrine of free will. For nothing has been said to suggest that where the character trait can be predicated the action will invariably follow; it has not been supposed that a man who can truly be said to be generous never acts ungenerously even under given conditions.

Keeping the relevant sense of "determinism" in mind, we may now start to discuss the view that free will requires determinism. The first version which I shall consider is that put forward by Hobart, who suggests that an action which is not determined cannot properly be called an *action* at all, being something that happened to the agent rather than something he *did*. Hobart says, "*In proportion* as it [the action] is undetermined, it is just as if his legs should suddenly spring up and carry him off where he did not prefer to go." To see how odd this suggestion is we have only to ask when we would say that a man's legs were carrying him off where he did not prefer to go. One can imagine the scene: he is sitting quietly in his chair and has said that he is going to go on reading his book; suddenly he cries, "Good heavens, I can't control my legs!" and as he moves across the room, he hangs on to the furniture or asks someone else to hold him. Here indeed his legs are carrying him where he does not want to go, but what has this to do with indeterminism, and what has the ordinary case, where he walks across the room, to do with determinism? Perhaps Hobart thinks that when a man does something meaning to do it, he does what he wants to do, and so his action is determined by his desire. But to do something meaning to do it is to do it in a certain way, not to do it as the result of the operation of a causal law. When one means to do something, one does not call out for help in preventing the movement of one's limbs; on the contrary, one is likely to stop other people from interfering, saying, "I want to do this." It is by such factors that walking across the room is distinguished from being carried off by one's legs. It is to be explained in terms of the things said and done by the agent, not in terms of some force,

there could be an empirical law connecting wanting with acting under a particular set of conditions. The mistake lies not in the idea that such laws are *possible* but in the thought that there is a reference to them in the statement that a man did one thing because he wanted something else.

So far we have been dealing only with cases in which a question about a motive was answered by specifying something aimed at or wanted. Now we should turn to the cases in which the motive is said to be kindness, vanity, ambition, meanness, jealousy, and so on, to see whether determinism is involved.

It is easy to show that a motive is not a cause in Russell's sense, for it is clearly not an antecedent cause. Professor Gilbert Ryle has pointed out that a man who acts out of vanity is not a man who had a feeling of vanity immediately before he acted, and if it is objected that the vanity which preceded the action need not have manifested itself in a feeling, one may ask what else *would* count as the vanity which was causing him to act. A man's motives are not given by what was happening to him immediately before he started to act. Nor do we discover some independent condition cotemporaneous with the action and a law linking the two, for again there is nothing which would count as vanity except the tendency to do this kind of thing.

So much is implied in what Ryle says about acting out of vanity, but his own account of what it is to do so still uses something which is objectionably like a causal model. The analogy which he thinks apt is that between saying a man acted out of vanity and saying a piece of glass broke because it was brittle: "To explain an act as done from a certain motive is not analogous to saying that the glass broke because a stone hit it, but to the quite different type of statement that the glass broke, when the stone hit it, because the glass was brittle."[10] The positive part of this statement seems to me mistaken. Acting out of vanity is not so closely connected with being vain as Ryle must suppose it to be. Let us suppose that his account of what it is to be vain is entirely correct; to say that a man is vain is to say that he tends to behave in certain ways, to feel aggrieved in particular situations, and so on.[11] It does not follow that ascribing vanity as a motive for an action is bringing this action under the "lawlike" proposition that the agent is a man who tends to do these things. For it makes sense to say that a man acts out of vanity on a particular occasion although he is not in general vain, or even vain about this kind of thing. It cannot therefore be true that when we speak of an agent's motive for a particular action we are explaining it in terms of his character, as Ryle suggests; we are not saying "he *would* do that." It is of course possible to give a motive *and* to say that the agent has the character trait concerned, but the latter cannot be included in an account of what it is to assign a motive to a particular action.

The explanation of why Ryle says what he does seems to lie in the fact that he has taken a false example of explaining an action by giving a motive. He considers as his example the explanation, "He boasted because he is vain,"

---

[10] *Concept of Mind* (London, 1949), pp. 86-87.
[11] *Ibid.*, p. 86.

which is not in fact an explanation of the right type; considered as a statement assigning a motive to a particular action it would be uninformative, for except in very special cases *boasting is* acting out of vanity. It is not surprising that this particular sentence has a different function—that of relating this act of vanity to the character trait. What Ryle says about the example is correct, but it is not an example of the kind of thing he is trying to describe.

It might seem as if we could reformulate the theory to meet the objection about the man who acts out of vanity on one occasion by saying that a man's acting out of vanity is like glass breaking because of a brittleness which could be temporary. "He acted out of vanity" would then be explained as meaning that at that particular time he tended to react in the ways described by Ryle. (If he finds a chance of securing the admiration and envy of others, he does whatever he thinks will produce this admiration and envy.) This is wrong because, whereas glass which is even temporarily brittle has all the reactions which go by this name, a man who is temporarily acting out of vanity is not liable to do other things of this kind. To find concepts which this model would fit one must turn to such descriptions as "a boastful mood," "a savage frame of mind," or "a fit of bad temper."

Assigning a motive to an action is not bringing it under any law; it is rather saying something about the kind of action it was, the direction in which it was tending, or what it was done *as*. A possible comparison would be with the explanation of a movement in a dance which consisted in saying what was being danced. Often in diagnosing motives we should look to purposes—to what the action was done for. This we should discover if we found out what the agent was prepared to go without and what he insisted on having; the fact that visitors are made to admire a garden even in the rain is strong evidence that they were invited out of vanity rather than kindness. In other cases finding the motive will be better described as finding what was being done—finding, for instance, that someone was *taking revenge*. We should take it that a man's motive was revenge if we discovered that he was intentionally harming someone and that his doing so was conditional on his believing that that person had injured him. In the same way we should take it that someone was acting out of gratitude if he (1) intended to confer a benefit and (2) saw this as called for by a past kindness. The fact that it is only the character of the particular action which is involved shows how far we are from anything which could involve motives as determining causes.

We have now considered two suggestions: (1) that an undetermined action would not be one which could properly be attributed to an agent as something that he *did* and (2) that an undetermined action would not be the action of a *rational* agent. A third version, the one put forward by Hume, suggests that an undetermined action would be one for which it would be impossible to praise or blame, punish or reward a man, because it would be connected with nothing permanent in his nature.

> 'Tis only [Hume says] upon the principles of necessity, that a person acquires any merit or demerit from his actions. . . . Actions are by their very

nature temporary and perishing; and where they proceed not from some cause in the characters and disposition of the person, who perform'd them, they infix not themselves upon him, and can neither redound to his honour, if good, nor infamy, if evil. The action in itself may be blameable. . . . But the person is not responsible for it; and as it proceeded from nothing in him, that is durable and constant, and leaves nothing of that nature behind it, 'tis impossible he can, upon its account, become the object of punishment or vengeance.[12]

Hume is surely wrong in saying that we could not praise or blame, punish or reward, a person in whose character there was nothing "permanent or durable." As he was the first to point out, we do not need any *unchanging* element in order to say that a person is the same person throughout a period of time, and our concept of merit is framed to fit our concept of personal identity. We honor people as well as nations for what they have done in the past and do not consider what has been done merely as an indication of what may be expected in the future. Moreover, it is perfectly rational to punish people for what they have done, even if there is no reason to think that they would be likely to do it again. The argument that it will be a different *me* who will be beaten tomorrow carries no weight, for "different" or not the back which will be beaten is the one about which I am concerned today. So we have no reason to invent something durable and constant underlying the actions which we punish or reward. And it is not in fact our practice to pick out for praise or blame only those actions for which something of the kind can be found. It would be possible, of course, that we should do this, punishing the cruel action of the cruel man but not that of one usually kind. But even in such a situation there would be no argument against the man who said that moral responsibility depended upon indeterminism; for a motive is not a determining cause, nor is an habitual motive. If we say that a man constantly acts out of cruelty, we no more say that his actions are determined than if we say that he acts out of cruelty on a particular occasion. There could of course be a law to the effect that no one who has been cruel for thirty years can turn to kindness after that, and this would throw responsibility back from the later to the earlier acts. But it is clear that this is a special assumption in no way involved in the statement that cruelty is a "durable and constant" element in someone's character.

I have already mentioned Ayer's argument that moral responsibility cannot be defended on the basis of indeterminism and will now consider his version in detail. Ayer says that the absence of a cause will not give the moralist what he wants, because "if it is a matter of pure chance that a man should act in one way rather than another, he may be free but he can hardly be responsible."[13] To the suggestion that "my actions are the result of my own free choice," Ayer will reply with a question about how I came to make my choice:

Either it is an accident that I choose to act as I do or it is not. If it is an accident, then it is merely a matter of chance that I did not choose otherwise; and if it is merely a matter of chance that I did not choose otherwise, it is

[12] *Treatise*, bk. II, pt. III, sec. 2.
[13] *Philosophical Essays*, p. 275.

surely irrational to hold me morally responsible for choosing as I did. But if it is not an accident that I choose to do one thing rather than another, then presumably there is some causal explanation of my choice: and in that case we are led back to determinism.[14]

The "presumably" seems to be the weak link in the argument, which assumes a straightforward opposition between causality and chance that does not in general exist. It is not at all clear that when actions or choices are called "chance" or "accidental" this has anything to do with the absence of causes, and if it has not we will not be saying that they are in the ordinary sense a matter of chance if we say that they are undetermined.

When should we say that it was a matter of chance that a man did what he did? A typical example would be the case in which a man killed someone with a bullet which glanced off some object in a totally unforseeable way; here he could disclaim responsibility for the act. But in this instance, and that of something done "by accident," we are dealing with what is done unintentionally, and this is not the case which Ayer has in mind. We may turn, as he does, to the actions which could be said to have been "chosen" and ask how the words "chance" and "accident" apply to choices. Ayer says, "Either it is an accident that I choose to act as I do, or it is not." The notion of choosing by accident to do something is on the face of it puzzling; for usually choosing to do something is opposed to doing it by accident. What does it mean to say that the choice itself was accidental? The only application I can think of for the words "I chose by accident" is in a case such as the following. I choose a firm with which to have dealings without meaning to pick on one run by an international crook. I can now rebut the charge of *choosing a firm run by an international crook* by saying that I chose it by accident. I cannot be held responsible for this but only for any carelessness which may have been involved. But this is because the relevant action—the one with which I am being charged—was unintentional; it is for this reason and not because my action was uncaused that I can rebut the charge. Nothing is said about my action being uncaused, and if it were, this could not be argued on my behalf; the absence of causes would not give me the same right to make the excuse.

Nor does it make any difference if we substitute "chance" for "accident." If I say that it was a matter of chance that I chose to do something, I rebut the suggestion that I chose it for this reason or for that, and this can be a plea against an accusation which has to do with my reasons. But I do not imply that there was no reason for my doing what I did, and I say nothing whatsoever about my choice being undetermined. If we use "chance" and "accident" as Ayer wants to use them, to signify the absence of causes, we shall have moved over to a totally different sense of the words, and "I chose it by chance" can no longer be used to disclaim responsibility.

[14] *Ibid.*

SARTRE

Having opened the section with Aristotle, who defends the view that all men have a common nature or "essence," it is appropriate that we should close with Jean-Paul Sartre's forceful rejection of that traditional doctrine. Sartre (1905–), one of the most gifted French philosophers since Descartes, is an exponent of the doctrine known as Existentialism. Like Plato, Sartre uses a variety of literary forms to present his philosophy. In addition to essays and treatises, Sartre has written a number of highly successful plays and short stories.

It is interesting to compare Sartre's views with those expressed by the originator of existentialism, Sören Kierkegaard, in the first section of this book. Despite the fact that Kierkegaard is a devout Christian and Sartre is a defiant atheist, the two men agree on the primacy of the isolated, subjective individual. Neither Kierkegaard nor Sartre is willing to submit to the authority of others; each feels that he must find his own salvation, whether in this world or beyond. In this respect, they both reflect the revolution wrought by Descartes in his Meditations.

Existence Precedes Essence

. . . What is meant by the term *existentialism?*

Most people who use the word would be rather embarrassed if they had to explain it, since, now that the word is all the rage, even the work of a musician or painter is being called existentialist. A gossip columnist in *Clartés* signs himself *The Existentialist*, so that by this time the word has been so stretched and has taken on so broad a meaning, that it no longer means anything at all. It seems that for want of an advanced-guard doctrine analogous to surrealism, the kind of people who are eager for scandal and flurry turn to this philosophy which in other respects does not at all serve their purposes in this sphere.

Actually, it is the least scandalous, the most austere of doctrines. It is intended strictly for specialists and philosophers. Yet it can be defined easily. What complicates matters is that there are two kinds of existentialists; first,

From "The Humanism of Existentialism" in *Essays in Existentialism* by Jean-Paul Sartre, ed. Wade Baskin. New York: Citadel Press, 1968, pp. 33–37, 41, 50, 52–53. © 1965 by Philosophical Library, Inc. Reprinted by permission of Philosophical Library, Inc.

those who are Christian, among whom I would include Jaspers and Gabriel Marcel, both Catholic; and on the other hand the atheistic existentialists among whom I class Heidegger, and then the French existentialists and myself. What they have in common is that they think that existence precedes essence, or, if you prefer, that subjectivity must be the starting point.

Just what does that mean? Let us consider some object that is manufactured, for example, a book or a paper-cutter: here is an object which has been made by an artisan whose inspiration came from a concept. He referred to the concept of what a paper-cutter is and likewise to a known method of production, which is part of the concept, something which is, by and large, a routine. Thus, the paper-cutter is at once an object produced in a certain way and, on the other hand, one having a specific use; and one can not postulate a man who produces a paper-cutter but does not know what it is used for. Therefore, let us say that, for the paper-cutter, essence—that is, the ensemble of both the production routines and the properties which enable it to be both produced and defined—precedes existence. Thus, the presence of the paper-cutter or book in front of me is determined. Therefore, we have here a technical view of the world whereby it can be said that production precedes existence.

When we conceive God as the Creator, He is generally thought of as a superior sort of artisan. Whatever doctrine we may be considering, whether one like that of Descartes or that of Leibniz, we always grant that will more or less follows understanding or, at the very least, accompanies it, and that when God creates He knows exactly what He is creating. Thus, the concept of man in the mind of God is comparable to the concept of a paper-cutter in the mind of the manufacturer, and, following certain techniques and a conception, God produces man, just as the artisan, following a definition and a technique, makes a paper-cutter. Thus, the individual man is the realization of a certain concept in the divine intelligence.

In the eighteenth century, the atheism of the *philosophers* discarded the idea of God, but not so much for the notion that essence precedes existence. To a certain extent, this idea is found everywhere; we find it in Diderot, in Voltaire, and even in Kant. Man has a human nature; this human nature, which is the concept of the human, is found in all men, which means that each man is a particular example of a universal concept, man. In Kant, the result of this universality is that the wild-man, the natural man, as well as the bourgeois, are circumscribed by the same definition and have the same basic qualities. Thus, here too the essence of man precedes the historical existence that we find in nature.

Atheistic existentialism, which I represent, is more coherent. It states that if God does not exist, there is at least one being in whom existence precedes essence, a being who exists before he can be defined by any concept, and that this being is man, or, as Heidegger says, human reality. What is meant here by saying that existence precedes essence? It means that, first of all, man exists, turns up, appears on the scene, and, only afterwards, defines himself. If man, as the existentialist conceives him, is indefinable, it is because at first he is nothing. Only afterward will he be something, and he himself will have made what he will be. Thus, there is no human nature, since there is no God to conceive it. Not only is man what he conceives himself to be, but he is also only what he wills himself to be after this thrust toward existence.

Man is nothing else but what he makes of himself. Such is the first principle of existentialism. It is also what is called subjectivity, the name we are labeled with when charges are brought against us. But what do we mean by this, if not that man has a greater dignity than a stone or table? For we mean that man first exists, that is, that man first of all is the being who hurls himself toward a future and who is conscious of imagining himself as being in the future. Man is at the start a plan which is aware of itself, rather than a patch of moss, a piece of garbage, or a cauliflower; nothing exists prior to this plan; there is nothing in heaven; man will be what he will have planned to be. Not what he will want to be. Because by the word "will" we generally mean a conscious decision, which is subsequent to what we have already made of ourselves. I may want to belong to a political party, write a book, get married; but all that is only a manifestation of an earlier, more spontaneous choice that is called "will." But if existence really does precede essence, man is responsible for what he is. Thus, existentialism's first move is to make every man aware of what he is and to make the full responsibility of his existence rest on him. And when we say that a man is responsible for himself, we do not only mean that he is responsible for his own individuality, but that he is responsible for all men.

The word subjectivism has two meanings, and our opponents play on the two. Subjectivism means, on the one hand, that an individual chooses and makes himself; and, on the other, that it is impossible for man to transcend human subjectivity. The second of these is the essential meaning of existentialism. When we say that man chooses his own self, we mean that every one of us does likewise; but we also mean by that that in making this choice he also chooses all men. In fact, in creating the man that we want to be, there is not a single one of our acts which does not at the same time create an image of man as we think he ought to be. To choose to be this or that is to affirm at the same time the value of what we choose, because we can never choose evil. We always choose the good, and nothing can be good for us without being good for all.

If, on the other hand, existence precedes essence, and if we grant that we exist and fashion our image at one and the same time, the image is valid for everybody and for our whole age. Thus, our responsibility is much greater than we might have supposed, because it involves all mankind. If I am a workingman and choose to join a Christian trade-union rather than be a communist, and if by being a member I want to show that the best thing for man is resignation, that the kingdom of man is not of this world, I am not only involving my own case—I want to be resigned for everyone. As a result, my action has involved all humanity. To take a more individual matter, if I want to marry, to have children; even if this marriage depends solely on my own circumstances or passion or wish, I am involving all humanity in monogamy and not merely myself. Therefore, I am responsible for myself and for everyone else. I am creating a certain image of man of my own choosing. In choosing myself, I choose man. . . .

If existence really does precede essence, there is no explaining things away by reference to a fixed and given human nature. In other words, there is no determinism, man is free, man is freedom. On the other hand, if God does not exist, we find no values or commands to turn to which legitimize our conduct. So, in the bright realm of values, we have no excuse behind us, nor justification before us. We are alone, with no excuses.

That is the idea I shall try to convey when I say that man is condemned to be free. Condemned, because he did not create himself, yet, in other respects is free; because, once thrown into the world, he is responsible for everything he does. The existentialist does not believe in the power of passion. He will never agree that a sweeping passion is a ravaging torrent which fatally leads a man to certain acts and is therefore an excuse. He thinks that man is responsible for his passion. . . .

"After all, these people are so spineless, how are you going to make heroes out of them?" This objection almost makes me laugh, for it assumes that people are born heroes. That's what people really want to think. If you're born cowardly, you may set your mind perfectly at rest; there's nothing you can do about it; you'll be cowardly all your life, whatever you may do. If you're born a hero, you may set your mind just as much at rest; you'll be a hero all your life; you'll drink like a hero and eat like a hero. What the existentialist says is that the coward makes himself cowardly, that the hero makes himself heroic. There's always a possibility for the coward not to be cowardly any more and for the hero to stop being heroic. What counts is total involvement; some one particular action or set of circumstances is not total involvement. . . .

. . . If it is impossible to find in every man some universal essence which would be human nature, yet there does exist a universal human condition. It's not by chance that today's thinkers speak more readily of man's condition than of his nature. By condition they mean, more or less definitely, the *a priori* limits which outline man's fundamental situation in the universe. Historical situations vary; a man may be born a slave in a pagan society or a feudal lord or a proletarian. What does not vary is the necessity for him to exist in the world, to be at work there, to be there in the midst of other people, and to be mortal there. The limits are neither subjective nor objective, or, rather, they have an objective and a subjective side. Objective because they are to be found every-where and are recognizable everywhere; subjective because they are *lived* and are nothing if man does not live them, that is, freely determine his existence with reference to them. And though the configurations may differ, at least none of them are completely strange to me, because they all appear as attempts either to pass beyond these limits or recede from them or deny them or adapt to them. Consequently, every configuration, however individual it may be, has a universal value. . . .

In this sense we may say that there is a universality of man; but it is not given, it is perpetually being made. I build the universal in choosing myself; I build it in understanding the configuration of every other man, whatever age he might have lived in. This absoluteness of choice does not do away with the relativeness of each epoch. At heart, what existentialism shows is the connection between the absolute character of free involvement, by virtue of which every man realizes himself in realizing a type of mankind, an involvement always comprehensible in any age whatsoever and by any person whosoever, and the relativeness of the cultural ensemble which may result from such a choice; it must be stressed that the relativity of Cartesianism and the absolute character of Cartesian involvement go together. In this sense, you may, if you like, say that each of us performs an absolute act in breathing, eating, sleeping, or behaving in any way whatever. There is no difference between being free, like a configuration, like an existence which chooses its essence, and being absolute. There is no difference between being an absolute temporarily localized, that is, localized in history, and being universally comprehensible.

AFTERWORD

The more deeply we go into the problem of freedom and determinism, the farther we are from a solution. On first glance, it seems easy enough to distinguish the ordinary cases, in which men can justly be held responsible for their acts, from those unusual circumstances in which some mitigation or total excuse from responsibility is called for. Aristotle's sensible, matter-of-fact discussion very nicely captures our customary attitudes, even though it was written more than two thousand years ago. But as we work our way through the arguments of Augustine, Descartes, Hume, and the others, we find ourselves moving farther and farther from our original commonsense convictions.

It makes sense to excuse a man for failing to know something which he could not reasonably have been expected to know; but how do we determine what it is reasonable to expect? We all agree that a man should be blamed only for those acts which he has freely chosen to do; but on closer examination, "freedom" looks very much like mere chance, or accident, which is not quite what we thought we meant by a **responsible** act. On the one hand, the ability to predict what a man will do seems to imply that he cannot help doing it, and so is not responsible. On the other hand, the most evil actions are just those which flow from the settled policies of consistently wicked personalities, and hence are quite easy to predict.

The problem, it seems to me, is that our commonsense notion of the line between responsibility and nonresponsibility shifts as we accumulate more detailed knowledge of human behavior. Before anything was known of brain tumors and epileptic seizures, we blamed men for acts which today are seen to be quite involuntary. With the growth of systematic psychiatric knowledge, we progressively withdraw praise and blame from compulsive or psychotic behavior which, only a century ago, was thought to be voluntary and hence culpable.

Now, it is tempting to tell ourselves that we have discovered the true limits of the voluntary and the involuntary, and hence that we now know enough to define a valid legal test for responsibility. But surely it is foolish to build a moral or legal theory on such a shaky foundation. Can anyone doubt that the coming years will bring more knowledge of human behavior? That at some time in the future, for example, by use of electroencephelograms or biochemical tests or what-not, we shall be able to predict which men are likely to commit murder? And as our knowledge expands, will there not be a natural and quite reasonable tendency for the sphere of legal responsibility to contract?

Some way must be found to reconcile our scientific understanding of human behavior with our moral evaluations of individual responsibility. What guidance do our seven authors offer?

Aristotle, as we have seen, merely restates with elegant clarity the sorts of distinctions and rules of thumb to which we usually appeal in our moral and legal arguments about responsibility. His discussion is a good place to start, but it does not really answer any of the doubts we have about the legitimacy of holding men responsible for their actions.

St. Augustine's reconciliation of divine omniscience with individual freedom will appeal to persons of strong religious conviction who are troubled by the apparent contradictions of the Christian doctrine. Nevertheless, a very large measure of faith is required to accept the notion that I am responsible for an action which God foresaw from all eternity.

Descartes' rather simple solution to the problem is appealing, in a way, for it explains immoral actions as being much like unwarranted beliefs. If I were as wise as I am free, I would never do what I oughtn't. But because my capacity for action reaches farther than my knowledge and understanding, I sometimes step out blindly, rushing in where wise men fear to tread. The principal difficulty with Descartes' account is the absence of any sense of the **moral** dimension of freedom. He makes an immoral action sound very much like a mathematical error. Indeed, if our reason is limited, why should we be blamed for acting beyond our capacity to understand. Isn't that like blaming a beginner for making a mistake that only an expert would avoid?

Hume very considerably complicates the problem by showing us the connection between praise and blame on the one hand and predictability on the other. The extended debate between Hume, Broad, and Foot carries us to a level of understanding more sophisticated than that attained by Aristotle, Augustine, and Descartes. In the light of their arguments, it seems to me that we must seriously consider whether questions of moral responsibility should be completely divorced from questions of praise, blame, and social evaluation. We tend to take it for granted that each man sees himself in the same way that others see him. Perhaps we should distinguish between the individual's subjective awareness of his own freedom and responsibility, and society's perception of him as causally determined by factors outside his own control. There is surely some truth in Sartre's insistence that men create themselves through their free choices. Others may perceive me as no more than an instance of biological and social laws, but in some inward manner I know myself to be a unique person, not an instance of any type.

III
THEORY OF KNOWLEDGE

ESP:
   The Criteria of
      Empirical Knowledge

INTRODUCTION TO THE CONTEMPORARY ISSUE

Some controversies are serious and urgent, like drugs or the supposed repressiveness of American society. Some are merely intriguing or provocative, and we argue about them for the fun of it, not because we feel morally obliged to resolve them. The old dispute about extrasensory perception, or ESP, is one of the fun controversies. All of us wonder, from time to time, whether there isn't perhaps a little something to the stories about mental telepathy, precognition, psychokinesis, and the other "strange powers of the mind." Seances, haunted houses, levitation—it would be a dull person who hadn't thought to himself, "perhaps it **is** true!" In many non-Western societies, these occult mental capacities are openly and widely believed in, and serious affairs of state are even decided by consulting astrologers or mystics.

Strange as it may seem, a number of sober, terribly serious, quite rational philosophers have been convinced of the existence of some sort of extrasensory perception—some means, that is, of perceiving the world or communicating with others which makes no use of the familiar five senses. Some of you may have heard of Prof. J. B. Rhine, the Duke University psychologist who has explored ESP under experimental conditions. But how many of you know that there is, in England, a Society for Psychical Research whose members include many of the most distinguished British academics, and whose first president was one of the leading philosophers of the late nineteenth century!

To set the stage for the debate over ESP, you will read three selections. The first is the inaugural address delivered by that distinguished philosopher, Henry Sidgwick, to the first meeting of the Society for Psychical Research in 1882. Note the almost painful sobriety of Sidgwick's tone. He seems determined to persuade his audience that psychical research is no laughing matter.

The second selection, from a book by Hereward Carrington, is a survey of research procedures in psychical science by a believer, one of those who has become convinced that men do have mental powers not recognized by the practitioners of ordinary science.

To reestablish the light touch which threatens to disappear beneath the weight of Sidgwick's ponderous objectivity and Carrington's earnestness, we conclude with a recent look at the subject by a journalist, Daniel Cohen. Mr. Cohen's piece reminds us of the frequency with which apparently well-documented cases of extrasensory perception have turned out, on closer examination, to be mere hoax.

For those students of an experimental turn of mind, may I recommend the following simple test: Take an ordinary deck of cards and shuffle it thoroughly. Try as hard as you can to guess the suit of the top card. Turn it up to see whether you were correct. Shuffle the cards thoroughly and repeat the process. Keeping a record of your results, continue the experiment for one hundred times. If you are correct in more than thirty or thirty-five of the one hundred cases, write a letter to the Society for Psychic Research. You may possess powers of extrasensory perception.

HENRY SIDGWICK

Address to the Society for Psychical Research

Before we proceed to what has been marked out as the business of this meeting, as it is the first general meeting of our new Society since the time it was definitely constituted, it has been thought that I should make a few brief remarks on the aims and methods of the Society, which will form a kind of explanation in supplement to our prospectus defining those aims and methods, —which, I suppose, has been seen by all the members, and perhaps by some who are not as yet members. This prospectus has not been subjected to much instructive public criticism. It has been received, either with entire cordiality, or with guarded neutrality, or with uninstructive contempt. Still, several private criticisms on that prospectus and questions suggested by it have come to my notice; and it seems to me that I might perhaps employ the few minutes of your time that I wish to take up in no better way than in replying to these criticisms and objections.

The first question I have heard is, Why form a Society for Psychical Research at all at this time, including in its scope not merely the phenomena of thought-reading (to which your attention will be directed chiefly this afternoon), but also those of clairvoyance and mesmerism, and the mass of obscure phenomena commonly known as Spiritualistic? Well, in answering this, the first question, I shall be able to say something on which I hope we shall all agree; meaning by "we," not merely we who are in this room, but we and the scientific world outside; and as, unfortunately, I have but few obser-vations to make on which so much agreement can be hoped for, it may be as well to bring this into prominence, namely, that we are all agreed that the present state of things is a scandal to the enlightened age in which we live. That the dispute as to the reality of these marvellous phenomena,—of which it is quite impossible to exaggerate the scientific importance, if only a tenth part of what has been alleged by generally credible witnesses could be shewn to be true,—I say it is a scandal that the dispute as to the reality of these phenomena should still be going on, that so many competent witnesses should have de-clared their belief in them, that so many others should be profoundly interested

President's Address, July 17, 1882. From *Proceedings of the Society for Psychical Research.*

in having the question determined, and yet that the educated world, as a body, should still be simply in the attitude of incredulity.

Now the primary aim of our Society, the thing which we all unite to promote, whether as believers or non-believers, is to make a sustained and systematic attempt to remove this scandal in one way or another. Some of those whom I address feel, no doubt, that this attempt can only lead to the proof of most of the alleged phenomena; some, again, think it probable that most of the alleged phenomena; some, again, think it probable that most, if not all, will be disproved; but regarded as a Society, we are quite unpledged, and as individuals, we are all agreed that any particular investigation that we may make should be carried on with a single-minded desire to ascertain the facts, and without any foregone conclusion as to their nature.

But then here comes the second question, which I have had put by many who are by no means unfriendly to our efforts,—that is, Why should this attempt succeed more than so many others that have been made during the last thirty years? To this question there are several answers. The first is, that the work has to go on. The matter is far too important to be left where it now is, and, indeed, considering the importance of the questions still in dispute, which we hope to try to solve, as compared with other scientific problems on which years of patient and unbroken investigation have been employed, we may say that no proportionate amount of labour has yet been devoted to our problems; so that even if we were to grant that previous efforts had completely failed, that would still be no adequate reason for not renewing them. But, again, I should say that previous efforts have not failed; it is only true that they have not completely succeeded. Important evidence has been accumulated, important experience has been gained, and important effects have been produced upon the public mind.

I say that important evidence has been accumulated; and here I should like to answer a criticism that I have privately heard which tends to place the work of our Society in a rather invidious aspect. It is supposed that we throw aside *en bloc* the results of previous inquiries as untrustworthy, and arrogate to ourselves a superior knowledge of scientific method or intrinsically greater trustworthiness—that we hope to be believed, whatever conclusions we may come to, by the scientific world, though previous inquirers have been uniformly distrusted. Certainly I am conscious of making no assumption of this kind. I do not presume to suppose that I could produce evidence better in quality than much that has been laid before the world by writers of indubitable scientific repute—men like Mr. Crookes, Mr. Wallace, and the late Professor de Morgan. But it is clear that from what I have defined as the aim of the Society, however good some of its evidence may be in quality, we require a great deal more of it. I do not mean to dispute,—it is not now the time to dispute,—with any individual who holds that reasonable persons, who have looked carefully into the evidence that has been so far obtained, ought to be convinced by that evidence; but the educated world, including many who have given much time and thought to this subject, are not yet convinced, and therefore we want more evidence.

If anyone asks me what I mean by, or how I define, sufficient scientific proof of thought-reading, clairvoyance, or the phenomena called Spiritualistic, I should ask to be allowed to evade the difficulties of determining in the abstract what constitutes adequate evidence. What I mean by *sufficient evidence* is evidence that will convince the scientific world, and for that we obviously require a good deal more than we have so far obtained. I do not mean that some effect in this direction has not been produced: if that were so we could not hope to do much. I think that something has been done; that the advocates of obstinate incredulity—I mean the incredulity that waives the whole affair aside as undeserving of any attention from rational beings—feel their case to be not *primâ facie* so strong now as it was.

Thirty years ago it was thought that want of scientific culture was an adequate explanation of the vulgar belief in mesmerism and table-turning. Then, as one man of scientific repute after another came forward with the results of individual investigation, there was a quite ludicrous ingenuity exercised in finding reasons for discrediting his scientific culture. He was said to be an amateur, not a professional; or a specialist without adequate generality of view and training; or a mere discoverer not acquainted with the strict methods of experimental research; or he was not a Fellow of the Royal Society, or if he was it was by an unfortunate accident. Or again, national distrust came in; it was chiefly in America that these things went on; or as I was told myself, in Germany, some years ago, it was only in England, or America, or France, or Italy, or Russia, or some half-educated country, but not in the land of *Geist*. Well, these things are changed now, and though I do not think this kind of argument has quite gone out of use yet it has on the whole been found more difficult to work; and our obstinately incredulous friends, I think, are now generally content to regard the interest that men of undisputed scientific culture take in these phenomena as an unexplained mystery, like the phenomena themselves.

Then again, to turn to a different class of objectors, I think, though I do not wish to overrate the change, that the attitude of the clergy has sensibly altered. A generation ago the investigator of the phenomena of Spiritualism was in danger of being assailed by a formidable alliance of scientific orthodoxy and religious orthodoxy; but I think that this alliance is now harder to bring about. Several of the more enlightened clergy and laity who attend to the state of religious evidences have come to feel that the general principles on which incredulous science explains off-hand the evidence for these modern marvels are at least equally cogent against the records of ancient miracles, that the two bodies of evidence must *primâ facie* stand or fall together, or at least must be dealt with by the same methods.

Then, again, a generation ago we were directed to go to the conjurers, and told that we should see that the whole thing was conjuring. I quite think that this direction was to a great extent just and important: it is highly desirable that the investigation of these matters should be carried on by men who have tried to acquaint themselves with the performances of conjurers. But we can no longer be told off-hand that all the marvels recorded by Mr. Crookes, Professor Zöllner, and others, are easy conjuring tricks, because we have the incontrovertible testimony of conjurers to the contrary. They may be conjuring tricks, but they are at any rate tricks that conjurers cannot find out.

For these various reasons I think we may say that on the whole matters are now more favourable for an impartial reception of the results of our investigation, so far as we can succeed in obtaining any positive results, than they were twenty years ago. In saying this I do not in the least wish to ignore or make light of the evidence that has been accumulated in recent years to shew that at least a great part of the extraordinary phenomena referred to Spiritual agency by Spiritualists in England and America are really due to trickery and fraud of some kind. I had this view when I said just now that important experience had been gained by preceding investigations. This is certainly part of the experience, and I believe that no Spiritualist denies its importance. It would, however, be a mistake to suppose that investigators, or even believers in mesmerism or Spiritualistic phenomena, had not their eyes open twenty years ago to the part played in these phenomena by fraud.

My interest in this subject dates back for nearly twenty years, and I quite remember that when I began to look into the matter, nearly every educated Spiritualist that I came across, however firmly convinced, warned me against fraud, and emphasised his warning by impressive anecdotes. It is merely a question of degree, and I think it would be generally admitted that recent experiences have changed the view of many Spiritualists with regard to the degree. I think that even educated and scientific Spiritualists were not quite prepared for the amount of fraud which has recently come to light, nor for the obstinacy with which the mediums against whom fraud has been proved have been afterwards defended, and have in fact been able to go on with what I may, without offence, call their trade, after exposure no less than before.

And this leads me to the point which is chiefly characteristic of the method of investigation which our Society will, I hope, in the main use. Though it would be a mistake to lay down a hard and fast rule that we may not avail ourselves of the services of paid performers or paid mediums, still we shall, as much as possible, direct our investigation to phenomena where no ordinary motives to fraud,—at any rate I may say no pecuniary motives,—can come in. There has, of course, always been a mass of evidence of this kind. In fact, I think everyone who has become convinced of the reality of the phenomena, or has become strongly and persistently convinced that there is a *primâ facie* case for investigation, has had his attention first attracted by narratives of what has gone on in private families or private circles where none but relatives or intimate friends have been concerned.

Now, the great gain that I hope may accrue from the formation of this

Society is that the occurrence of phenomena—*primâ facie* inexplicable by any ordinary natural laws—may be more rapidly and more extensively communicated to us who desire to give our time to the investigation, so that in the first instance we may carefully sift the evidence, and guard against the danger of illusion or deception which even here may, of course, come in; and then, when the evidence has been sifted by accumulation of personal experiments, make it more available for the purpose of producing general conviction.

As I said before, I do not mean to claim for myself or my colleagues either any special aptitude for investigation, or any special claim to the credence of mankind, as compared with the members of private households or circles of friends where the phenomena may in the first instance occur. But in a matter so strange to ordinary experience I think we may say that it is only gradually that a man learns the complicated precautions that have to be taken in order to exclude all conceivable possibility of illusion or deception. Certainly my own experience is that I only learnt what had to be done in this way, and had to be guarded against, in a gradual way, by repeated experiments.

As regards the question of credibility, the important point to bear in mind is that every additional witness who, as De Morgan said, has a fair stock of credit to draw upon, is an important gain. Though his credit alone is not likely to suffice for the demand that is made on it, his draft will help. For we must not expect any decisive effect in the direction at which we primarily aim, on the common sense of mankind, from any single piece of evidence, however complete it has been made. Scientific incredulity has been so long in growing, and has so many and so strong roots, that we shall only kill it, if we are able to kill it at all as regards any of those questions, by burying it alive under a heap of facts. We must keep "pegging away," as Lincoln said; we must accumulate fact upon fact, and add experiment upon experiment, and, I should say, not wrangle too much with incredulous outsiders about the conclusiveness of any one, but trust to the mass of evidence for conviction. The highest degree of demonstrative force that we can obtain out of any single record of investigation is, of course, limited by the trustworthiness of the investigator. We have done all that we can when the critic has nothing left to allege except that the investigator is in the trick. But when he has nothing else left to allege he will allege that.

We shall, I hope, make a point of bringing no evidence before the public until we have got it to this pitch of cogency. I think it is desirable on various grounds, but one ground is, I think, this: It is due to the private families or private circles of friends whom we hope to persuade to allow us to take part in their experiments, not to leave the subject or the medium of the phenomena—when we have convinced ourselves, by our own methods, of the genuineness of the phenomena—to bear alone the injurious suggestions of any incredulous materialist who may find it needful to attack our experiments. We must drive the objector into the position of being forced either to admit the phenomena as inexplicable, at least by him, or to accuse the investigators either of lying or cheating or of a blindness or forgetfulness incompatible with any intellectual condition except absolute idiocy.

I am glad to say that this result, in my opinion, has been satisfactorily attained in the investigation of thought-reading.

HEREWARD CARRINGTON   *Psychical Research*

The Meaning
of Psychical Research

Psychical Research may be defined as the scientific investigation of supernormal phenomena—meaning by "supernormal" unusual or extraordinary, and not necessarily "supernatural." We no longer believe that the "supernatural" exists, in the generally accepted meaning of that term, for if any phenomena occur, they must necessarily be natural and belong to the order of nature—though perhaps to a more extended order of nature than we have been in the habit of considering. We live in a materialistic age; modern science is fast becoming mechanistic in many of its branches, and this conception is even dominating the sciences of biology and psychology. From the strictly mechanistic point-of-view, of course, psychic phenomena do not and could not occur; they would be absolutely "impossible." It is because of this outlook upon the Universe that many men of science refuse even to consider the evidence advanced by psychical researchers. From their philosophic viewpoint, such manifestations could not *possibly* happen—and therefore they *do not* occur! But there is such a thing as being unduly dogmatic, even in science. The *odium scientificum* may be as unjustifiable and as intolerant as the *odium theologicum*. If certain *facts* occur, they must be accepted *as such*—whether we can "explain" them or not, and whether or not they happen to fit into the particular scheme of things which we may hold at the time. True science must ever be open-minded, willing to accept new evidence, new facts, no matter how contrary to accepted teaching they may appear at the time. The facts must be established first, and hypotheses to account for these facts may follow later.

The term "Psychic *Science*" may arouse antagonism in certain minds, who would contend that this subject is not a "science" at all, but merely an ill-advised attempt to investigate certain alleged "phenomena," which are mainly non-existent, or are based upon superstition, illusion and fraud. Such,

Part I, "Introductory," from *The Story of Psychic Science* by Hereward Carrington. New York: Ives Washburn, 1931. Reprinted by permission of David McKay Company, Inc. for Ives Washburn, Inc.

however, is not the opinion of many of the leading minds in the world to-day. Sir William Crookes spoke of Psychical Research as "a science which, though still in a purely nascent stage, seems to me at least as important as any other science whatever." Sir Oliver Lodge has referred to it as "a new science"; and Dr. Geley contends that it is "the most complex of all the sciences." One must always remember that science consists not so much in a body of facts as in a *method*; the *facts* of science are constantly changing, the *method* never! It is quite possible, for example, to be "scientific" in the investigation of a "haunted house," and quite unscientific in the investigation of the composition of table salt. It all depends upon the approach—the manner in which any particular subject is treated. I shall hope to prove . . . that the method employed by psychical researchers, in their inquiries, is quite scientific, and that many of these phenomena may be said to have been thoroughly established.

It must not be thought that the modern scientific investigator is insensible to the trend of thought to-day—the evidences of evolution, the spread of rationalism in religion, the mechanistic advances and theories of the various branches of science. He realizes these quite as fully as the most confirmed skeptic. At the same time, he reveres, above all else, *facts;* and believes that if mechanistic philosophy is founded upon a view of life which entirely ignores a whole body of phenomena, then that philosophy will have to be remoulded so as to include them. The old adage, "if the facts do not agree with my philosophy, then so much the worse for the facts!" is perhaps a case of putting the cart before the horse. The facts are the really essential things. Modern physiology contends, it is true, that thought is a function of the brain, and consequently that it cannot exist without it; but if certain observed phenomena prove the contrary, this view must be given up. If mind and thought can be shown to exist apart from the brain, then some new theory as to their relationship must evidently be formulated.

A word, perhaps, should be said regarding the relationship of this subject to religion. Here, psychical researchers are invariably "between the Devil and the deep sea!" On the one hand, the orthodox attack the subject because it is not in conformity with their Teachings. Many orthodox persons, for instance, contend that spiritualistic manifestations are contrary to the teachings of the Bible. Spiritualists, on the other hand, contend that the Bible is full of psychic phenomena, from beginning to end, and that there is a striking similarity between the older manifestations and the newer phenomena. Moses Hull, for example, has written a 400-page book, *An Encyclopædia of Biblical Spiritualism*, in which he endeavours to prove this at great length. Dr. B. F. Austin, again, the Editor of *Reason*—a spiritualistic magazine—has compiled a long list, or table, giving chapter and verse references to such phenomena as materialization, independent writing and speaking voices, trance, psychic healing, levitation, clairvoyant and prophetic dreams, speaking with tongues, etc. It can hardly be doubted that these reported instances bear a striking analogy to the newer cases of the same type; and I see no reason to doubt that the same psychic powers were in operation then as now. On the other hand, the rationalist attacks psychic science for "fostering superstition" and endeavouring to turn men's minds back to worn-out and effete theological conceptions. Both of these attitudes are unjust. In the first place, psychic investigation—strictly speaking— has nothing to do with religion; it is purely a scientific question: an inquiry into the reality of certain odd phenomena which are alleged to occur, and an endeavour to ascertain their causes and laws, should they be proved to exist. Spiritualism, it is true, *is* a religion—as Sir Arthur Conan Doyle and others have insisted. It is a religio-philosophical system, based upon a certain set of alleged facts; but with that system psychical research has nothing to do. It confines itself to the investigation of the facts themselves, and should these indirectly afford some support for religious beliefs (as Lodge, Myers, and others have contended) that is purely incidental, and merely happens to be the case.[1] From which the reader will see the very clear distinction made between "Spiritualism," on the one hand, and "Psychic Research," on the other. The former is a religion, the latter a science. This I shall hope to render more clear as we proceed.

Traditional orthodox theology, on the other hand, has nothing more definite to offer than its bare assertions, coupled with its claim of divine inspiration. It is practically devoid of evidence. Those who may choose to believe its teachings are of course privileged to do so, but the scientist wants facts. He says, "Where is your *evidence* that any such thing as a soul exists at all? I fail to find evidence for it anywhere in nature!" And, apart from these psychical and spiritualistic phenomena, *there is no evidence!* No direct proof is otherwise obtainable. Only by isolating an individual, spiritual entity, and proving its separate existence and independence,—by means of direct contact with it,— can such proof of its reality be obtained. There is no other way. When Sir William Ramsay isolated Argon in the atmosphere, he proved its existence by thus isolating it, and saying, "Here it is!" Similarly, we can prove only the reality of spirit by thus isolating it, and obtaining proof of its continued existence and personal identity. This can only be done by some method of direct communication. We must not begin by assuming the existence—or non-existence—of some spiritual world, and then arguing as to the nature, or possibilities, of communication subsequently. We must prove the existence of such a world by reason of these very communications; and, if they should prove not to be such, we must give up the idea of a spiritual world altogether.

I have spoken of "proof." It is true that this is often an ambiguous term, and proof is often hard to obtain. Conclusive proof of the authenticity of any

---

[1] The criticism is frequently heard that psychical researchers often become spiritualists because of the strong "will to believe." It might be replied that skeptics remain such because of the strong "will to *dis*believe!" It is an interesting fact, in this connection, that Prof. F. C. S. Schiller conducted a statistical inquiry, some years ago, as to the belief in a future life, and the result was quite surprising: a very large percentage of those asked had no particular interest in the subject one way or the other! (*See Proceedings of the Society for Psychical Research*, Vol. XV, Part 36.) It seems probable, therefore, that this is not so important a factor as generally imagined.

psychical phenomenon is admittedly an extraordinarily difficult thing. Even a simple physical phenomenon—such as the levitation of a table—has been subject to endless controversy, and it is probable that relatively few persons are even yet convinced of its actuality! When it comes to subtle, psychological problems, the task is more difficult still. The average man is used to the concept "table," but he is totally at a loss when one begins to discuss a "stream of consciousness!" Verification by the senses is no longer possible. Our criteria are here purely mental. How, then, gauge the validity of a purely mental phenomenon in another? . . . Largely by the conditions of the experiment. If these are completely satisfactory, the results are considered valid. But when we come to supernormal phenomena, and particularly proof of survival (the *crux* of spiritualism), it is obviously far more difficult to arrive at any definite decision, since only one side of the circle (so to say) is known to us; the other side must remain forever invisible, embedded in the mental or spiritual realm. We can only control the conditions to a very limited extent (in mental tests), and must accept and judge the results as we obtain them. The evidence desired is obviously the most conclusive possible,—under test conditions the most stringent. *Proof of personal identity* is chiefly desired—coupled with such additional *data* as may be secured, serving to substantiate the chief claims made. Such proof of personal identity can only be obtained from the mind or "spirit" claiming to communicate. The question of "proof" here becomes very difficult; it becomes, in fact, largely a question of the *balance of probability*. In view of all the circumstances, is it more rational to believe this or that? Probably any final decision can only be reached when the weight of the evidence becomes so great that one alternative so strongly outweighs the other that any rational man would accept it, under the circumstances.

It must be remembered, in all that I have said, that I have been speaking throughout of the purely mental or psychic phenomena, to the exclusion of the physical. The latter are also subject to scientific investigation. Psychic phenomena, therefore, fall into two groups or categories: the mental and the physical. Raps, lights, materializations, movements of objects without contact —all those phenomena which affect the material world in which we live—these are the so-called *physical* manifestations. Telepathy, clairvoyance, premonitions, apparitions, dreams, trance phenomena, etc.,—these are purely *psychic* or *mental*. However, there is a certain over-lapping to be noted here. Thus, when unaccountable "rappings" are heard, these are classed as physical phenomena; but if these rappings spell-out certain words, according to a given code,—seemingly displaying an intelligence behind them,—we have here mental concomitants as well. This commingling of manifestations is frequently to be observed in psychic investigation.

As to the physical phenomena themselves—*qua* phenomena—these are now being studied in various psychical laboratories, by means of suitable apparatus, and we thus are initiating a proper, instrumental method of registering and recording these facts. We shall also discuss this question at some length later on.

Psychic phenomena may be either *spontaneous* or *experimental*. The former may occur to anyone, at any time, even in a seemingly normal condition. The latter are *induced*, and are usually observed in the presence of mediums,—amateur or professional. The former can only be observed, just as many natural phenomena must be observed, and cannot be induced at will (meteors, fire-balls, freaks of lightning, etc.). The latter may be studied by the experimental method, and much important work is now being done in psychic laboratories, as we shall presently see. This branch of psychic investigation is in fact fast becoming a "science," in every sense of the word.

While many of the spontaneous phenomena have occurred while the receiver, or so-called "percipient," is in a normal condition (as I have said), the majority of the experimental manifestations are only noted when the medium or subject is entranced, or in some unusual state. This state need not necessarily be "abnormal," as many seem to think,—in the sense of *sub*normal. It is probably true that a certain dissociation of the mind occurs in most mediumship. But this is only *one* of the conditions involved, and there are many others,—of which we know very little. Further, it must be remembered that the mere fact of dissociation in no way serves to explain the supernormal phenomena which are manifested at the time. The abnormal and the supernormal are doubtless in some way inter-connected, but they are not the same thing—merely coincidental, and the abnormal state does not at all explain the added mediumistic powers displayed.

In all psychic investigations, we must enter upon the subject with a perfectly open mind—free from theological dogma, on the one hand, and scientific dogma, on the other. We should be governed, as Prof. Flournoy pointed out long ago, by two maxims:

1. All is possible.
2. The strength of the evidence must be proportioned to the strangeness of the facts.

Now, many of these psychic phenomena are "most strange," and the evidence for their occurrence should accordingly be proportionately strong. The more striking the evidence, the greater the pains which should be exercised in order to make the case completely fraud-proof. It may be said that this has been the ideal invariably sought for by competent investigators.

Prejudice, intolerance, and ignorance are the three chief enemies of Psychical Research. These have existed throughout the ages, and are still with us! They have invariably opposed any new fact or theory radically at variance with accepted teaching. As Mr. Stanley de Brath says, in his "Foreword" to Mrs. Helen C. Lambert's *General Survey of Psychic Phenomena:*

> History shows that even in the case of normal and verifiable physical facts involving a departure from habitual modes of thought, a period of two generations usually elapses between the first verification and the general acceptance. Copernicus published his *Treatise* in A.D. 1540. It remained in abey-

ance till Galileo took it up in 1613; and showed in his telescope that the moon is a sphere, and established the chief laws of gravitation. The Professors of Padua refused even to look through the instrument, and his views were condemned by Catholics and Reformers alike. Curiously enough another period of seventy-three years elapsed before Newton published the *Principles* in 1686, in which the gravitational explanation was mathematically demonstrated. Even with the mathematical support, this took close on seventy years to obtain general recognition, and the opposition he had to face was so bitter that he nearly came to the resolution to publish nothing more; "for," said he, "I see that a man must either resolve to put out nothing new, or become a slave to defend it." Harvey's discovery of the circulation of the blood, and Lyell's *Elements of Geology* had a similar, though shorter, record of opposition; and Darwin's *Origin of Species*, published in 1859, has not even yet,—as a recent trial has reminded us—passed into uncontroverted acceptance.

Excessive credulity, on the one hand, and excessive incredulity, on the other, are alike enemies to scientific psychic investigation. The credulous spiritualist, who sees "spirits" in every knock or in every fold of the curtain is as harmful as the blatant skeptic, who believes that everything is fraud and illusion. Cool, dispassionate, open-minded, yet critical investigation is the hardest thing in the world to obtain. The ideal psychic investigator is indeed a *rara avis*, and must be born, as well as made. He must be impervious to attacks and criticism alike, for he is sure to be vilified, slandered and lied-about, distrusted and disbelieved: for, in this subject, the greater the "authority" one is, the bigger the fool—in public estimation! One can only continue his work and his investigations quite unperturbed by such criticisms, sustained only by his love of truth, and by his conviction that it is mighty, and shall at last prevail!

One criticism must be answered here, however, in view of the fact that it is so often heard. It is this: Even granting the genuineness of certain of these phenomena, of what practical *use* are they? Of what benefit to mankind? Well, in the first place, a fact is a fact, and truth is truth, whether it may be obviously useful or not. One might reply: Of what *use* is a comet or a sunspot? Nevertheless men of science spend years of their lives and thousands of dollars in studying these very phenomena. To the man-in-the-street, the ultimate structure of the Atom or the truth of Relativity makes not the smallest difference: he can make money, eat, drink, and sleep just as well if one theory be true as the other. Yet there is not a man of science in the world who would accept this superficial view-point. To him, these scientific matters are of the very greatest importance, and of absorbing interest—even if they are lacking in any dollars-and-cents returns. So, in this investigation, these phenomena are of extreme interest,—if they be true. Is the discovery of hitherto unknown and unsuspected physical and biological facts of no interest or value? Is the possible proof of "survival" useless? Is the proof that we possess unused and undeveloped powers within ourselves useless? Is the possible application of all this to our daily lives also useless? It would be foolish indeed to think so! When Michael Faraday was asked (regarding induction), "What is the use of this discovery?" he answered, "What is the use of a child—it grows to be a man!" Surely, nothing could be more apropos the case in point!

Psychical Research is one of the oldest, and at the same time, the newest of the sciences. These curious manifestations have been recorded throughout all history,—yet, it is only within our own day that they have been studied for the first time scientifically. "Faith," as Dr. Hyslop has reminded us, "no longer charms with her magic wand, save among those who do not accept or appreciate scientific method, but whose flimsy standards afford no criteria for defence against illusion and deception." We are only now emerging from the period of the childhood of the race. We know but little; there is much yet to be discovered, much to be learned. As Professor William James has so forcibly reminded us:

> . . . An audience of some five or six score people, if each person in it could speak for his own generation, would carry us away to the black unknown of the human species, to days without a document or monument to tell their tale. Is it creditable that such a mushroom knowledge, such a growth overnight as this, *can* represent more than the minutest glimpse of what the universe will really prove to be when adequately understood? No! Our science is a drop, our ignorance a sea. Whatever else be certain, this at least is certain: that the world of our present natural knowledge *is* enveloped in a larger world of *some* sort of whose residual properties we at present can have no positive idea.[2]

And did not Newton himself say: "To myself I seem to have been as a child playing on the seashore, while the immense ocean of Truth lay unexplored before me."

The Reality of the Invisible

One fact should, perhaps, be insisted upon at once, inasmuch as it is so frequently overlooked by the ordinary skeptical individual. It is that the invisible is *real*—in fact, the greatest of all realities, inasmuch as it represents our true inner being. There is an old saying that "no man hath seen God." It is equally true that no man hath seen man! No one has ever seen anyone else. You see his clothes, his hair, his eyes, his skin; but the invisible personality with whom you are conversing—*that* you never see and never can in life. Locked in the dark chamber of the skull, this invisible entity resides, always intangible, silent, invisible. Yet it is very real! It merely becomes a question of evidence, therefore, whether this entity (1) possesses unknown powers, of which we are normally ignorant; and (2) whether it can survive the shock called death, and continue its active existence in some other mental (invisible) world. It is purely a question of evidence, of fact, and that is one of the questions with which psychical research concerns itself,—merely because of the fact that cer-

[2] *The Will to Believe*, etc., pp. 53-54.

tain phenomena seem to force this possibility upon us. The more deeply we penetrate this mysterious region—this borderland between life and death—between mind and matter—the more extraordinary and significant do these phenomena become; the nearer do we seem to approach reality. In the stirring words of Sir William Crookes:

> Steadily, unflinchingly, we strive to pierce the inmost heart of Nature, from what she is, to reconstruct what she has been, and to prophesy what she yet shall be. Veil after veil we have lifted, and her face grows more beautiful, august, and wonderful, with every barrier that is withdrawn.

The Personality of the Investigator

It must be acknowledged that, in all psychic investigation, much depends upon the general character and personality of the man observing the alleged phenomena and rendering the report. There is a certain "personal factor" always involved, and this is freely acknowledged by all experienced researchers, and the reports of some men necessarily considered of more value than those of others, on this account. A specialized training is necessary for this work; our ideal investigator must have a thorough knowledge of the literature of the subject; he must have a good grounding in normal and abnormal psychology; in physics, chemistry, biology, photography, and some laboratory experience; he must be a keen observer, a good judge of human nature and its motives; he must be well trained in magic and sleight-of-hand; he must be shrewd, quick of thought and action, ever on the alert, patient, resourceful, open-minded, tolerant, rapid in his observations and deductions, sympathetic, and have a sense of humour! He must be free from superstition, and at the same time unswayed by bigotry,—theological or scientific. In short, an ideal psychic investigator is hard to find, and it is probable that such a man is born rather than made. Some men are by nature more cautious than others, and this characteristic is true of nations no less than individuals. All this being true, the relative value of published cases and reports must vary, to some extent; those emanating from certain individuals are of greater weight and authority than those reported by others.

The point I wish to make, however, is this: That every Tom, Dick, and Harry is not entitled to set himself up as a critic of this evidence, much as he may think so. Psychic investigation has now become a highly specialized study, and calls for a combination of temperament and knowledge hard to find, as I trust I have shown.

All this is true; but it must be emphasized that the status of the various leaders of scientific research, the world over, is excellent, and their standards high. Few cases ever officially endorsed and published have had to be retracted. The charge of insincerity or dishonesty has never, to the best of my knowledge, been brought against a single investigator of note. Yet, so exasperated have some critics become, when attacking this subject, that they have scarcely scrupled at hinting that the investigator himself is not to be trusted!

This situation was foreseen by Professor Sidgwick, however, and in his very *first* presidential address before the Society (on July 17, 1882) he said:

> We must drive the objector into the position of being forced either to admit the phenomena as inexplicable, at least by him, or to accuse the investigators either of lying or cheating or of a blindness or forgetfulness incompatible with any intellectual condition except absolute idiocy. . . . We have done all that we can when the critic has nothing left to allege except that the investigator is in the trick. But when he has nothing else left to allege he will allege that. . . .[3]

It is hardly necessary to point out that the social and scientific standing of the majority of investigators places them quite beyond criticism of this sort. The only recourse for the skeptic is to allege that the investigators were hallucinated or in some way tricked.

DANIEL COHEN   *ESP: Science or Delusion?*

A few months ago the writer and critic Marya Mannes said on radio that Russia had eight large laboratories experimenting with extrasensory perception, and that they were getting remarkable results. Thus another wild ESP story was kept spinning. This one, which has been around for three years, seemed to come from an unimpeachable source.

A *Chicago Tribune* feature writer, Norma Lee Browning, first mentioned the eight centers early in 1963. She said that they "conducted experiments which, if the results are half as good as the Russians claim, indicate that they may be the first to put a human thought in orbit or achieve mind-to-mind communication with men on the moon." This sort of journalism is not calculated to blow up much of a scientific storm, but Dr. Eugene B. Konecci, director of Biotechnology and Human Research for NASA, repeated Miss Browning's remarks almost word for word but without giving credit—and thus seemed to give NASA endorsement to the report. Unfortunately, the story isn't true. The Soviet Union has one small ESP or parapsychology laboratory, and if the results are even twice as good as the Russians claim, they are still not very good at all.

Another well-circulated ESP rumor is that the U.S. atomic submarine *Nautilus* has engaged in highly successful ship-to-shore telepathy experiments. This one started in the usually reliable French publication *Science et Vie*. Not only is the story unconfirmed; it has been flatly denied by absolutely everyone

---

[3] Sidgwick's address, from which this quotation has been taken, is reprinted in this volume. The quotation has been rearranged by the author.—ED.

"ESP: Science or Delusion" by Daniel Cohen. *The Nation*, No. 19 (May 9, 1966), 550–53. © 1966 by Nation Associates, Inc. Reprinted by permission of the author.

who could have been connected with such experiments, and the *Nautilus* itself was in dry dock at Portsmouth, N.H., when the alleged experiments took place.

A source of continued embarrassment to the interesting little field of ESP is the fact that too many people find it much too interesting. Enthusiasts suspend disbelief so quickly that they accept the wildest exaggerations, misconceptions and downright hoaxes. Since serious study of ESP began late in the 19th century, the field has been a gathering place for crooked mediums, phony psychics, fraudulent mind readers and an assortment of public crackpots.

Small wonder that most scientists are wary of ESP; they do not want to be caught in bed with the table tippers and ghost chasers. Universities, foundations and the government are also conventional to the point of disliking to hand out other people's money for bizarre-sounding research projects—particularly when these projects are certain to be publicized. The press swings between regarding ESP as an established fact and treating it as a big joke, but in either case the stories get published.

In 1963, the Air Force Cambridge Research Laboratories began a project aimed at testing for extrasensory perception with a machine. It was a small project, just a beginning really, and the results were inconclusive; but it made newspapers all over the country. Today, as far as can be determined, no government or military ESP work is going on, and government scientists are unwilling to talk publicly about the subject. In private they admit that they are still interested and rather wistfully hope that somewhere, someone will appropriate the money for further research.

The small number of Soviet scientists interested in parapsychology have been even more embarrassed. Late in 1963, they announced that they found a woman, Rosa Kuleshova, who could read newspapers with her fingers while blindfolded. Soon three other "finger-tip readers" were found. Although finger reading is the least spectacular of all the presumed extrasensory abilities, the fact that the experiments had been performed by supposedly hardheaded, materialistic Russians made a good story. It inspired Dr. Richard P. Youtz, a psychology professor at Barnard College, to search for the same abilities here in America. He found a Flint, Mich., housewife, Mrs. Patricia Stanley, who could identify colors with her finger tips. He told the Eastern Psychological Association that "eyeless vision" was a "real phenomenon." A few weeks later *Life* was giving its readers do-it-yourself finger-tip vision tests.

All sorts of explanations were offered for eyeless vision. The most common was that the women were able to detect subtle heat differences between different colors or between printed and nonprinted portions of a piece of paper. A magician friend who looked at the photographs of the Soviet tests in progress offered another explanation. "It's a fraud," he said flatly. He thought it would be almost childishly simple for the women to see through or around the blindfolds. Magicians, he pointed out, were able to do the same thing with much more elaborate eye coverings. "Scientists are not conjurers; they are very naive about tricks. I have seen them fooled many times."

Within months Lev Teplov, science reporter for the Novosti press agency, had come to the same conclusion. He arranged controlled tests for Rosa Kuleshova and her three imitators. Those who agreed to take Teplov's tests failed miserably. He wrote: "It would be wrong to treat all of these 'phenomena' as sheer deceit. Apparently these cases are related to symptoms of hysteria." It turned out that one of the women was a known swindler and another a patient in a mental institution. Teplov's comments on the gullibility of the scientists were cruel.

Dr. Youtz's claims were less sensational and his tests more carefully controlled, but when he retested Mrs. Stanley, after initial successful and well-publicized experiments, he found her ability had fled. My magician friend was critical of Dr. Youtz's techniques and pointed out that it was quite possible for a subject to receive unconscious sensory clues and thus deceive without being aware of it.

References to eyeless vision have been dropped from the most recent articles announcing that ESP has finally been proved. The new excitement centers upon an experiment performed by Drs. T. D. Duane and Thomas Behrendt of Jefferson Medical College, Philadelphia. They reported the unexplainable occurrence of a particular brain-wave pattern among pairs of identical twins. Sets of such twins were seated about 15 feet apart in separate rooms. Each had electrodes attached to his scalp to register the pattern of his brain waves. One twin was told to close his eyes, thus producing the alpha rhythms characteristic of this sort of activity. Fifteen sets of twins were tested and Duane and Behrendt noted that in two sets the alpha rhythm appeared in the other twin, though his eyes were open. Interesting, but hardly cause for breaking out the champagne to celebrate the long-awaited laboratory confirmation of ESP.

Since the invention of the electroencephalograph by Hans Berger in 1929, a great deal of ESP research has centered on brain waves. Berger himself thought his instruments could be used to record the energy responsible for extrasensory perception. To date this hope remains unfulfilled. The brain does generate electrical pulses and in theory it might be possible for one brain to receive and interpret these impulses from another. But there is little experimental evidence to support this theory and a good deal that points in the other direction.

Westinghouse tried to test brain-to-brain communication without success. Dr. Edmond Dewan of the Cambridge Research Laboratories was actually able to open and close electrical circuits with alpha waves from his brain. However, he had electrodes attached to his scalp, and even then he was able to send messages only by means of a light or buzzer at the rate of one letter every twenty seconds. This is a very long way from brain-to-brain communication.

Clearly, no physical basis for telepathy has been established. For other

for over forty years) but also because of his unquestionable honesty. When his methods were criticized, as they often were, he tried to correct them. If the results suffered—so be it. He has been almost as open about his failures as he has about his successes.

This dedication to scientific principles is curiously impressive when one realizes that Rhine is absolutely convinced that ESP is a supernatural or spiritual force. He has said it "liberates the sciences from the confinement of a materialist metaphysics."

Rhine once considered becoming a minister, but turned to psychical research after attending a lecture on spiritualism by Sir Arthur Conan Doyle. (Doyle, creator of that relentless logician, Sherlock Holmes, became one of the most gullible mystics in history.) Rhine is basically a religious man, but religious leaders have rarely displayed a mutual attraction for psychical (psi) research. Rhine has complained: "It is in the very nature of orthodoxy not to welcome, let alone support, an experimental invasion of the domain of authority and faith." However, a few churchmen, particularly in England, have associated themselves with psychical organizations.

Rhine's frankly spiritual outlook embarrasses some of the more physically or psychologically oriented members of the psychical research fraternity. He was all right in his day, they confide, but now we must have more sensitive and accurate tests. A brave ambition; unfortunately, no one has yet devised such tests.

Rhine's experiments have also been criticized by the other wing of the psychical research field. These radicals see little use in all the card shuffling and statistics. Who cares if someone can guess eight correct cards rather than five, out of a pack of twenty-five. The really exciting things are the prophetic dreams and the dog that howls at the moment his master dies a thousand miles away. These "spontaneous psychical occurrences" are the touchstone of interest in ESP; any attempt to "quantify" psi in the laboratory is not only doomed, it will lead the field astray. Strange stories are obviously more fun than dry statistics, and many striking and even startling psi events seem well documented. But tales of this type inevitably contain an unacceptable vagueness, and just collecting such oddities, in the manner of Robert Ripley, will lead nowhere. Articles will be published in Sunday supplements, but not in *Science*.

Every year serious conferences are held at which important people proclaim that ESP has arrived—or almost. It has been going on now for more than fifty years. In the early 1900s, William James said that psi investigation would be the most important part of psychology in the decades to follow. He was the first in a long and often distinguished line of investigators to sight a false dawn.

It is tempting, therefore, to conclude that the whole soggy business is utter nonsense and be done with all the irritating enthusiasts and their wild stories. But there are those niggling little bits of evidence—not conclusive, not even persuasive, but damn persistent and interesting. For if it were true . . .

COMMENTARY ON THE CONTEMPORARY ISSUE

As usual, many philosophical problems are embedded in our contemporary dispute; the ESP controversy might lead us quite naturally into a discussion of the nature of the mind, the relationship of mind to body, the possibility of a life beyond bodily death, or even—by a slight stretch of our philosophical imagination—the individual's right to privacy. In this section we shall focus on what philosophers call the "epistemological" problems raised by ESP—the problems, that is, concerning the nature, limits, criteria, and evidence of our **knowledge** of the world around us.

The dramatic reports of remarkable happenings which Sidgwick, Carrington, and Cohen recount immediately raise questions in our minds. The most obvious question is simply: Did it happen? Or is it a pure hoax, a fake, a bag of tricks? If a man appears to be able to guess a series of playing cards which his collaborator is looking at in the next room, is he really guessing, or is he receiving hidden clues from a tiny radio set fitted in the frames of his glasses? Are the voices from beyond the grave in a seance merely cleverly concealed recordings triggered by a button under the spirit medium's foot? A great deal of the time and effort expended by "psychic researchers" goes to this rudimentary task of separating the hoaxes from the genuinely puzzling instances. (A similar sorting problem with regard to flying saucers, or UFOs, cost the Air Force a fortune before it finally decided to forget the whole matter.)

Once the reports have been verified, a deeper question is posed: What do they prove? If I really heard voices at the seance—indeed, if they can even be recorded and replayed—does that or does that not constitute evidence of life after death? If a "psychic" really can guess cards in a deck with a degree of accuracy that defies the laws of probability, may we reasonably infer that he has some power of perception or intuition which the rest of us lack? Does **any** amount of such evidence justify the belief that the laws of nature have been broken? Or does it, perhaps, show only that there are natural laws whose existence we have not suspected?

We arrive finally, by this progressive deepening of the question, at one of the central issues of all Western philosophy: What are the sources and criteria of knowledge? An examination of the works of those philosophers who have earned the right to be called "great" reveals that, almost without exception, they grappled with this problem of the principles of knowledge. In the last four centuries, epistemology or theory of knowledge has been the heart and soul of Western philosophy. Descartes, Spinoza, Leibniz, Kant, Locke, Berkeley, Hume, Mill—all have concentrated their best energies on analyzing the knowledge which is supposedly found in logic, in mathematics, in the natural and social sciences, or merely in everyday experience.

The five selections included in this section do not begin to cover the full range of issues and viewpoints in epistemology. Nevertheless, in the classical writings of Leibniz, Hume, and James, and in the contemporary discussions of Ayer and Chisholm a number of major themes are developed. The introductory remarks for each selection will suggest some of the philosophical questions which you might ask yourself as you read. Before you begin, however, let me sketch some of the broad outlines of the theory of knowledge in modern philosophical literature.

Modern epistemology begins with the dramatic challenge posed by Descartes' sceptical arguments in his First Meditation. That passage, which you read in Section I, called into question virtually everything which men thought they had some reason to believe: religion, science, mathematics, history, even the testimony of their senses. For the next 300 years, Western philosophers devoted a considerable portion of their energies to criticizing and defending man's capacity for knowledge.

Broadly speaking, two major positions were developed in the continuing debate over the limits and sources of knowledge. On one side was the school of thought known as "Rationalism." Descartes himself adopted the rationalist position, as did Benedict Spinoza, Gottfried Leibniz, and Christian Wolff after him. The rationalists held that the primary source of knowledge is man's rational faculty, his capacity for formal argumentation. By simplifying matters a good deal, we can summarize the rationalist doctrine in four key propositions:

1. Reason itself is the source of the concepts which play a central role in our cognition—concepts such as "necessity," "possibility," "cause," "substance," and "being."

2. Through the correct employment of those concepts, reason can arrive at systematic and complete knowledge of the existence of God, the nature of the universe, and man's relation to both God and nature.

3. Our knowledge is characterized by universality and certainty. What we know, we know with absolute assurance. Any cognition which possesses less than certainty is mere belief, not true knowledge.

4. Pure mathematics, mathematical physics, and rational theology are the branches of human knowledge which most perfectly exemplify the cognitive ideal. Other knowledge claims are to be accepted or rejected according to whether they measure up to that ideal.

On the other side of the epistemological debate was the empiricist school, frequently called "British Empiricism" because John Locke, George Berkeley, and David Hume, the three most important empiricists, were all British subjects. Empiricism followed a much more sceptical line of argument moving farther away from the confident conviction that knowledge is possible for man. In order to contrast the empiricist with the rationalist positions, we may summarize it also in four parallel propositions:

1. All our concepts are derived from the sights, sounds, tastes, smells, and feels that we receive through our senses. Reason itself is not the source of any concepts; it merely combines and manipu-

lates the materials provided by sensation. If concepts like "cause" and "necessity" cannot be traced back to an origin in sense-experience, then they must be mere empty words, referring to nothing.

2. We can have no knowledge of God's existence, and only limited knowledge **at best** of the universe and man's place in it.

3. Only the trivial tautologies of logic and pure mathematics ever achieve the universality and certainty so prized by the rationalists. If we do have real knowledge of the world, it is a knowledge of probabilities only. All substantive knowledge is fragmentary, corrigible, and incomplete.

4. The immediate testimony of the senses is the knowledge which comes closest to the cognitive ideal. If anything at all is certain, it is the evidence of my eyes and ears, not the abstract principles of physics.

As you can see, the rationalists and empiricists square off against one another on a number of questions, three of which are central to a study of the theory of knowledge. These questions are: First, what is the **source** of our knowledge of the world; Second, what are the characteristics or **criteria** of that knowledge; and Third, what are its **limits?**

In the readings selected for this section, Leibniz expresses the rationalist view and Hume represents British Empiricism. William James follows in the empiricist tradition, although his theory of Pragmatism also has roots in the post-Kantian German School of Idealism. Logical Positivism, as defended here by A. J. Ayer, is in many ways an attempt to combine some of the insights of both the empiricist and the rationalist philosophers. Like Hume, Ayer insists that all our concepts be traced to their origins in sense-experience. But he agrees with the rationalists that mathematics and physics are the appropriate models of knowledge.

The last selection, from a recent book by Prof. Roderick Chisholm of Brown University, reflects the dramatic change that has taken place in recent years in Anglo-American discussions of the theory of knowledge. After three centuries of debate over the questions raised by Descartes, many philosophers concluded that the indecisiveness of the argument might have its source in the unclarity of the key term "to know." Professor Chisholm's painstaking dissection of the terms "know" and "believe" shows us how much more there is to these familiar notions than we might have suspected. Despite the manifest brilliance of Leibniz, Hume, and the other great participants of the rationalist empiricist debate, it is doubtful that they realized the full complexity of the concept of knowledge.

LEIBNIZ

Gottfried Wilhelm Freiherr von Leibniz (1646–1716) is one of the authentic geniuses of modern European civilization. A man of prodigious energy and breadth of interest, he combined a career of creative work in logic, mathematics, physics, philosophy, and linguistics with such diverse projects as a genealogy of the royal house of Hanover, a proposal for a Catholic mission to the Far East, and a variety of proposals for academies of arts and sciences in a number of European countries.

Leibniz tackles two associated questions in this selection: first, whether all of our concepts and knowledge come from the evidence of our eyes, ears, and other senses; and second, whether there is anything in the world besides matter. In reply to both questions, he takes what has come to be called the Rationalist line. We do have other sources of knowledge than the senses, and there is something besides matter in the universe. (Both answers, of course, are relevant to the dispute over ESP.)

Leibniz is opposed to the simple experimental or observational approach of collecting instances and then generalizing from them. Mere accumulations of observations never by themselves provide us with the sort of inner, theoretical understanding of the universe which deserves the name "knowledge." The gross empiricist is like the medicine man who knows, from experience, which herbs will help a sick patient, but yet has no idea why they help. Modern medicine offers an elaborate biochemical theory which genuinely explains the inner nature of both the illness and the drug. We might compare Leibniz to the modern theoretical physicist whose work is done on the blackboard rather than in a laboratory.

We can imagine the sort of objection Leibniz might offer to the evidence piled up by psychic researchers. It is not enough to guess cards ten thousand times and then compute probabilities, he might have said; until you have a theory of psychic communication which explains the phenomena you have observed, you will know nothing. Do not simply scurry about looking for remarkable cases. Try to explain how such cases occur. Only then will your knowledge acquire the certainty and necessity which distinguish truly rational cognition.

Reason and the Senses
as Sources of Knowledge

LETTER TO QUEEN CHARLOTTE OF PRUSSIA, 1702

Madame:

The letter written not long since from Paris to Osnabruck and which I recently read, by your order, at Hanover, seemed to me truly ingenious and beautiful. And as it treats of the two important questions, *Whether there is something in our thoughts which does not come from the senses, and Whether there is something in nature which is not material,* concerning which I acknowledge that I am not altogether of the opinion of the author of the letter, I should like to be able to explain myself with the same grace as he, in order to obey the commands and to satisfy the curiosity of your Majesty.

We use the external senses as, to use the comparison of one of the ancients, a blind man does a stick, and they make us know their particular objects, which are colors, sounds, odors, flavors, and the qualities of touch. But they do not make us know what these sensible qualities are or in what they consist. For example, whether red is the revolving of certain small globules which it is claimed cause light; whether heat is the whirling of a very fine dust; whether sound is made in the air as circles in the water when a stone is thrown into it, as certain philosophers claim; this is what we do not see. And we could not even understand how this revolving, these whirlings and these circles, if they should be real, should cause exactly these perceptions which we have of red, of heat, of noise. Thus it may be said that *sensible qualities* are in fact *occult qualities*, and that there must be others *more manifest* which can render the former more explicable. And far from understanding only sensible things, it is exactly these which we understand the least. And although they are familiar to us we do not understand them the better for that; as a pilot understands no better than another person the nature of the magnetic needle which turns toward the north, although he has it always before his eyes in the compass, and although he does not admire it any the more for that reason.

I do not deny that many discoveries have been made concerning the nature of these occult qualities, as, for example, we know by what kind of refraction blue and yellow are formed, and that these two colors mixed form green; but for all this we cannot yet understand how the perception which we have of these three colors results from these causes. Also we have not even nominal definitions of such qualities by which to explain the terms. The purpose of nominal definitions is to give sufficient marks by which the thing may be recognized; for example, assayers have marks by which they distinguish gold from every other metal, and even if a man had never seen gold these signs

From *The Philosophical Works of Leibniz,* trans. by George Martin Duncan.

might be taught him so that he would infallibly recognize it if he should some day meet with it. But it is not the same with these sensible qualities; and marks to recognize blue, for example, could not be given if we had never seen it. So that blue is its own mark, and in order that a man may know what blue is it must necessarily be shown to him.

It is for this reason that we are accustomed to say that the *notions* of these qualities are *clear*, for they serve to recognize them; but that these same notions are not *distinct*, because we cannot distinguish or develop that which they include. It is an *I know not what* of which we are conscious, but for which we cannot account. Whereas we can make another understand what a thing is of which we have some description or nominal definition, even although we should not have the thing itself at hand to show him. However, we must do the senses the justice to say that, in addition to these occult qualities, they make us know other qualities which are more manifest and which furnish more distinct notions. And these are those which we ascribe to the *common sense*, because there is no external sense to which they are particularly attached and belong. And here definitions of the terms or words employed may be given. Such is the idea of *numbers*, which is found equally in sounds, colors, and touches. It is thus that we perceive also *figures*, which are common to colors and to touches, but which we do not notice in sounds. Although it is true that in order to conceive distinctly numbers and even figures, and to form sciences of them, we must come to something which the senses cannot furnish, and which the understanding adds to the senses.

As therefore our soul compares (for example) the numbers and figures which are in colors with the numbers and figures which are found by touch, there must be an *internal sense*, in which the perceptions of these different external senses are found united. This is what is called the *imagination*, which comprises at once the *notions of the particular senses*, which are *clear* but *confused*, and the *notions of the common sense*, which are clear and distinct. And these clear and distinct ideas which are subject to the imagination are the objects of the *mathematical sciences*, namely of arithmetic and geometry, which are *pure* mathematical sciences, and of the application of these sciences to nature, forming mixed mathematics. It is evident also that particular sensible qualities are susceptible of explanations and of reasonings only in so far as they involve what is common to the objects of several external senses, and belong to the internal sense. For those who try to explain sensible qualities distinctly always have recourse to the ideas of mathematics, and these ideas always involve *size* or multitude of parts. It is true that the mathematical sciences would not be demonstrative, and would consist in a simple induction or observation, which would never assure us of the perfect generality of the truths there found, if something higher and which intelligence alone can furnish did not come to the aid of the *imagination* and the *senses*.

There are, therefore, objects of still other nature, which are not included at all in what is observed in the objects of the senses in particular or in common, and which consequently are not objects of the imagination either. Thus besides the *sensible* and *imageable*, there is that which is purely *intelligible*, as being the *object of the understanding alone*, and such is the object of my thought when I think of myself.

━ This thought of the *Ego*, which informs me of sensible objects, and of my own action resulting therefrom, adds something to the objects of the senses. To think a color and to observe that one thinks it, are two very different thoughts, as different as the color is from the Ego which thinks it. And as I conceive that other beings may also have the right to say *I*, or that it could be said for them, it is through this that I conceive what is called *substance* in general, and it is also the consideration of the Ego itself which furnishes other *metaphysical* notions, such as cause, effect, action, similarity, etc., and even those of *logic* and of *ethics*. Thus it can be said that there is nothing in the understanding which does not come from the senses, except the understanding itself, or that which understands.

There are then three grades of notions: the *sensible only*, which are the objects appropriate to each sense in particular; the *sensible and at the same time intelligible*, which pertain to the common sense; and the *intelligible only*, which belong to the understanding. The first and the second are both imageable, but the third are above the imagination. The second and third are intelligible and distinct; but the first are confused, although they are clear or recognizable.

Being itself and *truth* are not known wholly through the senses; for it would not be impossible for a creature to have long and orderly dreams, resembling our *life*, of such a sort that everything which it thought it perceived through the senses would be but mere *appearances*. There must therefore be something beyond the senses, which distinguishes the true from the apparent. But the truth of the demonstrative sciences is exempt from these doubts, and must even serve for judging of the truth of sensible things. For as able philosophers, ancient and modern, have already well remarked:—if all that I should think that I see should be but a dream, it would always be true that I who think while dreaming, would be something, and would actually think in many ways, for which there must always be some reason.

Thus what the ancient Platonists have observed is very true, and is very worthy of being considered, that the existence of sensible things and particularly of the *Ego* which thinks and which is called spirit or soul, is incomparably more sure than the existence of sensible things; and that thus it would not be impossible, speaking with metaphysical rigor, that there should be at bottom only these intelligible substances, and that sensible things should be but appearances. While on the other hand our lack of attention makes us take sensible things for the only true things. It is well also to observe that if I should discover any demonstrative truth, mathematical or other, while dreaming (as might in fact be), it would be just as certain as if I had been awake. This shows us how intelligible truth is independent of the truth or of the existence outside of us of sensible and material things.

This conception of *being* and of *truth* is found therefore in the Ego and in the understanding, rather than in the external senses and in the perception of external objects.

There we find also what it is to affirm, to deny, to doubt, to will, to act. But above all we find there the *force of the consequences* of reasoning, which are a part of what is called the *natural light*. For example, from this premise, that *no wise man is wicked*, we may, by reversing the terms, draw this conclusion, that *no wicked man is wise*. Whereas from this sentence, that *every wise man is praiseworthy*, we cannot conclude by converting it, that *every one praiseworthy is wise* but only that *some praiseworthy ones are wise*. Although we may always convert particular affirmative propositions, for example, if *some wise man is rich* it must also be that *some rich men are wise*, this cannot be done in particular negatives. For example, we may say that *there are charitable persons who are not just*, which happens when charity is not sufficiently regulated; but we cannot infer from this that *there are just persons who are not charitable;* for in justice are included at the same time charity and the rule of reason.

It is also by this *natural light* that the *axioms* of mathematics are recognized; for example, that *if from two equal things the same quantity be taken away the things which remain are equal;* likewise that *if in a balance everything is equal on the one side and on the other, neither will incline*, a thing which we foresee without ever having experienced it. It is upon such foundations that we construct arithmetic, geometry, mechanics and the other demonstrative sciences; in which, in truth, the senses are very necessary, in order to have certain ideas of sensible things, and experiments are necessary to establish certain facts, and even useful to verify reasonings as by a kind of proof. But the force of the demonstrations depends upon intelligible notions and truths, which alone are capable of making us discern what is necessary, and which, in the conjectural sciences, are even capable of determining demonstratively the degree of probability upon certain given suppositions, in order that we may choose rationally among opposite appearances, the one which is greatest. Nevertheless this part of the art of reasoning has not yet been cultivated as much as it ought to be.

But to return to *necessary truths*, it is generally true that we know them only by this natural light, and not at all by the experiences of the senses. For the senses can very well make known, in some sort, what is, but they cannot make known what *ought to be* or could not be otherwise.

For example, although we may have experienced numberless times that every massive body tends toward the centre of the earth and is not sustained in the air, we are not sure that this is necessary as long as we do not understand the reason of it. Thus we could not be sure that the same thing would occur in air at a higher altitude, at a hundred or more leagues above us; and there are philosophers who imagine that the earth is a magnet, and as the ordinary magnet does not attract the needle when a little removed from it, they think that the attractive force of the earth does not extend very far either. I do not say that they are right, but I do say that one cannot go very certainly beyond the experiences one has had, when one is not aided by reason.

This is why the geometricians have always considered that what is only proved by *induction* or by examples, in geometry or in arithmetic, is never perfectly proved. For example, experience teaches us that odd numbers continuously added together produce the square numbers, that is to say, those which come from multiplying a number by itself. Thus 1 and 3 make 4, that is to say 2 times 2. And 1 and 3 and 5 make 9, that is to say 3 times 3. And 1 and 3 and 5 and 7 make 16, that is 4 times 4. And 1 and 3 and 5 and 7 and 9 make 25, that is 5 times 5. And so on.

1	1	1	1
3	3	3	3
–	5	5	5
4	–	7	7
	9	–	9
		16	–
			25
2	3	4	5
x	x	x	x
2	3	4	5
4	9	16	25

However, if one should experience it a hundred thousand times, continuing the calculation very far, he may reasonably think that this will always follow; but he does not therefore have absolute certainty of it, unless he learns the demonstrative reason which the mathematicians found out long ago. And it is on this foundation of the uncertainty of inductions, but carried a little too far, that an Englishman has lately wished to maintain that we can avoid death. For (said he) the inference is not good: my father, my grandfather, my great-grandfather are dead and all the others who have lived before us; therefore we shall also die. For their death has no influence on us. The trouble is that we resemble them a little too much in this respect that the causes of their death subsist also in us. For the resemblance would not suffice to draw sure consequences without the consideration of the same reasons.

In truth there are *experiments* which succeed numberless times and ordinarily, and yet it is found in some extraordinary cases that there are *instances* where the experiment does not succeed. For example, if we should have found a hundred thousand times that iron put all alone on the surface of water goes to the bottom, we are not sure that this must always happen. And without recurring to the miracle of the prophet Elisha, who made iron float, we know that an iron pot may be made so hollow that it floats, and that it can even carry besides a considerable weight, as do boats of copper or of tin. And even the abstract sciences like geometry furnish cases in which what ordinarily occurs occurs no longer. For example, we ordinarily find that two lines which continually approach each other finally meet, and many people will almost swear that this could never be otherwise. And nevertheless geometry furnishes us with extraordinary lines, which are for this reason called *asymptotes*, which prolonged *ad infinitum* continually approach each other, and nevertheless never meet.

This consideration shows also that there is a *light born within us*. For since the senses and inductions could never teach us truths which are thoroughly universal, nor that which is absolutely necessary, but only that which is, and that which is found in particular examples; and since we nevertheless know necessary and universal truths of the sciences, a privilege which we have above the brutes; it follows that we have derived these truths in part from what is within us. Thus we may lead a child to these by simple interrogations, after the manner of Socrates, without telling him anything, and without making him experiment at all upon the truth of what is asked him. And this could very easily be practiced in numbers and other similar matters.

I agree, nevertheless, that in the present state the external senses are necessary to us for thinking, and that, if we had none, we could not think. But that which is necessary for something does not for all that constitute its essence. Air is necessary for life, but our life is something else than air. The senses furnish us the matter for reasoning, and we never have thoughts so abstract that something from the senses is not mingled therewith; but reasoning requires something else in addition to what is from the senses.

As to the *second question*, whether there are *immaterial substances*, in order to solve it, it is first necessary to explain one's self. Hitherto by matter has been understood that which includes only notions purely passive and indifferent, namely, extension and impenetrability, which need to be determined by something else to some form or action. Thus when it is said that there are immaterial substances, it is thereby meant that there are substances which include other notions, namely, perception and the principle of action or of change, which could not be explained either by extension or by impenetrability. These beings, when they have feeling, are called *souls*, and when they are capable of reason, they are called spirits. Thus if one says that force and perception are essential to matter, he takes matter for corporeal substance which is complete, which includes form and matter, or the soul with the organs. It is as if it were said that there were souls everywhere. This might be true, and would not be contrary to the doctrine of immaterial substances. For it is not intended that these souls be separate from matter, but simply that they are something more than matter, and are not produced nor destroyed by the changes which matter undergoes, nor subject to dissolution, since they are not composed of parts.

Nevertheless it must be avowed also that there is *substance separated from matter.* And to see this, one has only to consider that there are number-less forms which matter might have received in place of the series of variations which it has actually received. For it is clear, for example, that the stars could move quite otherwise, space and matter being indifferent to every kind of motion and figure.

Hence the reason or universal determining cause whereby things are, and are as they are rather than otherwise, must be outside of matter. And even the existence of matter depends thereon, since we do not find in its notion that it carries with it the reason of its existence.

Now this ultimate reason of things, which is common to them all and universal by reason of the connection existing between all parts of nature, is what we call *God,* who must necessarily be an infinite and absolutely perfect substance. I am inclined to think that all immaterial finite substances (even the genii or angels according to the opinion of the ancient Church Fathers) are united to organs, and accompany matter, and even that souls or active forms are everywhere found in it. And matter, in order to constitute a substance which is complete, cannot do without them, since force and action are found everywhere in it, and since the laws of force depend on certain remarkable metaphysical reasons or intelligible notions, and cannot be explained by notions which are merely material or mathematical or which belong to the sphere of the imagination.

Perception also could not be explained by any mechanism whatsoever. We may therefore conclude that there is in addition something immaterial everywhere in these creatures, and particularly in us, in whom this force is accompanied by a sufficiently distinct perception, and even by that light, of which I have spoken above, which makes us resemble in miniature the Divinity, as well by knowledge of the order, as by the ordering which we ourselves know how to give to the things which are within our reach, in imitation of that which God gives to the universe. It is in this also that our *virtue* and per-fection consist, as our *felicity* consists in the pleasure which we take therein.

And since every time we penetrate into the depths of things, we find there the most beautiful order we could wish, even surpassing what we have therein imagined, as all those know who have fathomed the sciences; we may conclude that it is the same in all the rest, and that not only immaterial sub-stances subsist always, but also that their lives, progress and changes are regu-lated for advance toward a certain end, or rather to approach more and more thereto, as do the asymptotes. And although we sometimes recoil, like lines which retrograde, advancement none the less finally prevails and wins.

The natural light of reason does not suffice for knowing the detail thereof, and our experiences are still too limited to catch a glimpse of the laws of this order. The revealed light guides us meanwhile through faith, but there is room to believe that in the course of time we shall know them even more by experience, and that there are spirits that know them already more than we do.

Meanwhile the philosophers and the poets, for want of this, have betaken themselves to the fictions of metempsychosis or of the Elysian Fields, in order to give some ideas which might strike the populace. But the consideration of the perfection of things or (what is the same thing) of the sovereign power, wisdom and goodness of God, who does all for the best, that to say, in the greatest order, suffices to render content those who are reasonable, and to make us believe that the contentment ought to be greater, according as we are more disposed to follow order or reason.

HUME

You have already met David Hume in Section II, talking about free-dom of the will. Hume was very discouraged by the poor reception of his Treatise of Human Nature, *and he decided therefore to re-write it in a more popular style. Ten years later, in 1748, he pub-lished two short works containing what he felt to be the heart of his work of theory and knowledge and ethics. The first work, en-titled* Enquiry Concerning the Human Understanding, *set forth his sceptical attacks on scientific and everyday beliefs about the world around us. Hume argued very persuasively that just about all of our beliefs are absolutely groundless. History, science, even common sense, he said, are just accumulations of habit, prejudice, and unwar-ranted conviction. Needless to say, Hume was not received by the public with open arms, and his sceptical attacks on religious belief especially earned him a good many enemies.*

In the present selection, Hume takes as his target the Christian belief in miracles. *Hume argues as follows: Even if we grant that science can give us knowledge of laws of nature—which of course Hume didn't grant—still we must draw the line at any nonsense about miracles. The problem with miracles is that they are logically impossible. A miracle is, by definition, an event which violates the laws of nature (and hence reveals the workings of a divine being). But the only evidence we have of the laws of nature is our observa-tion of past and present events. (Notice that Hume disagrees here with Leibniz.) Now there are two possibilities. If we are convinced that the so-called "miracle" really happened, then that just shows us that we must revise our conception of the laws of nature. If, on the other hand, we are convinced of the laws of nature, then we will conclude that the "miracle" never really happened (the reports are exaggerated, the observers were hallucinating, etc.). But, Hume con-cludes, the evidence cannot* possibly *prove* both *that the laws are correct* and *that an exception has taken place.*

The relevance of this argument to the ESP debate is obvious. Many orthodox scientists reject the work of the psychic research-ers because it looks to them too much like reports of miracles and other strange, "unnatural" events.

Empirical Evidence and
the Impossibility of Miracles

I

There is, in Dr. Tillotson's writings, an argument against the *real presence* which is as concise and elegant and strong as any argument can possibly be supposed against a doctrine so little worthy of a serious refutation. It is acknowledged on all hands, says that learned prelate, that the authority either of the Scripture or of tradition is founded merely on the testimony of the Apostles, who were eyewitnesses to those miracles of our Saviour by which He proved His divine mission. Our evidence, then, for the truth of the *Christian* religion is less than the evidence for the truth of our senses, because even in the first authors of our religion it was no greater, and it is evident it must diminish in passing from them to their disciples; nor can anyone rest such confidence in their testimony as in the immediate object of his senses. But a weaker evidence can never destroy a stronger; and therefore, were the doctrine of the real presence ever so clearly revealed in Scripture, it were directly contrary to the rules of just reasoning to give our assent to it. It contradicts sense, though both the Scripture and tradition, on which it is supposed to be built, carry not such evidence with them as sense when they are considered merely as external evidences, and are not brought home to everyone's breast by the immediate operation of the Holy Spirit.

Nothing is so convenient as a decisive argument of this kind, which must at least *silence* the most arrogant bigotry and superstition, and free us from their impertinent solicitations. I flatter myself that I have discovered an argument of a like nature which, if just, will, with the wise and learned, be an everlasting check to all kinds of superstitious delusion, and consequently will be useful as long as the world endures. For so long, I presume, will the accounts of miracles and prodigies be found in all history, sacred and profane.

Though experience be our only guide in reasoning concerning matters of fact, it must be acknowledged that this guide is not altogether infallible, but in some cases is apt to lead us into errors. One who in our climate should expect better weather in any week of June than in one of December would reason justly and conformably to experience, but it is certain that he may happen, in the event, to find himself mistaken. However, we may observe that in such a case he would have no cause to complain of experience, because it commonly informs us beforehand of the uncertainty by that contrariety of events which we may learn from a diligent observation. All effects follow not with like certainty from their supposed causes. Some events are found, in all countries

Section X, "Of Miracles." From *Inquiry Concerning Human Understanding* by David Hume. Originally published in 1748.

and all ages, to have been constantly conjoined together; others are found to have been more variable, and sometimes to disappoint our expectations, so that in our reasonings concerning matter of fact there are all imaginable degrees of assurance, from the highest certainty to the lowest species of moral evidence.

A wise man, therefore, proportions his belief to the evidence. In such conclusions as are founded on an infallible experience, he expects the event with the last degree of assurance, and regards his past experience as a full *proof* of the future existence of that event. In other cases he proceeds with more caution: he weighs the opposite experiments; he considers which side is supported by the greater number of experiments; to that side he inclines, with doubt and hesitation; and when at last he fixes his judgment, the evidence exceeds not what we properly call *probability*. All probability, then, supposes an opposition of experiments and observations, where the one side is found to overbalance the other and to produce a degree of evidence proportioned to the superiority. A hundred instances or experiments on one side, and fifty on another, afford a doubtful expectation of any event, though a hundred uniform experiments, with only one that is contradictory, reasonably beget a pretty strong degree of assurance. In all cases we must balance the opposite experiments where they are opposite, and deduct the smaller number from the greater in order to know the exact force of the superior evidence.

To apply these principles to a particular instance, we may observe that there is no species of reasoning more common, more useful, and even necessary to human life than that which is derived from the testimony of men and the reports of eyewitnesses and spectators. This species of reasoning, perhaps, one may deny to be founded on the relation of cause and effect. I shall not dispute about a word. It will be sufficient to observe that our assurance in any argument of this kind is derived from no other principle than our observation of the veracity of human testimony and of the usual conformity of facts to the report of witnesses. It being a general maxim that no objects have any discoverable connection together, and that all the inferences which we can draw from one to another are founded merely on our experience of their constant and regular conjunction, it is evident that we ought not to make an exception to this maxim in favor of human testimony, whose connection with any event seems in itself as little necessary as any other. Were not the memory tenacious to a certain degree, had not men commonly an inclination to truth and a principle of probity, were they not sensible to shame when detected in a falsehood, were not these, I say, discovered by *experience* to be qualities inherent in human nature, we should never repose the least confidence in human testimony. A man delirious or noted for falsehood and villainy has no manner of authority with us.

And as the evidence derived from witnesses and human testimony is founded on past experience, so it varies with the experience and is regarded either as a *proof* or a *probability*, according as the conjunction between any particular kind of report and any kind of object has been found to be constant or variable. There are a number of circumstances to be taken into consideration in all judgments of this kind, and the ultimate standard by which we determine all disputes that may arise concerning them is always derived from experience and observation. Where this experience is not entirely uniform on any side, it is attended with an unavoidable contrariety in our judgments and with the same opposition and mutual destruction of argument as in every other kind of evidence. We frequently hesitate concerning the reports of others. We balance the opposite circumstances which cause any doubt or uncertainty; and when we discover a superiority on any side, we incline to it, but still with a diminution of assurance, in proportion to the force of its antagonist.

This contrariety of evidence, in the present case, may be derived from several different causes: from the opposition of contrary testimony, from the character or number of the witnesses, from the manner of their delivering their testimony, or from the union of all these circumstances. We entertain a suspicion concerning any matter of fact when the witnesses contradict each other, when they are but few or of a doubtful character, when they have an interest in what they affirm, when they deliver their testimony with hesitation, or on the contrary with too violent asseverations. There are many other particulars of the same kind which may diminish or destroy the force of any argument derived from human testimony.

Suppose, for instance, that the fact which the testimony endeavors to establish partakes of the extraordinary and the marvelous; in that case the evidence resulting from the testimony admits of a diminution, greater or less, in proportion as the fact is more or less unusual. The reason why we place any credit in witnesses and historians is not derived from any *connection* which we perceive *a priori* between testimony and reality, but because we are accustomed to find a conformity between them. But when the fact attested is such a one as has seldom fallen under our observation, here is a contest of two opposite experiences, of which the one destroys the other as far as its force goes, and the superior can only operate on the mind by the force which remains. The very same principle of experience which gives us a certain degree of assurance in the testimony of witnesses gives us also, in this case, another degree of assurance against the fact which they endeavor to establish; from which contradiction there necessarily arises a counterpoise and mutual destruction of belief and authority.

I should not believe such a story were it told me by Cato was a proverbial saying in Rome, even during the lifetime of that philosophical patriot. The incredibility of a fact, it was allowed, might invalidate so great an authority.

The Indian prince who refused to believe the first relations concerning the effects of frost reasoned justly, and it naturally required very strong testimony to engage his assent to facts that arose from a state of nature with which he was unacquainted, and which bore so little analogy to those events of which he had had constant and uniform experience. Though they were not contrary to his experience, they were not conformable to it.[1]

But in order to increase the probability against the testimony of witnesses, let us suppose that the fact which they affirm, instead of being only marvelous, is really miraculous, and suppose also that the testimony, considered apart and in itself, amounts to an entire proof; in that case there is proof against proof, of which the strongest must prevail, but still with a diminution of its force, in proportion to that of its antagonist.

A miracle is a violation of the laws of nature; and as a firm and unalterable experience has established these laws, the proof against a miracle, from the very nature of the fact, is as entire as any argument from experience can possibly be imagined. Why is it more than probable that all men must die, that lead cannot of itself remain suspended in the air, that fire consumes wood and is extinguished by water, unless it be that these events are found agreeable to the laws of nature, and there is required a violation of these laws, or in other words a miracle, to prevent them? Nothing is esteemed a miracle if it ever happen in the common course of nature. It is no miracle that a man, seemingly in good health, should die on a sudden, because such a kind of death, though more unusual than any other, has yet been frequently observed to happen. But it is a miracle that a dead man should come to life, because that has never been observed in any age or country. There must, therefore, be a uniform experience against every miraculous event, otherwise the event would not merit that appellation. And as a uniform experience amounts to a proof, there is here a direct and full *proof*, from the nature of the fact, against the existence of any miracle; nor can such a proof be destroyed or the miracle rendered credible but by an opposite proof which is superior.[2]

The plain consequence is (and it is a general maxim worthy of our atten-

---

[1] No Indian, it is evident, could have experience that water did not freeze in cold climates. This is placing nature in a situation quite unknown to him, and it is impossible for him to tell *a priori* what will result from it. It is making a new experiment, the consequence of which is always uncertain. One may sometimes conjecture from analogy what will follow, but still this is but conjecture. And it must be confessed that, in the present case of freezing, the event follows contrary to the rules of analogy and is such as a rational Indian would not look for. The operations of cold upon water are not gradual, according to the degrees of cold, but whenever it comes to the freezing point, the water passes in a moment from the utmost liquidity to perfect hardness. Such an event, therefore, may be denominated *extraordinary* and requires a pretty strong testimony to render it credible to people in a warm climate. But still it is not *miraculous*, nor contrary to uniform experience of the course of nature in cases where all the circumstances are the same. The inhabitants of Sumatra have always seen water fluid in their own climate, and the freezing of their rivers ought to be deemed a prodigy. But they never saw water in Muscovy during the winter, and therefore they cannot reasonably be positive what would there be the consequence.

[2] Sometimes an event may not, *in itself*, seem to be contrary to the laws of nature, and yet if it were real it might, by reason of some circumstances, be denominated a miracle,

tion) that no testimony is sufficient to establish a miracle unless the testimony be of such a kind that its falsehood would be more miraculous than the fact which it endeavors to establish. And even in that case there is a mutual destruction of arguments, and the superior only gives us an assurance suitable to that degree of force which remains after deducting the inferior. When anyone tells me that he saw a dead man restored to life, I immediately consider with myself whether it be more probable that this person should either deceive or be deceived, or that the fact which he relates should really have happened. I weigh the one miracle against the other, and according to the superiority which I discover I pronounce my decision, and always reject the greater miracle. If the falsehood of his testimony would be more miraculous than the event which he relates, then, and not till then, can he pretend to command my belief or opinion.

II

In the foregoing reasoning we have supposed that the testimony upon which a miracle is founded may possibly amount to an entire proof, and that the falsehood of that testimony would be a real prodigy. But it is easy to show that we have been a great deal too liberal in our concession, and that there never was a miraculous event established on so full an evidence.

For *first*, there is not to be found in all history any miracle attested by a sufficient number of men of such unquestioned good sense, education, and learning as to secure us against all delusion in themselves, of such undoubted integrity as to place them beyond all suspicion of any design to deceive others, of such credit and reputation in the eyes of mankind as to have a great deal to lose in case of their being detected in any falsehood, and at the same time attesting facts performed in such a public manner and in so celebrated a part of the world as to render the detection unavoidable; all which circumstances are requisite to give us a full assurance in the testimony of men.

because in *fact* it is contrary to these laws. Thus if a person claiming a divine authority should command a sick person to be well, a healthful man to fall down dead, the clouds to pour rain, the winds to blow, in short, should order many natural events, which immediately follow upon his command, these might justly be esteemed miracles, because they are really, in this case, contrary to the laws of nature. For if any suspicion remain that the event and command concurred by accident, there is no miracle and no transgression of the laws of nature. If this suspicion be removed, there is evidently a miracle and a transgression of these laws, because nothing can be more contrary to nature than that the voice or command of a man should have such an influence. A miracle may be accurately defined, *a transgression of a law of nature by a particular volition of the Deity, or by the interposition of some invisible agent.* A miracle may either be discoverable by men or not. This alters not its nature and essence. The raising of a house or ship into the air is a visible miracle. The raising of a feather, when the wind wants ever so little of a force requisite for that purpose, is as real a miracle, though not so sensible with regard to us.

Secondly, we may observe in human nature a principle which, if strictly examined, will be found to diminish extremely the assurance which we might, from human testimony, have in any kind of prodigy. The maxim by which we commonly conduct ourselves in our reasonings is that the objects of which we have no experience resemble those of which we have; that what we have found to be most usual is always most probable; and that where there is an opposition of arguments, we ought to give the preference to such as are founded on the greatest number of past observations. But though, in proceeding by this rule, we readily reject any fact which is unusual and incredible in an ordinary degree, yet in advancing further, the mind observes not always the same rule, but when anything is affirmed utterly absurd and miraculous, it rather the more readily admits of such a fact upon account of that very circumstance which ought to destroy all its authority. The passion of *surprise* and *wonder*, arising from miracles, being an agreeable emotion, gives a sensible tendency toward the belief of those events from which it is derived. And this goes so far that even those who cannot enjoy this pleasure immediately, nor can believe those miraculous events of which they are informed, yet love to partake of the satisfaction at second hand or by rebound, and place a pride and delight in exciting the admiration of others.

With what greediness are the miraculous accounts of travelers received, their descriptions of sea and land monsters, their relations of wonderful adventures, strange men, and uncouth manners? But if the spirit of religion join itself to the love of wonder, there is an end of common sense, and human testimony in these circumstances loses all pretensions to authority. A religionist may be an enthusiast and imagine he sees what has no reality. He may know his narrative to be false, and yet persevere in it with the best intentions in the world, for the sake of promoting so holy a cause. Or even where this delusion has not place, vanity, excited by so strong a temptation, operates on him more powerfully than on the rest of mankind in any other circumstances, and self-interest with equal force. His auditors may not have, and commonly have not, sufficient judgment to canvass his evidence. What judgment they have, they renounce by principle, in these sublime and mysterious subjects. Or if they were ever so willing to employ it, passion and a heated imagination disturb the regularity of its operations. Their credulity increases his impudence, and his impudence overpowers their credulity.

Eloquence, when at its highest pitch, leaves little room for reason or reflection, but addressing itself entirely to the fancy or the affections, captivates the willing hearers, and subdues their understanding. Happily, this pitch it seldom attains. But what a Tully or a Demosthenes could scarcely effect over a Roman or Athenian audience, every *Capuchin*, every itinerant or stationary teacher can perform over the generality of mankind, and in a higher degree, by touching such gross and vulgar passions.

The many instances of forged miracles and prophecies and supernatural events which, in all ages, have either been detected by contrary evidence or which detect themselves by their absurdity, prove sufficiently the strong propensity of mankind to the extraordinary and the marvelous, and ought reasonably to beget a suspicion against all relations of this kind. This is our natural way of thinking, even with regard to the most common and most credible events. For instance, there is no kind of report which arises so easily and spreads so quickly, especially in country places and provincial towns, as those concerning marriages, insomuch that two young persons of equal condition never see each other twice, but the whole neighborhood immediately join them together. The pleasure of telling a piece of news so interesting, of propagating it, and of being the first reporters of it spreads the intelligence. And this is so well known that no man of sense gives attention to these reports till he find them confirmed by some greater evidence. Do not the same passions, and others still stronger, incline the generality of mankind to believe and report, with the greatest vehemence and assurance, all religious miracles?

Thirdly, it forms a strong presumption against all supernatural and miraculous relations that they are observed chiefly to abound among ignorant and barbarous nations; or if a civilized people has ever given admission to any of them, that people will be found to have received them from ignorant and barbarous ancestors, who transmitted them with that inviolable sanction and authority which always attend received opinions. When we peruse the first histories of all nations, we are apt to imagine ourselves transported into some new world, where the whole frame of nature is disjointed and every element performs its operations in a different manner from what it does at present. Battles, revolutions, pestilence, famine, and death are never the effect of those natural causes which we experience. Prodigies, omens, oracles, judgments quite obscure the few natural events that are intermingled with them. But as the former grow thinner every page, in proportion as we advance nearer the enlightened ages, we soon learn that there is nothing mysterious or supernatural in the case, but that all proceeds from the usual propensity of mankind toward the marvelous, and that, though this inclination may at intervals receive a check from sense and learning, it can never be thoroughly extirpated from human nature.

It is strange, a judicious reader is apt to say upon the perusal of these wonderful historians, *that such prodigious events never happen in our days*. But it is nothing strange, I hope, that men should lie in all ages. You must surely have seen instances enough of that frailty. You have yourself heard many such marvelous relations started, which being treated with scorn by all the wise and judicious, have at last been abandoned even by the vulgar. Be assured that those renowned lies which have spread and flourished to such a monstrous height arose from like beginnings, but being sown in a more proper soil shot up at last into prodigies almost equal to those which they relate.

It was a wise policy in that false prophet Alexander, who, though now forgotten, was once so famous, to lay the first scene of his impostures in Paphlagonia, where, as Lucian tells us, the people were extremely ignorant and stupid, and ready to swallow even the grossest delusion. People at a distance, who are weak enough to think the matter at all worth inquiry, have no opportunity of receiving better information. The stories come magnified to them by a hundred circumstances. Fools are industrious in propagating the imposture, while the wise and learned are contented, in general, to deride its absurdity, without informing themselves of the particular facts by which it may be distinctly refuted. And thus the impostor above-mentioned was enabled to proceed from his ignorant Paphlagonians to the enlisting of votaries, even among the Grecian philosophers and men of the most eminent rank and distinction in Rome, nay, could engage the attention of that sage emperor Marcus Aurelius so far as to make him trust the success of a military expedition to his delusive prophecies.

The advantages are so great of starting an imposture among an ignorant people that, even though the delusion should be too gross to impose on the generality of them (*which, though seldom, is sometimes the case*), it has a much better chance for succeeding in remote countries than if the first scene had been laid in a city renowned for arts and knowledge. The most ignorant and barbarous of these barbarians carry the report abroad. None of their countrymen have a large correspondence, or sufficient credit and authority to contradict and beat down the delusion. Men's inclination to the marvelous has full opportunity to display itself. And thus a story which is universally exploded in the place where it was first started shall pass for certain at a thousand miles distance. But had Alexander fixed his residence at Athens, the philosophers at that renowned mart of learning had immediately spread throughout the whole Roman empire their sense of the matter, which, being supported by so great authority and displayed by all the force of reason and eloquence, had entirely opened the eyes of mankind. It is true, Lucian, passing by chance through Paphlagonia, had an opportunity of performing this good office. But, though much to be wished, it does not always happen that every Alexander meets with a Lucian, ready to expose and detect his impostures.

I may add as a *fourth* reason which diminishes the authority of prodigies, that there is no testimony for any, even those which have not been expressly detected, that is not opposed by an infinite number of witnesses, so that not only the miracle destroys the credit of testimony, but the testimony destroys itself. To make this the better understood, let us consider that in matters of religion whatever is different is contrary, and that it is impossible the religions of ancient Rome, of Turkey, of Siam, and of China should all of them be established on any solid foundation. Every miracle, therefore, pretended to have been wrought in any of these religions (and all of them abound in miracles), as its direct scope is to establish the particular system to which it is attributed, so has it the same force, though more indirectly, to overthrow every other system. In destroying a rival system, it likewise destroys the credit of those miracles on which that system was established, so that all the prodigies of different religions are to be regarded as contrary facts, and the evidences of these prodigies, whether weak or strong, as opposite to each other. According to this method of reasoning, when we believe any miracle of Mahomet or his successors, we have for our warrant the testimony of a few barbarous Arabians. And on the other hand, we are to regard the authority of Titus Livius, Plutarch, Tacitus, and, in short, of all the authors and witnesses, Grecian, Chinese, and Roman Catholic, who have related any miracle in their particular religion—I say, we are to regard their testimony in the same light as if they had mentioned the Mahometan miracle and had in express terms contradicted it with the same certainty as they have for the miracle they relate. This argument may appear oversubtle and refined, but is not in reality different from the reasoning of a judge who supposes that the credit of two witnesses maintaining a crime against anyone is destroyed by the testimony of two others who affirm him to have been two hundred leagues distant at the same instant when the crime is said to have been committed.

One of the best-attested miracles in all profane history is that which Tacitus reports of Vespasian, who cured a blind man in Alexandria by means of his spittle, and a lame man by the mere touch of his foot, in obedience to a vision of the god Serapis, who had enjoined them to have recourse to the Emperor for these miraculous cures. The story may be seen in that fine historian[3] where every circumstance seems to add weight to the testimony, and might be displayed at large with all the force of argument and eloquence, if anyone were now concerned to enforce the evidence of that exploded and idolatrous superstition. The gravity, solidity, age, and probity of so great an emperor, who, through the whole course of his life, conversed in a familiar manner with his friends and courtiers, and never affected those extraordinary airs of divinity assumed by Alexander and Demetrius. The historian, a contemporary writer noted for candor and veracity, and withal the greatest and most penetrating genius perhaps of all antiquity, and so free from any tendency to credulity that he even lies under the contrary imputation of atheism and profaneness. The persons from whose authority he related the miracle, of established character for judgment and veracity, as we may well presume; eyewitnesses of the fact, and confirming their testimony after the Flavian family was despoiled of the empire and could no longer give any reward as the price of a lie. *Utrumque qui interfuere nunc quoque memorant, postquam nullum mendacio pretium.*[4] To which, if we add the public nature of the facts, as related, it will appear that no evidence can well be supposed stronger for so gross and so palpable a falsehood.

There is also a memorable story related by Cardinal De Retz, which may well deserve our consideration. When that intriguing politician fled into Spain to avoid the persecution of his enemies, he passed through Saragossa, the capital of Aragon, where he was shown, in the cathedral, a man who had served

---

[3] *Hist.*, lib. iv. cap. 81. Suetonius gives nearly the same account in *vita Vesp.*
[4] [Both facts are told by eyewitnesses even now when falsehood brings no reward.]

seven years as a doorkeeper and was well known to everybody in town that had ever paid his devotions at that church. He had been seen for so long a time wanting a leg, but recovered that limb by the rubbing of holy oil upon the stump, and the Cardinal assures us that he saw him with two legs. This miracle was vouched by all the canons of the church, and the whole company in town were appealed to for a confirmation of the fact, whom the Cardinal found, by their zealous devotion, to be thorough believers of the miracle. Here the relater was also contemporary to the supposed prodigy, of an incredulous and libertine character as well as of great genius, the miracle of so *singular* a nature as could scarcely admit of a counterfeit, and the witnesses very numerous, and all of them in a manner spectators of the fact to which they gave their testimony. And what adds mightily to the force of the evidence and may double our surprise on this occasion is that the Cardinal himself, who relates the story, seems not to give any credit to it, and consequently cannot be suspected of any concurrence in the holy fraud. He considered justly that it was not requisite, in order to reject a fact of this nature, to be able accurately to disprove the testimony and to trace its falsehood through all the circumstances of knavery and credulity which produced it. He knew that, as this was commonly altogether impossible at any small distance of time and place, so was it extremely difficult, even where one was immediately present, by reason of the bigotry, ignorance, cunning, and roguery of a great part of mankind. He therefore concluded, like a just reasoner, that such an evidence carried falsehood upon the very face of it, and that a miracle supported by any human testimony was more properly a subject of derision than of argument.

There surely never was a greater number of miracles ascribed to one person than those which were lately said to have been wrought in France upon the tomb of Abbé Paris, the famous Jansenist, with whose sanctity the people were so long deluded. The curing of the sick, giving hearing to the deaf and sight to the blind, were everywhere talked of as the usual effects of that holy sepulcher. But what is more extraordinary, many of the miracles were immediately proved upon the spot, before judges of unquestioned integrity, attested by witnesses of credit and distinction, in a learned age, and on the most eminent theater that is now in the world. Nor is this all: a relation of them was published and dispersed everywhere, nor were the *Jesuits*, though a learned body supported by the civil magistrate, and determined enemies to those opinions in whose favor the miracles were said to have been wrought, ever able distinctly to refute or detect them.[5] Where shall we find such a number of circumstances agreeing to the corroboration of one fact? And what have we to oppose to such a cloud of witnesses but the absolute impossibility or miraculous nature of the events which they relate? And this surely, in the

---

[5] This book was written by Mons. Montgeron, counsel or judge of the parliament of Paris, a man of figure and character, who was also a martyr to the cause, and is now said to be somewhere in a dungeon on account of his book.

eyes of all responsible people, will alone be regarded as a sufficient refutation.

Is the consequence just, because some human testimony has the utmost force and authority in some cases, when it relates the battles of Philippi or Pharsalia for instance, that therefore all kinds of testimony must in all cases have equal force and authority? Suppose that the Caesarean and Pompeian factions had, each of them, claimed the victory in these battles, and that the historians of each party had uniformly ascribed the advantage to their own side; how could mankind, at this distance, have been able to determine between them? The contrariety is equally strong between the miracles related by Herodotus or Plutarch, and those delivered by Mariana, Bede, or any monkish historian.

The wise lend a very academic faith to every report which favors the passion of the reported, whether it magnifies his country, his family, or himself, or in any other way strikes in with his natural inclinations and propensities. But what greater temptation than to appear a missionary, a prophet, an ambassador from heaven? Who would not encounter many dangers and difficulties in order to attain so sublime a character? Or if, by the help of vanity and a heated imagination, a man has first made a convert of himself and entered seriously into the delusion, who ever scruples to make use of pious frauds in support of so holy and meritorious a cause?

The smallest spark may here kindle into the greatest flame, because the materials are always prepared for it. The *avidum genus auricularum*,[6] the gazing populace, receive greedily without examination, whatever soothes superstition and promotes wonder.

How many stories of this nature have, in all ages, been detected and exploded in their infancy? How many more have been celebrated for a time, and have afterwards sunk into neglect and oblivion? Where such reports, therefore, fly about, the solution of the phenomenon is obvious, and we judge in conformity to regular experience and observation when we account for it by the known and natural principles of credulity and delusion. And shall we, rather than have recourse to so natural a solution, allow of a miraculous violation of the most established laws of nature?

I need not mention the difficulty of detecting a falsehood in any private or even public history at the place where it is said to happen, much more when the scene is removed to ever so small a distance. Even a court of judicature, with all the authority, accuracy, and judgment which they can employ, find themselves often at a loss to distinguish between truth and falsehood in the most recent actions. But the matter never comes to any issue if trusted to the common method of altercation and debate and flying rumors, especially when men's passions have taken part on either side.

In the infancy of new religions, the wise and learned commonly esteem the matter too inconsiderable to deserve their attention or regard. And when

---

[6] Lucretius.

afterwards they would willingly detect the cheat, in order to undeceive the deluded multitude, the season is now past, and the records and witnesses which might clear up the matter have perished beyond recovery.

No means of detection remain but those which must be drawn from the very testimony itself of the reporters; and these, though always sufficient with the judicious and knowing, are commonly too fine to fall under the comprehension of the vulgar.

Upon the whole, then, it appears that no testimony for any kind of miracle has ever amounted to a probability, much less to a proof; and that, even supposing it amounted to a proof, it would be opposed by another proof derived from the very nature of the fact which it would endeavor to establish. It is experience only which gives authority to human testimony, and it is the same experience which assures us of the laws of nature. When, therefore, these two kinds of experience are contrary, we have nothing to do but subtract the one from the other and embrace an opinion either on one side or the other with that assurance which arises from the remainder. But according to the principle here explained, this subtraction, with regard to all popular religions, amounts to an entire annihilation; and therefore we may establish it as a maxim that no human testimony can have such force as to prove a miracle, and make it a just foundation for any such system of religion.

I beg the limitations here made may be remarked, when I say that a miracle can never be proved so as to be the foundation of a system of religion. For I own that otherwise there may possibly be miracles or violations of the usual course of nature, of such a kind as to admit of proof from human testimony, though perhaps it will be impossible to find any such in all the records of history. Thus suppose all authors in all languages agree that from the first of January, 1600, there was a total darkness over the whole earth for eight days; suppose that the tradition of this extraordinary event is still strong and lively among the people; that all travelers who return from foreign countries bring us accounts of the same tradition without the least variation or contradiction; it is evident that our present philosophers, instead of doubting the fact, ought to receive it as certain and ought to search for the causes whence it might be derived. The decay, corruption, and dissolution of nature is an event rendered probable by so many analogies that any phenomenon which seems to have a tendency toward that catastrophe comes within the reach of human testimony, if that testimony be very extensive and uniform.

But suppose that all the historians who treat of England should agree that on the first of January, 1600, Queen Elizabeth died; that both before and after her death she was seen by her physicians and the whole court, as is usual with persons of her rank; that her successor was acknowledged and proclaimed by the Parliament; and that, after being interred for a month, she again appeared, resumed the throne, and governed England for three years; I must confess that I should be surprised at the concurrence of so many odd circumstances, but should not have the least inclination to believe so miraculous an event. I should not doubt of her pretended death and of those other public circumstances that followed it; I should only assert it to have been pretended, and that it neither was, nor possibly could be, real. You would in vain object to me the difficulty and almost impossibility of deceiving the world in an affair of such consequence, the wisdom and solid judgment of that renowned Queen, with the little or no advantage which she could reap from so poor an artifice. All this might astonish me, but I would still reply that the knavery and folly of men are such common phenomena that I should rather believe the most extraordinary events to arise from their concurrence than admit of so signal a violation of the laws of nature.

But should this miracle be ascribed to any new system of religion, men in all ages have been so much imposed on by ridiculous stories of that kind that this very circumstance would be a full proof of a cheat, and sufficient, with all men of sense, not only to make them reject the fact but even reject it without further examination. Though the being to whom the miracle is ascribed be in this case almighty, it does not, upon that account, become a whit more probable, since it is impossible for us to know the attributes or actions of such a being otherwise than from the experience which we have of his productions in the usual course of nature. This still reduces us to past observation, and obliges us to compare the instances of the violation of truth in the testimony of men with those of the violation of the laws of nature by miracles, in order to judge which of them is most likely and probable. As the violations of truth are more common in the testimony concerning religious miracles than in that concerning any other matter of fact, this must diminish very much the authority of the former testimony and make us form a general resolution never to lend any attention to it, with whatever specious pretense it may be covered.

Lord Bacon seems to have embraced the same principles of reasoning.

> We ought [says he] to make a collection or particular history of all monsters and prodigious births or productions, and in a word of everything new, rare, and extraordinary in nature. But this must be done with the most severe scrutiny, lest we depart from truth. Above all, every relation must be considered as suspicious which depends in any degree upon religion, as the prodigies of Livy. And no less so, everything that is to be found in the writers of natural magic or alchemy, or such authors who seem, all of them, to have an unconquerable appetite for falsehood and fable.[7]

I am the better pleased with the method of reasoning here delivered, as I think it may serve to confound those dangerous friends or disguised enemies to the *Christian religion* who have undertaken to defend it by the principles of human reason. Our most holy religion is founded on *faith*, not on reason, and it is a sure method of exposing it to put it to such a trial as it is by no means fitted to endure. To make this more evident, let us examine those miracles re-

---

[7] *Nov. Org.,* lib. ii. aph. 29.

lated in Scripture, and not to lose ourselves in too wide a field, let us confine ourselves to such as we find in the *Pentateuch*, which we shall examine according to the principles of these pretended Christians, not as the word or testimony of God himself, but as the production of a mere human writer and historian. Here then we are first to consider a book presented to us by a barbarous and ignorant people, written in an age when they were still more barbarous, and in all probability long after the facts which it relates, corroborated by no concurring testimony, and resembling those fabulous accounts which every nation gives of its origin. Upon reading this book we find it full of prodigies and miracles. It gives an account of a state of the world and of human nature entirely different from the present, of our fall from that state, of the age of man extended to near a thousand years, of the destruction of the world by a deluge, of the arbitrary choice of one people as the favorites of heaven, and that people the countrymen of the author, of their deliverance from bondage by prodigies the most astonishing imaginable. I desire anyone to lay his hand upon his heart and after a serious consideration declare whether he thinks that the falsehood of such a book, supported by such a testimony, would be more extraordinary and miraculous than all the miracles it relates, which is, however, necessary to make it be received, according to the measures of probability above established.

What we have said of miracles may be applied, without any variation, to prophecies, and indeed all prophecies are real miracles and as such only can be admitted as proofs of any revelation. If it did not exceed the capacity of human nature to foretell future events, it would be absurd to employ any prophecy as an argument for a divine mission or authority from heaven. So that, upon the whole, we may conclude that the *Christian religion* not only was at first attended with miracles, but even at this day cannot be believed by any reasonable person without one. Mere reason is insufficient to convince us of its veracity. And whoever is moved by *faith* to assent to it is conscious of a continued miracle in his own person, which subverts all the principles of his understanding and gives him a determination to believe what is most contrary to custom and experience.

JAMES

Pragmatism is the only major philosophical school which has its origin in America, and William James (1842–1910) can fairly be called its leading spokesman. In this famous essay, James sets forth the pragmatic theory of truth and meaning on which the entire doctrine rests.

The familiar slogan of pragmatism is "It's true if it works." Somewhat more precisely, James holds that the test of the truth of a proposition is its success or failure in predicting new sense experiences. For example, when I assert that whales are mammals, I am—according to James—implicitly making a number of predictions about sense experiences which I would have under various circumstances. Thus, if I dissect a whale (a herculean task!) I shall discover that it has a vertebrate skeletal structure and mammalian reproductive organs; if I follow a pregnant whale around, I shall eventually see it give birth to a live baby whale, and so forth. More complex statements about electron fields, genetic encoding, social institutions, or ancient civilizations, all turn out—or so James says—to be testable by reference to some possible future experience. If a proposition does not make predictions which we can at least in principle test, then pragmatists say it is simply meaningless. (In the next selection, you will find the positivist A. J. Ayer defending a very similar position.)

James conceived his own philosophy as tough-minded—a no-nonsense, observationally based, hardheaded look at the facts. One might therefore expect him to be extremely hostile to the claims of the psychic researchers. But just the opposite is the case, as you will find in the concluding section of this book. Precisely because he believed in looking the facts squarely in the face, James took a lively interest in religious experiences, mystical visions, and all manner of "facts" which might not fit the preconceptions of a dogmatic empiricist. It is up to you to decide whether those reports meet the standards of meaningfulness and truth laid down by James in this essay.

Pragmatism's Conception
of Truth

When Clerk-Maxwell was a child it is written that he had a mania for having everything explained to him, and that when people put him off with vague verbal accounts of any phenomenon he would interrupt them impatiently by saying, "Yes; but I want you to tell me the *particular go* of it!" Had his question been about truth, only a pragmatist could have told him the particular go of it. I believe that our contemporary pragmatists, especially Messrs. Schiller and Dewey, have given the only tenable account of this subject. It is a very ticklish subject, sending subtle rootlets into all kinds of crannies, and hard to treat in the sketchy way that alone befits a public lecture. But the Schiller-Dewey view of truth has been so ferociously attacked by rationalistic philosophers, and so abominably misunderstood, that here, if anywhere, is the point where a clear and simple statement should be made.

I fully expect to see the pragmatist view of truth run through the classic stages of a theory's career. First, you know, a new theory is attacked as absurd; then it is admitted to be true, but obvious and insignificant; finally it is seen to be so important that its adversaries claim that they themselves discovered it. Our doctrine of truth is at present in the first of these three stages, with symptoms of the second stage having begun in certain quarters. I wish that this lecture might help it beyond the first stage in the eyes of many of you.

Truth, as any dictionary will tell you, is a property of certain of our ideas. It means their "agreement," as falsity means their disagreement, with "reality." Pragmatists and intellectualists both accept this definition as a matter of course. They begin to quarrel only after the question is raised as to what may precisely be meant by the term "agreement," and what by the term "reality," when reality is taken as something for our ideas to agree with.

In answering these questions the pragmatists are more analytic and painstaking, the intellectualists more offhand and irreflective. The popular notion is that a true idea must copy its reality. Like other popular views, this one follows the analogy of the most usual experience. Our true ideas of sensible things do indeed copy them. Shut your eyes and think of yonder clock on the wall, and you get just such a true picture or copy of its dial. But your idea of its "works" (unless you are a clockmaker) is much less of a copy, yet it passes muster, for it in no way clashes with the reality. Even though it should shrink to the mere word "works," that word still serves you truly; and when you speak of the "time-keeping function" of the clock, or of its spring's "elasticity," it is hard to see exactly what your ideas can copy.

You perceive that there is a problem here. Where our ideas cannot copy definitely their object, what does agreement with that object mean? Some

Lecture VI from *Pragmatism* by William James, 1907.

idealists seem to say that they are true whenever they are what God means that we ought to think about that object. Others hold the copy-view all through, and speak as if our ideas possessed truth just in proportion as they approach to being copies of the Absolute's eternal way of thinking.

These views, you see, invite pragmatistic discussion. But the great assumption of the intellectualists is that truth means essentially an inert static relation. When you've got your true idea of anything, there's an end of the matter. You're in possession; you *know;* you have fulfilled your thinking destiny. You are where you ought to be mentally; you have obeyed your categorical imperative; and nothing more need follow on that climax of your rational destiny. Epistemologically you are in stable equilibrium.

Pragmatism, on the other hand, asks its usual question. "Grant an idea or belief to be true," it says, "what concrete difference will its being true make in any one's actual life? How will the truth be realized? What experiences will be different from those which would obtain if the belief were false? What, in short, is the truth's cash-value in experiential terms?"

The moment pragmatism asks this question, it sees the answer: *True ideas are those that we can assimilate, validate, corroborate and verify. False ideas are those that we can not.* That is the practical difference it makes to us to have true ideas; that, therefore, is the meaning of truth, for it is all that truth is known-as.

This thesis is what I have to defend. The truth of an idea is not a stagnant property inherent in it. Truth *happens* to an idea. It *becomes* true, is *made* true by events. Its verity *is* in fact an event, a process: the process namely of its verifying itself, its veri-*fication.* Its validity is the process of its valid-*ation.*

But what do the words verification and validation themselves pragmatically mean? They again signify certain practical consequences of the verified and validated idea. It is hard to find any one phrase that characterizes these consequences better than the ordinary agreement-formula—just such consequences being what we have in mind whenever we say that our ideas "agree" with reality. They lead us, namely, through the acts and other ideas which they instigate, into or up to, or towards, other parts of experience with which we feel all the while—such feeling being among our potentialities—that the original ideas remain in agreement. The connexions and transitions come to us from point to point as being progressive, harmonious, satisfactory. This function of agreeable leading is what we mean by an idea's verification. Such an account is vague and it sounds at first quite trivial, but it has results which it will take the rest of my hour to explain.

Let me begin by reminding you of the fact that the possession of true thoughts means everywhere the possession of invaluable instruments of action; and that our duty to gain truth, so far from being a blank command from out

of the blue, or a "stunt" self-imposed by our intellect, can account for itself
by excellent practical reasons.

The importance to human life of having true beliefs about matters of fact
is a thing too notorious. We live in a world of realities that can be infinitely
useful or infinitely harmful. Ideas that tell us which of them to expect count
as the true ideas in all this primary sphere of verification, and the pursuit of
such ideas is a primary human duty. The possession of truth, so far from being
here an end in itself, is only a preliminary means towards other vital satisfactions. If I am lost in the woods and starved, and find what looks like a cowpath, it is of the utmost importance that I should think of a human habitation
at the end of it, for if I do so and follow it, I save myself. The true thought is
useful here because the house which is its object is useful. The practical value
of true ideas is thus primarily derived from the practical importance of their
objects to us. Their objects are, indeed, not important at all times. I may on
another occasion have no use for the house; and then my idea of it, however
verifiable, will be practically irrelevant, and had better remain latent. Yet since
almost any object may some day become temporarily important, the advantage
of having a general stock of *extra* truths, of ideas that shall be true of merely
possible situations, is obvious. We store such extra truths away in our memories, and with the overflow we fill our books of reference. Whenever such
an extra truth becomes practically relevant to one of our emergencies, it
passes from cold-storage to do work in the world and our belief in it grows
active. You can say of it then either that "it is useful because it is true" or that
"it is true because it is useful." Both these phrases mean exactly the same
thing, namely that here is an idea that gets fulfilled and can be verified. True
is the name for whatever idea starts the verification-process, useful is the name
for its completed function in experience. True ideas would never have been
singled out as such, would never have acquired a class-name, least of all a
name suggesting value, unless they had been useful from the outset in this
way.

From this simple cue pragmatism gets her general notion of truth as
something essentially bound up with the way in which one moment in our
experience may lead us towards other moments which it will be worth while
to have been led to. Primarily, and on the commonsense level, the truth of a
state of mind means this function of *a leading that is worth while*. When a
moment in our experience, of any kind whatever, inspires us with a thought
that is true, that means that sooner or later we dip by that thought's guidance
into the particulars of experience again and make advantageous connexion with
them. This is a vague enough statement, but I beg you to retain it, for it is
essential.

Our experience meanwhile is all shot through with regularities. One bit
of it can warn us to get ready for another bit, can "intend" or be "significant
of" that remoter object. The object's advent is the significance's verification.

Truth, in these cases, meaning nothing but eventual verification, is manifestly incompatible with waywardness on our part. Woe to him whose beliefs play fast and loose with the order which realities follow in his experience; they will lead him nowhere or else make false connexions.

By "realities" or "objects" here, we mean either things of common sense, sensibly present, or else common-sense relations, such as dates, places, distances, kinds, activities. Following our mental image of a house along the cowpath, we actually come to see the house; we get the image's full verification. *Such simply and fully verified leadings are certainly the originals and prototypes of the truth-process.* Experience offers indeed other forms of truth-process, but they are all conceivable as being primary verifications arrested, multiplied or substituted one for another.

Take, for instance, yonder object on the wall. You and I consider it to be a "clock," altho no one of us has seen the hidden works that make it one. We let our notion pass for true without attempting to verify. If truths mean verification-process essentially, ought we then to call such unverified truths as this abortive? No, for they form the overwhelmingly large number of the truths we live by. Indirect as well as direct verifications pass muster. Where circumstantial evidence is sufficient, we can go without eye-witnessing. Just as we here assume Japan to exist without ever having been there, because it *works* to do so, everything we know conspiring with the belief, and nothing interfering, so we assume that thing to be a clock. We *use* it as a clock, regulating the length of our lecture by it. The verification of the assumption here means its leading to no frustration or contradiction. Verifi*ability* of wheels and weights and pendulum is as good as verification. For one truth-process completed there are a million in our lives that function in this state of nascency. They turn us *towards* direct verification; lead us into the *surroundings* of the objects they envisage; and then, if everything runs on harmoniously, we are so sure that verification is possible that we omit it, and are usually justified by all that happens.

Truth lives, in fact, for the most part on a credit system. Our thoughts and beliefs "pass," so long as nothing challenges them, just as bank-notes pass so long as nobody refuses them. But this all points to direct face-to-face verifications somewhere, without which the fabric of truth collapses like a financial system with no cash-basis whatever. You accept my verification of one thing, I yours of another. We trade on each other's truth. But beliefs verified concretely by *somebody* are the posts of the whole superstructure.

Another great reason—beside economy of time—for waiving complete verification in the usual business of life is that all things exist in kinds and not singly. Our world is found once for all to have that peculiarity. So that when we have once directly verified our ideas about one specimen of a kind, we consider ourselves free to apply them to other specimens without verification. A mind that habitually discerns the kind of thing before it, and acts by the law of the kind immediately, without pausing to verify, will be a "true" mind in ninety-nine out of a hundred emergencies, proved so by its conduct fitting everything it meets, and getting no refutation.

Indirectly or only potentially verifying processes may thus be true as well as full verification-processes. They work as true processes would work, give us the same advantages, and claim our recognition for the same reasons. All this on the common-sense level of matters of fact, which we are alone considering.

But matters of fact are not our only stock in trade. *Relations among purely mental ideas* form another sphere where true and false beliefs obtain, and here the beliefs are absolute, or unconditional. When they are true they bear the name either of definitions or of principles. It is either a principle or a definition that 1 and 1 make 2, that 2 and 1 make 3, and so on; that white differs less from gray than it does from black; that when the cause begins to act the effect also commences. Such propositions hold of all possible "ones," of all conceivable "whites" and "grays" and "causes." The objects here are mental objects. Their relations are perceptually obvious at a glance, and no sense-verification is necessary. Moreover, once true, always true, of those same mental objects. Truth here has an "eternal" character. If you can find a concrete thing anywhere that is "one" or "white" or "gray" or an "effect," then your principles will everlastingly apply to it. It is but a case of ascertaining the kind, and then applying the law of its kind to the particular object. You are sure to get truth if you can but name the kind rightly, for your mental relations hold good of everything of that kind without exception. If you, then, nevertheless, failed to get truth concretely, you would say that you had classed your real objects wrongly.

In this realm of mental relations, truth again is an affair of leading. We relate one abstract idea with another, framing in the end great systems of logical and mathematical truth, under the respective terms of which the sensible facts of experience eventually arrange themselves, so that our eternal truths hold good of realities also. The marriage of fact and theory is endlessly fertile. What we say is here already true in advance of special verification, *if we have subsumed our objects rightly.* Our ready-made ideal framework for all sorts of possible objects follows from the very structure of our thinking. We can no more play fast and loose with these abstract relations than we can do with our sense-experiences. They coerce us; we must treat them consistently, whether or not we like the results. The rules of addition apply to our debts as rigorously as to our assets. The hundredth decimal of π, the ratio of the circumference to its diameter, is predetermined ideally now, tho no one may have computed it. If we should ever need the figure in our dealings with an actual circle we should need to have it given rightly, calculated by the usual rules; for it is the same kind of truth that those rules elsewhere calculate.

Between the coercions of the sensible order and those of the ideal order, our mind is thus wedged tightly. Our ideas must agree with realities, be such realities concrete or abstract; be they facts or be they principles, under penalty of endless inconsistency and frustration.

So far, intellectualists can raise no protest. They can only say that we have barely touched the skin of the matter.

Realities mean, then, either concrete facts, or abstract kinds of thing and relations perceived intuitively between them. They furthermore and thirdly mean, as things that new ideas of ours must no less take account of, the whole body of other truths already in our possession. But what now does "agreement" with such threefold realities mean?—to use again the definition that is current.

Here it is that pragmatism and intellectualism began to part company. Primarily, no doubt, to agree means to copy, but we saw that the mere word "clock" would do instead of a mental picture of its works, and that of many realities our ideas can only be symbols and not copies. "Past time," "power," "spontaneity,"—how can our mind copy such realities?

To "agree" in the widest sense with a reality *can only mean to be guided either straight up to it or into its surroundings, or to be put into such working touch with it as to handle either it or something connected with it better than if we disagreed.* Better either intellectually or practically! And often agreement will only mean that nothing contradictory from the quarter of that reality comes to interfere with the way in which our ideas guide us elsewhere. To copy a reality is, indeed, one very important way of agreeing with it, but it is far from being essential. The essential thing is the process of being guided. Any idea that helps us to *deal*, whether practically or intellectually, with either the reality or its belongings, that doesn't entangle our progress in frustrations, that *fits*, in fact, and adapts our life to the reality's whole setting, will agree sufficiently to meet the requirement. It will hold true of that reality.

Thus, *names* are just as "true" or "false" as definite mental pictures are. They set up similar verification-processes, and lead to fully equivalent practical results.

All human thinking gets discursified; we exchange ideas; we lend and borrow verifications, get them from one another by means of social intercourse. All truth thus gets verbally built out, stored up, and made available for every one. Hence, we must *talk* consistently just as we must *think* consistently: for both in talk and thought we deal with kinds. Names are arbitrary, but once understood they must be kept to. We musn't now call Abel "Cain" or Cain "Abel." If we do, we ungear ourselves from the whole book of Genesis, and from all its connexions with the universe of speech and fact down to the present time. We throw ourselves out of whatever truth that entire system of speech and fact may embody.

The overwhelming majority of our true ideas admit of no direct or face-to-face verification—those of past history, for example, as of Cain and Abel. The stream of time can be remounted only verbally, or verified indirectly by the present prolongations or effects of what the past harbored. Yet if they agree with these verbalities and effects, we can know that our ideas of the past are true. *As true as past time itself was,* so true was Julius Cæsar, so true were antediluvian monsters, all in their proper dates and settings. That past time itself was, is guaranteed by its coherence with everything that's present. True as the present *is,* the past *was* also.

Agreement thus turns out to be essentially an affair of leading—leading that is useful because it is into quarters that contain objects that are important. True ideas lead us into useful verbal and conceptual quarters as well as directly up to useful sensible termini. They lead to consistency, stability and flowing human intercourse. They lead away from excentricity and isolation, from foiled and barren thinking. The untrammelled flowing of the leading-process, its general freedom from clash and contradiction, passes for its indirect verification; but all roads lead to Rome, and in the end and eventually, all true processes must lead to the face of directly verifying sensible experiences *somewhere,* which somebody's ideas have copied.

Such is the large loose way in which the pragmatist interprets the word agreement. He treats it altogether practically. He lets it cover any process of conduction from a present idea to a future terminus, provided only it run prosperously. It is only thus that "scientific" ideas, flying as they do beyond common sense, can be said to agree with their realities. It is, as I have already said, *as if* reality were made of ether, atoms or electrons, but we must n't think so literally. The term "energy" does n't even pretend to stand for anything "objective." It is only a way of measuring the surface of phenomena so as to string their changes on a simple formula.

Yet in the choice of these man-made formulas we can not be capricious with impunity any more than we can be capricious on the common-sense practical level. We must find a theory that will *work;* and that means something extremely difficult; for our theory must mediate between all previous truths and certain new experiences. It must derange common sense and previous belief as little as possible, and it must lead to some sensible terminus or other that can be verified exactly. To "work" means both these things; and the squeeze is so tight that there is little loose play for any hypothesis. Our theories are wedged and controlled as nothing else is. Yet sometimes alternative theoretic formulas are equally compatible with all the truths we know, and then we choose between them for subjective reasons. We choose the kind of theory to which we are already partial; we follow "elegance" or "economy." Clerk-Maxwell somewhere says it would be "poor scientific taste" to choose the more complicated of two equally well-evidenced conceptions; and you will all agree with him. Truth in science is what gives us the maximum possible sum of satisfactions, taste included, but consistency both with previous truth and with novel fact is always the most imperious claimant.

I have led you through a very sandy desert. But now, if I may be allowed so vulgar an expression, we begin to taste the milk in the cocoanut. Our rationalist critics here discharge their batteries upon us, and to reply to them will take us out from all this dryness into full sight of a momentous philosophical alternative.

Our account of truth is an account of truths in the plural, of processes of leading, realized *in rebus*, and having only this quality in common, that they *pay*. They pay by guiding us into or towards some part of a system that dips at numerous points into sense-percepts, which we may copy mentally or not, but with which at any rate we are now in the kind of commerce vaguely designated as verification. Truth for us is simply a collective name for verification-processes, just as health, wealth, strength, etc., are names for other processes connected with life, and also pursued because it pays to pursue them. Truth is *made*, just as health, wealth and strength are made, in the course of experience.

Here rationalism is instantaneously up in arms against us. I can imagine a rationalist to talk as follows:

"Truth is not made," he will say; "it absolutely obtains, being a unique relation that does not wait upon any process, but shoots straight over the head of experience, and hits its reality every time. Our belief that yon thing on the wall is a clock is true already, altho no one in the whole history of the world should verify it. The bare quality of standing in that transcendent relation is what makes any thought true that possesses it, whether or not there be verification. You pragmatists put the cart before the horse in making truth's being reside in verification-processes. These are merely signs of its being, merely our lame ways of ascertaining after the fact, which of our ideas already has possessed the wondrous quality. The quality itself is timeless, like all essences and natures. Thoughts partake of it directly, as they partake of falsity or of irrelevancy. It can't be analyzed away into pragmatic consequences."

The whole plausibility of this rationalist tirade is due to the fact to which we have already paid so much attention. In our world, namely, abounding as it does in things of similar kinds and similarly associated, one verification serves for others of its kind, and one great use of knowing things is to be led not so much to them as to their associates, especially to human talk about them. The quality of truth, obtaining *ante rem*, pragmatically means, then, the fact that in such a world innumerable ideas work better by their indirect or possible than by their direct and actual verification. Truth *ante rem* means only verifiability, then; or else it is a case of the stock rationalist trick of treating the *name* of a concrete phenomenal reality as an independent prior entity, and placing it behind the reality as its explanation. Professor Mach quotes somewhere an epigram of Lessing's:

Sagt Hänschen Schlau zu Vetter Fritz,
"Wie kommt es, Vetter Fritzen,
Dass grad' die Reichsten in der Welt,
Das meiste Geld besitzen?"*

Hänschen Schlau here treats the principle "wealth" as something distinct from the facts denoted by the man's being rich. It antedates them; the facts become only a sort of secondary coincidence with the rich man's essential nature.

In the case of "wealth" we all see the fallacy. We know that wealth is but a name for concrete processes that certain men's lives play a part in, and not a natural excellence found in Messrs. Rockefeller and Carnegie, but not in the rest of us.

Like wealth, health also lives *in rebus*. It is a name for processes, as digestion, circulation, sleep, etc., that go on happily, tho in this instance we are more inclined to think of it as a principle and to say the man digests and sleeps so well *because* he is so healthy.

With "strength" we are, I think, more rationalistic still, and decidedly inclined to treat it as an excellence pre-existing in the man and explanatory of the herculean performances of his muscles.

With "truth" most people go over the border entirely, and treat the rationalistic account as self-evident. But really all these words in *th* are exactly similar. Truth exists *ante rem* just as much and as little as the other things do.

The scholastics, following Aristotle, made much of the distinction between habit and act. Health *in actu* means, among other things, good sleeping and digesting. But a healthy man need not always be sleeping, or always digesting, any more than a wealthy man need be always handling money, or a strong man always lifting weights. All such qualities sink to the status of "habits" between their times of exercise; and similarly truth becomes a habit of certain of our ideas and beliefs in their intervals of rest from their verifying activities. But those activities are the root of the whole matter, and the condition of their being any habit to exist in the intervals.

"The true," to put it very briefly, is only the expedient in the way of our thinking, just as "the right" is only the expedient in the way of our behaving. Expedient in almost any fashion; and expedient in the long run and on the whole of course; for what meets expediently all the experience in sight won't necessarily meet all farther experiences equally satisfactorily. Experience, as we know, has ways of *boiling over*, and making us correct our present formulas.

The "absolutely" true, meaning what no farther experience will ever alter, is that ideal vanishing-point towards which we imagine that all our temporary

---

* Said crafty Hans to Cousin Fritz,
  "Why is it, Cousin Fritz,
  That those ranked richest in the world,
  The most wealth do possess?"—Ed.

truths will some day converge. It runs on all fours with the perfectly wise man, and with the absolutely complete experience; and, if these ideals are ever realized, they will all be realized together. Meanwhile we have to live to-day by what truth we can get to-day, and be ready to-morrow to call it falsehood. Ptolemaic astronomy, euclidean space, aristotelian logic, scholastic metaphysics, were expedient for centuries, but human experience has boiled over those limits, and we now call these things only relatively true, or true within those borders of experience. "Absolutely" they are false; for we know that those limits were casual, and might have been transcended by past theorists just as they are by present thinkers.

When new experiences lead to retrospective judgments, using the past tense, what these judgments utter *was* true, even tho no past thinker had been led there. We live forwards, a Danish thinker has said, but we understand backwards. The present sheds a backward light on the world's previous processes. They may have been truth-processes for the actors in them. They are not so for one who knows the later revelations of the story.

This regulative notion of a potential better truth to be established later, possibly to be established some day absolutely, and having powers of retroactive legislation, turns its face, like all pragmatist notions, towards concreteness of fact, and towards the future. Like the half-truths, the absolute truth will have to be *made*, made as a relation incidental to the growth of a mass of verification-experience to which the half-true ideas are all along contributing their quota.

I have already insisted on the fact that truth is made largely out of previous truths. Men's beliefs at any time are so much experience *funded*. But the beliefs are themselves parts of the sum total of the world's experience, and become matter, therefore, for the next day's funding operations. So far as reality means experienceable reality, both it and the truths men gain about it are everlastingly in process of mutation—mutation towards a definite goal, it may be—but still mutation.

Mathematicians can solve problems with two variables. On the Newtonian theory, for instance, acceleration varies with distance, but distance also varies with acceleration. In the realm of truth-processes facts come independently and determine our beliefs provisionally. But these beliefs make us act, and as fast as they do so, they bring into sight or into existence new facts which re-determine the beliefs accordingly. So the whole coil and ball of truth, as it rolls up, is the product of a double influence. Truths emerge from facts; but they dip forward into facts again and add to them; which facts again create or reveal new truth (the word is indifferent) and so on indefinitely. The "facts" themselves meanwhile are not *true*. They simply *are*. Truth is the function of the beliefs that start and terminate among them.

The case is like a snowball's growth, due as it is to the distribution of the snow on the one hand, and to the successive pushes of the boys on the other, with these factors co-determining each other incessantly.

The most fateful point of difference between being a rationalist and being a pragmatist is now fully in sight. Experience is in mutation, and our psychological ascertainments of truth are in mutation—so much rationalism will allow; but never that either reality itself or truth itself is mutable. Reality stands complete and ready-made from all eternity, rationalism insists, and the agreement of our ideas with it is that unique unanalyzable virtue in them of which she has already told us. As that intrinsic excellence, their truth has nothing to do with our experiences. It adds nothing to the content of experience. It makes no difference to reality itself; it is supervenient, inert, static, a reflexion merely. It doesn't *exist*, it *holds* or *obtains*, it belongs to another dimension from that of either facts or fact-relations, belongs, in short, to the epistemological dimension—and with that big word rationalism closes the discussion.

Thus, just as pragmatism faces forward to the future, so does rationalism here again face backward to a past eternity. True to her inveterate habit, rationalism reverts to "principles," and thinks that when an abstraction once is named, we own an oracular solution.

The tremendous pregnancy in the way of consequences for life of this radical difference of outlook will only become apparent in my later lectures. I wish meanwhile to close this lecture by showing that rationalism's sublimity does not save it from inanity.

When, namely, you ask rationalists, instead of accusing pragmatism of desecrating the notion of truth, to define it themselves by saying exactly what *they* understand by it, the only positive attempts I can think of are these two:

1. "Truth is the system of propositions which have an unconditional claim to be recognized as valid."[1]
2. Truth is a name for all those judgments which we find ourselves under obligation to make by a kind of imperative duty.[2]

The first thing that strikes one in such definitions is their unutterable triviality. They are absolutely true, of course, but absolutely insignificant until you handle them pragmatically. What do you mean by "claim" here, and what do you mean by "duty"? As summary names for the concrete reasons why thinking in true ways is overwhelmingly expedient and good for mortal men, it is all right to talk of claims on reality's part to be agreed with, and of obligations on our part to agree. We feel both the claims and the obligations, and we feel them for just those reasons.

But the rationalists who talk of claim and obligation *expressly say that they have nothing to do with our practical interests or personal reasons.* Our reasons for agreeing are psychological facts, they say, relative to each thinker, and to the accidents of his life. They are his evidence merely, they are no part

---

[1] A. E. Taylor, *Philosophical Review*, vol. xiv, p. 288.
[2] H. Rickert, *Der Gegenstand der Erkenntniss*, chapter on "Die Urtheilsnothwendigkeit."

of the life of truth itself. That life transacts itself in a purely logical or epistemological, as distinguished from a psychological, dimension, and its claims antedate and exceed all personal motivations whatsoever. Tho neither man nor God should ever ascertain truth, the word would still have to be defined as that which *ought* to be ascertained and recognized.

There never was a more exquisite example of an idea abstracted from the concretes of experience and then used to oppose and negate what it was abstracted from.

Philosophy and common life abound in similar instances. The "sentimentalist fallacy" is to shed tears over abstract justice and generosity, beauty, etc., and never to know these qualities when you meet them in the street, because the circumstances make them vulgar. Thus I read in the privately printed biography of an eminently rationalistic mind: "It was strange that with such admiration for beauty in the abstract, my brother had no enthusiasm for fine architecture, for beautiful painting, or for flowers." And in almost the last philosophic work I have read, I find such passages as the following: "Justice is ideal, solely ideal. Reason conceives that it ought to exist, but experience shows that it can not. . . . Truth, which ought to be, can not be. . . . Reason is deformed by experience. As soon as reason enters experience it becomes contrary to reason."

The rationalist's fallacy here is exactly like the sentimentalist's. Both extract a quality from the muddy particulars of experience, and find it so pure when extracted that they contrast it with each and all its muddy instances as an opposite and higher nature. All the while it is *their* nature. It is the nature of truths to be validated, verified. It pays for our ideas to be validated. Our obligation to seek truth is part of our general obligation to do what pays. The payments true ideas bring are the sole why of our duty to follow them. Identical whys exist in the case of wealth and health.

Truth makes no other kind of claim and imposes no other kind of ought than health and wealth do. All these claims are conditional; the concrete benefits we gain are what we mean by calling the pursuit a duty. In the case of truth, untrue beliefs work as perniciously in the long run as true beliefs work beneficially. Talking abstractly, the quality "true" may thus be said to grow absolutely precious and the quality "untrue" absolutely damnable: the one may be called good, the other bad, unconditionally. We ought to think the true, we ought to shun the false, imperatively.

But if we treat all this abstraction literally and oppose it to its mother soil in experience, see what a preposterous position we work ourselves into.

We can not then take a step forward in our actual thinking. When shall I acknowledge this truth and when that? Shall the acknowledgment be loud?— or silent? If sometimes loud, sometimes silent, which *now?* When may a truth go into cold-storage in the encyclopedia? and when shall it come out for battle? Must I constantly be repeating the truth "twice two are four" because of its eternal claim on recognition? or is it sometimes irrelevant? Must my thoughts dwell night and day on my personal sins and blemishes, because I truly have them?—or may I sink and ignore them in order to be a decent social unit, and not a mass of morbid melancholy and apology?

It is quite evident that our obligation to acknowledge truth, so far from being unconditional, is tremendously conditioned. Truth with a big T, and in the singular, claims abstractly to be recognized, of course; but concrete truths in the plural need be recognized only when their recognition is expedient. A truth must always be preferred to a falsehood when both relate to the situation; but when neither does, truth is as little of a duty as falsehood. If you ask me what o'clock it is and I tell you that I live at 95 Irving Street, my answer may indeed be true, but you don't see why it is my duty to give it. A false address would be as much to the purpose.

With this admission that there are conditions that limit the application of the abstract imperative, *the pragmatistic treatment of truth sweeps back upon us in its fulness*. Our duty to agree with reality is seen to be grounded in a perfect jungle of concrete expediencies.

When Berkeley had explained what people meant by matter, people thought that he denied matter's existence. When Messrs. Schiller and Dewey now explain what people mean by truth, they are accused of denying *its* existence. These pragmatists destroy all objective standards, critics say, and put foolishness and wisdom on one level. A favorite formula for describing Mr. Schiller's doctrines and mine is that we are persons who think that by saying whatever you find it pleasant to say and calling it truth you fulfil every pragmatistic requirement.

I leave it to you to judge whether this be not an impudent slander. Pent in, as the pragmatist more than any one else sees himself to be, between the whole body of funded truths squeezed from the past and the coercions of the world of sense about him, who so well as he feels the immense pressure of objective control under which our minds perform their operations? If any one imagines that this law is lax, let him keep its commandment one day, says Emerson. We have heard much of late of the uses of the imagination in science. It is high time to urge the use of a little imagination in philosophy. The unwillingness of some of our critics to read any but the silliest of possible meanings into our statements is as discreditable to their imaginations as anything I know in recent philosophic history. Schiller says the true is that which "works." Thereupon he is treated as one who limits verification to the lowest material utilities. Dewey says truth is what gives "satisfaction." He is treated as one who believes in calling everything true which, if it were true, would be pleasant.

Our critics certainly need more imagination of realities. I have honestly tried to stretch my own imagination and to read the best possible meaning into the rationalist conception, but I have to confess that it still completely baffles me. The notion of a reality calling on us to "agree" with it, and that for no reasons, but simply because its claims is "unconditional" or "transcendent," is one that I can make neither head nor tail of. I try to imagine myself as the sole reality in the world, and then to imagine what more I would "claim" if I were allowed to. If you suggest the possibility of my claiming that a mind should come into being from out of the void inane and stand and *copy* me, I can indeed imagine what the copying might mean, but I can conjure up no motive. What good it would do me to be copied, or what good it would do that mind to copy me, if further consequences are expressly and in principle ruled out as motives for the claim (as they are by our rationalist authorities) I can not fathom. When the Irishman's admirers ran him along to the place of banquet in a sedan chair with no bottom, he said, "Faith, if it wasn't for the honor of the thing, I might as well have come on foot." So here: but for the honor of the thing, I might as well have remained uncopied. Copying is one genuine mode of knowing (which for some strange reason our contemporary transcendentalists seem to be tumbling over each other to repudiate); but when we get beyond copying, and fall back on unnamed forms of agreeing that are expressly denied to be either copyings or leadings or fittings, or any other processes pragmatically definable, the *what* of the "agreement" claimed becomes as unintelligible as the why of it. Neither content nor motive can be imagined for it. It is an absolutely meaningless abstraction.[3]

Surely in this field of truth it is the pragmatists and not the rationalists who are the more genuine defenders of the universe's rationality.

[3] I am not forgetting that Professor Rickert long ago gave up the whole notion of truth being founded on agreement with reality. Reality according to him, is whatever agrees with truth, and truth is founded solely on our primal duty. This fantastic flight, together with Mr. Joachim's candid confession of failure in his book *The Nature of Truth*, seems to me to mark the bankruptcy of rationalism when dealing with this subject. Rickert deals with part of the pragmatistic position under the head of what he calls "Relativismus." I can not discuss his text here. Suffice it to say that his argumentation in that chapter is so feeble as to seem almost incredible in so generally able a writer.

AYER

To the layman, "Logical Positivism" vies with "Existentialism" as the best-known philosophical label in twentieth-century thought. In philosophical circles, the statement of the logical positivist position most often referred to is A. J. Ayer's Language, Truth, and Logic. *The movement known as Logical Positivism had its start in Vienna in the 1920s, where a group of philosophically inclined scientists and scientifically inclined philosophers met to discuss the implications of the new science and mathematical logic which was then being developed. Drawing on philosophical traditions going back to Hume in England and Kant in Germany, they formulated a comprehensive theory of language, meaning, and truth which could serve to illuminate the nature of* a priori *and empirical knowledge. Writing in England in 1936, Ayer (1910–   ) sums up the principal doctrines of the so-called Vienna circle with a force and conviction rare in philosophical works. To this day, Ayer's little book remains the classical exposition of logical positivist doctrine.*

One good way to read Ayer is to view him as attacking the doctrines advanced by Leibniz in the first selection in this section. Ayer insists that no *nontrivial proposition can ever be known with the certainty that Leibniz demanded. The most we can ever achieve, he argues, is a probability judgment based on an accumulation of empirical evidence. Furthermore, contrary to Leibniz, the positivists claim that the testimony of our senses is the ultimate basis for any knowledge claims about the world.*

Ayer combines Hume's emphasis on sense evidence with Leibniz's concern for a priori *truth, but he is very much closer to Hume in his philosophical orientation. Like Hume, Ayer denies that reason alone can teach us anything about the world; the most that we can learn by unaided reason is the content of our own ideas. As we shall see in a later section, Ayer's strongly empiricist learnings make him extremely hostile to the cognitive claims of metaphysics, ethics, and religion.*

Positivism's Conception
of Truth

Having shown how the validity of *a priori* propositions is determined, we shall now put forward the criterion which is used to determine the validity of empirical propositions. In this way we shall complete our theory of truth. For it is easy to see that the purpose of a "theory of truth" is simply to describe the criteria by which the validity of the various kinds of propositions is determined. And as all propositions are either empirical or *a priori*, and we have already dealt with the *a priori*, all that is now required to complete our theory of truth is an indication of the way in which we determine the validity of empirical propositions. And this we shall shortly proceed to give.

But first of all we ought, perhaps, to justify our assumption that the object of a "theory of truth" can only be to show how propositions are validated. For it is commonly supposed that the business of the philosopher who concerns himself with "truth" is to answer the question "What is truth?" and that it is only an answer to this question that can fairly be said to constitute a "theory of truth." But when we come to consider what this famous question actually entails, we find that it is not a question which gives rise to any genuine problem; and consequently that no theory can be required to deal with it.

We have already remarked that all questions of the form, "What is the nature of *x*?" are requests for a definition of a symbol in use, and that to ask for a definition of a symbol *x* in use is to ask how the sentences in which *x* occurs are to be translated into equivalent sentences, which do not contain *x* or any of its synonyms. Applying this to the case of "truth" we find that to ask, "What is truth?" is to ask for such a translation of the sentence "(the proposition) *p* is true."

It may be objected here that we are ignoring the fact that it is not merely propositions that can be said to be true or false, but also statements and assertions and judgements and assumptions and opinions and beliefs. But the answer to this is that to say that a belief, or a statement, or a judgement, is true is always an elliptical way of ascribing truth to a proposition, which is believed, or stated, or judged. Thus, if I say that the Marxists' belief that capitalism leads to war is true, what I am saying is that the proposition, believed by Marxists, that capitalism leads to war is true; and the illustration holds good when the word "opinion" or "assumption," or any of the others in the list, is substituted for the word "belief." And, further, it must be made clear that we are not hereby committing ourselves to the metaphysical doctrine that propositions are real entities. Regarding classes as a species of logical constructions, we may define a proposition as a class of sentences which have the same intensional significance for anyone who understands them. Thus, the sentences, "I am ill," "Ich bin krank," "Je suis malade," are all elements of the proposition "I am ill." And what we have previously said about logical constructions should make it clear that we are not asserting that a proposition is a collection of sentences, but rather than to speak about a given proposition is a way of speaking about certain sentences, just as to speak about sentences, in this usage, is a way of speaking about particular signs.

Reverting to the analysis of truth, we find that in all sentences of the form "p is true," the phrase "is true" is logically superfluous. When, for example, one says that the proposition "Queen Anne is dead" is true, all that one is saying is that Queen Anne is dead. And similarly, when one says that the proposition "Oxford is the capital of England" is false, all that one is saying is that Oxford is not the capital of England. Thus, to say that a proposition is true is just to assert it, and to say that it is false is just to assert its contradictory. And this indicates that the terms "true" and "false" connote nothing, but function in the sentence simply as marks of assertion and denial. And in that case there can be no sense in asking us to analyse the concept of "truth."

This point seems almost too obvious to mention, yet the preoccupation of philosophers with the "problem of truth" shows that they have overlooked it. Their excuse is that references to truth generally occur in sentences whose grammatical forms suggest that the word "true" does stand for a genuine quality or relation. And a superficial consideration of these sentences might lead one to suppose that there was something more in the question "What is truth?" than a demand for the analysis of the sentence "p is true." But when one comes to analyse the sentences in question, one always finds that they contain sub-sentences of the form "p is true" or "p is false," and that when they are translated in such a way as to make these sub-sentences explicit, they contain no other mention of truth. Thus, to take two typical examples, the sentence "A proposition is not made true by being believed" is equivalent to "for no value of p or x, is 'p is true' entailed by 'x believes p'": and the sentence "Truth is sometimes stranger than fiction" is equivalent to "There are values of p and q such that p is true and q is false and p is more surprising than q." And the same result would be yielded by any other example one cared to take. In every case the analysis of the sentence would confirm our assumption that the question "What is truth?" is reducible to the question "What is the analysis of the sentence 'p is true'?" And it is plain that this question raises no genuine problem, since we have shown that to say that p is true is simply a way of asserting p.

We conclude, then, that there is no problem of truth as it is ordinarily conceived. The traditional conception of truth as a "real quality" or a "real relation" is due, like most philosophical mistakes, to a failure to analyse sentences correctly. There are sentences, such as the two we have just analysed, in which the word "truth" seems to stand for something real; and this leads the speculative philosopher to enquire what this "something" is. Naturally he fails to obtain a satisfactory answer, since his question is illegitimate. For our analysis has shown that the word "truth" does not stand for anything, in the way which such a question requires.

It follows that if all theories of truth were theories about the "real quality" or the "real relation," which the word "truth" is naïvely supposed to stand for, they would be all nonsense. But in fact they are for the most part theories of an entirely different sort. Whatever question their authors may think that they are discussing, what they are really discussing most of the time is the question "What makes a proposition true or false?" And this is a loose way of expressing the question "With regard to any proposition p, what are the conditions in which p (is true) and what are the conditions in which not-p?" In other words, it is a way of asking how propositions are validated. And this is the question which we were considering when we embarked on our digression about the analysis of truth.

In saying that we propose to show "how propositions are validated," we do not of course mean to suggest that all propositions are validated in the same way. On the contrary we lay stress on the fact that the criterion by which we determine the validity of an *a priori* or analytic proposition is not sufficient to determine the validity of an empirical or synthetic proposition. For it is characteristic of empirical propositions that their validity is not purely formal. To say that a geometrical proposition, or a system of geometrical propositions, is false is to say that it is self-contradictory. But an empirical proposition, or a system of empirical propositions, may be free from contradiction, and still be false. It is said to be false, not because it is formally defective, but because it fails to satisfy some material criterion. And it is our business to discover what this criterion is.

We have been assuming so far that empirical propositions, though they differ from *a priori* propositions in their method of validation, do not differ in this respect among themselves. Having found that all *a priori* propositions are validated in the same way, we have taken it for granted that this holds good of empirical propositions also. But this assumption would be challenged by a great many philosophers who agree with us in most other respects. They would say that among empirical propositions, there was a special class of propositions whose validity consisted in the fact that they directly recorded an immediate experience. They maintain that these propositions, which we may call "ostensive" propositions, are not mere hypotheses but are absolutely certain. For they are supposed to be purely demonstrative in character, and so incapable of being refuted by any subsequent experience. And they are, on this view, the only empirical propositions which are certain. The rest are hypotheses which derive what validity they have from their relationship to the ostensive propositions. For their probability is held to be determined by the number and variety of the ostensive propositions which can be deduced from them.

That no synthetic proposition which is not purely ostensive can be logically indubitable, may be granted without further ado. What we cannot admit is that any synthetic proposition can be purely ostensive. For a notion of an ostensive proposition appears to involve a contradiction in terms. It implies that there could be a sentence which consisted of purely demonstrative symbols and was at the same time intelligible. And this is not even a logical possibility. A sentence which consisted of demonstrative symbols would not express a genuine proposition. It would be a mere ejaculation, in no way characterizing that to which it was supposed to refer.

The fact is that one cannot in language point to an object without describing it. If a sentence is to express a proposition, it cannot merely name a situation; it must say something about it. And in describing a situation, one is not merely "registering" a sense-content; one is classifying it in some way or other, and this means going beyond what is immediately given. But a proposition would be ostensive only if it recorded what was immediately experienced, without referring in any way beyond. And as this is not possible, it follows that no genuine synthetic proposition can be ostensive, and consequently that none can be absolutely certain.

Accordingly we hold not merely that no ostensive propositions ever are expressed, but that it is inconceivable that any ostensive proposition ever should be expressed. That no ostensive propositions ever are expressed might be admitted even by those who believe in them. They might allow that in actual practice one never limits oneself to describing the qualities of an immediately presented sense-content, but always treats it as if it were a material thing. And it is obvious that the propositions in which we formulate our ordinary judgements about material things are not ostensive, referring as they do to an infinite series of actual and possible sense-contents. But it is in principle possible to formulate propositions which simply describe the qualities of sense-contents without expressing perceptual judgments. And it is claimed that these artificial propositions would be genuinely ostensive. It should be clear from what we have already said that this claim is unjustified. And if any doubt on this point still remains, we may remove it with the help of an example.

Let us suppose that I assert the proposition "This is white," and my words are taken to refer, not, as they normally would, to some material thing, but to a sense-content. Then what I am saying about this sense-content is that it is an element in the class of sense-contents which constitutes "white" for me; or in other words that it is similar in colour to certain other sense-contents, namely those which I should call, or actually have called, white. And I think I am saying also that it corresponds in some fashion to the sense-contents which go to constitute "white" for other people: so that if I discovered that I had an abnormal colour-sense, I should admit that the sense-content in question was not white. But even if we exclude all reference to other people, it is still possible to think of a situation which would lead me to suppose that my classification of a sense-content was mistaken. I might, for example, have discovered that whenever I sensed a sense-content of a certain quality, I made some distinctive overt bodily movement; and I might on one occasion be presented with a sense-content which I asserted to be of that quality, and then fail to make the bodily reaction which I had come to associate with it. In such a case I should probably abandon the hypothesis that sense-contents of that quality always called out in me the bodily reaction in question. But I should not, logically, be obliged to abandon it. If I found it more convenient, I could save this hypothesis by assuming that I really did make the reaction, although I did not notice it, or, alternatively, that the sense-content did not have the quality I asserted it to have. The fact that this course is a possible one, that it involves no logical contradiction, proves that a proposition which describes the quality of a presented sense-content may as legitimately be doubted as any other empirical proposition.[1] And this shows that such a proposition is not ostensive, for we have seen that an ostensive proposition could not legitimately be doubted. But propositions describing the actual qualities of presented sense-contents are the only examples of ostensive propositions which those who believe in ostensive propositions have ever ventured to give. And if these propositions are not ostensive, it is certain that none are.

In denying the possibility of ostensive propositions, we are not of course denying that there really is a "given" element in each of our sense-experiences. Nor are we suggesting that our sensations are themselves doubtful. Indeed such a suggestion would be nonsensical. A sensation is not the sort of thing which can be doubtful or not doubtful. A sensation simply occurs. What are doubtful are the propositions which refer to our sensations, including the propositions which describe the qualities of a presented sense-content, or assert that a certain sense-content has occurred. To identify a proposition of this sort with the sensation itself would clearly be a gross logical blunder. Yet I fancy that the doctrine of ostensive propositions is the outcome of such a tacit identification. It is difficult to account for it in any other way.

However, we shall not waste time speculating about the origins of this false philosophical doctrine. Such questions may be left to the historian. Our business is to show that the doctrine is false, and this we may fairly claim to have done. It should now be clear that there are no absolutely certain empirical propositions. It is only tautologies that are certain. Empirical propositions are one and all hypotheses, which may be confirmed or discredited in actual sense-experience. And the propositions in which we record the observations that verify these hypotheses are themselves hypotheses which are subject to the test of further sense-experience. Thus there are no final propositions. When we set about verifying a hypothesis we may make an observation which satisfies us at the time. But the very next moment we may doubt whether the

---

[1] Of course those who believe in "ostensive" propositions do not maintain that such a proposition as "This is white" is valid in virtue of its form alone. What they assert is that I am entitled to regard the proposition "This is white" as objectively certain when I am actually experiencing a white sense-content. But can it really be the case that they mean to assert no more than the trivial tautology that when I am seeing something white, then I am seeing something white?

observation really did take place, and require a fresh process of verification in order to be reassured. And, logically, there is no reason why this procedure should not continue indefinitely, each act of verification supplying us with a new hypothesis, which in turn leads to a further series of acts of verification. In practice we assume that certain types of observation are trustworthy, and admit the hypothesis that they have occurred, without bothering to embark on a process of verification. But we do this, not from obedience to any logical necessity, but from a purely pragmatic motive, the nature of which will shortly be explained.

When one speaks of hypotheses being verified in experience, it is important to bear in mind that it is never just a single hypothesis which an observation confirms or discredits, but always a system of hypotheses. Suppose that we have devised an experiment to test the validity of a scientific "law." The law states that in certain conditions a certain type of observation will always be forthcoming. It may happen in this particular instance that we make the observation as our law predicts. Then it is not only the law itself that is substantiated, but also the hypotheses which assert the existence of the requisite conditions. For it is only by assuming the existence of these conditions that we can hold that our observation is relevant to the law. Alternatively, we may fail to make the expected observation. And in that case we may conclude that the law is invalidated by our experiment. But we are not obliged to adopt this conclusion. If we wish to preserve our law, we may do so by abandoning one or more of the other relevant hypotheses. We may say that the conditions were really not what they seemed to be, and construct a theory to explain how we came to be mistaken about them; or we may say that some factor which we had dismissed as irrelevant was really relevant, and support this view with supplementary hypotheses. We may even assume that the experiment was really not unfavourable, and that our negative observation was hallucinatory. And in that case we must bring the hypotheses which record the conditions that are deemed necessary for the occurrence of a hallucination into line with the hypotheses which describe the conditions in which this observation is supposed to have taken place. Otherwise we shall be maintaining incompatible hypotheses. And this is the one thing that we may not do. But, so long as we take suitable steps to keep our system of hypotheses free from self-contradiction, we may adopt any explanation of our observations that we choose. In practice our choice of an explanation is guided by certain considerations, which we shall presently describe. And these considerations have the effect of limiting our freedom in the matter of preserving and rejecting hypotheses. But logically our freedom is unlimited. Any procedure which is self-consistent will satisfy the requirements of logic.

It appears, then, that the "facts of experience" can never compel us to abandon a hypothesis. A man can always sustain his convictions in the face of apparently hostile evidence if he is prepared to make the necessary *ad hoc* assumptions. But although any particular instance in which a cherished hypothesis appears to be refuted can always be explained away, there must still remain the possibility that the hypothesis will ultimately be abandoned. Otherwise it is not a genuine hypothesis. For a proposition whose validity we are resolved to maintain in the face of any experience is not a hypothesis at all, but a definition. In other words, it is not a synthetic but an analytic proposition.

That some of our most hallowed "laws of nature" are merely disguised definitions is, I think, incontestable, but this is not a question that we can go into here.[2] It is sufficient for us to point out that there is a danger of mistaking such definitions for genuine hypotheses, a danger which is increased by the fact that the same form of words may at one time, or for one set of people, express a synthetic proposition, and at another time, or for another set of people, express a tautology. For our definitions of things are not immutable. And if experience leads us to entertain a very strong belief that everything of the kind A has the property of being a B, we tend to make the possession of this property a defining characteristic of the kind. Ultimately we may refuse to call anything A unless it is also a B. And in that case the sentence "All A's are B's," which originally expressed a synthetic generalization, would come to express a plain tautology.

One good reason for drawing attention to this possibility is that the neglect of it by philosophers is responsible for much of the confusion that infects their treatment of general propositions. Consider the stock example, "All men are mortal." We are told that this is not a doubtful hypothesis, as Hume maintained, but an instance of a necessary connection. And if we ask what it is that is here necessarily connected, the only answer that appears possible to us is that it is the concept of "man" and the concept of "being mortal." But the only meaning which we attach to the statement that two concepts are necessarily connected is that the sense of one concept is contained in that of the other. Thus to say that "All men are mortal" is an instance of a necessary connection is to say that the concept of being mortal is contained in the concept of man, and this amounts to saying that "All men are mortal" is a tautology. Now the philosopher may use the word "man" in such a way that he would refuse to call anything a man unless it were mortal. And in that case the sentence "All men are mortal" will, as far as he is concerned, express a tautology. But this does not mean that the proposition which we ordinarily express by that sentence is a tautology. Even for our philosopher, it remains a genuine empirical hypothesis. Only he cannot now express it in the form, "All men are mortal." Instead, he must say that everything which has the other defining properties of a man also has the property of being mortal, or something to that effect. Thus we may create tautologies by a suitable adjustment of our definitions: but we cannot solve empirical problems merely by juggling with the meanings of words.

Of course, when a philosopher says that the proposition "All men are

---

[2] For an elaboration of this view, see H. Poincaré, *La Science et l'Hypothèse*.

mortal" is an instance of a necessary connection, he does not intend to say that it is a tautology. It is left to us to point out that this is all he can be saying, if his words are to bear their ordinary sense and at the same time express a significant proposition. But I think that he finds it possible to hold that this general proposition is both synthetic and necessary, only because he identifies it tacitly with the tautology which might, given suitable conventions, be expressed by the same form of words. And the same applies to all other general propositions of law. We may turn the sentences which now express them into expressions of definitions. And then these sentences will express necessary propositions. But these will be different propositions from the original generalizations. They, as Hume saw, can never be necessary. However firmly we believe them, it is always conceivable that a future experience will lead us to abandon them.

This brings us once more to the question, What are the considerations that determine in any given situation which of the relevant hypotheses shall be preserved and which shall be abandoned? It is sometimes suggested that we are guided solely by the principle of economy, or, in other words, by our desire to make the least possible alteration in our previously accepted system of hypotheses. But though we undoubtedly have this desire, and are influenced by it to some extent, it is not the sole, or even the dominant, factor in our procedure. If our concern was simply to keep our existing system of hypotheses intact, we should not feel obliged to take any notice of an unfavourable observation. We should not feel the need to account for it in any way whatsoever—not even by introducing the hypothesis that we had just had a hallucination. We should simply ignore it. But, in fact, we do not disregard inconvenient observations. Their occurrence always causes us to make some alteration in our system of hypotheses in spite of our desire to keep it intact. Why is this so? If we can answer this question, and show why we find it necessary to alter our systems of hypotheses at all, we shall be in a better position to decide what are the principles according to which such alterations are actually carried out.

What we must do to solve this problem is to ask ourselves, What is the purpose of formulating hypotheses? Why do we construct these systems in the first place? The answer is that they are designed to enable us to anticipate the course of our sensations. The function of a system of hypotheses is to warn us beforehand what will be our experience in a certain field—to enable us to make accurate predictions. The hypothesis may therefore be described as rules which govern our expectation of future experience. There is no need to say why we require such rules. It is plain that on our ability to make successful predictions depends the satisfaction of even our simplest desires, including the desire to survive.

Now the essential feature of our procedure with regard to the formulation of these rules is the use of past experience as a guide to the future. We have already remarked upon this, when discussing the so-called problem of induction, and we have seen that there is no sense in asking for a theoretical justification of this policy. The philosopher must be content to record the facts of scientific procedure. If he seeks to justify it, beyond showing that it is self-consistent, he will find himself involved in spurious problems. This is a point which we stressed earlier on, and we shall not trouble to argue it over again.

We remark, then, as a fact that our forecasts of future experience are in some way determined by what we have experienced in the past. And this fact explains why science, which is essentially predictive, is also to some extent a description of our experience.[3] But it is noticeable that we tend to ignore those features of our experience which cannot be made the basis of fruitful generalizations. And, furthermore, that which we do describe, we describe with some latitude. As Poincaré puts it: "One does not limit oneself to generalizing experience, one corrects it; and the physicist who consented to abstain from these corrections and really be satisfied with bare experience would be obliged to promulgate the most extraordinary laws."[4]

But even if we do not follow past experience slavishly in making our predictions, we are guided by it to a very large extent. And this explains why we do not simply disregard the conclusion of an unfavourable experiment. We assume that a system of hypotheses which has broken down once is likely to break down again. We could, of course, assume that it had not broken down at all, but we believe that this assumption would not pay us so well as the recognition that the system had really failed us, and therefore required some alteration if it was not to fail us again. We alter our system because we think that by altering it we shall make it a more efficient instrument for the anticipation of experience. And this belief is derived from our guiding principle that, broadly speaking, the future course of our sensations will be in accordance with the past.

This desire of ours to have an efficient set of rules for our predictions, which causes us to take notice of unfavourable observations, is also the factor which primarily determines how we adjust our system to cover the new data. It is true that we are infected with a spirit of conservatism and would rather make small alterations than large ones. It is disagreeable and troublesome for us to admit that our existing system is radically defective. And it is true that, other things being equal, we prefer simple to complex hypotheses, again from the desire to save ourselves trouble. But if experience leads us to suppose that radical changes are necessary, then we are prepared to make them, even though they do complicate our system, as the recent history of physics shows. When

[3] It will be seen that even "descriptions of past experience" are in a sense predictive since they function as "rules for the anticipation of future experience." See the end of this chapter for an elaboration of this point.

[4] *La Science et l'Hypothèse*, Part IV, Chapter ix, p. 170.

an observation runs counter to our most confident expectations, the easiest course is to ignore it, or at any rate to explain it away. If we do not do this, it is because we think that, if we leave our system as it is, we shall suffer further disappointments. We think it will increase the efficiency of our system as an instrument of prediction if we make it compatible with the hypothesis that the unexpected observation occurred. Whether we are right in thinking this is a question which cannot be settled by argument. We can only wait and see if our new system is successful in practice. If it is not, we alter it once again.

We have now obtained the information in order to answer our original question, "What is the criterion by which we test the validity of an empirical proposition?" The answer is that we test the validity of an empirical hypothesis by seeing whether it actually fulfils the function which it is designed to fulfil. And we have seen that the function of an empirical hypothesis is to enable us to anticipate experience. Accordingly, if an observation to which a given proposition is relevant conforms to our expectations, the truth of that proposition is confirmed. One cannot say that the proposition has been proved absolutely valid, because it is still possible that a future observation will discredit it. But one can say that its probability has been increased. If the observation is contrary to our expectations, then the status of the proposition is jeopardised. We may preserve it by adopting or abandoning other hypotheses: or we may consider it to have been confuted. But even if it is rejected in consequence of an unfavourable observation, one cannot say that it has been invalidated absolutely. For it is still possible that future observations will lead us to reinstate it. One can say only that its probability has been diminished.

It is necessary now to make clear what is meant in this context by the term "probability." In referring to the probability of a proposition, we are not, as is sometimes supposed, referring to an intrinsic property of it, or even to an unanalysable logical relation which holds between it and other propositions. Roughly speaking, all that we mean by saying that an observation increases the probability of a proposition is that it increases our confidence in the proposition, as measured by our willingness to rely on it in practice as a forecast of our sensations, and to retain it in preference to other hypotheses in face of an unfavourable experience. And, similarly, to say of an observation that it diminishes the probability of a proposition is to say that it decreases our willingness to include the proposition in the system of accepted hypotheses which serve us as guides to the future.[5]

As it stands, this account of the notion of probability is somewhat over-simplified. For it assumes that we deal with all hypotheses in a uniform self-consistent fashion, and this is unfortunately not the case. In practice, we do not always relate belief to observation in the way which is generally recognized

---

[5] This definition is not, of course, intended to apply to the mathematical usage of the term "probability."

to be the most reliable. Although we acknowledge that certain standards of evidence ought always to be observed in the formation of our beliefs, we do not always observe them. In other words, we are not always rational. For to be rational is simply to employ a self-consistent accredited procedure in the formation of all one's beliefs. The fact that the procedure, by reference to which we now determine whether a belief is rational, may subsequently forfeit our confidence, does not in any way detract from the rationality of adopting it now. For we define a rational belief as one which is arrived at by the methods which we now consider reliable. There is no absolute standard of rationality, just as there is no method of constructing hypotheses which is guaranteed to be reliable. We trust the methods of contemporary science because they have been successful in practice. If in the future we were to adopt different methods, then beliefs which are now rational might become irrational from the standpoint of these new methods. But the fact that this is possible has no bearing on the fact that these beliefs are rational now.

This definition of rationality enables us to amend our account of what is meant by the term "probability," in the usage with which we are now concerned. To say that an observation increases the probability of a hypothesis is not always equivalent to saying that it increases the degree of confidence with which we actually entertain the hypothesis, as measured by our readiness to act upon it: for we may be behaving irrationally. It is equivalent to saying that the observation increases the degree of confidence with which it is rational to entertain the hypothesis. And here we may repeat that the rationality of a belief is defined, not by reference to any absolute standard, but by reference to part of our own actual practice.

The obvious objection to our original definition of probability was that it was incompatible with the fact that one is sometimes mistaken about the probability of a proposition—that one can believe it to be more or less probable than it really is. It is plain that our amended definition escapes this objection. For, according to it, the probability of a proposition is determined both by the nature of our observations and by our conception of rationality. So that when a man relates belief to observation in a way which is inconsistent with the accredited scientific method of evaluating hypotheses, it is compatible with our definition of probability to say that he is mistaken about the probability of the propositions which he believes.

With this account of probability we complete our discussion of the validity of empirical propositions. The point which we must finally stress is that our remarks apply to all empirical propositions without exception, whether they are singular, or, particular, or universal. Every synthetic proposition is a rule for the anticipation of future experience, and is distinguished in content from other synthetic propositions by the fact that it is relevant to different situations. So that the fact that propositions referring to the past have the same hypothetical character as those which refer to the present, and those which refer to the future, in no way entails that these three types of proposition are not distinct. For they are verified by, and so serve to predict, different experiences.

It may be their failure to appreciate this point which has caused certain philosophers to deny that propositions about the past are hypotheses in the same sense as the laws of a natural science are hypotheses. For they have not been able to support their view by any substantial arguments, or to say what propositions about the past are, if they are not hypotheses, of the sort we have just described. For my own part, I do not find anything excesively paradoxical in the view that propositions about the past are rules for the prediction of those "historical" experiences which are commonly said to verify them, and I do not see how else "our knowledge of the past" is to be analysed. And I suspect, moreover, that those who object to our pragmatic treatment of history are really basing their objections on a tacit, or explicit, assumption that the past is somehow "objectively there" to be corresponded to—that it is "real" in the metaphysical sense of the term. And from what we have remarked concerning the metaphysical issue of idealism and realism, it is clear that such an assumption is not a genuine hypothesis.

CHISHOLM

For three hundred years after the publication of Descartes' Medita-
tions, philosophers of knowledge concerned themselves almost ex-
clusively with the problem of scepticism and certainty generated
by the doubts expressed in the First Meditation. Only recently has
there been a resurgence of interest in the explication of the rep-
ertory of epistemic concepts ("know," "believe," "probable,"
"reasonable," "evident") which men use in evaluating their everyday
experience of the world. In this selection by the American philos-
opher Roderick Chisholm (1916–), problems first raised in Plato's
dialogues are taken up again from a modern perspective.

At first reading, it may seem that Chisholm is merely articu-
lating a number of definitions, and we may wonder how much can
possibly depend on the way we use terms. But a closer look shows
us that Chisholm is attacking the reductionist, exclusive, mathe-
matics- and logic-oriented epistemology of such philosophers as
A. J. Ayer, as well as the scepticism of a David Hume. Chisholm
sketches a view of knowledge and belief which makes it quite
correct to call our experience of the world "knowledge." When
we say that we know something, we are not necessarily employing
a special faculty of the mind ("reason"), as Leibniz claims; nor
are we merely reporting the patterns of regularity in our sense
experience, as Hume asserts. Rather, we are evaluating the grounds
of our belief and judging their adequacy. Only a philosopher
hypnotised by pure mathematics will be so foolish as to demand
absolute certainty where none can be found.

As you read Chisholm's essay, notice that he couches his dis-
cussion in terms of the meanings of certain key words ("know,"
"believe"). One of the disputed issues of contemporary philosophy
is whether this shift from the material mode (talking about things)
to the formal mode (talking about words) makes any genuine philo-
sophical difference in the end.

The Problem of the Theatetus

In Plato's dialogue, the *Meno*, Socrates remarks: "That there is a difference between right opinion and knowledge is not at all a conjecture with me but something I would particularly assert that I know. There are not many things of which I would say that, but this one, at any rate, I will include among those that I know." The distinction would seem to be obvious. If one has knowledge, then one also has right or true opinion. But the converse is not true: one may have right or true opinion without having knowledge. Thus, we may guess correctly today, and therefore, have true opinion, but not know until tomorrow. Or we may have true opinion and never know at all.

In the *Theatetus*, Plato poses the following question: What is the distinction between knowledge and true, or right, opinion? He then sets out to "bring the many sorts of knowledge under one definition." It is doubtful that he succeeded and it is certain that we cannot do any better. But we may throw some light upon "the many sorts of knowledge," if we consider the difficulties that are involved in answering Plato's question.

One approach to the question, which Plato himself suggests, is to assume, first, that if one man knows and another man has true opinion but does not know, then the first man has everything that the second man has and something else as well. Then, having made this assumption, we ask: What is that which, when added to true opinion, yields knowledge? This approach to Plato's question may be put more schematically. The expression "*S* knows that *h* is true," where "*S*" may be replaced by a name or description of some person and where "*h* is true" may be replaced by a sentence such as "It is raining" or "Anaxagoras was a Greek philosopher," is assumed to tell us three different things:

1. *S* believes that *h*
   e.g., the person in question believes that it is raining, or believes that Anaxagoras was a Greek philosopher. It also tells us that
2. *h* is true
   e.g., that it is raining, or that Anaxagoras was a Greek philosopher. And finally, it tells us something else:
3. ———.

Thus, we have a blank to fill. What shall we say of 3?

Chapter 1 from *Theory of Knowledge* by Roderick M. Chisholm. Englewood Cliffs, N.J.: Prentice-Hall, Inc., 1966. © 1966 by Prentice-Hall, Inc. Reprinted by permission of Prentice-Hall, Inc.

We may begin by approaching our problem in this way, keeping in mind the possibility that we should have begun in some other way.

We will find that most of the expressions that come to mind as possible candidates for 3 will be expressions that seem to leave us with our problem. For when we try to say what *they* mean, we again come back to "know."

Adequate Evidence

It is often said that *adequate evidence* is that which, when added to true opinion, yields knowledge. May we fill in our blank, then, by saying "*S* has adequate evidence for *h*"?

Some have objected to this type of definition by saying: "Consider a man who has adequate evidence (not only has he heard the opinions of all the experts, but he has also had access to all of the evidence that they have had) and who believes what he does not because of the evidence that he has, but for some entirely frivolous reason (he follows what the tea leaves say). However good his evidence may be, such a man surely cannot be said to know, even if what he believes is true, for he hasn't recognized his evidence for what it's worth." But what this objection shows us, one could argue, is not that it is possible for a man with a true belief to have adequate evidence and at the same time not to know; it shows us, rather, that it is possible for such a man to have adequate evidence, and therefore, to know, but without *knowing* that he knows.

There are other reasons, however, for rejecting the definition.

For one thing, it is possible to add adequate evidence to true belief or opinion without obtaining knowledge. Many of those who predicted the election results correctly had adequate evidence—even at an early point in the campaign—for what they believed and predicted, but no one, at that time, knew that the predictions were true.

And for another thing, the expression "adequate evidence," as it is ordinarily interpreted, presupposes the concept of *knowledge*—knowledge, not of that for which we are said to *have* adequate evidence, but of something else. If a man says, for example, that we have adequate evidence for the hypothesis that no one can live on the planet Mercury, he is likely to mean that on the basis of what we know, there is very good reason to believe that no one can live on the planet Mercury. Or in slightly more technical language, he is saying that in relation to what is known, it is highly improbable that there can be life on Mercury.

We may say of this type of definition, then, what Socrates said of the attempt to define knowledge in terms of reason or explanation: "If, my boy, the command to add reason or explanation means learning to know and not merely getting an opinion . . . our splendid definition of knowledge would be a fine affair! For learning to know is acquiring knowledge, is it not?" [*Theatetus*]

Probability

The concept of adequate evidence presupposes the concept of knowledge, but the concept of probability need not do so. May we say, then, that *probability* is that which, when added to true opinion, yields knowledge?

The term "probability," as it is ordinarily used, may be taken in a variety of senses. Of these, the most common are the *statistical* sense, the *inductive* sense, and the *absolute* sense. Whichever of these interpretations we adopt, we will find that the concept of probability does not provide us with the solution to Plato's problem.

(1) Taking the term in its statistical sense, we may say with Aristotle that the probable is "that which happens for the most part." Probability statements, when taken in this way, tell us something about the relative frequency with which a given property or event (say, death before the age of 100) occurs within a certain reference class or population (say, the class of men, or of philosophers, or of ancient Greek philosophers). Thus, the statement "It is highly probable that a given ancient Greek philosopher, for example, Anaxagoras, died before he reached 100," when taken in this way, will tell us that Anaxagoras was a member of a certain class of entities (ancient Greek philosophers), the vast majority of which died before they reached 100. Statistical probability statements, which may be arithmetically more complex, are analogous.

But just how are we to go about defining knowledge in terms of statistical probability? Let us allow ourselves to say that if a man believes something, then *what* he believes is a proposition. Then, we shall try to say something of this sort: If a man knows a given proposition to be true, then the proposition is a member of a certain wider class of propositions, the vast majority of which have a certain further property P. And we will hope to find a property P which is such that if a proposition is a member of a class of propositions, the vast majority of which have that property P, then the proposition is one that can be said to be *known* to be true—but *what* class of propositions, and what additional property P? It will not be enough to say that the class of propositions is the class of propositions that S believes and that P is the property of being true, for in this case we shall not have made any distinction between knowledge and true opinion. And it will be too much to say that the class is the class of true propositions that S believes and that the additional property P is the property of being *known* to be true, for in this case we will be presupposing the distinction we are trying to define.

(2) The *inductive* sense of "probable" may seem to be more promising. If, once again, we allow ourselves the term "proposition," then we may say that "probable," in its inductive sense, refers to a certain logical relation that holds between propositions. Two propositions, e and h, may be so related logically that the proposition h may be said to be probable—that is, more probable than not—in relation to the proposition *e*. In such a case, *h* may be said to be *probable in relation to e*. If the reader can identify a good inductive argument, then he will have no trouble in identifying this relation. For to say that *h* is probable in relation to *e* is tantamount to saying that an argument having *e* as premise (*e* may be a conjunction of many propositions) and *h* as conclusion, would be a good inductive argument in favor of *h*. Let us say, for example, that "Anaxagoras lived to be 500 years old" is probable in relation to "Anaxagoras was an ancient Greek philosopher, and the vast majority of Greek philosophers lived to be 500 years old." The latter proposition, if we knew it to be true, would provide good inductive support for the former. Unfortunately, however, the question "What is a good inductive argument?" is at least as difficult as the question "What is the distinction between knowledge and true opinion?" And even if this were not so, inductive probability would not provide us with the answer to our question.

If we attempt to draw the distinction between knowledge and true opinion by reference to the inductive sense of "probable," then presumably we will say that our subject *S* knows the proposition *h* to be true, provided that *h* is probable in relation to a certain other proposition *e*. But *what* other proposition *e*? It will not be enough to say that there is a certain *true* proposition *e* which is such that *h* is probable on the basis of *e*, for in this case we will not be able to draw the distinction between knowledge and true opinion. We must say not only that *e* is true, but also that *e* has some further property as well. And what could this further property be—except that of being *known* by *S* to be true? Hence, the problem of the *Theatetus* recurs, this time with respect to *e* instead of *h*. How are we to define "*S* knows that *e* is true"?

(3) When the term "probable" is used in the *absolute* sense, and this would seem to be its most frequent use, it is closely related to what is intended by the term "know." The phrase "in all probability" is often used to express the absolute sense of "probable." Thus, if we say "In all probability it will rain tomorrow," we mean that the hypothesis or proposition that it will rain tomorrow is more probable than not, in the inductive sense of "probable" just considered, in relation to those propositions that are *known* to be true or that could, very readily, be known to be true. We may be relating the hypothesis to what it is we happen to know ourselves; or we may be relating it to what it is we believe the experts happen to know (as we would be doing if we said "In all probability, a man will be landed on the moon before the century is over"); or we may be relating the hypothesis to the knowledge of some subclass of experts who are indicated by the context of utterance.

In its most straightforward sense, the concept of absolute probability might be defined in this way: A proposition *h* is *probable in the absolute sense* for a given subject *S*, provided that *h* is probable in the inductive sense, in relation to the conjunction of all those propositions that *S* knows to be true.[1]

---

[1] The following definition would achieve the same end without referring to "the conjunction of all those propositions that *S* knows to be true." A proposition *h* is probable

(Hence, we may equate what is expressed by "*h* is probable in the absolute sense for *S*" with what is expressed by "*S* has adequate evidence for *h*.") Since we must appeal to the concept of knowledge to explicate the concept of absolute probability, we cannot make use of the concept of absolute probability in order to complete our definition of knowledge.[2]

Observation

In writings on the philosophy of science, it is often assumed (1) that knowledge may be defined in terms of *observation* and (2) that observation, being a concept of physiology and psychology, can be defined in terms of those sciences and without reference to knowledge. In support of the first contention, one might formulate the following definition: To say of someone *S* that *S* knows a certain proposition *h* to be true to say that *S* has true opinion with respect to *h* and that *h* is an observation proposition for *S*. And in support of the second, one might point out that to say of a man that he observes a cat, for example, is to say that a cat is, for him, a stimulus object, that it has caused him to have a certain sensation, and perhaps also that it has "entered into his field of vision."

This approach to Plato's question will not serve to "bring the many sorts of knowledge under one definition," for as we shall see later in some detail, there are many sorts of knowledge of logic and mathematics and our knowledge of some of our own states of mind. But there is another difficulty that is even more serious.

The term "observation" is a member of a certain family of terms (compare "perceive," "see," "hear," "feel") each of which is subject to two quite different types of interpretation. If we interpret any one of these terms in such a way that, on that interpretation, one of the two contentions comprising the present suggestion will be true (and we may do this), then, on that interpretation of the term, the other contention will be false.

We may say of a man simply that he observes a cat on the roof. Or we may say of him that he observes *that* a cat is on the roof. In the second case, the verb "observe" takes a "that"-clause, a propositional clause, as its grammatical object. We may distinguish, therefore, between a "propositional" and a "nonpropositional" use of the term "observe," and we may make an analogous distinction for "perceive," "see," "hear," and "feel."

---

in the absolute sense for *S* provided: there is a conjunction *e* of propositions that *S* knows to be true; *h* is probable in relation to *e;* and there is no proposition *i* such that both (1) *S* knows *i* to be true and (2) *h* is not probable in relation to the conjunction of *e* and *i*.

[2] The distinction between the inductive and statistical senses of "probable" is clearly drawn by Rudolf Carnap in *The Logical Foundations of Probability* (Chicago: University of Chicago Press, 1950). The expression "absolute probability," interpreted somewhat as here, was used by Bernard Bolzano in his *Wissenschaftslehre*, III (Leipzig: Felix Meiner, 1930), 267–68; this work was first published in 1837. Still another sense of "probable" is distinguished in footnote 16 of this chapter.

If we take the verb "observe" propositionally, saying of the man that he observes that a cat is on the roof, or that he observes a cat to be on the roof, then we may also say of him that he *knows* that a cat is on the roof; for in the propositional sense of "observe," observation may be said to imply knowledge. But if we take the verb nonpropositionally, saying of the man only that he observes a cat which is on the roof, then what we say will not imply that he knows that there is a cat on the roof. For a man may be said to observe a cat, to see a cat, or hear a cat, in the nonpropositional sense of these terms, without his knowing that a cat is what it is that he is observing, or seeing, or hearing. "It wasn't until the following day that I found out that what I saw was only a cat."

The distinction between these two senses of "observe" and the other related terms may also be illustrated by the following passage in *Robinson Crusoe:* "When, one morning the day broke, and all unexpectedly before their eyes a ship stood, what it was was evident at a glance to Crusoe. . . . But how was it with Friday? As younger and uncivilized, his eyes were presumably better than those of his master. That is, Friday saw the ship really the best of the two; and yet he could hardly be said to see it at all." Using "see" non-propositionally, we may say that Friday not only saw the ship, but saw it better than Crusoe did; using it propositionally, we may say that Crusoe, but not Friday, saw *that* it was a ship and hence, that Friday hardly saw a ship at all.

We can define the Friday, nonpropositional sense of "observe" by means of the terms of psychology and physiology. But this sense of observation does not imply knowledge, and we cannot use it to complete our definition of knowledge. We must appeal instead to the Crusoe, propositional sense of "observe." What, then, did Crusoe have that Friday did not have?

The obvious answer is that Crusoe had *knowledge.* His senses enabled him to *know,* with the result that "what it was was evident at a glance." This sense of "observation," therefore, must be defined in terms of knowledge, and so we are left, once again, with Plato's problem.

Knowledge as an Ethical Concept

If we are to solve the problem, we must find a definition of *knowledge* that is not patently circular. We cannot be content to define knowledge by reference, say, to "that which falls within our cognizance." Nor will it do merely to introduce some technical term and then resolve to use it in the way in which we ordinarily use the word "knowledge." We may say, if we like, that to constitute knowledge, a true opinion must also be one that is "evident," but we must not suppose that the introduction of the technical term is itself sufficient to throw any light upon our problem.

Let us consider, then, the possibility of defining knowledge in ethical terms. To know that *h* is true will be not only to have true opinion with respect to *h*, but also to have a certain right or duty with respect to *h*. Whether such a definition will turn out to be circular will depend upon how we specify the right or duty in question. The terms "right" and "duty" are not technical terms invented merely in order to complete our definition. We may assume that "right" and "duty" are correlative terms: A man has a right to perform a certain act A if, and only if, he does not have the right to refrain from performing A. Instead of saying "He has a duty to perform A," we may also say "He ought to perform A."

One may object that any such definition would throw no light upon the concept of knowledge, for what it is to have a right or duty is at least as obscure as what it is to know. The obvious reply is: The philosopher is indeed confronted not only with the difficult concept of knowledge, but also with the difficult concept of a right or a duty; but if he can succeed in defining one of these by reference to the other, then he will have progressed at least to the extent of finding himself with one difficult concept, where formerly he had found himself with two.[3]

What right or duty, then, does the knower have with respect to that which he knows? A simple answer would be: If a man knows that a certain proposition is true, then he has the duty to accept or believe that proposition. More exactly, S knows that h is true, provided that (1) S accepts or believes h; (2) h is true; and (3) S has the duty to accept or believe h. Would this be an adequate definition?

The term "duty" must be taken in its ordinary sense if the definition is to be of any significance. But "duty," as we ordinarily understand the term, is used in connection with actions, or possible actions, that are within the agent's power and for which he can be held responsible if he performs them. ("'Ought' implies 'can.'") But are beliefs actions, or possible actions, that are within anyone's power?[4] And can a man be held responsible for what he believes, or fails to believe? (We often speak of what a man ought to know, but seldom, if ever, of what a man ought to believe.)

---

[3] Thus, some moral philosophers have attempted to define "duty" in terms of "know" —e.g., in terms of what an "ideal oberver" would approve if only he knew all of the relevant facts. See Francis Hutcheson, *An Essay on the Nature and Conduct of the Passions, with Illustrations upon the Moral Sense* (1728); see also, Roderick Firth, "Ethical Absolutism and the Ideal Observer," *Philosophy and Phenomenological Research*, XII (1952), 317–45. This way of defining "duty," however, involves difficulties analogous to those encountered in trying to define "know." If the characteristics that would make an observer "ideal" include certain moral qualifications, then an "ideal-observer" definition of "duty" may become circular; and if they do not, then it may be impossible to determine what such an observer would approve, in which case the definition would be inapplicable.

[4] Descartes assumed that beliefs are acts which are within our power, and Spinoza, that they are not. This general problem is discussed in: C. S. Peirce, *Collected Papers*, ed. Charles Hartshorne and Paul Weiss, I (Cambridge: Harvard University Press, 1931), 331–34; H. H. Price, "Belief and Will," *Aristotelian Society Supplementary Volume*, XXVIII (1954), 1–26; C. I. Lewis, *The Ground and Nature of the Right*, "Right Believing and Right Concluding" (New York: Columbia University Press, 1955), Chap. 2; and Stuart Hampshire, *Thought and Action* (New York: The Viking Press, Inc., 1959), Chap. 2.

There is a difficulty that is even more serious: If beliefs—more exactly, believings—are actions for which we can be held responsible, then the proposed definition would imply that to turn a man's true opinion into knowledge, it would be sufficient to make the holding of that opinion a duty. But it is at least conceivable that a man may have the duty to accept a true proposition which he does not know to be true. For example, a man may have the duty to believe that the members of his family are honest or faithful without in fact knowing that they are. Or a sick man, who has various unfulfilled obligations, may have the duty to accept certain propositions if, by accepting them, he can make himself well and useful once again. The proposed definition would have the consequence that, if these duties to believe are fulfilled, and if the propositions thus believed happen to be true, then the believer, *ipso facto,* knows that they are true. And this is absurd.[5]

Analogous considerations hold if we define knowing in terms of "the right to believe," instead of "the duty to believe."

Let us consider, then, another type of right or duty, one that is more closely related to the concept of knowing—the right or duty that we have, in certain cases, to take precautions. Taking precautions is a kind of activity. When a man takes precautions, he prepares for the worst, even though he may not expect it to happen. For example, he may not believe that his house will burn, but he takes precautions by buying fire insurance. But if he *knows* that a given proposition is true, then, it would seem, there is no point in taking any precautions against the possibility that the proposition is false. If, somehow, he knew that his house would never burn, then, it would seem, there would be no point in his insuring the house against fire or otherwise taking precautions against the possibility that his house might burn. Suppose, then, we say that a man knows *h* to be true, provided that no matter what he may do, he has the right to rely upon *h*—that is to say, no matter what he may do, he does not have the duty to take precautions against the possibility that *h* is false.

This definition has been suggested by a familiar doctrine of scholastic philosophy: If a man *knows*, then he need have no "fear of error," and so far as what is known is concerned, his intellect may be in "a state of repose."[6] A. J. Ayer has suggested a similar definition, saying that the man who knows, as contrasted with the man who merely has true opinion, is the man who has the "right to be sure."[7]

But here, too, there are difficulties. The duty to take precautions in any particular case is a function not only of what is known, but also of what happens to be at stake—if not, indeed, of what is *known* to be at stake. Where the

[5] See Roderick Firth, "Chisholm and the Ethics of Belief," *Philosophical Review,* LXVIII (1959), 493–506.

[6] See D. J. Mercier, *Critériologie générale, ou Théorie générale de la certitude,* 8th ed. (Paris: Felix Alcan, 1923), pp. 420–21; P. Coffey, *Epistemology, or the Theory of Knowledge,* I (London: Longmans, Green & Company, Ltd., 1917), 54–55.

[7] *The Problem of Knowledge* (New York: St. Martin's Press, Inc., 1955), pp. 31–35.

stakes are small, there may be no need to take precautions—whether or not one knows. And where the stakes are large, there may be a duty to take precautions—whether or not one knows. Moreover, the duty to take precautions may arise in still other ways. Even if a captain knows that his ship is seaworthy, he may yet have the obligation to provide lifeboats and to take other precautions against the possibility that it is not. For he may have the obligation to reassure his passengers; or he may have sworn to obey the law and thus have acquired the obligation to take precautions with every sailing.

Again, there are circumstances under which a man may be said to have the duty to rely upon certain propositions about his friends, or upon certain propositions that his friends have assured him are true, even though he does not know these propositions to be true. One of the duties of the Christian, for example, is said to be that of faith—where faith is a matter of trust, a matter of relying upon the several tenets that make up the doctrine of Christianity. The virtue of having faith is thought by some Christians to lie in the very fact that the tenets of the faith are propositions which are *not* known to be true and which, indeed, are extremely unreasonable.[8] If it is the duty of the Christian to have faith, and if the tenets of that faith happen to be true, then, according to the proposed definition of knowledge, it will follow from these facts alone that the Christian *knows* these tenets to be true.

It is not enough, then, to define "*S* knows that *h* is true" by reference merely to the right not to take precautions against the possibility that *h* is false. For *S* may know that *h* is true and yet not have this right; or he may have the right (for he may have the duty, and if he has the duty he has the right) and yet not know that *h* is true.

By introducing proper qualifications, we could conceivably formulate an ethical definition of "know" that would not be subject to such difficulties. But no one has yet been able to formulate satisfactorily just what the qualifications are that are needed. At the present time, then, we do not have an ethical definition that will constitute a solution to the problem of the *Theatetus*.[9]

---

[8] Cf. the following passage from Kierkegaard's *Concluding Unscientific Postscript:* "Suppose a man who wishes to acquire faith; let the comedy begin. He wishes to have faith, but he wishes also to safeguard himself by means of an objective inquiry and its approximation process. What happens? With the help of the approximation process the absurd becomes something different: it becomes probable, it becomes increasingly probable, it becomes extremely and emphatically probable. Now he is ready to believe it, and he ventures to claim for himself that he does not believe as shoemakers and tailors and simple folk believe, but only after long deliberation. Now he is ready to believe it [i.e., to accept it on faith]; and lo, now it has become precisely impossible to believe it. Anything that is almost probable, is something he can almost know, or as good as know, or extremely and emphatically almost *know*—but it is impossible to *believe*. For the absurd is the object of faith, and the only object that can be believed." From *A Kierkegaard Anthology*, ed. Robert Bretall (Princeton: Princeton University Press, 1947), pp. 220–21.

[9] Still other difficulties are noted by Herbert Heidelberger in, "On Defining Epistemic Expressions," *Journal of Philosophy*, LX (1963), 344–48.

"Performative Utterances"

It may well be asked, at this point, whether our problem has not been misconceived—whether what we take to be a problem may not actually rest upon a false presupposition. We have been supposing all along that there is something x such that, when x is added to true opinion, the result is knowledge, and we have sought, so far in vain, for this something x. But is it necessary to make any such supposition in order to make the distinction between knowledge and true opinion?

There are those who believe that if we note certain ways in which people use the *word* "know," we will then be able to see that the supposition in question is mistaken. One source of this belief is an influential paper by J. L. Austin, in which he describes what he calls the "performative" function of "I know."[10]

The concept of a "performative" function may be illustrated by referring to the ordinary use of the expression "I promise." Usually, when a man utters the words "I promise," the point of his utterance is not to report anything; the man's concern is to make the promise, not to describe himself as making a promise. To utter the words "I promise," under ordinary conditions, is to promise. "I request" is similar. Thus, if a man uses the word "request" in the third person, saying "He requests," then he is describing or reporting what some other person is doing; or if he uses the word in the first person, but in the past tense, saying "I requested," then he is describing or reporting something that he himself was doing; but if he uses the word in the first person and in the present tense, saying "I request," then his point is not to report or describe himself as requesting—his point is to make a request. The same thing holds for such verbs as "order," "warn," "guarantee," and "baptize." (One indication of a performative use, Austin remarks, is the fact that "the little word 'hereby' actually occurs or might naturally be inserted"—as in "Trespassers are hereby warned that cars will be towed away at owner's expense.")

The expression "I know," Austin points out, performs a function very similar to that of "I promise." When a man utters the words "I promise" he provides a guarantee; he stakes his reputation and binds himself to others—and similarly, for saying "I know." Saying "I know," Austin writes, "is *not* saying 'I have performed a specially striking feat of cognition, superior, in the same scale as believing and being sure, even to being merely quite sure': for there *is* nothing in that scale superior to being quite sure. Just as promising is not something superior, in the same scale as hoping and intending, even to merely fully intending: for there *is* nothing in that scale superior to fully intending. When I say 'I know,' *I give others my word: I give others my authority* for

[10] "Other Minds," *Proceedings of the Aristotelian Society,* Supplementary Volume XX (1946); reprinted in Austin's *Philosophical Papers,* ed. J. O. Urmson and G. J. Warnock (New York: Oxford University Press, 1961), pp. 44–84.

saying that '*S* is *P*.' "[11] And Austin concludes: "To suppose 'I know' is a descriptive phrase, is only one example of the *descriptive fallacy*, so common in philosophy."[12]

It is in the spirit of these observations also to note that where "I know" performs the function of giving assurance, "I believe" may perform that of taking it away. For to say "I believe," under certain circumstances, is tantamount to saying "Don't take *my* word for it—I won't be responsible." How, then, could "knowing" ever be thought to imply "believing"—if the function of the one is to give, and that of the other, to take away?

On the basis of such considerations, some philosophers have concluded that the problem of the *Theatetus* is a psuedo-problem. It is said to be a pseudo-problem because it is thought to be based upon a false assumption, the assumption, namely, that there *is* a state which may be described or reported by means of the word "know." And it is by committing the "descriptive fallacy" that one is led to make this assumption.

But let us look more carefully at the concept of a "performative utterance."

Almost every utterance may be said to be performative in at least one respect, for almost every utterance is intended to have effects other than those of simply describing or reporting. What, then, is the peculiarity of the particular expressions that Austin calls "performative"? Austin did not provide a clear definition of the concept, but I think that "performative utterances" might be described as follows.

There are certain acts—e.g., requesting, ordering, guaranteeing, baptizing —which have this characteristic: When the circumstances are right, then to perform the act it is enough to make an utterance containing words which the speaker commonly uses to designate such an act. A standard way of making a request, among English-speaking people, is to make an utterance beginning with "I request" (the same thing holds for promising, ordering, guaranteeing, baptizing). Let us say, then, of anyone who performs an act in this way, that his utterance is a "performative utterance"—in what we may call the strict sense of this term.

An utterance beginning with "I want" is not performative in this strict sense, for it cannot be said to be an "act" of wanting. But "I want" is often used to accomplish what one might accomplish by means of the strict performative "I request." Let us say, then, that "I want" may be a "performative utterance" in an *extended* sense of the latter expression.

In which of these senses may an utterance of "I know" be said to be performative? Clearly, "I know" is not performative in what I have called the strict sense of the term, for knowing is not an "act" that can be performed by saying "I know." To say "I *promise* that *p*," at least under certain circumstances, *is* to promise that *p*; but to say "I know that *p*" is not itself to know that *p*. (One may say "I hereby promise," but not "I hereby know.") "I know"

---

[11] *Philosophical Papers*, p. 67. Cf. C. S. Peirce, *Collected Papers*, V (1932), 383–87.
[12] *Ibid.*, p. 71.

is related to "I guarantee" and "I give you my word" in the way in which "I want" is related to "I request." For "I know" is often used to accomplish what one may accomplish by the strict performative "I guarantee" or "I give you my word." Hence, "I know" may be performative in an extended sense of the term.

"I want" is not always a substitute for "I request." I may tell you what I want, and thus, describe my psychological state, even when I know there is no possibility of your helping me in getting what I want. And "I know" is not always a substitute for "I guarantee." I may tell you—confess or boast to you—that I know some of the things that you also know, and on an occasion when you neither need nor want my guarantee. ("I believe," similarly, is not always a substitute for "I can't provide you with any guarantees," for I may tell you what I believe on occasion when I *am* prepared to give you guarantees.)

What, then, of Austin's remark "To suppose 'I know' is a descriptive phrase, is only one example of the *descriptive fallacy*, so common in philosophy"? It looks very much as though Austin was assuming mistakenly that "I know" is performative in the strict sense and not merely in the extended sense. Yet, just as an utterance of "I want" may serve *both* to say something about me and to get you to do something, an utterance of "I know" may serve both to say something about me and to provide you with guarantees. To suppose that the performance of the nondescriptive function is inconsistent with a simultaneous performance of the descriptive function might be called, therefore, an example of the *performative fallacy*.

The expression "I know" is not to be taken lightly, and therefore, if we are philosophers, we may ask what the conditions are that entitle one to say it. Thus, Austin says: "If you say you *know* something, the most immediate challenge takes the form of asking 'Are you in a position to know?': that is, you must undertake to show, not merely that you are sure of it, but that it is *within your cognizance*."[13]

If a man is entitled to say "I know that *h*," it may well be that he has performed no striking feat of cognition, but *h* does "fall within his cognizance." And if *h* does thus fall within his cognizance, then surely, whether or not he *says* "I know," he *does* know. ("He knows but he isn't saying.") Hence, it would seem there *is* a state, after all, that may be described or reported by means of the word "know."[14] It is by committing the "performative fallacy" that one is led to suppose that there is not.

---

[13] *Philosophical Papers*, p. 68. I have italicized the final three words.

[14] J. O. Urmson proposed an account of the use of "I know" similar to Austin's and then attempted to extend the account to second and third persons and to other tenses in the following way: To say, for example, that Mr. Jones *knew* some proposition to be true is to say that Mr. Jones was "in a position in which he was entitled to say 'I know.'" And what is it to be "in a position in which one is entitled to say 'I know'"? According to Urmson, it is to be in the position of having "all the *evidence* one could need"—which brings us back to the point at which we began our discussion of Plato's problem. See "Parenthetical Verbs," in *Essays in Conceptual Analysis*, ed. A. G. N. Flew (New York: St. Martin's Press, Inc., 1956), p. 199; the italics are mine.

Other Epistemic Terms

"Know" is one of a family of terms—we might call them terms of epistemic appraisal—which present us with essentially similar problems. We can throw some light upon "know" by noting its relations to other members of the same family.

Just as we may say of a man that he *knows* a certain hypothesis or proposition to be true, we may also say: a certain hypothesis is *evident* to him; it is *reasonable* of him to accept a certain hypothesis; one hypothesis is, for him, *more reasonable* than another; a certain hypothesis is for him *gratuitous*, or *indifferent*, or *acceptable*, or *unacceptable*.

If we say that a certain hypothesis or proposition is "unacceptable," where "unacceptable" is to be taken as a term of epistemic appraisal, we mean not that the proposition is incapable of being accepted, but rather, that epistemically it is unworthy of being accepted. The negation of any proposition that a man knows to be true, or of any proposition that is evident to him, could be said to be a proposition that is, for him, unacceptable. Hence, for most of us, "Chicago is not on Lake Michigan" would be unacceptable. Other propositions may be unacceptable even though their negations are not evident or not known to be true. For there are some propositions which are such that both they and their negations are unacceptable. These are the propositions which in the terms of the ancient sceptics, any reasonable man would *withhold;* he would neither believe them nor disbelieve them, neither affirm them nor deny them. Obvious examples of such propositions are those that generate paradox, e.g., Russell's "The class of all classes that are not members of themselves is a member of itself." According to the rigid ethics of belief advocated by W. K. Clifford, every proposition for which there is "insufficient evidence" is also unacceptable.[15] According to positivistic philosophers, some propositions that are unverifiable and all propositions that have a metaphysical subject matter may also be said to be unacceptable.

A "gratuitous" proposition may be described as one which there is no point in accepting. If we could say that an unacceptable proposition is one that ought not to be accepted, then we could say that a gratuitous proposition is one that need not be accepted. Hence, the charge of gratuitousness is less serious than that of unacceptability: Every unacceptable proposition is gratuitous, but some gratuitous propositions (unless Clifford is right) are not unacceptable. The astronomy of Copernicus, according to some, makes that of Ptolemy gratuitous, but it does not make it unacceptable. The Ptolemaic astronomy is not unacceptable, but since it is needlessly complex, it is gratuitous.

Sometimes propositions are said to be epistemically "indifferent," but we must distinguish two quite different uses of this term. (1) Will it rain in Balti-

---

[15] See "The Ethics of Belief," in *Lectures and Essays,* II (London: Macmillan & Co., Ltd., 1879), 163-205.

more a year from today? For most of us, the proposition is epistemically "in-different" in that there is as much, or as little, reason for believing it as there is for disbelieving it. Any proposition that has a probability of .5 in relation to everything that is known could be said to be indifferent in this first sense of the term. (2) An act is said to be morally indifferent if performance of the act is permissible and if nonperformance is also permissible. It is sometimes said analogously that a proposition is epistemically indifferent if the proposition is acceptable and if its negation is also acceptable.

If a proposition is indifferent in the first of these two senses of the term, then it is not indifferent in the second. For if there is no ground for choosing between the proposition and its negation, then suspension of belief would seem to be the reasonable course, in which case neither the proposition nor its nega-tion would be acceptable. It may well be, in fact, that no proposition is in-different in the second sense of the term.

Some propositions are "beyond reasonable doubt." Or as we may also say, they are such that it is "reasonable" for a man to believe them. These include those propositions for which he has adequate evidence (in the sense of "ade-quate evidence" discussed earlier). For presumably, it is reasonable for a man to believe any proposition that is more probable than not in relation to the totality of what he knows. (This is the epistemic thesis that is sometimes ex-pressed by saying "induction is justified."[16]) An important epistemological question concerns whether or not there are any *other* propositions which it is reasonable for a man to accept.

Some propositions are "evident" as well as reasonable. Any proposition that a man knows to be true is one that may be said to be evident for him. But it may be that some propositions that are evident for him are not propositions that he knows to be true. Thus, it has been held that whatever is logically entailed by what is evident, is itself evident. But some of the propositions that are logically entailed by what a man knows may be such that he does not know that they are entailed by what he knows, and they may even be propositions which he does not accept (he may know that all philosophers are men and yet refrain from believing that everything that is not a man is something that is not a philosopher). In this case, he will refrain from accepting or believing certain propositions which are evident for him; and an evident proposition that is not

---

16 We have been using "*h* is probable for *S*," in its *absolute* sense, to mean that *h* is inductively supported by (is more probable than not in relation to) what is known by *S*. But sometimes the expression is used *epistemically* to mean merely that *h* is a proposition which is reasonable for *S* to accept. This ambiguity seems to have misled some philosophers into supposing that they can easily demonstrate the justifiability of induction. Taking "probable" in its epistemic sense, they note that a probable proposition is one that is reasonable; then, taking "probable" in its *absolute* sense, they note that a probable propo-sition is one that is inductively supported by what is known; and finally, by committing the fallacy of equivocation, they deduce that if a proposition is inductively supported by what is known, then it is one that it is reasonable to accept.

accepted cannot be said to be a proposition that is known. Again, any proposition that is both evident and false would be a proposition that is evident but not known; whether there are any such propositions is an extraordinarily difficult question to which we shall return.

Hence, there are important differences between saying that a certain proposition is "evident" for a man and saying that he has "adequate evidence" for that proposition. We may note three such differences: (1) A man may have adequate evidence for a proposition that is not evident to him. If he happens to know, for example, that there are 1,000 balls in the urn and that 999 of them are red, and if he knows further that one of them will be drawn at random, then he might be said to have adequate evidence for the proposition that the ball to be drawn will be red; but before the ball is drawn it will not be evident for him that it is red. (2) The "logic" of the concept of the evident differs from that of the concept of adequate evidence. Thus, if the balls in the urn are to be taken out one at a time, and none of them returned, perhaps we may say that the man now has adequate evidence, with respect to *each* particular drawing, that the ball drawn on that particular occasion will be red, but he does not have adequate evidence for the proposition that, on every occasion, the ball that is drawn will be red. But if, somehow, it were *evident* for him, with respect to *each* occasion, that on that occasion a red ball would be drawn, then it would also be evident for him that on *every* occasion a red ball would be drawn. (3) There may be propositions that are evident for a man, but which are such that he cannot properly be said to *have* adequate evidence for them. For if we follow ordinary usage, we will say of such propositions as "I seem to remember having been in this place before," that they are propositions which may *be* evident for a man at a given time, but not that they are propositions for which he *has* evidence at that time. Thus, if I *have* evidence for a given proposition, then I will be able to cite certain *other* propositions as being my evidence for that proposition; but even though it is evident for me that I seem to remember having been in this place before, there are no other propositions I could cite as being my *evidence* for the proposition that I seem to remember having been in this place before.[17]

Some Definitions

If "know" and the other epistemic terms we have been discussing can all be defined in terms of one epistemic term or locution, then perhaps it can be said that we have provided a partial solution to Plato's problem.

Let us remind ourselves, first, that we may take one of three different attitudes toward any given proposition: we may believe or accept the proposi-

[17] For further discussion of some of these points, cf. Herbert Heidelberger, "Knowledge, Certainty, and Probability," *Inquiry*, VI (1963), 242–50.

tion; we may disbelieve or reject the proposition (and this is the same as believing or accepting the negation of the proposition); or we may "withhold" the proposition—that is, we may refrain from believing it and we may also refrain from disbelieving it. And secondly, let us remind ourselves that for any proposition and any person, some of these attitudes will be *more reasonable*, at any given time, than others. Thus, St. Augustine suggested that even though there might be ground to question the reliability of the senses, it would be more reasonable for most of us most of the time to believe that we could rely upon them than to believe that we could not. Presumably, for most of us at the present time, it is more reasonable to withhold the proposition that there is life on Venus than it is to accept it; but it is more reasonable to accept the proposition that there is life on Venus than it is to accept the proposition that there is life on Mercury. What is suggested when we say of one of these attitudes that it is more reasonable than another, is this: If the person in question were a rational being, if his concerns were purely intellectual, and if he were to choose between the two attitudes, then he would choose the more reasonable in preference to the less reasonable.[18]

By reference to this concept of one epistemic attitude being more reasonable than another for a given subject at a given time, we can define and systematize our various epistemic concepts. A proposition is *reasonable* or "beyond reasonable doubt," if believing it is more reasonable than withholding it; it is *gratuitous* if believing it is not more reasonable than withholding it; it is *unacceptable* if withholding it is more reasonable than believing it; and it is *acceptable* if withholding it is not more reasonable than believing it.[19] And a proposition *h* may be said to be *evident* for a subject *S* provided (1) that *h* is reasonable for *S* and (2) that there is no proposition *i* such that it is more reasonable for *S* to believe *i* than it is for him to believe *h*. We thus have a hierarchy of epistemic terms: Every proposition that is evident is reasonable, but

[18] The following observation by William James reminds us that such a person—a rational being whose concerns are purely intellectual—would not be motivated merely by the desire to play it safe. "There are two ways of looking at our duty in the matter of opinion,—ways entirely different, and yet ways about whose difference the theory of knowledge seems hitherto to have shown very little concern. We *must know the truth:* and *we must avoid error*—these are our first and great commandments as would-be knowers; but they are not two ways of stating an identical commandment, they are two separable laws. . . . By choosing between them we may end by coloring differently our whole intellectual life. . . . For my part, I can believe that worse things than being duped may happen to a man." From *The Will to Believe and Other Essays in Popular Philosophy* (New York: David McKay Co., Inc., 1911), pp. 17-19.

[19] Of the two senses of "indifferent" distinguished above, a proposition could be said to be *indifferent*, in the first sense, if believing it is not more reasonable than disbelieving it and if disbelieving it is not more reasonable than believing it. It would be indifferent, in the second sense, if both it and its negation were acceptable; but as we have noted, there is ground for questioning whether any proposition is indifferent in this second sense.

not conversely; and every proposition that is reasonable is acceptable, but not conversely.[20]. . .

Having defined the evident, we may now return to the problem of the *Theatetus* and to the definition with which we began.

> *S knows* at *t* that *h* is true, provided: (1) *S* believes *h* at *t;* (2) *h* is true; and (3) *h* is evident at *t* for *S*.[21]

We thus have a partial solution to the problem. We have defined "know" in terms of "evident." And we have defined "evident" in terms of "more reasonable." The definition of "evident" is not completely empty, for we have seen that "more reasonable" is also adequate for the definition of other basic terms of epistemic appraisal. Our definition, therefore, enables us to see the ways in which these various concepts are related. We may leave unanswered the important question of whether it is possible to define "more reasonable" in strictly ethical terms. . . .

[20] An "epistemic logic," exhibiting the logical relations among these concepts, could be developed on the basis of these three assumptions: (1) If one attitude is more reasonable than another and the other more reasonable than a third, then the first is more reasonable than the third. (2) If one attitude is more reasonable than another, then the other is not more reasonable than it. (3) If withholding a given proposition is not more reasonable than believing it, then believing it is more reasonable than disbelieving it (e.g., if agnosticism is not more reasonable than theism, then theism is more reasonable than atheism).

[21] If we countenance the possibility that some propositions are both evident and false, we must add a qualification to the definition in order to remove a difficulty pointed out by Edmund L. Gettier in "Is Justified True Belief Knowledge?" *Analysis*, XXV (1963), 121-23. Suppose "I see a sheep in the field" is a false proposition *i* that is evident for *S* (he mistakes a dog for a sheep); then "A sheep is in the field" (*h*) will also be evident for *S*. Suppose further that there happens to be a sheep in the field that *S* does not see. This situation, obviously, would not warrant our saying *S knows* that there is a sheep in the field; yet it satisfies the conditions of our definition, for *S* believes *h*, *h* is true, and *h* is evident for *S*. To rule out this type of situation, it would be necessary to add a qualification to our definition of "know."

Let us say that a proposition *e* "justifies" a proposition *h* provided *e* and *h* are such that, for any subject and any time, if *e* is evident to that subject at that time then *h* is evident to that subject at that time; and let us say that a "basic proposition" is an evident proposition such that the only evident propositions that thus justify it are propositions that entail it. To meet the difficulty, we might consider adding the following clause which would make our definition of "know" recursive:

"Either (1) *h* is a basic proposition for *S* at *t*, or (2) *h* is entailed by a set of propositions that are known by *S* at *t*, or (3) a proposition that is known by *S* at *t* and that does not justify any false proposition justifies *h*."

. . . If it is necessary to add such a fourth clause to our definition of "know," then *knowing that one knows*, i.e., being certain, is considerably more difficult than merely knowing. For discussions of this latter question, see Jaakko Hintikka, *Knowledge and Belief* (Ithaca: Cornell University Press, 1962), Chap. 5, and Roderick M. Chisholm, "The Logic of Knowing," *Journal of Philosophy*, LX (1963), 775-95.

AFTERWORD

If you have done your card guessing and you have accumulated a pile of raw data, the time has come to ask what it all proves? Is there some extrasensory form of communication? Are telepathy, precognition, psychokinesis, and the rest ever possible? And what of astrology and all the other "sciences" which claim to open up new and exciting paths to knowledge? What can our philosophers tell us about such matters?

As I have remarked before, we must not expect philosophy to give us detailed answers to particular questions. Nevertheless, I think a very clear message is communicated by Leibniz, Hume, James, Ayer, and Chisholm, despite their many differences. It is that every knowledge claim that is advanced—whether from the natural sciences, psychic research, astrology, or everyday experience—must meet the same test of meaningfulness, verifiability, and reasonableness before it can be accepted. There are no miracles, no privileged spheres of superior knowledge, no short cuts bypassing the hard road of observation, experiment, and reasoning. Henry Sidgwick and Hereward Carrington obviously believed that legitimate empirical evidence could be found for the existence of extrasensory perception. None of our five philosophers would rule that possibility out in advance. But among them, the five would insist upon **three** criteria which ESP claims must meet to be accepted as genuine empirical knowledge:

1. The claims must assert something about the world that is capable of being confirmed or disconfirmed in our experience.

2. The claims must fit into a larger body of scientific knowledge which relates ESP to other scientifically verifiable phenomena (such as electromagnetic radiation or brain-state potentials).

3. The claims must be reasonable, according to criteria of reasonableness that apply evenhandedly to all knowledge claims whatsoever.

Measured against these three criteria, it seems to me that astrology is patently without any merit, that flying-saucer theories are at best implausible, and that the reports of the extremely varied events known as "psychic phenomena" must be awarded the Scottish verdict, "not proved." Of one thing we may be certain, however. If it is adequately demonstrated that telepathy or psychokinesis is a genuine human power, we shall not thereby have discovered a method for transcending the limits of scientific knowledge. We shall merely have discovered some more things in heaven or earth that were not dreamt of in our philosophy.

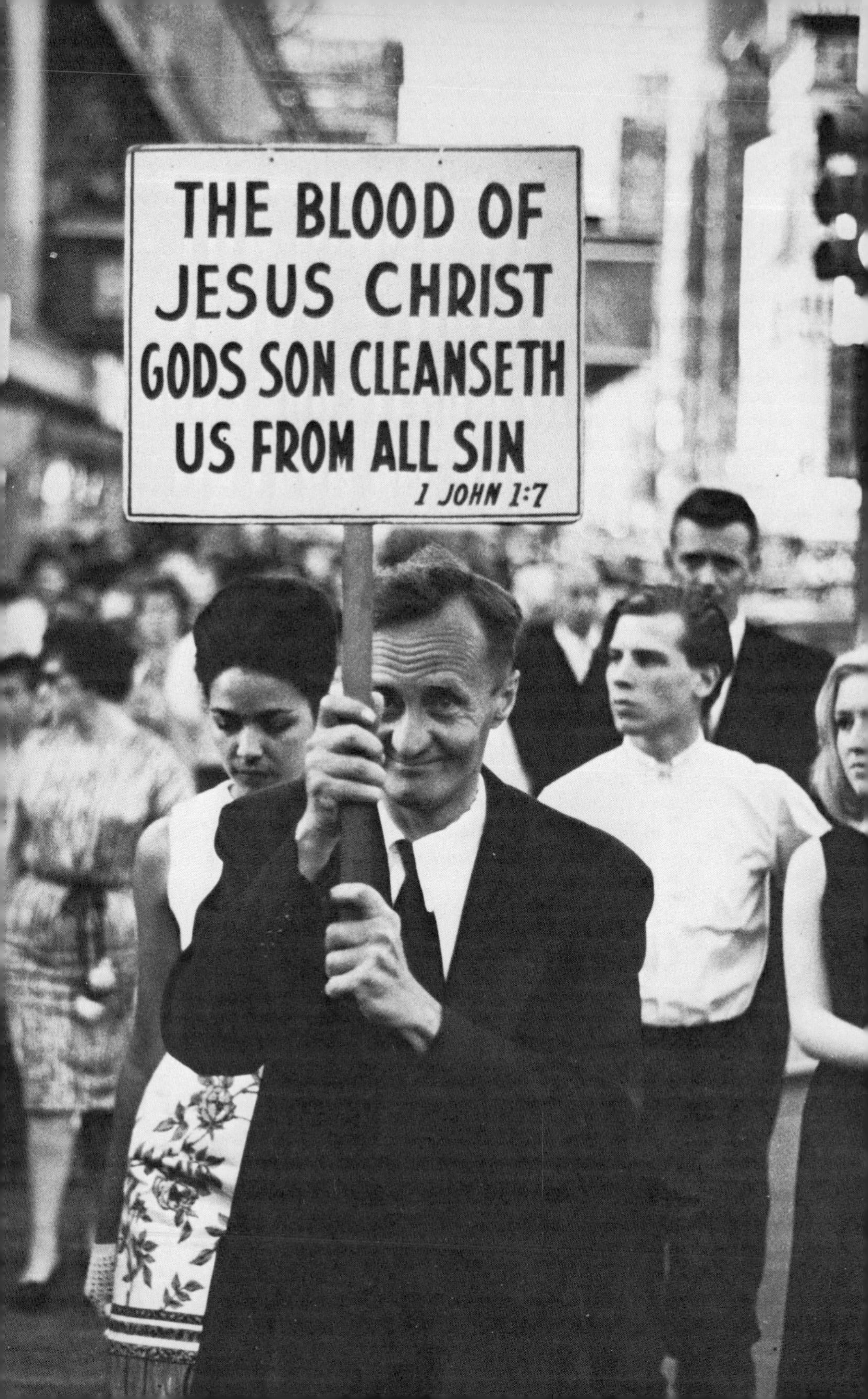
THE BLOOD OF
JESUS CHRIST
GODS SON CLEANSETH
US FROM ALL SIN
1 JOHN 1:7

IV
ETHICS

*Christ
and Nietzsche:
The Principles of Morals*

A NOTE OF EXPLANATION BY THE EDITOR

This section of the book is devoted to a number of problems in the field of Ethics or Moral Philosophy. One of the oldest and most frequently debated issues in Ethics is the opposition between selfishness and self-sacrifice, or "egoism" and "altruism." Most "official" or establishment moralists simply assume that selfishness is bad and that sacrificing oneself for others is the highest form of virtue. Yet all of us, I suspect, have a secret feeling that the martyr is a bit peculiar, and that maybe it isn't all that terrible to put yourself first now and then.

The best-known contemporary defender of selfishness as right, justified, indeed even **virtuous,** is the widely read novelist Ayn Rand. In her best-selling works, **The Fountainhead** and **Atlas Shrugged,** Miss Rand expounds a philosophy of "objectivism," according to which absolute, uncompromising self-interest is the highest moral principle. Because she has a large following, and also because she writes so vividly, I had hoped to include a selection from one of Miss Rand's novels in the opening pages of this section. What better way, I thought, to pose the moral dilemma with force and contemporary relevance.

Now, the law requires me to obtain permission from the copyright-holder of any selection I wish to reprint. I wrote to Random House, Inc., the publishers of Miss Rand's novel **Atlas Shrugged,** requesting that permission. The Random House permissions department replied as follows:

> We will have to obtain Miss Rand's approval of your use of selections from **For the New Intellectual.** Before she grants approval, she would like to see those portions of your manuscript which contain any comments about her and/or her philosophy and she would also like to see the context in which the selections from her work will be used.

I was absolutely astonished by this extraordinary demand. In all my years as an author and editor, I had never seen anything even remotely like it. What made the matter worse, Miss Rand is the apostle of absolute liberty, the high priestess of individualism. In order to submit to her demand, I would have to violate every tenet of her own philosophy. Accordingly, I wrote the following letter to Miss Rand:

> Dear Miss Rand:
> The Permissions Department of Random House informs me that in order to obtain permission to reprint a selection from John Galt's speech in an introduction to Philosophy that I am editing, I must submit to you "those portions of the manuscript which contain any comments about you and/or your philosophy" together with an indication of the context in which the selection will be used. As I am sure you will understand, I cannot possibly submit to so humiliating an enslavement of my intellect. During my entire adult life, I have permitted no one to censor what I wrote or said, either directly or indirectly. As I have not yet written the editorial material which would accompany the selections from your writings, I cannot now be certain what it will contain, but when I come to write it, I will say what I have to say without overtly or covertly trimming my remarks to meet the approval of any other person.

As it happens, I disagree completely with your philosophy. And, indeed, that is one of the reasons why I wish to include a statement of it in my book. I would, of course, be happy to show you a copy of the selections I would like to use, so you may be sure that I have not distorted your thought in the process of selecting. However, if you do not have enough confidence in the power of your own ideas to stand behind them, no matter what the surrounding contexts or their position, then I am afraid that I really don't want you in my book at all.

I hope that you will agree to my request for permission to reprint a selection from John Galt's speech. Awaiting your reply, I am,

Yours sincerely,
Robert Paul Wolff

Not even according me the courtesy of a direct reply, Miss Rand informed me through her lawyer that she would not give her permission to reprint John Galt's speech. When I called her lawyer for an explanation, he refused to come to the phone.

Well, the law is the law, so you will not read anything by Ayn Rand in this book. Instead, I have chosen a very pungent passage from the nineteenth-century philosopher who has clearly influenced Miss Rand's thought, namely, Friedrich Nietzsche. If you wish to confront "objectivism" directly, you will have to buy one of Ayn Rand's books.

INTRODUCTION TO THE CONTEMPORARY ISSUE

As I explained in the preceding note, this section somewhat breaks the pattern which has been established in Sections I through III. We begin, as before, with a dispute which leads us into a number of deeper philosophical questions, but the authors of our introductory selections are not quite "contemporary" in the usual sense. Nietzsche was a nineteenth-century German philosopher, and Jesus lived almost two thousand years ago. Still, I agree with Kierkegaard that we are as close to Jesus—or as far from Him— as the men and women who gathered round Him on that hill in Galilee. If the New Testament has ever been relevant at all, then it is as relevant today as it was when the Sermon on the Mount was first preached.

The Bible is familiar to you all, but you might find it useful to have a few words of explanation of the passage from Nietzsche's **Geneology of Morals.** Nietzsche writes very bitterly about the Jews as the authors of what he calls "slave morality," and it would be easy to read him as simply a bigoted anti-Semite. On closer inspection, however, it is clear that Nietzsche's real target is not the Jews themselves, but the ethic of humility, self-sacrifice, and nonviolence which all the great religions have preached. For Nietzsche, Christianity is as bad as Judaism, and we may assume that he would be equally opposed to Buddhism, Hinduism, and the moral teachings of Confucius.

Nietzsche's great strength is his deep insight into the hidden emotional wellsprings of the ethics of altruism and humility. He insists that frustrated hostility lurks behind the meekness of Jesus' beatitudes. The low and weak of the earth, unable to express their natural aggression toward others, make a virtue of their impotence and celebrate the goodness of the underdog. But in their fantasies of a life after death, Nietzsche claims, they reveal the intensity of their bitterness; they comfort themselves that God will do to their enemies, in Hell, what they cannot do to those enemies on earth.

Underlying Nietzsche's attacks on established morality is an argument which can be summarized in the form of a syllogism:

> In human affairs, what is contrary to human
> nature is evil.
> Meekness, humility, self-sacrifice are all
> contrary to human nature.
> Therefore, these "Christian" virtues are all evil,
> and their opposites are really good.

We can dispute Nietzsche's psychology, of course, as it is expressed in the minor premise. But even before we do that, we must question the major premise that nature is the true standard of good and evil. The theological doctrine of original sin is, among other things, a challenge to the reassuring belief that man is naturally good, and that only culture, or religion, or philosophy corrupts him. For all his shocking defiance of accepted morality, Nietzsche is perhaps really a romantic with an idealized conception of morality.

. . . (25) And there followed him great multitudes of people from Galilee, and *from* Decapolis, and *from* Jerusalem, and *from* Judea, and *from* beyond Jordan.

Chapter 5

And seeing the multitudes, he went up into a mountain: and when he was set, his disciples came unto him: (2) And he opened his mouth, and taught them, saying, (3) Blessed *are* the poor in spirit: for theirs is the kingdom of heaven. (4) Blessed *are* they that mourn: for they shall be comforted. (5) Blessed *are* the meek: for they shall inherit the earth. (6) Blessed *are* they which do hunger and thirst after righteousness: for they shall be filled. (7) Blessed *are* the merciful: for they shall obtain mercy. (8) Blessed *are* the pure in heart: for they shall see God. (9) Blessed *are* the peacemakers: for they shall be called the children of God. (10) Blessed *are* they which are persecuted for righteousness' sake: for theirs is the kingdom of heaven. (11) Blessed are *ye*, when *men* shall revile you, and persecute *you*, and shall say all manner of evil against you falsely, for my sake. (12) Rejoice, and be exceeding glad: for great *is* your reward in heaven: for so persecuted they the prophets which were before you.

(13) Ye are the salt of the earth: but if the salt have lost his savor, wherewith shall it be salted? it is thenceforth good for nothing, but to be cast out, and to be trodden under foot of men. (14) Ye are the light of the world. A city that is set on a hill cannot be hid. (15) Neither do men light a candle, and put it under a bushel, but on a candlestick; and it giveth light unto all that are in the house. (16) Let your light so shine before men, that they may see your good works, and glorify your Father which is in heaven.

(17) Think not that I am come to destroy the law, or the prophets: I am not come to destroy, but to fulfil. (18) For verily I say unto you, Till heaven and earth pass, one jot or one tittle shall in no wise pass from the law, till all be fulfilled. (19) Whosoever therefore shall break one of these least commandments, and shall teach men so, he shall be called the least in the kingdom of heaven: but whosoever shall do and teach *them*, the same shall be called great in the kingdom of heaven. (20) For I say unto you, That except your righteousness shall exceed *the righteousness* of the scribes and Pharisees, ye shall in no case enter into the kingdom of heaven.

(21) Ye have heard that it was said by them of old time, Thou shalt not kill; and whosoever shall kill shall be in danger of the judgment: (22) But I say unto you, That whosoever is angry with his brother without a cause shall be in

Matthew 4:25–7. *King James Version.*

danger of the judgment: and whosoever shall say to his brother, Raca, shall be in danger of the council: but whosoever shall say, Thou fool, shall be in danger of hell fire. (23) Therefore if thou bring thy gift to the altar, and there rememberest that thy brother hath aught against thee; (24) Leave there thy gift before the altar, and go thy way; first be reconciled to thy brother, and then come and offer thy gift. (25) Agree with thine adversary quickly, while thou art in the way with him; lest at any time the adversary deliver thee to the judge, and the judge deliver thee to the officer, and thou be cast into prison. (26) Verily I say unto thee, Thou shalt by no means come out thence, till thou hast paid the uttermost farthing.

(27) Ye have heard that it was said by them of old time, Thou shalt not commit adultery: (28) But I say unto you, That whosoever looketh on a woman to lust after her hath committed adultery with her already in his heart. (29) And if thy right eye offend thee, pluck it out, and cast *it* from thee: for it is profitable for thee that one of thy members should perish, and not *that* thy whole body should be cast into hell. (30) And if thy right hand offend thee, cut it off, and cast *it* from thee: for it is profitable for thee that one of thy members should perish, and not *that* thy whole body should be cast into hell. (31) It hath been said, Whosoever shall put away his wife, let him give her a writing of divorcement: (32) But I say unto you, That whosoever shall put away his wife, saving for the cause of fornication, causeth her to commit adultery: and whosoever shall marry her that is divorced committeth adultery.

(33) Again, ye have heard that it hath been said by them of old time, Thou shalt not forswear thyself, but shalt perform unto the Lord thine oaths: (34) But I say unto you, Swear not at all; neither by heaven; for it is God's throne: (35) Nor by the earth; for it is his footstool: neither by Jerusalem; for it is the city of the great King. (36) Neither shalt thou swear by thy head, because thou canst not make one hair white or black. (37) But let your communication be, Yea, yea; Nay, nay: for whatsoever is more than these cometh of evil.

(38) Ye have heard that it hath been said, An eye for an eye, and a tooth for a tooth: (39) But I say unto you, That ye resist not evil: but whosoever shall smite thee on thy right cheek, turn to him the other also. (40) And if any man will sue thee at the law, and take away thy coat, let him have *thy* cloak also. (41) And whosoever shall compel thee to go a mile, go with him twain. (42) Give to him that asketh thee, and from him that would borrow of thee turn not thou away.

(43) Ye have heard that it hath been said, Thou shalt love thy neighbor, and hate thine enemy. (44) But I say unto you, Love your enemies, bless them that curse you, do good to them that hate you, and pray for them which despitefully use you, and persecute you; (45) That ye may be the children of your Father which is in heaven: for he maketh his sun to rise on the evil and on the good, and sendeth rain on the just and on the unjust. (46) For if ye love them which love you, what reward have ye? do not even the publicans

the same? (47) And if ye salute your brethren only, what do ye more *than others?* do not even the publicans so? (48) Be ye therefore perfect, even as your Father which is in heaven is perfect.

Chapter 6

Take heed that ye do not your alms before men, to be seen of them: otherwise ye have no reward of your Father which is in heaven. (2) Therefore when thou doest *thine* alms, do not sound a trumpet before thee, as the hypocrites do in the synagogues and in the streets, that they may have glory of men. Verily I say unto you, They have their reward. (3) But when thou doest alms, let not thy left hand know what thy right hand doeth: (4) That thine alms may be in secret: and thy Father which seeth in secret himself shall reward thee openly.

(5) And when thou prayest, thou shalt not be as the hypocrites *are:* for they love to pray standing in the synagogues and in the corners of the streets, that they may be seen of men. Verily I say unto you, They have their reward. (6) But thou, when thou prayest, enter into thy closet, and when thou hast shut thy door, pray to thy Father which is in secret; and thy Father which seeth in secret shall reward thee openly. (7) But when ye pray, use not vain repetitions, as the heathen *do:* for they think that they shall be heard for their much speaking. (8) Be not ye therefore like unto them: for your Father knoweth what things ye have need of, before ye ask him. (9) After this manner therefore pray ye: Our Father which art in heaven, Hallowed be thy name. (10) Thy kingdom come. Thy will be done in earth, as *it is* in heaven. (11) Give us this day our daily bread. (12) And forgive us our debts, as we forgive our debtors. (13) And lead us not into temptation, but deliver us from evil: For thine is the kingdom, and the power, and the glory, for ever. Amen. (14) For if ye forgive men their trespasses, your heavenly Father will also forgive you: (15) But if ye forgive not men their trespasses, neither will your Father forgive your trespasses.

(16) Moreover when ye fast, be not as the hypocrites, of a sad countenance: for they disfigure their faces, that they may appear unto men to fast. Verily I say unto you, They have their reward. (17) But thou, when thou fastest, anoint thine head, and wash thy face; (18) That thou appear not unto men to fast, but unto thy Father which is in secret: and thy Father which seeth in secret shall reward thee openly.

(19) Lay not up for yourselves treasures upon earth, where moth and rust doth corrupt, and where thieves break through and steal: (20) But lay up for yourselves treasures in heaven, where neither moth nor rust doth corrupt, and where thieves do not break through nor steal: (21) For where your treasure is, there will your heart be also. (22) The light of the body is the eye: if therefore thine eye be single, thy whole body shall be full of light. (23) But if

thine eye be evil, thy whole body shall be full of darkness. If therefore the light that is in thee be darkness, how great *is* that darkness!

(24) No man can serve two masters: for either he will hate the one, and love the other; or else he will hold to the one, and despise the other. Ye cannot serve God and mammon. (25) Therefore I say unto you, Take no thought for your life, what ye shall eat or what ye shall drink; nor yet for your body, what ye shall put on. Is not the life more than meat, and the body than raiment? (26) Behold the fowls of the air: for they sow not, neither do they reap, nor gather into barns; yet your heavenly Father feedeth them. Are ye not much better than they? (27) Which of you by taking thought can add one cubit unto his stature? (28) And why take ye thought for raiment? Consider the lilies of the field, how they grow; they toil not, neither do they spin: (29) And yet I say unto you, That even Solomon in all his glory was not arrayed like one of these. (30) Wherefore, if God so clothe the grass of the field, which to-day is, and to-morrow is cast into the oven, *shall he* not much more *clothe* you, O ye of little faith? (31) Therefore take no thought, saying, What shall we eat? or, What shall we drink? or, Wherewithal shall we be clothed? (32) (For after all these things do the Gentiles seek:) for your heavenly Father knoweth that ye have need of all these things. (33) But seek ye first the kingdom of God and his righteousness; and all these things shall be added unto you. (34) Take therefore no thought for the morrow: for the morrow shall take thought for the things of itself. Sufficient unto the day *is* the evil thereof.

Chapter 7

Judge not, that ye be not judged. (2) For with what judgment ye judge, ye shall be judged: and with what measure ye mete, it shall be measured to you again. (3) And why beholdest thou the mote that is in thy brother's eye, but considerest not the beam that is in thine own eye? (4) Or how wilt thou say to thy brother, Let me pull out the mote out of thine eye; and, behold, a beam *is* in thine own eye? (5) Thou hypocrite, first cast out the beam out of thine own eye; and then shall thou see clearly to cast out the mote out of thy brother's eye.

(6) Give not that which is holy unto the dogs, neither cast ye your pearls before swine, lest they trample them under their feet, and turn again and rend you.

(7) Ask, and it shall be given you; seek, and ye shall find; knock, and it shall be opened unto you: (8) For every one that asketh receiveth; and he that seeketh findeth; and to him that knocketh it shall be opened. (9) Or what man is there of you, whom if his son ask bread, will he give him a stone? (10) Or if he ask a fish, will he give him a serpent? (11) If ye then, being evil, know how to give good gifts unto your children, how much more shall your Father which is in heaven give good things to them that ask him? (12) Therefore all

things whatsoever ye would that men should do to you, do ye even so to them: for this is the law and the prophets.

(13) Enter ye in at the strait gate: for wide *is* the gate, and broad *is* the way, that leadeth to destruction, and many there be which go in thereat: (14) Because strait *is* the gate, and narrow *is* the way, which leadeth unto life, and few there be that find it.

(15) Beware of false prophets, which come to you in sheep's clothing, but inwardly they are ravening wolves. (16) Ye shall know them by their fruits. Do men gather grapes of thorns, or figs of thistles? (17) Even so every good tree bringeth forth good fruit; but a corrupt tree bringeth forth evil fruit. (18) A good tree cannot bring forth evil fruit, neither *can* a corrupt tree bring forth good fruit. (19) Every tree that bringeth not forth good fruit is hewn down, and cast into the fire. (20) Wherefore by their fruits ye shall know them.

(21) Not every one that saith unto me, Lord, Lord, shall enter into the kingdom of heaven; but he that doeth the will of my Father which is in heaven. (22) Many will say to me in that day, Lord, Lord, have we not prophesied in thy name? and in thy name have cast out devils? and in thy name done many wonderful works? (23) And then will I profess unto them, I never knew you: depart from me, ye that work iniquity.

(24) Therefore whosoever heareth these sayings of mine, and doeth them, I will liken him unto a wise man, which built his house upon a rock: (25) And the rain descended, and the floods came, and the winds blew, and beat upon that house; and it fell not: for it was founded upon a rock. (26) And every one that heareth these sayings of mine, and doeth them not, shall be likened unto a foolish man, which built his house upon the sand: (27) And the rain descended, and the floods came, and the winds blew, and beat upon that house; and it fell: and great was the fall of it. (28) And it came to pass, when Jesus had ended these sayings, the people were astonished at his doctrine: (29) For he taught them as *one* having authority, and not as the scribes.

FRIEDRICH NIETZSCHE

The Christian
Transvaluation of Values

The reader will have already surmised with what ease the priestly mode of valuation can branch off from the knightly aristocratic mode, and then develop into the very antithesis of the latter: special impetus is given to this opposition,

From *Genealogy of Morals* by Friedrich Nietzsche, First Essay, Sections 7-9. Trans. by Horace B. Samuel.

by every occasion when the castes of the priests and warriors confront each other with mutual jealousy and cannot agree over the prize. The knightly-aristocratic "values" are based on a careful cult of the physical, on a flowering, rich, and even effervescing healthiness, that goes considerably beyond what is necessary for maintaining life, on war, adventure, the chase, the dance, the tourney—on everything, in fact, which is contained in strong, free, and joyous action. The priestly-aristocratic mode of valuation is—we have seen—based on other hypotheses: it is bad enough for this class when it is a question of war! Yet the priests are, as is notorious, *the worst enemies*—why? Because they are the weakest. Their weakness causes their hate to expand into a monstrous and sinister shape, a shape which is most crafty and most poisonous. The really great haters in the history of the world have always been priests, who are also the cleverest haters—in comparison with the cleverness of priestly revenge, every other piece of cleverness is practically negligible. Human history would be too fatuous for anything were it not for the cleverness imported into it by the weak—take at once the most important instance. All the world's efforts against the "aristocrats," the "mighty," the "masters," the "holders of power" are negligible by comparison with what has been accomplished against those classes by *the Jews*—the Jews, that priestly nation which eventually realised that the one method of effecting satisfaction on its enemies and tyrants was by means of a radical transvaluation of values, which was at the same time an act of the *cleverest revenge*. Yet the method was only appropriate to a nation of priests, to a nation of the most jealously nursed priestly revengefulness. It was the Jews who, in opposition to the aristocratic equation (good = aristocratic = beautiful = happy = loved by the gods), dared with a terrifying logic to suggest the contrary equation, and indeed to maintain with the teeth of the most profound hatred (the hatred of weakness) this contrary equation, namely, "the wretched are alone the good; the poor, the weak, the lowly, are alone the good; the suffering, the needy, the sick, the loathsome, are the only ones who are pious, the only ones who are blessed, for them alone is salvation—but you, on the other hand, you aristocrats, you men of power, you are to all eternity the evil, the horrible, the covetous, the insatiate, the godless; eternally also shall you be the unblessed, the cursed, the damned!" We know who it was who reaped the heritage of this Jewish transvaluation. In the context of the monstrous and inordinately fateful initiative which the Jews have exhibited in connection with this most fundamental of all declarations of war, I remember the passage which came to my pen on another occasion (*Beyond Good and Evil*, Aph. 195)—that it was, in fact, with the Jews that the *revolt of the slaves* begins in the sphere *of morals;* that revolt which has behind it a history of two millennia, and which at the present day has only moved out of our sight, because it—has achieved victory.

But you understand this not? You have no eyes for a force which has taken two thousand years to achieve victory?—There is nothing wonderful in this: all *lengthy* processes are hard to see and to realise. But *this* is what took place: from the trunk of that tree of revenge and hate, Jewish hate,—that most profound and sublime hate, which creates ideals and changes old values to new creations, the like of which has never been on earth,—there grew a phenomenon which was equally incomparable, *a new love*, the most profound and sublime of all kinds of love;—and from what other trunk could it have grown? But beware of supposing that this love has soared on its upward growth, as in any way a real negation of that thirst for revenge, as an antithesis to the Jewish hate! No, the contrary is the truth! This love grew out of that hate, as its crown, as its triumphant crown, circling wider and wider amid the clarity and fulness of the sun, and pursuing in the very kingdom of light and height its goal of hatred, its victory, its spoil, its strategy, with the same intensity with which the roots of that tree of hate sank into everything which was deep and evil with increasing stability and increasing desire. This Jesus of Nazareth, the incarnate gospel of love, this "Redeemer" bringing salvation and victory to the poor, the sick, the sinful—was he not really temptation in its most sinister and irresistible form, temptation to take the tortuous path to those very *Jewish* values and those very Jewish ideals? Has not Israel really obtained the final goal of its sublime revenge, by the tortuous paths of this "Redeemer," for all that he might pose as Israel's adversary and Israel's destroyer? Is it not due to the black magic of a really *great* policy of revenge, of a far-seeing, burrowing revenge, both acting and calculating with slowness, that Israel himself must repudiate before all the world the actual instrument of his own revenge and nail it to the cross, so that all the world—that is, all the enemies of Israel—could nibble without suspicion at this very bait? Could, moreover, any human mind with all its elaborate ingenuity invent a bait that was more truly *dangerous?* Anything that was even equivalent in the power of its seductive, intoxicating, defiling, and corrupting influence to that symbol of the holy cross, to that awful paradox of a "god on the cross," to that mystery of the unthinkable, supreme, and utter horror of the self-crucifixion of a god for the *salvation of man?* It is at least certain that *sub hoc signo* Israel, with its revenge and transvaluation of all values, has up to the present always triumphed again over all other ideals, over all more aristocratic ideals.

"But why do you talk of nobler ideals? Let us submit to the facts; that the people have triumphed—or the slaves, or the populace, or the herd, or whatever name you care to give them—if this has happened through the Jews, so be it! In that case no nation ever had a greater mission in the world's history. The 'masters' have been done away with; the morality of the vulgar man has triumphed. This triumph may also be called a blood-poisoning (it has mutually fused the races)—I do not dispute it; but there is no doubt but that this intoxication has succeeded. The 'redemption' of the human race (that is, from the masters) is progressing swimmingly; everything is obviously becoming Judaised, or Christianised, or vulgarised (what is there in the words?). It seems impossible to stop the course of this poisoning through the whole body politic of mankind—but its *tempo* and pace may from the present time be slower, more delicate, quieter, more discreet—there is time enough. In view of this context has the Church nowadays any necessary purpose? Has it, in fact, a right to live? Or could man get on without it? *Quæritur.* It seems that it fetters and retards this tendency, instead of accelerating it. Well, even that might be its utility. The Church certainly is a crude and boorish institution, that is repugnant to an intelligence with any pretence at delicacy, to a really modern taste. Should it not at any rate learn to be somewhat more subtle? It alienates nowadays, more than it allures. Which of us would, forsooth, be a freethinker if there were no Church? It is the Church which repels us, *not* its poison—apart from the Church we like the poison." This is the epilogue of a freethinker to my discourse, of an honourable animal (as he has given abundant proof), and a democrat to boot, he had up to that time listened to me, and could not endure my silence, but for me, indeed, with regard to this topic there is much on which to be silent.

COMMENTARY ON THE CONTEMPORARY ISSUE

It isn't completely fair to Nietzsche to put him up against the Sermon on the Mount—a man would have to be more than just a great philosopher to be a match for the Bible! Nevertheless, the pair of readings poses starkly one of the great dilemmas of the moral life: the conflict between the concerns of the self and the needs, interests, and welfare of **others.** Drawing on the Latin words for "I" (**ego**) and "other" (**alter**), philosophers label this the problem of **egoism** versus **altruism.** Some philosophers describe the problem as a conflict between the call of duty and the lure of inclination, for they assume that we are naturally inclined to serve our own self-interests, whereas duty tells us to make allowance for the interests of others.

In their attempts to settle such ethical disputes as the conflict between egotism and altruism, philosophers have frequently searched for some First Principle of morals, to which all parties could make appeal in cases of disagreement. Some of the first principles which have been proposed lay great emphasis on the effects of our actions. Look to the consequences, they say, if you wish to know whether an action is right or wrong. Other candidates for the title of First Principle concentrate instead on the reasons which men have for their actions. These principles tell us to look at the motives, not the consequences.

In this section, both approaches are represented by their most famous champions. The consequence-oriented, or "teleological," position is expressed by John Stuart Mill in his classic exposition of the "Greatest Happiness" Principle of Utilitarianism. According to Mill, the moral value of an act is determined by estimating the total amount of happiness and unhappiness that it is likely to produce in everyone who is affected by it. The crucial point, of course, is that we are to count everyone's feelings, not just our own.

Totally opposed to utilitarianism is the motive-oriented "Formalism" of Immanuel Kant. Kant's Categorical Imperative commands us to judge actions by the logical consistency and rationality of the reasons which guide them, rather than by their consequences. The dispute between the teleological and formalist positions, as represented here by Mill and Kant, is as absolute a disagreement as one will find in philosophical writings.

When philosophers confront one another in this apparently irreconcilable fashion, they often turn to an examination of the terms of the dispute, in an effort to see whether the dispute grows out of a conceptual confusion. They try to **dissolve** the controversy when they find that they cannot **solve** it.

Both Edward Westermarck and Alfred J. Ayer try this tactic in order to bring the ancient ethical disputes to a close. Westermarck, relying heavily on anthropological evidence of cultural variations in norms, insists that all ethical judgements are relative to the culture of the speaker. When two men differ on the rightness of capital punishment or the bindingness of promises, they are likely to be merely expressing the different norms of their societies. The search for transcultural moral principles is fruitless, Westermarck insists.

Ayer carries the process of dissolving even further. According to the "Emotive Theory" of ethical language, which Ayer espouses, moral judgments are not strictly statements at all. They assert nothing, and hence cannot be either true or false. All the old ethical arguments are therefore mere pseudo-arguments, or confusions.

The opening selection by Bishop Butler speaks directly to the dispute between egoism and altruism. By clarifying both notions and sweeping away certain common errors concerning self-love, Butler prepares the way for the deeper arguments of Kant and Mill. The concluding essay, by the modern American novelist and philosopher William Gass, pulls us up short in our ethical reasonings and reminds us, in a thoroughly healthy way, that beneath the philosophical disputes lie living, breathing human beings.

BUTLER

In this well-known sermon, Bishop Joseph Butler (1692–1752) refutes the old cynical saying that men act only from a motive of self-love, that beneath the surface of generosity, sympathy, or benevolence, there always lurks the egoistic thought: "Will I get pleasure from this act?" As we shall see later, Jeremy Bentham made this egoistic law of human psychology the foundation of his utilitarian philosophy.

Oddly enough, defenders of the doctrine of egoism tend to forget that hatred is as much a form of altruism as love. People who refuse to believe that I could ever help *another person out of genuine friendship or love, nevertheless are perfectly willing to grant that I might* hurt *someone out of hatred. Yet both cases are equally in contradiction with the egoistic theory.*

Butler's lengthy analysis of egoism and altruism turns on a single fundamental distinction. It is one thing to say that a man gets pleasure from accomplishing the end of his action, and quite another to say that the expectation of that pleasure is his reason for *acting. For example, I frequently eat because I am hungry. I may get pleasure from the food, but that is not my reason for eating. Sometimes, however, I eat even though I am not hungry, because I like the food that is offered and hope to get pleasure from eating it. Butler argues that it is wrong to confuse these two cases and claim that I* always *eat in order to get pleasure.*

Exactly the same distinction can be made in actions directed toward others. When I give a friend a birthday present, I may get pleasure from the fact that he likes it. But my reason for *giving the present is to give* him *pleasure. That is why I make sure to choose something he will like.*

Now, the egoist replies that I only give the present in order to get the pleasure which comes from watching my friend's face light up. But this is a mistake, for if I did not really want my friend to be pleased, I would not myself get pleasure from his reaction. In other words, the fact that I get pleasure from causing someone else to be happy proves that I genuinely wanted him to be happy. And that is all the altruist is claiming.

Upon the Love of
Our Neighbour

Every man hath a general desire of his own happiness; and likewise a variety of particular affections, passions, and appetites, to particular external objects. The former proceeds from, or is, self-love, and seems inseparable from all sensible creatures, who can reflect upon themselves and their own interest or happiness, so as to have that interest an object to their minds: what is to be said of the latter is, that they proceed from, or together make up, that particular nature, according to which man is made. The object the former pursues is somewhat internal, our own happiness, enjoyment, satisfaction; whether we have or have not a distinct particular perception what it is, or wherein it consists: the objects of the latter are this or that particular external thing, which the affections tend towards, and of which it hath always a particular idea or perception. The principle we call self-love never seeks anything external for the sake of the thing, but only as a means of happiness or good: particular affections rest in the external things themselves. One belongs to man as a reasonable creature reflecting upon his own interest or happiness; the other, though quite distinct from reason, are as much a part of human nature.

That all particular appetites and passions are towards *external things themselves*, distinct from the *pleasure arising from them*, is manifested from hence, that there could not be this pleasure, were it not for that prior suitableness between the object and the passion: there could be no enjoyment or delight for one thing more than another, from eating food more than from swallowing a stone, if there were not an affection or appetite to one thing more than another.

Every particular affection, even the love of our neighbour, is as really our own affection, as self-love; and the pleasure arising from its gratification is as much my own pleasure, as the pleasure self-love would have from knowing I myself should be happy some time hence, would be my own pleasure. And if, because every particular affection is a man's own, and the pleasure arising from its gratification his own pleasure, or pleasure to himself, such particular affection must be called self-love. According to this way of speaking, no creature whatever can possibly act but merely from self-love; and every action and every affection whatever is to be resolved up into this one principle. But then this is not the language of mankind: or, if it were, we should want words to express the difference between the principle of an action, proceeding from cool consideration that it will be to my own advantage; and an action, suppose of revenge, or of friendship, by which a man runs upon certain ruin, to do evil or good to another. It is manifest the principles of these actions are totally

Sermon XI, preached on Advent Sunday, from *Fifteen Sermons upon Human Nature* by Joseph Butler. London, 1726.

different, and so want different words to be distinguished by: all that they agree in is, that they both proceed from, and are done to gratify an inclination in a man's self. But the principle or inclination in one case is self-love; in the other, hatred, or love of another. There is then a distinction between the cool principle of self-love, or general desire of our own happiness, as one part of our nature, and one principle of action; and the particular affections towards particular external objects, as another part of our nature, and another principle of action. How much soever, therefore, is to be allowed to self-love, yet it cannot be allowed to be the whole of our inward constitution; because, you see, there are other parts or principles which come into it.

Further, private happiness or good is all which self-love can make us desire or be concerned about. In having this consists its gratification; it is an affection to ourselves—a regard to our own interest, happiness, and private good: and in the proportion a man hath this, he is interested, or a lover of himself. Let this be kept in mind, because there is commonly, as I shall presently have occasion to observe, another sense put upon these words. On the other hand, particular affections tend towards particular external things; these are their objects; having these is their end; in this consists their gratification: no matter whether it be, or be not, upon the whole, our interest or happiness. An action, done from the former of these principles, is called an interested action. An action, proceeding from any of the latter, has its denomination of passionate, ambitious, friendly, revengeful, or any other, from the particular appetite or affection from which it proceeds. Thus self-love, as one part of human nature, and the several particular principles as the other part, are themselves, their objects, and ends, stated and shown.

From hence it will be easy to see how far, and in what ways, each of these can contribute and be subservient to the private good of the individual. Happiness does not consist in self-love. The desire of happiness is no more the thing itself, than the desire of riches is the possession or enjoyment of them. People may love themselves with the most entire and unbounded affection, and yet be extremely miserable. Neither can self-love any way help them out, but by setting them on work to get rid of the causes of their misery, to gain or make use of those objects which are by nature adapted to afford satisfaction. Happiness or satisfaction consists only in the enjoyment of those objects which are by nature suited to our several particular appetites, passions, and affections. So that if self-love wholly engrosses us, and leaves no room for any other principle, there can be absolutely no such thing at all as happiness or enjoyment of any kind whatever; since happiness consists in the gratification of particular passions, which supposes the having of them. Self-love then does not constitute *this* or *that* to be our interest or good; but our interest of good being constituted by nature and supposed self-love, only puts us upon obtaining and securing it. Therefore, if it be possible that self-love may prevail and exert itself in a degree or manner which is not subservient to this end, then it will not follow that our interest will be promoted in proportion to the degree in which that principle engrosses us, and prevails over others. Nay, further, the private and contracted affection, when it is not subservient to this end, private good, may, for anything that appears, have a direct contrary tendency and effect. And if we will consider the matter, we shall see that it often really has. Disengagement is absolutely necessary to enjoyment; and a person may have so steady and fixed an eye upon his own interest, whatever he places it in, as may hinder him from attending to many gratifications within his reach, which others have their minds free and open to. Overfondness for a child is not generally thought to be for its advantage; and, if there be any guess to be made from appearances, surely that character we call *selfish* is not the most promising for happiness. Such a temper may plainly be, and exert itself in a degree and manner which may give unnecessary and useless solicitude and anxiety, in a degree and manner which may prevent obtaining the means and materials of enjoyment, as well as the making use of them. Immoderate self-love does very ill consult its own interest; and how much soever a paradox it may appear, it is certainly true, that, even from self-love, we should endeavour to get over all inordinate regard to, and consideration of, ourselves. Every one of our passions and affections hath its natural stint and bound, which may easily be exceeded; whereas our enjoyments can possibly be but in a determinate measure and degree. Therefore such excess of the affection, since it cannot procure any enjoyment, must in all cases be useless, but is generally attended with inconveniences, and often is down-right pain and misery. This holds as much with regard to self-love as to all other affections. The natural degree of it, so far as it sets us on work to gain and make use of the materials of satisfaction, may be to our real advantage: but beyond or beside this, it is in several respects an inconvenience and disadvantage. Thus it appears that private interest is so far from being likely to be promoted in proportion to the degree in which self-love engrosses us, and prevails over all other principles, that *the contracted affection may be so prevalent as to disappoint itself and even contradict its own end, private good.*

"But who, except the most sordidly covetous, ever thought there was any rivalship between the love of greatness, honour, power, or between sensual appetites, and self-love? No; there is a perfect harmony between them. It is by means of these particular appetites and affections that self-love is gratified in enjoyment, happiness, and satisfaction. The competition and rivalship is between self-love and the love of our neighbour. That affection which leads us out of ourselves, makes us regardless of our own interest, and substitute that of another in its stead." Whether then there be any peculiar competition and contrariety in this case, shall now be considered.

Self-love and interestedness was stated to consist in or be an affection to ourselves, a regard to our own private good: it is, therefore, distinct from benevolence, which is an affection to the good of our fellow-creatures. But that benevolence is distinct from, that is, not the same thing with self-love, is no reason for its being looked upon with any peculiar suspicion, because every principle whatever, by means of which self-love is gratified, is distinct from

it. And all things, which are distinct from each other, are equally so. A man has
an affection or aversion to another: that one of these tends to, and is gratified
by doing good, that the other tends to, and is gratified by doing harm, does not
in the least alter the respect which either one or the other of these inward
feelings has to self-love. We use the word *property* so as to exclude any other
persons having an interest in that, of which we say a particular man has the
property: and we often use the word *selfish* so as to exclude in the same manner all regards to the good of others. But the cases are not parallel: for though
that exclusion is really part of the idea of property, yet such positive exclusion,
or bringing this peculiar disregard to the good of others into the idea of self-
love, is in reality adding to the idea, or changing it from what it was before
stated to consist in, namely, in an affection to ourselves. This being the whole
idea of self-love, it can no otherwise exclude good-will or love of others, than
merely by not including it, no otherwise than it excludes love of arts, or
reputation, or of anything else. Neither, on the other hand, does benevolence,
any more than love of arts or reputation, exclude self-love. Love of our neighbour, then has just the same respect to, is no more distant from self-love, than
hatred of our neighbour, or than love and hatred of anything else. Thus the
principles, from which men rush upon certain ruin for the destruction of an
enemy, and for the preservation of a friend, have the same respect to the
private affection, are equally interested, or equally disinterested; and it is of no
avail, whether they are said to be one or the other. Therefore, to those who
are shocked to hear virtue spoken of as disinterested, it may be allowed, that it
is indeed absurd to speak thus of it; unless hatred, several particular instances of
vice, and all the common affections and aversions in mankind, are acknowledged to be disinterested too. Is there any less inconsistence between the love
of inanimate things, or of creatures merely sensitive, and self-love, than between self-love, and the love of our neighbour? Is desire of, and delight in the
happiness of another any more a diminution of self-love, than desire of and
delight in the esteem of another? They are both equally desire of and delight
in somewhat external to ourselves: either both or neither are so. The object of
self-love is expressed in the term self: and every appetite of sense, and every
particular affection of the heart, are equally interested or disinterested, because
the objects of them are all equally self or somewhat else. Whatever ridicule,
therefore, the mention of a disinterested principle or action may be supposed
to lie open to, must, upon the matter being thus stated, relate to ambition, and
every appetite and particular affection, as much as to benevolence. And indeed all the ridicule, and all the grave perplexity, of which this subject hath
had its full share, is merely from words. The most intelligible way of speaking
of it seems to be this: that self-love, and the actions done in consequence of
it (for these will presently appear to be the same as to this question), are interested; that particular affections toward external objects, and the actions
done in consequence of those affections, are not so. But every one is at liberty
to use words as he pleases. All that is here insisted upon is, that ambition,

revenge, benevolence, all particular passions whatever, and the actions they produce, are equally interested or disinterested.

Thus it appears, that there is no peculiar contrariety between self-love and benevolence; no greater competition between these, than between any other particular affections and self-love. This relates to the affections themselves. Let us now see whether there be any peculiar contrariety between the respective courses of life which these affections lead to; whether there be any greater competition between the pursuit of private and of public good, than between any other particular pursuits and that of private good.

There seems no other reason to suspect that there is any such peculiar contrariety, but only that the course of action which benevolence leads to, has a more direct tendency to promote the good of others, than that course of action, which love of reputation, suppose, or any other particular affection, leads to. But that any affection tends to the happiness of another, does not hinder its tending to one's own happiness too. That others enjoy the benefit of the air and the light of the sun, does not hinder but that these are as much one's own private advantage now, as they would be if we had the property of them exclusive of all others. So a pursuit which tends to promote the good of another, yet may have as great tendency to promote private interest, as a pursuit which does not tend to the good of another at all, or which is mischievous to him. All particular affections whatever, resentment, benevolence, love of the arts, equally lead to a course of action for their own gratification, *i. e.*, the gratification of ourselves: and the gratification of each gives delight: so far, then, it is manifest they have all the same respect to private interest. Now, take into consideration further, concerning these three pursuits, that the end of the first is the harm; of the second, the good of another; of the last, somewhat indifferent: and is there any necessity, that these additional considerations should alter the respect which we before saw these three pursuits had to private interest; or render any one of them less conducive to it than any other? Thus, one man's affection is to honour, as his end; in order to obtain which, he thinks no pains too great. Suppose another, with such a singularity of mind, as to have the same affection to public good, as his end, which he endeavours with the same labour to obtain. In case of success, surely the man of benevolence hath as great enjoyment as the man of ambition; they both equally having the end, their affections, in the same degree, tended to; but in case of disappointment, the benevolent man has clearly the advantage; since endeavouring to do good, considered as a various pursuit, is gratified by his own consciousness, *i. e.*, is in a degree its own reward.

And as to these two, or benevolence and any other particular passions whatever, considered in a further view, as forming a general temper, which more or less disposes us for enjoyment of all the common blessings of life, distinct from their own gratification: is benevolence less the temper of tranquility and freedom, than ambition or covetousness? Does the benevolent man appear less easy with himself, from his love to his neighbour? Does he less relish his being? Is there any peculiar gloom seated on his face? Is his mind less open to entertainment, or to any particular gratification? Nothing is more manifest, than that being in good humour, which is benevolence whilst it lasts, is itself the temper of satisfaction and enjoyment.

Suppose, then, a man sitting down to consider how he might become most easy to himself, and attain the greatest pleasure he could; all that which is his real natural happiness; this can only consist in the enjoyment of those objects which are by nature adapted to our several faculties. These particular enjoyments make up the sum total of our happiness, and they are supposed to arise from riches, honours, and the gratification of sensual appetites. Be it so: yet none profess themselves so completely happy in these enjoyments, but that there is room left in the mind for others, if they were presented to them. Nay, these, as much as they engage us, are not thought so high, but that human nature is capable even of greater. Now there have been persons in all ages, who have professed that they found satisfaction in the exercise of charity, in the love of their neighbour, in endeavouring to promote the happiness of all they had to do with, and in the pursuit of what is just, and right, and good, as the general bent of their mind and end of their life; and that doing an action of baseness or cruelty, would be as great violence to *their* self, as much breaking in upon their nature, as any external force. Persons of this character would add, if they might be heard, that they consider themselves as acting in the view of an infinite Being, who is in a much higher sense the object of reverence and of love, than all the world besides; and, therefore, they could have no more enjoyment from a wicked action done under his eye, than the persons to whom they are making their apology could, if all mankind were the spectators of it; and that the satisfaction of approving themselves to his unerring judgment, to whom they thus refer all their actions, is a more continued settled satisfaction than any this world can afford; as also that they have, no less than others, a mind free and open to all the common innocent gratifications of it such as they are. And, if we go no further, does there appear any absurdity in this? Will any one take upon him to say, that a man cannot find his account in this general course of life, as much as in the most unbounded ambition, or the excesses of pleasure? Or that such a person has not consulted so well for himself, for the satisfaction and peace of his own mind, as the ambitious or dissolute man? And though the consideration, that God himself will in the end justify their taste, and support their cause, is not formally to be insisted upon here; yet this much comes in, that all enjoyments whatever are much more clear and unmixed, from the assurance that they will end well. It is certain, then, that there is nothing in these pretensions to happiness, especially when there are not wanting persons, who have supported themselves with satisfactions of this kind in sickness, poverty, disgrace, and in the very pangs of death? whereas, it is manifest all other enjoyments fail in these circumstances. This surely looks suspicious of having somewhat in it. Self-love, methinks, should be alarmed. May she not possibly pass over greater pleasures, than those she is so wholly taken up with?

The short of the matter is no more than this. Happiness consists in the gratification of certain affections, appetites, passions, with objects which are by nature adapted to them. Self-love may indeed set us on work to gratify these: but happiness or enjoyment has no immediate connexion with self-love, but arises from such gratification alone. Love of our neighbour is one of those affections. This, considered as a virtuous principle, is gratified by a consciousness of endeavouring to promote the good of others: but considered as a natural affection, its gratification consists in the actual accomplishment of this endeavour. Now, indulgence or gratification of this affection, whether in that consciousness, or this accomplishment, has the same respect to interest, as indulgence of any other affection; they equally proceed from, or do not proceed from, self-love; they equally include, or equally exclude, this principle. Thus it appears, that "benevolence and the pursuit of public good have at least as great respect to self-love and the pursuit of private good, as any other particular passions, and their respective pursuits."

Neither is covetousness, whether as a temper or pursuit, any exception to this. For if by covetousness is meant the desire and pursuit of riches for their own sake, without any regard to or consideration of the uses of them; this hath as little to do with self-love, as benevolence hath. But by this word is usually meant, not such madness and total distraction of mind, but immoderate affection to and pursuit of riches as possessions, in order to some further end; namely, satisfaction, interest, or good. This, therefore, is not a particular affection, or particular pursuit, but it is the general principle of self-love, and the general pursuit of our own interest; for which reason, the word *selfish* is by every one appropriated to this temper and pursuit. Now, as it is ridiculous to assert that self-love and the love of our neighbour are the same; so neither is it asserted that following these different affections hath the same tendency and respect to our own interest. The comparison is not between self-love and the love of our neighbour; between pursuit of our own interest, and the interest of others; but between the several particular affections in human nature towards external objects, as one part of the comparison; and the one particular affection to the good of our neighbour, as the one part of it: and it has been shown, that all these have the same respect to self-love and private interest.

There is indeed frequently an inconsistence, or interfering between self-love or private interest, and the several particular appetites, passions, affections, or the pursuits they lead to. But this competition or interfering is merely accidental, and happens much oftener between pride, revenge, sensual gratifications, and private interest, than between private interest and benevolence. For nothing is more common than to see men give themselves up to a passion or an affection to their known prejudice and ruin, and in direct contradiction to manifest and real interest, and the loudest calls of self-love: whereas the seeming competitions and interfering between benevolence and private interest, relate much more to the materials or means of enjoyment, than to enjoyment itself. There is often an interfering in the former, where there is none in the latter. Thus, as to riches: so much money as a man gives away, so much less will remain in his possession. Here is a real interfering. But though a man cannot possibly give without lessening his fortune, yet there are multitudes might give without lessening their own enjoyment; because they may have more than they can turn to any real use or advantage to themselves. Thus, the more thought and time any one employs about the interests and good of others, he must necessarily have less to attend his own; but he may have so ready and large a supply of his own wants, that such thought might be really useless to himself, though of great service and assistance to others.

The general mistake, that there is some greater inconsistence between endeavouring to promote the good of another and self-interest, than between self-interest and pursuing anything else, seems, as hath already been hinted to arise from our notions of property; and to be carried on by this property's being supposed to be itself our happiness or good. People are so very much taken up with this one subject, that they seem from it to have formed a general way of thinking, which they apply to other things that they have nothing to do with. Hence, in a confused and slight way, it might well be taken for granted, that another's having no interest in affection (*i. e.*, his good not being the object of it), renders, as one may speak, the proprietor's interest in it greater; and that if another had an interest in it, this would render his less, or occasion that such affection could not be so friendly to self-love, or conducive to private good, as an affection or pursuit which has not a regard to the good of another. This, I say, might be taken for granted, whilst it was not attended to, that the object of every particular affection is equally somewhat external to ourselves: and whether it be the good of another person, or whether it be any other external thing, makes no alteration with regard to its being one's own affection, and the gratification of it one's own private enjoyment. And so far as it is taken for granted, that barely having the means and materials of enjoyment is what constitutes interest and happiness; that our interest and good consists in possessions themselves, in having the property of riches, houses, lands, gardens, not in the enjoyment of them; so far it will even more strongly be taken for granted, in the way already explained, that an affection's conducing to the good of another, must even necessarily occasion it to conduce less to private good, if not to be positively detrimental to it. For, if property and happiness are one and the same thing, as by increasing the property of another, you lessen your own property, so by promoting the happiness of another, you must lessen your own happiness. But whatever occasioned the mistake, I hope it has been fully proved to be one; as it has been proved, that there is no peculiar rivalship or competition between self-love and benevolence; that as there may be a competition between these two, so there may also between any particular affection whatever and self-love; that every particular affection, benevolence among the rest, is subservient to self-love, by being the instrument of private enjoyment; and that in one respect benevolence contributes more to private interest, *i. e.*, enjoyment or satisfaction, than any other of the particular common affections, as it is in a degree its own gratification.

And to all these things may be added, that religion, from whence arises our strongest obligation to benevolence, so far from disowning the principle of self-love, that it often addresses itself to that very principle, and always to the mind in that state when reason presides; and there can no access be had to the understanding, but by convincing men, that the course of life we would persuade them to is not contrary to their interest. It may be allowed, without any prejudice to the cause of virtue and religion, that our ideas of happiness and misery are, of all our ideas, the nearest and most important to us; that they will, nay, if you please, that they ought to prevail over those of order, and beauty, and harmony, and proportion, if there should ever be, as it is impossible there ever should be, any inconsistency between them; though these last, too, as expressing the fitness of action, are real as truth itself. Let it be allowed, though virtue or moral rectitude does indeed consist in affection to and pursuit of what is right and good, as such: yet that, when we sit down in a cool hour, we can either justify to ourselves this or any other pursuit, till we are convinced that it will be for our happiness, or at least not contrary to it.

KANT

The three most famous ethical principles in all of Western thought are the Golden Rule, the Greatest Happiness—or Utilitarian—Principle, and the Categorical Imperative of Immanuel Kant. Despite Kant's modest denial that his ethical theory contained anything new or original, I think it may fairly be said that no other single work has had so great an impact on moral philosophy as his short book, Foundations of the Metaphysics of Morals.

Kant's aim in the Foundations *is to discover a general moral principle which is absolutely universal in its application, unconditionally necessary in its rigor, and completely independent of the accidental particularities of time, place, or human nature. In short, Kant sought a moral principle which would be as binding on all rational creatures as the very laws of logic themselves. He thought he had found such a principle, which he called the Categorical Imperative. With this principle as a touchstone, Kant held that he could test the particular rules or maxims by which we live, in order to see whether they accord with the requirements of morality.*

The argument of the Foundation *is very difficult, and you will not be able to grasp its complete structure from the selection included here. A few introductory remarks may help you to see what Kant is driving at, so that you can form a preliminary opinion about the merits of his theory.*

Kant's central thesis is that men deserve to be praised or blamed for their actions on the basis of their motives or reasons for acting, rather than on the basis of the good or bad consequences which their actions produce. We are all familiar with the man who does the right thing for the wrong reasons—the philanthropist who gives money to charity in order to get his name in the paper rather than to help the needy, or, to use Kant's example, the grocer who is honest because it brings him business, rather than because one ought to pay one's debts. Kant insists that an action has moral worth only if it is done for the right reasons.

When we give reasons for anything, we are always implicitly appealing to some sort of general rule governing all the cases similar to the present one. For example, if I say that I am drinking water because I am thirsty (that is my reason), I am implying that water in general relieves thirst. Therefore, being thirsty would be a good reason for someone else to drink water. In other words, whatever is a good reason for one person must be an equally good reason for all other persons who find themselves in similar circumstances with similar purposes.

Now, suppose we ignore all the ways in which men differ from one another—some are old, others young; some are hungry, others are not; some like privacy, others crave company, and so forth. In short, let us abstract *from the particular characteristics of individuals, and focus* only *on the traits they have in common. What rule for action can we formulate which would be a good rule for all men—in fact, for all rational agents—irrespective of their different tastes, needs, desires, and circumstances? Obviously, there is only one answer, and it is a pretty general one at that: Act only on reasons which would be equally good reasons for all rational agents. Or, as Kant puts it in the* Foundations of the Metaphysics of Morals,

> *Act only according to that maxim by which you can at the same time will that it should become a universal law.*

This doesn't look as though it tells you very much about right and wrong, so Kant sets out some examples to show you how to apply the Categorical Imperative. The fourth example is especially relevant to our debate in this section, because it concerns our duty to help our fellow men.

The Categorical Imperative

Nothing in the world—indeed nothing even beyond the world—can possibly be conceived which could be called good without qualification except a *good will*. Intelligence, wit, judgment, and the other talents of the mind, however they may be named, or courage, resoluteness, and perseverance as qualities of temperament, are doubtless in many respects good and desirable. But they can become extremely bad and harmful if the will, which is to make use of these gifts of nature and which in its special constitution is called character, is not good. It is the same with the gifts of fortune. Power, riches, honor, even health, general well-being, and the contentment with one's condition which is called happiness, make for pride and even arrogance if there is not a good

From Immanuel Kant: *Foundations of the Metaphysics of Morals* trans. by Lewis White Beck. Indianapolis: Bobbs-Merrill Co. Copyright © 1959 by the Library of Liberal Arts, Inc. Reprinted by permission of the Liberal Arts Press Division of the Bobbs-Merrill Company, Inc.

will to correct their influence on the mind and on its principles of action so as to make it universally comfortable to its end. It need hardly be mentioned that the sight of being adorned with no feature of a pure and good will, yet enjoying uninterrupted prosperity, can never give pleasure to a rational impartial observer. Thus the good will seems to constitute the indispensable condition even of worthiness to be happy.

Some qualities seem to be conducive to this good will and can facilitate its action, but, in spite of that, they have no intrinsic unconditional worth. They rather presuppose a good will, which limits the high esteem which one otherwise rightly has for them and prevents their being held to be absolutely good. Moderation in emotions and passions, self-control, and calm deliberation not only are good in many respects but even seem to constitute a part of the inner worth of the person. But however unconditionally they were esteemed by the ancients, they are far from being good without qualification. For without the principle of good will they can become extremely bad, and the coolness of a villain makes him not only far more dangerous but also more directly abominable in our eyes than he would have seemed without it.

The good will is not good because of what it effects or accomplishes or because of its adequacy to achieve some proposed end; it is good only because of its willing, i.e., it is good of itself. And, regarded for itself, it is to be esteemed incomparably higher than anything which could be brought about by it in favor of any inclination or even of the sum total of all inclinations. Even if it should happen that, by a particularly unfortunate fate or by the niggardly provision of a stepmotherly nature, this will should be wholly lacking in power to accomplish its purpose, and if even the greatest effort should not avail it to achieve anything of its end, and if there remained only the good will (not as a mere wish but as the summoning of all the means in our power), it would sparkle like a jewel in its own right, as something that had its full worth in itself. Usefulness or fruitlessness can neither diminish nor augment this worth. Its usefulness would be only its setting, as it were, so as to enable us to handle it more conveniently in commerce or to attract the attention of those who are not yet connoisseurs, but not to recommend it to those who are experts or to determine its worth.

But there is something so strange in this idea of the absolute worth of the will alone, in which no account is taken of any use, that, not withstanding the agreement even of common sense, the suspicion must arise that perhaps only high-flown fancy is its hidden basis, and that we may have misunderstood the purpose of nature in its appointment of reason as the ruler of our will. We shall therefore examine this idea from this point of view.

In the natural constitution of an organized being, i.e., one suitably adapted to life, we assume as an axiom that no organ will be found for any purpose which is not the fittest and best adapted to that purpose. Now if its preservation, its welfare—in a word, its happiness—were the real end of nature in a being having reason and will, then nature would have hit upon a very poor arrangement in appointing the reason of the creature to be the executor of this purpose. For all the actions which the creature has to perform with this intention, and the entire rule of its conduct, would be dictated much more exactly by instinct, and that end would be far more certainly attained by instinct than it ever could be by reason. And if, over and above this, reason should have been granted to the favored creature, it would have served only to let it contemplate the happy constitution of its nature, to admire it, to rejoice in it, and to be grateful for it to its beneficent cause. But reason would not have been given in order that the being should subject its faculty of desire to that weak and delusive guidance and to meddle with the purpose of nature. In a word, nature would have taken care that reason did not break forth into practical use nor have the presumption, with its weak insight, to think out for itself the plan of happiness and the means of attaining it. Nature would have taken over not only the choice of ends but also that of the means, and with wise foresight she would have entrusted both to instinct alone.

And, in fact, we find that the more a cultivated reason deliberately devotes itself to the enjoyment of life and happiness, the more the man falls short of true contentment. From this fact there arises in many persons, if only they are candid enough to admit it, a certain degree of misology, hatred of reason. This is particularly the case with those who are most experienced in its use. After counting all the advantages which they draw—I will not say from the invention of the arts of common luxury—from the sciences (which in the end seem to be also a luxury of the understanding), they nevertheless find that they have actually brought more trouble on their shoulders instead of gaining in happiness; they finally envy, rather than despise, the common run of men who are better guided by mere natural instinct and who do not permit their reason much influence on their conduct. And we must at least admit that a morose attitude or ingratitude to the goodness with which the world is governed is by no means found always among those who temper or refute the boasting eulogies which are given of the advantages of happiness and contentment with which reason is supposed to supply us. Rather their judgment is based on the idea of another and far more worthy purpose of their existence for which, instead of happiness, their reason is properly intended, this purpose, therefore, being the supreme condition to which the private purposes of men must for the most part defer.

Reason is not, however, competent to guide the will safely with regard to its objects and the satisfaction of all our needs (which it in part multiplies), and to this end an innate instinct would have led with far more certainty. But reason is given to us as a practical faculty, i.e., one which is meant to have an influence on the will. As nature has elsewhere distributed capacities suitable to the functions they are to perform, reason's proper function must be to produce a will good in itself and not one good merely as a means, for to the former reason is absolutely essential. This will must indeed not be the sole and complete good but the highest good and the condition of all others, even of the desire for happiness. In this case it is entirely compatible with the wisdom of nature that the cultivation of reason, which is required for the former uncon- ditional purpose, at least in this life restricts in many ways—indeed can reduce to less than nothing—the achievement of the latter conditional purpose, happiness. For one perceives that nature here does not proceed unsuitably to its purpose, because reason, which recognizes its highest practical vocation in the establishment of a good will, is capable of a contentment of its own kind, i.e., one that springs from the attainment of a purpose which is determined by reason, even though this injures the ends of inclination.

We have, then, to develop the concept of a will which is to be esteemed as good of itself without regard to anything else. It dwells already in the nat- ural sound understanding and does not need so much to be taught as only to be brought to light. In the estimation of the total worth of our actions it always takes first place and is the condition of everything else. In order to show this, we shall take the concept of duty. It contains that of a good will, though with certain subjective restrictions and hindrances; but these are far from concealing it and making it unrecognizable, for they rather bring it out by contrast and make it shine forth all the brighter.

I here omit all actions which are recognized as opposed to duty, even though they may be useful in one respect or another, for with these the ques- tion does not arise at all as to whether they may be carried out *from* duty, since they conflict with it. I also pass over the actions which are really in accordance with duty and to which one has no direct inclination, rather ex- ecuting them because impelled to do so by another inclination. For it is easily decided whether an action in accord with duty is performed from duty or for some selfish purpose. It is far more difficult to note this difference when the action is in accordance with duty and, in addition, the subject has a direct inclination to do it. For example, it is in fact in accordance with duty that a dealer should not overcharge an inexperienced customer, and wherever there is much business the prudent merchant does not do so, having a fixed price for everyone, so that a child may buy of him as cheaply as any other. Thus the customer is honestly served. But this is far from sufficient to justify the belief that the merchant has behaved in this way from duty and principles of honesty. His own advantage required this behavior; but it cannot be assumed that over and above that he had a direct inclination to the purchaser and that, out of love, as it were, he gave none an advantage in price over another. There- fore the action was done neither from duty nor from direct inclination but only for a selfish purpose.

On the other hand, it is a duty to preserve one's life, and moreover every- one has a direct inclination to do so. But for that reason the often anxious care which most men take of it has no intrinsic worth, and the maxim of doing so has no moral import. They preserve their lives according to duty, but not from duty. But if adversities and hopeless sorrow completely take away the relish for life, if an unfortunate man, strong in soul, is indignant rather than despondent or dejected over his fate and wishes for death, and yet preserves his life without loving it and from neither inclination nor fear but from duty—then his maxim has a moral import.

To be kind where one can is duty, and there are, moreover, many persons so sympathetically constituted that without any motive of vanity or selfishness they find an inner satisfaction in spreading joy, and rejoice in the contentment of others which they have made possible. But I say that, however dutiful and amiable it may be, that kind of action has no true moral worth. It is on a level with [actions arising from] other inclinations, such as the inclination to honor, which, if fortunately directed to what in fact accords with duty and is generally useful and thus honorable, deserve praise and encouragement but no esteem. For the maxim lacks the moral import of an action done not from inclination but from duty. But assume that the mind of that friend to mankind was clouded by a sorrow of his own which extinguished all sympathy with the lot of others and that he still had the power to benefit others in distress, but that their need left him untouched because he was preoccupied with his own need. And now suppose him to tear himself, unsolicited by inclination, out of this dead insensibility and to perform this action only from duty and without any inclination—then for the first time his action has genuine moral worth. Furthermore, if nature has put little sympathy in the heart of a man, and if he, though an honest man, is by temperament cold and indifferent to the sufferings of others, perhaps because he is provided with special gifts of patience and fortitude and expects or even requires that others should have the same—and such a man would certainly not be the meanest product of nature —would not he find himself a source from which to give himself a far higher worth than he could have got by having a good-natured temperament? This is unquestionably true even though nature did not make him philanthropic, for it is just here that the worth of the character is brought out, which is morally and incomparably the highest of all: he is beneficent not from inclination but from duty.

To secure one's own happiness is at least indirectly a duty, for discontent with one's condition under pressure from many cares and amid unsatisfied wants could easily become a great temptation to transgress duties. But without any view to duty all men have the strongest and deepest inclination to happiness, because in this idea all inclinations are summed up. But the precept of happiness is often so formulated that it definitely thwarts some inclinations, and men can make no definite and certain concept of the sum of satisfaction of all inclinations which goes under the name of happiness. It is not to be wondered at, therefore, that a single inclination, definite as to what it promises and as to the time at which it can be satisfied, can outweigh a fluctuating idea, and that, for example, a man with the gout can choose to enjoy what he likes and to suffer what he may, because according to his calculations at least on this occasion he has not sacrificed the enjoyment of the present moment to a perhaps groundless expectation of a happiness supposed to lie in health. But even in this case, if the universal inclination to happiness did not determine his will, and if health were not at least for him a necessary factor in these calculations, there yet would remain, as in all other cases, a law that he ought to promote his happiness, not from inclination but from duty. Only from this law would his conduct have true moral worth.

It is in this way, undoubtedly, that we should understand those passages of Scripture which command us to love our neighbor and even our enemy, for love as an inclination cannot be commanded. But beneficence from duty, when no inclination impels it and even when it is opposed by a natural and unconquerable aversion, is practical love, not pathological love; it resides in the will and not in the propensities of feeling, in principles of action and not in tender sympathy; and it alone can be commanded.

[Thus the first proposition of morality is that to have moral worth an action must be done from duty.] The second proposition is: An action performed from duty does not have its moral worth in the purpose which is to be achieved through it but in the maxim by which it is determined. Its moral value, therefore, does not depend on the realization of the object of the action but merely on the principle of volition by which the action is done, without any regard to the objects of the faculty of desire. From the preceding discussion it is clear that the purposes we may have for our actions and their effects as ends and incentives of the will cannot give the actions any unconditional and moral worth. Wherein, then, can this worth lie, if it is not in the will in relation to its hoped-for effect? It can lie nowhere else than in the principle of the will, irrespective of the ends which can be realized by such action. For the will stands, as it were, at the crossroads halfway between its a priori principle which is formal and its a posteriori incentive which is material. Since it must be determined by something, if it is done from duty it must be determined by the formal principle of volition as such since every material principle has been withdrawn from it.

The third principle, as a consequence of the two preceding, I would express as follows: Duty is the necessity of an action executed from respect for law. I can certainly have an inclination to the object as an effect of the proposed action, but I can never have respect for it precisely because it is a mere effect and not an activity of a will. Similarly, I can have no respect for any inclination whatsoever, whether my own or that of another; in the former case I can at most approve of it and in the latter I can even love it, i.e., see it as favorable to my own advantage. But that which is connected with my will merely as ground and not as consequence, that which does not serve my inclination but overpowers it or at least excludes it from being considered in making a choice—in a word, law itself—can be an object of respect and thus a command. Now as an act from duty wholly excludes the influence of inclination and therewith every object of the will, nothing remains which can determine the will objectively except the law, and nothing subjectively except pure respect for this practical law. This subjective element is the maxim[1] that I ought to follow such a law even if it thwarts all my inclinations.

Thus the moral worth of an action does not lie in the effect which is expected from it or in any principle of action which has to borrow its motive from this expected effect. For all these effects (agreeableness of my own condition, indeed even the promotion of the happiness of others) could be brought about through other causes and would not require the will of a rational being, while the highest and unconditional good can be found only in such a will. Therefore, the pre-eminent good can consist only in the conception of the law in itself (which can be present only in a rational being) so far as this conception and not the hoped-for effect is the determining ground of the will. This pre-eminent good, which we call moral, is already present in the person who acts according to this conception, and we do not have to look for it first in the result.[2]

But what kind of a law can that be, the conception of which must determine the will without reference to the expected result? Under this condition alone the will can be called absolutely good without qualification. Since I have robbed the will of all impulses which could come to it from obedience to any law, nothing remains to serve as a principle of the will except universal conformity of its action to law as such. That is, I should never act in such a way that I could not also will that my maxim should be a universal law. Mere conformity to law as such (without assuming any particular law applicable to certain actions) serves as the principle of the will, and it must serve as such a

---

[1] A maxim is the subjective principle of volition. The objective principle (i.e., that which would serve all rational beings also subjectively as a practical principle if reason had full power over the faculty of desire) is the practical law.

[2] It might be objected that I seek to take refuge in an obscure feeling behind the word "respect," instead of clearly resolving the question with a concept of reason. But though respect is a feeling, it is not one received through any [outer] influence but is self-wrought by a rational concept; thus it differs specifically from all feelings of the former kind which may be referred to inclination or fear. What I recognize directly as a law for myself I recognize with respect, which means merely the consciousness of the submission of my will to a law without the intervention of other influences on my mind. The direct determination of the will by the law and the consciousness of this determination is respect; thus respect can be regarded as the effect of the law on the subject and not as the cause of the law. Respect is properly the conception of a worth which thwarts my self-love. Thus it is regarded as an object neither of inclination nor of fear, though it has something analogous to both. The only object of respect is the law, and indeed only the law which we impose on ourselves and yet recognize as necessary in itself. As a law, we are subject to it without consulting self-love; as imposed on us by ourselves, it is a consequence of our will. In the former respect it is analogous to fear and in the latter to inclination. All respect for a person is only respect for the law (of righteousness, etc.) of which the person provides an example. Because we see the improvement of our talents as a duty, we think of a person of talents as the example of a law, as it were (the law that we should by practice become like him in his talents), and that constitutes our respect. And so-called moral interest consists solely in respect for the law.

principle if duty is not to be a vain delusion and chimerical concept. The common reason of mankind in its practical judgments is in perfect agreement with this and has this principle constantly in view.

Let the question, for example, be: May I, when in distress, make a promise with the intention not to keep it? I easily distinguish the two meanings which the question can have, viz., whether it is prudent to make a false promise, or whether it conforms to my duty. Undoubtedly the former can often be the case, though I do see clearly that it is not sufficient merely to escape from the present difficulty by this expedient, but that I must consider whether inconveniences much greater than the present one may not later spring from this lie. Even with all my supposed cunning, the consequences cannot be so easily foreseen. Loss of credit might be far more disadvantageous than the misfortune I now seek to avoid, and it is hard to tell whether it might not be more prudent to act according to a universal maxim and to make it a habit not to promise anything without intending to fulfill it. But it is soon clear to me that such a maxim is based only on an apprehensive concern with consequences.

To be truthful from duty, however, is an entirely different thing from being truthful out of fear of disadvantageous consequences, for in the former case the concept of the action itself contains a law for me, while in the latter I must first look about to see what results for me may be connected with it. For to deviate from the principle of duty is certainly bad, but to be unfaithful to my maxim of prudence can sometimes be very advantageous to me, though it is certainly safer to abide by it. The shortest but most infallible way to find the answer to the question as to whether a deceitful promise is consistent with duty is to ask myself: Would I be content that my maxim (of extricating myself from difficulty by a false promise) should hold as a universal law for myself as well as for others? And could I say to myself that everyone may make a false promise when he is in a difficulty from which he otherwise cannot escape? I immediately see that I could will the lie but not a universal law to lie. For with such a law there would be no promises at all, inasmuch as it would be futile to make a pretense of my intention in regard to future actions to those who would not believe in this pretense or—if they overhastily did so—who would pay me back in my own coin. Thus my maxim would necessarily destroy itself as soon as it was made a universal law.

I do not, therefore, need any penetrating acuteness in order to discern what I have to do in order that my volition may be morally good. Inexperienced in the course of the world, incapable of being prepared for all its contingencies, I ask myself only: Can I will that my maxim become a universal law? If not, it must be rejected, not because of any disadvantage accruing to myself or even to others, but because it cannot enter as a principle into a possible universal legislation, and reason extorts from me an immediate respect for such legislation. I do not as yet discern on what it is grounded (a question the philosopher may investigate), but I at least understand that it is an estimation of the worth which far outweighs all the worth of whatever is recommended by the inclinations, and that the necessity of my actions from pure respect for the practical law constitutes duty. To duty every other motive must give place, because duty is the condition of a will good in itself, whose worth transcends everything. . . .

There is, therefore, only one categorical imperative. It is: Act only according to that maxim by which you can at the same time will that it should become a universal law.

Now if all imperatives of duty can be derived from this one imperative as a principle, we can at least show what we understand by the concept of duty and what it means, even though it remain undecided whether that which is called duty is an empty concept or not.

The universality of law according to which effects are produced constitutes what is properly called nature in the most general sense (as to form), i.e., the existence of things so far as it is determined by universal laws. [By analogy], then, the universal imperative of duty can be expressed as follows: Act as though the maxim of your action were by your will to become a universal law of nature.

We shall now enumerate some duties, adopting the usual division of them into duties to ourselves and to others and into perfect and imperfect duties.[3]

1. A man who is reduced to despair by a series of evils feels a weariness with life but is still in possession of his reason sufficiently to ask whether it would not be contrary to his duty to himself to take his own life. Now he asks whether the maxim of his action could become a universal law of nature. His maxim, however, is: For love of myself, I make it my principle to shorten my life when by a longer duration it threatens more evil than satisfaction. But it is questionable whether this principle of self-love could become a universal law of nature. One immediately sees a contradiction in a system of nature whose law would be to destroy life by the feeling whose special office is to impel the improvement of life. In this case it would not exist as nature; hence that maxim cannot obtain as a law of nature, and thus it wholly contradicts the supreme principle of all duty.

2. Another man finds himself forced by need to borrow money. He well knows that he will not be able to repay it, but he also sees that nothing will be loaned him if he does not firmly promise to repay it at a certain time. He desires to make such a promise, but he has enough conscience to ask himself whether it is not improper and opposed to duty to relieve his distress in such a way. Now, assuming he does decide to do so, the maxim of his action would be

---

[3] It must be noted here that I reserve the division of duties for a future *Metaphysics of Morals* and that the division here stands as only an arbitrary one (chosen in order to arrange my examples). For the rest, by a perfect duty I here understand a duty which permits no exception in the interest of inclination; thus I have not merely outer but also inner perfect duties. This runs contrary to the usage adopted in the schools, but I am not disposed to defend it here because it is all one to my purpose whether this is conceded or not.

as follows: When I believe myself to be in need of money, I will borrow money and promise to repay it, although I know I shall never do so. Now this principle of self-love or of his own benefit may very well be compatible with his whole future welfare, but the question is whether it is right. He changes the pretension of self-love into a universal law and then puts the question: How would it be if my maxim became a universal law? He immediately sees that it could never hold as a universal law of nature and be consistent with itself; rather it must necessarily contradict itself. For the universality of a law which says that anyone who believes himself to be in need could promise what he pleased with the intention of not fulfilling it would make the promise itself and the end to be accomplished by it impossible; no one would believe what was promised to him but would only laugh at any such assertion as vain pretense.

3. A third finds in himself a talent which could, by means of some cultivation, make him in many respects a useful man. But he finds himself in comfortable circumstances and prefers indulgence in pleasure to troubling himself with broadening and improving his fortunate natural gifts. Now, however, let him ask whether his maxim of neglecting his gifts, besides agreeing with his propensity to idle amusement, agrees also with what is called duty. He sees that a system of nature could indeed exist in accordance with such a law, even though man (like the inhabitants of the South Sea Islands) should let his talents rust and resolve to devote his life merely to idleness, indulgence, and propagation—in a word, to pleasure. But he cannot possibly will that this should become a universal law of nature or that it should be implanted in us by a natural instinct. For, as a rational being, he necessarily wills that all his faculties should be developed, inasmuch as they are given to him for all sorts of possible purposes.

4. A fourth man, for whom things are going well, sees that others (whom he could help) have to struggle with great hardships, and he asks, "What concern of mine is it? Let each one be as happy as heaven wills, or as he can make himself; I will not take anything from him or even envy him; but to his welfare or to his assistance in time of need I have no desire to contribute." If such a way of thinking were a universal law of nature, certainly the human race could exist, and without doubt even better than in a state where everyone talks of sympathy and good will, or even exerts himself occasionally to practice them while, on the other hand, he cheats when he can and betrays or otherwise violates the rights of man. Now although it is possible that a universal law of nature according to that maxim could exist, it is nevertheless impossible to will that such a principle should hold everywhere as a law of nature. For a will which resolved this would conflict with itself, since instances can often arise in which he would need the love and sympathy of others, and in which he would have robbed himself, by such a law of nature springing from his own will, of all hope of the aid he desires.

The foregoing are a few of the many actual duties, or at least of duties we hold to be actual, whose derivation from the one stated principle is clear. We must be able to will that a maxim of our action become a universal law; this is the canon of the moral estimation of our action generally. Some actions are of such a nature that their maxim cannot even be *thought* as a universal law of nature without contradiction, far from it being possible that one could will that it should be such. In others this internal impossibility is not found, though it is still impossible to *will* that their maxim should be raised to the universality of a law of nature, because such a will would contradict itself. We easily see that the former maxim conflicts with the stricter or narrower (imprescriptible) duty, the latter with broader (meritorious) duty. Thus all duties, so far as the kind of obligation (not the object of their action) is concerned, have been completely exhibited by these examples in their dependence on the one principle.

When we observe ourselves in any transgression of a duty, we find that we do not actually will that our maxim should become a universal law. That is impossible for us; rather, the contrary of this maxim should remain as a law generally, and we only take the liberty of making an exception to it for ourselves or for the sake of our inclination, and for this one occasion. Consequently, if we weighed everything from one and the same standpoint, namely, reason, we would come upon a contradiction in our own will, viz., that a certain principle is objectively necessary as a universal law and yet subjectively does not hold universally but rather admits exceptions. However, since we regard our action at one time from the point of view of a will wholly conformable to reason and then from that of a will affected by inclinations, there is actually no contradiction, but rather an opposition of inclination to the precept of reason (*antagonismus*). In this the universality of the principle (*universalitas*) is changed into mere generality (*generalitas*), whereby the practical principle of reason meets the maxim halfway. Although this cannot be justified in our own impartial judgment, it does show that we actually acknowledge the validity of the categorical imperative and allow ourselves (with all respect to it) only a few exceptions which seem to us to be unimportant and forced upon us. . . .

MILL

John Stuart Mill (1806–1873) was the godson of Jeremy Bentham and the son of one of Bentham's closest friends and associates, James Mill. From his infancy, the brilliant John Stuart was raised to be a defender of the Utilitarian philosophy. Mill fulfilled the hopes of his father and godfather, becoming the most important English philosopher of the nineteenth century, but he made significant alterations in the utilitarianism he expounded.

Bentham had insisted that only the quantity of pleasure and pain was to be considered in weighing the relative merits of alternative social policies. So long as pleasure was the result, it made no difference to Bentham whether a man read poetry or drank gin. But, Mill argues in the selection included here, there are qualitative differences between the higher pleasures of intellect and culture and the lower pleasures of the senses. What is more, Mill claimed, only a man who had experienced both sorts of pleasures could intelligently choose between them.

Now, this may seem like a small change in Bentham's utilitarianism, but it has very great moral implications. If Bentham is correct, then the poorest, least-educated working man in society is as good a judge of pleasures and pains as the wealthiest, most-cultivated aristocrat. But Mill's distinction between higher and lower pleasures suggests that there is a knowledgeable elite in society whose judgments should be given special weight in the councils of government. Since only the educated few know the joys of culture and intellect as well as the pleasures of the body, they are the only persons really capable of making wise decisions about such matters as public education, sponsorship of the arts, city planning, and so forth.

At the same time, we must not ignore the powerful egalitarian thrust of even Mill's revised utilitarianism. When all is said and done, Mill stands on the side of the individual man against the combined weight of tradition and social opinion. Each of us is the final judge of his own happiness, Mill insists, and as he argues in his famous essay On Liberty, *no one has a right to inflict his conception of the good life on another.*

Mill's emphasis on pleasure might seem to support the doctrine of selfishness expressed by Nietzsche, but he makes it very clear that he intends us to take everyone's happiness or unhappiness into account in making our calculations. Strictly speaking, utilitarianism preaches neither egoism nor altruism, for it tells us to give the same weight to our own interests as to the interests of others.

A passing remark is all that needs be given to the ignorant blunder of sup-posing that those who stand up for utility as the test of right and wrong use the term in that restricted and merely colloquial sense in which utility is opposed to pleasure. An apology is due to the philosophical opponents of utilitarianism for even the momentary appearance of confounding them with anyone capable of so absurd a misconception; which is the more extraordinary, inasmuch as the contrary accusation, of referring everything to pleasure, and that, too, in its grossest form, is another of the common charges against utilitarianism: and, as has been pointedly remarked by an able writer, the same sort of persons, and often the very same persons, denounce the theory "as impracticably dry when the word 'utility' precedes the word 'pleasure,' and as too practicably voluptuous when the word 'pleasure' precedes the word 'utility.' " Those who know anything about the matter are aware that every writer, from Epicurus to Bentham, who maintained the theory of utility meant by it, not something to be contradistinguished from pleasure, but pleasure itself, together with exemption from pain; and instead of opposing the useful to the agreeable or the ornamental, have always declared that the useful means these, among other things. Yet the common herd, including the herd of writers, not only in news-papers and periodicals, but in books of weight and pretension, are perpetually falling into this shallow mistake. Having caught up the word "utilitarian," while knowing nothing whatever about it but its sound, they habitually express by it the rejection or the neglect of pleasure in some of its forms: of beauty, of ornament, or of amusement. Nor is the term thus ignorantly misapplied solely in disparagement, but occasionally in compliment, as though it implied superiority to frivolity and the mere pleasures of the moment. And this per-verted use is the only one in which the word is popularly known, and the one from which the new generation are acquiring their sole notion of its meaning. Those who introduced the word, but who had for many years dis-continued it as a distinctive appellation, may well feel themselves called upon to resume it if by doing so they can hope to contribute anything toward res-cuing it from this utter degradation.[1]

The creed which accepts as the foundation of morals "utility" or the

Chapter II, "What Utilitarianism Is," from *Utilitarianism* by John Stuart Mill. Originally published in 1861.

[1] The author of this essay has reason for believing himself to be the first person who brought the word "utilitarian" into use. He did not invent it, but adopted it from a passing expression in Mr. Galt's *Annals of the Parish*. After using it as a designation for several years, he and others abandoned it from a growing dislike to anything resembling a badge or watchword of sectarian distinction. But as a name for one single opinion, not a set of opinions—to denote the recognition of utility as a standard, not any particular way of applying it—the term supplies a want in the language, and offers, in many cases, a con-venient mode of avoiding tiresome circumlocution.

"greatest happiness principle" holds that actions are right in proportion as they tend to promote happiness; wrong as they tend to produce the reverse of happiness. By happiness is intended pleasure and the absence of pain; by unhappiness, pain and the privation of pleasure. To give a clear view of the moral standard set up by the theory, much more requires to be said; in particular, what things it includes in the ideas of pain and pleasure, and to what extent this is left an open question. But these supplementary explanations do not affect the theory of life on which this theory of morality is grounded—namely, that pleasure and freedom from pain are the only things desirable as ends; and that all desirable things (which are as numerous in the utilitarian as in any other scheme) are desirable either for pleasure inherent in themselves or as means to the promotion of pleasure and the prevention of pain.

Now such a theory of life excites in many minds, and among them in some of the most estimable in feeling and purpose, inveterate dislike. To suppose that life has (as they express it) no higher end than pleasure—no better and nobler object of desire and pursuit—they designate as utterly mean and groveling, as a doctrine worthy only of swine, to whom the followers of Epicurus were, at a very early period, contemptuously likened; and modern holders of the doctrine are occasionally made the subject of equally polite comparisons by its German, French, and English assailants.

When thus attacked, the Epicureans have always answered that it is not they, but their accusers, who represent human nature in a degrading light, since the accusation supposes human beings to be capable of no pleasures except those of which swine are capable. If this supposition were true, the charge could not be gainsaid, but would then be no longer an imputation; for if the sources of pleasure were precisely the same to human beings and to swine, the rule of life which is good enough for the one would be good enough for the other. The comparison of the Epicurean life to that of beasts is felt as degrading, precisely because a beast's pleasures do not satisfy a human being's conceptions of happiness. Human beings have faculties more elevated than the animal appetites and, when once made conscious of them, do not regard anything as happiness which does not include their gratification. I do not, indeed, consider the Epicureans to have been by any means faultless in drawing out their scheme of consequences from the utilitarian principle. To do this in any sufficient manner, many Stoic, as well as Christian, elements require to be included. But there is no known Epicurean theory of life which does not assign to the pleasures of the intellect, of the feelings and imagination, and of the moral sentiments a much higher value as pleasures than to those of mere sensation. It must be admitted, however, that utilitarian writers in general have placed the superiority of mental over bodily pleasures chiefly in the greater permanency, safety, uncostliness, etc., of the former—that is, in their circumstantial advantages rather than in their intrinsic nature. And on all these points utilitarians have fully proved their case; but they might have taken the other and, as it may be called, higher ground with entire consistency. It is quite compatible with the principle of utility to recognize the fact that some kinds of pleasure are more desirable and more valuable than others. It would be absurd that, while in estimating all other things quality is considered as well as quantity, the estimation of pleasure should be supposed to depend on quantity alone.

If I am asked what I mean by difference of quality in pleasures, or what makes one pleasure more valuable than another, merely as a pleasure, except its being greater in amount, there is but one possible answer. Of two pleasures, if there be one to which all or almost all who have experience of both give a decided preference, irrespective of any feeling of moral obligation to prefer it, that is the more desirable pleasure. If one of the two is, by those who are competently acquainted with both, placed so far above the other that they prefer it, even though knowing it to be attended with a greater amount of discontent, and would not resign it for any quantity of the other pleasure which their nature is capable of, we are justified in ascribing to the preferred enjoyment a superiority in quality so far outweighing quantity as to render it, in comparison, of small account.

Now it is an unquestionable fact that those who are equally acquainted with and equally capable of appreciating and enjoying both do give a most marked preference to the manner of existence which employs their higher faculties. Few human creatures would consent to be changed into any of the lower animals for a promise of the fullest allowance of a beast's pleasures; no intelligent human being would consent to be a fool, no instructed person would be an ignoramus, no person of feeling and conscience would be selfish and base, even though they should be persuaded that the fool, the dunce, or the rascal is better satisfied with his lot than they are with theirs. They would not resign what they possess more than he for the most complete satisfaction of all the desires which they have in common with him. If they ever fancy they would, it is only in cases of unhappiness so extreme that to escape from it they would exchange their lot for almost any other, however undesirable in their own eyes. A being of higher faculties requires more to make him happy, is capable probably of more acute suffering, and certainly accessible to it at more points, than one of an inferior type; but in spite of these liabilities, he can never really wish to sink into what he feels to be a lower grade of existence. We may give what explanation we please of this unwillingness; we may attribute it to pride, a name which is given indiscriminately to some of the most and to some of the least estimable feelings of which mankind are capable; we may refer it to the love of liberty and personal independence, an appeal to which was with the Stoics one of the most effective means for the inculcation of it; to the love of power or to the love of excitement, both of which do really enter into and contribute to it; but its most appropriate appellation is a sense of dignity, which all human beings possess in one form or other, and in some, though by no means in exact, proportion to their higher faculties, and which is so essential a part of the happiness of those in whom it is strong that nothing which conflicts with it could be otherwise than momentarily an object of desire to them. Whoever supposes that this preference takes place at a sacrifice of happiness—that the superior being, in anything like equal circumstances, is not happier than the inferior—confounds the two very different ideas of happiness and content. It is indisputable that the being whose capacities of enjoyment are low has the greatest chance of having them fully satisfied; and a highly endowed being will always feel that any happiness which he can look for, as the world is constituted, is imperfect. But he can learn to bear its imperfections, if they are at all bearable; and they will not make him envy the being who is indeed unconscious of the imperfections, but only because he feels not at all the good which those imperfections qualify. It is better to be a human being dissatisfied than a pig satisfied; better to be Socrates dissatisfied than a fool satisfied. And if the fool, or the pig, are of a different opinion, it is because they only know their own side of the question. The other party to the comparison knows both sides.

It may be objected that many who are capable of the higher pleasures occasionally, under the influence of temptation, postpone them to the lower. But this is quite compatible with a full appreciation of the intrinsic superiority of the higher. Men often, from infirmity of character, make their election for the nearer good, though they know it to be the less valuable; and this no less when the choice is between two bodily pleasures than when it is between bodily and mental. They pursue sensual indulgences to the injury of health, though perfectly aware that health is the greater good. It may be further objected that many who begin with youthful enthusiasm for everything noble, as they advance in years, sink into indolence and selfishness. But I do not believe that those who undergo this very common change voluntarily choose the lower description of pleasures in preference to the higher. I believe that, before they devote themselves exclusively to the one, they have already become incapable of the other. Capacity for the nobler feelings is in most natures a very tender plant, easily killed, not only by hostile influences, but by mere want of sustenance; and in the majority of young persons it speedily dies away if the occupations to which their position in life has devoted them, and the society into which it has thrown them, are not favorable in keeping that higher capacity in exercise. Men lose their high aspirations as they lose their intellectual tastes, because they have not time or opportunity for indulging them; and they addict themselves to inferior pleasures, not because they deliberately prefer them, but because they are either the only ones to which they have access or the only ones which they are any longer capable of enjoying. It may be questioned whether anyone who has remained equally susceptible to both classes of pleasures ever knowingly and calmly preferred the lower, though many, in all ages, have broken down in an ineffectual attempt to combine both.

From this verdict of the only competent judges, I apprehend there can be no appeal. On a question which is the best worth having of two pleasures, or which of two modes of existence is the most grateful to the feelings, apart from its moral attributes and from its consequences, the judgment of those who are qualified by knowledge of both, or, if they differ, that of the majority among them, must be admitted as final. And there needs be the less hesitation to accept this judgment respecting the quality of pleasures, since there is no other tribunal to be referred to even on the question of quantity. What means are there of determining which is the acutest of two pains, or the intensest of two pleasurable sensations, except the general suffrage of those who are familiar with both? Neither pains nor pleasures are homogeneous, and pain is always heterogeneous with pleasure. What is there to decide whether a particular pleasure is worth purchasing at the cost of a particular pain, except the feelings and judgment of the experienced? When, therefore, those feelings and judgment declare the pleasures derived from the higher faculties to be preferable *in kind*, apart from the question of intensity, to those of which the animal nature, disjoined from the higher faculties, is susceptible, they are entitled on this subject to the same regard. . . .

WESTERMARCK

"It's all relative!" How often have we heard this bit of wisdom in an argument about morality? It is all relative to who you are, or to how you feel, or to the customs and convictions of your society, or to your religion, or to your political persuasion. Nothing more quickly unsettles the firm convictions of a true believer than the dismaying discovery that there are other true believers, equally confident of their truth, who totally disagree. Our belief in monogamy may survive an encounter with a rebel who refuses to settle down and get married to one and only one partner; but when we read of whole societies which regularly and respectably practice polygamy, something of the certainty goes out of our convictions.

In this selection from his book Ethical Relativity, *Edward Westermarck (1862–1939) sets forth the controversial thesis that all ethical judgments are subjective and hence no truths of ethics are to be discovered or defended. The implications of Westermarck's argument are dramatic and far-reaching, for virtually all of us engage in moral deliberations and disputes which presuppose the possibility of arriving at some ethical truth. Whether we are debating the morality of American foreign policy or attempting to resolve the competing claims of farmers, workers, and businessmen on the tax dollar, we talk as though there were right and wrong ways to act. If Westermarck is correct, then we are all mistaken, no matter which side of the issue we are on.*

To be sure, Westermarck grants that moral judgments do occur. It is a fact that men engage in moral deliberation, and a sociologist, anthropologist, or psychologist can certainly study the phenomenon of ethical judgment as a fact of human experience. But just as we may explore the phenomena of superstition without succumbing to a belief in the efficacy of rabbits' feet, so we may study men's moral beliefs without supposing that they are capable of being true or false.

Notice the extensive reference by Westermarck to other writers on ethical theory. This style of philosophical discussion, with much attention to "the literature," contrasts with the nonacademic style of Plato, Kierkegaard, Nietzsche, and others.

Ethics is generally looked upon as a "normative" science, the object of which is to find and formulate moral principles and rules possessing objective validity. The supposed objectivity of moral values, as understood in this treatise, implies that they have a real existence apart from any reference to a human mind, that what is said to be good or bad, right or wrong, cannot be reduced merely to what people think to be good or bad, right or wrong. It makes morality a matter of truth and falsity, and to say that a judgment is true obviously means something different from the statement that it is thought to be true. The objectivity of moral judgments does not presuppose the infallibility of the individual who pronounces such a judgment, nor even the accuracy of a general consensus of opinion; but if a certain course of conduct is objectively right, it must be thought to be right by all rational beings who judge truly of the matter and cannot, without error, be judged to be wrong.

In spite of the fervour with which the objectivity of moral judgments has been advocated by the exponents of normative ethics there is much diversity of opinion with regard to the principles underlying the various systems. This discord is as old as ethics itself. But while the evolution of other sciences has shown a tendency to increasing agreement on points of fundamental importance, the same can hardly be said to have been the case in the history of ethics, where the spirit of controversy has been much more conspicuous than the endeavour to add new truths to results already reached. Of course, if moral values are objective, only one of the conflicting theories can possibly be true. Each founder of a new theory hopes that it is he who has discovered the unique jewel of moral truth, and is naturally anxious to show that other theories are only false stones. But he must also by positive reasons make good his claim to the precious find.

These reasons are of great importance in a discussion of the question whether moral judgments really are objective or merely are supposed to be so; for if any one of the theories of normative ethics has been actually proved to be true, the objectivity of those judgments has *eo ipso* been established as an indisputable fact. I shall therefore proceed to an examination of the main evidence that has been produced in favour of the most typical of these theories.

I shall begin with hedonism, according to which actions are right in proportion as they tend to promote happiness, and wrong in proportion as they tend to produce the reverse of happiness. And by happiness is then meant "pleasure, and the absence of pain; by unhappiness, pain, and the privation of pleasure."[1] What is the evidence?

"The Supposed Objectivity of Moral Judgments." From Chaps. 1 and 2 of *Ethical Relativity* by Edward Westermarck. London: Routledge & Kegan Paul, Ltd., 1932. Reprinted by permission of the publisher.

[1] J. S. Mill, *Utilitarianism* (London, 1895), p. 10.

It has been said that the hedonistic principle requires no proof, because it is simply an analytic proposition, a mere definition. Because acts that are called right generally produce pleasure and acts that are called wrong generally produce pain, rightness and wrongness have been actually identified with the tendencies of acts to produce pleasure or pain. . . . Now the statement that a certain act has a tendency to promote happiness, or to cause unhappiness, is either true or false; and if rightness and wrongness are only other words for these tendencies, it is therefore obvious that the moral judgments also have objective validity. But it is impossible to doubt that anybody who sees sufficiently carefully into the matter must admit that the identification in question is due to a confusion between the meaning of terms and the use made of them when applied to acts on account of their tendencies to produce certain effects. Bentham himself seems to have felt something of the kind. For although he asserts that the rectitude of the principle of utility has been contested only by those who have not known what they have been meaning, he raises the question whether it is susceptible of any direct proof. And his answer is as follows:—"It should seem not: for that which is used to prove everything else, cannot itself be proved: a chain of proofs must have their commencement somewhere."[2] The question and the answer suggest that Bentham, after all, hardly looked upon the principle of utility or, as he also calls it, the greatest happiness principle, as strictly speaking a mere definition of rightness. . . .

Now the utilitarian standard is not the agent's own greatest happiness, but the greatest amount of happiness altogether. It may be defined as the rules and precepts for human conduct by the observance of which happiness might be, to the greatest extent possible, secured to all mankind; "and not to them only, but, so far as the nature of things admits, to the whole sentient creation."[3] How can this be proved? Mill argues that "no reason can be given why the general happiness is desirable, except that each person, so far as he believes it to be attainable, desires his own happiness. This, however, being a fact, we have not only all the proof which the case admits of, but all which it is possible to require, that happiness is a good: that each person's happiness is a good to that person, and the general happiness, therefore, a good to the aggregate of all persons."[4] But if a person desires his own happiness, and if what he desires is desirable in the sense that he ought to desire it, the standard of general happiness can only mean that each person ought to desire his own happiness. In other words, the premises in Mill's argument would lead to egotistic hedonism, not to utilitarianism or universalistic hedonism. . . .

It will perhaps be argued that even though this or that moral principle, or even all moral principles hitherto laid down, fail to be objectively valid or

[2] J. Bentham, *An Introduction to the Principles of Morals and Legislation* (Oxford, 1879), p. 4.
[3] Mill, p. 16 *sq.*
[4] *Ibid.*, p. 53.

express a moral truth, there may nevertheless be in the human mind some "faculty" which makes the pronouncement of objectively valid moral judgments possible. There are so many "theoretical" truths which have never been discovered, and yet we have in our intellect a "faculty" enabling us to pronounce judgments that are true. So also moralists of different normative schools of ethics maintain that we possess a faculty which can pronounce true moral judgments. This faculty has been called by names like "moral sense," "conscience," or "practical" or "moral reason," or been simply included under the general terms "reason" or "understanding.". . .

Butler calls "the moral faculty" conscience, but as a synonym for it he frequently uses the term "principle of reflection." It has two aspects, a purely cognitive and an authoritative, and on its cognitive side it "pronounces determinately some actions to be in themselves evil, wrong, unjust."[5] Sometimes he even calls it reason. But his dominant view seems to be that which lays stress on the instinctive intuition rather than the reflection.[6] He says:—"In all common ordinary cases we see intuitively at first view what is our duty. . . . This is the ground of the observation, that the first thought is often the best. In these cases doubt and deliberation is itself dishonesty. . . . That which is called considering what is our duty in a particular case, is very often nothing but endeavouring to explain it away."[7] But how, then, is it that different consciences so often issue conflicting orders? This question is never raised by Butler. He gives us no criterion of rightness and wrongness apart from the voice of conscience.[8]. . .

Since the days of Kant moral judgments have been referred to a special faculty or a part of the general faculty of reason, called "practical" or "moral" reason, as the source of the objective validity assigned to them; according to Kant the speculative and the practical reason "can ultimately be only one and the same reason which has to be distinguished merely in its application."[9] The very existence of this mysterious faculty presupposes that there really are self-evident or axiomatic moral propositions; hence if no such proposition can be

[5] J. Butler, *Sermon II.—Upon Human Nature*, § 8 (*Works*, i. [London, 1900], p. 45).

[6] *Cf.* J. Bonar, *Moral Sense* (London, 1930), p. 64.

[7] Butler, *Sermon VII.—Upon the Character of Balaam*, § 14 (*Works*, i. 100).

[8] *Cf.* J. M. Wilson and T. Fowler, *The Principles of Morals (Introductory Chapters)* (Oxford, 1886), p. 56; C. D. Broad, *Five Types of Ethical Theory* (London, 1930), p. 82 *sq.* Professor A. E. Taylor ("Some Features of Butler's Ethics," in *Mind*, N. S. xxxv. [London, 1926], p. 276 *sq.*) says that it is no fault of the *Sermons*, in which Butler's ethical doctrine is chiefly conveyed to us, that they did not consider the possibility of conflicting moral codes and the grounds on which a choice could be made between them, because the object of the preacher was to impress on his audience the necessity of conducting their lives virtuously, and they would be agreed, in all essentials, on the question what sort of conduct is right and wrong. But his disregard of the apparent or real variations in the deliverance of "conscience" certainly obscures his ethical theory in its most essential point.

[9] Kant, *Grundlegung zur Metaphysik der Sitten*, Vorrede (*Gesammelte Schriften*; iv [Berlin, 1911], p. 391; T. K. Abbott's translation in *Kant's Critique of Practical Reason and other Works on the Theory of Ethics* [London, 1898], p. 7).

shown to exist we have no right whatever to postulate that there is a faculty which ever could give us any. It is perfectly clear that Kant *assumed* the objectivity of duty, and that this assumption led him to the idea of a pure practical reason, not *vice versa*.[10] He needed a faculty to explain the moral law, which he regarded as a fact of pure reason, "of which we are *a priori* conscious, and which is apodictically certain," and the objective reality of which "cannot be proved by any deduction by any efforts of theoretical reason."[11]

The question to be answered, then, is whether any of the moral principles that have been regarded as self-evident really is so. If ethics is to be taken as the term for a normative science, I agree with Professor Moore's statement that "the fundamental principles of Ethics must be self-evident." I also agree with him when he says:—"The expression 'self-evident' means properly that the proposition so called is evident or true, *by itself* alone; that it is not an inference from some proposition other than *itself*. The expression does *not* mean that the proposition is true, because it is evident to you or me or all mankind, because in other words it appears to us to be true. That a proposition appears to be true can never be a valid argument that true it really is."[12] Just as the statement "this proposition is true" does not mean the same as to say, "I consider this proposition to be true," so also the statement "this moral principle is self-evident" does not mean the same as to say, "this moral principle appears self-evident to me." But how, then, can I know if a proposition is really self-evident or only supposed to be so? In the case of theoretical truths no truth is considered to have a claim to self-evidence which is not generally accepted as self-evident or axiomatic by all those whose intellect is sufficiently developed to have an opinion on the matter worthy of any consideration at all. It is true, as Kant said, that universal assent does not prove the objective validity of a judgment[13]—indeed, there are mathematical axioms that have been called in question although they have passed current for centuries; but, to speak with Sidgwick, the absence of disagreement between experts must be an indispensable negative condition of the certainty of our beliefs. In the case of moral principles enunciated as self-evident truths disagreement is rampant.

The great variability of moral judgments does not of course *eo ipso* disprove the possibility of self-evident moral intuitions. It is incompatible with that cruder kind of intuitionism which maintains that some moral faculty directly passes true moral judgments on particular courses of conduct at the moment of action. But what about the differences of opinion as regards the great moral principles that are supposed to be self-evident? . . . How can there be such a great diversity of opinion among "moral specialists" with regard to propositions that are assumed to be axioms? Some of these specialists say it is an

[10] *Cf.* A. Hägerström, *Kants Ethik* (Uppsala, 1902), p. 594.
[11] Kant, *Kritik der praktischen Vernunft*, i. 1. 1. 8 (v. 47; Abbott, p. 136).
[12] G. E. Moore, *Principia Ethica* (Cambridge, 1922), p. 143.
[13] Kant, *Kritik der praktischen Vernunft*, Vorrede (v. 12 *sq.*; Abbott, p. 98).

axiom that I ought not to prefer my own lesser good to the greater good of another; whilst others do not deny the self-evidence, but thoroughly disagree with the contents, of this proposition. According to Sidgwick the proposition that pleasure is the only rational ultimate end of action is an object of intuition; according to Dr. Moore, also a professor of moral philosophy, the untruth of this proposition is self-evident.[14]

There are no doubt moral propositions which really are certain and self-evident, for the simple reason that they are tautological, that the predicate is but a repetition of the subject; and moral philosophy contains a great number of such tautologies, from the days of Plato and Aristotle to the present times. But apart from such cases, which of course tell us nothing, I am not aware of any moral principle that could be said to be truly self-evident. The presumed self-evidence is only a matter of opinion; and in some cases one might even be inclined to quote Mr. Bertrand Russell's statement that "if self-evidence is alleged as a ground of belief, that implies that doubt has crept in, and that our self-evident proposition has not wholly resisted the assaults of scepticism."[15] None of the various theories of normative science can be said to have proved its case; none of them has proved that moral judgments possess objective validity, that there is anything truly good or bad, right or wrong, that moral principles express anything more than the opinions of those who believe in them.

But what, then, has made moralists believe that moral judgments possess an objective validity which none of them has been able to prove? What has induced them to construct their theories of normative ethics? What has allured them to invent a science the subject-matter of which—the objectively good or right—is not even known to exist? The answer is not difficult to find. It has often been remarked that there is much greater agreement among moralists on the question of moral practice than on the question of theory. When they are trying to define the ultimate end of right conduct or to find the essence of right and wrong, they give us the most contradictory definitions or explanations—as Leslie Stephen said, we find ourselves in a "region of perpetual antinomies, where controversy is everlasting, and opposite theories seem to be equally self-evident to different minds."[16] But when they pass to a discussion of what is right and wrong in concrete cases, in the various circumstances of life, the disagreement is reduced to a surprising extent. They all tell us that we should be kind to our neighbour, that we should respect his life and property, that we should speak the truth, that we should live in monogamy and

14 Moore, *op. cit.*, pp. 75, 144.

15 B. Russell, *The Analysis of Mind* (London, 1922), p. 263. See also H. H. Joachim, *The Nature of Truth* (Oxford, 1906), p. 55.

16 L. Stephen, *The Science of Ethics* (London, 1882), p. 2. *Cf.* H. Sidgwick, "My Station and Its Duties," in *International Journal of Ethics*, iv. (Philadelphia, etc., 1893), p. 13 *sq.*

be faithful husbands or wives, that we should be sober and temperate, and so forth. This is what makes books on ethics, when they come to the particular rules of life, so exceedingly monotonous and dull; for even the most controversial and pugnacious theorist becomes then quite tame and commonplace. And the reason for this is that all ethical theories are as a matter of fact based on the morality of common sense. . . . So also normative ethics has adopted the common sense idea that there *is* something right and wrong independently of what is thought to be right or wrong. People are not willing to admit that their moral convictions are a mere matter of opinion, and look upon convictions differing from their own as errors. If asked why there is so much diversity of opinion on moral questions, and consequently so many errors, they would probably argue that there *would* be unanimity as regards the rightness or wrongness of a given course of conduct *if* everybody possessed a sufficient knowledge of the case and all the attendant circumstances and *if*, at the same time, everybody had a sufficiently developed moral consciousness—which practically would mean a moral consciousness as enlightened and developed as their own. This characteristic of the moral judgments of common sense is shared by the judgments of philosophers, and is at the bottom of their reasoned arguments in favour of the objectivity of moral values.

The common sense idea that moral judgments possess objective validity is itself regarded as a proof of their really possessing such validity. It is argued that the moral judgment "claims objectivity," that it asserts a value which is found in that on which it is pronounced. "This is the meaning of the judgment," says Professor Sorley. "It is not about a feeling or attitude of, or any relation to, the subject who makes the judgment."[17] . . . The whole argument is really reduced to the assumption that an idea—in this case the idea of the validity of moral judgments—which is generally held, or held by more or less advanced minds, must be true: people claim objective validity for the moral judgment, therefore it must possess such validity. The only thing that may be said in favour of such an argument is, that if the definition of a moral proposition implies the claim to objectivity, a judgment that does not express this quality cannot be a moral judgment; but this by no means proves that moral propositions so defined are true—the predicated objectivity may be a sheer illusion.

Well then, it might be argued, if you do not admit that there is anything objectively right or wrong, you must not use these or any other moral predicates, because if you do, you assign to them a meaning that they do not possess. But what about other predicates which are also formally objective and yet, when we more carefully consider the matter are admitted to be merely subjective estimates? The aesthetic judgment makes claim to objectivity: when people say that something is beautiful, they generally mean something more than that it gives, or has a tendency to give, them aesthetic enjoyment; and

[17] W. R. Sorley, *Moral Values and the Idea of God* (Cambridge, 1924), p. 150.

there are also many philosophers who uphold the objectivity of beauty and maintain that the beauties of nature exist apart from a beholding eye or a hearing ear. But even those who agree with Hume that beauty is no quality in things themselves, but exists merely in the mind which contemplates them,[18] do not hesitate to speak of "beauty," and would consider it absurd to be taken to task for doing so. Sidgwick admits that if I say "the air is sweet" or "the food is disagreeable," it would not be exactly true that I mean no more than I like the one or dislike the other, although, if my statement is challenged, I shall probably content myself with affirming the existence of such feelings in my own mind. So also, if anybody calls a certain wine or cigar good, there is some objectivity implied in the judgment, and however willing he is to recognize that the so-called goodness is a mere matter of taste, he will certainly, even if he is a philosopher, continue to call the wine or cigar good, just as before. Or, to take an instance from the sphere of knowledge: Hume, in expounding his own view, still speaks with the man in the street of objects and processes in nature, although his very aim is to convince us that what we know is really limited to impressions and ideas. And every one of us makes use of the words sunrise and sunset, which are expressions from a time when people thought that the sun rose and set, though nobody now holds this view. Why, then, should not the ethical subjectivist be allowed to use the old terms for moral qualities, although he maintains that the objective validity generally implied in them is a mere illusion? . . .

There is thus a very general tendency to assign objectivity to our subjective experience, and this tendency is particularly strong and persistent with regard to our moral experience. Why we attribute validity to it is of course a matter that does not trouble the moral intuitionist any more than the mathematician looks for a ground for his axioms. He is not concerned with the question of origins. Professor Moore says that the questions as to the origin of people's moral feelings and ideas are of course "not without interest, and are subjects of legitimate curiosity," but "only form one special branch of Psychology or Anthropology."[19] And Professor Sorley remarks that when we ask, "Why do we assign validity to our moral approval and to moral ideas generally?" the history of their genesis gives us no answer.[20] For my own part I maintain, on the contrary, that an examination into the history of the moral consciousness of mankind gives us a clue to its supposed objectivity, as well as to its other characteristics. . . .

The authority assigned to conscience is really only an echo of the social or religious sanctions of conduct: it belongs to the "public" or the religious conscience, *vox populi* or *vox dei*. In theory it may be admitted that every man ought to act in accordance with his conscience. But this phrase is easily

18 D. Hume, "Essay xxiii.—Of the Standard of Taste," in *Philosophical Works*, iii. (London, 1875), p. 268.

19 G. E. Moore, *Ethics* (London, *s.d.*), p. 130 *sq.*

20 Sorley, *op. cit.*, p. 64.

forgotten when, in any matter of importance, the individual's conscience comes into conflict with the common sense of his community; or doubt may be thrown upon the sincerity of his professed convictions, or he may be blamed for having such a conscience as he has. There are philosophers, like Hobbes and Hegel, who have denied the citizen the right of having a private conscience. The other external source from which authority has been instilled into the moral law is the alliance between morality and religion. . . . It has been pointed out by Schopenhauer and others[21] that Kant's categorical imperative, with its mysteriousness and awfulness, is really an echo of the old religious formula "Thou shalt," though it is heard, not as the command of an external legislator, but as a voice coming from within. Schiller wrote to Goethe, "There still remains something in Kant, as in Luther, that makes one think of a monk who has left his monastery, but been unable to efface all traces of it."[22]

The theological argument in favour of the objective validity of moral judgments, which is based on belief in an all-good God who has revealed his will to mankind, contains, of course, an assumption that cannot be scientifically proved. But even if it could be proved, would that justify the conclusion drawn from it? Those who maintain that they in such a revelation possess an absolute moral standard and that, consequently, any mode of conduct which is in accordance with it must be objectively right, may be asked what they mean by an all-good God. If God were not supposed to be all-good, we might certainly be induced by prudence to obey his decrees, but they could not lay claim to *moral* validity; suppose the devil were to take over the government of the world, what influence would that have on the moral values—would it make the right wrong and the wrong right? It is only the all-goodness of God that can give his commandments absolute moral validity. But to say that something is good because it is in accordance with the will of an all-good God is to reason in a circle; if goodness means anything, it must have a meaning which is independent of his will. God is called good or righteous because he is supposed to possess certain qualities that we are used to call so: he is benevolent, he rewards virtue and punishes vice, and so forth. For such reasons we add the attributes goodness and righteousness to his other attributes, which express qualities of an objective character, and by calling him all-good we attribute to him perfect goodness. As a matter of fact, there are also many theologians who consider moral distinctions to be antecedent to the divine commands. Thomas Aquinas and his school maintain that the right is not right because God wills it, but that God wills it because it is right.

Before leaving this subject I must still mention a fact that has made moral-

---

[21] A. Schopenhauer, *Die Grundlage der Moral,* §§ 4, 6 (*Sämmtliche Werke,* iv.[2] [Leipzig, 1916], pp. 124–126, 133 *sqq.*). F. Paulsen, *Immanuel Kant* (Stuttgart, 1899), p. 345 *sq.* J. Rehmke, *Grundlegung der Ethik als Wissenschaft* (Leipzig, 1925), p. 58. *Cf.* Kant, *Von der Einwohnung des bösen Princips neben dem guten,* Anmerkung (vi. 23 n.†; Abbott, p. 330 n.1), where he speaks of the majesty of the law "like that on Sinai."

[22] *Briefwechsel zwischen Schiller und Goethe in den Jahren 1794 bis 1805,* ii. (Stuttgart & Augsburg, 1856), p. 167.

ists so anxious to prove the objectivity of our moral judgments, namely, the belief that ethical subjectivism is an extremely dangerous doctrine. In a little book called *Is Conscience an Emotion?*, largely written to oppose views held either by Professor McDougall or myself, Dr. Rashdall remarks that "the scientific spirit does not require us to blind ourselves to the practical consequences which hang upon the solution of not a few scientific problems," and that "assuredly there is no scientific problem upon which so much depends as upon the answer we give to the question whether the distinction which we are accustomed to draw between right and wrong belongs to the region of objective truth like the laws of mathematics and of physical science, or whether it is based upon an actual emotional constitution of individual human beings."[23] He maintains that the emotionalist theory of ethics, which leads to a denial of the objective validity of moral judgments, "is fatal to the deepest spiritual convictions and to the highest spiritual aspirations of the human race," and that it therefore is "a matter of great practical as well as intellectual importance" that it should be rejected. "To deny the validity of the idea of duty," he says, "has a strong tendency to impair its practical influence on the individual's life"; and "the belief in the objectivity of our moral judgments is a necessary premiss for any valid argument for the belief either in God, if by that be understood a morally good or perfect Being, or in Immortality."[24] The last statement is astounding. In another place Dean Rashdall argues that objective morality presupposes the belief in God, and now we are told that any valid argument for the belief in God presupposes objective morality. These two statements combined lead to the logical conclusion that there is no valid evidence *either* for the existence of God *or* for the objectivity of moral judgments.

It is needless to say that a scientific theory is not invalidated by the mere fact that it is likely to cause mischief. The unfortunate circumstance that there do exist dangerous things in the world, proves that something may be dangerous and yet true. Another question is whether the ethical subjectivism I am here advocating really is a danger to morality. It cannot be depreciated by the same inference as was drawn from the teaching of the ancient Sophists, namely, that if that which appears to each man as right or good stands for that which is right or good, then everybody has the natural right to follow his caprice and inclinations and to hinder him doing so is an infringement on his rights. My moral judgments spring from my own moral consciousness; they judge of the conduct of other men not from their point of view but from mine, not in accordance with their feelings and opinions about right and wrong but according to my own. And these are not arbitrary. We approve and disapprove because we cannot do otherwise; our moral consciousness belongs to our mental constitution, which we cannot change as we please. Can we help feeling pain when the fire burns us? Can we help sympathizing with our friends? Are these

---

[23] H. Rashdall, *Is Conscience an Emotion?* (London, 1914), p. 199 *sq.*
[24] *Ibid.*, pp. 126, 127, 194.

facts less necessary or less powerful in their consequences, because they fall within the subjective sphere of our experience? So also, why should the moral law command less obedience because it forms a part of ourselves?

I think that ethical writers are often inclined to overrate the influence of moral theory upon moral practice, but if there is any such influence at all, it seems to me that ethical subjectivism, instead of being a danger, is more likely to be an advantage to morality. Could it be brought home to people that there is no absolute standard in morality, they would perhaps be on the one hand more tolerant and on the other hand more critical in their judgments. Emotions depend on cognitions and are apt to vary according as the cognitions vary; hence a theory which leads to an examination of the psychological and historical origin of people's moral opinions should be more useful than a theory which postulates moral truths enunciated by self-evident intuitions that are unchangeable. In every society the traditional notions as to what is good or bad, obligatory or indifferent, are commonly accepted by the majority of people without further reflection. By tracing them to their source it will be found that not a few of these notions have their origin in ignorance and superstition or in sentimental likes or dislikes, to which a scrutinizing judge can attach little importance; and, on the other hand, he must condemn many an act or omission which public opinion, out of thoughtlessness, treats with indifference. It will, moreover, appear that moral estimates often survive the causes from which they sprang. And what unprejudiced person can help changing his views if he be persuaded that they have no foundation in existing facts?

I have thus arrived at the conclusion that neither the attempts of moral philosophers or theologians to prove the objective validity of moral judgments, nor the common sense assumption to the same effect, give us any right at all to accept such a validity as a fact. So far, however, I have only tried to show that it has not been proved; now I am prepared to take a step further and assert that it cannot exist. The reason for this is that in my opinion the predicates of all moral judgments, all moral concepts, are ultimately based on emotions, and that, as is very commonly admitted,[25] no objectivity can come from an emotion. It is of course true or not that we in a given moment have a certain emotion; but in no other sense can the antithesis of true and false be applied to it. The belief that gives rise to an emotion, the cognitive basis of it, is either

---

[25] See, *e.g.*, Rashdall, *The Theory of Good and Evil* (London, 1924), i. 145 *sq.*, ii. 195; *Idem, Is Conscience an Emotion?*, pp. 30, 36; Sorley, *op. cit.*, p. 54; C. Hebler, *Philosophische Aufsätze* (Leipzig, 1869), p. 48; J. Watson, *Hedonistic Theories from Aristippus to Spencer* (Glasgow, 1895), p. 135; H. Maier, *Psychologie des emotionalen Denkens* (Tübingen, 1908), pp. 789, 790, 800; H. Münsterberg, *Philosophie der Werte* (Leipzig, 1908), p. 28; H. Höffding, *Etik* (Köbenhavn & Kristiania, 1913), p. 51; L. T. Hobhouse, *The Rational Good* (London, 1921), p. 16; R. Müller-Freienfels, *Irrationalismus* (Leipzig, 1922), p. 226; *Idem, Metaphysik des Irrationalen* (Leipzig, 1927), p. 400; J. Laird, *The Idea of Value* (Cambridge, 1929), pp. 247, 315.

true or false; in the latter case the emotion may be said to be felt "by mistake" —as when a person is frightened by some object in the dark which he takes for a ghost, or is indignant with a person to whom he imputes a wrong that has been committed by somebody else; but this does not alter the nature of the emotion itself. We may call the emotion of another individual "unjustified," if we feel that we ourselves should not have experienced the same emotion had we been in his place, or, as in the case of moral approval or disapproval, if we cannot share his emotion. But to speak, as Brentano does,[26] of "right" and "wrong" emotions, springing from self-evident intuitions and having the same validity as truth and error, is only another futile attempt to objectivize our moral judgments. . . .

If there are no moral truths it cannot be the object of a science of ethics to lay down rules for human conduct, since the aim of all science is the discovery of some truth. Professor Höffding argues that the subjectivity of our moral valuations does not prevent ethics from being a science any more than the subjectivity of our sensations renders a science of physics impossible, because both are concerned with finding the external facts that correspond to the subjective processes.[27] It may, of course, be a subject for scientific inquiry to investigate the means which are conducive to human happiness or welfare, and the results of such a study may also be usefully applied by moralists, but it forms no more a part of ethics than physics is a part of psychology. If the word "ethics" is to be used as the name for a science, the object of that science can only be to study the moral consciousness as a fact.

[26] F. Brentano, *Vom Ursprung sittlicher Erkenntnis* (Leipzig, 1921), p. 18 *sqq.*
[27] Höffding, *op. cit.,* p. 68.

AYER

The most powerful attack on ethics as a branch of philosophy comes from the logical positivists, who insist that our supposed moral judgments simply have no coherent meaning at all. In this selection from A. J. Ayer's classic work, Language, Truth, and Logic, *we see how the positivists' verification theory of meaning is used to undermine the claims of virtually every previous ethical theory.*

The heart of Ayer's attack is the claim that moral judgments do not, properly speaking, assert any proposition whatsoever. The statement "lying is wrong" looks very much like the statement "lead is metallic." Both sentences seem to assert that something (lying, lead) has a certain characteristic or property (is wrong, is metallic). Presumably, therefore, it makes sense to ask in each case whether the sentence is true or false, what evidence we can produce in support of our conclusion, and so on. But the appearance of similarity is an illusion—a grammatical illusion, we might say, produced by the similarity of the syntax of the two statements. "Lying is wrong" does not assert anything at all, according to Ayer. It merely gives voice to, or expresses, my disapproval of lying. "Lying is wrong" is actually a good deal more like "Hurrah!" or "Ugh!" than it is like "Lead is metallic." If someone cheers for the opposing team at a football game, it wouldn't make much sense to tell him that he was mistaken. The best we can do is simply to cheer louder for our own team.

This expressive, or "emotive," interpretation of ethical judgments is, to put it mildly, unsettling. Can this really be all we are doing when we engage in lengthy moral debates? Are the great disputes over slavery, poverty, war, and civil liberties nothing more than highly complicated cheering contests? Certainly the men and women who have argued moral questions through the ages have not thought so! And yet, it is not enough to reject Ayer's views out of hand and retreat to common sense. If we are convinced that there is more to moral discourse than the expression of attitudes, then it is up to us to put forward an analysis of that discourse which can meet the very powerful arguments of the positivists.

The Positivist Critique
of Ethics

There is still one objection to be met before we can claim to have justified our views that all synthetic propositions are empirical hypotheses. This objection is based on the common supposition that our speculative knowledge is of two distinct kinds—that which relates to questions of empirical fact, and that which relates to questions of value. It will be said that "statements of value" are genuine synthetic propositions, but that they cannot with any show of justice be represented as hypotheses, which are used to predict the course of our sensations; and, accordingly, that the existence of ethics and æsthetics as branches of speculative knowledge presents an insuperable objection to our radical empiricist thesis.

In face of this objection, it is our business to give an account of "judgements of value" which is both satisfactory in itself and consistent with our general empiricist principles. We shall set ourselves to show that in so far as statements of value are significant, they are ordinary "scientific" statements; and that in so far as they are not scientific, they are not in the literal sense significant, but are simply expressions of emotion which can be neither true nor false. In maintaining this view, we may confine ourselves for the present to the case of ethical statements. What is said about them will be found to apply, *mutatis mutandis*, to the case of æsthetic statements also.

The ordinary system of ethics, as elaborated in the works of ethical philosophers, is very far from being a homogeneous whole. Not only is it apt to contain pieces of metaphysics, and analyses of non-ethical concepts: its actual ethical contents are themselves of very different kinds. We may divide them, indeed, into four main classes. There are, first of all, propositions which express definitions of ethical terms, or judgments about the legitimacy or possibility of certain definitions. Secondly, there are propositions describing the phenomena of moral experience, and their causes. Thirdly, there are exhortations to moral virtue. And, lastly, there are actual ethical judgements. It is unfortunately the case that the distinction between these four classes, plain as it is, is commonly ignored by ethical philosophers; with the result that it is often very difficult to tell from their works what it is that they are seeking to discover or prove.

In fact, it is easy to see that only the first of our four classes, namely that which comprises the propositions relating to the definitions of ethical terms, can be said to constitute ethical philosophy. The propositions which describe the phenomena of moral experience, and their causes, must be assigned to the science of psychology, or sociology. The exhortations to moral virtue are not

From "Critique of Ethics," Chap. 6 of *Language, Truth, and Logic* by Alfred J. Ayer. New York: Dover Publications, Inc. © 1946 Dover Publications, Inc., and Victor Gollancz, Ltd. Reprinted by permission of the publishers.

propositions at all, but ejaculations or commands which are designed to provoke the reader to action of a certain sort. Accordingly, they do not belong to any branch of philosophy or science. As for the expressions of ethical judgements, we have not yet determined how they should be classified. But inasmuch as they are certainly neither definitions nor comments upon definitions, nor quotations, we may say decisively that they do not belong to ethical philosophy. A strictly philosophical treatise on ethics should therefore make no ethical pronouncements. But it should, by giving an analysis of ethical terms, show what is the category to which all such pronouncements belong. And this is what we are now about to do.

A question which is often discussed by ethical philosophers is whether it is possible to find definitions which would reduce all ethical terms to one or two fundamental terms. But this question, though it undeniably belongs to ethical philosophy, is not relevant to our present enquiry. We are not now concerned to discover which term, within the sphere of ethical terms, is to be taken as fundamental; whether, for example, "good" can be defined in terms of "right" or "right" in terms of "good," or both in terms of "value." What we are interested in is the possibility of reducing the whole sphere of ethical terms to non-ethical terms. We are enquiring whether statements of ethical value can be translated into statements of empirical fact.

That they can be so translated is the contention of those ethical philosophers who are commonly called subjectivists, and of those who are known as utilitarians. For the utilitarian defines the rightness of actions, and the goodness of ends, in terms of the pleasure, or happiness, or satisfaction, to which they give rise; the subjectivist, in terms of the feelings of approval which a certain person, or group of people, has towards them. Each of these types of definition makes moral judgements into a sub-class of psychological or sociological judgements; and for this reason they are very attractive to us. For, if either was correct, it would follow that ethical assertions were not generically different from the factual assertions which are ordinarily contrasted with them; and the account which we have already given of empirical hypotheses would apply to them also.

Nevertheless we shall not adopt either a subjectivist or a utilitarian analysis of ethical terms. We reject the subjectivist view that to call an action right, or a thing good, is to say that it is generally approved of, because it is not self-contradictory to assert that some actions which are generally approved of are not right, or that some things which are generally approved of are not good. And we reject the alternative subjectivist view that a man who asserts that a certain action is right, or that a certain thing is good, is saying that he himself approves of it, on the ground that a man who confessed that he sometimes approved of what was bad or wrong would not be contradicting himself. And a similar argument is fatal to utilitarianism. We cannot agree that to call an action right is to say that of all the actions possible in the circumstances it would cause, or be likely to cause, the greatest happiness, or the greatest balance of pleasure over pain, or the greatest balance of satisfied over unsatisfied desire, because we find that it is not self-contradictory to say that it is some-times wrong to perform the action which would actually or probably cause the greatest happiness, or the greatest balance of pleasure over pain, or of satisfied over unsatisfied desire. And since it is not self-contradictory to say that some pleasant things are not good, or that some bad things are desired, it can-not be the case that the sentence "*x* is good" is equivalent to "*x* is pleasant," or to "*x* is desired." And to every other variant of utilitarianism with which I am acquainted the same objection can be made. And therefore we should, I think, conclude that the validity of ethical judgements is not determined by the feli-cific tendencies of actions, any more than by the nature of people's feelings; but that it must be regarded as "absolute" or "intrinsic," and not empirically calculable.

If we say this, we are not, of course, denying that it is possible to invent a language in which all ethical symbols are definable in non-ethical terms, or even that it is desirable to invent such a language and adopt it in place of our own; what we are denying is that the suggested reduction of ethical to non-ethical statements is consistent with the conventions of our actual language. That is, we reject utilitarianism and subjectivism, not as proposals to replace our existing ethical notions by new ones, but as analyses of our existing ethical notions. Our contention is simply that, in our language, sentences which con-tain normative ethical symbols are not equivalent to sentences which express psychological propositions, or indeed empirical propositions of any kind.

It is advisable here to make it plain that it is only normative ethical symbols, and not descriptive ethical symbols, that are held by us to be indefinable in factual terms. There is a danger of confusing these two types of symbols, be-cause they are commonly constituted by signs of the same sensible form. Thus a complex sign of the form "*x* is wrong" may constitute a sentence which expresses a moral judgement concerning a certain type of conduct, or it may constitute a sentence which states that a certain type of conduct is repugnant to the moral sense of a particular society. In the latter case, the symbol "wrong" is a descriptive ethical symbol, and the sentence in which it occurs expresses an ordinary sociological proposition; in the former case, the symbol "wrong" is a normative ethical symbol, and the sentence in which it occurs does not, we maintain, express an empirical proposition at all. It is only with normative ethics that we are at present concerned; so that whenever ethical symbols are used in the course of this argument without qualification, they are always to be interpreted as symbols of the normative type.

In admitting that normative ethical concepts are irreducible to empirical concepts, we seem to be leaving the way clear for the "absolutist" view of ethics—that is, the view that statements of value are not controlled by observa-tion, as ordinary empirical propositions are, but only by a mysterious "intel-lectual intuition." A feature of this theory, which is seldom recognized by its advocates, is that it makes statements of value unverifiable. For it is notorious that what seems intuitively certain to one person may seem doubtful, or even false, to another. So that unless it is possible to provide some criterion by which one may decide between conflicting intuitions, a mere appeal to intuition is worthless as a test of a proposition's validity. But in the case of moral judgements, no such criterion can be given. Some moralists claim to settle the matter by saying that they "know" that their own moral judgements are correct. But such an assertion is of purely psychological interest, and has not the slightest tendency to prove the validity of any moral judgement. For dissentient moralists may equally well "know" that their ethical views are correct. And, as far as subjective certainty goes, there will be nothing to choose between them. When such differences of opinion arise in connection with an ordinary empirical proposition, one may attempt to resolve them by referring to, or actually carrying out, some relevant empirical test. But with regard to ethical statements, there is, on the "absolutist" or "intuitionist" theory, no relevant empirical test. We are therefore justified in saying that on this theory ethical statements are held to be unverifiable. They are, of course, also held to be genuine synthetic propositions.

Considering the use which we have made of the principle that a synthetic proposition is significant only if it is empirically verifiable, it is clear that the acceptance of an "absolutist" theory of ethics would undermine the whole of our main argument. And as we have already rejected the "naturalistic" theories which are commonly supposed to provide the only alternative to "absolutism" in ethics, we seem to have reached a difficult position. We shall meet the difficulty by showing that the correct treatment of ethical statements is afforded by a third theory, which is wholly compatible with our radical empiricism.

We begin by admitting that the fundamental ethical concepts are unanalysable, inasmuch as there is no criterion by which one can test the validity of the judgements in which they occur. So far we are in agreement with the absolutists. But, unlike the absolutists, we are able to give an explanation of this fact about ethical concepts. We say that the reason why they are unanalysable is that they are mere pseudo-concepts. The presence of an ethical symbol in a proposition adds nothing to its factual content. Thus if I say to someone, "You acted wrongly in stealing that money," I am not stating anything more than if I had simply said, "You stole that money." In adding that this action is wrong I am not making any further statement about it. I am simply evincing my moral disapproval of it. It is as if I had said, "You stole that money," in a peculiar tone of horror, or written it with the addition of some special exclamation marks. The tone, or the exclamation marks, adds nothing to the literal meaning of the sentence. It merely serves to show that the expression of it is attended by certain feelings in the speaker.

If now I generalise my previous statement and say, "Stealing money is wrong," I produce a sentence which has no factual meaning—that is, expresses no proposition which can be either true or false. It is as if I had written "Stealing money!!"—where the shape and thickness of the exclamation marks show, by a suitable convention, that a special sort of moral disapproval is the feeling which is being expressed. It is clear that there is nothing said here which can be true or false. Another man may disagree with me about the wrongness of stealing, in the sense that he may not have the same feelings about stealing as I have, and he may quarrel with me on account of my moral sentiments. But he cannot, strictly speaking, contradict me. For in saying that a certain type of action is right or wrong, I am not making any factual statement, not even a statement about my own state of mind. I am merely expressing certain moral sentiments. And the man who is ostensibly contradicting me is merely expressing his moral sentiments. So that there is plainly no sense in asking which of us is in the right. For neither of us is asserting a genuine proposition.

What we have just been saying about the symbol "wrong" applies to all normative ethical symbols. Sometimes they occur in sentences which record ordinary empirical facts besides expressing ethical feeling about those facts: sometimes they occur in sentences which simply express ethical feeling about a certain type of action, or situation, without making any statement of fact. But in every case in which one would commonly be said to be making an ethical judgement, the function of the relevant ethical word is purely "emotive." It is used to express feeling about certain objects, but not to make any assertion about them.

It is worth mentioning that ethical terms do not serve only to express feeling. They are calculated also to arouse feeling, and so to stimulate action. Indeed some of them are used in such a way as to give the sentences in which they occur the effect of commands. Thus the sentence "It is your duty to tell the truth" may be regarded both as the expression of a certain sort of ethical feeling about truthfulness and as the expression of the command "Tell the truth." The sentence "You ought to tell the truth" also involves the command "Tell the truth," but here the tone of the command is less emphatic. In the sentence "It is good to tell the truth" the command has become little more than a suggestion. And thus the "meaning" of the word "good," in its ethical usage, is differentiated from that of the word "duty" or the word "ought." In fact we may define the meaning of the various ethical words in terms both of the different feelings they are ordinarily taken to express, and also the different responses which they are calculated to provoke.

We can now see why it is impossible to find a criterion for determining the validity of ethical judgements. It is not because they have an "absolute" validity which is mysteriously independent of ordinary sense-experience, but because they have no objective validity whatsoever. If a sentence makes no statement at all, there is obviously no sense in asking whether what it says is true or false. And we have seen that sentences which simply express moral judgements do not say anything. They are pure expressions of feeling and as such do not come under the category of truth and falsehood. They are un-verifiable for the same reason as a cry of pain or a word of command is un-verifiable—because they do not express genuine propositions.

Thus, although our theory of ethics might fairly be said to be radically subjectivist, it differs in a very important respect from the orthodox subjectivist theory. For the orthodox subjectivist does not deny, as we do, that the sentences of a moralizer express genuine propositions. All he denies is that they express propositions of a unique non-empirical character. His own view is that they express propositions about the speaker's feelings. If this were so, ethical judgements clearly would be capable of being true or false. They would be true if the speaker had the relevant feelings, and false if he had not. And this is a matter which is, in principle, empirically verifiable. Furthermore they could be significantly contradicted. For if I say, "Tolerance is a virtue," and someone answers, "You don't approve of it," he would, on the ordinary subjectivist theory, be contradicting me. On our theory, he would not be contradicting me, because, in saying that tolerance was a virtue, I should not be making any statement about my own feelings or about anything else. I should simply be evincing my feelings, which is not at all the same thing as saying that I have them.

The distinction between the expression of feeling and the assertion of feeling is complicated by the fact that the assertion that one has a certain feeling often accompanies the expression of that feeling, and is then, indeed, a factor in the expression of that feeling. Thus I may simultaneously express boredom and say that I am bored, and in that case my utterance of the words, "I am bored," is one of the circumstances which make it true to say that I am expressing or evincing boredom. But I can express boredom without actually saying that I am bored. I can express it by my tone and gestures, while making a statement about something wholly unconnected with it, or by an ejaculation, or without uttering any words at all. So that even if the assertion that one has a certain feeling always involves the expression of that feeling, the expression of a feeling assuredly does not always involve the assertion that one has it. And this is the important point to grasp in considering the distinction between our theory and the ordinary subjectivist theory. For whereas the subjectivist holds that ethical statements actually assert the existence of certain feelings, we hold that ethical statements are expressions and excitants of feeling which do not necessarily involve any assertions.

We have already remarked that the main objection to the ordinary subjectivist theory is that the validity of ethical judgements is not determined by the nature of their author's feelings. And this is an objection which our theory escapes. For it does not imply that the existence of any feelings is a necessary and sufficient condition of the validity of an ethical judgement. It implies, on the contrary, that ethical judgements have no validity.

There is, however, a celebrated argument against subjectivist theories which our theory does not escape. It has been pointed out by Moore that if ethical statements were simply statements about the speaker's feelings, it would be impossible to argue about questions of value.[1] To take a typical example: if a man said that thrift was a virtue, and another replied that it was a vice, they would not, on this theory, be disputing with one another. One would be saying that he approved of thrift, and the other that *he* didn't; and there is no reason why both these statements should not be true. Now Moore held it to be obvi-

[1] Cf. *Philosophical Studies*, "The Nature of Moral Philosophy."

ous that we do dispute about questions of value, and accordingly concluded that the particular form of subjectivism which he was discussing was false.

It is plain that the conclusion that it is impossible to dispute about questions of value follows from our theory also. For as we hold that such sentences as "Thrift is a virtue" and "Thrift is a vice" do not express propositions at all, we clearly cannot hold that they express incompatible propositions. We must therefore admit that if Moore's argument really refutes the ordinary subjectivist theory, it also refutes ours. But, in fact, we deny that it does refute even the ordinary subjectivist theory. For we hold that one really never does dispute about questions of value.

This may seem, at first sight, to be a very paradoxical assertion. For we certainly do engage in disputes which are ordinarily regarded as disputes about questions of value. But, in all such cases, we find, if we consider the matter closely, that the dispute is not really about a question of value, but about a question of fact. When someone disagrees with us about the moral value of a certain action or type of action, we do admittedly resort to argument in order to win him over to our way of thinking. But we do not attempt to show by our arguments that he has the "wrong" ethical feeling towards a situation whose nature he has correctly apprehended. What we attempt to show is that he is mistaken about the facts of the case. We argue that he has misconceived the agent's motive: or that he has misjudged the effects of the action, or its probable effects in view of the agent's knowledge; or that he has failed to take into account the special circumstances in which the agent was placed. Or else we employ more general arguments about the effects which actions of a certain type tend to produce, or the qualities which are usually manifested in their performance. We do this in the hope that we have only to get our opponent to agree with us about the nature of the empirical facts for him to adopt the same moral attitude towards them as we do. And as the people with whom we argue have generally received the same moral education as ourselves, and live in the same social order, our expectation is usually justified. But if our opponent happens to have undergone a different process of moral "conditioning" from ourselves, so that, even when he acknowledges all the facts, he still disagrees with us about the moral value of the actions under discussion, then we abandon the attempt to convince him by argument. We say that it is impossible to argue with him because he has a distorted or underdeveloped moral sense; which signifies merely that he employs a different set of values from our own. We feel that our own system of values is superior, and therefore speak in such derogatory terms of his. But we cannot bring forward any arguments to show that our system is superior. For our judgement that it is so is itself a judgement of value, and accordingly outside the scope of argument. It is because argument fails us when we come to deal with pure questions of value, as distinct from questions of fact, that we finally resort to mere abuse.

In short, we find that argument is possible on moral questions only if some system of values is presupposed. If our opponent concurs with us in expressing moral disapproval of all actions of a given type *t*, then we may get him to condemn a particular action A, by bringing forward arguments to show that A is of type *t*. For the question whether A does or does not belong to that type is a plain question of fact. Given that a man has certain moral principles, we argue that he must, in order to be consistent, react morally to certain things in a certain way. What we do not and cannot argue about is the validity of these moral principles. We merely praise or condemn them in the light of our own feelings.

If anyone doubts the accuracy of this account of moral disputes, let him try to construct even an imaginary argument on a question of value which does not reduce itself to an argument about a question of logic or about an empirical matter of fact. I am confident that he will not succeed in producing a single example. And if that is the case, he must allow that its involving the impossibility of purely ethical arguments is not, as Moore thought, a ground of objection to our theory, but rather a point in favour of it.

Having upheld our theory against the only criticism which appeared to threaten it, we may now use it to define the nature of all ethical enquiries. We find that ethical philosophy consists simply in saying that ethical concepts are pseudo-concepts and therefore unanalysable. The further task of describing the different feelings that the different ethical terms are used to express, and the different reactions that they customarily provoke, is a task for the psychologist. There cannot be such a thing as ethical science, if by ethical science one means the elaboration of a "true" system of morals. For we have seen that, as ethical judgements are mere expressions of feeling, there can be no way of determining the validity of any ethical system, and, indeed, no sense in asking whether any such system is true. All that one may legitimately enquire in this connection is, What are the moral habits of a given person or group of people, and what causes them to have precisely those habits and feelings? And this enquiry falls wholly within the scope of the existing social sciences.

It appears, then, that ethics, as a branch of knowledge, is nothing more than a department of psychology and sociology. And in case anyone thinks that we are overlooking the existence of casuistry, we may remark that casuistry is not a science, but is a purely analytical investigation of the structure of a given moral system. In other words, it is an exercise in formal logic.

When one comes to pursue the psychological enquiries which constitute ethical science, one is immediately enabled to account for the Kantian and hedonistic theories of morals. For one finds that one of the chief causes of moral behaviour is fear, both conscious and unconscious, of a god's displeasure, and fear of the enmity of society. And this, indeed, is the reason why moral precepts present themselves to some people as "categorical" commands. And one finds, also, that the moral code of a society is partly determined by the beliefs of that society concerning the conditions of its own happiness—or, in other words, that a society tends to encourage or discourage a given type of conduct by the use of moral sanctions according as it appears to promote or detract from the contentment of the society as a whole. And this is the reason why altruism is recommended in most moral codes and egotism condemned. It is from the observation of this connection between morality and happiness that hedonistic or eudæmonistic theories of morals ultimately spring, just as the moral theory of Kant is based on the fact, previously explained, that moral precepts have for some people the force of inexorable commands. As each of these theories ignores the fact which lies at the root of the other, both may be criticized as being onesided; but this is not the main objection to either of them. Their essential defect is that they treat propositions which refer to the causes and attributes of our ethical feelings as if they were definitions of ethical concepts. And thus they fail to recognise that ethical concepts are pseudo-concepts and consequently indefinable.

As we have already said, our conclusions about the nature of ethics apply to æsthetics also. Æsthetic terms are used in exactly the same way as ethical terms. Such æsthetic words as "beautiful" and "hideous" are employed, as ethical words are employed, not to make statements of fact, but simply to express certain feelings and evoke a certain response. It follows, as in ethics, that there is no sense in attributing objective validity to æsthetic judgements, and no possibility of arguing about questions of value in æsthetics, but only about questions of fact. A scientific treatment of æsthetics would show us what in general were the causes of æsthetic feeling, why various societies produced and admired the works of art they did, why taste varies as it does within a given society, and so forth. And these are ordinary psychological or sociological questions. They have, of course, little or nothing to do with æsthetic criticism as we understand it. But that is because the purpose of æsthetic criticism is not so much to give knowledge as to communicate emotion. The critic, by calling attention to certain features of the work under review, and expressing his own feelings about them, endeavours to make us share his attitude towards the work as a whole. The only relevant propositions that he formulates are propositions describing the nature of the work. And these are plain records of fact. We conclude, therefore, that there is nothing in æsthetics, any more than there is in ethics, to justify the view that it embodies a unique type of knowledge.

It should now be clear that the only information which we can legitimately derive from the study of our æsthetic and moral experiences is information about our own mental and physical make-up. We take note of these experiences as providing data for our psychological and sociological generalisations. And this is the only way in which they serve to increase our knowledge. It follows that any attempt to make our use of ethical and æsthetic concepts the basis of a metaphysical theory concerning the existence of a world of values, as distinct from the world of facts, involves a false analysis of these concepts. Our own analysis has shown that the phenomena of moral experience cannot fairly be used to support any rationalist or metaphysical doctrine whatsoever. In particular, they cannot, as Kant hoped, be used to establish the existence of a transcendent god. . . .

GASS

I have no complicated explanation for my decision to include this selection in the present section. Suffice it to say that it is, in my opinion, one of the most delightful and original essays on ethics to appear in a philosophical journal for many years. William Gass (1924–) is a novelist as well as a philosopher, and his command of language shows itself in the wit of his exposition.

Gass's message is simple but very profound. We are wrong to suppose that particular moral situations are merely instances of general principles, and that we understand what is wrong (or right) with a particular act only after we have brought it under a general heading. So Kant is wrongheaded in trying to show that promise-keeping is an instance of the Categorical Imperative; and Mill is wrongheaded in trying to show that generosity falls under the Greatest Happiness Principle. The truth is really the other way round: We have confidence in the Categorical Imperative or a Utilitarian Principle only because we observe that they fit what we already know to be right or wrong.

In an odd way, Gass agrees with A. J. Ayer up to a point, for both of them say that moral judgment fits neither the deductive pattern of logic and mathematics nor the inductive pattern of the natural sciences. But of course they very soon part company, for Ayer is prepared to reject ethics on the basis of his theory of meaning, whereas Gass thinks only a madman would give up his deepest beliefs for an uncertain bit of meta-philosophy.

I think we can view this essay as an antidote for the disease of overtheorizing. It is good and proper to seek general principles and theoretical overviews, but when we begin to lose touch with the moral convictions which guided us into a study of ethics in the first place, then the time has come to insist upon the priority of the real, the human, and the immediate.

The Case of
the Obliging Stranger

I

Imagine I approach a stranger on the street and say to him, "If you please, sir, I desire to perform an experiment with your aid." The stranger is obliging, and I lead him away. In a dark place conveniently by, I strike his head with the broad of an axe and cart him home. I place him, buttered and trussed, in an ample electric oven. The thermostat reads 450° F. Thereupon I go off to play poker with friends and forget all about the obliging stranger in the stove. When I return, I realize I have overbaked my specimen, and the experiment, alas, is ruined.

Something has been done wrong. Or something wrong has been done.

Any ethic that does not roundly condemn my action is vicious. It is interesting that none is vicious for this reason. It is also interesting that no more convincing refutation of any ethic could be given than by showing that it approved of my baking the obliging stranger.

This is really all I have to say, but I shall not stop on that account. Indeed, I shall begin again.

II

The geometer cannot demonstrate that a line is beautiful. The beauty of lines is not his concern. We do not chide him when he fails to observe uprightness in his verticals, when he discovers no passions between sinuosities. We would not judge it otherwise than foolish to berate him for neglecting to employ the methods successful in biology or botany merely because those methods dealt fairly with lichens and fishes. Nor do we despair of him because he cannot give us reasons for doing geometry which will equally well justify our drilling holes in teeth. There is a limit, as Aristotle said, to the questions which we may sensibly put to each man of science; and however much we may desire to find unity in the purposes, methods, and results of every fruitful sort of inquiry, we must not allow that desire to make mush of their necessary differences.

Historically, with respect to the fundamental problems of ethics, this limit has not been observed. Moreover, the analogy between mathematics and morals, or between the methods of empirical science and the good life, has

"The Case of the Obliging Stranger" by William H. Gass. *Philosophical Review*, LXVI (1957), 193–204.

always been unfairly one-sided. Geometers never counsel their lines to be moral, but moralists advise men to be like lines and go straight. There are triangles of lovers, but no triangles in love. And who says the organism is a state?

For it is true that the customary methods for solving moral problems are the methods which have won honors by leaping mathematical hurdles on the one hand or scientific and physical ones on the other: the intuitive and deductive method and the empirical and inductive one. Nobody seems to have minded very much that the moral hurdle has dunked them both in the pool beyond the wall, for they can privately laugh at each other for fools, and together they can exclaim how frightfully hard is the course.

The difficulty for the mathematical method is the discovery of indubitable moral first premises which do not themselves rest on any inductive foundation and which are still applicable to the complicated tissue of factors that make up moral behavior. The result is that the premises are usually drawn from metaphysical speculations having no intimate relation to moral issues or from rational or mystical revelations which only the intuiter and his followers are willing to credit. For the purposes of deduction, the premises have to be so broad and, to satisfy intuition, so categorically certain, that they become too thin for touch and too heavy for bearing. All negative instances are pruned as unreal or parasitic. Consequently, the truth of the ultimate premises is constantly called into question by those who have intuited differently or have men and actions in mind that they want to call good and right but cannot.

Empirical solutions, so runs the common complaint, lop off the normative branch altogether and make ethics a matter of expediency, taste, or conformity to the moral etiquette of the time. One is told what people do, not what they ought to do; and those philosophers who still wish to know what people ought to do are told, by some of the more uncompromising, that they can have no help from empiricism and are asking a silly question. Philosophers, otherwise empiricists, who admit that moral ends lie beyond the reach of factual debate turn to moral sentiment or some other *bonum ex machina*, thus generously embracing the perplexities of both methods.

III

Questions to which investigators return again and again without success are very likely improperly framed. It is important to observe that the ethical question put so directly as "What is good?" or "What is right?"[1] aims in its answer not, as one might immediately suppose, at a catalogue of the world's good, right things. The moralist is not asking for a list of sheep and goats. The

---

[1] The order in which these questions are asked depends on one's view of the logical primacy of moral predicates. I shall not discriminate among them since I intend my remarks to be indiscriminate.

case of the obliging stranger is a case of immoral action, but this admission is not an answer, even partially, to the question, "What is wrong?"

Furthermore, the ethical question is distressingly short. "Big" questions, it would seem, ought to be themselves big, but they almost never are; and they tend to grow big simply by becoming short—too short, in fact, ever to receive an answer. I might address, to any ear that should hear me, the rather less profound-sounding, but none the less similar question, "Who won?" or perhaps the snappier, "What's a winner?" I should have to ask this question often because, if I were critical, I should never find an answer that would suit me; while at the same time there would be a remarkable lot of answers that suited a remarkable lot of people. The more answers I had—the more occasions on which I asked the question—the more difficult, the more important, the more "big" the question would become.

If the moralist does not want to hear such words as "Samson," "money," or "brains" when he asks his question, "What is good?", what does he want to hear? He wants to hear a word like "power." He wants to know what is good in the things that are good that makes them good. It should be perfectly clear it is not the things themselves that he thinks good or bad but the qualities they possess, the relations they enter into, or the consequences they produce. Even an intuitionist, who claims to perceive goodness directly, perceives a property of things when he perceives goodness, and not any *thing*, except incidentally. The wrong done the obliging stranger was not the act of cooking him but was something belonging to the act in some one of many possible ways. It is not I who am evil (if I am not mad) but something which I *have* that is; and while, of course, I may be adjudged wicked for having whatever it is I have that is bad, it is only because I have it that I am wicked—as if I owned a vicious and unruly dog.

I think that so long as I look on my act in this way, I wrong the obliging stranger a second time.

The moralist, then, is looking for the ingredient that perfects or spoils the stew. He wants to hear the word "power." He wants to know what is good in what is good that makes it good; and the whole wretched difficulty is that one is forced to reply either that what is good in what is good makes the good in what is good good, or that it is, in fact, made good by things which are not in the least good at all. So the next question, which is always, "And why is power good?" is answered by saying that it is good because it is power and power is good; or it is put off by the promise that power leads to things worth much; or it is shrugged aside with the exclamation, "Well, that's life!" This last is usually accompanied by an exhortation not to oppose the inevitable course of nature.

You cannot ask questions forever. Sooner or later the questioning process is brought up short by statements of an apparently dogmatic sort. Pleasure is sought for pleasure's sake. The principle of utility is susceptible of no demonstration. Every act and every inquiry aims at well-being. The nonnatural property of goodness fastens itself to its object and will remain there whatever world the present world may madly become. Frustrated desires give rise to problems, and problems are bad. We confer the title of The Good upon our natural necessities.

I fail to see why, if one is going to call a halt in this way, the halt cannot be called early, and the evident, the obvious, the axiomatic, the indemonstrable, the intrinsic, or whatever one wants to name it, be deemed those clear cases of moral goodness, badness, obligation, or wrong which no theory can cloud, and for which men are prepared to fight to the last ditch. For if someone asks me, now I am repentant, why I regard my act of baking the obliging stranger as wrong, what can I do but point again to the circumstances comprising the act? "Well, I put this fellow in an oven, you see. The oven was on, don't you know." And if my questioner persists, saying: "Of course, I know all about *that*; but what I want to know is, why is *that* wrong?", I should recognize there is no use in replying that it is wrong because of the kind of act it is, a wrong one, for my questioner is clearly suffering from a sort of *folie de doute morale* which forbids him to accept any final answer this early in the game, although he will have to accept precisely the same kind of answer at some time or other.

Presumably there is some advantage in postponing the stop, and this advantage lies in the explanatory power of the higher-level answer. It cannot be that my baking the stranger is wrong for no reason at all. It would then be inexplicable. I do not think this is so, however. It is not inexplicable; it is transparent. Furthermore, the feeling of elucidation, of greater insight or knowledge, is a feeling only. It results, I suspect, from the satisfaction one takes in having an open mind. The explanatory factor is always more inscrutable than the event it explains. The same questions can be asked of it as were asked of the original occasion. It is either found in the situation and brought forward to account for all, as one might advance pain, in this case, out of the roaster; or it resides there mysteriously, like an essence, the witch in the oven; or it hovers, like a coil of smoke, as hovers the greatest unhappiness of the greatest number.

But how ludicrous are the moralist's "reasons" for condemning my baking the obliging stranger. They sound queerly unfamiliar and out of place. This is partly because they intrude where one expects to find denunciation only and because it is true they are seldom if ever *used*. But their strangeness is largely due to the humor in them.

Consider:

My act produced more pain than pleasure.

Baking this fellow did not serve the greatest good to the greatest number.

I acted wrongly because I could not consistently will that the maxim of my action become a universal law.

God forbade me, but I paid no heed.

Anyone can apprehend the property of wrongness sticking plainly to the whole affair.

Decent men remark it and are moved to tears.

But I should say that my act was wrong even if my stranger were tickled into laughter while he cooked; or even if his baking did the utmost good it could; or if, in spite of all, I could consistently will that whatever maxim I might have had might become a universal law; or even if God had spoken from a bush to me, "Thou shalt!" How redundant the property of wrongness, as if one needed *that*, in such a case! And would the act be right if the whole world howled its glee? Moralists can say, with conviction, that the act is wrong; but none can *show* it.

Such cases, like that of the obliging stranger, are cases I call clear. They have the characteristic of moral transparency, and they comprise the core of our moral experience. When we try to explain why they are instances of good or bad, of right or wrong, we sound comic, as anyone does who gives elaborate reasons for the obvious, especially when these reasons are so shamefaced before reality, so miserably beside the point. What we must explain is not why these cases have the moral nature they have, for that needs no explaining, but *why they are so clear*. It is an interesting situation: any moralist will throw over his theory if it reverses the decision on cases like the obliging stranger's. The most persuasive criticism of any ethical system has always been the demonstration, on the critic's part, that the system countenances moral absurdities, despite the fact that, in the light of the whole theoretical enterprise, such criticisms beg the question. Although the philosopher who is caught by a criticism of this sort may protest its circularity or even manfully swallow the dreadful conclusion, his system has been scotched, if it has not been killed.

Not all cases are clear. But the moralist will furrow his brow before even this one. He will pursue principles which do not apply. He does not believe in clear cases. He refuses to believe in clear cases. Why?

IV ✓

His disbelief is an absolute presupposition with him. It is a part of his methodological commitments and a part of his notion of profundity and of the nature of philosophy. It is a part of his reverence for intellectual humility. It is a part of his fear of being arbitrary. So he will put the question bravely to the clear cases, even though no state of fact but only his state of mind brings the question up, and even though putting the question, revealing the doubt, destroys immediately the validity of any answer he has posed the question to announce.

Three children are killed by a drunken driver. A family perishes in a sudden fire. Crowded bleachers collapse. Who is puzzled, asking why these things are terrible, why these things are wrong? When is such a question asked? It is asked when the case is not clear, when one is in doubt about it. "Those impious creatures! . . . At the movies . . . today, . . . which is the Lord's!" Is that so bad? Is being impious, even, so bad? I do not know. It is unclear, so I ask why. Or I disagree to pick a quarrel. Or I am a philosopher whose business it is to be puzzled. But do I imagine there is nothing the matter when three children are run over by drunkenness, or when a family goes up in smoke, or when there is a crush of people under timbers under people? There is no lack of clarity here, there is only the philosopher: patient, persistent as the dung beetle, pushing his "whys" up his hillocks with his nose. His doubts are never of the present case. They are always general. They are doubts in legion, regiment, and principle.

The obliging stranger is overbaked. I wonder whether this is bad or not. I ask about it. Presumably there is a reason for my wonderment. What is it? Well, of course there is not any reason that is a reason about the obliging stranger. There is only a reason because I am a fallibilist, or because one must not be arbitrary, or because all certainties in particular cases are certain only when deduced from greater, grander certainties. The reason I advance may be advanced upon itself. The entire moral structure tumbles at once. It is a test of the clarity of cases that objections to them are objections in principle; that the principle applies as well to all cases as to any one; and that these reasons for doubt devour themselves with equal right and the same appetite. That is why the moralist is really prepared to fight for the clear cases to the last ditch; why, when he questions them, he does so to display his philosophical breeding, because it is good form: he knows that if these cases are not clear, none are, and if none are, the game is up.

If there are clear cases, and if every moralist, at bottom, behaves as if there were, why does he still, at the top, behave as if there were none?

V

He may do so because he is an empiricist practicing induction. He believes, with Peirce, that "the inductive method springs directly out of dissatisfaction with existing knowledge." To get more knowledge he must become dissatisfied with what he has, all of it, by and large, often for no reason whatever. Our knowledge is limited, and what we do know, we know inexactly. In the sphere of morals the moralist has discovered how difficult it is to proceed from facts to values, and although he has not given up, his difficulties persuade him not that no one knows but that no one can be sure.

Above all, the empiricist has a hatred of certainty. His reasons are not entirely methodological. Most are political: certainty is evil; it is dictatorial; it is undemocratic; all cases should be scrutinized equally; there should be no favoritism; the philosopher is fearless. "Thought looks into the pit of hell and is not afraid."

The moralist may behave as if there were no clear cases because he is a rationalist practicing deduction. He knows all about the infinite regress. He is familiar with the unquestioned status of first principles. He is beguiled by the precision, rigor, and unarguable moves of logical demonstration. Moreover, he is such an accomplished doubter of the significance of sensation that he has persuaded the empiricist also to doubt that significance. He regards the empiricist as a crass, anti-intellectual booby, a smuggler where he is not an honest skeptic, since no fact, or set of facts, will account for the value we place on the obliging stranger unless we are satisfied to recount again the precise nature of the case.

Suppose our case concerned toads. And suppose we were asking of the toads, "Why? Why are you toads?" They would be unable to reply, being toads. How far should we get in answering our own question if we were never sure of any particular toad that he was one? How far should we get with our deductions if we were going to deduce one from self-evident toadyisms? What is self-evident about toads except that some are toads? And if we had a toad before us, and we were about to investigate him, and someone doubted that we had a toad before us, we could only say our creature was tailless and clumsy and yellow-green and made warts. So if someone still wanted to doubt our toad, he would have to change the definition of "toad," and someone might want to do that; but who wants to change our understanding of the word "immoral" so that the baking of the obliging stranger is not to be called immoral?

The empiricist is right: the deductive ethic rests upon arbitrary postulation. The rationalist is right: the inductive ethic does not exist; or worse, it consists of arbitrary values disguised as facts. Both are guilty of the most elaborate and flagrant rationalizations. Both know precisely what it is they wish to save. Neither is going to be surprised in the least by what turns out to be good or bad. They are asking of their methods answers that their methods cannot give.

VI

It is confusion which gives rise to doubt. What about the unclear cases? I shall be satisfied to show that there are clear ones, but the unclear ones are more interesting, and there are more of them. How do we decide about blue laws, supposing that there is nothing to decide about the obliging stranger except how to prevent the occurrence from happening again? How do we arbitrate conflicts of duty where each duty, even, may be clear? What of principles, after all? Are there none? Are they not used by people? Well, they talk about them more than they use them, but they use them a little.

I should like to try to answer these questions another time. I can only indicate, quite briefly, the form these answers will take.

I think we decide cases where there is some doubt by stating what it is about them that puzzles us. We hunt for more facts, hoping that the case will clear:

"She left her husband with a broken hand and took the children."

"She did!"

"He broke his hand on her head."

"Dear me; but even so!"

"He beat her every Thursday after tea and she finally couldn't stand it any longer."

"Ah, of course, but the poor children?"

"He beat them, too."

"My, my, and was there no other way?"

"The court would grant her no injunction."

"Why not?"

"Judge Bridlegoose is a fool."

"Ah, of course, she did right, no doubt about it."

If more facts do not clear the case, we redescribe it, emphasizing first this fact and then that until it is clear, or until we have several clear versions of the original muddle. Many ethical disputes are due to the possession, by the contending parties, of different accounts of the same occasion, all satisfactorily clear, and this circumstance gives the disputants a deep feeling for the undoubted rightness of each of their versions. Such disputes are particularly acrimonious, and they cannot be settled until an agreement is reached about the true description of the case.

There are, of course, conflicts of duty which are perfectly clear. I have promised to meet you at four to bowl, but when four arrives I am busy rescuing a baby from the jaws of a Bengal tiger and cannot come. Unclear conflicts we try to clarify. And it sometimes happens that the tug of obligations is so equal as to provide no reasonable solution. If some cases are clear, others are undecidable.

It is perfectly true that principles are employed in moral decisions—popular principles, I mean, like the golden rule and the laws of God. Principles really obscure matters as often as they clear them. They are generally flags and slogans to which the individual is greatly attached. Attack the principle and you attack the owner: his good name, his reputation, his sense of righteousness. Love me, love my maxims. People have been wrongly persuaded that principles decide cases and that a principle which fails in one case fails in all. So principles are usually vehicles for especially powerful feelings and frequently get in the way of good sense. We have all observed the angry arguer who grasps the nettle of absurdity to justify his bragging about the toughness of his skin.

I should regard useful principles as summaries of what may be present generally in clear cases, as for instance: cases where pain is present are more often adjudged bad than not. We might, if the reverse were true for pleasure, express our principle briefly in hedonistic terms: pleasure is the good. But there may be lots of principles of this sort, as there may be lots of rather common factors in clear cases. Principles state more or less prevalent identifying marks, as cardinals usually nest in low trees, although there is nothing to prevent them from nesting elsewhere, and the location of the nest is not the essence of the bird. When I appeal to a principle, then, the meaning of my appeal consists of the fact that before me is a case about which I can reach no direct decision; of the fact that the principle I invoke is relevant, since not every principle is (the laws of God do not cover everything, for instance). In this way I affirm my loyalty to those clear cases the principle so roughly summarizes and express my desire to remain consistent with them.

VII

Insofar as present moral theories have any relevance to our experience, they are elaborate systems designed to protect the certainty of the moralist's last-ditch data. Although he may imagine he is gathering his principles from the purest vapors of the mind, the moralist will in fact be prepared to announce as such serenities only those which support his most cherished goods. And if he is not careful to do just this, he will risk being charged with irrelevancy by those who will employ the emptiness and generality of his principles to demonstrate the value of trivialities: as for example, the criticism of the categorical imperative that claims one can universally will all teeth be brushed with powder in the morning, and so on in like manner.

Ethics, I wish to say, is about something, and in the rush to establish principles, to elicit distinctions from a recalcitrant language, and to discover "laws," those lovely things and honored people, those vile seducers and ruddy villains our principles and laws are supposed to be based upon and our ethical theories to be about are overlooked and forgotten.

AFTERWORD

We began with the conflict between the Judeo-Christian ethic of humility, love, and brotherhood and the romantic Nietzschean celebration of the superior egocentric individual. The search for some answers to this and other ethical dilemmas has led us very deep into problems of truth, meaning, and language. Probably no branch of philosophy has generated such persistent and vigorous disagreements as ethics.

If I were to try to mediate the disputes between Kant and Mill, or Ayer and Gass, I would simply end up writing yet another ethical theory. Since these concluding remarks to Section IV are hardly the place for so ambitious an enterprise, let me restrict myself to a few general observations about the views of our authors.

If we read Nietzsche with a measure of understanding, I think we shall see that he is not so far from Jesus' sermon as he first appears. Nietzsche hated the hypocrisy and the smugness of nineteenth-century established morality, but Jesus probably would have felt the same way. Certainly He had little patience for the wealthy, the powerful, and the self-satisfied in His own society. What Nietzsche cannot see is the possibility of a pacifism which is not merely a cover for impotent rage. He recognizes that aggression can be joyous, but fails to perceive the same joy in Jesus' love of His fellow men. The New Testament makes it quite clear that Jesus felt—and expressed—righteous anger. But that anger need not lead to destruction, nor need it rest on contempt for those who are weak and ill-favored.

Whatever we decide about the validity of the Categorical Imperative, on one issue Kant is clearly correct. If there are any valid moral principles at all, then surely they must be valid a priori, as the laws of logic are. Kant's great contribution to our understanding of ethics is his uncompromising insistence upon the a priori status of moral principles. We do not discover what is right by performing experiments or making observations—though the knowledge gained from observation and experiment may be invaluable in applying moral principles to particular cases. (By now you all will realize that these general remarks, which I express with such confidence, are themselves open to dispute among philosophers. It is even very difficult for a philosopher to say "Good Morning" without having **someone** rise up in disagreement).

As for the cautionary essay by William Gass, I can only say in agreement that if my moral theory gives me permission to roast obliging strangers, then something must be wrong with my theory. There must be **some** limit on how far a philosopher will proceed on theory alone before his sense of reality tells him that he has gone wrong.

V
PHILOSOPHICAL
ANTHROPOLOGY

Repression in America:
Politics and
Human Nature

INTRODUCTION TO THE CONTEMPORARY ISSUE

Is America the land of the free and the home of the brave, a nation dedicated to liberty and justice for all its citizens, a nation—with all its faults—that can truly be called the last, best hope for mankind? Or is America a violent, repressive, racist, imperialist nation which manipulates its subjects at home and destroys the legitimate aspirations of hundreds of millions of men and women abroad? When all is said and done, is this country of ours **good** or **bad**? Should we love it, even as we might love an errant but basically decent friend? Or should we hate it as only an enemy can be hated?

At no time since the great Civil War a century ago—perhaps at no time in our entire history—have these questions seemed as real to Americans as they do today. The great majority of our citizens, even among the young, would probably insist that the United States, with all its faults, remains the freest, most just nation on earth. But a growing number of thoughtful and articulate persons have lost this patriotic faith. More and more men and women are unable to identify their own deepest moral convictions with the policies and goals of the American state. They see this country as repressive, destructive, pervasively, and perhaps irremediably unjust.

The treatment of black men and women is undoubtedly the most visible cause of this growing disillusionment, and certainly America's involvement in Vietnam has played a major role. But just as it is not clear whether the radical condemnation of America is justified by the social injustices which we all admit to exist, so it is far from certain that the faith of the dissenters would be restored by significant improvements in those areas. The fundamental problem is that the two sides in the dispute see American society in absolutely opposed and irreconcilable ways.

Many native voices have articulated the negative view of America, but by a strange trick of historical accident, the leading critic of our society is a foreign-born professor trained in the Hegelian tradition of continental Europe, Herbert Marcuse. In a series of scholarly books, Marcuse has developed the insights of Hegel, Marx, and Freud, and applied them to the unprecedented conditions of modern technological society. Technical though he is, Marcuse has won an international audience among radical young people who rightly sense that he is a kindred spirit. In the first chapter of his most influential book, **One-Dimensional Man,** Marcuse mounts a systematic attack on contemporary American life and politics. Some of you will find yourselves nodding in agreement as you read his descriptions of the totalitarian repressiveness of our affluent society. Others will wonder whether he is talking about the America you live in.

In order to give some balance to the debate, I have reprinted a review of a related book by Marcuse, **An Essay on Liberation.** The reviewer is Prof. Sidney Hook, one of America's most distinguished political philosophers. Hook himself was a radical socialist in his youth, but in scores of books and articles he has hammered away at what he feels are the hypocrisies, confusions, and contradictions of the radical critique.

The New Forms
of Control

A comfortable, smooth, reasonable, democratic unfreedom prevails in advanced industrial civilization, a token of technical progress. Indeed, what could be more rational than the suppression of individuality in the mechanization of socially necessary but painful performances; the concentration of individual enterprises in more effective, more productive corporations; the regulation of free competition among unequally equipped economic subjects; the curtailment of prerogatives and national sovereignties which impede the international organization of resources. That this technological order also involves a political and intellectual coordination may be a regrettable and yet promising development.

The rights and liberties which were such vital factors in the origins and earlier stages of industrial society yield to a higher stage of this society: they are losing their traditional rationale and content. Freedom of thought, speech, and conscience were—just as free enterprise, which they served to promote and protect—essentially *critical* ideas, designed to replace an obsolescent material and intellectual culture by a more productive and rational one. Once institutionalized, these rights and liberties shared the fate of the society of which they had become an integral part. The achievement cancels the premises.

To the degree to which freedom from want, the concrete substance of all freedom, is becoming a real possibility, the liberties which pertain to a state of lower productivity are losing their former content. Independence of thought, autonomy, and the right to political opposition are being deprived of their basic critical function in a society which seems increasingly capable of satisfying the needs of the individuals through the way in which it is organized. Such a society may justly demand acceptance of its principles and institutions, and reduce the opposition to the discussion and promotion of alternative policies *within* the status quo. In this respect, it seems to make little difference whether the increasing satisfaction of needs is accomplished by an authoritarian or a non-authoritarian system. Under the conditions of a rising standard of living, non-conformity with the system itself appears to be socially useless, and the more so when it entails tangible economic and political disadvantages and threatens the smooth operation of the whole. Indeed, at least in so far as the necessities of life are involved, there seems to be no reason why the production and distribution of goods and services should proceed through the competitive concurrence of individual liberties.

Freedom of enterprise was from the beginning not altogether a blessing.

As the liberty to work or to starve, it spelled toil, insecurity, and fear for the vast majority of the population. If the individual were no longer compelled to prove himself on the market, as a free economic subject, the disappearance of this kind of freedom would be one of the greatest achievements of civilization. The technological processes of mechanization and standardization might release individual energy into a yet uncharted realm of freedom beyond necessity. The very structure of human existence would be altered; the individual would be liberated from the work world's imposing upon him alien needs and alien possibilities. The individual would be free to exert autonomy over a life that would be his own. If the productive apparatus could be organized and directed toward the satisfaction of the vital needs, its control might well be centralized; such control would not prevent individual autonomy, but render it possible.

This is a goal within the capabilities of advanced industrial civilization, the "end" of technological rationality. In actual fact, however, the contrary trend operates: the apparatus imposes its economic and political requirements for defense and expansion on labor time and free time, on the material and intellectual culture. By virtue of the way it has organized its technological base, contemporary industrial society tends to be totalitarian. For "totalitarian" is not only a terroristic political coordination of society, but also a non-terroristic economic-technical coordination which operates through the manipulation of needs by vested interests. It thus precludes the emergence of an effective opposition against the whole. Not only a specific form of government or party rule makes for totalitarianism, but also a specific system of production and distribution which may well be compatible with a "pluralism" of parties, newspapers, "countervailing powers," etc.

Today political power asserts itself through its power over the machine process and over the technological organization of the apparatus. The government of advanced and advancing industrial societies can maintain and secure itself only when it succeeds in mobilizing, organizing, and exploiting the technical, scientific, and mechanical productivity available to industrial civilization. And this productivity mobilizes society as a whole, above and beyond any particular individual or group interests. The brute fact that the machine's physical (only physical?) power surpasses that of the individual, and of any particular group of individuals, makes the machine the most effective political instrument in any society whose basic organization is that of the machine process. But the political trend may be reversed; essentially the power of the machine is only the stored-up and projected power of man. To the extent to which the work world is conceived of as a machine and mechanized accordingly, it becomes the *potential* basis of a new freedom for man.

Contemporary industrial civilization demonstrates that it has reached the stage at which "the free society" can no longer be adequately defined in the traditional terms of economic, political, and intellectual liberties, not because these liberties have become insignificant, but because they are too significant to be combined within the traditional forms. New modes of realization are needed, corresponding to the new capabilities of society.

Such new modes can be indicated only in negative terms because they would amount to the negation of the prevailing modes. Thus economic freedom would mean freedom *from* the economy—from being controlled by economic forces and relationships; freedom from the daily struggle for existence, from earning a living. Political freedom would mean liberation of the individuals *from* politics over which they have no effective control. Similarly, intellectual freedom would mean the restoration of individual thought now absorbed by mass communication and indoctrination, abolition of "public opinion" together with its makers. The unrealistic sound of these propositions is indicative, not of their utopian character, but of the strength of the forces which prevent their realization. The most effective and enduring form of warfare against liberation is the implanting of material and intellectual needs that perpetuate obsolete forms of the struggle for existence.

The intensity, the satisfaction and even the character of human needs, beyond the biological level, have always been preconditioned. Whether or not the possibility of doing or leaving, enjoying or destroying, possessing or rejecting something is seized as a *need* depends on whether or not it can be seen as desirable and necessary for the prevailing societal institutions and interests. In this sense, human needs are historical needs and, to the extent to which the society demands the repressive development of the individual, his needs themselves and their claim for satisfaction are subject to overriding critical standards.

We may distinguish both true and false needs. "False" are those which are superimposed upon the individual by particular social interests in his repression: the needs which perpetuate toil, aggressiveness, misery, and injustice. Their satisfaction might be most gratifying to the individual, but this happiness is not a condition which has to be maintained and protected if it serves to arrest the development of the ability (his own and others) to recognize the disease of the whole and grasp the chances of curing the disease. The result then is euphoria in unhappiness. Most of the prevailing needs to relax, to have fun, to behave and consume in accordance with the advertisements, to love and hate what others love and hate, belong to this category of false needs.

Such needs have a societal content and function which are determined by external powers over which the individual has no control; the development and satisfaction of these needs is heteronomous. No matter how much such needs may have become the individual's own, reproduced and fortified by the conditions of his existence; no matter how much he identifies himself with them and finds himself in their satisfaction, they continue to be what they were from the beginning—products of a society whose dominant interest demands repression.

The prevalence of repressive needs is an accomplished fact, accepted in ignorance and defeat, but a fact that must be undone in the interest of the happy individual as well as all those whose misery is the price of his satisfaction. The only needs that have an unqualified claim for satisfaction are the vital ones—nourishment, clothing, lodging at the attainable level of culture. The satisfaction of all these needs is the prerequisite for the realization of *all* needs, of the unsublimated as well as the sublimated ones.

For any consciousness and conscience, for any experience which does not accept the prevailing societal interest as the supreme law of thought and behavior, the established universe of needs and satisfactions is a fact to be questioned—questioned in terms of truth and falsehood. These terms are historical throughout, and their objectivity is historical. The judgment of needs and their satisfaction, under the given conditions, involves standards of *priority*— standards which refer to the optimal development of the individual, of all individuals, under the optimal utilization of the material and intellectual resources available to man. The resources are calculable. "Truth" and "falsehood" of needs designate objective conditions to the extent to which the universal satisfaction of vital needs and, beyond it, the progressive alleviation of toil and poverty, are universally valid standards. But as historical standards, they do not only vary according to area and stage of development, they also can be defined only in (greater or lesser) *contradiction* to the prevailing ones. What tribunal can possibly claim the authority of decision?

In the last analysis, the question of what are true and false needs must be answered by the individuals themselves, but only in the last analysis; that is, if and when they are free to give their own answer. As long as they are kept incapable of being autonomous, as long as they are indoctrinated and manipulated (down to their very instincts), their answer to this question cannot be taken as their own. By the same token, however, no tribunal can justly arrogate to itself the right to decide which needs should be developed and satisfied. Any such tribunal is reprehensible, although our revulsion does not do away with the question: how can the people who have been the object of effective and productive domination by themselves create the conditions of freedom?

The more rational, productive, technical, and total the repressive administration of society becomes, the more unimaginable the means and ways by which the administered individuals might break their servitude and seize their own liberation. To be sure, to impose Reason upon an entire society is a paradoxical and scandalous idea—although one might dispute the righteousness of a society which ridicules this idea while making its own population into objects of total administration. All liberation depends on the consciousness of servitude, and the emergence of this consciousness is always hampered by the predominance of needs and satisfactions which, to a great extent, have become the individual's own. The process always replaces one system of preconditioning by another; the optimal goal is the replacement of false needs by true ones, the abandonment of repressive satisfaction.

The distinguishing feature of advanced industrial society is its effective suffocation of those needs which demand liberation—liberation also from that which is tolerable and rewarding and comfortable—while it sustains and absolves the destructive power and repressive function of the affluent society. Here, the social controls exact the overwhelming need for the production and consumption of waste; the need for stupefying work where it is no longer a real necessity; the need for modes of relaxation which soothe and prolong this stupefication; the need for maintaining such deceptive liberties as free competition at administered prices, a free press which censors itself, free choice between brands and gadgets.

Under the rule of a repressive whole, liberty can be made into a powerful instrument of domination. The range of choice open to an individual is not the decisive factor in determining the degree of human freedom, but *what* can be chosen and what *is* chosen by the individual. The criterion for free choice can never be an absolute one, but neither is it entirely relative. Free election of masters does not abolish the masters or the slaves. Free choice among a wide variety of goods and services does not signify freedom if these goods and services sustain social controls over a life of toil and fear—that is, if they sustain alienation. And the spontaneous reproduction of superimposed needs by the individual does not establish autonomy; it only testifies to the efficacy of the controls.

Our insistence on the depth and efficacy of these controls is open to the objection that we overrate greatly the indoctrinating power of the "media," and that by themselves the people would feel and satisfy the needs which are now imposed upon them. The objection misses the point. The preconditioning does not start with the mass production of radio and television and with the centralization of their control. The people enter this stage as preconditioned receptacles of long standing: the decisive difference is in the flattening out of the contrast (or conflict) between the given and the possible, between the satisfied and the unsatisfied needs. Here, the so-called equalization of class distinctions reveals its ideological function. If the worker and his boss enjoy the same television program and visit the same resort places, if the typist is as attractively made up as the daughter of her employer, if the Negro owns a Cadillac, if they all read the same newspaper, then this assimilation indicates not the disappearance of classes, but the extent to which the needs and satisfactions that serve the preservation of the Establishment are shared by the underlying population.

Indeed, in the most highly developed areas of contemporary society, the transplantation of social into individual needs is so effective that the difference between them seems to be purely theoretical. Can one really distinguish between the mass media as instruments of information and entertainment, and as agents of manipulation and indoctrination? Between the automobile as nuisance and as convenience? Between the horrors and the comforts of functional architecture? Between the work for national defense and the work for corporate gain? Between the private pleasure and the commercial and political utility involved in increasing the birth rate?

We are again confronted with one of the most vexing aspects of advanced industrial civilization: the rational character of its irrationality. Its productivity and efficiency, its capacity to increase and spread comforts, to turn waste into need, and destruction into construction, the extent to which this civilization transforms the object world into an extension of man's mind and body makes the very notion of alienation questionable. The people recognize themselves in their commodities; they find their soul in their automobile, hi-fi set, split-level home, kitchen equipment. The very mechanism which ties the individual to his society has changed, and social control is anchored in the new needs which it has produced.

The prevailing forms of social control are technological in a new sense. To be sure, the technical structure and efficacy of the productive and destructive apparatus has been a major instrumentality for subjecting the population to the established social division of labor throughout the modern period. Moreover, such integration has always been accompanied by more obvious forms of compulsion: loss of livelihood, the administration of justice, the police, the armed forces. It still is. But in the contemporary period, the technological controls appear to be the very embodiment of Reason for the benefit of all social groups and interests—to such an extent that all contradiction seems irrational and all counteraction impossible.

No wonder then that, in the most advanced areas of this civilization, the social controls have been introjected to the point where even the individual protest is affected at its roots. The intellectual and emotional refusal "to go along" appears neurotic and impotent. This is the socio-psychological aspect of the political event that marks the contemporary period: the passing of the historical forces which, at the preceding stage of industrial society, seemed to represent the possibility of new forms of existence.

But the term "introjection" perhaps no longer describes the way in which the individual by himself reproduces and perpetuates the external controls exercised by his society. Introjection suggests a variety of relatively spontaneous processes by which a Self (Ego) transposes the "outer" into the "inner." Thus introjection implies the existence of an inner dimension distinguished from and even antagonistic to the external exigencies—an individual consciousness and an individual unconscious *apart from* public opinion and behavior.[1] The idea of "inner freedom" here has its reality: it designates the private space in which man may become and remain "himself."

Today this private space has been invaded and whittled down by tech-

[1] The change in the function of the family here plays a decisive role: its "socializing" functions are increasingly taken over by outside groups and media. See my *Eros and Civilization* (Boston: Beacon Press, 1955), pp. 96 ff.

nological reality. Mass production and mass distribution claim the *entire* individual, and industrial psychology has long since ceased to be confined to the factory. The manifold processes of introjection seem to be ossified in almost mechanical reactions. The result is, not adjustment but *mimesis:* an immediate identification of the individual with *his* society and, through it, with the society as a whole.

This immediate, automatic identification (which may have been characteristic of primitive forms of association) reappears in high industrial civilization; its new "immediacy," however, is the product of a sophisticated, scientific management and organization. In this process, the "inner" dimension of the mind in which opposition to the status quo can take root is whittled down. The loss of this dimension, in which the power of negative thinking—the critical power of Reason—is at home, is the ideological counterpart to the very material process in which advanced industrial society silences and reconciles the opposition. The impact of progress turns Reason into submission to the facts of life, and to the dynamic capability of producing more and bigger facts of the same sort of life. The efficiency of the system blunts the individuals' recognition that it contains no facts which do not communicate the repressive power of the whole. If the individuals find themselves in the things which shape their life, they do so, not by giving, but by accepting the law of things—not the law of physics but the law of their society.

I have just suggested that the concept of alienation seems to become questionable when the individuals identify themselves with the existence which is imposed upon them and have in it their own development and satisfaction. This identification is not illusion but reality. However, the reality constitutes a more progressive stage of alienation. The latter has become entirely objective; the subject which is alienated is swallowed up by its alienated existence. There is only one dimension, and it is everywhere and in all forms. The achievements of progress defy ideological indictment as well as justification; before their tribunal, the "false consciousness" of their rationality becomes the true consciousness.

This absorption of ideology into reality does not, however, signify the "end of ideology." On the contrary, in a specific sense advanced industrial culture is *more* ideological than its predecessor, inasmuch as today the ideology is in the process of production itself. In a provocative form, this proposition reveals the political aspects of the prevailing technological rationality. The productive apparatus and the goods and services which it produces "sell" or impose the social system as a whole. The means of mass transportation and communication, the commodities of lodging, food, and clothing, the irresistible output of the entertainment and information industry carry with them prescribed attitudes and habits, certain intellectual and emotional reactions which bind the consumers more or less pleasantly to the producers and, through the latter, to the whole. The products indoctrinate and manipulate; they promote a false consciousness which is immune against its falsehood. And as these beneficial products become available to more individuals in more social classes, the indoctrination they carry ceases to be publicity; it becomes a way of life. It is a good way of life—much better than before—and as a good way of life, it militates against qualitative change. Thus emerges a pattern of *one-dimensional thought and behavior* in which ideas, aspirations, and objectives that, by their content, transcend the established universe of discourse and action are either repelled or reduced to terms of this universe. They are redefined by the rationality of the given system and of its quantitative extension.

The trend may be related to a development in scientific method: operationalism in the physical, behaviorism in the social sciences. The common feature is a total empiricism in the treatment of concepts; their meaning is restricted to the representation of particular operations and behavior. The operational point of view is well illustrated by P. W. Bridgman's analysis of the concept of length.[2]

> We evidently know what we mean by length if we can tell what the length of any and every object is, and for the physicist nothing more is required. To find the length of an object, we have to perform certain physical operations. The concept of length is therefore fixed when the operations by which length is measured are fixed: that is, the concept of length involves as much and nothing more than the set of operations by which length is determined. In general, we mean by any concept nothing more than a set of operations; *the concept is synonymous with the corresponding set of operations.*

Bridgman has seen the wide implications of this mode of thought for the society at large:[3]

> To adopt the operational point of view involves much more than a mere restriction of the sense in which we understand "concept," but means a far-reaching change in all our habits of thought, in that we shall no longer permit ourselves to use as tools in our thinking concepts of which we cannot give an adequate account in terms of operations.

Bridgman's prediction has come true. The new mode of thought is today the predominant tendency in philosophy, psychology, sociology, and other fields. Many of the most seriously troublesome concepts are being "eliminated" by showing that no adequate account of them in terms of operations or behavior can be given. The radical empiricist onslaught . . . thus provides the meth-

---

[2] P. W. Bridgman, *The Logic of Modern Physics* (New York: Macmillan, 1928), p. 5. The operational doctrine has since been refined and qualified. Bridgman himself has extended the concept of "operation" to include the "paper-and-pencil" operations of the theorist (in Philipp J. Frank, *The Validation of Scientific Theories* [Boston: Beacon Press, 1954], Chap. II). The main impetus remains the same: it is "desirable" that the paper-and-pencil operations "be capable of eventual contact, although perhaps indirectly, with instrumental operations."

[3] P. W. Bridgman, *The Logic of Modern Physics*, loc. cit., p. 31.

odological justification for the debunking of the mind by the intellectuals—a positivism which, in its denial of the transcending elements of Reason, forms the academic counterpart of the socially required behavior.

Outside the academic establishment, the "far-reaching change in all our habits of thought" is more serious. It serves to coordinate ideas and goals with those exacted by the prevailing system, to enclose them in the system, and to repel those which are irreconcilable with the system. The reign of such a one-dimensional reality does not mean that materialism rules, and that the spiritual, metaphysical, and bohemian occupations are petering out. On the contrary, there is a great deal of "Worship together this week," "Why not try God," Zen, existentialism, and beat ways of life, etc. But such modes of protest and transcendence are no longer contradictory to the status quo and no longer negative. They are rather the ceremonial part of practical behaviorism, its harmless negation, and are quickly digested by the status quo as part of its healthy diet.

One-dimensional thought is systematically promoted by the makers of politics and their purveyors of mass information. Their universe of discourse is populated by self-validating hypotheses which, incessantly and monopolistically repeated, become hypnotic definitions or dictations. For example, "free" are the institutions which operate (and are operated on) in the countries of the Free World; other transcending modes of freedom are by definition either anarchism, communism, or propaganda. "Socialistic" are all encroachments on private enterprises not undertaken by private enterprise itself (or by government contracts), such as universal and comprehensive health insurance, or the protection of nature from all too sweeping commercialization, or the establishment of public services which may hurt private profit. This totalitarian logic of accomplished facts has its Eastern counterpart. There, freedom is the way of life instituted by a communist regime, and all other transcending modes of freedom are either capitalistic, or revisionist, or leftist sectarianism. In both camps, ideas are non-behavioral and subversive. The movement of thought is stopped at barriers which appear as the limits of Reason itself.

Such limitation of thought is certainly not new. Ascending modern rationalism, in its speculative as well as empirical form, shows a striking contrast between extreme critical radicalism in scientific and philosophic method on the one hand, and an uncritical quietism in the attitude toward established and functioning social institutions. Thus Descartes' *ego cogitans* was to leave the "great public bodies" untouched, and Hobbes held that "the present ought always to be preferred, maintained, and accounted best." Kant agreed with Locke in justifying revolution *if and when* it has succeeded in organizing the whole and in preventing subversion.

However, these accommodating concepts of Reason were always contradicted by the evident misery and injustice of the "great public bodies" and the effective, more or less conscious rebellion against them. Societal conditions existed which provoked and permitted real dissociation from the established state of affairs; a private as well as political dimension was present in which dissociation could develop into effective opposition, testing its strength and the validity of its objectives.

With the gradual closing of this dimension by the society, the self-limitation of thought assumes a larger significance. The interrelation between scientific-philosophical and societal processes, between theoretical and practical Reason, asserts itself "behind the back" of the scientists and philosophers. The society bars a whole type of oppositional operations and behavior; consequently, the concepts pertaining to them are rendered illusory or meaningless. Historical transcendence appears as metaphysical transcendence, not acceptable to science and scientific thought. The operational and behavioral point of view, practiced as a "habit of thought" at large, becomes the view of the established universe of discourse and action, needs and aspirations. The "cunning of Reason" works, as it so often did, in the interest of the powers that be. The insistence on operational and behavioral concepts turns against the efforts to free thought and behavior *from* the given reality and *for* the suppressed alternatives. Theoretical and practical Reason, academic and social behaviorism meet on common ground: that of an advanced society which makes scientific and technical progress into an instrument of domination.

"Progress" is not a neutral term; it moves toward specific ends, and these ends are defined by the possibilities of ameliorating the human condition. Advanced industrial society is approaching the stage where continued progress would demand the radical subversion of the prevailing direction and organization of progress. This stage would be reached when material production (including the necessary services) becomes automated to the extent that all vital needs can be satisfied while necessary labor time is reduced to marginal time. From this point on, technical progress would transcend the realm of necessity, where it served as the instrument of domination and exploitation which thereby limited its rationality; technology would become subject to the free play of faculties in the struggle for the pacification of nature and of society.

Such a state is envisioned in Marx's notion of the "abolition of labor." The term "pacification of existence" seems better suited to designate the historical alternative of a world which—through an international conflict which transforms and suspends the contradictions within the established societies— advances on the brink of a global war. "Pacification of existence" means the development of man's struggle with man and with nature, under conditions where the competing needs, desires, and aspirations are no longer organized by vested interests in domination and scarcity—an organization which perpetuates the destructive forms of this struggle.

Today's fight against this historical alternative finds a firm, mass basis in the underlying population, and finds its ideology in the rigid orientation of thought and behavior to the given universe of facts. Validated by the accomplishments of science and technology, justified by its growing productivity, the status quo defies all transcendence. Faced with the possibility of pacification on the grounds of its technical and intellectual achievements, the mature industrial society closes itself against this alternative. Operationalism, in theory and practice, becomes the theory and practice of *containment*. Underneath its obvious dynamics, this society is a thoroughly static system of life: self-propelling in its oppressive productivity and in its beneficial coordination. Containment of technical progress goes hand in hand with its growth in the established direction. In spite of the political fetters imposed by the status quo, the more technology appears capable of creating the conditions for pacification, the more are the minds and bodies of man organized against this alternative.

The most advanced areas of industrial society exhibit throughout these two features: a trend toward consummation of technological rationality, and intensive efforts to contain this trend within the established institutions. Here is the internal contradiction of this civilization: the irrational element in its rationality. It is the token of its achievements. The industrial society which makes technology and science its own is organized for the ever-more-effective domination of man and nature, for the ever-more-effective utilization of its resources. It becomes irrational when the success of these efforts opens new dimensions of human realization. Organization for peace is different from organization for war; the institutions which served the struggle for existence cannot serve the pacification of existence. Life as an end is qualitatively different from life as a means.

Such a qualitatively new mode of existence can never be envisaged as the mere by-product of economic and political changes, as the more or less spontaneous effect of the new institutions which constitute the necessary prerequisite. Qualitative change also involves a change in the *technical* basis on which this society rests—one which sustains the economic and political institutions through which the "second nature" of man as an aggressive object of administration is stabilized. The techniques of industrialization are political techniques; as such, they prejudge the possibilities of Reason and Freedom.

To be sure, labor must precede the reduction of labor, and industrialization must precede the development of human needs and satisfactions. But as all freedom depends on the conquest of alien necessity, the realization of freedom depends on the *techniques* of this conquest. The highest productivity of labor can be used for the perpetuation of labor, and the most efficient industrialization can serve the restriction and manipulation of needs.

When this point is reached, domination—in the guise of affluence and liberty—extends to all spheres of private and public existence, integrates all authentic opposition, absorbs all alternatives. Technological rationality reveals its political character as it becomes the great vehicle of better domination, creating a truly totalitarian universe in which society and nature, mind and body are kept in a state of permanent mobilization for the defense of this universe.

SIDNEY HOOK

Review of Marcuse's
An Essay on Liberation

Although Marx was a prophet of social revolution, his predictions about when, where and how it would occur were not confirmed. Nor did he foresee the rise of Fascism and the welfare state. Actually, it was the advent of the welfare state that eroded the doctrinaire and revolutionary character of Western Marxism. For it showed that democratic political processes could affect the operation of the economic system, abolish some of its worst evils and open a perspective for profound change in the power relations of different classes.

The very success of reform brings despair to the heart of those who, like Herbert Marcuse, wish to revolutionize the entire basis of human society and abolish all injustice. The main reason for their despair is the belief that the workers, who should have been the carriers of social revolution, have become part of the Establishment in all the developed economies of the West. Corrupted by the sorry affluence of their society, striving for the same values, goods and services of the middle-classes, the workers, declares Marcuse, are now a "conservative, even counter-revolutionary force." The situation is hardly remediable, because the vested interest of the workers in the System extends to their very nerve endings, to their biological make-up.

Who, then, will be the carriers of the revolution? For not all the scientific and technical advances in the world will by themselves bring liberation. That can now be achieved, Marcuse asserts, only by "a new type of man" with "a new sensibility" whose "biological dimension" will render him forever immune to the degrading seductions of an affluent society. The new, biological type of man is not the new type of Soviet man—who seems to want the same things in life as the workers corrupted by capitalist prosperity, who misguidedly strive for the same high standard of living as their employers. The new man must be instinctually different, "A type of man with a different sensitivity as well as consciousness; men who would speak a different language, have different gestures, follow different impulses; men who have developed an instinctual barrier against cruelty, brutality, and ugliness."

Where can such a new man—really superman—be found? We obviously cannot rely on biological mutations. Marcuse is very unclear on this point. He tells us that the construction of a new society "presupposes" such a man, and that the new sensibility must "precede" the revolution. But he also asserts that the new man cannot be "envisaged" except through revolution. All this makes the prospect of human liberation very dubious.

It does, however, reveal the spirit of Marcuse's thought. Convinced that he has gone beyond Marx, he has actually returned to the Utopian, undemo-

Review of *An Essay on Liberation* by Herbert Marcuse, April 20, 1969 from *The New York Times Book Review*, Sidney Hook. © 1969 by The New York Times Company. Reprinted by permission of The New York Times and the author.

cratic positions Marx criticized as playing into the hands of reaction. For Marx, the emancipation of the working class depended upon its own historical struggles to improve its lot; it could not be effected by an élite party or group of supermen. And the view that genuine revolutionary social change must be preceded by "the revolution within," whether spiritual or biological, was for Marx the oldest text of social illusion. Human nature may be a historical variable, but this emphasis upon developing "a new type of man" reeks of totalitarianism. It brings to mind the horrid definition of the intellectual, attributed to Stalin, as "the engineer of the human soul."

Disappointed with the workers, Marcuse finds his last best hope for a truly free society—described as if it were a sexy heaven on earth—in active minorities, "mainly among the young middle-class intelligentsia and the ghetto population." Although a minority, they represent "the common interest" of the oppressed majority, and are therefore justified in acting in its name. Marcuse leaves it far from clear that these groups have escaped the contagion of their society; and by his own account of their behavior they seem rather a comedown from the kindly supermen of the "new sensibility."

So far, Marcuse's ideas are a rehash of discredited fantasies. But when he begins to apply them to politics, they become mischievous. Absurdities in the marketplace tend to prepare the way for atrocities. Marcuse admits that existing democracy "provides the most favorable ground for the development and organization of dissent." But he scorns it. The very reforms, concessions and freedoms that democracy makes possible lull the majority into endorsing decisions not in its best interests, as Marcuse understands those interests. What good is its freedom if the majority chooses wrongly—as it must do in a class society? Therefore, he concludes, social change must take place not through "the rules and methods of democratic legality" but through extra-parliamentary "rebellion."

Among the reasons he offers for rejecting existing democracy as spurious is that government is "factually exercised" by élites. But this is true of any representative system. The relevant questions are: To whom are élites responsible? Is their power limited by other powers, judicial and social? Can they be changed or dismissed by expressions of the majority will? Disregard these questions, as Marcuse does, and the whole distinction between dictatorship and democracy becomes meaningless, and Orwell's double-speak becomes the public idiom.

Marcuse frankly acknowledges that he is prepared to replace the present existing élite by another governing élite which does *not* have majority support. He follows Lenin and Stalin here, not Marx. One naturally asks: What guarantee is there that the regime of his undemocratic élite will not be as repressive as Stalin's or Hitler's? Marcuse's response is hardly reassuring:

> Our entire discussion was based on the proposition that the revolution would be liberating only if it were carried out by the non-repressive forces stirring in existing society. The proposition is no more, and no less, than a hope.

For this forlorn hope—since the "new man" is still in the limbo of the unborn—Marcuse is willing to incite to rebellion and insurrection despite their tragic costs.

In selecting those who are to revolt, Marcuse's élitism is at its most arrogant. He pins his hope for rebellions on some student groups, some elements among the *lumpenproletariat*, but mainly on the Negroes. In the past, when the civil-rights movement showed that black people wanted the same goods and services as whites, Marcuse sneered at their capitulation to middle-class values, and was indifferent to whether they had the right to vote. Since the ghetto riots, he has discovered their force for rebellion. "The ghetto population of the United States constitutes such a force. Confined to small areas of living and dying, it can be more easily organized and directed." (sic!)

It is not likely that the black population will permit itself to be directed by Marcuse or anyone else in behalf of a forlorn hope.

The spirit that pervades this book, and most of Marcuse's writings, is more Prussian than Marxist. He doesn't argue his positions as much as he proclaims them. Confused by Hegel, the law of contradiction has no terrors for him. Inconvenient facts are simply ignored. He writes, for example, "as the common Enemy of all capitalism, communism promoted the organization of a common interest superseding the inter-capitalist differences and conflicts." How, then, account for capitalist England and capitalist America making common cause with Communist Russia against capitalist Germany in World War II? Although he speaks of the direct democracy of the rebels, of the "new men," he has no conception of the ethics of democracy, for he unqualifiedly endorses Castro's regime and "the Chinese cultural revolution." Apparently insensate, mindless glorification of Mao is an illustration of "biological solidarity" at work; and the breaking of the fingers of musicians who play Western music in China is an expression of "instinctual creative force." This is pure Orwell.

In the interests of a libertarian society, Marcuse would ruthlessly repress all who differ with him about how to make man and society freer. He enjoys rights in this spurious democracy he is frank to admit he would deny to others. The most effective response to his dogmatic intolerance is not to subject him to the repressions he would visit upon others, nor to deprive him of the rewards, comforts and protection of the welfare state to which he clings with as great a tenacity as those whom he denounces for their spiritual corruption, but rather to expose his views most widely to the criticism and laughter they deserve.

For Marcuse's reputation as a thinker is not likely to survive a careful reading of this book.

COMMENTARY ON THE CONTEMPORARY ISSUE

By now, it should be obvious to you that many philosophical problems are embedded in Marcuse's controversial attacks on American society. He himself calls attention to the connection between operationalist and logical positivist theories of meaning on the one hand, and a politically conservative defense of established institutions on the other. But underlying this and other philosophical disputes in Marcuse's thought is a fundamental, not very clearly exposed theory of human nature itself—a theory about what man **is,** and what he could **become.** In this section, I should like you to examine a number of different theories of human nature in order to see how they give rise to equally diverse political doctrines.

When Marcuse says that modern technological capitalist society is repressive, what does he mean? If we say that Germany under Hitler was repressive, it is clear what we mean—critics of Nazi policies were fired from their jobs, or thrown in jail, or even killed. Millions of German citizens were herded into concentration camps and executed because of their religion of their ethnic background. In short, when we describe a regime or a society as "repressive," we are saying that it holds people down, thwarts their legitimate desires, makes them miserable—and that it does all this by threats, by force, against their wishes.

Now, we all know that there are still millions of Americans who live in poverty, millions who suffer discrimination because of their race or religion. Even with our elaborate system of constitutional safeguards, there are still men and women whose rights are violated because of their unpopular opinions. So we might naturally suppose that Marcuse had these manifest inadequacies of American society in mind when he described it as "repressive." But as we read him, we discover that that isn't what he means at all. When he talks about the way America oppresses its citizens, he means the well-paid, unionized, secure auto and steel workers **as well as** the migrant fruit pickers or unemployed ghetto youths. He even means the comfortable, middle-class, suburban professional men with their split-level homes and three-car garages! What on earth can it mean to say that such people are "repressed"? They have wealth, security, privacy, education, political influence—how can they possibly be put in the same category as Russian political exiles in Siberia or overworked wage slaves in early capitalist factories?

To see what Marcuse is driving at, let us take an analogy from medicine. Suppose that a team of doctors from the World Health Organization were to visit a primitive tribe in a remote region near the headwaters of the Amazon River. After winning the confidence of the natives and giving them all physical examinations, the team might conclude that **all** the members of the tribe were suffering a serious dietary deficiency which weakened their health and shortened their lifespan.

Now, imagine the chief of the tribe being told that he and all his people were sick. "Nonsense!" he might reply. "Some of my people fall ill from time to time; some even die from sickness. But how can you say that the strongest and healthiest of my warriors are sick?"

The doctors, of course, would have no trouble answering the question. As medical experts, they would have a clear idea of what constituted a **healthy** condition for the human body. Hence, they could compare the physical condition of the natives to that standard or ideal and draw the conclusion that the entire tribe was unwell. Those "healthy" natives who didn't think they were ill would simply be wrong. In matters of medicine, the patient doesn't always know best. If a man has never seen a really healthy human being, if he has no scientifically grounded conception of the natural lifespan of the human race, then he may simply not know that his own health is impaired.

Let us return to Marcuse and draw the analogy. A social critic is like a doctor. He has a theory of human nature and human happiness which he uses as a standard against which to evaluate the condition of men and women in his society. His theory may be derived from observation, from systematic experiment, from reflections on his own experience, or even from religion or pure reason. Whatever the source, it tells him what the good, or healthy, or happy human condition is. When he looks at society, he uses his theory to judge that some people are psychologically unfulfilled—that their personalities are thwarted or stunted or warped by their social environment, so that they cannot achieve real emotional health. In short, he judges that they are **unhappy.** We might say that a social critic diagnoses the spiritual ills of society, just as a public health expert diagnoses its physical ills.

As we noted, most men know when they are physically unwell, but sometimes an individual may be unaware that he is not in good health, and under special circumstances even an entire society may suffer from illness or poor health without knowing it. The social critic would extend the analogy and agree that although most men know when they are unhappy, it sometimes happens that a man is unhappy—or psychologically ill—without realizing it. What is more, a society may have such a limited conception of man's spiritual potential that it simply can't recognize its own psychological inadequacies. Imagine, if you can, a society which had no art whatsoever. An observer from another culture would be able to see this cultural impoverishment even though those **in** the society could not perceive that there was something missing from their lives.

Marcuse and the many other radical critics of American society are saying, in effect, that Americans are spiritually sick without knowing it. Even though we may **think** we are reasonably happy—as happy as men can expect to be in this life—still we are unfulfilled and spiritually warped by our social institutions. Hence, the radicals argue, we **all** need to be liberated—the rich as well as the poor, the powerful as well as the weak. To return to the hypothetical example of the South American tribe, the chief and his warriors, as well as the poor or maimed in the tribe, are physically sick, although they may not know it.

As I am sure you can imagine, there are a great many arguments against Marcuse's position, and against the attempt in general to base a critique of society on a theory of human nature. One particularly vulnerable point is, of course, the analogy between the health of the body and the health of the soul. This analogy has a long history, going all the way back to Plato's **Republic** and **Gorgias,** but in philosophy age does not confer dignity or authority on an argument, and we must decide for ourselves whether it makes sense to talk of Americans as suffering from a spiritual or psychological malady which they themselves are unaware of.

In the second section, you read an attack by Dr. Thomas Szasz on the legal defense, "not guilty by reason of insanity." Dr. Szasz explicitly repudiated the notions of mental health and mental illness, claiming that the conflicts which psychiatry treats as diseases are really "problems in living." If Szasz is correct, then Plato, Marx, Marcuse, and many other social critics must find some other foundation for their analyses of the human condition.

As you read the selections in this section, see whether you can discover the ways in which the authors draw political conclusions from their conceptions of human nature. See too whether the authors provide us with any evidence or argument to support their views of man. One way to test your grasp of the selection is to figure out the opinion which each author would have formed of modern American society on the basis of his theory of man. Would Aristotle consider our society a good place for men to realize their human potential? Would Bentham, or Mill, or Marx, or Nietzsche, or Skinner? If not, what changes would each propose?

The most important question, needless to say, is what **you** think. Is this a society in which you want to live? How would you change it? And **why?** For a philosopher, remember, the **why** is always as important as the **how** or the **what.** Whether you are a defender or a critic of American society, you should have reasoned arguments to support your position.

ARISTOTLE

For Aristotle, the complete development of man's nature requires a socio-political setting in which he can play an active role in the affairs of his polis, or political community. Man is a rational creature, and reason is—among other things—the power to deliberate on the ends of our action and to choose what we judge to be best. However, any state which denies men the opportunity to participate in the affairs of government must necessarily leave them thwarted and unfulfilled. Sometimes, of course, men are conscious of this exclusion from the government of their society, and they may demand a greater role, as the American revolutionaries did. But often the subjects of a tyranny do not fully realize what they are missing. Their capacity for self-rule is atrophied, like the eyes of fish which dwell in cave ponds and never see the light. Such men, Aristotle might say, would be repressed and thwarted without knowing it.

However, Aristotle is no lover of democracy, for he firmly believes that only part of mankind has sufficient rational power to engage in true self-rule. In his famous attempt to justify the ancient Greek institution of slavery, Aristotle argues that only some men have the rational capacity necessary for successful self-rule. These few are the "natural masters." The rest of mankind are "natural slaves," whose wisest course is to submit to the rule of the masters. The basis for Aristotle's distinction is the variation in the distribution of intellectual ability, and so in a sense we might view him as arguing for rule by the intelligent or the well-educated.

We are all so conditioned to respond negatively to the idea of "slavery" that we may fail to notice the great similarity between Aristotle's theory and the views of many modern American political scientists. It is common today to distinguish between the "politically active" and "politically passive" segments of the population. The former run for office, join organizations, work in campaigns, write to their representatives, and involve themselves in the politics of their community. The latter merely vote on election days and concern themselves with other matters in between. Many political scientists consider the low level of active participation in American politics a sign of the health of the nation. What they are saying, in effect, is that we are better off with a small group of leaders, or "natural masters," and a mass of followers, or "natural slaves." But of course they do not say, as Aristotle most emphatically did, that only the political activists can live genuinely good lives.

Natural Slaves and
Natural Masters

I

Every state is a community of some kind, and every community is established with a view to some good; for mankind always act in order to obtain that which they think good. But, if all communities aim at some good, the state or political community, which is the highest of all, and which embraces all the rest, aims, and in a greater degree than any other, at the highest good.

Now there is an erroneous opinion that a statesman, king, householder, and master are the same, and that they differ, not in kind, but only in the number of their subjects. For example, the ruler over a few is called a master; over more, the manager of a household; over a still larger number, a statesman or king, as if there were no difference between a great household and a small state. The distinction which is made between the king and statesman is as follows: When the government is personal, the ruler is a king; when, according to the principles of the political science, the citizens rule and are ruled in turn, then he is called a statesman.

But all this is a mistake; for governments differ in kind, as will be evident to any one who considers the matter according to the method which has hitherto guided us. As in other departments of science, so in politics, the compound should always be resolved into the simple elements or least parts of the whole. We must therefore look at the elements of which the state is composed, in order that we may see in what they differ from one another, and whether any scientific distinction can be drawn between the different kinds of rule.

II

He who thus considers things in their first growth and origin, whether a state or anything else, will obtain the clearest view of them. In the first place (1) there must be a union of those who cannot exist without each other; for example, of male and female, that the race may continue; and this is a union which is formed, not of deliberate purpose, but because, in common with other animals and with plants, mankind have a natural desire to leave behind them an image of themselves. And (2) there must be a union of natural ruler and subject, that both may be preserved. For he who can foresee with his mind is by nature intended to be lord and master, and he who can work with his body is

Book 1 from *The Politics* by Aristotle, Chaps. 1–5. Trans. by Benjamin Jowett.

a subject, and by nature a slave; hence master and slave have the same interest. Nature, however, has distinguished between the female and the slave. For she is not niggardly, like the smith who fashions the Delphian knife for many uses; she makes each thing for a single use, and every instrument is best made when intended for one and not for many uses. But among barbarians no distinction is made between women and slaves, because there is no natural ruler among them: they are a community of slaves, male and female. Wherefore the poets say,—

It is meet that Hellenes should rule over barbarians;

as if they thought that the barbarian and the slave were by nature one.

Out of these two relationships between man and woman, master and slave, the family first arises, and Hesoid is right when he says,—

First house and wife and an ox for the plough,

for the ox is the poor man's slave. The family is the association established by nature for the supply of men's every-day wants, and the members of it are called by Charondas "companions of the cupboard," and by Epimenides the Cretan, "companions of the manger." But when several families are united, and the association aims at something more than the supply of daily needs, then comes into existence the village. And the most natural form of the village appears to be that of a colony from the family, composed of the children and grandchildren, who are said to be "suckled with the same milk." And this is the reason why Hellenic states were originally governed by kings; because the Hellenes were under royal rule before they came together, as the barbarians still are. Every family is ruled by the eldest, and therefore in the colonies of the family the kingly form of government prevailed because they were of the same blood. As Homer says [of the Cyclopes]:—

Each one gives law to his children and to his wives.

For they lived dispersedly, as was the manner in ancient times. Wherefore men say that the Gods have a king, because they themselves either are or were in ancient times under the rule of a king. For they imagine, not only the forms of the Gods, but their ways of life to be like their own.

When several villages are united in a single community, perfect and large enough to be nearly or quite self-sufficing, the state comes into existence, originating in the bare needs of life, and continuing in existence for the sake of a good life. And therefore, if the earlier forms of society are natural, so is the state, for it is the end of them, and the [completed] nature is the end. For what each thing is when fully developed, we call its nature, whether we are speaking of a man, a horse, or a family. Besides, the final cause and end of a thing is the best, and to be self-sufficing is the end and the best.

Hence it is evident that the state is a creation of nature, and that man is by nature a political animal. And he who by nature and not by mere accident is without a state, is either above humanity, or below it; he is the

Tribeless, lawless, hearthless one,

whom Homer denounces—the outcast who is a lover of war; he may be compared to an unprotected piece in the game of draughts.

Now the reason why man is more of a political animal than bees or any other gregarious animals is evident. Nature, as we often say, makes nothing in vain, and man is the only animal whom she has endowed with the gift of speech. And whereas mere sound is but an indication of pleasure or pain, and is therefore found in other animals (for their nature attains to the perception of pleasure and pain and the intimation of them to one another, and no further), the power of speech is intended to set forth the expedient and inexpedient, and likewise the just and the unjust. And it is a characteristic of man that he alone has any sense of good and evil, of just and unjust, and the association of living beings who have this sense makes a family and a state.

Thus the state is by nature clearly prior to the family and to the individual, since the whole is of necessity prior to the part; for example, if the whole body be destroyed, there will be no foot or hand, except in an equivocal sense, as we might speak of a stone hand; for when destroyed the hand will be no better. But things are defined by their working and power; and we ought not to say that they are the same when they are no longer the same, but only that they have the same name. The proof that the state is a creation of nature and prior to the individual is that the individual, when isolated, is not self-sufficing; and therefore he is like a part in relation to the whole. But he who is unable to live in society, or who has no need because he is sufficient for himself, must be either a beast or a god: he is no part of a state. A social instinct is implanted in all men by nature, and yet he who first founded the state was the greatest of benefactors. For man, when perfected, is the best of animals, but, when separated from law and justice, he is the worst of all; since armed injustice is the more dangerous, and he is equipped at birth with the arms of intelligence and with moral qualities which he may use for the worst ends. Wherefore, if he have not virtue, he is the most unholy and the most savage of animals, and the most full of lust and gluttony. But justice is the bond of men in states, and the administration of justice, which is the determination of what is just, is the principle of order in political society.

III

Seeing then that the state is made up of households, before speaking of the state we must speak of the management of the household. The parts of the household are the persons who compose it, and a complete household consists of slaves and freemen. Now we should begin by examining everything in its least elements; and the first and least parts of a family are master and slave, husband and wife, father and children. We have therefore to consider what each of these three relations is and ought to be:—I mean the relation of master and servant, of husband and wife, and thirdly of parent and child. . . . And there is another element of a household, the so-called art of money-making, which, according to some, is identical with household management, according to others, a principal part of it; the nature of this art will also have to be considered by us.

Let us first speak of master and slave, looking to the needs of practical life and also seeking to attain some better theory of their relation than exists at present. For some are of opinion that the rule of a master is a science, and that the management of a household, and the mastership of slaves, and the political and royal rule, as I was saying at the outset, are all the same. Others affirm that the rule of a master over slaves is contrary to nature, and that the distinction between slave and freeman exists by law only, and not by nature; and being an interference with nature is therefore unjust.

IV

Property is a part of the household, and therefore the art of acquiring property is a part of the art of managing the household; for no man can live well, or indeed live at all, unless he be provided with necessaries. And as in the arts which have a definite sphere the workers must have their own proper instruments for the accomplishment of their work, so it is in the management of a household. Now, instruments are of various sorts; some are living, others lifeless; in the rudder, the pilot of a ship has a lifeless, in the look-out man, a living instrument; for in the arts the servant is a kind of instrument. Thus, too, a possession is an instrument for maintaining life. And so, in the arrangement of the family, a slave is a living possession, and property a number of such instruments; and the servant is himself an instrument, which takes precedence of all other instruments. For if every instrument could accomplish its own work, obeying or anticipating the will of others, like the statues of Daedalus, or the tripods of Hephaestus, which, says the poet,

of their own accord entered the assembly of the Gods;

if, in like manner, the shuttle would weave and the plectrum touch the lyre without a hand to guide them, chief workmen would not want servants, nor masters slaves. Here, however, another distinction must be drawn: the instruments commonly so called are instruments of production, whilst a possession is an instrument of action. The shuttle, for example, is not only of use, but something else is made by it, whereas of a garment or of a bed there is only the use.

Further, as production and action are different in kind, and both require instruments, the instruments which they employ must likewise differ in kind. But life is action and not production, and therefore the slave is the minister of action [for he ministers to his master's life]. Again, a possession is spoken of as a part is spoken of; for the part is not only a part of something else, but wholly belongs to it; and this is also true of a possession. The master is only the master of the slave; he does not belong to him, whereas the slave is not only the slave of his master, but wholly belongs to him. Hence we see what is the nature and office of a slave; he who is by nature not his own but another's and yet a man, is by nature a slave; and he may be said to belong to another who, being a human being, is also a possession. And a possession may be defined as an instrument of action, separable from the possessor.

V

But is there any one thus intended by nature to be a slave, and for whom such a condition is expedient and right, or rather is not all slavery a violation of nature?

There is no difficulty in answering this question, on grounds both of reason and of fact. For that some should rule and others be ruled is a thing, not only necessary, but expedient; from the hour of their birth, some are marked out for subjection, others for rule.

And whereas there are many kinds both of rulers and subjects, that rule is the better which is exercised over better subjects—for example, to rule over men is better than to rule over wild beasts. The work is better which is executed by better workmen; and where one man rules and another is ruled, they may be said to have a work. In all things which form a composite whole and which are made up of parts, whether continuous or discrete, a distinction between the ruling and the subject elements comes to light. Such a duality exists in living creatures, but not in them only; it originates in the constitution of the universe; even in things which have no life, there is a ruling principle, as in musical harmony. But we are wandering from the subject. We will, therefore, restrict ourselves to the living creature which, in the first place, consists of soul and body: and of these two, the one is by nature the ruler, and the other the subject. But then we must look for the intentions of nature in things which retain their nature, and not in things which are corrupted. And therefore we must study the man who is in the most perfect state both of body and soul, for in him we shall see the true relation of the two; although in bad or corrupted natures the body will often appear to rule over the soul, because they are in an evil and unnatural condition. First then we may observe in living creatures both a despotical and a constitutional rule; for the soul rules the body with a despotical rule, whereas the intellect rules the appetites with a constitutional and royal rule. And it is clear that the rule of the soul over the body, and of the mind and the rational element over the passionate is natural and expedient; whereas the equality of the two or the rule of the inferior is always hurtful. The same holds good of animals as well as of men; for tame animals have a better nature than wild, and all tame animals are better off when they are ruled by man; for then they are preserved. Again, the male is by nature superior, and the female inferior; and the one rules, and the other is ruled; this principle, of necessity, extends to all mankind. Where then there is such a difference as that between soul and body, or between men and animals (as in the case of those whose business is to use their body, and who can do nothing better), the lower sort are by nature slaves, and it is better for them as for all inferiors that they should be under the rule of a master. For he who can be, and therefore is another's, and he who participates in reason enough to apprehend, but not to have, reason, is a slave by nature. Whereas the lower animals cannot even apprehend reason; they obey their instincts. And indeed the use made of slaves and of tame animals is not very different; for both with their bodies minister to the needs of life. Nature would like to distinguish between the bodies of freemen and slaves, making the one strong for servile labour, the other upright, and although useless for such services, useful for political life in the arts both of war and peace. But this does not hold universally: for some slaves have the souls and others have the bodies of freemen. And doubtless if men differed from one another in the mere forms of their bodies as much as the statues of the Gods do from men, all would acknowledge that the inferior class should be slaves of the superior. And if there is a difference in the body, how much more in the soul! But the beauty of the body is seen, whereas the beauty of the soul is not seen. It is clear, then, that some men are by nature free, and others slaves, and that for these latter slavery is both expedient and right. . . .

BENTHAM

It has been said that if you ask the average man in the street for his moral philosophy, nine times out of ten he will turn out to be a Utilitarian. There is no doubt that the Greatest Happiness Principle, first formulated by the eighteenth-century social reformer Jeremy Bentham (1748–1832), is by far the most natural and sensible-sounding moral principle in the literature of ethics. Always choose that action which promises to produce the greatest happiness for the greatest number of persons. What could be more reasonable? We all want to be happy, and surely each man's happiness should count for as much as his neighbor's. It is not hard to see that utilitarianism offers a convenient foundation for democratic politics, for it teaches that statesmen are to pursue the policies which will please the people, not themselves or some abstract and barren principle.

Bentham believes that happiness is simply pleasure and unhappiness is pain. Now, a man must surely know whether he is in pain, just as he must know whether he is feeling pleasure. So the utilitarian cannot claim, as Marcuse and Aristotle would, that men are unhappy without knowing it. Indeed, since Bentham holds that every man is directly aware of his own pleasures and pains, but only indirectly aware of the pleasures and pains of others, it follows as a logical necessity that each person is the best judge of his own happiness. Thus, the medical analogy breaks down, and the defenders of utilitarianism should allow no one to set himself up as a social doctor ready to diagnose the ills of society.

Nevertheless, utilitarianism readily admits that experts may know better than the general public how to produce pleasures and pains. After all, the proof of the pudding may be in the eating, but it still takes a master chef to make a good pudding. So utilitarianism leads naturally to a government which is controlled by the people and staffed by experts in various technical specialities. In short, utilitarianism seems to provide a justification for the sort of political system which has developed in America today.

In this section we are exploring the ways in which a social philosophy can rest on a theory of human nature. Jeremy Bentham's utilitarianism shows us quite clearly how a particular psychological account of happines, unhappiness, pleasure, and pain can support a political doctrine—in this case the theory of democracy.

I

MANKIND GOVERNED BY PAIN AND PLEASURE

Nature has placed mankind under the governance of two sovereign masters, *pain* and *pleasure*. It is for them alone to point out what we ought to do, as well as to determine what we shall do. On the one hand the standard of right and wrong, on the other the chain of causes and effects, are fastened to their throne. They govern us in all we do, in all we say, in all we think: every effort we can make to throw off our subjection, will serve but to demonstrate and confirm it. In words a man may pretend to abjure their empire: but in reality he will remain subject to it all the while. The *principle of utility*[1] recognises this subjection, and assumes it for the foundation of that system, the object of which is to rear the fabric of felicity by the hands of reason and of law. Systems which attempt to question it, deal in sounds instead of sense, in caprice instead of reason, in darkness instead of light.

But enough of metaphor and declamation: it is not by such means that moral science is to be improved.

II

PRINCIPLE OF UTILITY, WHAT

The principle of utility is the foundation of the present work: it will be proper therefore at the outset to give an explicit and determinate account of

Chapter I from *An Introduction to the Principles of Morals and Legislation* by Jeremy Bentham (1823 version).

[1] Note by the Author, July 1822.

To this denomination has of late been added, or substituted, the *greatest happiness* or *greatest felicity* principle: this for shortness, instead of saying at length *that principle* which states the greatest happiness of all those whose interest is in question, as being the right and proper, and only right and proper and universally desirable, end of human action: of human action in every situation, and in particular in that of a functionary or set of functionaries exercising the powers of Government. The word *utility* does not so clearly point to the ideas of *pleasure* and *pain* as the words *happiness* and *felicity* do: nor does it lead us to the consideration of the *number*, of the interests affected; to the *number*, as being the circumstance, which contributes, in the largest proportion, to the formation of the standard here in question; the *standard of right and wrong*, by which alone the propriety of human conduct, in every situation, can with propriety be tried. This want of a sufficiently manifest connexion between the ideas of *happiness* and *pleasure* on the one hand, and the idea of what is meant by it. By the principle[2] of utility is meant that principle which approves or disapproves of every action whatsoever, according to the tendency which it appears to have to augment or diminish the happiness of the party whose interest is in question: or, what is the same thing in other words, to promote or to oppose that happiness. I say of every action whatsoever; and therefore not only of every action of a private individual, but of every measure of government.

III

UTILITY WHAT

By utility is meant that property in any object, whereby it tends to produce benefit, advantage, pleasure, good, or happiness (all this in the present case comes to the same thing) or (what comes again to the same thing) to prevent the happening of mischief, pain, evil, or unhappiness to the party whose interest is considered: if that party be the community in general, then the happiness of the community: if a particular individual, then the happiness of that individual.

IV

INTEREST OF THE COMMUNITY, WHAT

The interest of the community is one of the most general expressions that can occur in the phraseology of morals: no wonder that the meaning of it is often lost. When it has a meaning, it is this. The community is a fictitious *body*, composed of the individual persons who are considered as constituting as it were its *members*. The interest of the community then is, what?—the sum of the interests of the several members who compose it.

---

utility on the other, I have every now and then found operating, and with but too much efficiency, as a bar to the acceptance, that might otherwise have been given, to this principle.

[2] The word principle is derived from the Latin *principium*: which seems to be compounded of the two words *primus*, first, or chief, and *cipium*, a termination which seems to be derived from *capio*, to take, as in *mancipium, municipium;* to which are analogous, *auceps, forceps,* and others. It is a term of very vague and very extensive signification: it is applied to any thing which is conceived to serve as a foundation or beginning to any series of operations: in some cases, of physical operations; but of mental operations in the present case.

The principle here in question may be taken for an act of the mind; a sentiment; a sentiment of approbation; a sentiment which, when applied to an action, approves of its utility, as that quality of it by which the measure of approbation or disapprobation bestowed upon it ought to be governed.

V

It is in vain to talk of the interest of the community, without understanding what is the interest of the individual.[3] A thing is said to promote the interest, or to be *for* the interest, of an individual, when it tends to add to the sum total of his pleasures: or, what comes to the same thing, to diminish the sum total of his pains.

VI

AN ACTION CONFORMABLE TO THE PRINCIPLE OF UTILITY, WHAT

An action then may be said to be conformable to the principle of utility, or, for shortness sake, to utility (meaning with respect to the community at large), when the tendency it has to augment the happiness of the community is greater than any it has to diminish it.

VII

A MEASURE OF GOVERNMENT CONFORMABLE TO THE PRINCIPLE OF UTILITY, WHAT

A measure of government (which is but a particular kind of action, performed by a particular person or persons) may be said to be conformable to or dictated by the principle of utility, when in like manner the tendency which it has to augment the happiness of the community is greater than any which it has to diminish it.

VIII

LAWS OR DICTATES OF UTILITY, WHAT

When an action, or in particular a measure of government, is supposed by a man to be conformable to the principle of utility, it may be convenient, for the purposes of discourse, to imagine a kind of law or dictate, called a law or dictate of utility: and to speak of the action in question, as being conformable to such law or dictate.

[3] Interest is one of those words, which not having any superior *genus*, cannot in the ordinary way be defined.

IX

A PARTIZAN OF THE PRINCIPLE OF UTILITY, WHO

A man may be said to be a partizan of the principle of utility, when the approbation or disapprobation he annexes to any action, or to any measure, is determined by and proportioned to the tendency which he conceives it to have to augment or to diminish the happiness of the community: or in other words, to its conformity or unconformity to the laws or dictates of utility.

X

OUGHT, OUGHT NOT, RIGHT AND WRONG, &C. HOW TO BE UNDERSTOOD

Of an action that is conformable to the principle of utility one may always say either that it is one that ought to be done, or at least that it is not one that ought not to be done. One may say also, that it is right it should be done; at least that it is not wrong it should be done: that it is a right action; at least that it is not a wrong action. When thus interpreted, the words *ought*, and *right* and *wrong*, and others of that stamp, have a meaning: when otherwise, they have none.

XI

TO PROVE THE RECTITUDE OF THIS PRINCIPLE
IS AT ONCE UNNECESSARY AND IMPOSSIBLE

Has the rectitude of this principle been ever formally contested? It should seem that it had, by those who have not known what they have been meaning. Is it susceptible of any direct proof? it should seem not: for that which is used to prove every thing else, cannot itself be proved: a chain of proofs must have their commencement somewhere. To give such proof is as impossible as it is needless.

XII

IT HAS SELDOM, HOWEVER, AS YET BEEN CONSISTENTLY PURSUED

Not that there is or ever has been that human creature breathing, however stupid or perverse, who has not on many, perhaps on most occasions of his life, deferred to it. By the natural constitution of the human frame, on most occasions of their lives men in general embrace this principle, without think-ing of it: if not for the ordering of their own actions, yet for the trying of their own actions, as well as of those of other men. There have been, at the same time, not many, perhaps, even of the most intelligent, who have been disposed to embrace it purely and without reserve. There are even few who have not taken some occasion or other to quarrel with it, either on account of their not understanding always how to apply it, or on account of some preju-dice or other which they were afraid to examine into, or could not bear to part with. For such is the stuff that man is made of: in principle and in practice, in a right track and in a wrong one, the rarest of all human qualities is consistency.

XIII

IT CAN NEVER BE CONSISTENTLY COMBATED

When a man attempts to combat the principle of utility, it is with reasons drawn, without his being aware of it, from that very principle itself.[4] His argu-

---

[4] "The principle of utility (I have heard it said) is a dangerous principle: it is dangerous on certain occasions to consult it." This is as much as to say, what? that it is not consonant to utility, to consult utility: in short, that it is *not* consulting it, to consult it.

Addition by the Author, July 1822.

Not long after the publication of the Fragment on Government, anno 1776, in which, in the character of an all-comprehensive and all-commanding principle, the principle of *utility* was brought to view, one person by whom observation to the above effect was made was *Alexander Wedderburn*, at that time Attorney or Solicitor General, afterwards successively Chief Justice of the Common Pleas, and Chancellor of England, under the successive titles of Lord Loughborough and Earl of Rosslyn. It was made—not indeed in my hearing, but in the hearing of a person by whom it was almost immediately communi-cated to me. So far from being self-contradictory, it was a shrewd and perfectly true one. By that distinguished functionary, the state of the Government was thoroughly understood: by the obscure individual, at that time not so much as supposed to be so: his disquisitions had not been as yet applied, with any thing like a comprehensive view, to the field of Constitutional Law, nor therefore to those features of the English Government, by which the greatest happiness of the ruling *one* with or without that of a favoured few, are now so plainly seen to be the only ends to which the course of it has at any time been directed. The *principle of utility* was an appellative, at that time employed—employed by me, as it had been by others, to designate that which, in a more perspicuous and instructive manner, may, as above, be designated by the name of the *greatest happiness principle*. "This prin-ciple (said Wedderburn) is a dangerous one." Saying so, he said that which, to a certain extent, is strictly true: a principle, which lays down, as the only *right* and justifiable end of Government, the greatest happiness of the greatest number—how can it be denied to be a dangerous one? dangerous it unquestionably is, to every government which has for its *actual* end or object, the greatest happiness of a certain *one*, with or without the addition of some comparatively small number of others, which it is matter of pleasure or accommo-dation to him to admit, each of them, to a share in the concern, on the footing of so many junior partners. *Dangerous* it therefore really was, to the interest—the sinister interest—of all those functionaries, himself included, whose interest it was, to maximize delay, vexation, and expense, in judicial and other modes of procedure, for the sake of the profit, extractible

ments, if they prove any thing, prove not that the principle is *wrong*, but that, according to the applications he supposes to be made of it, it is *misapplied*. Is it possible for a man to move the earth? Yes; but he must first find out another earth to stand upon.

XIV

COURSE TO BE TAKEN FOR SURMOUNTING PREJUDICES THAT MAY HAVE BEEN ENTERTAINED AGAINST IT

To disprove the propriety of it by arguments is impossible; but, from the causes that have been mentioned, or from some confused or partial view of it, a man may happen to be disposed not to relish it. Where this is the case, if he thinks the settling of his opinions on such a subject worth the trouble, let him take the following steps, and at length, perhaps, he may come to reconcile himself to it.

1. Let him settle with himself, whether he would wish to discard this principle altogether; if so, let him consider what it is that all his reasonings (in matters of politics especially) can amount to?

2. If he would, let him settle with himself, whether he would judge and act without any principle, or whether there is any other he would judge and act by?

3. If there be, let him examine and satisfy himself whether the principle he thinks he has found is really any separate intelligible principle; or whether it be not a mere principle in words, a kind of phrase, which at bottom expresses neither more nor less than the mere averment of his own unfounded sentiments; that is, what in another person he might be apt to call caprice?

4. If he is inclined to think that his own approbation or disapprobation, annexed to the idea of an act, without any regard to its consequences, is a sufficient foundation for him to judge and act upon, let him ask himself whether his sentiment is to be a standard of right and wrong, with respect to every other man, or whether every man's sentiment has the same privilege of being a standard to itself?

5. In the first case, let him ask himself whether his principle is not despotical, and hostile to all the rest of human race?

6. In the second case, whether it is not anarchial, and whether at this

---

out of the expense. In a Government which had for its end in view the greatest happiness of the greatest number, Alexander Wedderburn might have been Attorney General and then Chancellor: but he would not have been Attorney General with £15,000 a year, nor Chancellor, with a peerage with a veto upon all justice, with £25,000 a year, and with 500 sinecures at his disposal, under the name of Ecclesiastical Benefices, besides *et cæteras*.

rate there are not as many different standards of right and wrong as there are men? and whether even to the same man, the same thing, which is right to-day, may not (without the least change in its nature) be wrong to-morrow? and whether the same thing is not right and wrong in the same place at the same time? and in either case, whether all argument is not at an end? and whether, when two men have said, "I like this," and "I don't like it," they can (upon such a principle) have any thing more to say?

7. If he should have said to himself, No: for that the sentiment which he proposes as a standard must be grounded on reflection, let him say on what particulars the reflection is to turn? if on particulars having relation to the utility of the act, then let him say whether this is not deserting his own principle, and borrowing assistance from that very one in opposition to which he sets it up: or if not on those particulars, on what other particulars?

8. If he should be for compounding the matter, and adopting his own principal in part, and the principle of utility in part, let him say how far he will adopt it?

9. When he has settled with himself where he will stop, then let him ask himself how he justifies to himself the adopting it so far? and why he will not adopt it any farther?

10. Admitting any other principle than the principle of utility to be a right principle, a principle that it is right for a man to pursue; admitting (what is not true) that the word *right* can have a meaning without reference to utility, let him say whether there is any such thing as a *motive* that a man can have to pursue the dictates of it: if there is, let him say what that motive is, and how it is to be distinguished from those which enforce the dictates of utility: if not, then lastly let him say what it is this other principle can be good for?

MARX

As masters of ceremonies like to say, Karl Marx (1818–1883) needs no introduction. In the past two centuries only Hegel, Freud, and Einstein have had an equivalent impact on the shape of Western thought. With the appearance in the twentieth century of entire subcontinents committed at least officially to his doctrine, we can safely say that Marx is the most influential political and social thinker of the modern world. Until quite recently, only Marx's maturer writings were available to us—his three-volume economic work on Capital, *the provocative and dramatic* Communist Manifesto, *and so on. Now, however, we can read some of the essays which Marx wrote when he was still in his twenties and very much under the influence of the German metaphysician Hegel. In the so-called* Economic-Philosophic Manuscripts *of 1844, from which the present selection on alienation is taken, we find Marx expounding a theory of human nature and human fulfillment which provides a moral and psychological dimension to his critique of early capitalist society.*

Marx begins with the premise that man is a socially productive animal. *Contrary to Aristotle, who located man's essential nature in his capacity for reason, Marx argues that man distinguishes himself from the animals by his ability to transform the environment to meet his needs for food, clothing, and shelter. This transformation, or "production," is a social, not an individual, activity, and so men develop systematic relationships with one another which shape their entire lives. Some men hunt or farm while others make useful objects from wood, stone, animal skins, and metal. Exchanges take place and regular economic patterns emerge. Legal and political institutions, religious practices, artistic expression all make their appearance, and all—Marx claims—are influenced by the basic, underlying productive processes by which men collectively transform their environment.*

The productive process is not merely a useful means to the end of satisfying our wants, however. Marx believes that men need productive activity or work in order to develop their inner nature to the fullest. Contrary to the philosophers known as Hedonists, Marx insists that a life of pure leisure and consumption would be ultimately unsatisfying. Men need to be active, to do, *not merely to* consume. *Just as an artist derives satisfaction from actually creating a picture or a statue, so all of us—Marx says—gain fulfillment from making the world fruitful and beautiful through our efforts. A farmer looking at a field of grain can say, "I did that! I cleared that land, tilled the soil, and raised that wheat." He does not merely see a profit or loss.*

In the course of history, Marx asserts, it inevitably happens that some men gain control of the land, the tools, and the raw materials which other men need in order to do productive work. The owners then can coerce the others into paying for the privilege of working, and they can even force the workers to make whatever commodities the owners want. In this way, private property becomes an instrument of exploitation and coercion.

Now, men must eat to live, so when the landowner or factory owner sets conditions which men must meet in order to work, the workers have no choice but to submit. The price they pay, of course, is in the first instance a share of what they produce. The landowner takes part of the farmer's crop; the factory owner takes the goods which the worker has made and pays him only a fraction of their value in wages, pocketing the rest as profits.

The worker loses a share of his product. But he also loses the chance to regulate his own work activity, to develop his productive powers as he sees fit, to establish cooperative relationships with the other workers. To use Marx's term, he becomes "alienated," from his product, from himself, from the work process, and from other men. In short, men under capitalism are denied the opportunity to develop their true human nature.

Obviously, a theory of this sort provides a ready-made basis for social criticism. Most of Marx's writings present an indictment of capitalist society as well as a program for the future. As is often the case with social critics, he is clearer and more detailed about the evils of the present than he is about the alternatives for the future. Nevertheless, you should be able to decide, on the basis of this reading, whether you agree with Marx that a truly happy and fulfilling life requires a commitment to cooperative, productive, autonomous work.

Alienated Labour

XXII

We have begun from the presuppositions of political economy. We have accepted its terminology and its laws. We presupposed private property; the

From *Karl Marx: Early Writings*, trans. and ed. by T. B. Bottomore. New York: McGraw-Hill Book Company, 1963. © 1963 by T. B. Bottomore. Used with permission of McGraw-Hill Book Company and C. A. Watts & Co., Ltd.

separation of labour, capital and land, as also of wages, profit and rent; the division of labour; competition; the concept of exchange value, etc. From political economy itself, in its own words, we have shown that the worker sinks to the level of a commodity, and to a most miserable commodity; that the misery of the worker increases with the power and volume of his production; that the necessary result of competition is the accumulation of capital in a few hands, and thus a restoration of monopoly in a more terrible form; and finally that the distinction between capitalist and landlord, and between agricultural labourer and industrial worker, must disappear, and the whole of society divide into the two classes of property *owners* and *propertyless* workers.

Political economy begins with the fact of private property; it does not explain it. It conceives the *material* process of private property, as this occurs in reality, in general and abstract formulas which then serve it as laws. It does not *comprehend* these laws; that is, it does not show how they arise out of the nature of private property. Political economy provides no explanation of the basis for the distinction of labour from capital, of capital from land. When, for example, the relation of wages to profits is defined, this is explained in terms of the interests of capitalists; in other words, what should be explained is assumed. Similarly, competition is referred to at every point and is explained in terms of external conditions. Political economy tells us nothing about the extent to which these external and apparently accidental conditions are simply the expression of a necessary development. We have seen how exchange itself seems an accidental fact. The only motive forces which political economy recognizes are *avarice* and the *war between the avaricious, competition.*

Just because political economy fails to understand the interconnexions within this movement it was possible to oppose the doctrine of competition to that of monopoly, the doctrine of freedom of the crafts to that of the guilds, the doctrine of the division of landed property to that of the great estates; for competition, freedom of crafts, and the division of landed property were conceived only as accidental consequences brought about by will and force, rather than as necessary, inevitable and natural consequences of monopoly, the guild system and feudal property.

Thus we have now to grasp the real connexion between this whole system of alienation—private property, acquisitiveness, the separation of labour, capital and land, exchange and competition, value and the devaluation of man, monopoly and competition—and the system of *money.*

Let us not begin our explanation as does the economist, from a legendary primordial condition. Such a primordial condition does not explain anything; it merely removes the question into a grey and nebulous distance. It asserts as a fact or event what it should deduce, namely, the necessary relation between two things; for example, between the division of labour and exchange. In the same way theology explains the origin of evil by the fall of man; that is, it asserts as a historical fact what it should explain.

We shall begin from a *contemporary* economic fact. The worker becomes poorer the more wealth he produces and the more his production increases in power and extent. The worker becomes an ever cheaper commodity the more goods he creates. The *devaluation* of the human world increases in direct relation with the *increase in value* of the world of things. Labour does not only create goods; it also produces itself and the worker as a *commodity*, and indeed in the same proportion as it produces goods.

This fact simply implies that the object produced by labour, its product, now stands opposed to it as an *alien being*, as a *power independent* of the producer. The product of labour is labour which has been embodied in an object and turned into a physical thing; this product is an *objectification* of labour. The performance of work is at the same time its objectification. The performance of work appears in the sphere of political economy as a *vitiation* of the worker, objectification as a *loss* and as *servitude to the object*, and appropriation as *alienation*.

So much does the performance of work appear as vitiation that the worker is vitiated to the point of starvation. So much does objectification appear as loss of the object that the worker is deprived of the most essential things not only of life but also of work. Labour itself becomes an object which he can acquire only by the greatest effort and with unpredictable interruptions. So much does the appropriation of the object appear as alienation that the more objects the worker produces the fewer he can possess and the more he falls under the domination of his product, of capital.

All these consequences follow from the fact that the worker is related to the *product of his labour* as to an *alien* object. For it is clear on this presupposition that the more the worker expends himself in work the more powerful becomes the world of objects which he creates in face of himself, the poorer he becomes in his inner life, and the less he belongs to himself. It is just the same as in religion. The more of himself man attributes to God the less he has left in himself. The worker puts his life into the object, and his life then belongs no longer to himself but to the object. The greater his activity, therefore, the less he possesses. What is embodied in the product of his labour is no longer his own. The greater this product is, therefore, the more he is diminished. The *alienation* of the worker in his product means not only that his labour becomes an object, assumes an *external* existence, but that it exists independently, *outside himself*, and alien to him, and that it stands opposed to him as an autonomous power. The life which he has given to the object sets itself against him as an alien and hostile force.

XXIII

Let us now examine more closely the phenomenon of *objectification;* the worker's production and the *alienation* and *loss* of the object it produces, which is involved in it. The worker can create nothing without *nature*, without the *sensuous external world*. The latter is the material in which his labour is realized, in which it is active, out of which and through which it produces things.

But just as nature affords the *means of existence* of labour, in the sense that labour cannot *live* without objects upon which it can be exercised, so also it provides the *means of existence* in a narrower sense; namely the means of physical existence for the *worker* himself. Thus, the more the worker *appropriates* the external world of sensuous nature by his labour the more he deprives himself of *means of existence*, in two respects: first, that the sensuous external world becomes progressively less an object belonging to his labour or a means of existence of his labour, and secondly, that it becomes progressively less a means of existence in the direct sense, a means for the physical subsistence of the worker.

In both respects, therefore, the worker becomes a slave of the object; first, in that he receives an *object of work*, i.e. receives *work*, and secondly, in that he receives *means of subsistence*. Thus the object enables him to exist, first as a *worker* and secondly, as a *physical subject*. The culmination of this enslavement is that he can only maintain himself as a *physical subject* so far as he is a *worker*, and that it is only as a *physical subject* that he is a worker.

(The alienation of the worker in his object is expressed as follows in the laws of political economy: the more the worker produces the less he has to consume; the more value he creates the more worthless he becomes; the more refined his product the more crude and misshapen the worker; the more civilized the product the more barbarous the worker; the more powerful the work the more feeble the worker; the more the work manifests intelligence the more the worker declines in intelligence and becomes a slave of nature.)

Political economy conceals the alienation in the nature of labour in so far as it does not examine the direct relationship between the worker (work) and production. Labour certainly produces marvels for the rich but it produces privation for the worker. It produces palaces, but hovels for the worker. It produces beauty, but deformity for the worker. It replaces labour by machinery, but it casts some of the workers back into a barbarous kind of work and turns the others into machines. It produces intelligence, but also stupidity and cretinism for the workers.

The direct relationship of labour to its products is the relationship of the worker to the objects of his production. The relationship of property owners to the objects of production and to production itself is merely a *consequence* of this first relationship and confirms it. We shall consider this second aspect later.

Thus, when we ask what is the important relationship of labour, we are concerned with the relationship of the *worker* to production.

So far we have considered the alienation of the work only from one aspect; namely, *his relationship with the products of his labour*. However, alienation appears not merely in the result but also in the *process of production*, within *productive activity* itself. How could the worker stand in an alien relationship to the product of his activity if he did not alienate himself in the act of production itself? The product is indeed only the *résumé* of activity, of production. Consequently, if the product of labour is alienation, production itself must be active alienation—the alienation of activity and the activity of alienation. The alienation of the object of labour merely summarizes the alienation in the work activity itself.

What constitutes the alienation of labour? First, that the work is *external* to the worker, that it is not part of his nature; and that, consequently, he does not fulfil himself in his work but denies himself, has a feeling of misery rather than well-being, does not develop freely his mental and physical energies but is physically exhausted and mentally debased. The worker, therefore, feels himself at home only during his leisure time, whereas at work he feels homeless. His work is not voluntary but imposed, *forced labour*. It is not the satisfaction of a need, but only a *means* for satisfying other needs. Its alien character is clearly shown by the fact that as soon as there is no physical or other compulsion it is avoided like the plague. External labour, labour in which man alienates himself, is a labour of self-sacrifice, of mortification. Finally, the external character of work for the worker is shown by the fact that it is not his own work but work for someone else, that in work he does not belong to himself but to another person.

Just as in religion the spontaneous activity of human fantasy, of the human brain and heart, reacts independently as an alien activity of gods or devils upon the individual, so the activity of the worker is not his own spontaneous activity. It is another's activity and a loss of his own spontaneity.

We arrive at the result that man (the worker) feels himself to be freely active only in his animal functions—eating, drinking and procreating, or at most also in his dwelling and in personal adornment—while in his human functions he is reduced to an animal. The animal becomes human and the human becomes animal.

Eating, drinking and procreating are of course also genuine human functions. But abstractly considered, apart from the environment of human activities, and turned into final and sole ends, they are animal functions.

We have now considered the act of alienation of practical human activity, labour, from two aspects: (1) the relationship of the worker to the *product of labour* as an alien object which dominates him. This relationship is at the same time the relationship to the sensuous external world, to natural objects, as an alien and hostile world; (2) the relationship of labour to the *act of production* within *labour*. This is the relationship of the worker to his own activity as something alien and not belonging to him, activity as suffering (passivity), strength as powerlessness, creation as emasculation, the *personal* physical and mental energy of the worker, his personal life (for what is life but activity?), as an activity which is directed against himself, independent of him and not belonging to him. This is *self-alienation* as against the above-mentioned alienation of the *thing*.

XXIV

We have now to infer a third characteristic of *alienated labour* from the two we have considered.

Man is a species-being not only in the sense that he makes the community (his own as well as those of other things) his object both practically and theoretically, but also (and this is simply another expression for the same thing) in the sense that he treats himself as the present, living species, as a *universal* and consequently free being.[1]

Species-life, for man as for animals, has its physical basis in the fact that man (like animals) lives from inorganic nature, and since man is more universal than an animal so the range of inorganic nature from which he lives is more universal. Plants, animals, minerals, air, light, etc. constitute, from the theoretical aspect, a part of human consciousness as objects of natural science and art; they are man's spiritual inorganic nature, his intellectual means of life, which he must first prepare for enjoyment and perpetuation. So also, from the practical aspect, they form a part of human life and activity. In practice man lives only from these natural products, whether in the form of food, heating, clothing, housing, etc. The universality of man appears in practice in the universality which makes the whole of nature into his inorganic body: (1) as a direct means of life; and equally (2) as the material object and instrument of his life activity. Nature is the inorganic body of man; that is to say nature, excluding the human body itself. To say that man *lives* from nature means that nature is his *body* with which he must remain in a continuous interchange in order not to die. The statement that the physical and mental life of man, and nature, are interdependent means simply that nature is interdependent with itself, for man is a part of nature.

Since alienated labour: (1) alienates nature from man; and (2) alienates man from himself, from his own active function, his life activity; so it alienates him from the species. It makes *species-life* into a means of individual life. In the first place it alienates species-life and individual life, and secondly, it turns the latter, as an abstraction, into the purpose of the former, also in its abstract and alienated form.

For labour, *life activity, productive life*, now appear to man only as *means* for the satisfaction of a need, the need to maintain his physical existence. Productive life is, however, species-life. It is life creating life. In the type of life activity resides the whole character of a species, its species-character; and free, conscious activity is the species-character of human beings. Life itself appears only as a *means of life*.

The animal is one with its life activity. It does not distinguish the activity

---

[1] In this passage Marx reproduces Feuerbach's argument in *Das Wesen des Christentums*. [T.B.B.]

from itself. It is *its activity*. But man makes his life activity itself an object of his will and consciousness. He has a conscious life activity. It is not a determination with which he is completely identified. Conscious life activity distinguishes man from the life activity of animals. Only for this reason is he a species-being. Or rather, he is only a self-conscious being, i.e. his own life is an object for him, because he is a species-being. Only for this reason is his activity free activity. Alienated labour reverses the relationship, in that man because he is a self-conscious being makes his life activity, his *being*, only a means for his *existence*.

The practical construction of an *objective world*, the *manipulation* of inorganic nature, is the confirmation of man as a conscious species-being, i.e. a being who treats the species as his own being or himself as a species-being. Of course, animals also produce. They construct nests, dwellings, as in the case of bees, beavers, ants, etc. But they only produce what is strictly necessary for themselves or their young. They produce only in a single direction, while man produces universally. They produce only under the compulsion of direct physical needs, while man produces when he is free from physical need and only truly produces in freedom from such need. Animals produce only themselves, while man reproduces the whole of nature. The products of animal production belong directly to their physical bodies, while man is free in face of his product. Animals construct only in accordance with the standards and needs of the species to which they belong, while man knows how to produce in accordance with the standards of every species and knows how to apply the appropriate standard to the object. Thus man constructs also in accordance with the laws of beauty.

It is just in his work upon the objective world that man really proves himself as a *species-being*. This production is his active species-life. By means of it nature appears as *his* work and his reality. The object of labour is, therefore, the *objectification of man's species-life;* for he no longer reproduces himself merely intellectually, as in consciousness, but actively and in a real sense, and he sees his own reflection in a world which he has constructed. While, therefore, alienated labour takes away the object of production from man, it also takes away his *species-life,* his real objectivity as a species-being, and changes his advantage over animals into a disadvantage in so far as his inorganic body, nature, is taken from him.

Just as alienated labour transforms free and self-directed activity into a means, so it transforms the species-life of man into a means of physical existence.

Consciousness, which man has from his species, is transformed through alienation so that species-life becomes only a means for him. (3) Thus alienated labour turns the *species-life of man,* and also nature as his mental species-property, into an *alien* being and into a *means* for his *individual existence*. It alienates from man his own body, external nature, his mental life and his *human* life. (4) A direct consequence of the alienation of man from the product of his labour, from his life activity and from his species-life, is that *man* is *alienated* from other *men*. When man confronts himself he also confronts *other* men. What is true of man's relationship to his work, to the product of his work and to himself, is also true of his relationship to other men, to their labour and to the objects of their labour.

In general, the statement that man is alienated from his species-life means that each man is alienated from others, and that each of the others is likewise alienated from human life.

Human alienation, and above all the relation of man to himself, is first realized and expressed in the relationship between each man and other men. Thus in the relationship of alienated labour every man regards other men according to the standards and relationships in which he finds himself placed as a worker.

XXV

We began with an economic fact, the alienation of the worker and his production. We have expressed this fact in conceptual terms as *alienated labour*, and in analysing the concept we have merely analysed an economic fact.

Let us now examine further how this concept of alienated labour must express and reveal itself in reality. If the product of labour is alien to me and confronts me as an alien power, to whom does it belong? If my own activity does not belong to me but is an alien, forced activity, to whom does it belong? To a being *other* than myself. And who is this being? The *gods?* It is apparent in the earliest stages of advanced production, e.g. temple building, etc. in Egypt, India, Mexico, and in the service rendered to gods, that the product belonged to the gods. But the gods alone were never the lords of labour. And no more was *nature*. What a contradiction it would be if the more man subjugates nature by his labour, and the more the marvels of the gods are rendered superfluous by the marvels of industry, the more he should abstain from his joy in producing and his enjoyment of the product for love of these powers.

The *alien* being to whom labour and the product of labour belong, to whose service labour is devoted, and to whose enjoyment the product of labour goes, can only be *man* himself. If the product of labour does not belong to the worker, but confronts him as an alien power, this can only be because it belongs to *a man other than the worker*. If his activity is a torment to him it must be a source of *enjoyment* and pleasure to another. Not the gods, nor nature, but only man himself can be this alien power over men.

Consider the earlier statement that the relation of man to himself is first *realized, objectified*, through his relation to other men. If he is related to the product of his labour, his objectified labour, as to an *alien*, hostile, powerful and independent object, he is related in such a way that another alien, hostile, powerful and independent man is the lord of this object. If he is related to his own activity as to unfree activity, then he is related to it as activity in the service, and under the domination, coercion and yoke, of another man.

Every self-alienation of man, from himself and from nature, appears in the relation which he postulates between other men and himself and nature. Thus religious self-alienation is necessarily exemplified in the relation between laity and priest, or, since it is here a question of the spiritual world, between the laity and a mediator. In the real world of practice this self-alienation can only be expressed in the real, practical relation of man to his fellow men. The medium through which alienation occurs is itself a *practical* one. Through alienated labour, therefore, man not only produces his relation to the object and to the process of production as to alien and hostile men; he also produces the relation of other men to his production and his product, and the relation between himself and other men. Just as he creates his own production as a vitiation, a punishment, and his own product as a loss, as a product which does not belong to him, so he creates the domination of the non-producer over production and its product. As he alienates his own activity, so he bestows upon the stranger an activity which is not his own.

We have so far considered this relation only from the side of the worker, and later on we shall consider it also from the side of the non-worker.

Thus, through alienated labour the worker creates the relation of another man, who does not work and is outside the work process, to this labour. The relation of the worker to work also produces the relation of the capitalist (or whatever one likes to call the lord of labour) to work. *Private property* is, therefore, the product, the necessary result, of *alienated labour*, of the external relation of the worker to nature and to himself.

Private property is thus derived from the analysis of the concept of *alienated labour;* that is, alienated man, alienated labour, alienated life, and estranged man.

We have, of course, derived the concept of *alienated labour* (*alienated life*) from political economy, from an analysis of the *movement of private property*. But the analysis of this concept shows that although private property appears to be the basis and cause of alienated labour, it is rather a consequence of the latter, just as the gods are *fundamentally* not the cause but the product of confusions of human reason. At a later stage, however, there is a reciprocal influence.

Only in the final stage of the development of private property is its secret revealed, namely, that it is on one hand the *product* of alienated labour, and on the other hand the *means* by which labour is alienated, *the realization of this alienation.*

This elucidation throws light upon several unresolved controversies—

  1. Political economy begins with labour as the real soul of production and then goes on to attribute nothing to labour and everything to

private property. Proudhon, faced by this contradiction, has decided in favour of labour against private property. We perceive, however, that this apparent contradiction is the contradiction of *alienated labour* with itself and that political economy has merely formulated the laws of alienated labour.

We also observe, therefore, that *wages* and *private property* are identical, for wages, like the product or object of labour, labour itself remunerated, are only a necessary consequence of the alienation of labour. In the wage system labour appears not as an end in itself but as the servant of wages. We shall develop this point later on and here only bring out some of the [XXVI] consequences.

An enforced *increase in wages* (disregarding the other difficulties, and especially that such an anomaly could only be maintained by force) would be nothing more than a *better remuneration of slaves*, and would not restore, either to the worker or to the work, their human significance and worth.

Even the *equality of incomes* which Proudhon demands would only change the relation of the present-day worker to his work into a relation of all men to work. Society would then be conceived as an abstract capitalist.

2. From the relation of alienated labour to private property it also follows that the emancipation of society from private property, from servitude, takes the political form of the *emancipation of the workers;* not in the sense that only the latter's emancipation is involved, but because this emancipation includes the emancipation of humanity as a whole. For all human servitude is involved in the relation of the worker to production, and all the types of servitude are only modifications or consequences of this relation.

As we have discovered the concept of *private property* by an *analysis* of the concept of *alienated labour,* so with the aid of these two factors we can evolve all the *categories* of political economy, and in every category, e.g. trade, competition, capital, money, we shall discover only a particular and developed expression of these fundamental elements.

However before considering this structure let us attempt to solve two problems.

1. To determine the general nature of *private property* as it has resulted from alienated labour, in its relation to *genuine human and social property.*

2. We have taken as a fact and analysed the *alienation of labour.* How does it happen, we may ask, that *man alienates his labour?* How is this alienation founded in the nature of human development? We have already done much to solve the problem in so far as we have *trans-*

formed the question concerning the *origin of private property* into a question about the relation between *alienated labour* and the process of development of mankind. For in speaking of private property one believes oneself to be dealing with something external to mankind. But in speaking of labour one deals directly with mankind itself. This new formulation of the problem already contains its solution.

We have resolved alienated labour into two parts, which mutually determine each other, or rather, which constitute two different expressions of one and the same relation. *Appropriation* appears as *alienation* and *alienation* as *appropriation*, alienation as genuine acceptance in the community.

We have considered one aspect, *alienated* labour, in its bearing upon the *worker* himself, i.e. *the relation of alienated labour to itself*. And we have found as the necessary consequence of this relation the *property relation* of the *non-worker* to the *worker* and to labour. *Private property* as the material, summarized expression of alienated labour includes both relations; *the relation of the worker to labour, to the product of his labour and to the non-worker*, and the relation of the *non-worker to the worker and to the product of the latter's labour*.

We have already seen that in relation to the worker, who *appropriates* nature by his labour, appropriation appears as alienation, self-activity as activity for another and of another, living as the sacrifice of life, and production of the object as loss of the object to an alien power, an alien man. Let us now consider the relation of this *alien* man to the worker, to labour, and to the object of labour.

It should be noted first that every thing which appears to the worker as an *activity of alienation*, appears to the non-worker as a *condition of alienation*. Secondly, the *real, practical* attitude (as a state of mind) of the worker in production and to the product appears to the non-worker who confronts him as a *theoretical* attitude.

XXVII

Thirdly, the non-worker does everything against the worker which the latter does against himself, but he does not do against himself what he does against the worker.

Let us examine these three relationships more closely.[2]

---

[2] The manuscript breaks off unfinished at this point. [T.B.B.]

NIETZSCHE

Friedrich Nietzsche (1844–1900) is the black sheep of philosophy. Brilliant, erratic, contrary, provocative, he deliberately states his perceptive insights in ways which are designed to irritate and arouse his readers. Nietzsche was one of the first students of human nature to perceive the twisted complexity of the received morality of the Christian tradition. Anticipating the work of Freud, he called attention to the wellsprings of resentment and anger from which much supposedly sweet and charitable moralizing flows.

Nietzsche set himself against the entire Judeo-Christian ethical position, opting instead for what he believed to be the healthier, more natural pagan views contained in the barbarian traditions of early Europe. On the surface, Nietzsche seems to extol brutality and to condemn civilization, but if you look a bit deeper you will see that he is really defending the amoral artist of the Romantic period against the dull, constricting negativism of bourgeois society. Strange as it may seem, Nietzsche, the great author of the cry "God is dead," has much in common with the god-intoxicated Kierkegaard.

The keynote to Nietzsche's attack on Christian morality is the insistence that aggression is human, natural, and good. Only when it is bottled up and denied expression does it become resentment, guilt, bitterness, and self-hatred. Like Freud after him, Nietzsche saw that we do not eliminate our aggressive impulses by repressing them. They return to bedevil us in forms which are ultimately destructive of the human spirit. What is more, we should not even wish to eliminate the aggressive component in human nature, for it is a source of great creative power. Indeed, Nietzsche would argue, a race of men who were genuinely molded in the image of Jesus would be sterile, tedious, and unworthy to walk the face of the earth!

It is not hard to imagine what Nietzsche would say of modern American society: Conformist, routinized, tame, overcivilized, it thwarts the creative impulses of men. Paradoxically, this very repression is the cause of the aimless, irrational violence which corrupts our social fabric. In the end, Nietzsche believes, more inhuman acts are committed in the name of morality and religion than in the name of egotistical self-interest or creative aggression. The barbarian lays about him with his sword until the blood lust is sated, killing in the process a handful of warriors; the civilized man presses buttons at his desk which kill millions, and then goes quietly home to dinner. Who is really the greater threat to human welfare?

What sort of political order is implied by Nietzsche's philosophy? It is hard to say. The Nazis claimed him as their philosophical ancestor, but Nietzsche would probably have viewed Hitler as a jumped-up petty bourgeois imposter, not as an heir to the noble barbarians of Germany's past. Ayn Rand's romantic celebration of superior individuals owes a great debt to Nietzsche, but her obsession with capitalism would surely have seemed to him the final victory of the hated Judeo-Christian ethos.

Slaves and Masters
Once More

The revolt of the slaves in morals begins in the very principle of *resentment* becoming creative and giving birth to values—a resentment experienced by creatures who, deprived as they are of the proper outlet of action, are forced to find their compensation in an imaginary revenge. While every aristocratic morality springs from a triumphant affirmation of its own demands, the slave morality says "no" from the very outset to what is "outside itself," "different from itself," and "not itself": and this "no" is its creative deed. This volte-face of the valuing standpoint—this *inevitable* gravitation to the objective instead of back to the subjective—is typical of "resentment": the slave-morality requires as the condition of its existence an external and objective world, to employ physiological terminology, it requires objective stimuli to be capable of action at all—its action is fundamentally a reaction. The contrary is the case when we come to the aristocrat's system of values: it acts and grows spontaneously, it merely seeks its antithesis in order to pronounce a more grateful and exultant "yes" to its own self;—its negative conception, "low," "vulgar," "bad," is merely a pale late-born foil in comparison with its positive and fundamental conception (saturated as it is with life and passion), of "we aristocrats, we good ones, we beautiful ones, we happy ones."

When the aristocratic morality goes astray and commits sacrilege on reality, this is limited to that particular sphere with which it is *not* sufficiently acquainted—a sphere, in fact, from the real knowledge of which it disdainfully defends itself. It misjudges, in some cases, the sphere which it despises,

First Essay, No. 10. From *Genealogy of Morals* by Friedrich Nietzsche. Trans. by Horace B. Samuel.

the sphere of the common vulgar man and the low people: on the other hand, due weight should be given to the consideration that in any case the mood of contempt, of disdain, of superciliousness, even on the supposition that it *falsely* portrays the object of its contempt, will always be far removed from that degree of falsity which will always characterise the attacks—in effigy, of course—of the vindictive hatred and revengefulness of the weak in onslaughts on their enemies. In point of fact, there is in contempt too strong an admixture of nonchalance, of casualness, of boredom, of impatience, even of personal exultation, for it to be capable of distorting its victim into a real caricature or a real monstrosity. Attention again should be paid to the almost benevolent *nuances* which, for instance, the Greek nobility imports into all the words by which it distinguishes the common people from itself; note how continuously a kind of pity, care, and consideration imparts its honeyed *flavour*, until at last almost all the words which are applied to the vulgar man survive finally as expressions for "unhappy," "worthy of pity" (compare δειλός, δείλαιος, πονηρός, μοχθηρός; the latter two names really denoting the vulgar man as labour-slave and beast of burden)—and how, conversely, "bad," "low," "unhappy" have never ceased to ring in the Greek ear with a tone in which "unhappy" is the predominant note: this is a heritage of the old noble aristocratic morality, which remains true to itself even in contempt (let philologists remember the sense in which ὀϊζυρός, ἄνολβος, τλήμων, δυστυχεῖν, ξυμφορά used to be employed. The "well-born" simply *felt* themselves the "happy"; they did not have to manufacture their happiness artificially through looking at their enemies, or in cases to talk and lie themselves into happiness (as is the custom with all resentful men); and similarly, complete men as they were, exuberant with strength, and consequently *necessarily* energetic, they were too wise to dissociate happiness from action—activity becomes in their minds necessarily counted as happiness (that is the etymology of εὖπράττειν)—all in sharp contrast to the "happiness" of the weak and the oppressed, with their festering venom and malignity, among whom happiness appears essentially as a narcotic, a deadening, a quietude, a peace, a "Sabbath," an enervation of the mind and relaxation of the limbs,—in short, a purely *passive* phenomenon. While the aristocratic man lived in confidence and openness with himself (γενναῖος, "noble-born," emphasises the nuance "sincere," and perhaps also "naïf"), the resentful man, on the other hand, is neither sincere nor naïf, nor honest and candid with himself. His soul *squints;* his mind loves hidden crannies, tortuous paths and backdoors, everything secret appeals to him as *his* world, *his* safety, *his* balm; he is past master in silence, in not forgetting, in waiting, in provisional self-depreciation and self-abasement. A race of such *resentful* men will of necessity eventually prove more *prudent* than any aristocratic race, it will honour prudence on quite a distinct scale, as, in fact, a paramount condition of existence, while prudence among aristocratic men is apt to be tinged with a delicate flavour of luxury and refinement; so among them it plays nothing like so integral a part as that complete certainty of function of the governing *uncon-*

scious instincts or as indeed a certain lack of prudence, such as a vehement and valiant charge, whether against danger or the enemy, or as those ecstatic bursts of rage, love, reverence, gratitude, by which at all times noble souls have recognised each other. When the resentment of the aristocratic man manifests itself it fulfils and exhausts itself into an immediate reaction, and consequently instills no *venom:* on the other hand, it never manifests itself at all in countless instances, when in the case of the feeble and weak it would be inevitable. An inability to take seriously for any length of time their enemies, their disasters, their *misdeeds*—that is the sign of the full strong natures who possess a super-fluity of moulding a plastic force, that heals completely and produces forget-fulness: a good example of this in the modern world is Mirabeau, who had no memory for any insults and meannesses which were practised on him, and who was only incapable of forgiving because he forgot. Such a man indeed shakes off with a shrug many a worm which would have buried itself in another; it is only in characters like these that we see the possibility (supposing, of course, that there is such a possibility in the world) of the real *"love* of one's enemies." What respect for his enemies is found, forsooth, in an aristocratic man—and such a reverence is already a bridge to love! He insists on having his enemy to himself as his distinction. He tolerates no other enemy but a man in whose character there is nothing to despise and *much* to honour! On the other hand, imagine the "enemy" as the resentful man conceives him—and it is here exactly that we see his work, his creativeness; he has conceived "the evil enemy," the "evil one," and indeed that is the root idea from which he now evolves as a contrasting and corresponding figure a "good one," himself—his very self!

SKINNER

Our last author in this part, B. F. Skinner (1904–   ), is well known to students of psychology as the foremost living theoretician and defender of the doctrine known as Behaviorism. His experimental work on both animal and human subjects has gone far to demonstrate the possibility of a unified scientific explanation of behavior which makes no reference to intentions, ideas, beliefs, or other distinctly human cognitive processes. In his very influential "novel" Walden Two, Professor Skinner expounds the social and political consequences of his psychological theory in the form of a utopia, or portrait of an ideal community. Like Nietzsche, Skinner enjoys being provocative, and he deliberately states his views in a manner which is calculated to raise the blood pressure of a typical American reader.

There are several questions which we must answer before we can form an opinion about the political theory of Walden Two. *First of all, is Skinner's theory of behaviorism correct? Can we, even in theory, explain human actions by means of the same mechanism of stimulus, response, and conditioned reflex which we use to explain animal behavior? Many students of human nature, including Aristotle, Marx, and Freud, would insist that human action is different in kind from animal behavior. Only by referring to reasons, purposes, ends, and beliefs can we make sense of human action. Hence, they would argue, Skinner's program for utopian reform is defeated from the very start.*

But suppose Skinner were able to show that he could control our behavior and condition our responses by regulating the "inputs" or stimuli that we experience. A second question arises: Would it be right to do so, even for the purpose of making men happier? *John Stuart Mill didn't think so, as we have seen. Is happiness, however achieved, the highest good? Or are freedom and autonomy to be valued even above happiness? In these days of powerful government and centralized control of the means of education and communication, this may well be one of the burning issues of our society.*

The Utopia
of Behavioral Psychology

Castle got his chance to take up "general issues" that afternoon. A walk to the summit of Stone Hill had been planned for a large party, which included Mr. and Mrs. Meyerson and three or four children. It seemed unlikely that any serious discussion would be possible. But a storm had been threatening all morning, and at lunch we heard it break. The afternoon was again open. I detected a certain activity in the dining room as plans were changed. As we were finishing dinner two young people approached our table and spoke to Rodge, Steve, and the girls.

"Do you play? Cornet, sax, trombone? We're getting up a concert. We even have a lonely tuba."

"You play, Steve," said Mary.

"Steve was the best little old trombone in the Philippines," said Rodge.

"Good! Anybody else? It's strictly amateur."

It appeared that Barbara could play popular tunes on the piano, mostly by ear, and it was thought that something might be arranged. They departed for the theater to look over the common stock of instruments, and Frazier, Castle, and I were left alone.

Castle immediately began to warm up his motors. He picked up an empty cigarette package which Barbara had left on the table, tore it in two, placed the halves together, and tore them again. Various husky noises issued from his throat. It was obvious that something was about to happen, and Frazier and I waited in silence.

"Mr. Frazier," Castle said at last, in a sudden roar, "I accuse you of one of the most diabolical machinations in the history of mankind!" He looked as steadily as possible at Frazier, but he was trembling, and his eyes were popping.

"Shall we go to my room?" Frazier said quietly.

It was a trick of Frazier's to adopt a contrasting tone of voice, and in this instance it was devastating. Castle came down to earth with a humiliating bump. He had prepared himself for a verbal battle of heroic dimensions, but he found himself humbly carrying his tray to the service window and trailing Frazier along the Walk.

I was not sure of the line Castle was going to take. Apparently he had done some thinking since morning, probably during the service, but I could not guess the result. Frazier's manner was also puzzling. His suggestion that we go to his room had sounded a little as if he were inviting a truculent companion to "step outside and say that again!" He had apparently expected the attack from Castle and had prepared the defenses to his satisfaction.

When we had settled ourselves in Frazier's room, with Frazier full-length on the bed, over which he had hastily pulled a cover, Castle began again in an unsuccessful attempt to duplicate the surprise and force of his first assault.

"A modern, mechanized, managerial Machiavelli—that is my final estimate of you, Mr. Frazier," he said, with the same challenging stare.

"It must be gratifying to know that one has reached a 'final estimate,' " said Frazier.

"An artist in power," Castle continued, "whose greatest art is to conceal art. The silent despot."

"Since we are dealing in 'M's,' why not sum it all up and say 'Mephistophelian'?" said Frazier, curiously reviving my fears of the preceding afternoon.

"I'm willing to do that!" said Castle. "And unless God is very sure of himself, I suspect He's by no means easy about this latest turn in the war of the angels. So far as I can see, you've blocked every path through which man was to struggle upward toward salvation. Intelligence, initiative—you have filled their places with a sort of degraded instinct, engineered compulsion. Walden Two is a marvel of efficient coordination—as efficient as an anthill!"

"Replacing intelligence with instinct—" muttered Frazier. "I had never thought of that. It's an interesting possibility. How's it done?" It was a crude maneuver. The question was a digression, intended to spoil Castle's timing and to direct our attention to practical affairs in which Frazier was more at home.

"The behavior of your members is carefully shaped in advance by a Plan," said Castle, not to be taken in, "and it's shaped to perpetuate that Plan. Intellectually Walden Two is quite as incapable of a spontaneous change of course as the life within a beehive."

"I see what you mean," said Frazier distantly. But he returned to his strategy. "And have you discovered the machinery of my power?"

"I have, indeed. We were looking in the wrong place. There's no *current* contact between you and the members of Walden Two. You threw us off the track very skillfully on that point last night. But you were behaving as a despot when you first laid your plans—when you designed the social structure and drew up the contract between community and member, when you worked out your educational practices and your guarantees against despotism—What a joke! Don't tell me you weren't in control *then!* Burris saw the point. What about your career as organizer? *There* was leadership! And the most damnable leadership in history, because you were setting the stage for the withdrawal of yourself as a personal force, knowing full well that everything that happened would still be your doing. Hundreds—you predicted millions—of unsuspecting souls were to fall within the scope of your ambitious scheme."

Castle was driving his argument home with great excitement, but Frazier was lying in exaggerated relaxation, staring at the ceiling, his hands cupped behind his head.

"Very good, Mr. Castle," he said softly. "I gave you the clue, of course, when we parted last night."

"You did, indeed. And I've wondered why. Were you led into that fatal error by your conceit? Perhaps that's the ultimate answer to your form of despotism. No one could enjoy the power you have seized without wishing to display it from time to time."

"I've admitted neither power nor despotism. But you're quite right in saying that I've exerted an influence and in one sense will continue to exert it forever. I believe you called me a *primum mobile*—not quite correctly, as I found upon looking the term up last night. But I did plan Walden Two—not as an architect plans a building, but as a scientist plans a long-term experiment, uncertain of the conditions he will meet but knowing how he will deal with them when they arise. In a sense, Walden Two is predetermined, but not as the behavior of a beehive is determined. Intelligence, no matter how much it may be shaped and extended by our educational system, will still function as intelligence. It will be used to puzzle out solutions to problems to which a beehive would quickly succumb. What the plan does is to keep intelligence on the right track, for the good of society rather than of the intelligent individual—or for the eventual rather than the immediate good of the individual. It does this by making sure that the individual will not forget his personal stake in the welfare of society."

"But you are forestalling many possibly useful acts of intelligence which aren't encompassed by your plan. You have ruled out points of view which may be more productive. You are implying that T. E. Frazier, looking at the world from the middle of the twentieth century, understands the best course for mankind forever."

"Yes, I suppose I do."

"But that's absurd!"

"Not at all. I don't say I foresee the course man will take a hundred years hence, let alone forever, but I know which he should take now."

"How can you be sure of it? It's certainly not a question you have answered experimentally."

"I think we're in the course of answering it," said Frazier. "But that's beside the point. There's no alternative. We must take that course."

"But that's fantastic. You who are taking it are in a small minority."

Frazier sat up.

"And the majority are in a big quandary," he said. "They're not on the road at all, or they're scrambling back toward their starting point, or sidling from one side of the road to the other like so many crabs. What do you think two world wars have been about? Something as simple as boundaries or trade? Nonsense. The world is trying to adjust to a new conception of man in relation to men."

"Perhaps it's merely trying to adjust to despots whose ideas are incompatible with the real nature of man."

"Mr. Castle," said Frazier very earnestly, "let me ask you a question. I warn you, it will be the most terrifying question of your life. *What would you*

do if you found yourself in possession of an effective science of behavior?
Suppose you suddenly found it possible to control the behavior of men as you
wished. What would you do?"

"That's an assumption?"

"Take it as one if you like. *I* take it as a fact. And apparently you accept
it as a fact too. I can hardly be as despotic as you claim unless I hold the key
to an extensive practical control."

"What would I do?" said Castle thoughtfully. "I think I would dump
your science of behavior in the ocean."

"And deny men all the help you could otherwise give them?"

"And give them the freedom they would otherwise lose forever!"

"How could you give them freedom?"

"By refusing to control them!"

"But you would only be leaving the control in other hands."

"Whose?"

"The charlatan, the demagogue, the salesman, the ward heeler, the bully,
the cheat, the educator, the priest—all who are now in possession of the techniques of behavioral engineering."

"A pretty good share of the control would remain in the hands of the
individual himself."

"That's an assumption, too, and it's your only hope. It's your only possible chance to avoid the implications of a science of behavior. If man is
free, then a technology of behavior is impossible. But I'm asking you to consider the other case."

"Then my answer is that your assumption is contrary to fact and any
further consideration idle."

"And your accusations—?"

"—were in terms of intention, not of possible achievement."

Frazier sighed dramatically.

"It's a little late to be proving that a behavioral technology is well advanced. How can you deny it? Many of its methods and techniques are really
as old as the hills. Look at their frightful misuse in the hands of the Nazis! And
what about the techniques of the psychological clinic? What about education?
Or religion? Or practical politics? Or advertising and salesmanship? Bring them
all together and you have a sort of rule-of-thumb technology of vast power.
No, Mr. Castle, the science is there for the asking. But its techniques and
methods are in the wrong hands—they are used for personal aggrandizement in
a competitive world or, in the case of the psychologist and educator, for
futilely corrective purposes. My question is, have you the courage to take up
and wield the science of behavior for the good of mankind? You answer that
you would dump it in the ocean!"

"I'd want to take it out of the hands of the politicians and advertisers
and salesmen, too."

"And the psychologists and educators? You see, Mr. Castle, you can't have that kind of cake. The fact is, we not only *can* control human behavior, we *must*. But who's to do it, and what's to be done?"

"So long as a trace of personal freedom survives, I'll stick to my position," said Castle, very much out of countenance.

"Isn't it time we talked about freedom?" I said. "We parted a day or so ago on an agreement to let the question of freedom ring. It's time to answer, don't you think?"

"My answer is simple enough," said Frazier. "I deny that freedom exists at all. I must deny it—or my program would be absurd. You can't have a science about a subject matter which hops capriciously about. Perhaps we can never *prove* that man isn't free; it's an assumption. But the increasing success of a science of behavior makes it more and more plausible."

"On the contrary, a simple personal experience makes it untenable," said Castle. "The experience of freedom. I *know* that I'm free."

"It must be quite consoling," said Frazier.

"And what's more—you do, too," said Castle hotly. "When you deny your own freedom for the sake of playing with a science of behavior, you're acting in plain bad faith. That's the only way I can explain it." He tried to recover himself and shrugged his shoulders. "At least you'll grant that you *feel* free."

"The 'feeling of freedom' should deceive no one," said Frazier. "Give me a concrete case."

"Well, right now," Castle said. He picked up a book of matches. "I'm free to hold or drop these matches."

"You will, of course, do one or the other," said Frazier. "Linguistically or logically there seem to be two possibilities, but I submit there's only one in fact. The determining forces may be subtle but they are inexorable. I suggest that as an orderly person you will probably hold—ah! you drop them! Well, you see, that's all part of your behavior with respect to me. You couldn't resist the temptation to prove me wrong. It was all lawful. You had no choice. The deciding factor entered rather late, and naturally you couldn't foresee the result when you first held them up. There was no strong likelihood that you would act in either direction, and so you said you were free."

"That's entirely too glib," said Castle. "It's easy to argue lawfulness after the fact. But let's see you predict what I will do in advance. Then I'll agree there's law."

"I didn't say that behavior was predictable, any more than the weather is always predictable. There are often too many factors to be taken into account. We can't measure them all accurately, and we couldn't perform the mathematical operations needed to make a prediction if we had the measurements. The legality is usually an assumption—but none the less important in judging the issue at hand."

"Take a case where there's no choice, then," said Castle. "Certainly a man in jail isn't free in the sense in which I am free now."

"Good! That's an excellent start. Let us classify the kinds of determiners of human behavior. One class, as you suggest, is physical restraint—handcuffs, iron bars, forcible coercion. These are ways in which we shape human behavior according to our wishes. They're crude, and they sacrifice the affection of the controllee, but they often work. Now, what other ways are there of limiting freedom?"

Frazier had adopted a professional tone and Castle refused to answer.

"The threat of force would be one," I said.

"Right. And here again we shan't encourage any loyalty on the part of the controllee. He has perhaps a shade more of the feeling of freedom, since he can always 'choose to act and accept the consequences,' but he doesn't feel exactly free. He knows his behavior is being coerced. Now what else?"

I had no answer.

"Force or the threat of force—I see no other possibility," said Castle after a moment.

"Precisely," said Frazier.

"But certainly a large part of my behavior has no connection with force at all. There's my freedom!" said Castle.

"I wasn't agreeing that there was no other possibility—merely that *you* could see no other. Not being a good behaviorist—or a good Christian, for that matter—you have no feeling for a tremendous power of a different sort."

"What's that?"

"I shall have to be technical," said Frazier. "But only for a moment. It's what the science of behavior calls 'reinforcement theory.' The things that can happen to us fall into three classes. To some things we are indifferent. Other things we like—we want them to happen, and we take steps to make them happen again. Still other things we don't like—we don't want them to happen and we take steps to get rid of them or keep them from happening again.

"*Now,*" Frazier continued earnestly, "if it's in our power to create any of the situations which a person likes or to remove any situation he doesn't like, we can control his behavior. When he behaves as we want him to behave, we simply create a situation he likes, or remove one he doesn't like. As a result, the probability that he will behave that way again goes up, which is what we want. Technically it's called 'positive reinforcement.'

"The old school made the mistake of supposing that the reverse was true, that by removing a situation a person likes or setting up one he doesn't like—in other words by punishing him—it was possible to *reduce* the probability that he would behave in a given way again. That simply doesn't hold. It has been established beyond question. What is emerging at this critical stage in the evolution of society is a behavioral and cultural technology based on positive reinforcement alone. We are gradually discovering—at an untold cost in human suffering—that in the long run punishment doesn't reduce the probability that an act will occur. We have been so preoccupied with the contrary that we always take 'force' to mean punishment. We don't say we're using force when we send shiploads of food into a starving country, though we're displaying quite as much *power* as if we were sending troops and guns."

"I'm certainly not an advocate of force," said Castle. "But I can't agree that it's not effective."

"It's *temporarily* effective, that's the worst of it. That explains several thousand years of bloodshed. Even nature has been fooled. We 'instinctively' punish a person who doesn't behave as we like—we spank him if he's a child or strike him if he's a man. A nice distinction! The immediate effect of the blow teaches us to strike again. Retribution and revenge are the most natural things on earth. But in the long run the man we strike is no less likely to repeat his act."

"But he won't repeat it if we hit him hard enough," said Castle.

"He'll still *tend* to repeat it. He'll *want* to repeat it. We haven't really altered his potential behavior at all. That's the pity of it. If he doesn't repeat it in our presence, he will in the presence of someone else. Or it will be repeated in the disguise of a neurotic symptom. If we hit hard enough, we clear a little place for ourselves in the wilderness of civilization, but we make the rest of the wilderness still more terrible.

"Now, early forms of government are naturally based on punishment. It's the obvious technique when the physically strong control the weak. But we're in the throes of a great change to positive reinforcement—from a competitive society in which one man's reward is another man's punishment, to a cooperative society in which no one gains at the expense of anyone else.

"The change is slow and painful because the immediate, temporary effect of punishment overshadows the eventual advantage of positive reinforcement. We've all seen countless instances of the temporary effect of force, but clear evidence of the effect of not using force is rare. That's why I insist that Jesus, who was apparently the first to discover the power of refusing to punish, must have hit upon the principle by accident. He certainly had none of the experimental evidence which is available to us today, and I can't conceive that it was possible, no matter what the man's genius, to have discovered the principle from casual observation."

"A touch of revelation, perhaps?" said Castle.

"No, accident. Jesus discovered one principle because it had immediate consequences, and he got another thrown in for good measure."

I began to see light.

"You mean the principle of 'love your enemies'?" I said.

"Exactly! To 'do good to those who despitefully use you' has two unrelated consequences. You gain the peace of mind we talked about the other day. Let the stronger man push you around—at least you avoid the torture of your own rage. *That's* the immediate consequence. What an astonishing discovery it must have been to find that in the long run you could *control the stronger man* in the same way!"

"It's generous of you to give so much credit to your early colleague," said

Castle, "but why are we still in the throes of so much misery? Twenty centuries should have been enough for one piece of behavioral engineering."

"The conditions which made the principle difficult to discover made it difficult to teach. The history of the Christian Church doesn't reveal many cases of doing good to one's enemies. One must look outside the field of organized religion to find the principle in practice at all. Church governments are devotees of *power*, both temporal and bogus."

"But what has all this got to do with freedom?" I said hastily.

Frazier took time to reorganize his behavior. He looked steadily toward the window, against which the rain was beating heavily.

"Now that we *know* how positive reinforcement works and why negative doesn't," he said at last, "we can be more deliberate, and hence more successful, in our cultural design. We can achieve a sort of control under which the controlled, though they are following a code much more scrupulously than was ever the case under the old system, nevertheless *feel free*. They are doing what they want to do, not what they are forced to do. That's the source of the tremendous power of positive reinforcement—there's no restraint and no revolt. By a careful cultural design, we control not the final behavior, but the *inclination* to behave—the motives, the desires, the wishes.

"The curious thing is that in that case *the question of freedom never arises*. Mr. Castle was free to drop the matchbook in the sense that nothing was preventing him. If it had been securely bound to his hand he wouldn't have been free. Nor would he have been quite free if I'd covered him with a gun and threatened to shoot him if he let it fall. The question of freedom arises when there is restraint—either physical or psychological.

"But restraint is only one sort of control, and absence of restraint isn't freedom. It's not control that's lacking when one feels 'free,' but the objectionable control of force. Mr. Castle felt free to hold or drop the matches in the sense that he felt no restraint—no threat of punishment in taking either course of action. He neglected to examine his positive reasons for holding or letting go, in spite of the fact that these were more compelling in this instance than any threat of force.

"We have no vocabulary of freedom in dealing with what we want to do," Frazier went on. "The question never arises. When men strike for freedom, they strike against jails and the police, or the threat of them—against oppression. They never strike against forces which make them want to act the way they do. Yet, it seems to be understood that governments will operate only through force or the threat of force, and that all other principles of control will be left to education, religion, and commerce. If this continues to be the case, we may as well give up. A government can never create a free people with the techniques now allotted to it.

"The question is: Can men live in freedom and peace? And the answer is: Yes, if we can build a social structure which will satisfy the needs of everyone and in which everyone will want to observe the supporting code. But so far this has been achieved only in Walden Two. Your ruthless accusations to the contrary, Mr. Castle, this is the freest place on earth. And it is free precisely because we make no use of force or the threat of force. Every bit of our research, from the nursery through the psychological management of our adult membership, is directed toward that end—to exploit every alternative to forcible control. By skillful planning, by a wise choice of techniques we *increase* the feeling of freedom.

"It's not planning which infringes upon freedom, but planning which uses force. A sense of freedom was practically unknown in the planned society of Nazi Germany, because the planners made a fantastic use of force and the threat of force.

"No, Mr. Castle, when a science of behavior has once been achieved, there's no alternative to a planned society. We can't leave mankind to an accidental or biased control. But by using the principle of positive reinforcement —carefully avoiding force or the threat of force—we can preserve a personal sense of freedom."

Frazier threw himself back upon the bed and stared at the ceiling.

"But you haven't denied that you are in complete control," said Castle. "You are still the long-range dictator."

"As you will," said Frazier, waving his hands loosely in the air and then cupping them behind his head. "In fact, I'm inclined to agree. When you have once grasped the principle of positive reinforcement, you can enjoy a sense of unlimited power. It's enough to satisfy the thirstiest tyrant."

"There you are, then," said Castle. "That's my case."

"But it's a limited sort of despotism," Frazier went on. "And I don't think anyone should worry about it. The despot must wield his power for the good of others. If he takes any step which reduces the sum total of human happiness, his power is reduced by a like amount. What better check against a malevolent despotism could you ask for?"

"The check I ask for," said Castle, "is nothing less than democracy. Let the people rule and power will not be misused. I can't see that the nature of the power matters. As a matter of fact, couldn't this principle of 'positive reinforcement,' as you call it, be used by a democratic government just as well as by your dictatorship?"

"No principle is consistently used by a democratic government. What do you mean by democracy, anyway?"

"Government by the people or according to the will of the people, naturally," said Castle.

"As exemplified by current practices in the United States?"

"I suppose so. Yes, I'll take my stand on that. It's not a perfect democracy, but it's the best there is at the moment."

"Then I say that democracy is a pious fraud," said Frazier. "In what sense is it 'government by the people'?"

"In an obvious sense, I should say."

"It isn't obvious at all. How is the people's will ascertained? In an election. But what a travesty! In a small committee meeting, or even a town hall, I can see some point in voting, especially on a yes-or-no question. But fifty million voters choosing a president—that's quite another thing."

"I can't see that the number of voters changes the principle," said Castle.

"The chance that one man's vote will decide the issue in a national election," said Frazier, speaking very deliberately, "is less than the chance that he will be killed on his way to the polls. We pay no attention whatsoever to chances of that magnitude in our daily affairs. We should call a man a fool who bought a sweepstakes ticket with similar odds against him."

"It must mean something or people wouldn't vote," said Castle.

"How many of them would go on voting if they were free of a lot of extraneous pressures? Do you think a man goes to the polls because of any effect which casting a vote has ever had? By no means. He goes to avoid being talked about by his neighbors, or to 'knife' a candidate whom he dislikes, marking his X as he might defile a campaign poster—and with the same irrational spite. No, a man has no logical reason to vote whatsoever. The chances of affecting the issue are too small to alter his behavior in any appreciable way."

"I believe the mathematicians have a name for that fallacy," said Castle. "It's true that your chances of deciding the issue get smaller as the number of voters increases, but the stakes get larger at the same rate."

"But do they? Is a national election really an important issue? Does it really matter very much who wins? The platforms of the two parties are carefully made as much alike as possible, and when the election is over we're all advised to accept the result like good sports. Only a few voters go on caring very much after a week or two. The rest know there's no real threat. Things will go on pretty much the same. Elections are sometimes turned by a few million voters who can't make up their minds until election day. It can't be much of an issue if that's the case."

"Even so, it's important that the people *feel* they've chosen the government they want," said Castle.

"On the contrary, that's the worst of it. Voting is a device for blaming conditions on the people. The people aren't rulers, they're scapegoats. And they file to the polls every so often to renew their right to the title."

"I daresay there are defects in the machinery of democracy," said Castle. "No one wholly approves of the average presidential campaign. The will of the people is likely to be unduly influenced, and perhaps incorrectly determined. But that's a matter of technique. I think we will eventually work out a better system for ascertaining what the people want done. Democracy isn't a method of polling opinion, it's the assignment of power to that opinion. Let's assume that the will of the people can be ascertained. What then?"

"I should ask you that. What then, indeed? Are the people skilled governors? No. And they become less and less skilled, relatively speaking, as the science of government advances. It's the same point I raised in our discussion of the group nursery: when we've once acquired a behavioral technology, we can't leave the control of behavior to the unskilled. Your answer is to deny that the technology exists—a very feeble answer, it seems to me.

"The one thing the people know," Frazier continued, "and the one thing about which they should be heard is how they like the existing state of affairs, and perhaps how they would like some other state of affairs. What they conspicuously don't know is how to get what they want. That's a matter for specialists."

"But the people have solved some pretty important problems," I said.

"Have they, in fact? The actual practice in a democracy is to vote, not for a given state of affairs, but for a man who claims to be able to achieve that state. I'm not a historian"—Frazier laughed explosively—"quite the contrary—but I suspect that that's always what is meant by the rule of the people—rule by a man chosen by the people."

"Isn't that a possible way out, though?" said Castle. "Suppose we need experts. Why not elect them?"

"For a very simple reason. The people are in no position to evaluate experts. And elected experts are never able to act as they think best. They can't experiment. The amateur doesn't appreciate the need for experimentation. He wants his expert to *know*. And he's utterly incapable of sustaining the period of doubt during which an experiment works itself out. The experts must either disguise their experiments and pretend to know the outcome in advance or stop experimenting altogether and struggle to maintain the *status quo*."

" 'With all her faults, I love her still,' " said Castle. "I'll take democracy. We may have to muddle through. We may seem laughable to your streamlined Planners. But we have one thing on our side—freedom."

"I thought we had settled that," said Frazier.

"We had. But apparently not as you thought," said Castle, "I don't like despotism."

Frazier got up and went to the window. The rain had stopped, and the distant hills beyond the river had become visible. He stood with his back to us for perhaps a minute, which seemed very long against the energetic tempo of our conversation. Finally he turned.

"Can't I make you understand?" he said, holding out his hands in a gesture of appeal. "*I don't like despotism either!* I don't like the despotism of ignorance. I don't like the despotism of neglect, of irresponsibility, the despotism of accident, even. And I don't like the despotism of democracy!"

He turned back to the window.

"I don't think I follow you," said Castle, somewhat softened by Frazier's evident emotion.

"Democracy is the spawn of despotism," Frazier said, continuing to look out the window. "And like father, like son. Democracy is power and rule. It's not the will of the people, remember; it's the will of the majority." He turned and, in a husky voice which broke in flight like a tumbler pigeon on the word "out," he added, "My heart goes out to the everlasting minority." He seemed ready to cry, but I could not tell whether it was in sympathy for the oppressed or in rage at his failure to convince Castle.

"In a democracy," he went on, "there is *no* check against despotism, because the principle of democracy is supposed to be itself a check. But it guarantees only that the *majority* will not be despotically ruled."

"I don't agree that the minority has no say," said Castle. "But in any case it's better that at least half the people get what they want, instead of a small élite."

"There you are!" said Frazier, jumping up again just as he had started to sit down. "The majority are an élite. And they're despots. I want none of them! Let's have government for the benefit of all."

"But that isn't always possible," said Castle.

"It's possible much oftener than under a democracy. There are seldom any issues which have to be decided in an all-or-none fashion. A careful planner could work out a compromise which would be reasonably satisfying to everyone. But in a democracy, the majority solve the problem to their satisfaction, and the minority can be damned.

"The government of Walden Two," he continued, "has the virtues of democracy, but none of the defects. It's much closer to the theory or intent of democracy than the actual practice in America today. The will of the people is carefully ascertained. We have no election campaigns to falsify issues or obscure them with emotional appeals, but a careful study of the satisfaction of the membership is made. Every member has a direct channel through which he may protest to the Managers or even the Planners. And these protests are taken as seriously as the pilot of an airplane takes a sputtering engine. We don't need laws and a police force to compel a pilot to pay attention to a defective engine. Nor do we need laws to compel our Dairy manager to pay attention to an epidemic among his cows. Similarly, our Behavioral and Cultural Managers need not be compelled to consider grievances. A grievance is a wheel to be oiled, or a broken pipe line to be repaired.

"Most of the people in Walden Two take no active part in running the government. And they don't want an active part. The urge to have a say in how the country should be run is a recent thing. It was not part of early democracy. The original victory over tyranny was a constitutional guarantee of personal rights, including the right to protest if conditions were not satisfactory. But the business of ruling was left to somebody else. Nowadays, everybody fancies himself an expert in government and wants to have a say. Let's hope it's a temporary cultural pattern. I can remember when everyone could talk about the mechanical principles according to which his automobile ran or failed to run. Everyone was an automotive specialist and knew how to file the points of a magneto and take the shimmy out of front wheels. To suggest that these matters might be left to experts would have been called Fascism, if the term had been invented. But today no one knows how his car operates and I can't see that he's any the less happy.

"In Walden Two no one worries about the government except the few to whom that worry has been assigned. To suggest that everyone should take an interest would seem as fantastic as to suggest that everyone should become familiar with our Diesel engines. Even the constitutional rights of the members are seldom thought about, I'm sure. The only thing that matters is one's day-to-day happiness and a secure future. Any infringement there would undoubtedly 'arouse the electorate.' "

"I assume that your constitution at least can't be changed without a vote of the members," I said.

"Wrong again. It can be changed by a unanimous vote of the Planners and a two-thirds vote of the Managers. You're still thinking about government by the people. Get that out of your head. The people are in no better position to change the constitution than to decide upon current practices."

"Then what's to prevent your Planners from becoming despots?" I said. "Wouldn't it really be possible?"

"How?" said Frazier.

"Oh, in many ways, I imagine."

"Such as?"

"Well, if I were a Planner with a yen for despotism, I would begin by insinuating into the culture the notion that Planners were exceptional people. I would argue that they should be personally known to the members, and should therefore wear an identifying badge or uniform. This could be done under the guise of facilitating service to the members, but eventually the Planners would be set off as a separate caste. Then they'd be relieved from menial work on the ground that they were too busy with the affairs of the community. Then special quarters, perhaps quite luxurious, would be built for them. I'd bring the Managers around to this change in the constitution by giving them better quarters also. It would all be carefully propagandized, of course. Eventually more and more of the wealth of the community would be diverted to this élite, and I would come out with a true despotism. Isn't that possible?"

"If you mean, 'Isn't despotism possible?' the answer is yes," said Frazier. "Cultures which work for the advantage of a few last a long time. Look at India, where the oppressed aren't even aware that they are sick and miserable. But are the people strong, productive, progressive? If not, then the culture will eventually be replaced by competing cultures which work more efficiently. Our Planners know this. They know that any usurpation of power would weaken the community as a whole and eventually destroy the whole venture."

"A group of despotic planners might be willing to sacrifice the community," I said. "They wouldn't necessarily suffer if it failed. They could simply abscond with the funds."

"That would be a catastrophe. Like an earthquake, or a new and frightful epidemic, or a raid from another world. All we can do is take reasonable precautions. Your hypothetical case strikes me as implausible, that's all I can say."

"But isn't that just the weakness of your antidemocratic attitude?" Castle said. "Haven't you lost your guarantee against the usurpation of power?"

"There's no power to usurp," said Frazier. "There's no police, no military, no guns or bombs—tear-gas or atomic—to give strength to the few. In point of physical force the members are always clearly in power. Revolt is not only easy, it's inevitable if real dissatisfaction arises.

"And there's little real wealth to tempt anyone. It isn't true that the Planners could abscond with the funds. Our wealth is our happiness. The physical plant of the community would be practically worthless without the members.

"And then remember that the Planners are part of a noncompetitive culture in which a thirst for power is a curiosity. They have no reason to usurp. Their tradition is against it. Any gesture of personal domination would stand out as conspicuously as the theft of the bulletin board."

"But it's human to dominate," said Castle, "in any culture."

"That's an experimental question, Mr. Castle. You can't answer it from your armchair. But let's see what a usurpation of power would amount to. Insofar as the Planners rule at all, they do so through positive reinforcement. They don't use or threaten to use force. They have no machinery for that. In order to extend their power they would have to provide more and more satisfying conditions. A curious sort of despotism, Mr. Castle."

"But they might change to a different sort of power."

"That would require a unanimous vote. But the Planners are eventually demoted to simple citizenship. Their terms of office are staggered, and some of them are always so close to retirement that they wouldn't share in the selfish consequences. Why should they vote for the change?

"Usurpation of power is a threat only in a competitive culture," Frazier continued. "In Walden Two power is either destroyed or so diffused that usurpation is practically impossible. Personal ambition isn't essential in a good governor. As governmental technology advances, less and less is left to the decisions of governors, anyway. Eventually we shall have no use for Planners at all. The Managers will suffice."

Frazier turned to me in an open gesture of appeasement.

"Democracy is not a guarantee against despotism, Burris. Its virtues are of another sort. It has proved itself clearly superior to the despotic rule of a small élite. We have seen it survive in conflict with the despotic pattern in World War II. The democratic peoples proved themselves superior just because of their democracy. They could enlist the support of other peoples, who had less to fear from them than from an aggressive élite. They could marshal greater manpower in the long run because everyone had a stake in victory and few were suffering from the strain of forcible coercion. The despots couldn't convert the people they conquered while pretending to be a superior race. Every principle which seemed to strengthen the governmental structure of Fascism when the war began proved to be an eventual weakness.

"But the triumph of democracy doesn't mean it's the best government. It was merely the better in a contest with a conspicuously bad one. Let's not stop with democracy. It isn't, and can't be, the best form of government, because it's based on a scientifically invalid conception of man. It fails to take account of the fact that in the long run *man is determined by the state.* A *laissez-faire* philosophy which trusts to the inherent goodness and wisdom of the common man is incompatible with the observed fact that men are made good or bad and wise or foolish by the environment in which they grow."

"But which comes first," I asked, "the hen or the egg? Men build society and society builds men. Where do we start?"

"It isn't a question of starting. The start has been made. It's a question of what's to be done from now on."

"Then it's to be revolution, is that it?" said Castle. "If democracy can't change itself into something better—"

"Revolution? You're not a very rewarding pupil, Mr. Castle. The change won't come about through power politics at all. It will take place at another level altogether."

"What level?"

Frazier waved his hand toward the window, through which we could see the drenched landscape of Walden Two.

"Well," said Castle, "you'd better hurry up. It's not a job to be done on four hours a day."

"Four hours a day is exactly what it needs," said Frazier with a smile. He lay back upon the bed, looking rather tired.

"I can think of a conspicuous case in which the change you're advocating is coming about at the level of power politics," I said.

Frazier sat up quickly, with obvious effort. He looked at me suspiciously.

"Russia," I said.

"Ah, Russia," he said with relief. He showed no inclination to go on.

"What about Russia, though?"

"What about it, indeed?"

"Isn't there a considerable resemblance between Russian communism and your own philosophy?"

"Russia, Russia," Frazier murmured evasively. "Our visitors always ask that. Russia is our rival. It's very flattering—if you consider the resources and the numbers of people involved."

"But you're dodging my question. Hasn't Russia done what you're trying to do, but at the level of power politics? I can imagine what a Communist would say of your program at Walden Two. Wouldn't he simply tell you to drop the experiment and go to work for the Party?"

"He would and he does."

"And what's your answer?"

"I can see only four things wrong with Russia," Frazier said, clearly enjoying the condescension. "As originally conceived, it was a good try. It sprang from humanitarian impulses which are a commonplace in Walden Two. But it quickly developed certain weaknesses. There are four of them, and they were inevitable. They were inevitable just because the attempt was made at the level of power politics." He waited for me to ask him what the weaknesses were.

"The first," he said, as soon as I had done so, "is a decline in the experimental spirit. Many promising experiments have simply been dropped. The group care of children, the altered structure of the family, the abandonment of religion, new kinds of personal incentives—all these problems were 'solved' by dropping back to practices which have prevailed in capitalistic societies for centuries. It was the old difficulty. A government in power can't experiment. It must know the answers or at least pretend to know them. Today the Russians contend that an optimal cultural pattern has been achieved, if not yet fully implemented. They dare not admit to any serious need for improvement. Revolutionary experimentation is dead.

"In the second place, Russia has overpropagandized, both to its own people and to the outside world. Their propaganda is much more extensive than any which ever enslaved a working class. That's a serious defect, for it has made it impossible to evaluate their success. We don't know how much of the current vigor of Russian communism is due to a strong, satisfying way of life, and how much to indoctrination. You may call it a temporary expedient, to counteract the propaganda embedded in an older culture. But that need has long since passed, yet the propaganda continues. So long as it goes on, no valid data on the effectiveness of Russian communism can be obtained. For all we know, the whole culture would fall apart if the supporting attitudes were taken away. And what is worse, it's hard to see how they can ever be taken away. Propaganda makes it impossible to progress toward a form of society in which it is unnecessary.

"The third weakness of the Russian government is its use of heroes. The first function of the hero, in Russia as elsewhere, is to piece out a defective governmental structure. Important decisions aren't made by appeal to a set of principles; they are personal acts. The process of governing is an art, not a science, and the government is only as good or as long-lasting as the artist. As to the second function of the hero—how long would communism last if all the pictures of Lenin and Stalin were torn down? It's a question worth asking.

"But most important of all, the Russian experiment was based on power. You may argue that the seizure of power was also a temporary expedient, since the people who held it were intolerant and oppressive. But you can hardly defend the continued use of power in that way. The Russians are still a long way from a culture in which people behave as they *want* to behave, for their mutual good. In order to get its people to act as the communist pattern demands, the Russian government has had to use the techniques of capitalism. On the one hand it resorts to extravagant and uneven rewards. But an unequal distribution of wealth destroys more incentives than it creates. It obviously can't operate for the *common* good. On the other hand, the government also uses punishment or the threat of it. What kind of behavioral engineering do you call that?"

Frazier spat into the flowerpot in a gesture of disgust. Then he held out his hands with an exaggerated shrug and drew himself slowly to his feet. He had evidently had enough of Castle's "general issues."

AFTERWORD

In my editorial introductions to the selections in this section I have tried to indicate the ways in which the authors' theories of human nature would imply, or at least support, differing evaluations of American society. In these concluding remarks perhaps I can turn the question around and suggest the conceptions of man which would be appropriate for some of the political doctrines with which we are all familiar.

Let me begin with **three** political points of view which are very frequently confused with one another, and which are all labeled "conservative" or "right wing" in American public discussions. The first "conservative" view is that associated with the great eighteenth-century British writer Edmund Burke. Burke held—and many astute political philosophers have agreed—that man is a creation of passion as well as of reason, that no individual at any given moment in time can successfully deduce a viable system of social and political arrangements from abstract principles of pure logic. Hence, he concluded, we must rely heavily on the slowly accumulated wisdom of our forebears, as it is collected in our established institutions. The rage to tear down the old and build anew, which Burke viewed with horror in the French Revolution, can only result in greater harm than may have been suffered under the traditional arrangements. Believing that man's ties to society were emotional rather than rational, Burke urged his countrymen to cling to the symbols of authority and tradition, lest they irreparably damage the social organism in their haste to tinker with it. This deep-rooted scepticism about the possibility of rapid, thoroughgoing reform can be found in many experienced American public men, particularly in the Congress and the foreign service. It is probably the single greatest difference between the old and the young in this or any other time.

The second "conservative" or "right-wing" view is the extreme laissez-faire individualism associated with such public figures as Barry Goldwater and such academic theoreticians as the economist Milton Friedman. By an odd twist of language, this doctrine used to be known as liberalism, and in the late eighteenth century, when it first made its appearance, it was intended as a challenge to the conservatism of men like Burke. The "laissez-faire liberal" views man in the utilitarian mold as self-interested, rational, capable of making economic decisions on a pure profit-and-loss basis. Following Adam Smith, the laissez-faire theorists defend an unfettered capitalism as the most efficient way to maximize individual satisfactions. Any constraints on the marketplace, either from tradition or from the state, are seen as harmful distortions of the natural laws of economics. Classical "liberals" of this persuasion oppose any attempt to increase the power of the federal government. Their cry is, "Let the private sector do it!"

The third "conservative" position, exemplified by Nietzsche in this section and by such popular contemporary authors as Ortega y Gasset and Ayn Rand, is the elitist belief in the superiority of the intellectual and cultural minority of creative minds. On this view, there is not **one** human nature common to all men, but rather a type of mass man good only for following, and a higher type of creative individual who is a natural leader. (Note the similarity to Aristotle's doctrine of natural slaves and natural masters.)

Obviously, the traditional conservative, the laissez-faire liberal, and the elitist have very little in common. It is one of the oddities of American political life that they so often end up in the same political camp.

By contrast to the varieties of right-wing thought, the modern or welfare state liberal has a conception of man which is an amalgam of several different theories. Characteristically, the modern liberal sees men as potentially capable of rationally self-interested action, but he agrees with Burke's view that men need the nonrational ties of family, community, and state. The welfare state liberal is, in a sense, a theorist who tries to combine libertarian, individualist politics with communitarian, collectivist social science. So, for example, he insists on the individual's absolute right to privacy, but still calls on the state, in the name of the common welfare, to take collective action to remedy social ills. Welfare state liberals tend to lean very heavily on education as an instrument of social reform, for the root conviction of modern liberalism is that inside each socially conditioned, culturally determined member of society there is an old-style rational man trying to get out.

On the left, we again find several incompatible points of view being lumped together. The Marxian socialist, as we have seen, views man as essentially a **social** creature, whose happiness and personal fulfillment must come from his involvement with his fellow men. In this way, the socialist agrees with the Burkean conservative, against the laissez-faire liberal. Both conservatives and socialists criticize capitalist society for dehumanizing and alienating men, for destroying the natural bonds which tie men together in communities. The difference between the conservatives and the socialists, we might say, is that the conservatives look backward to a time when society was supposedly more organically whole and happy, while the socialists aim to create such a harmonious society in the future.

Allied on the left with the socialists, but basically opposed to them philosophically, are the **anarchists,** who espouse an extreme individualism and resist all claims to authority, whether by tradition, the state, or the "laws of history." Anarchists have a conception of human nature very much like that of the laissez-faire liberals, but they deny that capitalism is really an economic system in which men can be **free.**

This brief survey should make it clear why political debates are so confusing. Underlying the disputes about particular issues are several deep questions on which men disagree very strongly. Is man **rational** or **irrational?** Is he essentially an **individual** or a **part** of **society?** Are all men basically the same, or is there an elite which is markedly superior to the mass? Your answers to these questions will go a long way to determining where on the political spectrum you take your stand.

VI
POLITICAL
PHILOSOPHY

The Draft:
Foundations of
Political Obligation

INTRODUCTION TO THE CONTEMPORARY ISSUE

In this section of the book, I emerge temporarily from behind my mask of impartiality and become one of the combatants as well as the referee. As we all know, this violates every rule of law and fair play, so I shall have to try very hard to lean over backward in my editorial comments to do justice to my opponent.

No subject—not even drugs—touches America's college students more closely than the draft. Most of you have lived your entire lives in the shadow of involuntary military service. Your fathers fought in World War II and in Korea; your older brothers fought in Vietnam; and unless the world is totally transformed between my writing and your reading of those words, you too will face the prospect of being drafted into the Armed Forces of the United States. (Needless to say, those of you who are women will be affected almost as deeply, for your brothers, lovers, and husbands will be required to serve.)

The question poses itself therefore to each of you who is eligible: Shall I serve? Many factors will influence your decision, including patriotism, habit, fear, and self-interest. But one fundamental consideration lies at the heart of the matter: **Should** you serve? Do you have a **moral obligation** to obey the draft order and present yourself for induction when called? Does anyone ever have a right to evade the draft? To resist it openly? To flee the country? If the answer is yes, then what is the justification for evasion or resistance? Do you have a right to refuse to serve if you believe that the purposes of the government are wrong? Does it matter whether the government is a democracy or a dictatorship? Does a young man in Soviet Russia have a moral right to evade the draft if he can manage it? What about a young man in Cuba, in Spain, in England, in Greece?

If the answer to our question is **no**—if young American men have **no** right to evade or resist the draft—then what is the basis of their obligation? What arguments can be put forward to show that you morally **ought** to obey the order for induction?

You will read my answers to these questions in the essay which follows. There is no need for me to comment upon my own views. But it might help to balance the debate if I call your attention to a few of the key points in Justice Fortas's effective defense of the opposed position.

Note, first of all, that Justice Fortas's principal concern is with the processes of the law. Like a great many other champions of constitutional democracy, he sees our legal system as the chief means whereby the interests of the state can be made to coexist with the rights of the individual citizen. He will readily grant that the execution of the law is often capricious or unfair; he will even grant that the law itself is sometimes unjust. But beyond the law he sees only chaos, social misery, and ultimately much greater injustice. To the young man who refuses to fight in a war which the state has declared, Fortas poses a hard question: Can you be certain that the internal disorder which your rebellion promises is less evil than the war you reject? In the readings of this section, Thomas Hobbes offers a similar vision of the condition to which society would be reduced if disrespect for the law were to become common.

It is also important to remember that Justice Fortas links obedience to the law with an elaborate system of protection from its unjust exercise. He is prepared to grant the widest possible latitude to religious or moral pacifism, so long as the fundamental security of the state is preserved. But he draws the line at the individual who refuses to submit to the democratically chosen policies of the nation as a whole. To the dissenter who sets individual conscience above the dignity of the law, Fortas may well ask: If you will not abide by the freely determined will of a majority of the citizens of a democracy, then by what right do you live in society at all?

ROBERT PAUL WOLFF

Four Questions
On the Draft

Twenty-three hundred years ago, Callicles accused Socrates of wasting his life "whispering in a corner with a few boys," instead of entering the public arena where the affairs of the *polis* were being decided. Ever since, critics have charged philosophy with failing to deal with the issues of conscience which confront men in their real lives. For the most part, moral philosophers have responded with either bland assurances that the eternal verities have daily application or else with a modest denial that a lifetime of reflection on the right and the good confers any special wisdom on those who undertake it.

Recently, however, the heat has been on. Changes in the draft laws have lifted the immunity which once protected young men fortunate enough to go to college. The brightest and most morally concerned students have begun to ask hard questions about their political rights and obligations, and not surprisingly, they look to their professors for help in finding defensible answers. It would be easy for us to plead ignorance or to retreat behind the elaborate neutrality of the educational process, but the students would consider this a cop-out, and they would be right.

What I want to do, then, is to formulate some of the questions about the draft which have caused students the greatest concern, and to give reasoned, unequivocal answers to as many of them as possible. There are four questions which frequently arise when the subject of military obligations is debated:

1. Does a draft-eligible American man have a moral obligation to submit to induction and fight in the armed forces?

2. Does such a man have a *right* to resist the draft?

3. Does he have an *obligation* to resist the draft?
4. Does a draft resister have any sort of moral obligation to resist publicly? Does he have an obligation to accept legal punishment for his actions, or at least not to flee from it? Is it cowardly, reprehensible, or immoral to resist the draft clandestinely and to evade rather than challenge the government?

1. Does a draft-eligible American man have a moral obligation to submit to induction and fight in the armed forces?

I have couched this and the subsequent questions in terms of *moral* obligation because the issue for the students is what they *ought* to do, not merely what the law says they ought to do. Many persons never seem to take a distinction between legal and moral obligation. So long as the demands of the state do not too sharply conflict with their moral convictions, they go along from day to day assuming that what is legal is right. Nevertheless, the two are quite distinct, as men are reminded when governments become tyrannical or unjust. So we must ask whether there is any reason for a young American to believe that he ought to fight in the armed forces.

There are *three* arguments which might be offered to prove that Americans should serve when called. First, it might be said that our cause is a just cause, that we are fighting to suppress an evil foe or to defend a good and valiant friend, and therefore that men of all nations should join in the battle.

This is a familiar argument; when its premises are correct, it is a valid argument as well. Exactly such a call was issued by the earliest opponents of Nazism, and it was answered by thousands of brave young Americans even before the official entry of the United States into World War II. But not all wars are just, and no man has a duty to fight in those which are not. The Vietnam war is wicked and immoral; the invasion of the Dominican Republic was an act of naked imperialism; the attempted overthrow of the Castro government was only redeemed by its failure. The time is long past when a young man in the United States can assume that his government will only thrust itself into fights which are morally defensible.

To those who question the right of a young man to choose which wars he will fight and which he will refuse, we must answer that *selective* conscientious objection is the only sort of conscientious objection that makes any moral sense. If we can agree that all men have a fundamental obligation to fight *for* what is right and *against* what is wrong, then it should be obvious that absolute pacifism, like the principle "my country right or wrong," is simply an abdication of one's responsibility to distinguish just from unjust wars. When young draft resisters admit that they would have fought in World War II, it is taken by some as a devastating revelation of the inconsistency of their position.

In fact, it merely shows that they have the good sense to be able to distinguish a valiant defense of liberty from a wicked oppression of a victimized people.

Once we deny the justice of a war, defenders of the draft fall back on a second argument, the appeal to a debt of gratitude. America has nurtured you, the draft resisters are told. It has protected you, offered you the highest standards of living in the world, and conferred upon you all the advantages and benefits that flow from a rich society. Now your nation calls you to fight beneath its colors, to defend its shores and protect its interests. Only the most selfish, ungrateful, self-seeking young man could refuse such a call. Indeed, those of you who come from the wealthy and favored sectors of American society have enjoyed, not merely a fair share, but an overabundance of the good things America has to offer. Surely you owe something in return!

This, too, is an argument with merit, but that merit does not extend to any war whatsoever. Not by the widest stretch of a fevered ideological imagination could it be said that the security of the United States has been threatened in recent years. It is not *this country* that young men were called upon to defend in the 1960s, but only the immoral policy of the men who ruled its government. Perhaps if America were under attack, *even by a foe with justice on his side,* Americans might have some obligation, out of gratitude and loyalty, to defend her. But when our country actively pursues evil and aggressive policies, the greatest service any of us can possibly do is to oppose those policies so vigorously that the government is guided back onto a just course.

Finally, when the policy is seen to be immoral, and even the claims of gratitude prove unconvincing, defenders of the draft retreat to their innermost bastion of argument. Just or not, they say, the wars we fight are initiated by a democratically elected government. Say what you will of the policies of John Kennedy, Lyndon Johnson, Richard Nixon, or their successors, no one denies that they derive their authority from a free and secret ballot of all the people. The people are not always right, but in a true democracy their will is sovereign, right or wrong. The instruments exist for a recall of the administration and the election of a new president with new policies. Wrong as a war may be, no citizen is ever denied his right to speak against it. Those who oppose a war have every right to organize against it. But so long as this nation remains a democracy, minorities must abide by the will of the majority. Resistance is defensible, indeed even heroic, when directed against a tyranny. But resistance to the democratic will of the people is tyranny itself. Would the draft resisters deny the American people the right to determine the policy of the United States? Indeed, the principal resisters to the draft have not been those black youths who might most plausibly claim to have been denied their democratic rights; they are, instead, the sons of wealthy and politically active men and women, whose easy access to the instruments of political activity deprives them of any justification for resisting the democratically enacted laws of the land.

This argument rests on the assumption, that democracy is a legitimate form of political society. That is to say, it assumes that the citizens of a genuinely democratic state have a binding moral obligation to obey even those laws and governmental commands which are immoral, only as long as the laws have really been enacted by a majority of the citizens. This assumption is the foundation of the political ideology by which the United States is governed. So widespread is its acceptance that one can find very few serious political philosophers who even bother to question its truth.

After long reflection, I have come to the conclusion that the theory of democracy is wrong. No one, not even a citizen of a true democracy, has an obligation to obey the law as such, save under conditions so special and difficult of fulfillment as to hardly constitute an exception at all. In short, I have come to believe that the doctrine known as philosophical anarchism is true. There are no circumstances, real or hypothetical, under which a state can validly demand the obedience of its subjects.

This is a strong assertion, and I am well aware that I shall have difficulty persuading you of its truth. I have attempted to set forth my argument more fully in a book entitled *In Defense of Anarchism*, but even that work is incomplete, and will require further argument to support its conclusions. What I should like to do here is to sketch the outlines of my argument, so that you can form at least a preliminary opinion of its cogency.

The theory of government by consent of the governed was advanced as the solution to a conflict which seems on first examination to be utterly irresoluble. On the one hand, morality demands that each man freely and autonomously determine the guiding principles of his life and take full responsibility for the consequences of his own actions.

On the other hand, standing over and against this principle of autonomy is the authority claimed by the state. If autonomy means anything at all, it means making one's own decisions, being no man's servant. But if authority means anything at all, it means the right to command, which is to say, the right to be obeyed.

The problem faced by the early theorists of democracy was quite simply this: How can free and autonomous men submit to the authority of any state without truly losing their freedom?

The solution was thought to be in the nature of moral autonomy. The word "autonomous" literally means "giving laws to oneself," and so it was argued that the truly moral man was simultaneously a law-giver and a law-obeyer. To obey the laws handed down by another is slavish servility. To obey no law at all is irrational and irresponsible caprice. But to obey laws which one has legislated for oneself is the highest manifestation of human dignity. By the exercise of such autonomy, it was said, men earned the right to be treated, not as mere means or instruments, but as ends in themselves.

The extension of this doctrine to the political sphere is immediately obvious. When men submit to the commands of a ruler, they forfeit their freedom and become heteronomous slaves. When they submit to no laws at all, they sink into the caprice and chaos of anarchy. But when men submit to laws they have themselves made, then they are autonomous. Rule *of* the people is tyranny; rule *for* the people is at best benevolent tyranny. But rule *by* the people is *liberty*, which is to say, the union of individual autonomy with legitimate state authority.

This is a good argument. Indeed, I think it can be fairly described as the *only* good argument in the entire history of Western political theory. Unfortunately, although it is the best justification that has ever been offered for the authority claims of any form of political society, it is nonetheless—in my opinion—wrong. Save under very special circumstances, rule *by* the people violates the moral autonomy of the individual, just as rule *of* and rule *for* the people do.

Consider the original argument. If freedom requires that each man submit only to laws which he himself has legislated, then obviously unanimous consent must be obtained before any law can be put in force. Under these stringent constraints, it would literally be true that each man would obey only himself and remain as free as before. Unanimous direct democracy—the system in which every citizen votes on all the laws and a single negative vote defeats any measure—is thus a theoretical solution to the conflict between individual autonomy and the state's claim to authority.

But how are we to handle those situations in which a unanimous consensus does not miraculously emerge from the debate? The answer springs unbidden to every mind: Take a vote, of course, and let the state be guided by the will of the majority. We are, all of us, so accustomed to majority rule that it is very difficult for us even to notice that it is one distinctive way among many for settling disputes, and not the inevitable, natural, unquestionably obvious way. In the United States particularly, we are raised from the cradle as majoritarians. As soon as little children can count, they are taking votes. First-grade boys and girls in our public schools dutifully elect a class president, vice-president, and secretary-treasurer before they are old enough to write or carry money. I realize, therefore, that it will be difficult for me to get you to question the legitimacy of majority voting. Nevertheless, I must ask your indulgence, for this familiar rule is in fact the Achilles' heel of the defence of democracy. The entire theory of government by consent of the governed rests upon the principle of majority rule, and that principle is utterly without justification.

Let us remember the original purpose for which the theory of democracy was advanced. The problem was to find a form of political association that *free* men could join without losing their freedom. Government by unanimous consent met that requirement, and majority rule was then put forward to handle the situations in which unanimity could not be obtained. So the crucial question is this: Does majority rule provide a way of making collective decisions which preserves the moral autonomy, or liberty, of each member of the society?

Nobody denies that we *can* make decisions by majority rule. We can also make decisions by dictatorial rule of one man, or by rule of an elite minority, or even by putting all the alternatives in a fishbowl and pulling one out at random. The question is whether majority rule can preserve the union of individual freedom and state authority which unanimous democracy achieves.

Needless to say, the problem is with those persons who are in the minority. When a vote is taken, the majority are clearly bound by the outcome because they have directly willed the law which has been enacted. But the minority have voted *against* the law, presumably because they believed it to be unwise, or immoral, or contrary to the interests of the nation. If the theory of democracy is to have any plausibility at all—and if young men are to be morally obligated to obey laws of which they disapprove—then a proof must be found for the paradoxical proposition that in a majoritarian democracy the minority have a moral obligation to obey the majority. What is more, we must show that a member of the minority, in submitting to the majority, is not merely forfeiting his freedom and bowing his knee to tyranny.

The traditional answer is that majority rule is built into the original contract. When everyone first agrees to establish the state and submit to its laws, there is a clause in the agreement to the effect that henceforward a majority shall bind or oblige the whole. But this is not really any answer at all to the question we asked. No one denies that a man can bind himself by a promise; and he can quite obviously promise to obey the majority, just as he can promise to obey a king, a priest, or a slave master. The promise is equally binding in every instance. The question is whether a free man can promise to obey the majority without thereby forfeiting his freedom. We have already seen that he can make such a commitment to *unanimous* decision, because his consent is included in the collective will by which each law is enacted. Is there anything about majority rule which distinguishes it from all the various authoritarian or heteronomous forms of decision making, so that the moral liberty of the minority is preserved even though they, like the majority, have an absolute duty to obey validly enacted laws?

In the book which I mentioned earlier, I have canvassed the most prominent attempts to demonstrate the liberty-preserving character of majority rule. I can neither find nor think of a way of making majority rule compatible with the moral autonomy of the individual. The problem is always the same: Either the minority submit to the majority, thereby conforming to laws which they think are bad and against which they voted; or else the minority reserve to themselves the right to defy those laws which they consider too evil, in which case the fundamental authority of the state is negated.

Now, it goes without saying that a member of the minority may *choose* to go along with the majority on certain occasions, perhaps because he judges that the bad consequences of his acquiescence in an evil law are less serious than the general harm that would be caused by his defiance. But once he begins to reason in that manner, he has rejected the special claims of the democratic state, and is reduced to making his political decisions on the basis of considerations which would arise in any state, democratic or otherwise.

If all of this is correct, then no young man has any obligation whatsoever to submit to an induction order. Speaking more generally, if a man has not signed his freedom away by a rash promise to obey the commands of the majority, whatever they may be, and if he has not directly voted for the laws which have been enacted, then he does not stand under any moral obligation to obey those laws *as such*. As a moral agent, he is of course responsible for the consequences of his actions, and he must therefore consider what will result *both* from his conformity to the law *and* from his defiance of it. But after he has weighed the goods and evils to the best of his ability, no one can say to him: This is a democracy, and therefore irrespective of consequences you have a duty to obey the laws.

2. *Does a young American man have a right to resist the draft?*

The answer to this question follows immediately from the answer to the first. If a man has no obligation to fight, then he has a right to refuse to fight. The two are the obverse and reverse of the same coin.

3. *Does a young American man have an obligation to resist the draft?*

I hesitate to answer this question for two reasons. First, it is unseemly for those who are not in danger to urge hazardous actions on those who are, even in the name of morality. The world might be a better place if presidents agreed not to send young men to war and professors agreed not to send them to jail.

The second problem is that the individual draft resister has so little power in comparison with the state. There is no virtue in martyrdom, and when a young man can perceive no probable good result from his own resistance to the draft, it is difficult to argue that he is morally obligated to jeopardize his freedom and future. I hope I will not seem to be hedging if I say that this question must be left to the decision of the individual. Suffice it to say that he will certainly be doing something morally admirable if he chooses to resist the draft.

4. *Does a draft resister have any sort of moral obligation to resist publicly, to accept legal punishment or at least not to flee from it? Does he have a moral right to act clandestinely, to evade rather than to resist the draft?*

No question connected with the problem of draft resistance has caused more confusion and conflict than this. Even so solidly conservative a voice as *The New York Times* praised draft resisters like Dr. Spock, the Reverend

William Sloane Coffin, and their associates for publicly inviting legal retribution for their acts of resistance to the draft. A willingness to go to jail for one's belief is widely viewed in this country as evidence of moral sincerity, and even as a sort of argument for the position one is defending.

Now, tactically speaking, there is much to be said for legal martyrdom. As tyrannical governments are perpetually discovering, the sight of one's leader nailed to a cross has a marvelously bracing effect on the faithful members of a dissident sect. When the rulers are afflicted by the very principles they are violating, even the *threat* of self-sacrifice may force a government to its knees. So Gandhi proved.

But leaving tactics aside, no one has any moral obligation whatsoever to resist an unjust government openly rather than clandestinely. Nor has anyone a duty to invite and then to suffer unjust punishment. The choice is simple: if the law is just, obey it. If the law is unjust, evade it.

Indeed, the draft resister owes it to the government *not* to present himself for punishment. Since it is unjust to jail the opponents of the war, the submissive resister simply tempts the government to commit injustice. And inasmuch as it is morally worse to commit injustice than to suffer it, the resister who surrenders does the government more harm by permitting it to jail him that he suffers by going to jail himself. Simple charity dictates a policy of *evasion.* Let no one taunt the draft evader with accusations of cowardice. The myth of the hemlock-drinking Socrates is a trap laid by a reactionary Plato to ensnare those who would reject the authority of unjust governments. If we must compare the present-day draft evaders with some figure from history, let it be the runaway slave of ante-bellum days and his helpers along the underground railroad.

ABE FORTAS

The Limits of
Conscientious Objection

Conscientious Objectors

Youth's disaffection finds its most dramatic expression in the widespread opposition to the draft and the war in Vietnam. The right of the government to compel service in the armed forces is based upon Article I, Section 8, of the Constitution, which authorizes the Congress to raise armed

From *Concerning Dissent and Civil Disobedience* by Abe Fortas. Copyright © 1968 by Abe Fortas. Reprinted by arrangement with the New American Library, Inc., New York.

forces. From time immemorial, service in the armed forces, however onerous and distasteful, has been regarded as an obligation which the state may impose because of citizenship or residence.

From colonial times, however, there has been in this country general acceptance of the principle that while "conscientious objectors" are not exempt from the draft, they should not be forced into combat service. The special treatment of conscientious objectors was a natural and necessary corollary of our dedication to religious freedom. The exemption of conscientious objectors from combat service was debated in the Constitutional Convention, but it was not expressly written into the Constitution. It has been contended that the Constitution, because of the guarantees of religious freedom in the First Amendment, requires the exemption. But this has never been judicially established. The exemption has been included by the Congress in the various draft acts, and the decisions of the Supreme Court implementing the exemption have turned upon the construction of the statutory language.

Congress has stated the conscientious objector exemption in different terms at different times. The first Federal Conscription Law, enacted in 1863, did not refer to conscientious objectors, but it provided an escape from the draft. An individual could supply an acceptable substitute for himself or pay three hundred dollars to the War Department to use in procuring a substitute.

In the 1864 Draft Act, it was provided that persons who were "conscientiously opposed" to bearing arms and were prohibited from doing so by the articles of their "religious denomination," could secure exemption from combat. They then had the choice of hospital duty or of paying three hundred dollars to the benefit of sick and wounded soldiers.

The 1917 Draft Act restated the exemption and made it available to members of "any well-recognized religious sect" whose creed or principles forbade its members to "participate in war in any form." It eliminated the possibility of payment, but required noncombatant service as the President might prescribe. The Draft Act of 1940 eliminated the requirement of adherence to a recognized religious sect and granted exemption from combat to any person who by reason of "religious training and belief" was conscientiously opposed to war in any form.

Presently, the language is as follows:

> (j) Nothing contained in this title shall be construed to require any person to be subject to combatant training and service in the armed forces of the United States who, by reason of religious training and belief, is conscientiously opposed to participation in war in any form. Religious training and belief in this connection means an individual's belief in a relation to a Supreme Being involving duties superior to those arising from any human relation, but does not include essentially political, sociological, or philosophical views or a merely personal moral code.

The statute provides that the conscientious objector should be assigned to noncombatant service, or, if he is conscientiously opposed to participation even in that service, to "work of national importance under civilian direction."

In the famous Seeger case, decided in 1965, the Supreme Court had to consider whether the combat exemption was limited to persons who opposed war because of religious belief in the conventional sense—that is, centering upon belief in a Supreme Being. The Court ruled that the statutory provision could not be so restricted. It held that it also extended to persons who held a profound "belief that is sincere and meaningful" which "occupies a place in the life of its possessor parallel to that filled by the orthodox belief in God of one who clearly qualifies for the exemption."

This ruling equated profound moral beliefs with orthodox religious convictions for purposes of conscientious-objector status. But it did not modify the statute's admonition that the special status "does not include essentially political, sociological, or philosophical views or a merely personal moral code."

The principle of special status for conscientious objectors has never been extended to persons whose opposition to war is based only on intellectual grounds: for example, that war aids neither the victor nor the vanquished. As the Seeger decision emphasizes, the conscientious objection must proceed from a basic, general, moral philosophy or religious commitment which involves, as the statute says, opposition "to participation in war in any form." It has not been extended to persons whose moral conviction is that a particular war, rather than war generally, is abhorrent.

The needs of the state for manpower to wage war are always critical. Its ability to muster the needed soldiers may be the measure of its ability to survive. Even so, our government, as well as other states that reflect the ideals of civilization, recognizes and has always recognized that an individual's fundamental moral or religious commitments are entitled to prevail over the needs of the state. As Chief Justice Hughes said many years ago: "When one's belief collides with the power of the State, the latter is supreme within its sphere . . . But, in the forum of conscience, duty to a moral power higher than the State has always been maintained."

Relatively few of our people subscribe to a fundamental, philosophical, or religious rejection of all war. Despite all of the current clamor, as of 1966, conscientious objectors amounted to substantially less than 1 percent of all registrants in the Selective Service System. Most of our people recognize war as a savage inevitability in a world which is still far from being universally civilized.

Many of our young people, however, profoundly object to our participation in the war in Vietnam. Many of them say that our participation is "immoral"; and some believe that they should not be subject to induction or, if drafted, should be given conscientious-objector (noncombat) status because of their conscientious belief that our participation in this particular war is "immoral."

The attitude of these persons is entitled to respect, whether or not one agrees with it. It is not at all the same as that of the relatively few who sacrifice their self-respect by falsely claiming basic moral or religious objections to all war, which, if true, would entitle them to non-combat status. These persons, and those who counsel them in a self-degrading deceit, are not entitled to serious consideration. But that is not true of the thousands of young men who are seriously and honestly wrestling with the dilemma of rejecting not all wars, but their deep moral aversion to participation in a particular war.

We may respect their sincerity and sympathize with their problem, but in fact their claim that their profound rejection of a particular war should prevail over the state's needs is hardly consistent with the basic theory of organized society. By participating in the particular war, the state takes the position that the war *is* justified and moral. This is a governmental decision of the utmost gravity, and while the state can and should defer to the principle that a citizen may be excused from full participation in its consequences because of his duty "to a moral (or religious) power higher than the state," the state cannot acknowledge an individual's right to veto its decision that a particular war is right and necessary.

From the state's viewpoint, a disagreement about the morality of a particular war is a difference of judgment or policy; it is not and cannot be accepted as stemming from a moral or religious belief. In his First Inaugural Address, Jefferson said, "Not every difference of policy is a difference of principle." Once the state's decision has been made, and so long as the government adheres to it, it is not possible to exempt from its impact an individual who disagrees with that decision on the basis of a moral or intellectual judgment, as contrasted with an individual who is pledged to a general religious or moral philosophy which rejects war.

If the individual can veto his participation in the Vietnam war, he could also have declined to participate in World War II or the Korean conflict or a defense against invasion. This ability of the individual to choose his war, from the state's viewpoint, would destroy the state's ability to defend itself or to perform the obligations it has assumed, or to prevent the spread of attempts to conquer other nations of the world by outside-inspired and -aided subversion. The government having made this decision, the theory of the state insists that the individual must conform his conduct to it until the government's position is changed by congressional action or at the ballot box, or, indeed, by the persuasion of argument, protest, mass demonstration, and other methods safeguarded by the First Amendment.

Most of our wars have met bitter and violent condemnation as "immoral" and "barbarous." In the Revolutionary War, only about half of the people supported the revolution. Churchmen led the vocal opposition. Wealthy families bitterly assailed the politicians like George Washington whom they charged with base and selfish motivation.

The War of 1812 was first supported by a majority of the people. But in a short while, as we encountered difficulties and reverses, opposition became rampant. The nation had at first agreed that the war was necessary to prevent British depredations. However, after a time the war was attacked throughout

New England as "without justifiable cause and prosecuted in a manner which indicates that conquest and ambition are its real motives." Men and money were refused for the prosecution of the war. It was denounced by such persons as Chief Justice Marshall, Josiah Quincy, John Randolph of Virginia, William Ellery Channing, and William Cullen Bryant.

While the British army was at the very gates of New Orleans, the Hartford Convention was called to protest the war. This Convention included persons bearing the distinguished family names of Cabot, Lowell, Dwight, Lyman, Bigelow, Longfellow. The Governor of Massachusetts sent three commissioners to Washington to take the surrender, so he said, of a beaten administration and a defeated country. But while they were on their way, Jackson won the battle of New Orleans and the Treaty of Ghent was signed. There was an immediate reversal of public opinion. The Federalist party, which had opposed the war, soon disappeared.

The Mexican War was also popular at the start. But as it dragged on, it was bitterly denounced. Whig journals told Mexico that "her cause was just, that a majority of Americans detested the war, that our treasury could not bear the cost, that our government was incompetent . . . that our armies could not win the war, and that soon the Administration would be rebuked and its policies reversed." Congress passed a resolution condemning the war. Senator Webster charged President Polk with an "impeachable offense" in conducting the war. Henry Clay and others denounced the war. John Calhoun said it was unconstitutional because it was begun without a congressional declaration of war. A congressional resolution repeated the charge of unconstitutionality. Calhoun said, "There is no war, according to the sense of our Constitution," because Congress had not initially adopted a formal declaration of war. Newspapers urged immediate withdrawal. But after the Battle of Buena Vista, the same Whig journals hailed the "brilliant war," and General Taylor was chosen as the Whig candidate for President.

The Civil War, as we all know, was even more turbulent in these respects. President Lincoln was badgered by both hawks and doves. In 1863, *The New York Times* said that all that could save the North was immediate negotiation. It urged the appointment of a commission to negotiate with Jefferson Davis. In the spring of 1863, New York was convulsed by draft riots. Homes and buildings were burned; pitched battles were fought between police and rioters; over a thousand people were killed or wounded. A prominent congressman in the fall of 1863 echoed widespread sentiment in the North. He said, "Stop fighting. Make an armistice. Accept at once foreign mediation." A powerful movement began to force Lincoln not to stand for re-election. In August, 1864, Lincoln himself wrote that "this administration will not be re-elected," and the Democratic Party nominated General McClellan on a platform pledging that "immediate efforts be made for a cessation of hostilities . . . on the basis of a Federal Union of States."

World War I was strongly supported after Germany's declaration of unrestricted submarine warfare on January 29, 1917. But, even so, the left was vocal and tireless in its opposition. In World War II, isolationist sentiment in the country was strong, well-financed, and well-led until Pearl Harbor. It involved not only the right but also, after the Nazi-Soviet pact, the left. After Pearl Harbor, the country was fairly united.

The Korean War showed the familiar pattern: initial enthusiasm was followed by reaction, frustration, and criticism as time went on and the war was not won. In June, 1950, the Gallup poll found 81 percent favorable to Truman and the war. But after the initial defeats by the Chinese, a majority of the American people believed the intervention was a mistake, and felt that we should pull out. The Gallup poll showed a profound change of opinion: 66 percent for a pullout. By the spring of 1952, President Truman's popularity, according to the polls, had dropped from 81 percent to 26 percent.

Senator Taft branded the Korean conflict as "an utterly useless war." Senator Wherry said that Dean Acheson "has the blood of our boys in Korea on his hands." . . . Doves demanded withdrawal. . . . Truman was accused of news suppression. . . . Hawks condemned Truman's insistence upon a limited war. . . . But then, somehow, we were able to come through with success in achieving our limited objective of repelling the Communist aggression and enabling the creation of an independent South Korea. It cost us over 150,000 casualties. It took us more than three years. But I think it is fairly universal opinion in the Western world that the war was a necessary action; that if we had not taken on the sad and heavy burden of repelling the invasion of South Korea, no one else would or could have done so; and that the consequences of our default would have been greatly to increase the peril to the non-Communist nations of the world—including ourselves.

I do not cite any of this to denigrate the sincerity or integrity of those who oppose serving in combat roles in Vietnam for profound, moral reasons. It would be beside the point to argue that their judgment is questionable. The point that I make is that where their moral objection is solely to combat service in this particular war, it is not within the doctrine or theory of conscientious objection; and that it would indeed be difficult—perhaps anomalous —perhaps impossible—for the state to acknowledge moral objection to a particular war was as a basis for determining draft status, as distinguished from a general religious belief or moral code which rejects all wars.

Conclusion

The story of man is the history, first, of the acceptance and imposition of restraints necessary to permit communal life; and second, of the emancipation of the individual within that system of necessary restraints.

Conflict between the demands of ordered society and the desires and aspirations of the individual is the common theme of life's development. We find it in the family, where, first, the child is disciplined to accommodate himself to the needs of living with others; and then, as the years go by, he begins the painful process of achieving for himself relative freedom of action and a separate identity.

The same is true in any organized society. The achievement of liberty is man's indispensable condition of living; and yet, liberty cannot exist unless it is restrained and restricted. The instrument of balancing these two conflicting factors is the law.

So we must end as we began, with an acknowledgment that the rule of law is the essential condition of individual liberty as it is of the existence of the state.

We are now in the throes of a vast revolution. Considering its scope and depth, it has been relatively peaceful; I think that, even as of today, it is the most profound and pervasive revolution ever achieved by substantially peaceful means.

We have confessed that about twenty million people—Negroes—have been denied the rights and opportunities to which they are entitled. This national acknowledgment—typically American—is in itself a revolutionary achievement.

We have proclaimed our national obligation to repair the damage that this denial has inflicted. We have made a beginning—an important, substantial beginning—in the long, difficult, and enormously costly and disrupting task of reparation and reform.

At the same time, we have faced the revolt of the youth-generation. Our young people have dramatically challenged the authority of their elders. They have asserted the right of the youth-generation to frame its own standards and to a share of power in society.

For the United States, this assertion by the youth-generation of independence and of a claim to authority is relatively new and shocking. In a sense, it has been more disturbing than the Negro revolution to which it is dynamically related.

We have precedents for the trials and disorders that attend the economic and political breakthrough of a segment of the population. But the breakup of patterns of authority—of the straight line of march—is new. Our prior experience of youth's rebellion has been limited to explosions within the pattern. Presently, the design itself is challenged.

In both the Negro and the youth rebellions, the critical question is one of method, of procedure. The definition of objectives and the selection of those which will triumph are of fundamental importance to the quality of our society, of our own lives, and those of our descendants. But the survival of our society as a free, open, democratic community, will be determined not so much by the specific points achieved by the Negroes and the youth-generation as by the procedures—the rules of conduct, the methods, the practices—which survive the confrontations.

Procedure is the bone structure of a democratic society; and the quality of procedural standards which meet general acceptance—the quality of what is tolerable and permissible and acceptable conduct—determines the durability of the society and the survival possibilities of freedom within the society.

I have emphasized that our scheme of law affords great latitude for dissent and opposition. It compels wide tolerance not only for their expression but also for the organization of people and forces to bring about the acceptance of the dissenter's claim. Both our institutions and the characteristics of our national behavior make it possible for opposition to be translated into policy, for dissent to prevail. We have alternatives to violence.

Our present problems emerged as the result of militance and aggressiveness by the Negroes in pressing their dissent and demand. The forcefulness of their activity, in extent and depth, was new to our experience. The fundamental justice of their demands led to a national response, and produced substantial successes. These, in turn, fed the fires of dissent.

The disclosures of national discrimination against the Negroes and neglect of their demands, the example of their tactics, and the successes achieved, both stimulated and inspired the youth-generation. Enough young people had participated in the Negro revolution to provide a nucleus of activists for the youth revolt.

The youth-generation (except, of course, Negro youth) did not have specific grievances comparable to those of the Negroes; but they were stimulated to revolt by a breakup of established patterns in the arts and sciences; by the decline of the institution of the family; by the removal of most of the practical hazards of sex; and by the rude shattering of idealistic conceptions about their nation as a classless society in which all persons, regardless of race, were assured of basic rights and opportunity.

The war in Vietnam and the draft focused their anxieties and fears and their desperate hunger.

It would be idle and foolish to expect that these dissident groups—the Negroes and the youth-generation—would confine themselves to the polite procedures that the other segments of our society would wish. We can hardly claim that their deserving demands would be satisfied if they did not vigorously assert them. We certainly cannot claim that those demands would be satisfied just as soon without their strenuous insistence. But we can, I think, require that the methods which they adopt be within the limits which an organized, democratic society can endure.

An organized society cannot and will not long endure personal and property damage, whatever the reason, context, or occasion.

An organized society will not endure invasion of private premises or public offices, or interference with the work or activities of others if adequate facilities for protest and demonstration are otherwise available.

A democratic society should and must tolerate criticism, protest, demand for change, and organizations and demonstrations within the generally defined limits of the law to marshal support for dissent and change. It should and must make certain that facilities and protection where necessary are provided for these activities.

Protesters and change-seekers must adopt methods within the limits of the law. Despite the inability of anyone always to be certain of the line between the permissible and the forbidden, as a practical matter the lines are reasonably clear.

Violence must not be tolerated; damage to persons or property is intolerable. Any mass demonstration is dangerous, although it may be the most effective constitutional tool of dissent. But it must be kept within the limits of its permissible purpose. The functions of mass demonstrations, in the city or on the campus, are to communicate a point of view; to arouse enthusiasm and group cohesiveness among participants; to attract others to join; and to impress upon the public and the authorities the point advocated by the protesters, the urgency of their demand, and the power behind it. These functions do not include terror, riot, or pillage.

We must accept the discomforts necessarily implicit in a large, *lawful* demonstration because, in a sense, it is part of the dynamics of democracy which depends for its vitality upon the vigorous confrontation of opposing forces. But we cannot and should not endure physical assault upon person or property. This sort of assault is ultimately counter-productive. It polarizes society, and in any polarization, the minority group, although it may achieve initial, limited success, is likely to meet bitter reprisal and rejection of its demands.

In my judgment civil disobedience—the deliberate violation of law—is never justified in our nation, where the law being violated is not itself the focus or target of the protest. So long as our governments obey the mandate of the Constitution and assure facilities and protection for the powerful expression of individual and mass dissent, the disobedience of laws which are not themselves the target of the protest—the violation of law merely as a technique of demonstration—constitutes an act of rebellion, not merely of dissent.

Civil disobedience is violation of law. Any violation of law must be punished, whatever its purpose, as the theory of civil disobedience recognizes. But law violation directed not to the laws or practices that are the subject of dissent, but to unrelated laws which are disobeyed merely to dramatize dissent, may be morally as well as politically unacceptable.

At the beginning of this discussion, I presented the dilemma of obedience to law and the need that sometimes may arise to disobey profoundly immoral or unconstitutional laws. This is another kind of civil disobedience, and the only kind that, in my view, is ever truly defensible as a matter of social morality.

It is only in respect to such laws—laws that are basically offensive to fundamental values of life or the Constitution—that a moral (although not a legal) defense of law violation can possibly be urged. Anyone assuming to make the judgment that a law is in this category assumes a terrible burden. He has undertaken a fearful moral as well as legal responsibility. He should be prepared to submit to prosecution by the state for the violation of law and the imposition of punishment if he is wrong or unsuccessful. He should even admit the correctness of the state's action in seeking to enforce its laws, and he should acquiesce in the ultimate judgment of the courts.

For after all, each of us is a member of an organized society. Each of us benefits from its existence and its order. And each of us must be ready, like Socrates, to accept the verdict of its institutions if we violate their mandate and our challenge is not vindicated.

Animating all of this in our society is the principle of tolerance. The state must tolerate the individual's dissent, appropriately expressed. The individual must tolerate the majority's verdict when and as it is settled in accordance with the laws and the procedures that have been established. Dissent and dissenters have no monopoly on freedom. They must tolerate opposition. They must accept dissent from their dissent. And they must give it the respect and the latitude which they claim for themselves. Neither youth nor virtue can justify the disregard of this principle, in the classroom, the public hall, or on the streets. Protest does not justify hooliganism.

These are workable, viable principles in our nation, for we have alternatives to violence and alternatives to suppression. For the state, our constitutional principles, although they provide wide latitude for demonstration and dissent, permit strong and effective state response to violence. For the citizen, the guarantee of freedom of speech, of press, of peaceable assembly, of protest, of organization and dissent provides powerful instruments for effecting change. And ultimately, the all-important power of the vote—access to the ballot box—furnishes the most effective weapon in the citizen's arsenal.

The experience of these past few years shows, more vividly than any other episode in our history, how effective these alternatives are. It is through their use—and not through the sporadic incidents of violence—that we have effected the current social revolution; and it is through their use that we have begun to create a new and—hopefully—richer and better set of institutions and attitudes.

In short, we have shown that our democratic processes do indeed function, and that they can bring about fundamental response to fundamental demands, and can do this without revolution, and despite the occasional violence of those who either reject or have not attained the maturity and restraint to use, and not to abuse, their freedom. This is an extraordinary tribute to our institutions.

COMMENTARY ON THE CONTEMPORARY ISSUE

The legal obligation to serve in the armed forces is without doubt the most important burden of citizenship that can be laid upon a young man, but it is of course by no means the only burden. All of us, regardless of age, sex, or physical fitness, are confronted with a system of obligations and constraints which define our status as citizens. We are taxed, both directly and indirectly, at every level of government. Our economic activities are subject to elaborate licensing and regulation. Whenever we wish to build a home, drive an automobile, travel abroad, join a union, practice law or medicine, or even run for public office, we encounter the authority of the state. The problem posed by our contemporary debate—ought a young man submit to induction?—arises throughout our social existence. Do we have a moral obligation to obey the law? Why? Are there any limits to the authority of the state?

At least **three** different sorts of answers to this question of the authority of the state have been put forward by political philosophers. We may label these the arguments from the **source,** from the **procedure,** and from the **content** of the laws.

The most ancient justification of state authority rests on the nature of the source of the laws. Many religious philosophers have claimed that the state is merely the instrument of God, and that the laws are expressions of His divine will. The obligation to obey the laws, then, is merely an instance of the more general obligation to obey God. The Hebrew kings of biblical times, the Christian kings in the Middle Ages, and the rulers of Islam all based their authority on an appeal to divine mandate.

A similar justification is offered by those hereditary monarchs who possess the right to rule by virtue of their descent from legitimate rulers of an earlier time. Any movie buff is familiar with the dramatic scene in which the peasant lad reveals the royal birthmark which proves him to be the true son of the old king, **and therefore the rightful ruler of the realm.** We are not much impressed these days with the claims of primogeniture, but for many peoples throughout history, the oldest son of the reigning monarch has appeared to be the natural source of political authority.

Odd as it may seem, the youngest political theory—namely, democracy—falls into the same category as these ancient doctrines of divine and kingly role. The democrat holds that laws are binding **because they issue from the will of the people.** In other words, what is crucial is not **what** the law says, or **how** it is enacted and enforced, but **who** enacted it. "Why ought I to serve in the army?" asks the young man. "Because God wills it," says the theocrat. "Because the king commands it," says the monarchist. **"Because it is the will of the people,"** says the democrat.

In contrast to justification by appeal to the **source,** the second type of argument concentrates on the **procedures** through which laws are enacted and enforced. Modern theories of constitutional democracy, of the sort that Justice Fortas appeals to, place great emphasis on regularity and publicity of governmental procedures, on the existence of procedural safeguards against abuse of governmental authority. In effect, these theories maintain that a citizen has an obligation to obey the law so long as he has a genuine opportunity to appeal its application to himself when he feels that he has been unfairly treated. Proceduralists, as we may call these philosophers of politics, reject the narrow appeal to the classical principle of popular sovereignty. They talk instead of a complex system of judicial restraints, representative legislators, and informal interest-group lobbying, by means of which the interests of major social and economic groups are accommodated while the rights of the individual are protected.

The last type of justification of the state concentrates on the actual **content** or substantive effect of the laws. According to this line of argument, citizens are obliged to obey the state so long as it pursues what is truly good or right. In Plato's **Republic,** for example, the common citizens owe obedience to laws passed by the philosopher-kings **because those laws embody the good for man and society.** In Marxist theory, the citizens of the future proletarian state owe allegiance to the "dictatorship of the proletariat" because the welfare of mankind is advanced through the actions of the working class. In a somewhat more pessimistic vein, Hobbes insists that rational men will submit absolutely to the commands of the state because only in that way can they achieve social order and tranquility.

The four selections you will read in this section represent only a few of the many positions which have been taken over the centuries on this controversial issue. The truth may be difficult to discover, both in theory and in practice, but one thing is certain: When men and women cease to examine the reasons for obeying the state, tyranny will very quickly follow.

PLATO

Plato wrote four dialogues recording the last days and death of his great teacher Socrates. The Euthyphro *is a conversation between a young man with pretensions as a religious "expert," and Socrates, who is on his way to the law courts to be tried for "impiety." The* Apology *presents Socrates' famous defense of himself and his life of philosophical questioning, ending with his conviction by the jury. Having been condemned to death, Socrates was held in jail for a month before the sentence was carried out. The* Phaedo, *a discourse on the soul and immortality, describes the last night of his life. During that final month, a number of Socrates' friends and disciples sought to arrange his escape from prison. Among them was a wealthy businessman named Crito, who apparently could have managed to get Socrates out of jail and away from Athens. In the dialogue which bears his name, Crito tries unsuccessfully to persuade Socrates to flee. In the course of their argument, we are offered a powerful defense of the citizen's obligation to obey the law, even at the cost of his own life.*

Socrates bases his decision to remain in custody on two quite different arguments. First of all, he feels that he owes a debt of gratitude to Athens (and hence to "the laws" of Athens). He has spent his life within her walls. He has accepted her protection; in a manner of speaking, he is a child of Athens, and hence he owes a debt of filial obedience. In like manner, a modern Socrates might argue that he owes it to the United States to serve in the armed forces when called, inasmuch as he has for so many years accepted the benefits which the state has conferred upon him.

But over and above gratitude, Socrates says, he has a kind of contract with the state, and it would be dishonorable of him to break that contract when the state comes to collect. By remaining in Athens during his long life, Socrates has implicitly agreed to abide by her laws. To be sure, he never signed a formal document or made a formal promise, but his continued presence in the city constituted what lawyers call a "quasi-contract." If he had no intention of obeying the laws, he should have said so many years earlier and left Athens.

And so he stayed and drank the cup of hemlock and died. The argument did not die, however. With a few alterations to suit the time and place, the Crito *can stand today as a contemporary debate about the obligations of citizenship.*

Crito

PERSONS OF THE DIALOGUE

SCENE:—*The Prison of Socrates*

SOCRATES   CRITO

SOCRATES: Why have you come at this hour, Crito? it must be quite early?

CRITO: Yes, certainly.

SOCRATES: What is the exact time?

CRITO: The dawn is breaking.

SOCRATES: I wonder that the keeper of the prison would let you in.

CRITO: He knows me, because I often come, Socrates; moreover, I have done him a kindness.

SOCRATES: And are you only just come?

CRITO: No, I came some time ago.

SOCRATES: Then why did you sit and say nothing, instead of awakening me at once?

CRITO: Why, indeed, Socrates, I myself would rather not have all this sleeplessness and sorrow. But I have been wondering at your peaceful slumbers, and that was the reason why I did not awaken you, because I wanted you to be out of pain. I have always thought you happy in the calmness of your temperament; but never did I see the like of the easy, cheerful way in which you bear this calamity.

SOCRATES: Why, Crito, when a man has reached my age he ought not to be repining at the prospect of death.

CRITO: And yet other old men find themselves in similar misfortunes, and age does not prevent them from repining.

SOCRATES: That may be. But you have not told me why you come at this early hour.

CRITO: I come to bring you a message which is sad and painful; not, as I believe, to yourself, but to all of us who are your friends, and saddest of all to me.

SOCRATES: What! I suppose that the ship has come from Delos, on the arrival of which I am to die?

CRITO: No, the ship has not actually arrived, but she will probably be here to-

Crito, from *Dialogues* by Plato. Trans. by B. Jowett.

day, as persons who have come from Sunium tell me that they left her there; and therefore to-morrow, Socrates, will be the last day of your life.

SOCRATES: Very well, Crito; if such is the will of God, I am willing; but my belief is that there will be a delay of a day.

CRITO: Why do you say this?

SOCRATES: I will tell you. I am to die on the day after the arrival of the ship?

CRITO: Yes; that is what the authorities say.

SOCRATES: But I do not think that the ship will be here until to-morrow; this I gather from a vision which I had last night, or rather only just now, when you fortunately allowed me to sleep.

CRITO: And what was the nature of the vision?

SOCRATES: There came to me the likeness of a woman, fair and comely, clothed in white raiment, who called to me and said: O Socrates,

"The third day hence to Phthia shalt thou go."

CRITO: What a singular dream, Socrates!

SOCRATES: There can be no doubt about the meaning, Crito, I think.

CRITO: Yes, the meaning is only too clear. But, Oh! my beloved Socrates, let me entreat you once more to take my advice and escape. For if you die I shall not only lose a friend who can never be replaced, but there is another evil: people who do not know you and me will believe that I might have saved you if I had been willing to give money, but that I did not care. Now, can there be a worse disgrace than this—that I should be thought to value money more than the life of a friend? For the many will not be persuaded that I wanted you to escape, and that you refused.

SOCRATES: But why, my dear Crito, should we care about the opinion of the many? Good men, and they are the only persons who are worth considering, will think of these things truly as they happened.

CRITO: But do you see, Socrates, that the opinion of the many must be regarded, as is evident in your own case, because they can do the very greatest evil to any one who has lost their good opinion.

SOCRATES: I only wish, Crito, that they could; for then they could also do the greatest good, and that would be well. But the truth is, that they can do neither good nor evil: they cannot make a man wise or make him foolish; and whatever they do is the result of chance.

CRITO: Well, I will not dispute about that; but please to tell me, Socrates, whether you are not acting out of regard to me and your other friends: are you not afraid that if you escape hence we may get into trouble with the informers for having stolen you away, and lose either the whole or a great part of our property; or that even a worse evil may happen to us? Now, if this is your fear, be at ease; for in order to save you, we ought surely to run this, or even a greater risk; be persuaded, then, and do as I say.

SOCRATES: Yes, Crito, that is one fear which you mention, but by no means the only one.

CRITO: Fear not. There are persons who at no great cost are willing to save you and bring you out of prison; and as for the informers, you may observe that they are far from being exorbitant in their demands; a little money will satisfy them. My means, which, as I am sure, are ample, are at your service, and if you have a scruple about spending all mine, here are strangers who will give you the use of theirs; and one of them, Simmias the Theban, has brought a sum of money for this very purpose; and Cebes and many others are willing to spend their money too. I say therefore, do not on that account hesitate about making your escape, and do not say, as you did in the court, that you will have a difficulty in knowing what to do with yourself if you escape. For men will love you in other places to which you may go, and not in Athens only; there are friends of mine in Thessaly, if you like to go to them, who will value and protect you, and no Thessalian will give you any trouble. Nor can I think that you are justified, Socrates, in betraying your own life when you might be saved; this is playing into the hands of your enemies and destroyers; and moreover I should say that you were betraying your children; for you might bring them up and educate them; instead of which you go away and leave them, and they will have to take their chance; and if they do not meet with the usual fate of orphans, there will be small thanks to you. No man should bring children into the world who is unwilling to persevere to the end in their nurture and education. But you are choosing the easier part, as I think, not the better and manlier, which would rather have become one who professes virtue in all his actions, like yourself. And indeed, I am ashamed not only of you, but of us who are your friends, when I reflect that this entire business of yours will be attributed to our want of courage. The trial need never have come on, or might have been brought to another issue; and the end of all, which is the crowning absurdity, will seem to have been permitted by us, through cowardice and baseness, who might have saved you, as you might have saved yourself, if we had been good for anything (for there was no difficulty in escaping); and we did not see how disgraceful, Socrates, and also miserable all this will be to us as well as to you. Make your mind up then, or rather have your mind already made up, for the time of deliberation is over, and there is only one thing to be done, which must be done, if at all, this very night, and which any delay will render all but impossible; I beseech you therefore, Socrates, to be persuaded by me, and to do as I say.

SOCRATES: Dear Crito, your zeal is invaluable, if a right one; but if wrong, the greater the zeal the greater the evil; and therefore we ought to consider whether these things shall be done or not. For I am and always have been one of those natures who must be guided by reason, whatever the reason may be which upon reflection appears to me to be the best; and now that this fortune has come upon me, I cannot put away the reasons which I have before given: the principles which I have hitherto honoured and revered I still honour, and unless we can find other and better principles on the instant, I am certain not to agree with you; no, not even if the power of the multitude could inflict many more imprisonments, confiscations, deaths, frightening us like children with hobgoblin terrors. But what will be the fairest way of considering the question? Shall I return to your old argument about the opinions of men? some of which are to be regarded, and others, as we were saying, are not to be regarded. Now were we right in maintaining this before I was condemned? And has the argument which was once good now proved to be talk for the sake of talking;—in fact an amusement only, and altogether vanity? That is what I want to consider with your help, Crito:—whether, under my present circumstances, the argument appears to be in any way different or not; and is to be allowed by me or disallowed. That argument, which, as I believe, is maintained by many who assume to be authorities, was to the effect, as I was saying, that the opinions of some men are to be regarded, and of other men not to be regarded. Now you, Crito, are a disinterested person who are not going to die to-morrow—at least, there is no human probability of this, and you are therefore not liable to be deceived by the circumstances in which you are placed. Tell me then, whether I am right in saying that some opinions, and the opinions of some men only, are to be valued, and other opinions, and the opinions of other men, are not to be valued. I ask you whether I was right in maintaining this?

CRITO: Certainly.

SOCRATES: The good are to be regarded, and not the bad?

CRITO: Yes.

SOCRATES: And the opinions of the wise are good, and the opinions of the unwise are evil?

CRITO: Certainly.

SOCRATES: And what was said about another matter? Was the disciple in gymnastics supposed to attend to the praise and blame and opinion of every man, or of one man only—his physician or trainer, whoever that was?

CRITO: Of one man only.

SOCRATES: And he ought to fear the censure and welcome the praise of that one only, and not of the many?

CRITO: That is clear.

SOCRATES: And he ought to live and train, and eat and drink in the way which seems good to his single master who has understanding, rather than according to the opinion of all other men put together?

CRITO: True.

SOCRATES: And if he disobeys and disregards the opinion and approval of the one, and regards the opinion of the many who have no understanding, will he not suffer evil?

CRITO: Certainly he will.

SOCRATES: And what will the evil be, whither tending and what affecting, in the disobedient person?

CRITO: Clearly, affecting the body; that is what is destroyed by the evil.

SOCRATES: Very good; and is not this true, Crito, of other things which we need not separately enumerate? In the matter of just and unjust, fair and foul, good and evil, which are the subjects of our present consultation, ought we to follow the opinion of the many and to fear them; or the opinion of the one man who has understanding, and whom we ought to fear and reverence more than all the rest of the world: and whom deserting we shall destroy and injure that principle in us which may be assumed to be improved by justice and deteriorated by injustice;—is there not such a principle?

CRITO: Certainly there is, Socrates.

SOCRATES: Take a parallel instance:—if, acting under the advice of men who have no understanding, we destroy that which is improvable by health and deteriorated by disease—when that has been destroyed, I say, would life be worth having? And that is—the body?

CRITO: Yes.

SOCRATES: Could we live, having an evil and corrupted body?

CRITO: Certainly not.

SOCRATES: And will life be worth having, if that higher part of man be depraved, which is improved by justice and deteriorated by injustice? Do we suppose that principle, whatever it may be in man, which has to do with justice and injustice, to be inferior to the body?

CRITO: Certainly not.

SOCRATES: More honoured, then?

CRITO: Far more honoured.

SOCRATES: Then, my friend, we must not regard what the many say of us: but what he, the one man who has understanding of just and unjust, will say, and what the truth will say. And therefore you begin in error when you suggest that we should regard the opinion of the many about just and unjust, good and evil, honourable and dishonourable.—Well, some one will say, "but the many can kill us."

CRITO: Yes, Socrates; that will clearly be the answer.

SOCRATES: That is true: but still I find with surprise that the old argument is, as I conceive, unshaken as ever. And I should like to know whether I may say the same of another proposition—that not life, but a good life, is to be chiefly valued?

CRITO: Yes, that also remains.

SOCRATES: And a good life is equivalent to a just and honorable one—that holds also?

CRITO: Yes, that holds.

SOCRATES: From these premisses I proceed to argue the question whether I ought or ought not to try and escape without the consent of the Athenians: and if I am clearly right in escaping, then I will make the attempt; but if not, I will abstain. The other considerations which you mention, of money and loss of character and the duty of educating children, are, as I fear, only the doctrines of the multitude, who would be as ready to call people to life, if they were able, as they are to put them to death—and with as little reason. But now, since the argument has thus far prevailed, the only question which remains to be considered is, whether we shall do rightly either in escaping or in suffering others to aid in our escape and paying them in money and thanks, or whether we shall not do rightly; and if the latter, then death or any other calamity which may ensue on my remaining here must not be allowed to enter into the calculation.

CRITO: I think that you are right, Socrates; how then shall we proceed?

SOCRATES: Let us consider the matter together, and do you either refute me if you can, and I will be convinced; or else cease, my dear friend, from repeating to me that I ought to escape against the wishes of the Athenians: for I am extremely desirous to be persuaded by you, but not against my own better judgment. And now please to consider my first position, and do your best to answer me.

CRITO: I will do my best.

SOCRATES: Are we to say that we are never intentionally to do wrong, or that in one way we ought and in another way we ought not to do wrong, or is doing wrong always evil and dishonourable, as I was just now saying, and as has been already acknowledged by us? Are all our former admissions which were made within a few days to be thrown away? And have we, at our age, been earnestly discoursing with one another all our life long only to discover that we are no better than children? Or are we to rest assured, in spite of the opinion of the many, and in spite of consequences whether better or worse, of the truth of what was then said, that injustice is always an evil and dishonour to him who acts unjustly? Shall we affirm that?

CRITO: Yes.

SOCRATES: Then we must do no wrong?

CRITO: Certainly not.

SOCRATES: Nor when injured injure in return, as the many imagine; for we must injure no one at all?

CRITO: Clearly not.

SOCRATES: Again, Crito, may we do evil?

CRITO: Surely not, Socrates.

SOCRATES: And what of doing evil in return for evil, which is the morality of the many—is that just or not?

CRITO: Not just.

SOCRATES: For doing evil to another is the same as injuring him?

CRITO: Very true.

SOCRATES: Then we ought not to retaliate or render evil for evil to any one, whatever evil we may have suffered from him. But I would have you consider, Crito, whether you really mean what you are saying. For this opinion has never been held, and never will be held, by any considerable number of persons; and those who are agreed and those who are not agreed upon this point have no common ground, and can only despise one another when they see how widely they differ. Tell me, then, whether you agree with and assent to my first principle, that neither injury nor retaliation nor warding off evil by evil is ever right. And shall that be the premiss of our argument? Or do you decline and dissent from this? For this has been of old and is still my opinion; but, if you are of another opinion, let me hear what you have to say. If, however, you remain of the same mind as formerly, I will proceed to the next step.

CRITO: You may proceed, for I have not changed my mind.

SOCRATES: Then I will proceed to the next step, which may be put in the form of a question:—Ought a man to do what he admits to be right, or ought he to betray the right?

CRITO: He ought to do what he thinks right.

SOCRATES: But if this is true, what is the application? In leaving the prison against the will of the Athenians, do I wrong any? or rather do I not wrong those whom I ought least to wrong? Do I not desert the principles which were acknowledged by us to be just? What do you say?

CRITO: I cannot tell, Socrates; for I do not know.

SOCRATES: Then consider the matter in this way:—Imagine that I am about to play truant (you may call the proceeding by any name which you like), and the laws and the government come and interrogate me: "Tell us, Socrates," they say, "what are you about? are you going by an act of yours to overturn us—the laws and the whole state, as far as in you lies? Do you imagine that a state can subsist and not be overthrown, in which the decisions of law have no power, but are set aside and overthrown by individuals?" What will be our answer, Crito, to these and the like words? Any one, and especially a clever rhetorician, will have a good deal to urge about the evil of setting aside the law which requires a sentence to be carried out; and we might reply, "Yes; but the state has injured us and given an unjust sentence." Suppose I say that?

CRITO: Very good, Socrates.

SOCRATES: "And was that our agreement with you?" the law would say, "or were you to abide by the sentence of the state?" And if I were to express astonishment at their saying this, the law would probably add: "Answer, Socrates, instead of opening your eyes: you are in the habit of asking and answering questions. Tell us what complaint you have to make against us which justifies you in attempting to destroy us and the state? In the first place did we not bring you into existence? Your father married your mother by our aid and begat you. Say whether you have any objection to urge against those of us who regulate marriage?" None, I should reply. "Or against those of us who regulate the system of nurture and education of children in which you were trained? Were not the laws, who have the charge of this, right in commanding your father to train you in music and gymnastic?" Right, I should reply. "Well then, since you were brought into the world and nurtured and educated by us, can you deny in the first place that you are our child and slave, as your fathers were before you? And if this is true you are not on equal terms with us; nor can you think that you have a right to do to us what we are doing to you. Would you have any right to strike or revile or do any other evil to a father or to your master, if you had one, when you have been struck or reviled by him, or received some other evil at his hands?—you would not say this? And because we think right to destroy you, do you think that you have any right to destroy us in return, and your country as far as in you lies?

And will you, O professor of true virtue, say that you are justified in this? Has a philosopher like you failed to discover that our country is more to be valued and higher and holier far than mother or father or any ancestor, and more to be regarded in the eyes of the gods and of men of understanding? also to be soothed, and gently and reverently entreated when angry, even more than a father, and if not persuaded, obeyed? And when we are punished by her, whether with imprisonment or stripes, the punishment is to be endured in silence; and if she lead us to wounds or death in battle, thither we follow as is right; neither may any one yield or retreat or leave his rank, but whether in battle or in a court of law, or in any other place, he must do what his city and his country order him; or he must change their view of what is just: and if he may do no violence to his father or mother, much less may he do violence to his country." What answer shall we make to this, Crito? Do the laws speak truly, or do they not?

CRITO: I think that they do.

SOCRATES: Then the laws will say: "Consider, Socrates, if this is true, that in your present attempt you are going to do us wrong. For, after having brought you into the world, and nurtured and educated you, and given you and every other citizen a share in every good that we had to give, we further proclaim and give the right to every Athenian, that if he does not like us when he has come of age and has seen the ways of the city, and made our acquaintance, he may go where he pleases and take his goods with him; and none of us laws will forbid him or interfere with him. Any of you who does not like us and the city, and who wants to go to a colony or to any other city, may go where he likes, and take his goods with him. But he who has experience of the manner in which we order justice and administer the state, and still remains, has entered into an implied contract that he will do as we command him. And he who disobeys us is, as we maintain, thrice wrong: first, because in disobeying us he is disobeying his parents; secondly, because we are the authors of his education; thirdly, because he has made an agreement with us that he will duly obey our commands; and he neither obeys them nor convinces us that our commands are wrong; and we do not rudely impose them, but give him the alternative of obeying or convincing us;—that is what we offer, and he does neither. These are the sort of accusations to which, as we were saying, you, Socrates, will be exposed if you accomplish your intentions; you, above all other Athenians." Suppose I ask, why is this? they will justly retort upon me that I above all other men have acknowledged the agreement. "There is clear proof," they will say, "Socrates, that we and the city were not displeasing to you. Of all Athenians you have been the most constant resident in the city, which, as you never leave, you may be supposed to love. For you never went out of the city either to see the games, except once when you went to the Isthmus, or to any other place unless when you were on military service; nor did you travel as other men do. Nor had you any curiosity to know other states or their laws: your affections did not go beyond us and our state; we were your special favourites, and you acquiesced in our government of you; and this is the state in which you begat your children, which is a proof of your satisfaction. Moreover, you might, if you had liked, have fixed the penalty at banishment in the course of the trial—the state which refuses to let you go now would have let you go then. But you pretended that you preferred death to exile, and that you were not grieved at death. And now you have forgotten these fine sentiments, and pay no respect to us the laws, of whom you are the destroyer; and are doing what only a miserable slave would do, running away and turning your back upon the compacts and agreements which you made as a citizen. And first of all answer this very question: Are we right in saying that you agreed to be governed according to us in deed, and not in word only? Is that true or not?" How shall we answer that, Crito? Must we not agree?

CRITO: There is no help, Socrates.

SOCRATES: Then will they not say: "You, Socrates, are breaking the covenants and agreements which you made with us at your leisure, not in any haste or under any compulsion of deception, but having had seventy years to think of them, during which time you were at liberty to leave the city, if we were not to your mind, or if our covenants appeared to you to be unfair. You had your choice, and might have gone either to Lacedaemon or Crete, which you often praise for their good government, or to some other Hellenic or foreign state. Whereas you, above all other Athenians, seemed to be so fond of the state, or, in other words, of us her laws (for who would like a state that has no laws), that you never stirred out of her; the halt, the blind, the maimed were not more stationary in her than you were. And now you run away and forsake your agreements. Not so, Socrates, if you will take our advice; do not make yourself ridiculous by escaping out of the city.

"For just consider, if you transgress and err in this sort of way, what good will you do either to yourself or to your friends? That your friends will be driven into exile and deprived of citizenship, or will lose their property, is tolerably certain; and you yourself, if you fly to one of the neighbouring cities, as, for example, Thebes or Megara, both of which are well-governed cities, will come to them as an enemy, Socrates, and their government will be against you, and all patriotic citizens will cast an evil eye upon you as a subverter of the laws, and you will confirm in the minds of the judges the justice of their own condemnation of you. For he who is a corruptor of the laws is more than likely to be corruptor of the young and foolish portion of mankind. Will you then flee from well-ordered cities and virtuous men? and is existence worth having on these terms? Or will you go to them without shame, and talk to them, Socrates? And what will you say to them? What you say here about virtue and justice and institutions and laws being the best things among men. Would that be decent of you? Surely not. But if you go away from well-governed states to Crito's friends in Thessaly, where there is great disorder and licence, they will be charmed to have the tale of your escape from prison, set off with ludicrous particulars of the manner in which you were wrapped in a goatskin or some other disguise, and metamorphosed as the fashion of runaways is—that is very likely; but will there be no one to remind you that in your old age you violated the most sacred laws from a miserable desire of a little more life. Perhaps not, if you keep them in a good temper; but if they are out of temper you will hear many degrading things; you will live, but how?—as the flatterer of all men, and the servant of all men; and doing what?—eating and drinking in Thessaly, having gone abroad in order that you may get a dinner. And where will be your fine sentiments about justice and virtue then? Say that you wish to live for the sake of your children, that you may bring them up and educate them—will you take them into Thessaly and deprive them of Athenian citizenship? Is that the benefit which you would confer upon them? Or are you under the impression that they will be better cared for and educated here if you are still alive, although absent from them; for that your friends will take care of them? Do you fancy that if you are an inhabitant of Thessaly they will take care of them, and if you are an inhabitant of the other world they will not take care of them? Nay; but if they who call themselves friends are truly friends, they surely will.

"Listen, then, Socrates, to us who have brought you up. Think not of life and children first, and of justice afterwards, but of justice first, that you may be justified before the princes of the world below. For neither will you nor any that belong to you be happier or holier or juster in this life, or happier in another, if you do as Crito bids. Now you depart in innocence, a sufferer and not a doer of evil; a victim, not of the laws, but of men. But if you go forth, returning evil for evil, and injury for injury, breaking the covenants and agreements which you have made with us, and wronging those whom you ought least to wrong, that is to say, yourself, your friends, your country, and us, we shall be angry with you while you live, and our brethren, the laws in the world below, will receive you as an enemy; for they will know that you have done your best to destroy us. Listen, then, to us and not to Crito."

This is the voice which I seem to hear murmuring in my ears, like the sound of the flute in the ears of the mystic; that voice, I say, is humming in my ears, and prevents me from hearing any other. And I know that anything more which you may say will be vain. Yet speak, if you have anything to say.

CRITO: I have nothing to say, Socrates.

SOCRATES: Then let me follow the intimations of the will of God.

HOBBES

Thomas Hobbes (1588–1679) is the greatest of the English social contract theorists. In his famous study of the principles of the state, Leviathan, *Hobbes traces the absolute authority of the sovereign to a free contractual agreement, or covenant, entered into by the members of a society for their own protection. Elsewhere in* Leviathan, *Hobbes paints a dark and bitter picture of social life in the absence of an acknowledged political authority. A war of all against all blights every man's life, making some sort of pact of mutual protection necessary. In effect, Hobbes tells us that sensibly prudent men, finding themselves in the midst of social chaos, will decide to rescue themselves by setting up an absolute sovereign with authority to make and enforce a system of laws.*

Why ought each citizen to obey the laws enacted by the sovereign? The answer Hobbes offers is rational self-interest. Just as a prudent man submits to the dentist even though it hurts, knowing that the consequences of neglecting his teeth are even more painful, so the prudent citizen submits to the laws of the state, lest his disobedience, and that of his fellow citizens, lead back to the terrible disorder of the "state of nature."

Death is the very worst injury that can be done to a man. It makes no sense, therefore, to submit to death in order to avoid a "worse" evil. So, quite consistently, Hobbes says that every man has the right to resist death, even when it is to be inflicted in all justice by the state. A man might willingly pay a fine or go to jail, just as he willingly goes on a diet or has an operation, out of a self-interested calculation of the relative advantages of the alternatives open to him. But no rational man will accept death without a struggle, any more than a sick man would submit to an operation which was sure to kill him.

The pessimistic tone of Hobbes' language makes his theory sound a good deal more dictatorial and authoritarian than the social contract theories of Jean-Jacques Rousseau and John Locke. On close examination, however, we find that the doctrine of the Leviathan *is quite consistent with a rational anarchism. If Hobbes had had a somewhat more hopeful view of human affairs, he might have taken a very different direction in political theory.*

Of the Rights of Sovereigns
by Institution

The act of instituting a commonwealth, what. A *commonwealth* is said to be *instituted* when a *multitude* of men do agree and *covenant, every one with every one,* that to whatsoever *man* or *assembly of men* shall be given by the major part the *right* to *present* the person of them all—that is to say, to be their *representative*—every one, as well he that *voted for it* as he that *voted against it*, shall *authorize* all the actions and judgments of that man or assembly of men in the same manner as if they were his own, to the end to live peaceably among themselves and be protected against other men.

The consequences to such institutions, are: 1. *The subjects cannot change the form of government.* From this institution of a commonwealth are derived all the *rights* and *faculties* of him or them on whom the sovereign power is conferred by the consent of the people assembled. First, because they covenant, it is to be understood they are not obliged by former covenant to anything repugnant hereunto. And consequently they that have already instituted a commonwealth, being thereby bound by covenant to own the actions and judgments of one, cannot lawfully make a new covenant among themselves to be obedient to any other, in anything whatsoever, without his permission. And therefore, they that are subjects to a monarch cannot without his leave cast off monarchy and return to the confusion of a disunited multitude, nor transfer their person from him that bears it to another man or other assembly of men; for they are bound, every man to every man, to own and be reputed author of all that he that already is their sovereign shall do and judge fit to be done; so that any one man dissenting, all the rest should break their covenant made to that man, which is injustice; and they have also every man given the sovereignty to him that bears their person, and therefore if they depose him they take from him that which is his own, and so again it is injustice. Besides, if he that attempts to depose his sovereign be killed or punished by him for such attempt, he is author of his own punishment, as being by the institution author of all his sovereign shall do; and because it is injustice for a man to do anything for which he may be punished by his own authority, he is also upon that

Chapter 18 and selections from Chapter 21 from Part II of *Leviathan* by Thomas Hobbes. Originally published in English in 1651.

title unjust. And whereas some men have pretended for their disobedience to their sovereign a new covenant, made not with men but with God, this also is unjust; for there is no covenant with God but by mediation of somebody that represents God's person, which none does but God's lieutenant, who has the sovereignty under God. But this pretense of covenant with God is so evident a lie, even in the pretenders' own consciences, that it is not only an act of an unjust but also of a vile and unmanly disposition.

2. *Sovereign power cannot be forfeited.* Secondly, because the right of bearing the person of them all is given to him they make sovereign by covenant only of one to another and not of him to any of them, there can happen no breach of covenant on the part of the sovereign; and consequently none of his subjects, by any pretense of forfeiture, can be freed from his subjection. That he which is made sovereign makes no covenant with his subjects beforehand is manifest, because either he must make it with the whole multitude, as one party to the covenant, or he must make a several covenant with every man. With the whole, as one party, it is impossible because as yet they are not one person; and if he make so many several covenants as there be men, those covenants after he has the sovereignty are void because what act soever can be pretended by any one of them for breach thereof is the act both of himself and of all the rest, because done in the person and by the right of every one of them in particular. Besides, if any one or more of them pretend a breach of the covenant made by the sovereign at his institution, and others, or one other of his subjects, or himself alone, pretend there was no such breach, there is in this case no judge to decide the controversy; it returns therefore to the sword again, and every man recovers the right of protecting himself by his own strength, contrary to the design they had in the institution. It is therefore in vain to grant sovereignty by way of precedent covenant. The opinion that any monarch receives his power by covenant—that is to say, on condition—proceeds from want of understanding this easy truth: that covenants, being but words and breath, have no force to oblige, contain, constrain, or protect any man but what it has from the public sword—that is, from the untied hands of that man or assembly of men that has the sovereignty, and whose actions are avouched by them all and performed by the strength of them all in him united. But when an assembly of men is made sovereign, then no man imagines any such covenant to have passed in the institution; for no man is so dull as to say, for example, the people of Rome made a covenant with the Romans to hold the sovereignty on such or such conditions, which not performed, the Romans might lawfully depose the Roman people. That men see not the reason to be alike in a monarchy and in a popular government proceeds from the ambition of some that are kinder to the government of an assembly, whereof they may hope to participate, than of monarchy, which they despair to enjoy.

3. *No man can without injustice protest against the institution of the sovereign declared by the major part.* Thirdly, because the major part has by con-

senting voices declared a sovereign, he that dissented must now consent with the rest—that is, be contented to avow all the actions he shall do—or else justly be destroyed by the rest. For if he voluntarily entered into the congregation of them that were assembled, he sufficiently declared thereby his will, and therefore tacitly covenanted, to stand to what the major part should ordain; and therefore, if he refuse to stand thereto or make protestation against any of their decrees, he does contrary to his covenant, and therefore unjustly. And whether he be of the congregation or not, and whether his consent be asked or not, he must either submit to their decrees or be left in the condition of war he was in before, wherein he might without injustice be destroyed by any man whatsoever.

4. *The sovereign's actions cannot be justly accused by the subject.* Fourthly, because every subject is by this institution author of all the actions and judgments of the sovereign instituted, it follows that whatsoever he does, it can be no injury to any of his subjects; nor ought he to be by any of them accused of injustice. For he that does anything by authority from another does therein no injury to him by whose authority he acts; but by this institution of a commonwealth, every particular man is author of all the sovereign does; and consequently he that complains of injury from his sovereign complains of that whereof he himself is author, and therefore ought not to accuse any man but himself—no, nor himself of injury, because to do injury to one's self is impossible. It is true that they that have sovereign power may commit iniquity, but not injustice or injury in the proper signification.

5. *Whatsoever the sovereign does is unpunishable by the subject.* Fifthly, and consequently to that which was said last, no man that has sovereign power can justly be put to death or otherwise in any manner by his subjects punished. For seeing every subject is author of the actions of his sovereign, he punishes another for the actions committed by himself.

6. *The sovereign is judge of what is necessary for the peace and defense of his subjects.* And because the end of this institution is the peace and defense of them all, and whosoever has right to the end has right to the means, it belongs of right to whatsoever man or assembly that has the sovereignty to be judge both of the means of peace and defense and also of the hindrances and disturbances of the same, and to do whatsoever he shall think necessary to be done, both beforehand, for the preserving of peace and security by prevention of discord at home and hostility from abroad, and, when peace and security are lost, for the recovery of the same. And therefore,

And judge of what doctrines are fit to be taught them. Sixthly, it is annexed to the sovereignty to be judge of what opinions and doctrines are averse and what conducing to peace, and consequently on what occasions, how far, and what men are to be trusted withal in speaking to multitudes of people, and who shall examine the doctrines of all books before they be published. For the actions of men proceed from their opinions, and in the well-governing of opinions consists the well-governing of men's actions, in order to their peace and concord. And though in matter of doctrine nothing ought to be regarded but the truth, yet this is not repugnant to regulating the same by peace. For doctrine repugnant to peace can no more be true than peace and concord can be against the law of nature. It is true that in a commonwealth, where by the negligence or unskillfulness of governors and teachers false doctrines are by time generally received, the contrary truths may be generally offensive. Yet the most sudden and rough bustling in of a new truth that can be does never break the peace but only sometimes awake the war. For those men that are so remissly governed that they dare take up arms to defend or introduce an opinion are still in war, and their condition not peace but only a cessation of arms for fear of one another, and they live, as it were, in the precincts of battle continually. It belongs therefore to him that has the sovereign power to be judge or constitute all judges of opinions and doctrines as a thing necessary to peace, thereby to prevent discord and civil war.

7. *The right of making rules; whereby the subjects may every man know what is so his own, as no other subject can without injustice take it from him.* Seventhly is annexed to the sovereignty the whole power of prescribing the rules whereby every man may know what goods he may enjoy and what actions he may do without being molested by any of his fellow subjects; and this is it men call *propriety*. For before constitution of sovereign power, as has already been shown, all men had right to all things, which necessarily causes war; and therefore this propriety, being necessary to peace and depending on sovereign power, is the act of that power in order to the public peace. These rules of propriety, or *meum* and *tuum*, and of *good, evil, lawful*, and *unlawful* in the actions of subjects, are the civil laws—that is to say, the laws of each commonwealth in particular—though the name of civil law be now restrained to the ancient civil laws of the city of Rome, which being the head of a great part of the world, her laws at that time were in these parts the civil law.

8. *To him also belongs the right of all judicature and decision of controversy.* Eighthly is annexed to the sovereignty the right of judicature—that is to say, of hearing and deciding all controversies which may arise concerning law, either civil or natural, or concerning fact. For without the decision of controversies, there is no protection of one subject against the injuries of another; the laws concerning *meum* and *tuum* are in vain; and to every man remains, from the natural and necessary appetite of his own conservation, the right of protecting himself by his private strength, which is the condition of war and contrary to the end for which every commonwealth is instituted.

9. *And of making war and peace as he shall think best.* Ninthly is annexed to the sovereignty the right of making war and peace with other nations and commonwealths—that is to say, of judging when it is for the public good, and how great forces are to be assembled, armed, and paid for that end, and to

levy money upon the subjects to defray the expenses thereof. For the power by which the people are to be defended consists in their armies, and the strength of an army in the union of their strength under one command, which command the sovereign instituted therefore has; because the command of the *militia*, without other institution, makes him that has it sovereign. And therefore whosoever is made general of an army, he that has the sovereign power is always generalissimo.

10. *And of choosing all counselors and ministers, both of peace and war.* Tenthly is annexed to the sovereignty the choosing of all counselors, ministers, magistrates, and officers, both in peace and war. For seeing the sovereign is charged with the end, which is the common peace and defense, he is understood to have power to use such means as he shall think most fit for his discharge.

11. *And of rewarding and punishing, and that (where no former law has determined the measure of it) arbitrarily.* Eleventhly, to the sovereign is committed the power of rewarding with riches or honor, and of punishing with corporal or pecuniary punishment or with ignominy, every subject according to the law he has formerly made; or if there be no law made, according as he shall judge most to conduce to the encouraging of men to serve the commonwealth or deterring of them from doing disservice to the same.

12. *And of honor and order.* Lastly, considering what value men are naturally apt to set upon themselves, what respect they look for from others, and how little they value other men—from whence continually arise among them emulation, quarrels, factions, and at last war, to the destroying of one another and diminution of their strength against a common enemy—it is necessary that there be laws of honor and a public rate of the worth of such men as have deserved or are able to deserve well of the commonwealth, and that there be force in the hands of some or other to put those laws in execution. But it has already been shown that not only the whole *militia* or forces of the commonwealth, but also the judicature of all controversies is annexed to the sovereignty. To the sovereign therefore it belongs also to give titles of honor, and to appoint what order of place and dignity each man shall hold, and what signs of respect, in public or private meetings, they shall give to one another.

These rights are indivisible. These are the rights which make the essence of sovereignty, and which are the marks whereby a man may discern in what man or assembly of men the sovereign power is placed and resides. For these are incommunicable and inseparable. The power to coin money, to dispose of the estate and persons of infant heirs, to have preemption in markets, and all other statute prerogatives may be transferred by the sovereign, and yet the power to protect his subjects be retained. But if he transfer the *militia*, he retains the judicature in vain for want of execution of the laws; or if he grant away the power of raising money, the *militia* is in vain; or if he give away the government of doctrines, men will be frighted into rebellion with the fear of spirits. And so if we consider any one of the said rights, we shall presently see that the holding of all the rest will produce no effect in the conservation of peace and justice, the end for which all commonwealths are instituted. And this division is it whereof it is said *a kingdom divided in itself cannot stand;* for unless this division precede, division into opposite armies can never happen. If there had not first been an opinion received of the greatest part of England that these powers were divided between the King and the Lords and the House of Commons, the people had never been divided and fallen into this civil war— first between those that disagreed in politics and after between the dissenters about the liberty of religion—which has so instructed men in this point of sovereign right that there be few now in England that do not see that these rights are inseparable and will be so generally acknowledged at the next return of peace; and so continue till their miseries are forgotten, and no longer, except the vulgar be better taught than they have hitherto been.

And can by no grant pass away without direct renouncing of the sovereign power. And because they are essential and inseparable rights, it follows necessarily that in whatsoever words any of them seem to be granted away, yet if the sovereign power itself be not in direct terms renounced and the name of sovereign no more given by the grantees to him that grants them, the grant is void; for when he has granted all he can, if we grant back the sovereignty all is restored as inseparably annexed thereunto.

The power and honor of subjects vanishes in the presence of the power sovereign. This great authority being indivisible and inseparably annexed to the sovereignty, there is little ground for the opinion of them that say of sovereign kings, though they be *singulis majores,* of greater power than every one of their subjects, yet they be *universis minores,* or less power than them all together. For if by *all together* they mean not the collective body as one person, then *all together* and *every one* signify the same, and the speech is absurd. But if by *all together* they understand them as one person, which person the sovereign bears, then the power of all together is the same with the sovereign's power, and so again the speech is absurd; which absurdity they see well enough when the sovereignty is in an assembly of the people, but in a monarch they see is not; and yet the power of sovereignty is the same in whomsoever it be placed.

And as the power, so also the honor of the sovereign ought to be greater than that of any or all the subjects. For in the sovereignty is the fountain of honor. The dignities of lord, earl, duke, and prince are his creatures. As in the presence of the master the servants are equal, and without any honor at all, so are the subjects in the presence of the sovereign. And though they shine some more, some less, when they are out of his sight, yet in his presence they shine no more than the stars in the presence of the sun.

Sovereign power not so hurtful as the want of it, and the hurt proceeds for the greatest part from not submitting readily to a less. But a man may here object that the condition of subjects is very miserable, as being obnoxious to the lusts and other irregular passions of him or them that have so unlimited a power in their hands. And commonly they that live under a monarch think it the fault of monarchy, and they that live under the government of democracy or other sovereign assembly attribute all the inconvenience to that form of commonwealth, whereas the power in all forms, if they be perfect enough to protect them, is the same—not considering that the state of man can never be without some incommodity or other, and that the greatest that in any form of government can possibly happen to the people in general is scarce sensible in respect of the miseries and horrible calamities that accompany a civil war or that dissolute condition of masterless men, without subjection to laws and a co-ercive power to tie their hands from rapine and revenge; nor considering that the greatest pressure of sovereign governors proceeds not from any delight or profit they can expect in the damage or weakening of their subjects, in whose vigor consists their own strength and glory, but in the restiveness of themselves that, unwillingly contributing to their own defense, make it necessary for their governors to draw from them what they can in time of peace that they may have means on any emergent occasion or sudden need to resist or take advantage on their enemies. For all men are by nature provided of notable multiplying glasses—that is, their passions and self-love—through which every little payment appears a great grievance, but are destitute of those prospective glasses —namely, moral and civil science—to see afar off the miseries that hang over them and cannot without such payments be avoided.

Of the Liberty of Subjects

Liberty, what. Liberty, or freedom, signifies properly the absence of opposition—by opposition I mean external impediments of motion—and maybe applied no less to irrational and inanimate creatures than to rational. For whatsoever is so tied or environed as it cannot move but within a certain space, which space is determined by the opposition of some external body, we say it has not liberty to go farther. And so of all living creatures while they are imprisoned or restrained with walls or chains, and of the water while it is kept in by banks or vessels that otherwise would spread itself into a larger space, we use to say that they are not at liberty to move in such a manner as without those external impediments they would. But when the impediment of motion is in the constitution of the thing itself, we use not to say it wants the liberty but the power to move—as when a stone lies still or a man is fastened to his bed by sickness.

What it is to be free. And according to this proper and generally received meaning of the word, a FREEMAN *is he that in those things which by his strength and wit he is able to do is not hindered to do what he has a will to do.* But when the words *free* and *liberty* are applied to anything but *bodies,* they are abused, for that which is not subject to motion is not subject to impediment; and therefore, when it is said, for example, the way is free, no liberty of the way is signified but of those that walk in it without stop. And when we say a gift is free, there is not meant any liberty of the gift but of the giver, that was not bound by law or covenant to give it. So when we *speak freely*, it is not the liberty of voice or pronunciation but of the man, whom no law has obliged to speak otherwise than he did. Lastly, from the use of the word *free will*, no liberty can be inferred of the will, desire, or inclination but the liberty of the man, which consists in this: that he finds no stop in doing what he has the will, desire, or inclination to do.

Fear and liberty consistent. Fear and liberty are consistent, as when a man throws his goods into the sea for *fear* the ship should sink, he does it nevertheless very willingly, and may refuse to do it if he will: it is therefore the action of one that was *free;* so a man sometimes pays his debt only for *fear* of imprisonment, which, because nobody hindered him from detaining, was the action of a man at *liberty*. And generally all actions which men do in commonwealths for *fear* of the law are actions which the doers had *liberty* to omit.

Liberty and necessity consistent. *Liberty* and *necessity* are consistent, as in the water that has not only *liberty* but a *necessity* of descending by the channel; so likewise in the actions which men voluntarily do, which, because they proceed from their will, proceed from *liberty*, and yet—because every act of man's will and every desire and inclination proceeds from some cause, and that from another cause, in a continual chain whose first link is in the hand of God, the first of all causes—proceed from *necessity*. So that to him that could see the connection of those causes the *necessity* of all men's voluntary actions would appear manifest. And therefore God, that sees and disposes all things, sees also that the *liberty* of man in doing what he will is accompanied with the *necessity* of doing that which God will, and no more nor less. For though men may do many things which God does not command, nor is therefore author of them, yet they can have no passion nor appetite to anything of which God's will is not the cause. And did not his will assure the *necessity* of man's will, and consequently of all that on man's will depends, the *liberty* of men would be a contradiction and impediment to the omnipotence and *liberty* of God. And this shall suffice, as to the matter in hand, of the natural liberty which only is properly called *liberty*.

Artificial bonds or covenants. But as men, for the attaining of peace and conservation of themselves thereby, have made an artificial man, which we call a commonwealth, so also have they made artificial chains, called *civil laws*, which they themselves, by mutual covenants, have fastened at one end to the lips of that man or assembly to whom they have given the sovereign power, and at the other end to their own ears. These bonds, in their own nature but weak, may nevertheless be made to hold by the danger, though not by the difficulty, of breaking them. . . .

Liberty of subjects how to be measured. To come now to the particulars of the true liberty of a subject—that is to say, what are the things which, though commanded by the sovereign, he may nevertheless without injustice refuse to do —we are to consider what rights we pass away when we make a commonwealth, or, which is all one, what liberty we deny ourselves by owning all the actions, without exception, of the man or assembly we make our sovereign. For in the act of our *submission* consists both our *obligation* and our *liberty*, which must therefore be inferred by arguments taken from thence, there being no obligation on any man which arises not from some act of his own, for all men equally are by nature free. And because such arguments must either be drawn from the express words, *I authorize all his actions,* or from the intention of him that submits himself to power, which intention is to be understood by the end for which he so submits, the obligation and liberty of the subject is to be derived either from those words or others equivalent, or else from the end of the institution of sovereignty—namely, the peace of the subjects within themselves and their defense against a common enemy.

Subjects have liberty to defend their own bodies, even against them that lawfully invade them, and are not bound to hurt themselves. First, therefore, seeing sovereignty by institution is by covenant of every one to every one, and sovereignty by acquisition of covenants of the vanquished to the victor or child to the parent, it is manifest that every subject has liberty in all those things the right whereof cannot by covenant be transferred. I have shown before in the fourteenth chapter that covenants not to defend a man's own body are void. Therefore, if the sovereign command a man, though justly condemned, to kill, wound, or maim himself, or not to resist those that assault him, or to abstain from the use of food, air, medicine, or any other thing without which he cannot live, yet has that man the liberty to disobey.

If a man be interrogated by the sovereign or his authority concerning a crime done by himself, he is not bound, without assurance of pardon, to confess it; because no man, as I have shown in the same chapter, can be obliged by covenant to accuse himself.

Again, the consent of a subject to sovereign power is contained in these words: *I authorize, or take upon me, all his actions;* in which there is no restriction at all of his own former natural liberty, for by allowing him to *kill me* I am not bound to kill myself when he commands me. It is one thing to say: *kill me, or my fellow, if you please;* another thing to say, *I will kill myself, or my fellow.* It follows therefore, that—

No man is bound by the words themselves either to kill himself or any other man, and consequently that the obligation a man may sometimes have, upon the command of the sovereign, to execute any dangerous or dishonorable office depends not on the words of our submission but on the intention, which is to be understood by the end thereof. When, therefore, our refusal to obey frustrates the end for which the sovereignty was ordained, then there is no liberty to refuse; otherwise there is.

Nor to warfare, unless they voluntarily undertake it. Upon this ground, a man that is commanded as a soldier to fight against the enemy, though his sovereign have right enough to punish his refusal with death, may nevertheless in many cases refuse, without injustice—as when he substitutes a sufficient soldier in his place, for in this case he deserts not the service of the commonwealth. And there is allowance to be made for natural timorousness, not only to women, of whom no such dangerous duty is expected, but also to men of feminine courage. When armies fight, there is on one side or both a running away; yet when they do it not out of treachery but fear, they are not esteemed to do it unjustly but dishonorably. For the same reason, to avoid battle is not injustice but cowardice. But he that enrolls himself a soldier, or takes impressed money, takes away the excuse of a timorous nature, and is obliged not only to go to the battle but also not to run from it without his captain's leave. And when the defense of the commonwealth requires at once the help of all that are able to bear arms, everyone is obliged; because otherwise the institution of the commonwealth, which they have not the purpose or courage to preserve, was in vain.

To resist the sword of the commonwealth in defense of another man, guilty or innocent, no man has liberty; because such liberty takes away from the sovereign the means of protecting us, and is therefore destructive of the very essence of government. But in case a great many men together have already resisted the sovereign power unjustly, or committed some capital crime for which every one of them expects death, whether have they not the liberty then to join together and assist and defend one another? Certainly they have, for they but defend their lives, which the guilty man may as well do as the innocent. There was indeed injustice in the first breach of their duty; their bearing of arms subsequent to it, though it be to maintain what they have done, is no new unjust act. And if it be only to defend their persons, it is not unjust at all. But the offer of pardon takes from them to whom it is offered the plea of self-defense, and makes their perseverance in assisting or defending the rest unlawful. . . .

In what cases subjects are absolved of their obedience to their sovereign. The obligation of subjects to the sovereign is understood to last as long and no longer than the power lasts by which he is able to protect them. For the right men have by nature to protect themselves when none else can protect them can by no covenant be relinquished. The sovereignty is the soul of the commonwealth, which once departed from the body, the members do no more receive their motion from it. The end of obedience is protection, which, wheresoever a man sees it, either in his own or in another's sword, nature applies his obedience to it and his endeavor to maintain it. And though sovereignty, in the intention of them that make it, be immortal, yet it is in its own nature not only subject to violent death by foreign war, but also through the ignorance and passions of men, it has in it, from the very institution, many seeds of a natural mortality by intestine discord. . . .

LOCKE

If any single work can be considered the source of the political beliefs of our founding fathers, that work is the Second Treatise of Civil Government, *by John Locke. Locke (1632–1704) is best known in the history of philosophy for his long, rambling* Essay Concerning Human Understanding, *in which he laid down the fundamental principles of the empiricist philosophy which has dominated Anglo-American thought to the present day. The* Two Treatises of Civil Government *were published in 1689, a year after William of Orange ascended the throne of Great Britain in the upheaval known as the Glorious Revolution. Since Locke's* Treatises *argue for the sort of limited constitutional government which was instituted in 1688, scholars for many years assumed that he had written them in order to justify William of Orange's claims. Recently, an early draft of the* Treatises *was found, dating to 1681. As so often happens, philosophical ideas appropriate to the age were arrived at independently of public events. Nevertheless, Locke's great essay stands as a classic defense of the limitations on the authority of the state*

The key to Locke's argument is the connection he establishes between the purposes for which men set up a state and the conditions under which they are justified in overthrowing what they have set up. Locke, unlike Hobbes, takes a reasonably benign view of life in a pre-political social situation. There are strong reasons for collectively agreeing to obey a central authority, Locke believes, but those reasons are not so strong as to make revolution unthinkable. If the state ceases to protect the life, liberty, and property of individuals; if it exceeds its mandate so far as to tyrannize the very men who created it; if, in short, this instrument of other men's will becomes their enemy rather than their defender, then it is time for men to rise up and take the power of the state back into their own hands. One is reminded of Thomas Jefferson's remarkable statement that society would profit from a revolution every twenty years!

Both Hobbes and Locke view the state primarily as a maintainer of peace and order. In a sense, the state's functions are negative, for so long as men do not intrude upon one another's affairs in unjust ways, there is nothing for the state to do. By contrast, virtually all political factions these days see the state as playing a positive role in the affairs of society. The state is expected to regulate the economy, initiate projects in the public interest, and administer a wide spectrum of social welfare programs. It is worth asking how Hobbes and Locke would have to revise their political theories in order to make them relevant to modern conditions.

The Establishment
and Dissolution
of Political Societies

Of the Beginning
of Political Societies

Men being, as has been said, by nature all free, equal, and independent, no one can be put out of this estate, and subjected to the political power of another, without his own consent, which is done by agreeing with other men to join and unite into a community for their comfortable, safe, and peaceable living one amongst another, in a secure enjoyment of their properties, and a greater security against any that are not of it. This any number of men may do, because it injures not the freedom of the rest; they are left as they were in the liberty of the state of nature. When any number of men have so consented to make one community or government, they are thereby presently incorporated, and make one body politic, wherein the majority have a right to act and conclude the rest.

For when any number of men have, by the consent of every individual, made a community, they have thereby made that community one body, with a power to act as one body, which is only by the will and determination of the majority. For that which acts any community being only the consent of the individuals of it, and it being one body must move one way, it is necessary the body should move that way whither the greater force carries it, which is the consent of the majority; or else it is impossible it should act or continue one body, one community, which the consent of every individual that united into it agreed that it should; and so every one is bound by that consent to be concluded by the majority. And therefore we see that in assemblies empowered to act by positive laws, where no number is set by that positive law which empowers them, the act of majority passes for the act of the whole, and of course determines, as having by the law of nature and reason the power of the whole.

And thus every man, by consenting with others to make one body politic under one government, puts himself under an obligation to every one of that society, to submit to the determination of the majority, and to be concluded by it; or else this original compact, whereby he with others incorporates into one society, would signify nothing, and be no compact, if he be left free and under no other ties than he was in before in the state of nature. For what appearance would there be of any compact? What new engagement if he were no farther tied by any decrees of the society, then he himself thought fit, and

Chapter 8, sections 95–100, 119–22; chapter 9; chapter 19, sections 211–12, 220–30, 243. From *Of Civil Government: Second Treatise* by John Locke. First published England, 1689.

did actually consent to? This would be still as great a liberty as he himself had before his compact, or any one else in the state of nature hath, who may submit himself and consent to any acts of it if he thinks fit.

For if the consent of the majority shall not in reason be received as the act of the whole and conclude every individual, nothing but the consent of every individual can make anything to be the act of the whole which considering the infirmities of health and avocations of business, which in a number, though much less than that of a commonwealth, will necessarily keep many away from the public assembly, and the variety of opinions, and contrariety of interest, which unavoidably happen in all collections of men, 'tis next to impossible ever to be had. And therefore if the coming into society be upon such terms it will be only like Cato's coming into the theatre, *tantum ut exiret.*[1] Such a constitution as this would make the mighty leviathan of a shorter duration than the feeblest creatures, and not let it outlast the day it was born in; which cannot be supposed till we can think that rational creatures should desire and constitute societies only to be dissolved. For where the majority cannot conclude the rest, there they cannot act as one body, and consequently will be immediately dissolved again.

Whosoever therefore out of a state of nature unite into a community must be understood to give up all the power necessary to the ends for which they unite into society, to the majority of the community, unless they expressly agree in any number greater than the majority. And this is done by barely agreeing to unite into one political society, which is all the compact that is, or needs be, between the individuals that enter into or make up a commonwealth. And thus that which begins and actually constitutes any political society is nothing but the consent of a majority to unite and incorporate into such a society. And this is that, and that only, which did or could give beginning to any lawful government in the world.

To this I find two objections made.

First: That there are no instances to be found in story of a company of men independent, and equal one amongst another, that met together and in this way began to set up a government.

Secondly: 'Tis impossible of right that men should do so, because all men being born under government, they are to submit to that, and are not at liberty to begin a new one. . . .

Every man being, as has been shown, naturally free, and nothing being able to put him into subjection to any earthly power but only his own consent, it is to be considered what shall be understood to be sufficient declaration of a man's consent to make him subject to the laws of any government. There is a common distinction of an express and a tacit consent, which will concern our present case. Nobody doubts but an express consent of any man entering into any society makes him a perfect member of that society, a subject of that

---

[1] Only to leave.—Ed.

government. The difficulty is, what ought to be looked upon as a tacit consent, and how far it binds, *i.e.*, how far any one shall be looked on to have consented, and thereby submitted to any government, where he has made no expressions of it at all. And to this I say that every man that hath any possession or enjoyment of any part of the dominions of any government doth thereby give his tacit consent, and is as far forth obliged to obedience to the laws of that government during such enjoyment as any one under it; whether this his possession be of land to him and his heirs for ever, or a lodging for only a week; or whether it be barely travelling freely on the highway; and in effect it reaches as far as the very being of any one within the territories of that government.

To understand this better, it is fit to consider that every man when he at first incorporates himself into any commonwealth, he, by his uniting himself thereunto, annexes also, and submits to the community those possessions which he has or shall acquire that do not already belong to any other government; for it would be a direct contradiction for any one to enter into society with others for the securing and regulating of property, and yet to suppose his land, whose property is to be regulated by the laws of the society, should be exempt from the jurisdiction of that government to which he himself, and the property of the land, is a subject. By the same act, therefore, whereby, any one unites his person, which was before free, to any commonwealth, by the same he unites his possessions, which was before free, to it also; and they become, both of them, person and possession, subject to the government and dominion of that commonwealth as long as it hath a being. Whoever therefore from thenceforth by inheritance, purchases, permission, or otherwise, enjoys any part of the land so annexed to, and under the government of that commonwealth, must take it with the condition it is under, that is, of submitting to the government of the commonwealth under whose jurisdiction it is as far forth as any subject of it.

But since the government has a direct jurisdiction only over the land, and reaches the possessor of it (before he has actually incorporated himself in the society), only as he dwells upon, and enjoys that: the obligation any one is under, by virtue of such enjoyment, to submit to the government, begins and ends with the enjoyment; so that whenever the owner, who has given nothing but such a tacit consent to the government, will by donation, sale, or otherwise, quit the said possession, he is at liberty to go and incorporate himself into any other commonwealth, or to agree with others to begin a new one (*in vacuis locis*)[2] in any part of the world they can find free and unpossessed. Whereas he that has once by actual agreement and any express declaration given his consent to be of any commonweal is perpetually and indispensably obliged to be and remain unalterably a subject to it, and can never be again in the liberty of the state of nature; unless, by any calamity, the government he was under

[2] In an empty place.—Ed.

comes to be dissolved, or else by some public acts cuts him off from being any longer a member of it.

But submitting to the laws of any country, living quietly and enjoying privileges and protection under them makes not a man a member of that society. This is only a local protection and homage due to and from all those who, not being in the state of war, come within the territories belonging to any government to all parts whereof the force of its law extends. But this no more makes a man a member of that society a perpetual subject of that commonwealth, than it would make a man a subject to another in whose family he found it convenient to abide for some time; though whilst he continued in it he were obliged to comply with the laws, and submit to the government he found there. And thus we see, that foreigners by living all their lives under another government, and enjoying the privileges and protection of it, though they are bound even in conscience to submit to its administration as far forth as any denizen, yet do not thereby come to be subjects or members of that commonwealth. Nothing can make any man so, but his actually entering into it by positive engagement, and express promise and compact. This is that, which I think, concerning the beginning of political societies, and that consent which makes any one a member of any commonwealth.

Of the Ends
of Political Society
and Government

If man in the state of nature be so free, as has been said, if he be absolute lord of his own person and possessions, equal to the greatest, and subject to nobody, why will he part with his freedom, this empire, and subject himself to the dominion and control of any other power? To which, it is obvious to answer, that though in the state of nature he hath such a right, yet the enjoyment of it is very uncertain, and constantly exposed to the invasions of others. For all being kings as much as he, every man his equal, and the greater part no strict observers of equity and justice, the enjoyment of the property he has in this state is very unsafe, very unsecure. This makes him willing to quit this condition, which, however free, is full of fears and continual dangers; and it is not without reason that he seeks out and is willing to join in society with others, who are already united, or have a mind to unite, for the mutual preservation of their lives, liberties, and estates, which I call by the general name property.

The great and chief end, therefore, of men's uniting into commonwealths, and putting themselves under a government, is the preservation of their property; to which in the state of nature there are many things wanting.

First, There wants an established, settled, known law, received and allowed by common consent to be the standard of right and wrong, and the common measure to decide all controversies between them. For though the law of nature be plain and intelligible to all rational creatures; yet men, being biased by their interest, as well as ignorant for want of study of it, are not apt to allow of it as a law binding to them in the application of it to their particular cases.

Secondly, In the state of nature there wants a known and indifferent judge, with authority to determine all differences according to the established law. For every one in that state, being both judge and executioner of the law of nature, men being partial to themselves, passion and revenge is very apt to carry them too far, and with too much heat in their own cases, as well as negligence and unconcernedness, to make them too remiss in other men's.

Thirdly, In the state of nature there often wants power to back and support the sentence when right, and to give it due execution. They who by any injustice offend will seldom fail, where they are able by force to make good their injustice; such resistance many times makes the punishment dangerous, and frequently destructive to those who attempt it.

Thus mankind, notwithstanding all the privileges of the state of nature, being but in an ill condition, while they remain in it, are quickly driven into society. Hence it comes to pass that we seldom find any number of men live any time together in this state. The inconveniences that they are therein exposed to by the irregular and uncertain exercise of the power every man has of punishing the transgressions of others, make them take sanctuary under the established laws of government, and therein seek the preservation of their property. It is this makes them so willingly give up every one his single power of punishing, to be exercised by such alone, as shall be appointed to it amongst them; and by such rules as the community, or those authorised by them to that purpose, shall agree on. And in this we have the original right and rise of both the legislative and executive power, as well as of the governments and societies themselves.

For in the state of nature, to omit the liberty he has of innocent delights, a man has two powers.

The first is to do whatsoever he thinks fit for the preservation of himself, and others within the permission of the law of nature, by which law, common to them all, he and all the rest of mankind are of one community, make up one society, distinct from all other creatures. And were it not for the corruption and viciousness of degenerate men there would be no need of any other, no necessity that men should separate from this great and natural community, and associate into lesser combinations.

The other power a man has in the state of nature is the power to punish the crimes committed against that law. Both these he gives up when he joins in a private, if I may so call it, or particular political society, and incorporates into any commonwealth separate from the rest of mankind.

The first power, viz., of doing whatsoever he thought fit for the preservation of himself and the rest of mankind, he gives up to be regulated by laws made by the society, so far forth as the preservation of himself and the rest of that society shall require; which laws of the society in many things confine the liberty he had by the law of nature.

Secondly, The power of punishing he wholly gives up, and engages his natural force (which he might before employ in the execution of the law of nature, by his own single authority as he thought fit), to assist the executive power of the society, as the law thereof shall require. For being now in a new state, wherein he is to enjoy many conveniences, from the labour, assistance, and society of others in the same community, as well as protection from its whole strength; he has to part also with as much of his natural liberty, in providing for himself, as the good, prosperity and safety of the society shall require; which is not only necessary but just, since the other members of the society do the like.

But though men when they enter into society give up the equality, liberty and executive power they had in the state of nature into the hands of the society, to be so far disposed of by the legislative as the good of the society shall require; yet it being only with an intention in every one the better to preserve himself, his liberty and property (for no rational creature can be supposed to change his condition with an intention to be worse), the power of the society, or legislative constituted by them, can never be supposed to extend farther than the common good, but is obliged to secure every one's property by providing against those three defects above mentioned that made the state of nature so unsafe and uneasy. And so whoever has the legislative or supreme power of any commonwealth is bound to govern by established standing laws, promulgated and known to the people, and not by extemporary decrees; by indifferent and upright judges, who are to decide controversies by those laws; and to employ the force of the community at home only in the execution of such laws, or abroad, to prevent or redress foreign injuries, and secure the community from inroads and invasion. And all this to be directed to no other end but the peace, safety, and public good of the people.

Of the Dissolution of Government

He that will with any clearness speak of the dissolution of government ought, in the first place, to distinguish between the dissolution of the society and the dissolution of the government. That which makes the community, and brings men out of the loose state of nature into one politic society, is the agreement which every one has with the rest to incorporate and act as one body, and so be one distinct commonwealth. The usual and almost only way whereby this union is dissolved, is the inroad of foreign force making a conquest upon them. For in that case (not being able to maintain and support themselves as one entire and independent body) the union belonging to that body which consisted therein must necessarily cease, and so every one return to the state he was in before, with a liberty to shift for himself and provide for his own safety as he thinks fit in some other society. Whenever the society is dissolved, it is certain the government of that society cannot remain. Thus conquerors' swords often cut up governments by the roots, and mangle societies to pieces, separating the subdued or scattered multitude from the protection of and dependence on that society which ought to have preserved them from violence. The world is too well instructed in, and too forward to allow of this way of dissolving of governments, to need any more to be said of it; and there wants not much argument to prove that where the society is dissolved, the government cannot remain—that being as impossible as for the frame of a house to subsist when the materials of it are scattered and displaced by a whirlwind, or jumbled into a confused heap by an earthquake.

Besides this overturning from without, governments are dissolved from within.

First, When the legislative is altered. Civil society being a state of peace amongst those who are of it, from whom the state of war is excluded by the umpirage which they have provided in their legislative for the ending all differences that may rise amongst any of them, it is in their legislative that the members of a commonwealth are united and combined together in one coherent living body. This is the soul that gives form, life, and unity to the commonwealth. From hence the several members have their mutual influence, sympathy, and connection. And, therefore, when the legislative is broken or dissolved, dissolution and death follow. For the essence and union of the society consisting in having one will, the legislative, when once established by the majority, has the declaring and, as it were, keeping of, that will. The constitution of the legislative is the first and fundamental act of the society, whereby provision is made for the continuation of their union, under the direction of persons and bonds of laws made by persons authorised thereunto by the consent and appointment of the people, without which no one man or number of men amongst them can have authority of making laws that shall be binding to the rest. When any one or more shall take upon them to make laws, whom the people have not appointed so to do, they make laws without authority, which the people are not therefore bound to obey; by which means they come again to be one of subjection, and may constitute to themselves a new legislative, as they think best, being in full liberty to resist the force of those who without authority would impose anything upon them. Every one is at the disposure of his own will when those who had by the delegation of the society the declaring of the public will, are excluded from it, and others usurp the place who have no such authority or delegation. . . .

In these and the like cases, when the government is dissolved, the people are at liberty to provide for themselves by erecting a new legislative, differing from the other, by the change of persons, or form, or both, as they shall find it most for their safety and good. For the society can never, by the fault of another, lose the native and original right it has to preserve itself, which can only be done by a settled legislative, and a fair and impartial execution of the laws made by it. But the state of mankind is not so miserable that they are not capable of using this remedy, till it be too late to look for any. To tell people they may provide for themselves by erecting a new legislative, when by oppression, artifice, or being delivered over to a foreign power, their old one is gone, is only to tell them they may expect relief when it is too late, and the evil is past cure. This is in effect no more than to bid them first be slaves, and then to take care of their liberty; and when their chains are on tell them they may act like freemen. This, if barely so, is rather mockery than relief; and men can never be secure from tyranny if there be no means to escape it till they are perfectly under it. And therefore it is that they have not only a right to get out of it, but to prevent it.

There is therefore secondly another way whereby governments are dissolved, and that is when the legislative or the prince, either of them, act contrary to their trust.

First, The legislative acts against the trust reposed in them when they endeavour to invade the property of the subject, and to make themselves or any part of the community masters or arbitrary disposers of the lives, liberties, or fortunes of the people.

The reason why men enter into society is the preservation of their property; and the end why they choose and authorise a legislative is that there may be laws made, and rules set, as guards and fences to the properties of all the members of the society to limit the power and moderate the dominion of every part and member of the society. For since it can never be supposed to be the will of the society that the legislative should have a power to destroy that which every one designs secure by entering into society, and for which the people submitted themselves to legislators of their own making, whenever the legislators endeavour to take away and destroy the property of the people, or to reduce them to slavery under arbitrary power, they put themselves into a state of war with the people, who are thereupon absolved from any further obedience, and are left to the common refuge which God hath provided for all men against force and violence. Whensoever, therefore, the legislative shall transgress this fundamental rule of society, and either by ambition, fear, folly, or corruption, endeavour to grasp themselves or put into the hands of any other an absolute power over the lives, liberties, and estates of the people, by this breach of trust they forfeit the power the people had put into their hands, for quite contrary ends, and it devolves to the people, who have a right to resume their original liberty, and by the establishment of the new legislative (such as they shall think fit) provide for their own safety and security, which is the end for which they are in society. What I have said here concerning the legislative in general, holds true also concerning the supreme executor, who having a double trust put in him, both to have a part in the legislative and the supreme execution of the law, acts against both when he goes about to set up his own arbitrary will as the law of the society. He acts also contrary to his trust when he either employs the force, treasure, and offices of the society, to corrupt the representatives, and gain them to his purposes; or openly pre-engages the electors, and prescribes to their choice such whom he has by solicitations, threats, promises, or otherwise won to his designs, and employs them to bring in such, who have promised beforehand what to vote and what to enact. Thus to regulate candidates and electors, and new-model the ways of election, what is it but to cut up the government by the roots, and poison the very fountain of public security? For the people having reserved to themselves the choice of their representatives as the fence to their properties, could do it for no other end but that they might always be freely chosen, and, so chosen, freely act and advise as the necessity of the commonwealth and the public good should upon examination and mature debate be judged to require. This those who give their votes before they hear the debate, and have weighed the reason on all sides, are not capable of doing. To prepare such an assembly as this, and endeavour to set up the declared abettors of his own will for the true representatives of the people and the lawmakers of the society, is certainly as great a breach of trust and as perfect a declaration of a design to subvert the government as is possible to be met with. To which if one shall add rewards and punishments visibly employed to the same end and all the arts of perverted law made use of to take off and destroy all that stand in the way of such a design, and will not comply and consent to betray the liberties of their country, it will be past doubt what is doing. What power they ought to have in the society who thus employ it contrary to the trust that went along with it in its first institution is easy to determine; and one cannot but see that he who has once attempted any such thing as this cannot any longer be trusted.

To this perhaps it will be said that, the people being ignorant and always discontented, to lay the foundation of government in the unsteady opinion and uncertain humour of the people is to expose it to certain ruin; and no government will be able long to subsist if the people may set up a new legislative whenever they take offence at the old one. To this I answer: Quite the contrary. People are not so easily got out of their old forms as some are apt to suggest. They are hardly to be prevailed with to amend the acknowledged faults in the frame they have been accustomed to. And if there be any original defects, or adventitious ones introduced by time or corruption, it is not an easy thing to get them changed, even when all the world sees there is an opportunity for it. This slowness and aversion in the people to quit their old constitutions has, in the many revolutions which have been seen in this kingdom, in this and former ages still kept us to, or after some interval of fruitless attempts still brought us back again to our old legislative of King, Lords, and Commons. And whatever provocations have made the crown be taken from some of our princes' heads, they never carried the people so far as to place it in another line.

But it will be said, this hypothesis lays a ferment for frequent rebellion. To which I answer:

First, no more than any other hypothesis. For when the people are made miserable, and find themselves exposed to the ill-usage of arbitrary power, cry up their governors as much as you will for sons of Jupiter, let them be sacred and divine, descended, or authorised from heaven, give them out for whom or what you please, the same will happen. The people generally ill-treated, and contrary to right, will be ready upon any occasion to ease themselves of a burden that sits heavy upon them. They will wish and seek for the opportunity, which in the change, weakness, and accidents of human affairs seldom delays long to offer itself. He must have lived but a little while in the world who has not seen examples of this in his time, and he must have read very little who cannot produce examples of it in all sorts of governments in the world.

Secondly, I answer, such revolutions happen not upon every little mismanagement in public affairs. Great mistakes in the ruling part, many wrong and inconvenient laws, and all the slips of human frailty will be borne by the people without mutiny or murmur. But if a long train of abuses, prevarications and artifices, all tending the same way, make the design visible to the people—and they cannot but feel what they lie under, and see whither they are going—it is not to be wondered that they should then rouse themselves and endeavour to put the rule into such hands which may secure to them the ends for which government was at first erected, and without which ancient names and specious forms are so far from being better that they are much worse than the state of nature or pure anarchy; the inconveniences being all as great and as near, but the remedy farther off and more difficult.

Thirdly, I answer that this power in the people of providing for their safety anew by a new legislative when their legislators have acted contrary to their trust by invading their property, is the best fence against rebellion, and the probablest means to hinder it. For rebellion being an opposition, not to persons, but authority, which is founded only in the constitutions and laws of the government, those whoever they be who by force break through, and by force justify their violation of them, are truly and properly rebels. For when men by entering into society and civil government have excluded force, and introduced laws for the preservation of property, peace, and unity amongst themselves, those who set up force again in opposition to the laws do *rebellare* —that is, bring back again the state of war—and are properly rebels; which they who are in power (by pretence they have to authority, the temptation of force they have in their hands, and the flattery of those about them) being likeliest to do, the properest way to prevent the evil is to show them the danger and injustice of it who are under the greatest temptation to run into it.

In both the fore-mentioned cases, when either the legislative is changed or the legislators act contrary to the end for which they were constituted, those who are guilty are guilty of rebellion. For if anyone by force takes away the established legislative of any society, and the laws by them made pursuant to their trust, he thereby takes away the umpirage which everyone had consented to for a peaceable decision of all their controversies, and a bar to the state of war amongst them. They who remove or change the legislative, take away this decisive power, which nobody can have but by the appointment and consent of the people, and so destroying the authority which the people did, and nobody else can, set up; and introducing a power which the people hath not authorised, actually introduce a state of war which is that of force without authority. And thus by removing the legislative established by the society (in whose decisions the people acquiesced and united as to that of their own will), they untie the knot and expose the people anew to the state of war. And if those who by force take away the legislative are rebels, the legislators themselves, as has been shown, can be no less esteemed so, when they who were set up for the protection and preservation of the people, their liberties and properties, shall by force invade and endeavour to take them away; and so they, putting themselves into a state of war with those who made them the protectors and guardians of their peace, are properly and with the greatest aggravation *rebellants* (rebels).

But if they who say it lays a foundation for rebellion mean that it may occasion civil wars or intestine broils, to tell the people they are absolved from obedience when illegal attempts are made upon their liberties or properties, and may oppose the unlawful violence of those who were their magistrates when they invade their properties contrary to the trust put in them and that therefore this doctrine is not to be allowed, being so destructive to the peace of the world: they may as well say upon the same ground that honest men may not oppose robbers or pirates because this may occasion disorder or bloodshed. If any mischief come in such cases, it is not to be charged upon him who defends his own right, but on him that invades his neighbour's. If the innocent honest man must quietly quit all he has for peace's sake to him who will lay violent hands upon it, I desire it may be considered what a kind of peace there will be in the world which consists only in violence and rapine, and which is to be maintained only for the benefit of robbers and oppressors. Who would not think it an admirable peace betwixt the mighty and the mean when the lamb without resistance yielded his throat to be torn by the imperious wolf? Polyphemus's den gives us a perfect pattern of such a peace and such a government, wherein Ulysses and his companions had nothing to do but quietly to suffer themselves to be devoured. And no doubt Ulysses, who was a prudent man, preached up passive obedience, and exhorted them to a quiet submission by representing to them of what concernment peace was to mankind, and by showing the inconveniences which might happen if they should offer to resist Polyphemus, who had now the power over them.

The end of government is the good of mankind, and which is best for mankind, that the people should be always exposed to the boundless will of tyranny, or that the rulers should be sometimes liable to be opposed when they grow exorbitant in the use of their power, and employ it for the destruction and not the preservation of the properties of their people?

Nor let anyone say that mischief can arise from hence, as often as it shall please a busy head or turbulent spirit to desire the alteration of the government.

It is true such men may stir whenever they please, but it will be only to their own just ruin and perdition. For till the mischief be grown general, and the ill-designs of the rulers become visible, or their attempts sensible to the greater part, the people who are more disposed to suffer than right themselves by re-sistance are not apt to stir. The examples of particular injustice or oppression of here and there an unfortunate man, move them not. But if they universally have a persuasion grounded upon manifest evidence that designs are carrying on against their liberties, and the general course and tendency of things cannot but give them strong suspicions of the evil intention of their governors, who is to be blamed for it? Who can help it if they who might avoid it bring them-selves into this suspicion? Are the people to be blamed, if they have the sense of rational creatures, and can think of things no otherwise than as they find and feel them? And is it not rather their fault who put things into such a posture, that they would not have them thought to be as they are? I grant that the pride, ambition, and turbulency of private men have sometimes caused great disorders in commonwealths, and factions have been fatal to states and kingdoms. But whether the mischief hath oftener begun in the people's wanton-ness, and a desire to cast off the lawful authority of their rulers, or in the ruler's insolence, and endeavours to get and exercise an arbitrary power over their people; whether oppression or disobedience gave the first rise to the dis-order, I leave it to impartial history to determine. This I am sure, whoever, either ruler or subject, by force goes about to invade the rights of either prince or people, and lays the foundation for overturning the constitution and fame of any just government, he is guilty of the greatest crime I think a man is capable of, being to answer for all those mischiefs of blood, rapine, and desola-tion, which the breaking to pieces of governments brings on a country. And he who does it is justly to be esteemed the common enemy and pest of mankind, and is to be treated accordingly. . . .

To conclude, the power that every individual gave the society when he entered into it, can never revert to the individuals again as long as the society lasts, but will always remain in the community, because without this there can be no community, no commonwealth, which is contrary to the original agree-ment; so also when the society hath placed the legislative in any assembly of men to continue in them and their successors, with direction and authority for providing such successors, the legislative can never revert to the people whilst that government lasts, because having provided a legislative with power to con-tinue for ever, they have given up their political power to the legislative and cannot resume it. But if they have set limits to the duration of their legislative, and made this supreme power in any person or assembly only temporary; or else when by the miscarriages of those in authority it is forfeited; upon the forfeiture, or at the determination of the time set, it reverts to the society, and the people have a right to act as supreme, and continue the legislative in them-selves; or place it in a new form, or new hands as they think good.

VAN DEN HAAG

*This concluding essay by the distinguished conservative Ernest
van den Haag (1914–) accurately captures the uncertainty which
any thoughtful man must experience when faced with the conflict
between individual conscience and the social authority of the law.
First van den Haag states with great clarity and force the case
of obedience to the law, especially to law which issues from a
genuinely democratic majority. Then, with equal clarity and force,
he explains why neither he nor any other man of conscience can
agree unconditionally to obey whatever the majority should decide
to write into law.*

*Having posed a seemingly unsolvable problem, van den Haag
proceeds to analyze the types of disobedience to authority in an
attempt to develop some general principles for relating authority to
conscience. In the end, he confesses defeat, for after all the clarification and analysis have been done, the central question remains: What
shall I do when a legitimate democratic state commands me to do
what I know in my heart to be evil? Nothing could express the
intractability of this problem better than the anguished honesty
with which van den Haag admits his own failure.*

*Government, Conscience,
and Disobedience*

1. Is the Law Morally Binding?

If one greatly simplifies his views, Thomas Hobbes may be regarded
as having felt that any organization of society is better than none, and that
citizens for the sake of preserving it should obey all laws regardless of specific
justification for them. This view may have been shared by St. Paul.[1] The premise seems correct, but the conclusion does not follow. One may reason more

[1] Romans 13:1–10. John Locke, too, though on grounds of implicit consent, thought
that "no man in civil society can be exempt from the laws of it." *Of Civil Government*
(New York, 1924), p. 164.

cogently that obedience to penal law cannot ever be meant to be optional. The law peremptorily forbids some acts individuals might choose, regardless of whether they are motivated by a moral impulse or by anything else. If the law were not binding on all its subjects, regardless of the conscience of each, it would be an option and, therefore, not law. To claim the right to choose among laws and to disobey those one's conscience opposes is to deny the binding character of penal law. Yet this binding character is essential to the law's social function. Neither conscience alone nor power alone can replace it: options cannot regulate social life.

If one claims the moral right to disobey laws for the sake of one's conscience, one must grant to others as well the right to disobey laws opposed by their consciences (or to oppose interpretations of law or of the nature and source of their moral obligations). Unless the legal command coincides with that of his conscience, everyone would have a moral right to disobey any law. Segregationists could segregate, following their consciences, while desegregationists could desegregate, following theirs. Whenever opposed by conscience, taxes would be no more obligatory than national defense. Oppressors, following their consciences, could oppress; the oppressed, following theirs, could resist. Both would be entitled by their conscience to defy the law, and the stronger party would win in the ensuing nonviolent (?) conflict, which would be continuous and unending since no outcome could produce a rule morally binding any party. The law could not even temporarily settle conflicts among citizens, or limit their conduct. Relations among citizens would rest on their divergent consciences—and on whatever power each group might muster to make its conscience prevail. Such social order as there might be would depend on power alone; those who conformed to its rules owing but to compulsion would owe no allegiance to it except where it coincided with the impulses of their consciences. Once they are not regarded as morally binding, laws are hard to enforce without a police state.[2] (Police of course would follow their consciences in the methods of law enforcement, and in determining what laws to enforce.) The outcome would be a social organization depending on naked power alone, therefore exceedingly precarious as well as brutal, perhaps unviable, and certainly immoral. The superiority of conscience to law is usually advocated without awareness of these implications.[3] The paradoxical result—

[2] The principle which entitles the individual conscience to supersede law, although itself a moral principle, may be interpreted to deny the validity of moral norms as well. For moral norms must be universally binding if they are to be moral norms (though they may differ from laws with respect to enforcement or subject matter) and thus not superseded by individual conscience. But as a principle of nonuniversality the individual conscience cannot consistently claim universality. Further the individual conscience could no longer rest on moral principles once it denies universality.

[3] There are exceptions. Professor Staughton Lynd is partially aware of the implications, but unconcerned. In his *Civil Liberties in Wartime* (mimeographed) presented to the Biennial Conference of the Civil Liberties Union at Stony Brook, New York (1966), he

absolute reliance on conscience rather than law must end in absolute reliance on naked power—is seldom acknowledged. Explicating the implications makes refutation superfluous. But a positive statement of moral grounds for obeying the law remains necessary if possible qualifications are to be considered.

For a citizen to regard his government as legitimate is to grant it the authority to govern, and, thereby, to accept his obligation to obey its laws—the instrumentalities through which it governs—as superseding the will and conscience of individual citizens, including his own. One cannot claim the right to disobey, and thus to regard as illegitimate, the laws of a government to which one has granted the right to make them. If one accepts the government and its procedures as legitimate, and the law in question has been found legitimate by these procedures, one cannot deny one's obligation to obey it whether or not it is morally displeasing to do so—such a denial would deny the government the legislative power one has granted to it. Laws are made because unanimous agreement with, and voluntary assent to, the rule promulgated is *not* expected. The law obligates dissenters to obey—it does not give them the right to claim that their dissent exempts them from the obligation which is imposed precisely to create in action the unanimity lacking in opinion.

The government's authority to legislate and the citizen's obligation to obey the law can be rejected or qualified only on one or more of three grounds: (1) By regarding no government as legitimate and denying the binding character of any law. (This is the anarchist position.) (2) By regarding only some governments as legitimate. (This is the legitimist position vis-à-vis usurpation, the revolutionary position vis-à-vis a nonrevolutionary regime, and the democratic position vis-à-vis a nondemocratic regime. The laws of governments thought illegitimate are regarded as morally binding only when they do not essentially differ from those of a legitimate government, nor prevent its establishment.) (3) By regarding only some laws as legitimate; i.e., by regarding the legislative authority of all governments as limited by certain a priori principles whether or not explicitly stated. (This is the natural law position held on religious or philosophical grounds; and the natural rights position, held, e.g., by John Locke; but the position may be taken without relying on either.) Let us consider the three positions.

(1) "The life of a man" is not only "solitary, poor, nasty, brutish, and short" in the "state of nature"; it might be impossible, for no society is viable without accepted and enforced general rules. *Ubi societas, ibi jus.* Legislation, adjudication, and enforcement may be products of custom rather than of formal legal process, but this at best defeats the individual conscience—whether or not there is awareness of it—let alone justice, no less than formal judicial processes.

The belief that the individual conscience, unaided by law nor superseded

---

supports civil disobedience for both segregationists and desegregationists, as well as taxpayers, draftees, Negroes, *et al.* (even when motivated politically).

by it, could govern our actions, rests ultimately on a factual assertion, such as J. J. Rousseau's Pelagian: "Nature has made man happy and good—society corrupts him and causes his misery."[4] This is as patently wrong as wishful thinking ever can be.[5] The Augustinian belief in human depravity, in our corruption through the original *felix culpa*, clearly fits the facts, if not our wishes. It has been supported by Freud's observations about the id, the Oedipus complex, and the contribution of society—of internalized and constantly reinforced social rules—to the psychic developments that make us human, and sometimes moral: the ego and the superego. Actual observations of infants and of primitive tribes suggest that savages are not particularly "noble," "happy," or "free" and that infants are savages.[6] Conscience not only is a creature of society rather than of nature, but it requires constant reinforcement and realignment by penal law to remain effective and to make social life tolerable, or even possible. Thus any society, to continue as such, must recognize and enforce the moral obligation to obey its laws.

(2) I shall not defend the view that authority is always *ipso facto* legitimate. The legitimist regards as morally binding only the laws made by *legitimate* authority. Legitimacy may be established by the consent of the governed, by traditions and divine ordination, or by a revolutionary ethos. Thus, for a democrat the laws of a nondemocratic government are not morally binding—at least not when they function to stifle dissent and perpetuate the (illegitimate) nondemocratic authority. Further, laws enacted only because dissent was stifled are not morally binding, since they have been imposed by illegitimate power alone. On the other hand, laws which might have been consented to, even though no formal consent was given, as for example those dealing with theft, divorce, and murder, are binding even when the enacting authority is not legitimate. The law is tainted by the vice of the enacting authority only if it is clearly produced thereby, if no legitimate authority would have enacted it. In a tyranny, civil disobedience is justifiable for a democrat—though usually less effective and not more feasible than violent revolution. Revolution is justifiable in a system where the majority of citizens

---

[4] Of course Rousseau simply equates "nature" with the paradise of old described by the Bible and in Ovid's *Metamorphoses: "sponte sua sine lege fidem rectumque colebat . . . erant sine iudice tuti"* (everybody spontaneously, without law, kept promises and acted justly . . . [all] were secure without judges). Unlike anarchists, Ovid and the Bible acknowledged this happy state to be extrahistorical, and Rousseau himself inferred position (3) rather than (1) from his premise.

[5] Even if "nature" were that provident, we could not actually dispense with those laws which make indivisible value decisions, wherever the alternatives are not "good" and not "good" and "bad." See Ralph Ross and Ernest van den Haag, *The Fabric of Society* (New York: Harcourt, Brace and World, Inc., 1957), pp. 628–30.

[6] For a discussion of the utopian beliefs on which anarchism rests, and of what knowledge of reality psychoanalysis has given us, see Ernest van den Haag, "Psychoanalysis and Utopia," Freud Memorial Lecture, *Bulletin, Philadelphia Association for Psychoanalysis* (June, 1965).

are bereft of an effective right freely, peacefully, and by legitimate means to oust the government.[7] However, where the citizens do have the effective rights needed to oust the government legitimately, revolution cannot be justified from a democratic standpoint; it would necessarily replace democracy with tyranny.[8] Similarly, civil disobedience cannot be justified when there are law-abiding alternative ways of expressing dissent and urging change. But where there is no way of dissenting from a law except to violate it, where disobedience is the most effective way to argue against it and to urge a change, civil disobedience may be justified.

(3) According to the biblical tale, Abraham accepted God as so absolute a sovereign—*potestas legibus absoluta*—that he was ready to obey a divine command as immoral as it must have been contrary to his natural feeling: to sacrifice his son Isaac. At the last moment God stayed his hand. History since makes us chary of relying on God to stay our hands from carrying out immoral commands of a legislature. Outside of democracy, democrats may deny the legitimacy of the legislating authority and feel free to decide whether the law should be obeyed. And we can, of course, always resist, and at times we must, illegal commands in a democracy as well. But what about *legal* commands of legitimate authority when they are deeply contrary to our moral sense? How absolute is our obligation to obey the law made by legitimate process by the sovereign whom we grant the right to legislate? Fortunately actual and unequivocal cases cannot be cited to illustrate the dilemma I have in mind as it might occur in a democracy. But it can be imagined. Suppose a democratic government decrees that all circumcised people, or all redheaded or black-skinned people, are to be killed wantonly—without the justification that a worse evil is to be averted by the killing or evidence of individual guilt (though the majority may superstitiously think there is). The law is upheld by the highest court (or the constitution is changed by appropriate process to validate it). We continue to live in a democracy. I freely and publicly oppose the law; but my attempts to persuade fellow citizens, though undisturbed, are unavailing. The majority continues to vote for the immoral law, or for legislators favoring it. I would feel in duty bound not only to oppose, but also to disobey, so immoral a law. Else, I would have accepted democratic procedure as the ultimate arbiter, at least of collective moral questions. I do not propose to do so. If I have the courage, I might try to help victims escape. If I have friends,

---

[7] This right is "effective" when citizens can organize and persuade each other, so that the minority has the means to become a majority—though it may not succeed, of course.

[8] Even the attempt to persuade citizens to elect a government that would not allow itself to be peacefully ousted is not legitimate in a democracy and should be outlawed. See Ross and van den Haag, *op. cit.*, p. 632. Hence I continue to disagree with Sidney Hook, who in quoting me pushed fairness so far as to make my argument more persuasive than his own. Sidney Hook, *The Paradoxes of Freedom* (Berkeley: University of California Press, 1962), pp. 132 ff.

I might try to overthrow, by violence, so monstrous a majority government, in favor of a more humane minority government. Although acknowledging my general obligation to obey the law, I would feel a superior obligation to disobey this law, and even to overthrow the democratic majority whose right to govern and to make laws I generally uphold.[9] The difficulty arises because obedience to law, although generally best, is not always good, and democratic government, although on the whole most justifiable, is not always just. Here, both seem worse than disobedience and insurrection. Yet, to say as much is merely to state and not to solve a most troublesome dilemma: in conceivable, if unlikely, instances, one should disobey a law opposed by one's conscience, although the law is validly enacted by the legitimate authority to which one grants the right to enact laws superseding one's conscience.[10] How can we grant our government the right to make binding laws and yet reserve to ourselves the right to decide individually whether we are bound? For this last decision cannot in turn be made by law or by any social authority.

We cannot state a principle of sufficient specificity and generality to permit us to deduce from it when to follow law and when not to obey it. No principle can justify either conscience or law as a priori absolutes, so that, where they conflict, one must *always* follow either. If one could state a principle to tell when to disobey the law, the principle could be incorporated into the law: laws would have to be obeyed only if legitimate—if they conformed to the principle. Apart from general and vague appeals to "justice," "morality," "humanity," or "nature"—which do not help in specific cases—no such principle has been found. Even if it were not beyond the wit of man to formulate such principles with some specificity, they still would not solve the problem. If incorporated into law (if they are not, the problem only becomes harder)— as exemplified in our Constitution to some extent—they still have to be interpreted. Nothing interprets itself. By definition, interpretations of the law or constitution are needed because they cannot be anticipated with certainty by deduction. Thus, even if constitutional superlaw embodies all the principles one hopes will invalidate grossly immoral laws which the majority might otherwise make, the principles could be perversely (according to my conscience) interpreted by a supreme court and the immoral laws declared valid. The constitution itself might be changed too. Unless one is prepared always to subordinate one's own moral views to a procedural absolute, one might be confronted with laws one will feel oneself in duty bound to disobey, even if one recognizes a general obligation to obey.

---

[9] Note that John Locke grants the right to revolution when the government deprives citizens of their natural right to life, liberty, and property. But he envisages exclusively a democratic or at least majority revolution against the (minority) government and does not deal with a wrongful majority government. Locke, *op. cit.*, pp. 231, 203, *passim.*

[10] I neglect the comparatively trivial case of law-breaking to achieve the legislative intent, for the sake of focusing on law-breaking meant to defeat it.

To be sure, should I be unable to express my dissent and to try to persuade my fellow citizens, as a democrat I may cease to regard the government as legitimate and myself as obligated to obey laws not freely consented to. The moral right to decide which laws to follow would then revert to me. But the hard problem is what to do when a majority freely decides—and leaves dissent unimpeded—to do something so monstrous that my conscience rebels. Can I rely on my rebellious conscience then? I see no more reason to regard my conscience as an absolute than to so regard the law. Perhaps it is a less reliable guide than that of the majority. It seems unlikely that only I—and a few others —know what is right and the great majority does not. Yet, likely or not, it is conceivable, and some solution for the instances illustrated above is required. It is not enough to be guided by one's conscience, *or* by the law. We need a way of determining *when* either should prevail over the other, and why, and by what means.

The theoretical solutions historically offered—natural rights or natural law theories, theories relying on moral intuition, human nature, God, or conscience—state rather than solve the problem at best; at worst, they evade it. For the problem is not *whether* positive laws should be disobeyed whenever contrary to natural rights, laws, conscience, God, or any other principle. The problem is how to decide *when* they are. The problem of morally authoritative interpretation remains, however far we regress in search of a principle of validation (or invalidation) for positive law. By what authority other than individual conscience can "natural law" be safely interpreted? Yet individual consciences differ. Thus different individuals might engage in conflicting conduct—based on different consciences; we lack a binding *social* rule—yet we have just shown that even legitimate laws cannot always be morally binding, and that we cannot conceive of social authorities to decide when they are. The legislator, backed by the majority, thinks that his legislation conforms to natural law, conscience, and other accepted principles; but the individual conscience may think otherwise. No high tribunal can be assumed a priori to be morally right, or incapable of backing moral monstrosities; nor can the individual conscience be relied on.

We have come full circle. The law is needed to supersede individual consciences but cannot always be trusted to be right and binding. On the other hand, individual consciences cannot be trusted to decide rightly when to allow themselves to be superseded and bound, and when to disobey. When there is conflict the law must wholly supersede the individual conscience—yet cannot always do so: when the law is too immoral the individual conscience should rebel. But there can be no legal standard to indicate when the law should be rebelled against, and no other social standard. The tension between the law and the individual conscience is an aspect of the tension between the individual and the group and is unavoidable. It is as easy as it is futile to define this potential conflict away by redefining "law" or "morality" so that they must coincide, or so that they become irrelevant to each other. The conflict, however labeled, remains.[11]

2. Resistance to Law: Gradations

Since we can conceive of justifiable disobedience to law, let us consider the available types of disobedience. They may be graded according to the extent of the intended disruption of the legal order. In ascending order we have: (1) conscientious objection; (2) civil disobedience; (3) insurrection.

Usually the line between these means of resistance to law is not as clear in practice as it can be made in theory. Yet the distinctions—partly reflected in law—can be made, and the actions distinguished differ in degree of seriousness. Hence each type of action is appropriate to a class of circumstances.

(1) A refusal to follow a legal command, because of a fundamental moral or religious objection, is "conscientious objection." Examples are refusal to be drafted, to shoot at the enemy, to submit to vaccination. Our law actually exempts people at least from some legal duties when their consciences oppose them. But a democracy without such a privilege is entirely conceivable. (It is traditionally granted mainly in England and the United States.) Exemption can hardly be granted when, for example, failure to submit to vaccination endangers others who, though uninfected by moral scruples, may be infected by viruses. Even draft exemption could not be granted were it strongly infectious. When conscientious objectors are not exempted from the legal duty objected to, they often disobey the law.

Conscientious objection differs from civil disobedience because there need be no attempt to urge others to follow the course traced by the objector's conscience and there can be no attempts to compel others, or the government, to do so. The conscience of the objector prevents his participation in what it regards as wrong, but either it does not claim universal validity, or it does not claim the right to impose what it regards as universally valid on others. This

---

[11] Whereas I investigate principles to consider consistency and practical effects in the light of criteria of judgment such as the preservation of social order and of some moral imperatives, Professor Hook explores social practices in the light of criteria of judgment such as the preservation of liberty and of humanness. He develops the principles of permitted conduct through the desirability or undesirability of the observed practices. I congratulate myself upon finding that Professor Hook's conclusions differ from mine but in form, though he starts from the opposite end. By sticking to the concrete, Professor Hook is led to confront more immediately specific cases which he then uses to construct a pragmatic code which indicates where and to what extent and how conscience and law must limit each other and what forms their opposition may legitimately take. This Professor Hook has done magisterially in his "Social Protest and Civil Obedience," *The Humanist*, XXVII (Sept.–Dec., 1967), 5–6. The concreteness of his reasoning makes it possible for Professor Hook to avoid antinomies such as the one discussed in the text above.

conscience thus is solipsistic or rests on an entirely voluntaristic morality. Unlike civil disobedience, conscientious objection never involves more than violation of the law objected to (or, possibly, of laws not separable from it).

Conscientious objection is a psychic impediment, which might best be treated as though a physical impediment; *ultra posse nemo obligatur*,[12] though not meant for internal obstacles, may be applied by extension. Not that objectors are insane. But their conscience literally prevents them from doing what the law requires. If the evidence indicates that conscience is more than a pretext here and more than an opinion, for example if the objectors have been part of a group that has traditionally cultivated their conscientious objection, the best thing probably is to exempt them. If truly objectors, they are usually willing to accept alternative, and no less hazardous or hard, duties in war, or, in other cases, to help achieve a solution that both the community and their conscience can tolerate.

Conscientious (moral) objections must be sharply distinguished from political ones, if only by a sociological criterion. To prefer one's own political judgment to that of the majority is not conscientious objection. Refusal to serve in *any* war can be a moral matter. Refusal to serve in a *particular* war, against, for example, a Communist country, because one is a Communist, is a political matter. So is refusal to serve in any war because it is regarded as "unjust" or "aggressive," or because one has some grievance—racial or economic—against one's government. Not that ultimately the reasons for such refusal cannot be reduced to a moral judgment too. They can. Nevertheless, if such a refusal were recognized as "conscientious," the distinction between political and conscientious refusal would be lost. Anyone could refuse to serve or to pay taxes whenever his service, or his money, would be used for purposes he disapproved of. The individual conscience would become an absolute, the law an option. This would be worse than the law as an absolute.

The main effect of attempts to extend the legalization of conscientious objection might well be elimination of its legal status where it heretofore existed: If we grant people exemptions because in their political judgment a particular war is wrong, the most likely effect is the abolition of conscientious objection as a privilege. Should conscientious objection be so extended, it would be hard not to regard a convinced Nazi or Communist as a conscientious objector in the appropriate war, rather than, as the law hitherto has done, as someone who wrongfully gives his allegiance to a foreign sovereign, or disloyally disdains to do his duty.

In a democracy, conscientious objection is morally justifiable only when the majority decision (or the acts it requires from the citizen) altogether outrages—not merely offends—the religiously held *moral* principles of the objector, not merely his *political* views or ideology. The moral scruples must differ in kind, and exceed in intensity and depth, those we all may feel (about e.g.,

---

[12] No one is obligated beyond what is possible.—Ed.

killing a fellowman), and they must not depend on, or flow from, political allegiances.

Not much benefit is reaped by compelling a small group of people to act against religiously held convictions; and not much harm occurs by exempting them. However no society could survive at length if it permitted any citizen who opposed the social system as a whole or a policy of its government to refuse to perform the duties therefrom arising for all citizens. The opposition may oppose the majority government's decision to go to war; but if the opposition were allowed to refuse to serve, no wars could ever be won. A society which generally gives individual conscience priority over social decision clearly becomes self-defeating and bereft of social order or effective policy.

(2) Civil disobedience is a public protest against a law or policy regarded as morally wrong for all—not just the protesters. The protest may be meant to call attention to this wrong so that it may be corrected—legislators or other people are to be persuaded or coerced to change the practice objected to. The coercion or persuasion may be by a majority against a minority and also by a minority against a majority. The distinctive element is nonviolent disobedience for the purpose of persuading or compelling others to change or disobey laws or policies and, at times, to impede the attainment of the laws' purposes.

Thus, selective resistance to law enforcement without aggressive violence constitutes civil disobedience, when a law is deliberately disobeyed to publicly demonstrate opposition on moral grounds, to laws or policies of the government. Civil disobedience may be a means to bring down the government as a whole (it was so used in India), though more often it is intended to protest only against the specific laws disobeyed, against other laws, or against private actions tolerated by the government. Thus, the violation of laws against trespass may be a means of protest against draft laws, armament policies, private segregation, employment discrimination, or housing conditions. Civil disobedience may invite or resist but may not initiate or engage in violence; and it must rest not only on personal reluctance to obey the law but on a general moral principle which makes the object of the protest sufficiently objectionable to justify publicly defying a law in protest. Hence, a physician who, on moral grounds, performs an illegal abortion on a woman who has been raped does not engage in civil disobedience, because his purpose is to help the woman, and not to demonstratively defy any law. Civil disobedience is a public political act prompted by moral principle. The physician's violation, though prompted by moral feeling, is not intended to be public or political; it violates but does not defy the law and attempt to change it thereby.[13]

Civil disobedience, since it is disobedience to law with *mens rea*, is *ipso facto* unlawful—one cannot lawfully violate the law. If an act intended (or alleged) to be civil disobedience turns out not to have violated a law, be it that

[13] Of course, since both kinds of acts are law violations prompted by moral feeling, they both raise problems about the relationship of law to felt morality.

the act was not violative or that the "law" was not valid, it is not an act of civil disobedience. No act can be both obedient and disobedient to the same law. Thus civil disobedience is debatable in terms of the moral justification for the law, or for the disobedience to it, but not in terms of the legality of either: to defend the legality of an act is to deny that it is an act of civil disobedience, and thus to preclude debating it as such.

Whether a "law" is valid, or an act lawful, is known sometimes only a posteriori, when, upon challenge, the court of last resort has reached a decision.[14] If the "law" is not legal, or the "disobedience" is, there is a challenge to authority but no disobedience to law. To maintain, on the contrary, that to show that there was no actual disobedience to valid law is to vindicate disobedience to law, is to confuse lawful resistance to unlawful demands of an authority with unlawful resistance to lawful demands.

Even if the challenge fails and the law is found valid and the act violative, the unlawful act hardly is civil disobedience. The legal challenge *eo ipso* denies disobedience to and defiance of law, and avows that the defendant questioned the *legality* of an order enforced by a public authority. But civil disobedience is a deliberately unlawful act, avowed, intended, and carried out as such. Thus the defendant found innocent did not disobey the law; the defendant found guilty did, but, by his legal challenge, disavowed that he intended to commit civil (deliberate) disobedience. If a legal defense of the act is relied on, if legal guilt incurred for the sake of a moral principle is disavowed, there was no civil disobedience.[15]

Lawyers tend to confuse this basically simple issue because they can defend the civil disobedience of their clients only by arguing that it was not—that the client did not actually disobey a valid law.[16] Otherwise, they would be in the legally untenable position of admitting the unlawfulness of acts they defend as lawful. It may be the right and duty of defense counsel to deny the law violation. But they confuse their clients and the public when, having won or lost the case on this ground, they suggest that they struck a blow for civil disobedience—they did so no more than counsel for a person accused of any crime strikes a blow for crime, or its legality, when he denies that the act was committed, or was a crime.

Civil disobedience is socially more dangerous than conscientious objection and justifiable in even fewer instances. It is not only a personal refusal to obey

---

[14] I neglect procedural matters which may cause prosecution to fail independently.

[15] For the sake of brevity I neglect an original intent to defy the law, later changed, and an avowed intent frustrated by the law's invalidity—despite a plea of guilty.

[16] Again I neglect matters of procedure, which may moot the question of legal guilt. Note also that a "not guilty" plea is not always meant to be a denial of legal guilt. If the argument supporting it does not rely on intralegal (including constitutional) or factual reasoning, but on extralegal moral reasoning only, the "not guilty" plea is merely a device to publicize the moral reasoning which led to the defiance of the law, and not a denial of guilt from the standpoint of the law. It is also an abuse of the judicial process, at least in a democracy where the morality of the law can be attacked elsewhere.

the law, a small rent in the legal fabric, but an attempt to persuade or coerce others to disobey it—a dangerous opening of a seam. A man who "sits in" a draft board does not just protest conscription—this can be done by writing or speaking; nor does he just himself refuse to serve—this does not require sitting in. He wishes to coerce a modification of the law made by the representatives elected by the majority. To be sure, coercion and publicity seeking are not always clearly distinguishable. But neither are they always indistinguishable.[17]

When can civil disobedience be justified? Possibly to extend the democratic rights needed to participate in the process of political decision making. Thus, where the franchise is legally refused to any group, and the majority of those holding it cannot be persuaded to extend it to others as competent on the average as those having it, civil disobedience may both be justified and effective as a means, without creating evils greater than those objected to. Similarly, where citizens are legally prevented from exercising the franchise which is legally theirs, and legal processes do not effectively remove the illegality, civil disobedience may be justifiable and effective and may produce a net benefit. I would hesitate more about civil disobedience as a means of improving housing, or education, or removing segregation. Once the franchise can be exercised, obedience to law will serve deprived minorities better than disobedience. However, I can conceive cases for specific kinds of disobedience, as, for example, refusing to pay rent until repairs are made—but only if legal remedies have truly been exhausted and law-abiding political ones are hopeless. In such cases civil disobedience is used to enforce, albeit by illegal means, a morally or legally recognized right—not as a weapon in a clash of consciences.

Civil disobedience is hard to justify as a means to coerce others to disobey their consciences and to obey one's own instead. Thus, it is hard to justify the attempt by a minority to compel the majority to disobey their consciences and the law by, for example, disobeying a draft call, so as to obey the conscience of the minority which favors violating the draft law. "Sitting in" on a draft board or stopping military trains is such an attempt.

(3) Finally, insurrection may aim at bringing down the government as a whole, or at least achieving a comprehensive change in legislation and policy. In contrast to civil disobedience, violence is not shunned. The exclusive purpose is to compel rather than merely to urge the desired change.

Instances are conceivable in which a minority's attempt to coerce the majority even by violence seems justifiable in a democracy, let alone in other systems of government. If we revert to the, fortunately imaginary, case in which a democratic majority authorizes the wanton killing of a minority group, illegal self-defense of the group to be killed would be morally justifiable.

---

[17] Sometimes conscientious objection and civil disobedience seem similar. For example, "sitting in" at a luncheonette to be served with others is a personal refusal which cannot be separated from the attempt to coerce others (the owner of the luncheonette). But the purpose is clearly to modify the law or custom rather than a mere personal refusal to obey it.

So would insurrectionary action by other citizens to assist those to be killed. The illustration differs from the case of a war regarded as unjust by a minority, not only because the victims are citizens, but, more importantly, because the killing is wanton. Wars are not. I know of none where a factual judgment on the need to wage it for the achievement of some political purpose, other than wanton killing, does not play a role. The minority is not justified to impose its political judgment on the freely formed (i.e. democratic) majority.

I realize that this distinction is tenuous at best, and that it is not hard to imagine cases in which it could not be applied. I suggest it for largely practical reasons. It would take another paper to generalize these and to justify them theoretically. But in practical terms, agitation for insurrection, or sabotage, of an "unjust" war would weaken the war-making power of democracies—which are not likely to engage in wars of conquest—and thus in relative terms strengthen the hand of nondemocratic systems which would be exempt from such agitation in practice. These are more likely on the one hand to engage in wars of conquest, and on the other to bring about more oppression and injustice, should they be victorious. Thus, if democratic citizens in a democracy felt unbound by the decision of the majority to use military force when their conscience told them the war was unjust, democracy would be weaker, thus inviting wars of conquest, and more likely to be defeated, thereby inviting more injustice than I believe could be removed by morally authorizing a minority to refuse to serve, or to overthrow, a majority government engaged in an unjust war.

Although they are conceivable, I know of no actual laws passed in a democracy that would justify insurrectionary action. Even civil disobedience, in a democracy, is justifiable in my view mainly when democratic rights are illegally denied, or where democracy is legally (and hopelessly) restricted.

The conceivable, though unlikely, grossly immoral democratic legislation which might justify insurrection against the majority must involve irreversible and irreparable evils, such as the slaughtering of people. These must be distinguished from evils which, though irreversible, can be repaired, such as the imposition of unjust disabilities on a group. Such evils may, if no effective legal remedies are available, justify civil disobedience, if it promises to be effective and to create no greater evils than those protested against. Insurrection, however, would not be justified, for the democratic process is more likely than insurrection by a minority to remove the evils and to avoid their recurrence. The minority government would bring about greater though different evils. Thus, if the unjust law would wantonly require incarceration of redheads, I should favor civil disobedience over insurrection. But if execution were required, insurrection would be morally justified.

I contemplate this problem with a heavy heart, for although I may have clarified some aspects, and excluded some pseudosolutions, I have not been able to produce a social principle of moral validation or invalidation of legitimate and binding law. I have had to suggest that such a principle and such a procedure is necessary—yet impossible to produce.

AFTERWORD

Plato says **obey!** and offers us the martyred Socrates as a dramatic illustration. Hobbes says **obey!** and draws the line at submitting to execution. Locke says **obey if!,** and then spells out the conditions, limitations, and qualifications of that **if.** Van den Haag faces the problem squarely and admits defeat. Obedience seems necessary and defiance unavoidable when law and conscience conflict. What does all this say to the young man facing the draft?

Several points are clear enough, however cloudy the issue may be in general. First, any appeal to a social contract theory of political obligation must be strongly qualified by the fact that in the present day we are not free to decline the contract. If a young man opts to withdraw from the bargain by which he gains security at the cost of an obligation to serve, there is no way in which he can act on his choice. To be sure, he can emigrate to Canada or Australia, but once there he finds himself under the authority of another state which claims the same right of service. The time is past when a band of dissenters could set out for a new world and make their own social compact. In a sense, Plato's **Crito,** with its emphasis upon Socrates' debt of gratitude to the Athenian Laws, is more relevant to our present situation than the contract theories of Hobbes and Locke.

A second point: Van den Haag makes much of the terrible social disorder that would result if each man were to set himself up as judge of which laws to obey and which to defy. In this, he echoes Hobbes' fear of the "war of all against all." But one cannot prove that a proposition is false merely by showing how terrible it would be if everyone believed it. There might, after all, be some truths which it would be better to keep secret. Suppose it is true that human society can survive only if the generality of men believe in the legitimacy of their governments. Even so, it does not follow that the governments **are** legitimate. Perhaps it is only a myth of the Enlightenment that men will be happier for knowing the truth.

The central question to be answered is this: Does a citizen of a genuinely democratic state have an absolute, binding duty to obey all the laws which have been enacted by a majority in accordance with true democratic procedures? Justice Fortas says **yes.** I say **no.** Our four authors, while deepening our understanding of the problem, do not in the end offer us a definite answer.

ossellini Film Is Halted by City;
'he Miracle' Held 'Blasphemous'

By RICHARD H. PARKE

owings of an Italian picture,
Miracle," starring Anna
ani and directed by Roberto
llini, were stopped yesterday
oon at the Paris Theatre, 4
Fifty-eighth Street, at the
on of the city's Department
nses.

Lillian Gerard, the theatre's
ng director, said that Ed-
. McCaffrey, Commissioner
ses, told her in a
her on Fr
e film "of
blasphemou
cture, which
on Dec. 12,
iot woman
o, in a tran
motion, is se
who

The film, distributed in this
country by Joseph Burstyn, had
been passed by the New York
State Board of Censors and the
United States Customs and
ceived a high rating from th
tional Board of Review. I
shown at the Paris Theat
conjunction with two French
"A D
Country
omnibu

**4 ARE ARRESTED
IN FILM SEIZURE**

Judge Rules 'Censorship in
Denmark' to Be Obscene

H. LUBASCH

r and three
were arrested
criminal cour
authorized th
film "Censorshi
New Approach
by Judge Ja
prevents furth
the film in N
ty pending a tria
butor and the n
charges of promo

CALDWELL NOVEL BANNED

'God's Little Acre' Is Declared
Obscene in Massachusetts

BOSTON, July 26 (AP)—The novel
"God's Little Acre" by Erskine
Caldwell was banned from Massachusetts today by the full bench of
the Massachusetts Supreme Co
said it was "obscene
ruling by the s
turned the
rt ju

BAN ON PICTURE UPHELD

M. P. A. A. Directors Affirm the
Decision on 'Bicycle Thief'

The board of directors of the
Motion Picture Association of
America yesterday upheld the decision of its Production Code Administration in refusing to grant
its seal of approval to the Italian
film, "The Bicycle Thief,"
two scenes were eliminated.
The directors who met
ard room of Columbia Pic
Seventh Avenue, took a
viewing the picture and
from Joseph Burstyn,
and Joseph I. Bre
Code administrat
d's a

NOVEL OF ARMY B

Denver Librarian Ob
'Barracks-Room La

DENVER, March 18 (U
Jones' best-selling Ar
"From Here to Eter
anned temporarily from
Public Library tod
horities said "the a
free with his ba
age."

Malcolm Wyer,
d:

an author us
Jones const
whether it is
ok is abov
ny life in N
said the
volumes
cause

ecti
d b
d.

VII
AESTHETICS

*Pornography
and Censorship:
The Social Value of Art*

INTRODUCTION TO THE CONTEMPORARY ISSUE

Standards of decency, like hemlines, change from era to era, and few men today would turn their heads for that glimpse of an ankle that so interested our Victorian ancestors. But whether it is the fashion to say "limb" for "leg," or to speak in the most explicit manner about the forms and varieties of sexual activity, society always seem to draw a line between what is permissible and what is forbidden in speech and print. In the 1960s a number of court decisions so broadened the limits of what was allowable in books, films, and theater that American culture was overnight transformed. Books which the adventurous tourist had smuggled in from abroad began to appear in local bookstores; movies showed what novels had not dared even to describe; serious drama so far outstripped burlesque that the oldtime ecdysiasts took on the air of modest young ladies.

In the light of these changes in American standards of decency, it may seem a trifle quaint to go back two score years to the trial of James Joyce's great novel, **Ulysses.** To us today, **Ulysses** is a masterwork of fiction —it stands with the works of Richardson, Austen, Dickens, and the rest as one of the major novels in the English language. What can we possibly learn from a judicial hearing devoted to determining whether **Ulysses** is obscene?

The answer is that the opinions of the judges in the **Ulysses** case raise many important philosophical questions which will remain troubling and controversial long after James Joyce has achieved the status of an old master. As you shall see, both the majority opinion by Justice A. Hand and the dissent by Justice Manton appeal to the theory that art should serve certain social and moral ends. Although they disagree about the effect of the particular work of fiction before the court, the justices appear to share the ancient view that the artist must be judged by the social impact of his art. Needless to say, the view has not gone unchallenged in the history of philosophy, and in the readings of this section, you will encounter a number of quite diverse views on the relation of art to society, morality, and revolution.

Since the legal situation in the opening selection may be a bit obscure, let me explain briefly what was at stake. Random House, Inc., a publishing firm, attempted to import copies of Joyce's **Ulysses** for the purpose of selling them in the United States. The Customs officials seized the copies at the port of entry on the grounds that they were obscene, and filed suit to take possession of them (in order to destroy them). Random House went to court and won a reversal of the Bureau of Custom's decision. The government then appealed to the Circuit Court of Appeals, and the question was argued again. Random House once more won its case, and **Ulysses** was published and sold in America. The Appeals Court's decision was split, two to one, and we therefore have both the majority opinion and the dissent by Justice Manton. In effect, therefore, the court record provides us with a short debate on the merits of **Ulysses,** and on the larger issue of the standards of obscenity in literature.

United States v. One Book
Entitled Ulysses
by James Joyce

Appeal from the District Court of the United States for the Southern District of New York.

Libel by the United States for the forfeiture of one book entitled Ulysses, written by James Joyce, on the ground that it was an "obscene book" within the meaning of Tariff Act of 1930, section 305 (a), 19 USCA § 1305 (a), Random House, Inc., claimant. From a decree (5 F. Supp. 182) granting claimant's motion to dismiss the libel, the libelant appeals.

Affirmed.

Martin Conboy, U.S. Atty., of New York City (Martin Conboy, of New York City, Francis H. Horan, of Washington, D.C., and John F. Davidson, Asst. U.S. Attys., of New York City, of counsel), for libelant-appellant.

Greenbaum, Wolff & Ernst, of New York City (Morris L. Ernst and Alexander Lindey, both of New York City, of counsel), for claimant-appellee.

Before MANTON, L. HAND, and AUGUSTIN N. HAND, Circuit Judges.

AUGUSTUS N. HAND, CIRCUIT JUDGE

This appeal raises sharply the question of the proper interpretation of section 305 (a) of the Tariff Act of 1930, 19 USCA § 1305 (a). That section provides that "all persons are prohibited from importing into the United States from any foreign country . . . any obscene book, pamphlet, paper, writing, advertisement, circular, print, picture, drawing, or other representation, figure, or image on or of paper or other material, . . ." and directs that, upon the appearance of any such a book or matter at any customs office, the collector shall seize it and inform the district attorney, who shall institute proceedings for forfeiture. In accordance with the statute, the collector seized Ulysses, a book written by James Joyce, and the United States filed a libel for forfeiture. The claimant, Random House, Inc., the publisher of the American edition, intervened in the cause and filed its answer denying that the book was obscene and was subject to confiscation and praying that it be admitted into the United States. The case came on for trial before Woolsey, J., who found that the book, taken as a whole, "did not tend to excite sexual impulses or lustful thoughts but that its net effect . . . was only that of a somewhat tragic and very powerful commentary on the inner lives of men and women." He accordingly granted a decree adjudging that the book was "not of the character the entry of which is prohibited under the provision of section 305 of the Tariff

No. 459, Circuit Court of Appeals, Second Circuit, August 7, 1934. Reprinted from 72 *Federal Reporter,* 2nd Series, pp. 705–11.

Act of 1930 . . . and . . . dismissing the libel," from which this appeal has been taken.

James Joyce, the author of Ulysses, may be regarded as a pioneer among those writers who have adopted the "stream of consciousness" method of presenting fiction, which has attracted considerable attention in academic and literary circles. In this field Ulysses is rated as a book of considerable power by persons whose opinions are entitled to weight. Indeed it has become a sort of contemporary classic, dealing with a new subject-matter. It attempts to depict the thoughts and lay bare the souls of a number of people, some of them intellectuals and some social outcasts and nothing more, with a literalism that leaves nothing unsaid. Certain of its passages are of beauty and undoubted distinction, while others are of a vulgarity that is extreme and the book as a whole has a realism characteristic of the present age. It is supposed to portray the thoughts of the principal characters during a period of about eighteen hours.

We may discount the laudation of Ulysses by some of its admirers and reject the view that it will permanently stand among the great works of literature, but it is fair to say that it is a sincere portrayal with skillful artistry of the "streams of consciousness" of its characters. Though the depiction happily is not of the "stream of consciousness" of all men and perhaps of only those of a morbid type, it seems to be sincere, truthful, relevant to the subject, and executed with real art. Joyce, in the words of Paradise Lost, has dealt with "things unattempted yet in prose or rime"—with things that very likely might better have remained "unattempted"—but his book shows originality and is a work of symmetry and excellent craftsmanship of a sort. The question before us is whether such a book of artistic merit and scientific insight should be regarded as "obscene" within section 305 (a) of the Tariff Act.

That numerous long passages in Ulysses contain matter that is obscene under any fair definition of the word cannot be gainsaid; yet they are relevant to the purpose of depicting the thoughts of the characters and are introduced to give meaning to the whole, rather than to promote lust or portray filth for its own sake. The net effect even of portions most open to attack, such as the closing monologue of the wife of Leopold Bloom, is pitiful and tragic, rather than lustful. The book depicts the souls of men and women that are by turns bewildered and keenly apprehensive, sordid and aspiring, ugly and beautiful, hateful and loving. In the end one feels, more than anything else, pity and sorrow for the confusion, misery, and degradation of humanity. Page after page of the book is, or seems to be, incomprehensible. But many passages show the trained hand of an artist, who can at one moment adapt to perfection the style of an ancient chronicler, and at another become a veritable personification of Thomas Carlyle. In numerous places there are found originality, beauty, and distinction. The book as a whole is not pornographic, and, while in not a few spots it is coarse, blasphemous, and obscene, it does not, in our opinion, tend to promote lust. The erotic passages are submerged in the book as a whole and have little resultant effect. If these are to make the book subject to confiscation, by the same test Venus and Adonis, Hamlet, Romeo and Juliet, and the story told in the Eighth Book of the Odyssey by the bard Demodocus of how Ares and Aphrodite were entrapped in a net spread by the outraged Hephaestus amid the laughter of the immortal gods, as well as many other classics, would have to be suppressed. Indeed, it may be questioned whether the obscene passages in Romeo and Juliet were as necessary to the development of the play as those in the monologue of Mrs. Bloom are to the depiction of the latter's tortured soul.

It is unnecessary to add illustrations to show that, in the administration of statutes aimed at the suppression of immoral books, standard works of literature have not been barred merely because they contained *some* obscene passages, and that confiscation for such a reason would destroy much that is precious in order to benefit a few.

It is settled, at least so far as this court is concerned, that works of physiology, medicine, science, and sex instruction are not within the statute, though to some extent and among some persons they may tend to promote lustful thoughts. United States v. Dennett, 39 F.(2d) 564, 76 A. L. R. 1092. We think the same immunity should apply to literature as to science, where the presentation, when viewed objectively, is sincere, and the erotic matter is not introduced to promote lust and does not furnish the dominant note of the publication. The question in each case is whether a publication taken as a whole has a libidinous effect. The book before us has such portentous length, is written with such evident truthfulness in its depiction of certain types of humanity, and is so little erotic in its result, that it does not fall within the forbidden class.

In Halsey v. New York Society for Suppression of Vice, 234 N.Y. 1, 136 N.E. 219, 220, the New York Court of Appeals dealt with Mademoiselle de Maupin, by Theophile Gautier, for the sale of which the plaintiff had been prosecuted under a New York statute forbidding the sale of obscene books, upon the complaint of the defendant. After acquittal, the plaintiff sued for malicious prosecution, and a jury rendered a verdict in his favor. The Court of Appeals refused to disturb the judgment because the book had become a recognized French classic and its merits on the whole outweighed its objectionable qualities, though, as Judge Andrews said, it contained many paragraphs which, "taken by themselves," were "undoubtedly vulgar and indecent." In referring to the obscene passages, he remarked that: "No work may be judged from a selection of such paragraphs alone. Printed by themselves they might, as a matter of law, come within the prohibition of the statute. So might a similar selection from Aristophanes or Chaucer or Boccaccio, or even from the Bible. The book, however, must be considered broadly, as a whole." We think Judge Andrews was clearly right, and that the effect of the book as a whole is the test.

In the New York Supreme Court, Judge Morgan J. O'Brien declined to prohibit a receiver from selling Arabian Nights, Rabelais, Ovid's Art of Love, the Decameron of Boccaccio, the Heptameron of Queen Margaret of Navarre, or the Confessions of Rousseau. He remarked that a rule which would exclude them would bar "a very large proportion of the works of fiction of the most famous writers of the English language." In re Worthington Co. (Sup.) 30 N.Y.S. 361, 362, 24 L.R.A. 110. The main difference between many standard works and Ulysses is its far more abundant use of coarse and colloquial words and presentation of dirty scenes, rather than in any excess of prurient suggestion. We do not think that Ulysses, taken as a whole, tends to promote lust, and its criticised passages do this no more than scores of standard books that are constantly bought and sold. Indeed a book of physiology in the hands of adolescents may be more objectionable on this ground than almost anything else. . . .

It it true that the motive of an author to promote good morals is not the test of whether a book is obscene, and it may also be true that the applicability of the statute does not depend on the persons to whom a publication is likely to be distributed. The importation of obscene books is prohibited generally, and no provision is made permitting such importation because of the character of those to whom they are sold. While any construction of the statute that will fit all cases is difficult, we believe that the proper test of whether a given book is obscene is its dominant effect. In applying this test, relevancy of the objectionable parts to the theme, the established reputation of the work in the estimation of approved critics, if the book is modern, and the verdict of the past, if it is ancient, are persuasive pieces of evidence; for works of art are not likely to sustain a high position with no better warrant for their existence than their obscene content.

It may be that Ulysses will not last as a substantial contribution to literature, and it is certainly easy to believe that, in spite of the opinion of Joyce's laudators, the immortals will still reign, but the same thing may be said of current works of art and music and of many other serious efforts of the mind. Art certainly cannot advance under compulsion to traditional forms, and nothing in such a field is more stifling to progress than limitation of the right to experiment with a new technique. The foolish judgments of Lord Eldon about one hundred years ago, proscribing the works of Byron and Southey, and the finding of the jury under a charge by Lord Denman that the publication of Shelley's "Queen Mab" was an indictable offense are a warning to all who have to determine the limits of the field within which authors may exercise themselves. We think that Ulysses is a book of originality and sincerity of treatment and that it has not the effect of promoting lust. Accordingly it does not fall within the statute, even though it justly may offend many.

Decree affirmed.

MANTON, CIRCUIT JUDGE

I dissent. This libel, filed against the book Ulysses prays for a decree of forfeiture, and it is based upon the claim that the book's entry into the United States is prohibited by section 305 (a) of the Tariff Act of 1930, 19 USCA

1305 (a). On motion of appellee, the court below entered an order dismissing the libel, and the collector of customs was ordered to release the book. The motion was considered on the pleadings and a stipulation entered into by the parties.

The sole question presented is whether or not the book is obscene within section 305 (a) which provides:

"All persons are prohibited from importing into the United States from any foreign country . . . any obscene book, pamphlet, paper, writing, advertisement, circular, print, picture, drawing, or other representation, figure, or image on or of paper or other material. . . .

"Upon the appearance of any such book or matter at any customs office, the same shall be seized and held by the collector to await the judgment of the district court as hereinafter provided. . . . Upon the seizure of such book or matter the collector shall transmit information thereof to the district attorney of the district in which is situated the office at which such seizure has taken place, who shall institute proceedings in the district court for the forfeiture, confiscation, and destruction of the book or matter seized. . . .

"In any such proceeding any party in interest may upon demand have the facts at issue determined by a jury and any party may have an appeal or the right of review as in the case of ordinary actions or suits."

The parties agreed as to the facts in the stipulation. There is no conflicting evidence; the decision to be made is dependent entirely upon the reading matter found on the objectionable pages of the book (pages 173, 213, 214, 359, 361, 423, 424, 434, 467, 488, 498, 500, 509, 522, 526, 528, 551, 719, 724–727, 731, 738, 739, 745, 746, 754–756, 761, 762, 765, Random House Edition). The book itself was the only evidence offered. . . .

Who can doubt the obscenity of this book after a reading of the pages referred to, which are too indecent to add as a footnote to this opinion? Its characterization as obscene should be quite unanimous by all who read it. . . .

Ulysses is a work of fiction. It may not be compared with books involving medical subjects or description of certain physical or biological facts. It is written for alleged amusement of the reader only. The characters described in the thoughts of the author may in some instances be true, but, be it truthful or otherwise, a book that is obscene is not rendered less so by the statement of truthful fact. . . . It cannot be said that the test above has been rejected by United States v. Dennett (C.C.A.) 39 F.(2d) 564, 76 A.L.R. 1092, nor can that case be taken to mean that the book is to be judged as a whole. If anything, the case clearly recognizes that the book may be obscene because portions thereof are so, for pains are taken to justify and show not to be obscene portions to which objection is made. The gist of the holding is that a book is not to be declared obscene if it is "an accurate exposition of the relevant facts of the sex side of life in decent language and in manifestly serious and disinterested spirit." A work of obvious benefit to the community was never intended to be within the purview of the statute. No matter what may be said on the side of letters, the effect on the community can and must be the sole determining factor. "Laws of this character are made for society in the aggregate, and not in particular. So, while there may be individuals and societies of men and women of peculiar notions or idiosyncrasies, whose moral sense would neither be depraved nor offended, . . . yet the exceptional sensibility or want of sensibility, of such cannot be allowed as a standard." United States v. Harmon, supra.

In United States v. Kennerley (D.C.) 209 F. 119, the Bennett Case was followed despite the dictum objecting to a test which protected the "salacious" few. By the very argument used, to destroy a test which protects those most easily influenced, we can discard a test which would protect only the interests of the other comparatively small groups of society. If we disregard the protection of the morals of the susceptible, are we to consider merely the benefits and pleasures derived from letters by those who pose as the more highly developed and intelligent? To do so would show an utter disregard for the standards of decency of the community as a whole and an utter disregard for the effect of a book upon the average less sophisticated member of society, not to mention the adolescent. The court cannot indulge any instinct it may have to foster letters. The statute is designed to protect society at large, of that there can be no dispute; notwithstanding the deprivation of benefits to a few, a work must be condemned if it has a depraving influence.

And are we to refuse to enforce the statute Congress has enacted because of the argument that "obscenity is only the superstition of the day—the modern counterpart of ancient witchcraft"? Are we to be persuaded by the statement, set forth in the brief, made by the judge below in an interview with the press, "Education, not law, must solve problems of taste and choice (of books)," when the statute is clear and our duty plain?

The prevailing opinion states that classics would be excluded if the application of the statute here argued for prevailed. But the statute, Tariff Act 1930, § 305 (a), 19 USCA § 1305 (a), provides as to classics that they may be introduced into the commerce of the United States provided "that the Secretary of the Treasury . . . in his discretion, admit the so-called classics or books of recognized and established literary or scientific merit, but may, in his discretion, admit such classics or books only when imported for non-commercial purposes." The right to admission under this proviso was not sought nor is it justified by reason thereof in the prevailing opinion.

Congress passed this statute against obscenity for the protection of the great mass of our people; the unusual literator can, or thinks he can, protect himself. The people do not exist for the sake of literature, to give the author fame, the publisher wealth, and the book a market. On the contrary, literature exists for the sake of the people, to refresh the weary, to console the sad, to hearten the dull and downcast, to increase man's interest in the world, his joy of living, and his sympathy in all sorts and conditions of men. Art for art's sake is heartless and soon grows artless; art for the public market is not art at all, but commerce; art for the people's service is a noble, vital, and permanent element of human life.

The public is content with the standard of salability; the prigs with the standard of preciosity. The people need and deserve a moral standard; it should be a point of honor with men of letters to maintain it. Masterpieces have never been produced by men given to obscenity or lustful thoughts—men who have no Master. Reverence for good work is the foundation of literary character. A refusal to imitate obscenity or to load a book with it is an author's professional chastity.

Good work in literature has its permanent mark; it is like all good work, noble and lasting. It requires a human aim—to cheer, console, purify, or ennoble the life of people. Without this aim, literature has never sent an arrow close to the mark. It is by good work only that men of letters can justify their right to a place in the world.

Under the authoritative decision and considering the substance involved in this appeal, it is my opinion that the decree should be reversed.

COMMENTARY ON THE CONTEMPORARY ISSUE

Strictly speaking, the question before the court is simply whether Joyce's **Ulysses** is obscene within the meaning of the federal statutes governing the importation of literature from abroad, but the arguments of Justices Hand and Manton make it clear that a good deal more is at stake than a mere point of law. Just as the dispute over the legal criteria of insanity led us in Section II into the ancient philosophical argument over freedom of the will, so the problem of obscenity in literature raises one of the central issues of the philosophy of art, namely: What is the social role and social value of art?

There can be no question that artistic creation is one of the natural and universal activities of the human experience. No anthropological expedition or archeological excavation has ever discovered a human community from which all forms of dance, music, sculpture, painting, poetry, and decorative elaboration were entirely absent. From the cave paintings of the prehistoric Cro-Magnons to the high cultures of the past six thousand years, men have recorded, interpreted, and enhanced their lives with works of art.

But to say of a human activity that it is "natural and universal" is not yet to say that it is good or sociably desirable. After all, war is as common among men as art, and yet some persons at least would deny that warmaking should be encouraged or celebrated. So to the champions of the aesthetic, we may pose a question: Why art? What justification can you provide for society's encouraging and rewarding the activity of the artist?

One possible answer, of course, is that no justification is needed. Art is one of those things that is simply good in itself, like pleasure (as the utilitarians say). "Art for art's sake" is the banner under which the partisans of this view march; in the nineteenth century in Europe many students and practitioners of the aesthetic life took up this cry.

More often, however, the defenders of art have justified its existence by pointing to some function which art, and only art, can perform. Art has been called a medium through which men are put in touch with the divine. It has been described as the final fulfillment of the human spirit, as the bearer of social traditions, as the cement which binds individuals together into a harmonious and cohesive community. Judge Manton says that literature (and presumably other art as well) "exists for the sake of the people, to refresh the weary, to console the sad, to hearten the dull and downcast, to increase man's interest in the world, his joy of living, and his sympathy in all sorts and conditions of men." Art has even been assigned the role of a weapon in the revolutionary struggle of the proletariat.

Obviously, many important issues will remain to be settled even after we have ascertained the social value of art. What are the criteria of **beauty** in a work of art? Are they separate from the function of art as a social activity, or are the two related? Can an art work be **beautiful** even though it fails to fulfill a social function or even perverts the social purposes of art? In the case before us, could **Ulysses** be a beautiful work of literature and nevertheless serve socially harmful ends? Neither Justice Hand nor

Justice Manton addresses himself to that question, but obviously it must affect our attitude toward the government's censorship of art. It would be comforting to believe that when the state bans works as socially harmful, it is after all only proscribing **ugly** works, not beautiful ones.

The **Ulysses** decision raises yet another question which we shall deal with only tangentially in the readings of this section: Is it bad to "promote lust"? The champions of **Ulysses, Lady Chatterley's Lover,** and the other books which have come before the courts are so eager to demonstrate the psychological profundity, the higher moral purpose, the "redeeming social value" of the challenged works that it never seems to occur to them to meet the attack head-on. Is lust bad? When an author has labored hard to find just the words that will arouse his readers to a pitch of sexual heat, it seems a shame to argue in court that he really was writing an allegory of man's search for God or a metaphor of the artist's creative experience.

Our readings in this section make a rather odd assortment: A Greek, an American, two Russians, and an Englishman. You won't find all the possible positions on art in the selections from their writings, of course, but you ought to be able to get a pretty good argument going on the basis of the points of view they express.

PLATO

*Plato is far and away the greatest artist ever to set forth a philo-
sophical argument. It is therefore astonishing to discover him, at the
end of the* Republic, *calling for the banishment of all artists from the
ideal society. Are we to suppose that Plato would deny himself a
place in his own utopia? What reason can he have for a judgment
seemingly so perverse and contrary to the opinions of virtually all
cultured men?*

*Plato actually has two distinct arguments in support of his re-
jection of art. One of the arguments is metaphysical, drawing on the
Theory of Forms and appealing to the distinction between appearance and reality which you encountered in Section II. The other
argument is psychological and sociological; it derives from Plato's
experiences in the Athens of his day, and the conclusions he drew
concerning the conditions appropriate to the fostering of healthy
personalities. In the* Republic, Socrates *makes great efforts to demonstrate the connections between the metaphysical and the psychological levels of his theory. Whether he was successful is one of those
questions which readers of the Dialogues continue to debate.*

On the metaphysical level, Plato claims that art, as a kind of
mimesis *or imitation, merely carries us farther away from the reality
of the Forms. Just as physical objects are copies, in the realm of appearances, of the eternally real and immutable Forms, so a painting
or sculpture is the artist's copy of the physical object. When we
pursue philosophical wisdom, we move from appearance toward
reality. But when we admire a work of art, we are actually moving
in the opposite direction, toward the even less real and eternal. Thus,
on metaphysical grounds, Plato considers art to be a flight from
reality and true knowledge.*

*The psychological effects of art are equally disastrous, ac-
cording to Plato. Philosophy teaches us that in the healthy soul
reason rules and the passions submit to wise guidance. But music,
dance, theater, and poetry arouse the passions rather than dampen
them. Plato reminds his readers of the popular Greek belief that
artists are possessed by the Gods and speak in a kind of rapture. To
some, the ecstasy of creation may seem desirable, even admirable, but
to Plato it is a perversion of the just and healthy order of the soul.*

*In a certain sense, Plato views artists as a subversive element in
the ideal state. Their intensely personal vision, their rejection of
social norms and goals, and their appeal beyond the canons of reason, make them potentially dangerous to any government which
seeks a harmonious coordination of all the citizens of the state. Plato*

is too great an artist himself to deny the beauty of the works of the poets, but perhaps as a political philosopher he is wise to fear this disruptive influence.

The Banishment
of Art
from Utopia

Of the many excellences which I perceive in the order of our State, there is none which upon reflection pleases me better than the rule about poetry.

To what do you refer?

To the rejection of imitative poetry, which certainly ought not to be received; as I see far more clearly now that the parts of the soul have been distinguished.

What do you mean?

Speaking in confidence, for I should not like to have my words repeated to the tragedians and the rest of the imitative tribe—but I do not mind saying to you, that all poetical imitations are ruinous to the understanding of the hearers, and that the knowledge of their true nature is the only antidote to them.

Explain the purport of your remark.

Well, I will tell you, although I have always from my earliest youth had an awe and love of Homer, which even now makes the words falter on my lips, for he is the great captain and teacher of the whole of that charming tragic company; but a man is not to be reverenced more than the truth, and therefore I will speak out.

Very good, he said.

Listen to me then, or rather, answer me.

Put your question.

Can you tell me what imitation is? for I really do not know.

A likely thing, then, that I should know.

Why not? for the duller eye may often see a thing sooner than the keener.

Very true, he said; but in your presence, even if I had any faint notion, I could not muster courage to utter it. Will you inquire yourself?

Well then, shall we begin the inquiry in our usual manner: Whenever a

From Book 10 of *The Republic of Plato*, trans. by Benjamin Jowett.

number of individuals have a common name, we assume them to have also a corresponding idea or form:—do you understand me?

I do.

Let us take any common instance; there are beds and tables in the world —plenty of them, are there not?

Yes.

But there are only two ideas or forms of them—one the idea of a bed, the other of a table.

True.

And the maker of either of them makes a bed or he makes a table for our use, in accordance with the idea—that is our way of speaking in this and similar instances—but no artificer makes the ideas themselves: how could he?

Impossible.

And there is another artist,—I should like to know what you would say of him.

Who is he?

One who is the maker of all the works of all other workmen.

What an extraordinary man!

Wait a little, and there will be more reason for your saying so. For this is he who is able to make not only vessels of every kind, but plants and animals, himself and all other things—the earth and heaven, and the things which are in heaven or under the earth; he makes the gods also.

He must be a wizard and no mistake.

Oh! you are incredulous, are you? Do you mean that there is no such maker or creator, or that in one sense there might be a maker of all these things but in another not? Do you see that there is a way in which you could make them all yourself?

What way?

An easy way enough; or rather, there are many ways in which the feat might be quickly and easily accomplished, none quicker than that of turning a mirror round and round—you would soon enough make the sun and the heavens, and the earth and yourself, and other animals and plants, and all the other things of which we were just now speaking, in the mirror.

Yes, he said; but they would be appearances only.

Very good, I said, you are coming to the point now. And the painter too is, as I conceive, just another—a creator of appearances, is he not?

Of course.

But then I suppose you will say that what he creates is untrue. And yet there is a sense in which the painter also creates a bed?

Yes, he said, but not a real bed.

And what of the maker of the bed? were you not saying that he too makes, not the idea which, according to our view, is the essence of the bed, but only a particular bed?

Yes, I did.

Then if he does not make that which exists he cannot make true existence, but only some semblance of existence; and if any one were to say that the work of the maker of the bed, or of any other workman, has real existence, he could hardly be supposed to be speaking the truth.

At any rate, he replied, philosophers would say that he was not speaking the truth.

No wonder, then, that his work too is an indistinct expression of truth.

No wonder.

Suppose now that by the light of the examples just offered we inquire who this imitator is?

If you please.

Well then, here are three beds: one existing in nature, which is made by God, as I think that we may say—for no one else can be the maker?

No.

There is another which is the work of the carpenter?

Yes.

And the work of the painter is a third?

Yes.

Beds, then, are of three kinds, and there are three artists who superintend them: God, the maker of the bed, and the painter?

Yes, there are three of them.

God, whether from choice or from necessity, made one bed in nature and one only; two or more such ideal beds neither ever have been nor ever will be made by God.

Why is that?

Because even if He had made but two, a third would still appear behind them which both of them would have for their idea, and that would be the ideal bed and not the two others.

Very true, he said.

God knew this, and He desired to be the real maker of a real bed, not a particular maker of a particular bed, and therefore He created a bed which is essentially and by nature one only.

So we believe.

Shall we, then, speak of Him as the natural author or maker of the bed?

Yes, he replied; inasmuch as by the natural process of creation He is the author of this and of all other things.

And what shall we say of the carpenter—is not he also the maker of the bed?

Yes.

But would you call the painter a creator and maker?

Certainly not.

Yet if he is not the maker, what is he in relation to the bed?

I think, he said, that we may fairly designate him as the imitator of that which the others make.

Good, I said; then you call him who is third in the descent from nature an imitator?

Certainly, he said.

And the tragic poet is an imitator, and therefore, like all other imitators, he is thrice removed from the king and from the truth?

That appears to be so.

Then about the imitator we are agreed. And what about the painter?—I would like to know whether he may be thought to imitate that which originally exists in nature, or only the creations of artists?

The latter.

As they are or as they appear? you have still to determine this.

What do you mean?

I mean, that you may look at a bed from different points of view, obliquely or directly or from any other point of view, and the bed will appear different, but there is no difference in reality. And the same of all things.

Yes, he said, the difference is only apparent.

Now let me ask you another question: Which is the art of painting designed to be—an imitation of things as they are, or as they appear—of appearance or of reality?

Of appearance.

Then the imitator, I said, is a long way off the truth, and can do all things because he lightly touches on a small part of them, and that part an image. For example: A painter will paint a cobbler, carpenter, or any other artist, though he knows nothing of their arts; and, if he is a good artist, he may deceive children or simple persons, when he shows them his picture of a carpenter from a distance, and they will fancy that they are looking at a real carpenter.

Certainly.

And whenever any one informs us that he has found a man who knows all the arts, and all things else that anybody knows, and every single thing with a higher degree of accuracy than any other man—whoever tells us this, I think that we can only imagine him to be a simple creature who is likely to have been deceived by some wizard or actor whom he met, and whom he thought all-knowing, because he himself was unable to analyse the nature of knowledge and ignorance and imitation.

Most true.

And so, when we hear persons saying that the tragedians, and Homer, who is at their head, know all the arts and all things human, virtue as well as vice, and divine things too, for that the good poet cannot compose well unless he knows his subject, and that he who has not this knowledge can never be a poet, we ought to consider whether here also there may not be a similar illusion. Perhaps they may have come across imitators and been deceived by them; they may not have remembered when they saw their works that these were but imitations thrice removed from the truth, and could easily be made without any knowledge of the truth, because they are appearances only and not realities? Or, after all, they may be in the right, and poets do really know the things about which they seem to the many to speak so well?

The question, he said, should by all means be considered.

Now do you suppose that if a person were able to make the original as well as the image, he would seriously devote himself to the image-making branch? Would he allow imitation to be the ruling principle of his life, as if he had nothing higher in him?

I should say not.

The real artist, who knew what he was imitating, would be interested in realities and not in imitations; and would desire to leave as memorials of himself works many and fair; and, instead of being the author of encomiums, he would prefer to be the theme of them.

Yes, he said, that would be to him a source of much greater honour and profit.

Then, I said, we must put a question to Homer; not about medicine, or any of the arts to which his poems only incidentally refer: we are not going to ask him, or any other poet, whether he has cured patients like Asclepius, or left behind him a school of medicine such as the Asclepiads were, or whether he only talks about medicine and other arts at second-hand; but we have a right to know respecting military tactics, politics, education, which are the chiefest and noblest subjects of his poems, and we may fairly ask him about them. "Friend Homer," then we say to him "if you are only in the second remove from truth in what you say of virtue, and not in the third—not an image maker or imitator —and if you are able to discern what pursuits make men better or worse in private or public life, tell us what State was ever better governed by your help? The good order of Lacedaemon is due to Lycurgus, and many other cities great and small have been similarly benefited by others; but who says that you have been a good legislator to them and have done them any good? Italy and Sicily boast of Charondas, and there is Solon who is renowned among us; but what city has anything to say about you?" Is there any city which he might name?

I think not, said Glaucon; not even the Homerids themselves pretend that he was a legislator.

Well, but is there any war on record which was carried on successfully by him, or aided by his counsels, when he was alive?

There is not.

Or is there any invention of his, applicable to the arts or to human life, such as Thales the Milesian or Anarcharsis the Scythian, and other ingenious men have conceived, which is attributed to him?

There is absolutely nothing of the kind.

But, if Homer never did any public service, was he privately a guide or teacher of any? Had he in his lifetime friends who loved to associate with him, and who handed down to posterity an Homeric way of life, such as was established by Pythagoras who was so greatly beloved for his wisdom, and whose followers are to this day quite celebrated for the order which was named after him?

Nothing of the kind is recorded of him. For surely, Socrates, Creophylus, the companion of Homer, that child of flesh, whose name always makes us laugh, might be more justly ridiculed for his stupidity, if, as is said, Homer was greatly neglected by him and others in his own day when he was alive?

Yes, I replied, that is the tradition. But can you imagine, Glaucon, that if Homer had really been able to educate and improve mankind—if he had possessed knowledge and not been a mere imitator—can you imagine, I say, that he would not have had many followers, and been honoured and loved by them? Protagoras of Abdera, and Prodicus of Ceos, and a host of others, have only to whisper to their contemporaries: "You will never be able to manage either your house or your own State until you appoint us to be your ministers of education"—and this ingenious device of theirs has such an effect in making men love them that their companions all but carry them about on their shoulders. And is it conceivable that the contemporaries of Homer, or again of Hesiod, would have allowed either of them to go about as rhapsodists, if they had really been able to make mankind virtuous? Would they not have been as unwilling to part with them as with gold, and have compelled them to stay at home with them? Or, if the master would not stay, then the disciples would have followed him about everywhere, until they had got education enough?

Yes, Socrates, that, I think, is quite true.

Then must we not infer that all these poetical individuals, beginning with Homer, are only imitators; they copy images of virtue and the like, but the truth they never reach? The poet is like a painter who, as we have already observed, will make a likeness of a cobbler though he understands nothing of cobbling; and his picture is good enough for those who know no more than he does, and judge only by colours and figures.

Quite so.

In like manner the poet with his words and phrases may be said to lay on the colours of the several arts, himself understanding their nature only enough to imitate them; and other people, who are as ignorant as he is, and judge only from his words, imagine that if he speaks of cobbling, or of military tactics, or of anything else, in metre and harmony and rhythm, he speaks very well—such is the sweet influence which melody and rhythm by nature have. And I think that you must have observed again and again what a poor appearance the tales of poets make when stripped of the colours which music puts upon them, and recited in simple prose.

Yes, he said.

They are like faces which were never really beautiful, but only blooming; and now the bloom of youth has passed away from them?

Exactly.

Here is another point: The imitator or maker of the image knows nothing of true existence; he knows appearances only. Am I not right?

Yes.

Then let us have a clear understanding, and not be satisfied with half an explanation.

Proceed.

Of the painter we say that he will paint reins, and he will paint a bit?

Yes.

And the worker in leather and brass will make them?

Certainly.

But does the painter know the right form of the bit and reins? Nay, hardly even the workers in brass and leather who make them; only the horseman who knows how to use them—he knows their right form.

Most true.

And may we not say the same of all things?

What?

That there are three arts which are concerned with all things: one which uses, another which makes, a third which imitates them?

Yes.

And the excellence or beauty or truth of every structure, animate or inanimate, and of every action of man, is relative to the use for which nature or the artist has intended them.

True.

Then the user of them must have the greatest experience of them, and he must indicate to the maker the good or bad qualities which develop themselves in use; for example, the flute-player will tell the flute-maker which of his flutes is satisfactory to the performer; he will tell him how he ought to make them, and the other will attend to his instructions?

Of course.

The one knows and therefore speaks with authority about the goodness and badness of flutes, while the other, confiding in him, will do what he is told by him?

True.

The instrument is the same, but about the excellence or badness of it the maker will only attain to a correct belief; and this he will gain from him who knows, by talking to him and being compelled to hear what he has to say, whereas the user will have knowledge.

True.

But will the imitator have either? Will he know from use whether or not his drawing is correct or beautiful? or will he have right opinion from being compelled to associate with another who knows and gives him instructions about what he should draw?

Neither.

Then he will no more have true opinion than he will have knowledge about the goodness or badness of his imitations?

I suppose not.

The imitative artist will be in a brilliant state of intelligence about his own creations?

Nay, very much the reverse.

And still he will go on imitating without knowing what makes a thing good or bad, and may be expected therefore to imitate only that which appears to be good to the ignorant multitude?

Just so.

Thus far then we are pretty well agreed that the imitator has no knowledge worth mentioning of what he imitates. Imitation is only a kind of play or sport, and the tragic poets, whether they write in Iambic or in Heroic verse, are imitators in the highest degree?

Very true.

And now tell me, I conjure you, has not imitation been shown by us to be concerned with that which is thrice removed from the truth?

Certainly.

And what is the faculty in man to which imitation is addressed?

What do you mean?

I will explain: The body which is large when seen near, appears small when seen at a distance?

True.

And the same objects appear straight when looked at out of the water, and crooked when in the water; and the concave becomes convex, owing to the illusion about colours to which the sight is liable. Thus every sort of confusion is revealed within us; and this is that weakness of the human mind on which the art of conjuring and of deceiving by light and shadow and other ingenious devices imposes, having an effect upon us like magic.

True.

And the arts of measuring and numbering and weighing come to the rescue of the human understanding—there is the beauty of them—and the apparent greater or less, or more or heavier, no longer have the mastery over us, but give way before calculation and measure and weight?

Most true.

And this, surely, must be the work of the calculating and rational principle in the soul?

To be sure.

And when this principle measures and certifies that some things are equal, or that some are greater or less than others, there occurs an apparent contradiction?

True.

But were we not saying that such a contradiction is impossible—the same faculty cannot have contrary opinions at the same time about the same thing?

Very true.

Then that part of the soul which has an opinion contrary to measure is not the same with that which has an opinion in accordance with measure?

True.

And the better part of the soul is likely to be that which trusts to measure and calculation?

Certainly.

And that which is opposed to them is one of the inferior principles of the soul?

No doubt.

This was the conclusion at which I was seeking to arrive when I said that painting or drawing, and imitation in general, when doing their own proper work, are far removed from truth, and the companions and friends and associates of a principle within us which is equally removed from reason, and that they have no true or healthy aim.

Exactly.

The imitative art is an inferior who marries an inferior, and has inferior offspring.

Very true.

And is this confined to the sight only, or does it extend to the hearing also, relating in fact to what we term poetry?

Probably the same would be true of poetry.

Do not rely, I said, on a probability derived from the analogy of painting; but let us examine further and see whether the faculty with which poetical imitation is concerned is good or bad.

By all means.

We may state the question thus:—Imitation imitates the actions of men, whether voluntary or involuntary, on which, as they imagine, a good or bad result has ensued, and they rejoice or sorrow accordingly. Is there anything more?

No, there is nothing else.

But in all this variety of circumstances is the man at unity with himself—or rather, as in the instance of sight there was confusion and opposition in his opinions about the same things, so here also is there not strife and inconsistency in his life? Though I need hardly raise the question again, for I remember that all this has been already admitted; and the soul has been acknowledged by us to be full of these and ten thousand similar oppositions occurring at the same moment?

And we were right, he said.

Yes, I said, thus far we were right; but there was an omission which must now be supplied.

What was the omission?

Were we not saying that a good man, who has the misfortune to lose his son or anything else which is most dear to him, will bear the loss with more equanimity than another?

Yes.

But will he have no sorrow, or shall we say that although he cannot help sorrowing, he will moderate his sorrow?

The latter, he said, is the truer statement.

Tell me: will he be more likely to struggle and hold out against his sorrow when he is seen by his equals, or when he is alone?

It will make a great difference whether he is seen or not.

When he is by himself he will not mind saying or doing many things which he would be ashamed of any one hearing or seeing him do?

True.

There is a principle of law and reason in him which bids him resist, as well as a feeling of his misfortune which is forcing him to indulge his sorrow?

True.

But when a man is drawn in two opposite directions, to and from the same object, this, as we affirm, necessarily implies two distinct principles in him?

Certainly.

One of them is ready to follow the guidance of the law?

How do you mean?

The law would say that to be patient under suffering is best, and that we should not give way to impatience, as there is no knowing whether such things are good or evil; and nothing is gained by impatience; also, because no human thing is of serious importance, and grief stands in the way of that which at the moment is most required.

What is most required? he asked.

That we should take counsel about what has happened, and when the dice have been thrown order our affairs in the way which reason deems best; not, like children who have had a fall, keeping hold of the part struck and wasting time in setting up a howl, but always accustoming the soul forthwith to apply a remedy, raising up that which is sickly and fallen, banishing the cry of sorrow by the healing art.

Yes, he said, that is the true way of meeting the attacks of fortune.

Yes, I said; and the higher principle is ready to follow this suggestion of reason?

Clearly.

And the other principle, which inclines us to recollection of our troubles and to lamentation, and can never have enough of them, we may call irrational, useless, and cowardly?

Indeed, we may.

And does not the latter—I mean the rebellious principle—furnish a great variety of materials for imitation? Whereas the wise and calm temperament, being always nearly equable, is not easy to imitate or to appreciate when imitated, especially at a public festival when a promiscuous crowd is assembled in a theatre. For the feeling represented is one to which they are strangers.

Certainly.

Then the imitative poet who aims at being popular is not by nature made, nor is his art intended, to please or to affect the rational principle in the soul; but he will prefer the passionate and fitful temper, which is easily imitated?

Clearly.

And now we may fairly take him and place him by the side of the painter, for he is like him in two ways: first, inasmuch as his creations have an inferior degree of truth—in this, I say, he is like him; and he is also like him in being concerned with an inferior part of the soul; and therefore we shall be right in refusing to admit him into a well-ordered State, because he awakens and nourishes and strengthens the feelings and impairs the reason. As in a city when the evil are permitted to have authority and the good are put out of the way, so in the soul of man, as we maintain, the imitative poet implants an evil constitution, for he indulges the irrational nature which has no discernment of greater and less, but thinks the same thing at one time great and at another small—he is a manufacturer of images and is very far removed from the truth.

Exactly.

But we have not yet brought forward the heaviest count in our accusation:—the power which poetry has of harming even the good (and there are very few who are not harmed), is surely an awful thing?

Yes, certainly, if the effect is what you say.

Hear and judge: The best of us, as I conceive, when we listen to a passage of Homer, or one of the tragedians, in which he represents some pitiful hero who is drawling out his sorrows in a long oration, or weeping, and smiting his breast—the best of us, you know, delight in giving way to sympathy, and are in raptures at the excellence of the poet who stirs our feelings most.

Yes, of course I know.

But when any sorrow of our own happens to us, then you may observe that we pride ourselves on the opposite quality—we would fain be quiet and patient; this is the manly part, and the other which delighted us in the recitation is now deemed to be the part of a woman.

Very true, he said.

Now can we be right in praising and admiring another who is doing that which any one of us would abominate and be ashamed of in his own person?

No, he said, that is certainly not reasonable.

Nay, I said, quite reasonable from one point of view.

What point of view?

If you consider, I said, that when in misfortune we feel a natural hunger and desire to relieve our sorrow by weeping and lamentation, and that this feeling which is kept under control in our own calamities is satisfied and delighted by the poets;—the better nature in each of us, not having been sufficiently trained by reason or habit, allows the sympathetic element to break loose because the sorrow is another's; and the spectator fancies that there can be no disgrace to himself in praising and pitying any one who comes telling him what a good man he is, and making a fuss about his troubles; he thinks that the pleasure is a gain, and why should he be supercilious and lose this and the poem too? Few persons ever reflect, as I should imagine, that from the evil of other men something of evil is communicated to themselves. And so the feeling of sorrow which has gathered strength at the sight of the misfortunes of others is with difficulty repressed in our own.

How very true!

And does not the same hold also of the ridiculous? There are jests which you would be ashamed to make yourself, and yet on the comic stage, or indeed in private, when you hear them, you are greatly amused by them, and are not at all disgusted at their unseemliness;—the case of pity is repeated;—there is a principle in human nature which is disposed to raise a laugh, and this which you once restrained by reason, because you were afraid of being thought a buffoon, is now let out again; and having stimulated the risible faculty at the theatre, you are betrayed unconsciously to yourself into playing the comic poet at home.

Quite true, he said.

And the same may be said of lust and anger and all the other affections, of desire and pain and pleasure, which are held to be inseparable from every action—in all of them poetry feeds and waters the passions instead of drying them up; she lets them rule, although they ought to be controlled, if mankind are ever to increase in happiness and virtue.

I cannot deny it.

Therefore, Glaucon, I said, whenever you meet with any of the eulogists of Homer declaring that he has been the educator of Hellas, and that he is profitable for education and for the ordering of human things, and that you should take him up again and again and get to know him and regulate your whole life according to him, we may love and honour those who say these things—they are excellent people, as far as their lights extend; and we are ready to acknowledge that Homer is the greatest of poets and first of tragedy writers; but we must remain firm in our conviction that hymns to the gods and praises of famous men are the only poetry which ought to be admitted into our State. For if you go beyond this and allow the honeyed muse to enter, either in epic or lyric verse, not law and the reason of mankind, which by common consent have ever been deemed best, but pleasure and pain will be the rulers in our State.

That is most true, he said.

And now since we have reverted to the subject of poetry, let this our defence serve to show the reasonableness of our former judgment in sending away out of our State an art having the tendencies which we have described; for reason constrained us. But that she may not impute to us any harshness or want of politeness, let us tell her that there is an ancient quarrel between philosophy and poetry; of which there are many proofs, such as the saying of "the yelping hound howling at her lord," or of one "mighty in the vain talk of fools," and "the mob of sages circumventing Zeus," and the "subtle thinkers who are beggars after all"; and there are innumerable other signs of ancient enmity between them. Notwithstanding this, let us assure our sweet friend and the sister arts of imitation, that if she will only prove her title to exist in a well-ordered State we shall be delighted to receive her—we are very conscious of her charms; but we may not on that account betray the truth. I dare say, Glaucon, that you are as much charmed by her as I am, especially when she appears in Homer?

Yes, indeed, I am greatly charmed.

Shall I propose, then, that she be allowed to return from exile, but upon this condition only that she makes a defence of herself in lyrical or some other metre?

Certainly.

And we may further grant to those of her defenders who are lovers of poetry and yet not poets the permission to speak in prose on her behalf: let them show not only that she is pleasant but also useful to States and to human life, and we will listen in a kindly spirit; for if this can be proved we shall surely be the gainers—I mean, if there is a use in poetry as well as a delight?

Certainly, he said, we shall be the gainers.

If her defence fails, then, my dear friend, like other persons who are enamoured of something, but put a restraint upon themselves when they think their desires are opposed to their interests, so too must we after the manner of lovers give her up, though not without a struggle. We too are inspired by that love of poetry which the education of noble States has implanted in us, and therefore we would have her appear at her best and truest; but so long as she is unable to make good her defence, this argument of ours shall be a charm to us, which we will repeat to ourselves while we listen to her strains; that we may not fall away into the childish love of her which captivates the many. At all events we are well aware that poetry being such as we have described is not to be regarded seriously as attaining to the truth; and he who listens to her, fearing for the safety of the city which is within him, should be on his guard against her seductions and make our words his law.

Yes, he said, I quite agree with you.

Yes, I said, my dear Glaucon, for great is the issue at stake, greater than appears, whereas a man is to be good or bad. And what will any one be profited if under the influence of honour or money or power, aye, or under the excitement of poetry, he neglect justice and virtue?

Yes, he said; I have been convinced by the argument, as I believe that any one else would have been. . . .

SANTAYANA

George Santayana (1863–1952) is the most urbane, cultivated, and broadly literate philosopher to write and teach in the United States. Although he was born in Spain and spent his last forty years in Europe, he nevertheless spent the middle period of his life teaching philosophy at Harvard University.

This discussion of the justification of art, taken from Santayana's five-volume work The Life of Reason, exhibits both the breadth of his philosophical concerns and the spare elegance of his literary style. In this selection, you can find him touching on the metaphysical status of aesthetic objects, the relation of form to content in art, the psychological roots of aesthetic experience, the moral responsibility of the artist, and even the relation of art to politics, science, and religion.

In a sense, this is the pivotal reading of the section, for Santayana explicitly or implicitly comments upon all the positions defended by the other authors represented here. In each case, characteristically, he criticizes the position as it has been formulated for narrowness or a one-sided emphasis on a single dimension of art. Then, however, he acknowledges that the position, suitably restated, contains an element of truth. The key phrase in the reading, it seems to me, is Santayana's observation that the philosopher would need "intelligent sympathy" to mediate the dispute between poets and men of business or science. Santayana's entire life and work is a striving for just such an intelligent sympathy with every form of experience and activity.

This generous breadth of spirit is enormously attractive, but it is achieved at a price. The man who opens himself to all the diversity of human life tends to withdraw from any strong commitments to some one cause or community. Santayana was, during his entire life, an observer rather than a participant. It is this, perhaps, rather than his philosophical doctrines, that distinguishes him most from Plato, Tolstoy, and Trotsky.

Justification of Art

Art is subject to moral censorship. It is no longer the fashion among philosophers to decry art. Either its influence seems to them too slight to excite alarm, or their systems are too lax to subject anything to censure which has the least glamour or ideality about it. Tired, perhaps, of daily resolving the conflict between science and religion, they prefer to assume silently a harmony between morals and art. Moral harmonies, however, are not given; they have to be made. The curse of superstition is that it justifies and protracts their absence by proclaiming their invisible presence. Of course a rational religion could not conflict with a rational science; and similarly an art that was wholly admirable would necessarily play into the hands of progress. But as the real difficulty in the former case lies in saying what religion and what science would be truly rational, so here the problem is how far extant art is a benefit to mankind, and how far, perhaps, a vice or a burden.

Its initial or specific excellence is not enough. The art is *prima facie* and in itself a good cannot be doubted. It is a spontaneous activity, and that settles the question. Yet the function of ethics is precisely to revise *prima facie* judgments of this kind and to fix the ultimate resultant of all given interests, in so far as they can be combined. In the actual disarray of human life and desire, wisdom consists in knowing what goods to sacrifice and what simples to pour into the supreme mixture. The extent to which æsthetic values are allowed to colour the resultant or highest good is a point of great theoretic importance, not only for art but for general philosophy. If art is excluded altogether or given only a trivial rôle, perhaps as a necessary relaxation, we feel at once that a philosophy so judging human arts is ascetic or post-rational. It pretends to guide life from above and from without; it has discredited human nature and mortal interests, and has thereby undermined itself, since it is at best but a partial expression of that humanity which it strives to transcend. If, on the contrary, art is prized as something supreme and irresponsible, if the poetic and mystic glow which it may bring seems its own complete justification, then philosophy is evidently still prerational or, rather, nonexistent; for the beasts that listened to Orpheus belong to this school.

To be bewitched is not to be saved, though all the magicians and æsthetes in the world should pronounce it to be so. Intoxication is a sad business, at least for a philosopher; for you must either drown yourself altogether, or else when sober again you will feel somewhat fooled by yesterday's joys and somewhat lost in to-day's vacancy. The man who would emancipate art from discipline and reason is trying to elude rationality, not merely in art, but in all existence. He is vexed at conditions of excellence that make him conscious of his own incompetence and failure. Rather than consider his function, he pro-

From *Reason in Art*, Vol. IV of *The Life of Reason*.

claims his self-sufficiency. A way foolishness has of revenging itself is to excommunicate the world.

It is in the world, however, that art must find its level. It must vindicate its function in the human commonwealth. What direct acceptable contribution does it make to the highest good? What sacrifices, if any, does it impose? What indirect influence does it exert on other activities? Our answer to these questions will be our apology for art, our proof that art belongs to the Life of Reason.

All satisfactions, however hurtful, have an initial worth. When moralists deprecate passion and contrast it with reason, they do so, if they are themselves rational, only because passion is so often "guilty," because it works havoc so often in the surrounding world and leaves, among other ruins, "a heart high-sorrowful and cloyed." Were there no danger of such after-effects within and without the sufferer, no passion would be reprehensible. Nature is innocent, and so are all her impulses and moods when taken in isolation; it is only on meeting that they blush. If it be true that matter is sinful, the logic of this truth is far from being what the fanatics imagine who commonly propound it. Matter is sinful only because it is insufficient, or is wastefully distributed. There is not enough of it to go round among the legion of hungry ideas. To embody or enact an idea is the only way of making it actual; but its embodiment may mutilate it, if the material or the situation is not propitious. So an infant may be maimed at birth, when what injures him is not being brought forth, but being brought forth in the wrong manner. Matter has a double function in respect to existence; essentially it enables the spirit to be, yet chokes it incidentally. Men sadly misbegotten, or those who are thwarted at every step by the times' penury, may fall to thinking of matter only by its defect, ignoring the material ground of their own aspirations. All flesh will seem to them weak, except that forgotten piece of it which makes their own spiritual strength. Every impulse, however, had initially the same authority as this censorious one, by which the others are now judged and condemned.

But, on the whole, artistic activity is innocent. If a practice can point to its innocence, if it can absolve itself from concern for a world with which it does not interfere, it has justified itself to those who love it, though it may not yet have recommended itself to those who do not. Now art, more than any other considerable pursuit, more even than speculation, is abstract and inconsequential. Born of suspended attention, it ends in itself. It encourages sensuous abstraction, and nothing concerns it less than to influence the world. Nor does it really do so in a notable degree. Social changes do not reach artistic expression until after their momentum is acquired and their other collateral effects are fully predetermined. Scarcely is a school of art established, giving expression to prevailing sentiment, when this sentiment changes and makes that style seem empty and ridiculous. The expression has little or no power to maintain the movement it registers, as a waterfall has little or no power to bring more water down. Currents may indeed cut deep channels, but they cannot feed their own springs—at least not until the whole revolution of nature is taken into account.

In the individual, also, art registers passions without stimulating them; on the contrary, in stopping to depict them it steals away their life; and whatever interest and delight it transfers to their expression it subtracts from their vital energy. This appears unmistakably in erotic and in religious art. Though the artist's avowed purpose here be to arouse a practical impulse, he fails in so far as he is an artist in truth; for he then will seek to move the given passions only through beauty, but beauty is a rival object of passion in itself. Lascivious and pious works, when beauty has touched them, cease to give out what is wilful and disquieting in their subject and become altogether intellectual and sublime. There is a high breathlessness about beauty that cancels lust and superstition. The artist, in taking the latter for his theme, renders them innocent and interesting, because he looks at them from above, composes their attitudes and surroundings harmoniously, and makes them food for the mind. Accordingly it is only in a refined and secondary stage that active passions like to amuse themselves with their æsthetic expression. Unmitigated lustiness and raw fanaticism will snarl at pictures. Representations begin to interest when crude passions recede, and feel the need of conciliating liberal interests and adding some intellectual charm to their dumb attractions. Thus art, while by its subject it may betray the preoccupations among which it springs up, embodies a new and quite innocent interest.

It is liberal. This interest is more than innocent, it is liberal. Not being concerned with material reality so much as with the ideal, it knows neither ulterior motives nor quantitative limits; the more beauty there is the more there can be, and the higher one artist's imagination soars the better the whole flock flies. In æsthetic activity we have accordingly one side of rational life; sensuous experience is dominated there as mechanical or social realities ought to be dominated in science and politics. Such dominion comes of having faculties suited to their conditions and consequently finding an inherent satisfaction in their operation. The justification of life must be ultimately intrinsic; and wherever such self-justifying experience is attained, the ideal has been in so far embodied. To have realised it in a measure helps us to realise it further; for there is a cumulative fecundity in those goods which come not by increase of force or matter, but by a better organisation and form.

It is typical of perfect activity. Art has met, on the whole, with more success than science or morals. Beauty gives men the best hint of ultimate good which their experience as yet can offer; and the most lauded geniuses have been poets, as if people felt that those seers, rather than men of action or thought, had lived ideally and known what was worth knowing. That such should be the case, if the fact be admitted, would indeed prove the rudimentary state of human civilisation. The truly comprehensive life should be the statesman's, for whom perception and theory might be expressed and rewarded in action. The ideal dignity of art is therefore merely symbolic and vicarious. As some people study character in novels, and travel by reading tales of adventure, because real life is not yet so interesting to them as fiction, or because they find it cheaper to make their experiments in their dreams, so art in general is a rehearsal of rational living, and recasts in idea a world which we have no present means of recasting in reality. Yet this rehearsal reveals the glories of a possible performance better than do the miserable experiments until now executed on the reality.

When we consider the present distracted state of government and religion, there is much relief in turning from them to almost any art, where what is good is altogether and finally good, and what is bad is at least not treacherous. When we consider further the senseless rivalries, the vanities, the ignominy that reign in the "practical" world, how doubly blessed it becomes to find a sphere where limitation is an excellence, where diversity is a beauty, and where every man's ambition is consistent with every other man's and even favourable to it! It is indeed so in art; for we must not import into its blameless labours the bickerings and jealousies of criticism. Critics quarrel with other critics, and that is a part of philosophy. With an artist no sane man quarrels, any more than with the colour of a child's eyes. As nature, being full of seeds, rises into all sorts of crystallisations, each having its own ideal and potential life, each a nucleus of order and habitation for the absolute self, so art, though in a medium poorer than pregnant matter, and incapable of intrinsic life, generates a semblance of all conceivable beings. What nature does with existence, art does with appearance; and while the achievement leaves us, unhappily, much where we were before in all our efficacious relations, it entirely renews our vision and breeds a fresh world in fancy, where all form has the same inner justification that all life has in the real world. As no insect is without its rights and every cripple has his dream of happiness, so no artistic fact, no child of imagination, is without its small birthright of beauty. In this freer element, competition does not exist and everything is Olympian. Hungry generations do not tread down the ideal but only its spokesmen or embodiments, that have cast in their lot with other material things. Art supplies constantly to contemplation what nature seldom affords in concrete experience—the union of life and peace.

The ideal, when incarnate, becomes subject to civil society. The ideal, however, would not come down from the empyrean and be conceived unless somebody's thought were absorbed in the conception. Art actually segregates classes of men and masses of matter to serve its special interests. This involves expense; it impedes some possible activities and imposes others. On this ground, from the earliest times until our own, art has been occasionally attacked by moralists, who have felt that it fostered idolatry or luxury or irresponsible dreams.

Plato's strictures: he exaggerates the effect of myths. Of these attacks the most interesting is Plato's, because he was an artist by temperament, bred in the very focus of artistic life and discussion, and at the same time a consummate moral philosopher. His æsthetic sensibility was indeed so great that it led him, perhaps, into a relative error, in that he overestimated the influence which art can have on character and affairs. Homer's stories about the gods can hardly have demoralised the youths who recited them. No religion has ever given a picture of deity which men could have imitated without the grossest immorality. Yet these shocking representations have not had a bad effect on believers. The deity was opposed to their own vices; those it might itself be credited with offered no contagious example. In spite of the theologians, we know by instinct that in speaking of the gods we are dealing in myths and symbols. Some aspect of nature or some law of life, expressed in an attribute of deity, is what we really regard, and to regard such things, however sinister they may be, cannot but chasten and moralise us. The personal character that such a function would involve, if it were exercised willingly by a responsible being, is something that never enters our thoughts. No such painful image comes to perplex the plain sense of instinctive, poetic religion. To give moral importance to myths, as Plato tended to do, is to take them far too seriously and to belittle what they stand for. Left to themselves they float in an ineffectual stratum of the brain. They are understood and grow current precisely by not being pressed, like an idiom or a metaphor. The same æsthetic sterility appears at the other end of the scale, where fancy is anything but sacred. A Frenchman once saw in "Punch and Judy" a shocking proof of British brutality, destined further to demoralise the nation; and yet the scandal may pass. That black tragedy reflects not very pretty manners, but puppets exercise no suasion over men.

His deeper moral objections. To his supersensitive censure of myths Plato added strictures upon music and the drama: to excite passions idly was to enervate the soul. Only martial or religious strains should be heard in the ideal republic. Furthermore, art put before us a mere phantom of the good. True excellence was the function things had in use; the horseman knew the use and essence of a bridle better than the artisan did who put it together; but a painted bridle would lack even this relation to utility. It would rein in no horse, and was an impertinent sensuous reduplication of what, even when it had material being, was only an instrument and a means.

This reasoning has been little understood, because Platonists soon lost sight of their master's Socratic habit and moral intent. They turned the good into an existence, making it thereby unmeaning. Plato's dialectic, if we do not thus abolish the force of its terms, is perfectly cogent: representative art has indeed no utility, and, if the good has been identified with efficiency in a military state, it can have no justification. Plato's Republic was avowedly a fallen state, a church militant, coming sadly short of perfection; and the joy which Plato as much as any one could feel in sensuous art he postponed, as a man in mourning might, until life should be redeemed from baseness.

Their rightness. Never have art and beauty received a more glowing eulogy than is implied in Plato's censure. To him nothing was beautiful that was not beautiful to the core, and he would have thought to insult art—the remodelling of nature by reason—if he had given it a narrower field than all practice. As an architect who had fondly designed something impossible, or which might not please in execution, would at once erase it from the plan and abandon it for the love of perfect beauty and perfect art, so Plato wished to erase from pleasing appearance all that, when its operation was completed, would bring discord into the world. This was done in the ultimate interest of art and beauty, which in a cultivated mind are inseparable from the vitally good. It is mere barbarism to feel that a thing is æsthetically good but morally evil, or morally good but hateful to perception. Things partially evil or partially ugly may have to be chosen under stress of unfavourable circumstances, lest some worse thing come; but if a thing were ugly it would *thereby* not be wholly good, and if it were *altogether* good it would perforce be beautiful.

To criticise art on moral grounds is to pay it a high compliment by assuming that it aims to be adequate, and is addressed to a comprehensive mind. The only way in which art could disallow such criticism would be to protest its irresponsible infancy, and admit that it was more or less amiable blatancy in individuals, and not *art* at all. Young animals often gambol in a delightful fashion, and men also may, though hardly when they intend to do so. Sportive self-expression can be prized because human nature contains a certain elasticity and margin for experiment, in which waste activity is inevitable and may be precious: for this license may lead, amid a thousand failures, to some real discovery and advance. Art, like life, should be free, since both are experimental. But it is one thing to make room for genius and to respect the sudden madness of poets through which, possibly, some god may speak, and it is quite another not to judge the result by rational standards. The earth's bowels are full of all sorts of rumblings; which of the oracles drawn thence is true can be judged only by the light of day. If an artist's inspiration has been happy, it has been so because his work can sweeten or ennoble the mind and because its total effect will be beneficent. Art being a part of life, the criticism of art is a part of morals.

Importance of æsthetic alternatives. Maladjustments in human society are still so scandalous, they touch matters so much more pressing than fine art, that maladjustments in the latter are passed over with a smile, as if art were at any rate an irresponsible miraculous parasite that the legislator had better not meddle with. The day may come, however, if the state is ever reduced to a tolerable order, when questions of art will be the most urgent questions of morals, when genius at last will feel responsible, and the twist given to imagination will seem the most crucial thing in life. Under a thin disguise, the momentous character of imaginative choices has already been fully recognised by mankind. Men have passionately loved their special religions, languages, and manners, and preferred death to a life flowering in any other fashion. In justifying this attachment forensically, with arguments on the low level of men's named and consecrated interests, people have indeed said, and perhaps come to believe, that their imaginative interests were material interests at bottom, thinking thus to give them more weight and legitimacy; whereas in truth material life itself would be nothing worth, were it not, in its essence and its issue, ideal.

It was stupidly asserted, however, that if a man omitted the prescribed ceremonies or had unauthorised dreams about the gods, he would lose his battles in this world and go to hell in the other. He who runs can see that these expectations are not founded on any evidence, on any observation of what actually occurs; they are obviously a *mirage* arising from a direct ideal passion, that tries to justify itself by indirection and by falsehoods, as it has no need to do. We all read facts in the way most congruous with our intellectual habit, and when this habit drives us to effulgent creations, absorbing and expressing the whole current of our being, it not merely biases our reading of this world but carries us into another world altogether, which we posit instead of the real one, or beside it.

Grotesque as the blunder may seem by which we thus introduce our poetic tropes into the sequence of external events or existences, the blunder is intellectual only; morally, zeal for our special rhetoric may not be irrational. The lovely Phœbus is no fact for astronomy, nor does he stand behind the material sun, in some higher heaven, physically superintending its movements; but Phœbus is a fact in his own region, a token of man's joyful piety in the presence of the forces that really condition his welfare. In the region of symbols, in the world of poetry, Phœbus has his inalienable rights. Forms of poetry are forms of human life. Languages express national character and enshrine particular ways of seeing and valuating events. To make substitutions and extensions in expression is to give the soul, in her inmost substance, a somewhat new constitution. A method of apperception is a spontaneous variation in mind, perhaps the origin of a new moral species.

The value apperceptive methods have is of course largely representative, in that they serve more or less aptly to dominate the order of events and to guide action; but quite apart from this practical value, expressions possess a character of their own, a sort of vegetative life, as languages possess euphony. Two reports of the same fact may be equally trustworthy, equally useful as information, yet they may embody two types of mental rhetoric, and this diversity in genius may be of more intrinsic importance than the raw fact it works upon. The non-representative side of human perception may thus be the most momentous side of it, because it represents, or even constitutes, the man. After all, the chief interest we have in things lies in what we can make of them or what they can make of us. There is consequently nothing fitted to colour human happiness more pervasively than art does, nor to express more deeply the mind's internal habit. In educating the imagination art crowns all moral endeavour, which from the beginning is a species of art, and which becomes a fine art more completely as it works in a freer medium.

The importance of æsthetic goods varies with temperaments. How great a portion of human energies should be spent on art and its appreciation is a question to be answered variously by various persons and nations. There is no ideal *à priori;* an ideal can but express, if it is genuine, the balance of impulses and potentialities in a given soul. A mind at once sensuous and mobile will find its appropriate perfection in studying and reappear chiefly on the plane of perception, to render the circle of visions which makes up its life as delightful as possible. For such a man art will be the most satisfying, the most significant activity, and to load him with material riches or speculative truths or profound social loyalties will be to impede and depress him. The irrational is what does not justify itself in the end; and the born artist, repelled by the soberer and bitterer passions of the world, may justly call them irrational. They would not justify themselves in his experience; they make grievous demands and yield nothing in the end which is intelligible to him. His picture of them, if he be a dramatist, will hardly fail to be satirical; fate, frailty, illusion will be his constant themes. If his temperament could find political expression, he would minimise the machinery of life and deprecate any calculated prudence. He would trust the heart, enjoy nature, and not frown too angrily on inclination. Such a Bohemia he would regard as an ideal world in which humanity might flourish congenially.

The æsthetic temperament requires tutelage. A puritan moralist, before condemning such an infantile paradise, should remember that a commonwealth of butterflies actually exists. It is not any inherent wrongness in such an ideal that makes it unacceptable, but only the fact that human butterflies are not wholly mercurial and that even imperfect geniuses are but an extreme type in a society whose guiding ideal is based upon a broader humanity than the artist represents. Men of science or business will accuse the poet of folly, on the very grounds on which he accuses them of the same. Each will seem to the other to be obeying a barren obsession. The statesman or philosopher who should aspire to adjust their quarrel could do so only by force of intelligent sympathy with both sides, and in view of the common conditions in which they find themselves. What ought to be done is that which, when done, will most nearly justify itself to all concerned. Practical problems of morals are judicial and political problems. Justice can never be pronounced without hearing the parties and weighing the interests at stake.

Æsthetic values everywhere interfused. A circumstance that complicates such a calculation is this: æsthetic and other interests are not separable units, to be compared externally; they are rather standards interwoven in the texture of everything. Æsthetic sensibility colours every thought, qualifies every allegiance, and modifies every product of human labour. Consequently the love of beauty has to justify itself not merely intrinsically, or as a constituent part of life more or less to be insisted upon; it has to justify itself also as an influence. A hostile influence is the most odious of things. The enemy himself, the alien creature, lies in his own camp, and in a speculative moment we may put ourselves in his place and learn to think of him charitably; but his spirit in our own souls is like a private tempter, a treasonable voice weakening our allegiance to our own duty. A zealot might allow his neighbours to be damned in peace, did not a certain heretical odour emitted by them infect the sanctuary and disturb his own dogmatic calm. In the same way practical people might leave the artist alone in his oasis, and even grant him a pittance on which to live, as they feed the animals in a zoological garden, did he not intrude into their inmost con-clave and vitiate the abstract cogency of their designs. It is not so much art in its own field that men of science look askance upon, as the love of glitter and rhetoric and false finality trespassing upon scientific ground; while men of affairs may well deprecate a rooted habit of sensuous absorption and of sudden transit to imaginary worlds, a habit which must work havoc in their own sphere. In other words, there is an element of poetry inherent in thought, in conduct, in affection; and we must ask ourselves how far this ingredient is an obstacle to their proper development.

They are primordial. The fabled dove who complained, in flying, of the resistance of the air, was as wise as the philosopher who should lament the presence and influence of sense. Sense is the native element and substance of experience; all its refinements are still parts of it existentially; and whatever excellence belongs specifically to sense is a preliminary excellence, a value antecedent to any which thought or action can achieve. Science and morals have but representative authority; they are principles of ideal synthesis and safe transition; they are bridges from moment to moment of sentience. Their function is indeed universal and their value overwhelming, yet their office remains derivative or secondary, and what they serve to put in order has pre-viously its intrinsic worth. An æsthetic bias is native to sense, being indeed nothing but its form and potency; and the influence which æsthetic habits exer-cise on thought and action should not be regarded as an intrusion to be re-sented, but rather as an original interest to be built upon and developed. Sensibility contains the distinctions which reason afterward carries out and applies; it is sensibility that involves and supports primitive diversities, such as those between good and bad, here and there, fast and slow, light and darkness. There are complications and harmonies inherent in these oppositions, harmonies which æsthetic faculty proceeds to note; and from these we may then construct others, not immediately presentable, which we distinguish by attributing them to reason. Reason may well outflank and transform æsthetic judgments, but can never undermine them. Its own materials are the perceptions which if full and perfect are called beauties. Its function is to endow the parts of sentience with a consciousness of the system in which they lie, so that they may attain a mutual relevance and ideally support one another. But what could relevance or support be worth if the things to be buttressed were themselves worthless? It is not to organise pain, ugliness, and boredom that reason can be called into the world.

To superpose them adventitiously is to destroy them. When a practical or scientific man boasts that he has laid aside æsthetic prejudices and is following truth and utility with a single eye, he can mean, if he is judicious, only that he has not yielded to æsthetic preference after his problem was fixed, nor in an arbitrary and vexatious fashion. He has not consulted taste when it would have been in bad taste to do so. If he meant that he had rendered himself altogether insensible to æsthetic values, and that he had proceeded to organise conduct or thought in complete indifference to the beautiful, he would be simply proclaiming his inhumanity and incompetence. A right observance of æsthetic demands does not obstruct utility or logic; for utility and logic are themselves beautiful, while a sensuous beauty that ran counter to reason could never be, in the end, pleasing to an exquisite sense. Æsthetic vice is not favourable to æsthetic faculty: it is an impediment to the greatest æsthetic satisfactions. And so when by yielding to a blind passion for beauty we derange theory and practice, we cut ourselves off from those beauties which alone could have satisfied our passion. What we drag in so obstinately will bring but a cheap and unstable pleasure, while a double beauty will thereby be lost or obscured—first, the unlooked-for beauty which a genuine and stable system of things could not but betray, and secondly the coveted beauty itself, which, being imported here into the wrong context, will be rendered meretricious and offensive to good taste. If a jewel worn on the wrong finger sends a shiver through the flesh, how disgusting must not rhetoric be in diplomacy or unction in metaphysics!

They flow naturally from perfect function. The poetic element inherent in thought, affection, and conduct is prior to their prosaic development and altogether legitimate. Clear, well-digested perception and rational choices follow upon those primary creative impulses, and carry out their purpose systematically. At every stage in this development new and appropriate materials are offered for æsthetic contemplation. Straightness, for instance, symmetry, and rhythm are at first sensuously defined; they are characters arrested by æsthetic instinct; but they are the materials of mathematics. And long after these initial forms have disowned their sensuous values, and suffered a wholly dialectical expansion or analysis, mathematical objects again fall under the æsthetic eye, and surprise the senses by their emotional power. A mechanical system, such as astronomy in one region has already unveiled, is an inexhaustible field for æsthetic wonder. Similarly, in another sphere, sensuous affinity leads to friendship and love, and makes us huddle up to our fellows and feel their heart-beats; but when human society has thereupon established a legal and moral edifice, this new spectacle yields new imaginative transports, tragic, lyric, and religious. Æsthetic values everywhere precede and accompany rational activity, and life is, in one aspect, always a fine art; not by introducing inaptly æsthetic vetoes or æsthetic flourishes, but by giving to everything a form which, implying a structure, implies also an ideal and a possible perfection. This perfection, being felt, is also a beauty, since any process, though it may have become intellectual or practical, remains for all that a vital and sentient operation, with its inherent sensuous values. Whatever is to be representative in import must first be immediate in existence; whatever is transitive in operation must be at the same time actual in being. So that an æsthetic sanction sweetens all successful living; animal efficiency cannot be without grace, nor moral achievement without a sensible glory.

These vital harmonies are natural; they are neither perfect nor preordained. We often come upon beauties that need to be sacrificed, as we come upon events and practical necessities without number that are truly regrettable. There are a myriad of conflicts in practice and in thought, conflicts between rival possibilities, knocking inopportunely and in vain at the door of existence. Owing to the initial disorganisation of things, some demands continually prove to be incompatible with others arising no less naturally. Reason in such cases imposes real and inseparable sacrifices, but it brings a stable consolation if its discipline is accepted.

Even inhibited functions, when they fall into a new rhythm, yield new beauties. Decay, for instance, is a moral and æsthetic evil; but being a natural necessity it can become the basis for pathetic and magnificent harmonies, when once imagination is adjusted to it. The hatred of change and death is ineradicable while life lasts, since it expresses that self-sustaining organisation in a creature which we call its soul; yet this hatred of change and death is not so deeply seated in the nature of things as are death and change themselves, for the flux is deeper than the ideal. Discipline may attune our higher and more adaptable part to the harsh conditions of being, and the resulting sentiment, being the only one which can be maintained successfully, will express the greatest satisfactions which can be reached, though not the greatest that might be conceived or desired. To be interested in the changing seasons is, in this middling zone, a happier state of mind than to be hopelessly in love with spring. Wisdom discovers these possible accommodations, as circumstances impose them; and education ought to prepare men to accept them.

It is for want of education and discipline that a man so often insists petulantly on his random tastes, instead of cultivating those which might find some satisfaction in the world and might produce in him some pertinent culture. Untutored self-assertion may even lead him to deny some fact that should have been patent, and plunge him into needless calamity. His Utopias cheat him in the end, if indeed the barbarous taste he has indulged in clinging to them does not itself lapse before the dream is half formed.

He who loves beauty must chasten it. So men have feverishly conceived a heaven only to find it insipid, and a hell to find it ridiculous. Theodicies that were to demonstrate an absolute cosmic harmony have turned the universe into a tyrannous nightmare, from which we are glad to awake again in this unintentional and somewhat tractable world. Thus the fancies of effeminate poets in violating science are false to the highest art, and the products of sheer confusion, instigated by the love of beauty, turn out to be hideous. A rational severity in respect to art simply weeds the garden; it expresses a mature æsthetic choice and opens the way to supreme artistic achievements. To keep beauty in its place is to make all things beautiful.

TOLSTOY

According to the old jibe, "Those who can, do; those who can't, teach." The same shaft has been aimed at philosophers from time to time, particularly in the area of æsthetics. Artists tend to feel about philosophers of art the way authors feel about reviewers and playwrights about critics. It is therefore pleasant to come upon a thoughtful and provocative discussion of the theory of art by a man who is also one of the greatest literary artists of all time, namely, the nineteenth-century Russian novelist Leo Tolstoy (1828–1910).

All of us know of Tolstoy's majestic novel War and Peace *(1866), although probably not all of us have managed to get all the way through it. In an appendix to that work, Tolstoy gave evidence of his philosophical talents by developing a subtle theory of historical causation. Thirty years later, after undergoing a profound religious conversion to a primitive form of Christian mysticism, Tolstoy wrote the book from which the present selection is taken.*

As you will see, Tolstoy puts forward the claim that art, in order to be good, must communicate universal religious perceptions which will unite men and make them aware of their brotherhood under God. He is perfectly willing to insist that most of what cultured and sophisticated people admire in literature, painting, sculpture, and music is simply bad art. He even utters the prime aesthetic heresy by asserting that Beethoven's Ninth Symphony is bad art!

Tolstoy talks a great deal in this selection about religious *perceptions and feelings, specifically those of Christianity. But you should not lose sight of the fact that his primary concern is with uniting men through their common humanity. It would not be difficult to formulate a secular version of Tolstoy's aesthetic philosophy which drew the same conclusion about good and bad art without any reference to religion.*

The Religious Significance
of Art

What is art—if we put aside the conception of beauty, which confuses the whole matter? The latest and most comprehensible definitions of art, apart from the conception of beauty, are the following: (1) Art is an activity arising even in the animal kingdom, *a*, springing from sexual desire and the propensity to play (Schiller, Darwin, Spencer), and *b*, accompanied by a pleasurable excitement of the nervous system (Grant Allen). This is the physiological-evolutionary definition. (2) Art is the external manifestation by means of lines, colors, movements, sounds, or words, of emotions felt by man (Véron). This is the experimental definition. According to the very latest definition, (3) Art is "the production of some permanent object or passing action, which is fitted, not only to supply an active enjoyment to the producer, but to convey a pleasurable impression to a number of spectators or listeners, quite apart from any personal advantage to be derived from it" (Sully).

Notwithstanding the superiority of these definitions to the metaphysical definitions which depended on the conception of beauty, they are yet far from exact. The first, the physiological-evolutionary definition (1*a*), is inexact because, instead of speaking about the artistic activity itself, which is the real matter in hand, it treats of the derivation of art. The modification of it (1*b*), based on the physiological effects on the human organism, is inexact because within the limits of such definition many other human activities can be included, as has occurred in the neo-aesthetic theories, which reckon as art the preparation of handsome clothes, pleasant scents, and even victuals.

The experimental definition (2), which makes art consist in the expression of emotions, is inexact because a man may express his emotions by means of lines, colors, sounds, or words, and yet may not act on others by such expression, and then the manifestation of his emotions is not art.

The third definition (that of Sully) is inexact because in the production of objects or actions affording pleasure to the producer and a pleasant emotion to the spectators or hearers, apart from personal advantage, may be included the showing of conjuring tricks or gymnastic exercises and other activities which are not art. And further, many things, the production of which does not afford pleasure to the producer and the sensation received from which is unpleasant, such as gloomy, heartrending scenes in a poetic description or a play, may nevertheless be undoubted works of art.

The inaccuracy of all these definitions arises from the fact that in them all (as also in the metaphysical definitions) the object considered is the pleasure art may give, and not the purpose it may serve in the life of man and of humanity.

From Chapters 5, 15, and 16 of *What Is Art?* by Leo Tolstoy. Trans. by Almyer Maude (1899).

In order to correctly define art, it is necessary, first of all, to cease to consider it as a means to pleasure and to consider it as one of the conditions of human life. Viewing it in this way we cannot fail to observe that art is one of the means of intercourse between man and man.

Every work of art causes the receiver to enter into a certain kind of relationship both with him who produced, or is producing, the art, and with all those who, simultaneously, previously, or subsequently, receive the same artistic impression.

Speech, transmitting the thoughts and experiences of men, serves as a means of union among them, and art acts in a similar manner. The peculiarity of this latter means of intercourse, distinguishing it from intercourse by means of words, consists in this, that whereas by words a man transmits his thoughts to another, by means of art he transmits his thoughts to another, by means of art he transmits his feelings.

The activity of art is based on the fact that a man, receiving through his sense of hearing or sight another man's expression of feeling, is capable of experiencing the emotion which moved the man who expressed it. To take the simplest example: one man laughs, and another who hears becomes merry; or a man weeps, and another who hears feels sorrow. A man is excited or irritated, and another man seeing him comes to a similar state of mind. By his movements or by the sounds of his voice, a man expresses courage and determination or sadness and calmness, and this state of mind passes on to others. A man suffers, expressing his sufferings by groans and spasms, and this suffering transmits itself to other people; a man expresses his feelings of admiration, devotion, fear, respect, or love to certain objects, persons, or phenomena, and others are infected by the same feelings of admiration, devotion, fear, respect, or love to the same objects, persons, and phenomena.

And it is upon this capacity of man to receive another man's expression of feeling and experience those feelings himself, that the activity of art is based.

If a man infects another or others directly, immediately, by his appearance or by the sounds he gives vent to at the very time he experiences the feeling; if he causes another man to yawn when he himself cannot help yawning, or to laugh or cry when he himself is obliged to laugh or cry, or to suffer when he himself is suffering—that does not amount to art.

Art begins when one person, with the object of joining another or others to himself in one and the same feeling, expresses that feeling by certain external indications. To take the simplest example: a boy, having experienced, let us say, fear on encountering a wolf, relates that encounter; and, in order to evoke in others the feeling he has experienced, describes himself, his condition before the encounter, the surroundings, the wood, his own lightheartedness, and then the wolf's appearance, its movements, the distance between himself and the wolf, etc. All this, if only the boy, when telling the story, again experiences the feelings he had lived through and infects the hearers and compels them to feel what the narrator had experienced, is art. If even the boy had not seen a wolf but had frequently been afraid of one, and if, wishing to evoke in others the fear he had felt, he invented an encounter with a wolf and recounted it so as to make his hearers share the feelings he experienced when he feared the wolf, that also would be art. And just in the same way it is art if a man, having experienced either the fear of suffering or the attraction of enjoyment (whether in reality or in imagination), expresses these feelings on canvas or in marble so that others are infected by them. And it is also art if a man feels or imagines to himself feelings of delight, gladness, sorrow, despair, courage, or despondency and the transition from one to another of these feelings, and expresses these feelings by sounds so that the hearers are infected by them and experience them as they were experienced by the composer.

The feelings with which the artist infects others may be most various— very strong or very weak, very important or very insignificant, very bad or very good: feelings of love for one's own country, self-devotion and submission to fate or to God expressed in a drama, raptures of lovers described in a novel, feelings of voluptuousness expressed in a picture, courage expressed in a triumphal march, merriment evoked by a dance, humor evoked by a funny story, the feeling of quietness transmitted by an evening landscape or by a lullaby, or the feeling of admiration evoked by a beautiful arabesque—it is all art.

If only the spectators or auditors are infected by the feelings which the author has felt, it is art.

To evoke in oneself a feeling one has experienced, and having evoked it in oneself, then, by means of movements, lines, colors, sounds, or forms expressed in words, so to transmit that feeling that others may experience the same feeling—this is the activity of art.

Art is a human activity consisting in this, that one man consciously, by means of certain external signs, hands on to others feelings he has lived through, and that other people are infected by these feelings and also experience them.

Art is not, as the metaphysicians say, the manifestation of some mysterious Idea of beauty or God; it is not, as the aesthetical physiologists say, a game in which a man lets off his excess of stored-up energy; it is not the expression of man's emotions by external signs; it is not the production of pleasing objects; and, above all, it is not pleasure; but it is a means of union among men, joining them together in the same feelings, and indispensable for the life and progress toward well-being of individuals and of humanity.

As, thanks to man's capacity to express thoughts by words, every man may know all that has been done for him in the realms of thought by all humanity before his day, and can in the present, thanks to this capacity to understand the thoughts of others, become a sharer in their activity and can himself hand on to his contemporaries and descendants the thoughts he has assimilated from others, as well as those which have arisen within himself; so, thanks to man's capacity to be infected with the feelings of others by means of art, all that is being lived through by his contemporaries is accessible to him, as well as the feelings experienced by men thousands of years ago, and he has also the possibility of transmitting his own feelings to others.

If people lacked this capacity to receive the thoughts conceived by the men who preceded them and to pass on to others their own thoughts, men would be like wild beasts, or like Kaspar Hauser.[1]

And if men lacked this other capacity of being infected by art, people might be almost more savage still, and, above all, more separated from, and more hostile to, one another.

And therefore the activity of art is a most important one, as important as the activity of speech itself and as generally diffused.

We are accustomed to understand art to be only what we hear and see in theaters, concerts, and exhibitions, together with buildings, statues, poems, novels. . . . But all this is but the smallest part of the art by which we communicate with each other in life. All human life is filled with works of art of every kind—from cradlesong, jest, mimicry, the ornamentation of houses, dress, and utensils, up to church services, buildings, monuments, and triumphal processions. It is all artistic activity. So that by art, in the limited sense of the word, we do not mean all human activity transmitting feelings, but only that part which we for some reason select from it and to which we attach special importance.

This special importance has always been given by all men to that part of this activity which transmits feelings flowing from their religious perception, and this small part of art they have specifically called art, attaching to it the full meaning of the word.

That was how men of old—Socrates, Plato, and Aristotle—looked on art. Thus did the Hebrew prophets and the ancient Christians regard art; thus it was, and still is, understood by the Mohammedans, and thus it still is understood by religious folk among our own peasantry.

Some teachers of mankind—as Plato in his *Republic* and people such as the primitive Christians, the strict Mohammedans, and the Buddhists—have gone so far as to repudiate all art.

People viewing art in this way (in contradiction to the prevalent view of today which regards any art as good if only it affords pleasure) considered, and consider, that art (as contrasted with speech, which need not be listened to) is so highly dangerous in its power to infect people against their wills that mankind will lose far less by banishing all art than by tolerating each and every art.

Evidently such people were wrong in repudiating all art, for they denied that which cannot be denied—one of the indispensable means of communication,

---

[1] "The foundling of Nuremberg," found in the market-place of that town on May 26, 1828, apparently some sixteen years old. He spoke little and was almost totally ignorant even of common objects. He subsequently explained that he had been brought up in confinement underground and visited by only one man, whom he seldom saw.—Tr.

without which mankind could not exist. But not less wrong are the people of civilized European society of our class and day in favoring any art if it but serves beauty, i.e., gives people pleasure.

Formerly people feared lest among the works of art there might chance to be some causing corruption, and they prohibited art altogether. Now they only fear lest they should be deprived of any enjoyment art can afford, and patronize any art. And I think the last error is much grosser than the first and that its consequences are far more harmful.

Art, in our society, has been so perverted that not only has bad art come to be considered good, but even the very perception of what art really is has been lost. In order to be able to speak about the art of our society, it is, therefore, first of all necessary to distinguish art from counterfeit art.

There is one indubitable indication distinguishing real art from its counterfeit, namely, the infectiousness of art. If a man, without exercising effort and without altering his standpoint on reading, hearing, or seeing another man's work, experiences a mental condition which unites him with that man and with other people who also partake of that work of art, then the object evoking that condition is a work of art. And however poetical, realistic, effectful, or interesting a work may be, it is not a work of art if it does not evoke that feeling (quite distinct from all other feelings) of joy and of spiritual union with another (the author) and with others (those who are also infected by it).

It is true that this indication is an *internal* one, and that there are people who have forgotten what the action of real art is, who expect something else from art (in our society the great majority are in this state), and that therefore such people may mistake for this aesthetic feeling the feeling of diversion and a certain excitement which they receive from counterfeits of art. But though it is impossible to undeceive these people, just as it is impossible to convince a man suffering from "Daltonism"[2] that green is not red, yet, for all that, this indication remains perfectly definite to those whose feeling for art is neither perverted nor atrophied, and it clearly distinguishes the feeling produced by art from all other feelings.

The chief peculiarity of this feeling is that the receiver of a true artistic impression is so united to the artist that he feels as if the work were his own and not someone else's—as if what it expresses were just what he had long been wishing to express. A real work of art destroys, in the consciousness of the receiver, the separation between himself and the artist—not that alone, but also between himself and all whose minds receive this work of art. In this freeing of our personality from its separation and isolation, in this uniting of it with others, lies the chief characteristic and the great attractive force of art.

If a man is infected by the author's condition of soul, if he feels this emotion and this union with others, then the object which has effected this is

---

[2] A kind of color blindness discovered by John Dalton.—Ed.

art; but if there be no such infection, if there be not this union with the author and with others who are moved by the same work—then it is not art. And not only is infection a sure sign of art, but the degree of infectiousness is also the sole measure of excellence in art.

The stronger the infection, the better is the art as art, speaking now apart from its subject matter, i.e., not considering the quality of the feelings it transmits.

And the degree of infectiousness of art depends on three conditions:

1. On the greater or lesser individuality of the feeling transmitted;
2. on the greater or lesser clearness with which the feeling is transmitted;
3. on the sincerity of the artist, i.e., on the greater or lesser force with which the artist himself feels the emotion he transmits.

The more individual the feeling transmitted the more strongly does it act on the receiver; the more individual the state of soul into which he is transferred, the more pleasure does the receiver obtain, and therefore the more readily and strongly does he join in it.

The clearness of expression assists infection because the receiver, who mingles in consciousness with the author, is the better satisfied the more clearly the feeling is transmitted, which, as it seems to him, he has long known and felt, and for which he has only now found expression.

But most of all is the degree of infectiousness of art increased by the degree of sincerity in the artist. As soon as the spectator, hearer, or reader feels that the artist is infected by his own production, and writes, sings, or plays for himself, and not merely to act on others, this mental condition of the artist infects the receiver; and contrariwise, as soon as the spectator, reader, or hearer feels that the author is not writing, singing, or playing for his own satisfaction —does not himself feel what he wishes to express—but is doing it for him, the receiver, a resistance immediately springs up, and the most individual and the newest feelings and the cleverest technique not only fail to produce any infection but actually repel.

I have mentioned three conditions of contagiousness in art, but they may be all summed up into one, the last, sincerity, i.e., that the artist should be impelled by an inner need to express his feeling. That condition includes the first; for if the artist is sincere he will express the feeling as he experienced it. And as each man is different from every one else, his feeling will be individual for everyone else; and the more individual it is—the more the artist has drawn it from the depths of his nature—the more sympathetic and sincere it will be. And this same sincerity will impel the artist to find a clear expression of the feeling which he wishes to transmit.

Therefore this third condition—sincerity—is the most important of the three. It is always complied with in peasant art, and this explains why such art always acts so powerfully; but it is a condition almost entirely absent from our upper-class art, which is continually produced by artists actuated by personal aims of covetousness or vanity. . . .

The absence of any one of these conditions excludes a work from the category of art and relegates it to that of art's counterfeits. . . .

Thus is art divided from that which is not art, and thus is the quality of art as art decided, independently of its subject matter, i.e., apart from whether the feelings it transmits are good or bad.

But how are we to define good and bad art with reference to its subject matter?

Art, like speech, is a means of communication, and therefore of progress, i.e., of the movement of humanity forward toward perfection. Speech renders accessible to men of the latest generations all the knowledge discovered by the experience and reflection, both of preceding generations and of the best and foremost men of their own times; art renders accessible to men of the latest generations all the feelings experienced by their predecessors, and those also which are being felt by their best and foremost contemporaries. And as the evolution of knowledge proceeds by truer and more necessary knowledge, dislodging and replacing what is mistaken and unnecessary, so the evolution of feeling proceeds through art—feelings less kind and less needful for the well-being of mankind are replaced by others kinder and more needful for that end. That is the purpose of art. And, speaking now of its subject matter, the more art fulfills that purpose the better the art, and the less it fulfils it, the worse the art.

And the appraisement of feelings (i.e., the acknowledgment of these or those feelings as being more or less good, more or less necessary for the well-being of mankind) is made by the religious perception of the age.

In every period of history, and in every human society, there exists an understanding of the meaning of life which represents the highest level to which men of that society have attained, an understanding defining the highest good at which that society aims. And this understanding is the religious perception of the given time and society. And this religious perception is always clearly expressed by some advanced men, and more or less vividly perceived by all the members of the society. Such a religious perception and its corresponding expression exists always in every society. If it appears to us that in our society there is no religious perception, this is not because there really is none, but only because we do not want to see it. And we often wish not to see it because it exposes the fact that our life is inconsistent with that religious perception.

Religious perception in a society is like the direction of a flowing river. If the river flows at all, it must have a direction. If society lives, there must be a religious perception indicating the direction in which, more or less consciously, all its members tend. . . .

I know that according to an opinion current in our times religion is a superstition which humanity has outgrown, and that it is therefore assumed that no such thing exists as a religious perception, common to us all, by which art, in our time, can be evaluated. I know that this is the opinion current in the pseudo-cultured circles of today. People who do not acknowledge Christianity in its true meaning because it undermines all their social privileges, and who, therefore, invent all kinds of philosophic and aesthetic theories to hide from themselves the meaninglessness and wrongness of their lives, cannot think otherwise. These people intentionally, or sometimes unintentionally, confusing the conception of a religious perception think that by denying the cult they get rid of religious perception. But even the very attacks on religion and the attempts to establish a life-conception contrary to the religious perception of our times most clearly demonstrate the existence of a religious perception condemning the lives that are not in harmony with it.

If humanity progresses, i.e., moves forward, there must inevitably be a guide to the direction of that movement. And religions have always furnished that guide. All history shows that the progress of humanity is accomplished not otherwise than under the guidance of religion. But if the race cannot progress without the guidance of religion—and progress is always going on, and consequently also in our own times—then there must be a religion of our times. So that, whether it pleases or displeases the so-called cultured people of today, they must admit the existence of religion—not of a religious cult, Catholic, Protestant, or another, but of religious perception—which, even in our times, is the guide always present where there is any progress. And if a religious perception exists among us, then our art should be appraised on the basis of that religious perception; and, as has always and everywhere been the case, art transmitting feelings flowing from the religious perception of our time should be chosen from all the indifferent art, should be acknowledged, highly esteemed, and encouraged, while art running counter to that perception should be condemned and despised, and all the remaining indifferent art should neither be distinguished nor encouraged.

The religious perception of our time, in its widest and most practical application, is the consciousness that our well-being, both material and spiritual, individual and collective, temporal and eternal, lies in the growth of brotherhood among all men—in their loving harmony with one another. This perception is not only expressed by Christ and all the best men of past ages, it is not only repeated in the most varied forms and from most diverse sides by the best men of our own times, but it already serves as a clue to all the complex labor of humanity, consisting as this labor does, on the one hand, in the destruction of physical and moral obstacles to the union of men, and, on the other hand, in establishing the principles common to all men which can and should unite them into one universal brotherhood. And it is on the basis of this perception that we should appraise all the phenomena of our life, and, among the rest, our art also; choosing from all its realms whatever transmits feelings flowing from this religious perception, highly prizing and encouraging such art, rejecting whatever is contrary to this perception, and not attributing to the rest of art an importance not properly pertaining to it. . . .

It is true that art which satisfies the demands of the religious perception of our time is quite unlike former art, but, notwithstanding this dissimilarity, to a man who does not intentionally hide the truth from himself, it is very clear and definite what does form the religious art of our age. In former times, when the highest religious perception united only some people (who, even if they formed a large society, were yet but one society surrounded by others—Jews, or Athenian, or Roman citizens), the feelings transmitted by the art of that time flowed from a desire for the might, greatness, glory, and prosperity of that society, and the heroes of art might be people who contributed to that prosperity by strength, by craft, by fraud, or by cruelty (Ulysses, Jacob, David, Samson, Hercules, and all the heroes). But the religious perception of our times does not select any one society of men; on the contrary, it demands the union of all—absolutely of all people without exception—and above every other virtue it sets brotherly love to all men. And therefore, the feelings transmitted by the art of our time not only cannot coincide with the feelings transmitted by former art, but must run counter to them. . . .

Art, all art, has this characteristic, that it unites people. Every art causes those to whom the artist's feeling is transmitted to unite in soul with the artist, and also with all who receive the same impression. But non-Christian art, while uniting some people together, makes that very union a cause of separation between these united people and others; so that union of this kind is often a source, not only of division, but even of enmity toward others. Such is all patriotic art, with its anthems, poems, and monuments; such is all Church art, ie., the art of certain cults, with their images, statutes, processions, and other local ceremonies. Such art is belated and non-Christian art, uniting the people of one cult only to separate them yet more sharply from the members of other cults, and even to place them in relations of hostility to each other. Christian art is only such as tends to unite all without exception, either by evoking in them the perception that each man and all men stand in like relation toward God and toward their neighbor, or by evoking in them identical feelings which may even be the very simplest, provided only that they are not repugnant to Christianity and are natural to everyone without exception. . . .

Christian art, i.e., the art of our time, should be catholic in the original meaning of the word, i.e., universal, and therefore it should unite all men. And only two kinds of feeling do unite all men: first, feelings flowing from the perception of our sonship to God and of the brotherhood of man; and next, the simple feelings of common life, accessible to every one without exception—such as the feeling of merriment, of pity, of cheerfulness, of tranquillity, etc. Only these two kinds of feelings can now supply material for art good in its subject matter.

And the action of these two kinds of art, apparently so dissimilar, is one and the same. The feelings flowing from perception of our sonship to God and of the brotherhood of man—such as a feeling of sureness in truth, devotion to the will of God, self-sacrifice, respect for and love of man—evoked by Christian religious perception; and the simplest feelings—such as a softened or a merry mood caused by a song or an amusing jest intelligible to everyone, or by a touching story, or a drawing, or a little doll: both alike produce one and the same effect, the loving union of man with man. Sometimes people who are together are, if not hostile to one another, at least estranged in mood and feeling till perchance a story, a performance, a picture, or even a building, but most often of all music, unites them all as by an electric flash, and in place of their former isolation or even enmity they are all conscious of union and mutual love. Each is glad that another feels what he feels: glad of the communion established, not only between him and all present, but also with all now living who will yet share the same impression; and more than that, he feels the mysterious gladness of a communion which, reaching beyond the grave, unites us with all men of the past who have been moved by the same feelings, and with all men of the future who will yet be touched by them. And this effect is produced both by the religious art which transmits feelings of love to God and one's neighbor and by universal art transmitting the very simplest feelings common to all men.

The art of our time should be appraised differently from former art chiefly in this, that the art of our time, i.e., Christian art (basing itself on a religious perception which demands the union of man), excludes from the domain of art good in subject matter everything transmitting exclusive feelings which do not unite, but divide, men. It relegates such work to the category of art bad in its subject matter, while, on the other hand, it includes in the category of art good in subject matter a section not formerly admitted to deserve to be chosen out and respected, namely, universal art, transmitting even the most trifling and simple feelings if only they are accessible to all men without exception and therefore unite them. Such art cannot in our time but be esteemed good, for it attains the end which the religious perception of our time, i.e., Christianity, sets before humanity.

Christian art either evokes in men those feelings which, through love of God and of one's neighbor, draw them to greater and ever greater union and make them ready for and capable of such union, or evokes in them those feelings which show them that they are already united in the joys and sorrows of life. And therefore the Christian art of our time can be and is of two kinds: (1) art transmitting feelings flowing from a religious perception of man's position in the world in relation to God and to his neighbor—religious art in the limited meaning of the term; and (2) art transmitting the simplest feelings of common life, but such, always, as are accessible to all men in the whole world: the art of common life—the art of a people—universal art. Only these two kinds of art can be considered good art in our time. . . .

So there are only two kinds of good Christian art; all the rest of art not comprised in these two divisions should be acknowledged to be bad art, deserving not to be encouraged but to be driven out, denied, and despised as being art which does not unite, but divides, people. Such, in literary art, are all novels and poems which transmit Church or patriotic feelings, and also exclusive feelings pertaining only to the class of the idle rich such as aristocratic honor, satiety, spleen, pessimism, and refined and vicious feelings flowing from sex-love—quite incomprehensible to the great majority of mankind.

In painting we must similarly place in the class of bad art all the Church, patriotic, and exclusive pictures; all the pictures representing the amusements and allurements of a rich and idle life; all the so-called symbolic pictures, in which the very meaning of the symbol is comprehensible only to the people of a certain circle; and, above all, pictures with voluptuous subjects—all that odious female nudity which fills all the exhibitions and galleries. And to this class belongs almost all the chamber and opera music of our times, beginning especially from Beethoven (Schumann, Berlioz, Liszt, Wagner), by its subject matter devoted to the expression of feelings accessible only to people who have developed in themselves an unhealthy, nervous irritation evoked by this exclusive, artificial, and complex music.

"What! the *Ninth Symphony* not a good work of art!" I hear exclaimed by indignant voices.

And I reply, Most certainly it is not. All that I have written I have written with the sole purpose of finding a clear and reasonable criterion by which to judge the merits of works of art. And this criterion, coinciding with the indications of plain and sane sense, indubitably shows me that that symphony by Beethoven is not a good work of art. Of course, to people educated in the adoration of certain productions and of their authors, to people whose taste has been perverted just by being educated in such adoration, the acknowledgment that such a celebrated work is bad is amazing and strange. But how are we to escape the indications of reason and of common sense?

Beethoven's *Ninth Symphony* is considered a great work of art. To verify its claim to be such, I must first ask myself whether this work transmits the highest religious feeling. I reply in the negative, for music in itself cannot transmit those feelings; and therefore I ask myself next, Since this work does not belong to the highest kind of religious art, has it the other characteristic of the good art of our time—the quality of uniting all men in one common feeling: does it rank as Christian universal art? And again I have no option but to reply in the negative; for not only do I not see how the feelings transmitted by this work could unite people not specially trained to submit themselves to its complex hypnotism, but I am unable to imagine to myself a crowd of normal people who could understand anything of this long, confused, and artificial production, except short snatches which are lost in a sea of what is incomprehensible. And therefore, whether I like it or not, I am compelled to conclude that this work belongs to the rank of bad art. It is curious to note in this connection that attached to the end of this very symphony is a poem of Schiller's which (though somewhat obscurely) expresses this very thought, namely, that feeling (Schiller speaks only of the feeling of gladness) unites people and evokes love in them. But though this poem is sung at the end of the symphony, the music does not accord with the thought expressed in the verses; for the music is exclusive and does not unite all men, but unites only a few, dividing them off from the rest of mankind.

And just in this same way, in all branches of art, many and many works considered great by the upper classes of our society will have to be judged. By this one sure criterion we shall have to judge the celebrated *Divine Comedy* and *Jerusalem Delivered*, and a great part of Shakespeare's and Goethe's works, and in painting every representation of miracles, including Raphael's "Transfiguration," etc.

Whatever the work may be and however it may have been extolled, we have first to ask whether this work is one of real art or a counterfeit. Having acknowledged, on the basis of the indication of its infectiousness even to a small class of people, that a certain production belongs to the realm of art, it is necessary, on the basis of the indication of its accessibility, to decide the next question, Does this work belong to the category of bad, exclusive art, opposed to religious perception, or to Christian art uniting people? And having acknowledged an article to belong to real Christian art, we must then, according to whether it transmits the feelings flowing from love to God and man, or merely the simple feelings uniting all men, assign it a place in the ranks of religious art or in those of universal art.

Only on the basis of such verification shall we find it possible to select from the whole mass of what in our society claims to be art those works which form real, important, necessary spiritual food, and to separate them from all the harmful and useless art and from the counterfeits of art which surround us. Only on the basis of such verification shall we be able to rid ourselves of the pernicious results of harmful art and to avail ourselves of that beneficent action which is the purpose of true and good art and which is indispensable for the spiritual life of man and of humanity.

BELL

For Clive Bell (1881–1964), the aesthetic experience is intrinsically good, quite independently of any good or bad effects that it might produce in man, society, history, or religion. Bell is a defender of the doctrine that art is its own justification—"art for art's sake." He is particularly critical of the views of Tolstoy, but he would scarcely feel more sympathy with Plato's attempt to judge art on grounds of social utility.

Bell appeals to the ethical theories of the English philosopher G. E. Moore as support for his view that artistic experience has intrinsic value. He summarizes Moore's theory that goodness is a simple, nonnatural property analogous to such simple perceptional qualities as redness or yellowness. It is Bell's claim that aesthetic experience is intrinsically good, and that we can know this fact immediately and directly.

Bell's aim is to defend art as a human activity which is valuable in itself, needing no justification by appeal to religion or social harmony. But his reliance on Moore's theory of "nonnatural qualities" raises as many questions as it answers. For example, Moore insisted that no analysis could be given of the nature of goodness, because of its simplicity. Must we then conclude that no analysis can be given of the nature of beauty? Can there be no fruitful and intelligent debate about the artistic quality of a painting or poem? Are there really objective, intercultural, transhistorical standards of beauty, just as there are for such qualities as color? Such a claim is difficult enough to maintain in the sphere of ethics, as Westermarck showed. In the sphere of art it seems virtually paradoxical!

Art for Art's Sake

Between me and the pleasant places of history remains, however, one ugly barrier. I cannot dabble and paddle in the pools and shallows of the past until I have answered a question so absurd that the nicest people never tire of

Chapter 3, "Art and Ethics" from *Art* by Clive Bell. Reprinted by permission of G. P. Putnam's Sons and by Quentin Bell and Chatto and Windus Ltd.

asking it: "What is the moral justification of art?" Of course they are right who insist that the creation of art must be justified on ethical grounds: all human activities must be so justified. It is the philosopher's privilege to call upon the artist to show that what he is about is either good in itself or a means to good. It is the artist's duty to reply: "Art is good because it exalts to a state of ecstasy better far than anything a benumbed moralist can even guess at; so shut up." Philosophically he is quite right; only, philosophy is not so simple as that. Let us try to answer philosophically.

The moralist inquires whether art is either good in itself or a means to good. Before answering, we will ask what he means by the word "good," not because it is in the least doubtful, but to make him think. In fact, Mr. G. E. Moore has shown pretty conclusively in his *Principia Ethica* that by "good" everyone means just good. We all know quite well what we mean though we cannot define it. "Good" can no more be defined than "Red": no quality can be defined. Nevertheless we know perfectly well what we mean when we say that a thing is "good" or "red." This is so obviously true that its statement has greatly disconcerted, not to say enraged, the orthodox philosophers.

Orthodox philosophers are by no means agreed as to what we do mean by "good," only they are sure that we cannot mean what we say. They used to be fond of assuming that "good" meant pleasure; or, at any rate, that pleasure was the sole good as an end: two very different propositions. That "good" means "pleasure" and that pleasure is the sole good was the opinion of the Hedonists, and is still the opinion of any Utilitarians who may have lingered on into the twentieth century. They enjoy the honour of being the only ethical fallacies worth the powder and shot of a writer on art. I can imagine no more delicate or convincing piece of logic than that by which Mr. G. E. Moore disposes of both. But it is none of my business to do clumsily what Mr. Moore has done exquisitely. I have no mind by attempting to reproduce his dialectic to incur the merited ridicule of those familiar with the *Principia Ethica* or to spoil the pleasure of those who will be wise enough to run out this very minute and order a masterpiece with which they happen to be unacquainted. For my immediate purpose it is necessary only to borrow one shaft from that well-stocked armoury.

To him who believes that pleasure is the sole good, I will put this question: Does he, like John Stuart Mill, and everyone else I ever heard of, speak of "higher and lower" or "better and worse" or "superior and inferior" pleasures? And, if so, does he not perceive that he has given away his case? For, when he says that one pleasure is "higher" or "better" than another, he does not mean that it is greater in *quantity* but superior in *quality*.

On page 7 of *Utilitarianism*, J. S. Mill says:—

> If one of the two (pleasures) is, by those who are competently acquainted with both, placed so far above the other that they prefer it, even though knowing it to be attended with a greater amount of discontent, and would not resign it for any quantity of the other pleasure which their nature

is capable of, we are justified in ascribing to the preferred enjoyment a superiority in quality, so far outweighing quantity as to render it, in comparison, of small account.[1]

But if pleasure be the sole good, the only possible criterion of pleasures is quantity of pleasure. "Higher" or "better" can only mean containing more pleasure. To speak of "better pleasures" in any other sense is to make the goodness of the sole good as an end depend upon something which, *ex hypothesi*, is not good as an end. Mill is as one who, having set up sweetness as the sole good quality in jam, prefers Tiptree to Crosse and Blackwell, not because it is sweeter, but because it possesses a better kind of sweetness. To do so is to discard sweetness as an ultimate criterion and to set up something else in its place. So, when Mill, like everyone else, speaks of "better" or "higher" or "superior" pleasures, he discards pleasure as an ultimate criterion, and thereby admits that pleasure is not the sole good. He feels that some pleasures are better than others, and determines their respective values by the degree in which they possess that quality which all recognise but none can define—goodness. By higher and lower, superior and inferior pleasures we mean simply more good and less good pleasures. There are, therefore, two different qualities, Pleasantness and Goodness. Pleasure, amongst other things, may be good; but pleasure cannot mean good. By "good" we cannot mean "pleasureable"; for, as we see, there is a quality, "goodness," so distinct from pleasure that we speak of pleasures that are more or less good without meaning pleasures that are more or less pleasant. By "good," then, we do not mean "pleasure," neither is pleasure the sole good.

Mr. Moore goes on to inquire what things are good in themselves, as ends that is to say. He comes to a conclusion with which we all agree, but for which few could have found convincing and logical arguments: "states of mind," he shows, alone are good as ends.[2] People who have very little taste for logic will find a simple and satisfactory proof of this conclusion afforded by what is called "the method of isolation."

That which is good as an end will retain some, at any rate, of its value in complete isolation: it will retain all its value as an end. That which is good as a means only will lose all its value in isolation. That which is good as an end will remain valuable even when deprived of all its consequences and left with nothing but bare existence. Therefore, we can discover whether honestly we feel something to be good as an end, if only we can conceive it in complete isolation, and be sure that so isolated it remains valuable. Bread is good. Is bread good as an end or as a means? Conceive a loaf existing in an uninhabited and uninhabitable planet. Does it seem to lose its value? That is a little too easy. The physical universe appears to most people immensely good, for towards

---

[1] See the selection by Mill in Section IV of this volume.—ED.
[2] Formerly he held that inanimate beauty also was good in itself. But this tenet, I am glad to learn, he has discarded.

nature they feel violently that emotional reaction which brings to the lips the epithet "good"; but if the physical universe were not related to mind, if it were never to provoke an emotional reaction, if no mind were ever to be affected by it, and if it had no mind of its own, would it still appear good? There are two stars: one is, and ever will be, void of life, on the other exists a fragment of just living protoplasm which will never develop, will never become conscious. Can we say honestly that we feel one to be better than the other? Is life itself good as an end? A clear judgment is made difficult by the fact that one cannot conceive anything without feeling something for it; one's very conceptions provoke states of mind and thus acquire value as means. Let us ask ourselves, bluntly, can that which has no mind and affects no mind have value? Surely not. But anything which has a mind can have intrinsic value, and anything that affects a mind may become valuable as a means, since the state of mind produced may be valuable in itself. Isolate that mind. Isolate the state of mind of a man in love or rapt in contemplation; it does not seem to lose all its value. I do not say that its value is not decreased; obviously, it loses its value as a means to producing good states of mind in others. But a certain value does subsist—an intrinsic value. Populate the lone star with one human mind and every part of that star becomes potentially valuable as a means, because it may be a means to that which is good as an end—a good state of mind. The state of mind of a person in love or rapt in contemplation suffices in itself. We do not stay to inquire "What useful purpose does this serve, whom does it benefit, and how?" We say directly and with conviction—"This is good."

When we are challenged to justify our opinion that anything, other than a state of mind, is good, we, feeling it to be a means only, do very properly seek its good effects, and our last justification is always that it produces good states of mind. Thus, when asked why we call a patent fertiliser good, we may, if we can find a listener, show that the fertiliser is a means to good crops, good crops a means to food, food a means to life, and life a necessary condition of good states of mind. Further we cannot go. When asked why we hold a particular state of mind to be good, the state of aesthetic contemplation for instance, we can but reply that to us its goodness is self-evident. Some states of mind appear to be good independently of their consequences. No other things appear to be good in this way. We conclude, therefore, that good states of mind are alone good as ends.

To justify ethically any human activity, we must inquire—"Is this a means to good states of mind?" In the case of art our answer will be prompt and emphatic. Art is not only a means to good states of mind, but, perhaps, the most direct and potent that we possess. Nothing is more direct, because nothing affects the mind more immediately; nothing is more potent, because there is no state of mind more excellent or more intense than the state of aesthetic contemplation. This being so, to seek any other moral justification for art, to seek in art a means to anything less than good states of mind, is an act of wrong-headedness to be committed only by a fool or a man of genius.

Many fools have committed it and one man of genius has made it notorious. Never was cart put more obstructively before horse than when Tolstoi announced that the justification of art was its power of promoting good actions. As if actions were ends in themselves! There is neither virtue nor vice in running: but to run with good tidings is commendable, to run away with an old lady's purse is not. There is no merit in shouting: but to speak up for truth and justice is well, to deafen the world with charlatanry is damnable. Always it is the end in view that gives value to action; and, ultimately, the end of all good actions must be to create or encourage or make possible good states of mind. Therefore, inciting people to good actions by means of edifying images is a respectable trade and a roundabout means to good. Creating works of art is as direct a means to good as a human being can practise. Just in this fact lies the tremendous importance of art: there is no more direct means to good.

To pronounce anything a work of art is, therefore, to make a momentous moral judgment. It is to credit an object with being so direct and powerful a means to good that we need not trouble ourselves about any other of its possible consequences. But even were this not the case, the habit of introducing moral considerations into judgments between particular works of art would be inexcusable. Let the moralist make a judgment about art as a whole, let him assign it what he considers its proper place amongst means to good, but in aesthetic judgments, in judgments between members of the same class, in judgments between works of art considered as art, let him hold his tongue. If he esteem art anything less than equal to the greatest means to good he mistakes. But granting, for the sake of peace, its inferiority to some, I will yet remind him that his moral judgments about the value of particular works of art have nothing to do with their artistic value. The judge at Epsom is not permitted to disqualify the winner of the Derby in favour of the horse that finished last but one on the ground that the latter is just the animal for the Archbishop of Canterbury's brougham.

Define art as you please, preferably in accordance with my ideas; assign it what place you will in the moral system; and then discriminate between works of art according to their excellence in that quality, or those qualities, that you have laid down in your definition as essential and peculiar to works of art. You may, of course, make ethical judgments about particular works, not as works of art, but as members of some other class, or as independent and unclassified parts of the universe. You may hold that a particular picture by the President of the Royal Academy is a greater means to good than one by the glory of the New English Art Club, and that a penny bun is better than either. In such a case you will be making a moral and not an aesthetic judgment. Therefore it will be right to take into account the area of the canvases, the thickness of the frames, and the potential value of each as fuel or shelter against the rigours of our climate. In casting up accounts you should not neglect their possible effects on the middle-aged people who visit Burlington House and the Suffolk Street

Gallery; nor must you forget the consciences of those who handle the Chantry funds, or of those whom high prices provoke to emulation. You will be making a moral and not an aesthetic judgment; and if you have concluded that neither picture is a work of art, though you may be wasting your time, you will not be making yourself ridiculous. But when you treat a picture as a work of art, you have, unconsciously perhaps, made a far more important moral judgment. You have assigned it to a class of objects so powerful and direct as means to spiritual exaltation that all minor merits are inconsiderable. Paradoxical as it may seem, the only relevant qualities in a work of art, judged as art, are artistic qualities: judged as a means to good, no other qualities are worth considering; for there are no qualities of greater moral value than artistic qualities, since there is no greater means to good than art.

TROTSKY

The most brilliant of all the men who made the great Russian revolution of 1917 was undoubtedly Lev Davidovich Bronstein, known to history by his pseudonym Leon Trotsky (1877–1940). Trotsky was a skilled administrator, an impassioned public speaker, a profound student of politics, and—unlike his rival Joseph Stalin—a deeply cultured man in the old European style. Among his many writings was an essay on the relationship between Literature and Revolution *(1925), from which this excerpt is taken.*

Marx had argued that the art of a society, like its law, politics, and religion, is a reflection of the fundamental patterns of economic activity on which the life of the society rested. Hence, if one wished to understand the form and development of the art of the High Middle Ages, for example, the place to look was in the landholding arrangement known to us as feudalism, rather than in the history of artistic styles or the aesthetic consciousness of the individual artists.

To Marx's followers, among whom the Russian revolutionaries figured prominently, two questions were posed by this theory of "cultural superstructure" and "economic base." First, what role should art—and the artist—play in the revolutionary transition from capitalism to socialism? And second, what would art be like after the revolution, when socialism, and finally communism, had been firmly established?

Since the Soviet Union has not yet achieved the stage of communism of which Marx wrote, most of the attention of Stalin and his successors has been devoted to the first *question: What is art's role in the revolution? Trotsky devotes only a few words to the subject. "During the period of revolution," he writes, "only that literature which promotes the consolidation of the workers in their struggle against the exploiters is necessary and progressive." It is not difficult to see, in this single sentence, a formula for censorship quite as harsh as that proposed by Plato or Tolstoy.*

When he turns to the art of the post-revolutionary period, Trotsky's spirit soars. In one of the most beautiful passages in the corpus of Marxist writings, he describes the liberation of the human spirit that communism will bring. Trotsky's emphasis upon the control of nature and the merging of artistic creativity with industrial design has a remarkably American sound. Unlike many of our contemporary radical critics who champion unspoiled nature against the supposed inhumanity of the machine, Trotsky is in love with technology. He sees it only as a force for good, for creation and liberation.

> *Trotsky's optimistic faith in a communist technological society of the future contrasts sharply with the pessimistic forecasts of the environmental and population experts of our own day. Radicals and conservatives alike are agreed today in predicting a worldwide ecological disaster unless the unrestrained growth of technology is somehow contained. Trotsky, writing half a century after Marx, was nevertheless united with him by a faith in man's future. We today, yet another half-century further along, seem to be living in a different world.*

Art in a Socialist Society

Greater dynamics under Socialism. The "realism" of revolutionary art. Soviet comedy. Old and new tragedy. Art, technique and nature. The reshaping of Man.

When one speaks of revolutionary art, two kinds of artistic phenomena are meant: the works whose themes reflect the Revolution, and the works which are not connected with the Revolution in theme, but are thoroughly imbued with it, and are colored by the new consciousness arising out of the Revolution. These are phenomena which quite evidently belong, or could belong, in entirely different planes. Alexey Tolstoi, in his "The Road to Calvary," describes the period of the War and the Revolution. He belongs to the peaceful Yasnaya Polyana school, only his scale is infinitely smaller and his point of view narrower. And when he applies it to events of the greatest magnitude, it serves only as a cruel reminder that Yasnaya Polyana has been and is no more. But when the young poet, Tikhonov, without writing about the Revolution, writes about a little grocery store (he seems to be shy about writing of the Revolution), he perceives and reproduces its inertia and immobility with such fresh and passionate power as only a poet created by the dynamics of a new epoch can do. Thus if works about the Revolution and works of revolutionary art are not one and the same thing, they still have a point in common. The artists that are created by the Revolution cannot but want to speak of the Revolution. And, on the other hand, the art which will be filled with a great desire to speak of the Revolution, will inevitably reject the

Chapter 8, "Revolutionary and Socialist Art." From *Literature and Revolution* by Leon Trotsky. Trans. by Rose Strunsky.

Yasnaya Polyana point of view, whether it be the point of view of the Count or of the peasant.

There is no revolutionary art as yet. There are the elements of this art, there are hints and attempts at it, and, what is most important, there is the revolutionary man, who is forming the new generation in his own image and who is more and more in need of this art. How long will it take for such art to reveal itself clearly? It is difficult even to guess, because the process is intangible and incalculable, and we are limited to guesswork even when we try to time more tangible social processes. But why should not this art, at least its first big wave, come soon as the expression of the art of the young generation which was born in the Revolution and which carries it on?

Revolutionary art which inevitably reflects all the contradictions of a revolutionary social system, should not be confused with Socialist art for which no basis has as yet been made. On the other hand, one must not forget that Socialist art will grow out of the art of this transition period.

In insisting on such a distinction, we are not at all guided by a pedantic consideration of an abstract program. Not for nothing did Engels speak of the Socialist Revolution as a leap from the kingdom of necessity to the kingdom of freedom. The Revolution itself is not as yet the kingdom of freedom. On the contrary, it is developing the features of "necessity" to the greatest degree. Socialism will abolish class antagonisms, as well as classes, but the Revolution carries the class struggle to its highest tension. During the period of revolution, only that literature which promotes the consolidation of the workers in their struggle against the exploiters is necessary and progressive. Revolutionary literature cannot but be imbued with a spirit of social hatred, which is a creative historic factor in an epoch of proletarian dictatorship. Under Socialism, solidarity will be the basis of society. Literature and art will be tuned to a different key. All the emotions which we revolutionists, at the present time, feel apprehensive of naming—so much have they been worn thin by hypocrites and vulgarians—such as disinterested friendship, love for one's neighbor, sympathy, will be the mighty ringing chords of Socialist poetry.

However, does not an excess of solidarity, as the Nietzscheans fear, threaten to degenerate man into a sentimental, passive, herd animal? Not at all. The powerful force of competition which, in bourgeois society, has the character of market competition, will not disappear in a Socialist society, but, to use the language of psycho-analysis, will be sublimated, that is, will assume a higher and more fertile form. There will be the struggle for one's opinion, for one's project, for one's taste. In the measure in which political struggles will be eliminated—and in a society where there will be no classes, there will be no such struggles—the liberated passions will be channelized into technique, into construction which also includes art. Art then will become more general, will mature, will become tempered, and will become the most perfect method of the progressive building of life in every field. It will not be merely "pretty" without relation to anything else.

All forms of life, such as the cultivation of land, the planning of human habitations, the building of theaters, the methods of socially educating children, the solution of scientific problems, the creation of new styles, will vitally engross all and everybody. People will divide into "parties" over the question of a new gigantic canal, or the distribution of oases in the Sahara (such a question will exist too), over the regulation of the weather and the climate, over a new theater, over chemical hypotheses, over two competing tendencies in music, and over a best system of sports. Such parties will not be poisoned by the greed of class or caste. All will be equally interested in the success of the whole. The struggle will have a purely ideologic character. It will have no running after profits, it will have nothing mean, no betrayals, no bribery, none of the things that form the soul of "competition" in a society divided into classes. But this will in no way hinder the struggle from being absorbing, dramatic and passionate. And as all problems in a Socialist society—the problems of life which formerly were solved spontaneously and automatically, and the problems of art which were in the custody of special priestly castes—will become the property of all people, one can say with certainty that collective interests and passions and individual competition will have the widest scope and the most unlimited opportunity. Art, therefore, will not suffer the lack of any such explosions of collective, nervous energy, and of such collective psychic impulses which make for the creation of new artistic tendencies and for changes in style. It will be the æsthetic schools around which "parties" will collect, that is, associations of temperaments, of tastes and of moods. In a struggle so disinterested and tense, which will take place in a culture whose foundations are steadily rising, the human personality, with its invaluable basic trait of continual discontent, will grow and become polished at all its points. In truth, we have no reason to fear that there will be a decline of individuality or an impoverishment of art in a Socialist society.

Can we christen revolutionary art with any of the names that we have? Osinsky somewhere called it realistic. The thought here is true and significant, but there ought to be an agreement on a definition of this concept to prevent falling into a misunderstanding. . . .

What are we to understand under the term realism? At various periods, and by various methods, realism gave expression to the feelings and needs of different social groups. Each one of these realistic schools is subject to a separate and social literary definition, and a separate formal and literary estimation. What have they in common? A definite and important feeling for the world. It consists in a feeling for life as it is, in an artistic acceptance of reality, and not in a shrinking from it, in an active interest in the concrete stability and mobility of life. It is a striving either to picture life as it is or to idealize it, either to justify or to condemn it, either to photograph it or generalize and symbolize it. But it is always a preoccupation with our life of three dimensions as a sufficient and invaluable theme for art. In this large philosophic sense, and not in the narrow sense of a literary school, one may say with certainty that the new art will be realistic. The Revolution cannot live together with mysticism. Nor can the Revolution live together with romanticism, if that which Pilnyak, the Imagists and others call romanticism is, as it may be feared, mysticism shyly trying to establish itself under a new name. This is not being doctrinaire, this is an insuperable psychological fact. Our age cannot have a shy and portable mysticism, something like a pet dog that is carried along "with the rest." Our age wields an axe. Our life, cruel, violent and disturbed to its very bottom, says: "I must have an artist of a single love. Whatever way you take hold of me, whatever tools and instruments created by the development of art you choose, I leave to you, to your temperament and to your genius. But you must understand me as I am, you must take me as I will become, and there must be no one else besides me."

This means a realistic monism, in the sense of a philosophy of life, and not a "realism" in the sense of the traditional arsenal of literary schools. On the contrary, the new artist will need all the methods and processes evolved in the past, as well as a few supplementary ones, in order to grasp the new life. And this is not going to be artistic eclecticism, because the unity of art is created by an active world-attitude and active life-attitude. . . .

But can a great art be created out of our infidel epoch, ask certain mystics, who are willing to accept the Revolution if it can secure them immortality. Tragedy is a great and monumental form of literature. The tragedy of classic antiquity was deduced from its myths. All ancient tragedy is penetrated by a profound faith in fate which gave a meaning to life. The Christian myth unified the monumental art of the Middle Ages and gave a significance not only to the temples and the mysteries, but to all human relationships. The union of the religious point of view on life with an active participation in it, made possible a great art in those times. If one were to remove religious faith, not the vague, mystic buzzing that goes on in the soul of our modern intelligentsia, but the real religion, with God and a heavenly law and a church hierarchy, then life is left bare, without any place in it for supreme collisions of hero and destiny, of sin and expiation. The well-known mystic Stepun approaches art from this point of view in his article on "Tragedy and the Contemporary Life." He starts from the needs of art itself, tempts us with a new and monumental art, shows us a revival of tragedy in the distance, and, in conclusion, demands, in the name of art, that we submit to and obey the powers of heaven. There is an insinuating logic in Stepun's scheme. In fact, the author does not care for tragedy, because the laws of tragedy are nothing to him as compared to the laws of heaven. He only wishes to catch hold of our epoch by the small finger of tragic æsthetics in order to take hold of its entire hand. This is a purely Jesuitic approach. But from a dialectic point of view, Stepun's reasoning is formalistic and shallow. It ignores the materialistic and historical foundation from which the ancient drama and the Gothic art grew and from which a new art must grow.

The faith in an inevitable fate disclosed the narrow limits within which ancient man, clear in thought but poor in technique, was confined. He could not as yet undertake to conquer nature on the scale we do today, and nature hung over him like a fate. Fate is the limitation and the immobility of technical means, the voice of blood, of sickness, of death, of all that limits man, and that does not allow him to become "arrogant." Tragedy lay inherent in the contradiction between the awakened world of the mind, and the stagnant limitation of means. The myth did not create tragedy, it only expressed it in the language of man's childhood.

The bribe of spiritual expiation of the Middle Ages and, in general, the whole system of heavenly and earthly double bookkeeping, which followed from the dualism of religion, and especially of historic, positive Christianity, did not make the contradictions of life, but only reflected them and solved them fictitiously. Mediæval society overcame the growing contradictions by transferring the promissory note to the Son of God; the ruling classes signed this note, the Church hierarchy acted as endorser, and the oppressed masses prepared to discount it in the other world.

Bourgeois society broke up human relationships into atoms, and gave them unprecedented flexibility and mobility. Primitive unity of consciousness which was the foundation of a monumental religious art disappeared, and with it went primitive economic relationships. As a result of the Reformation, religion became individualistic. The religious symbols of art having had their cord cut from the heavens, fell on their heads and sought support in the uncertain mysticism of individual consciousness.

In the tragedies of Shakespeare, which would be entirely unthinkable without the Reformation, the fate of the ancients and the passions of the mediæval Christians are crowded out by individual human passions, such as love, jealousy, revengeful greediness, and spiritual dissension. But in every one of Shakespeare's dramas, the individual passion is carried to such a high degree of tension that it outgrows the individual, becomes super-personal, and is transformed into a fate of a certain kind. The jealousy of Othello, the ambition of Macbeth, the greed of Shylock, the love of Romeo and Juliet, the arrogance of Coriolanus, the spiritual wavering of Hamlet, are all of this kind. Tragedy in Shakespeare is individualistic, and in this sense has not the general significance of Œdipus Rex, which expresses the consciousness of a whole people. None the less, compared with Æschylus, Shakespeare represents a great step forward and not backward. Shakespeare's art is more human. At any rate, we shall no longer accept a tragedy in which God gives orders and man submits. Moreover, there will be no one to write such a tragedy.

Having broken up human relations into atoms, bourgeois society, during the period of its rise, had a great aim for itself. Personal emancipation was its name. Out of it grew the dramas of Shakespeare and Goethe's "Faust." Man placed himself in the center of the universe, and therefore in the center of art also. This theme sufficed for centuries. In reality, all modern literature has been nothing but an enlargement of this theme.

But to the degree in which the internal bankruptcy of bourgeois society was revealed as a result of its unbearable contradictions, the original purpose, the emancipation and qualification of the individual faded away and was relegated more and more into the sphere of a new mythology, without soul or spirit.

However the conflict between what is personal and what is beyond the personal, can take place, not only in the sphere of religion, but in the sphere of a human passion that is larger than the individual. The super-personal element is, above all, the social element. So long as man will not have mastered his social organization, the latter will hang over him as his fate. Whether at the same time society casts a religious shadow or not, is a secondary matter and depends upon the degree of man's helplessness. Babœuf's struggle for Communism in a society which was not yet ready for it, was a struggle of a classic hero with his fate. Babœuf's destiny had all the characteristics of true tragedy, just as the fate of the Gracchi had whose name Babœuf used.

Tragedy based on detached personal passions is too flat for our days. Why? Because we live in a period of social passions. The tragedy of our period lies in the conflict between the individual and the collectivity, or in the conflict between two hostile collectivities in the same individual. Our age is an age of great aims. This is what stamps it. But the grandeur of these aims lies in man's effort to free himself from mystic and from every other intellectual vagueness and in his effort to reconstruct society and himself in accord with his own plan. This, of course, is much bigger than the child's play of the ancients which was becoming to their childish age, or the mediæval ravings of monks, or the arrogance of individualism which tears personality away from the collectivity, and then, draining it to the very bottom, pushes it off into the abyss of pessimism, or sets it on all fours before the remounted bull Apis.

Tragedy is a high expression of literature because it implies the heroic tenacity of strivings, of limitless aims, of conflicts and sufferings. In this sense, Stepun was right when he characterized our "on the eve" art, as he called it, that is, the art which preceded the War and the Revolution, as insignificant.

Bourgeois society, individualism, the Reformation, the Shakespearean dramas, the great Revolution, these have made impossible the tragic significance of aims that come from without; great aims must live in the consciousness of a people or of a class which leads a people, if they are to arouse heroism or create a basis for great sentiments which inspire tragedy. The Tsarist War, whose purpose did not penetrate consciousness, gave birth to cheap verse only, with personal poetry trickling by its side, unable to rise to an objectivity and unable to form a great art.

If one were to regard the Decadent and the Symbolist schools, with all their off-shoots, from the point of view of the development of art as a social form, they would appear merely as scratches of the pen, as an exercise in craftsmanship, as a tuning up of instruments. The period in art when it was "on the eve" was without aims. Those who had aims had no time for art. At present, one has to carry out great aims by the means of art. One cannot tell whether revolutionary art will succeed in producing "high" revolutionary tragedy. But Socialist art will revive tragedy. Without God, of course. The new art will be atheist. It will also revive comedy, because the new man of the future will want to laugh. It will give new life to the novel. It will grant all rights to lyrics, because the new man will love in a better and stronger way than did the old people, and he will think about the problems of birth and death. The new art will revive all the old forms, which arose in the course of the development of the creative spirit. The disintegration and decline of these forms are not absolute, that is, they do not mean that these forms are absolutely incompatible with the spirit of the new age. All that is necessary is for the poet of the new epoch to re-think in a new way the thoughts of mankind, and to re-feel its feelings. . . .

There is no doubt that, in the future—and the farther we go, the more true it will be—such monumental tasks as the planning of city gardens, of model houses, of railroads, and of ports, will interest vitally not only engineering architects, participators in competitions, but the large popular masses as well. The imperceptible, ant-like piling up of quarters and streets, brick by brick, from generation to generation, will give way to titanic constructions of city-villages, with map and compass in hand. Around this compass will be formed true peoples' parties, the parties of the future for special technology and construction, which will agitate passionately, hold meetings and vote. In this struggle, architecture will again be filled with the spirit of mass feelings and moods, only on a much higher plane, and mankind will educate itself plastically, it will become accustomed to look at the world as submissive clay for sculpting the most perfect forms of life. The wall between art and industry will come down. The great style of the future will be formative, not ornamental. Here the Futurists are right. But it would be wrong to look at this as a liquidating of art, as a voluntary giving way to technique.

Take the penknife as an example. The combination of art and technique can proceed along two fundamental lines; either art embellishes the knife and pictures an elephant, a prize beauty, or the Eiffel Tower on its handle; or art helps technique to find an "ideal" form for the knife, that is, such a form which will correspond most adequately to the material of a knife and its purpose. To think that this task can be solved by purely technical means is incorrect, because purpose and material allow for an innumerable number of variations. To make an "ideal" knife, one must have, besides the knowledge of the properties of the material and the methods of its use, both imagination and taste. In accord with the entire tendency of industrial culture, we think that the artistic imagination in creating material objects will be directed towards working out the ideal form of a thing, as a thing, and not towards the embellishment of the thing as an æsthetic premium to itself. If this is true for penknives, it will be truer still for wearing apparel, furniture, theaters and cities. This does not mean the doing away with "machine-made" art, not even in the most distant future. But it seems that the direct coöperation between art and all branches of technique will become of paramount importance.

Does this mean that industry will absorb art, or that art will lift industry up to itself on Olympus? This question can be answered either way, depending on whether the problem is approached from the side of industry, or from the side of art. But in the object attained, there is no difference between either answer. Both answers signify a gigantic expansion of the scope and artistic quality of industry, and we understand here, under industry, the entire field without excepting the industrial activity of man; mechanical and electrified agriculture will also become part of industry.

The wall will fall not only between art and industry, but simultaneously between art and nature also. This is not meant in the sense of Jean-Jacques Rousseau, that art will come nearer to a state of nature, but that nature will become more "artificial." The present distribution of mountains and rivers, of fields, of meadows, of steppes, of forests, and of seashores, cannot be considered final. Man has already made changes in the map of nature that are not few nor insignificant. But they are mere pupils' practice in comparison with what is coming. Faith merely promises to move mountains; but technology, which takes nothing "on faith," is actually able to cut down mountains and move them. Up to now this was done for industrial purposes (mines) or for railways (tunnels); in the future this will be done on an immeasurably larger scale, according to a general industrial and artistic plan. Man will occupy himself with re-registering mountains and rivers, and will earnestly and repeatedly make improvements in nature. In the end, he will have rebuilt the earth, if not in his own image, at least according to his own taste. We have not the slightest fear that this taste will be bad.

The jealous, scowling Kliuev declares, in his quarrel with Mayakovsky, that "it does not behoove a maker of songs to bother about cranes," and that it is "only in the furnace of the heart, and in no other furnace, that the purple gold of life is melted." Ivanov-Razumnik, a populist, who was once a left Social-Revolutionist—and this tells the whole story—also took a hand in this quarrel. Ivanov-Razumnik declares that the poetry of the hammer and the machine, in whose name Mayakovsky speaks, is a transient episode, but that the poetry of "God-made Earth" is "the eternal poetry of the world." Earth and the machine are here contrasted as the eternal and temporary sources of poetry, and of course the eminent idealist, the tasteless and cautious semi-mystic Razumnik, prefers the eternal to the transient. But, in truth, this dualism of earth and machine is false; one can contrast a backward peasant field with a flour mill, either on a plantation, or in a Socialist society. The poetry of the earth is not eternal, but changeable, and man began to sing articulate songs only after he had placed between himself and the earth implements and instruments which were the first simple machines. There would have been no Koltzov without a scythe, a plow or a sickle. Does that mean that the earth with a scythe has the advantage of eternity over the earth with an electric plow? The new man, who is only now beginning to plan and to realize himself, will not contrast a barn-floor for grouse and a drag-net for sturgeons with a crane and a steam-hammer, as does Kliuev and Razumnik after him. Through the machine, man in Socialist society will command nature in its entirety, with its grouse and its sturgeons. He will point out places for mountains and for passes. He will change the course of the rivers, and he will lay down rules for the oceans. The idealist simpletons may say that this will be a bore, but that is why they are simpletons. Of course this does not mean that the entire globe will be marked off into boxes, that the forests will be turned into parks and gardens. Most likely, thickets and forests and grouse and tigers will remain, but only where man commands them to remain. And man will do it so well that the tiger won't even notice the machine, or feel the change, but will live as he lived in primeval times. The machine is not in opposition to the earth. The machine is the instrument of modern man in every field of life. The present-day city is transient. But it will not be dissolved back again into the old village. On the contrary, the village will rise in fundamentals to the plane of the city. Here lies the principal task. The city is transient, but it points to the future, and indicates the road. The present village is entirely of the past. That is why its æsthetics seem archaic, as if they were taken from a museum of folk art.

Mankind will come out of the period of civil wars much poorer from terrific destructions, even without the earthquakes of the kind that occurred in Japan. The effort to conquer poverty, hunger, want in all its forms, that is, to conquer nature, will be the dominant tendency for decades to come. The passion for mechanical improvements, as in America, will accompany the first stage of every new Socialist society. The passive enjoyment of nature will disappear from art. Technique will become a more powerful inspiration for artistic work, and later on the contradiction itself between technique and nature will be solved in a higher synthesis.

The personal dreams of a few enthusiasts today for making life more dramatic and for educating man himself rhythmically, find a proper and real place in this outlook. Having rationalized his economic system, that is, having saturated it with consciousness and planfulness, man will not leave a trace of the present stagnant and worm-eaten domestic life. The care for food and education, which lies like a millstone on the present-day family, will be removed, and will become the subject of social initiative and of an endless collective creativeness. Woman will at last free herself from her semi-servile condition. Side by side with technique, education, in the broad sense of the psycho-physical molding of new generations, will take its place as the crown of social thinking. Powerful "parties" will form themselves around pedagogic systems. Experiments in social education and an emulation of different methods will take place to a degree which has not been dreamed of before. Communist life will not be formed blindly, like coral islands, but will be built consciously, will be tested by thought, will be directed and corrected. Life will cease to be elemental, and for this reason stagnant. Man, who will learn how to move rivers and mountains, how to build peoples' palaces on the peaks of Mont Blanc and at the bottom of the Atlantic, will not only be able to add to his own life richness, brilliancy and intensity, but also a dynamic quality of the highest degree. The shell of life will hardly have time to form before it will burst open again under the pressure of new technical and cultural inventions and achievements. Life in the future will not be monotonous.

More than that. Man at last will begin to harmonize himself in earnest. He will make it his business to achieve beauty by giving the movement of his own limbs the utmost precision, purposefulness and economy in his work, his walk and his play. He will try to master first the semiconscious and then the subconscious processes in his own organism, such as breathing, the circulation of the blood, digestion, reproduction, and, within necessary limits, he will try to subordinate them to the control of reason and will. Even purely physiologic life will become subject to collective experiments. The human species, the coagulate*d homo sapiens,* will once more enter into a state of radical transformation, and, in his own hands, will become an object of the most complicated methods of artificial selection and psycho-physical training. This is entirely in accord with evolution. Man first drove the dark elements out of industry and ideology, by displacing barbarian routine by scientific technique, and religion by science. Afterwards he drove the unconscious out of politics, by overthrowing monarchy and class with democracy and rationalist parliamentarianism and then with the clear and open Soviet dictatorship. The blind elements have settled most heavily in economic relations, but man is driving them out from there also, by means of the Socialist organization of economic life. This makes it possible to reconstruct fundamentally the traditional family life. Finally, the nature of man himself is hidden in the deepest and darkest corner of the unconscious, of the elemental, of the sub-soil. Is it not self-evident that the greatest efforts of investigative thought and of creative initiative will be in that direction? The human race will not have ceased to crawl on all fours before God, kings and capital, in order later to submit humbly before the dark laws of heredity and a blind sexual selection! Emancipated man will want to attain a greater equilibrium in the work of his organs and a more proportional developing and wearing out of his tissues, in order to reduce the fear of death to a rational reaction of the organism towards danger. There can be no doubt that man's extreme anatomical and physiological disharmony, that is, the extreme disproportion in the growth and wearing out of organs and tissues, give the life instinct the form of a pinched, morbid and hysterical fear of death, which darkens reason and which feeds the stupid and humiliating fantasies about life after death.

Man will make it his purpose to master his own feelings, to raise his instincts to the heights of consciousness, to make them transparent, to extend the wires of his will into hidden recesses, and thereby to raise himself to a new plane, to create a higher social biologic type, or, if you please, a superman.

It is difficult to predict the extent of self-government which the man of the future may reach or the heights to which he may carry his technique. Social construction and psycho-physical self-education will become two aspects of one and the same process. All the arts—literature, drama, painting, music and architecture will lend this process beautiful form. More correctly, the shell in which the cultural construction and self-education of Communist man will be enclosed, will develop all the vital elements of contemporary art to the highest point. Man will become immeasurably stronger, wiser and subtler; his body will become more harmonized, his movements more rhythmic, his voice more musical. The forms of life will become dynamically dramatic. The average human type will rise to the heights of an Aristotle, a Goethe, or a Marx. And above this ridge new peaks will rise.

AFTERWORD

It may come as a surprise to discover that so many famous philosophers are either sympathetic to censorship of the arts or else downright opposed to art in general. As we have seen, Plato would drive the artists from his ideal city, Tolstoy refuses to acknowledge the aesthetic merit even of Shakespeare or Beethoven, and Trotsky has no use for art which fails to express the revolutionary spirit of the working class.

Since we live in a society which likes to think of itself as pluralist, tolerant, and open (whatever the reality may be), it may be hard for you even to imagine the frame of mind in which a man would seriously deny that Shakespeare and Beethoven are great artists. We tend these days to make celebrities of our creative artists, so that even minor talent or mere posturing is reported in the press, reviewed respectfully by critics, and paid very handsomely. Nevertheless, it is worth making the effort to understand the censor's point of view, for at the very least, the impulse to censor seems quite universal.

First of all, let us recognize that censorship arises most naturally when men are deeply committed to the importance of some point of view. What unites Plato, Tolstoy, and Trotsky is their absolute conviction that they are onto the real truth about life. Plato may find that truth in the eternal Forms, Tolstoy in primitive Christianity, and Trotsky in the revolutionary struggle of the proletariat, but they are one and all committed men. Since they believe that art can have a great impact on the passions of men, they quite naturally wish to ensure that only the right sorts of art are encouraged or permitted in society.

Now, of course, if you don't think art has the capacity to move men and shape their vision of life—if art is, for you, mere decoration or amusement—then you probably won't care very much what painters paint and writers write. But if you agree with Plato, Santayana, Bell, Tolstoy, and Trotsky that the artistic dimension of human existence is as powerful in its way as the material, will you not agree that in the interests of human welfare, some control must be exercised over what men see and hear and read?

The **Ulysses** case is in a way misleading, for it turns solely on the issue of obscenity. The legislators who wrote the law under which Joyce's novel was seized obviously believed that it was harmful to men to have certain of their sexual feelings aroused. Hence, we can view them as subscribing generally to the view that art should be judged by its social and psychological utility. But a defender of **Ulysses** could perfectly well argue for the book's release **without** rejecting the general principal of censorship. A critic might assert that **Ulysses** does **not** tend to "promote lust." Or he might even maintain that lust is a good thing to promote. That would still leave open the more general question whether works of art should be required to serve a social purpose.

Let us turn the question around. Why shouldn't art be required to serve a social purpose? We require doctors, lawyers, teachers, architects, industrialists, farmers, and merchants to serve social ends—or, at the very least, we demand that they avoid causing social harm. Why not artists? Is there any reason why the poet and painter should be exempted from the constraints which society has always imposed on the rest of its members?

Many of you are undoubtedly aware of John Stuart Mill's strong defense of freedom of speech and expression in his essay **On Liberty.** Mill argued that the advance of truth—which he believed would work to men's advantage and benefit—could best be encouraged by an absolute removal of all restraints on the right to speak and write what one wished, no matter how unpopular or distasteful to the majority. It is surprising (and perhaps upsetting), therefore, to find him arguing, in the last chapter of his **Principles of Political Economy,** for government regulation of culture. Here is the passage; it will serve as a provocative way to end our discussion:

> Now, the proposition that the consumer is a competent judge of the commodity, can be admitted only with numerous abatements and exceptions. He is generally the best judge (though even this is not true universally) of the material objects produced for his use. These are destined to supply some physical want, or gratify some taste or inclination, respecting which wants or inclinations there is no appeal from the person who feels them; or they are the means and appliances of some occupation, for the use of the persons engaged in it, who may be presumed to be judges of the things required in their habitual employment. But there are other things of the worth of which the demand of the market is by no means a test; things of which the utility does not consist in ministering to inclinations, nor in serving the daily uses of life, and the want of which is least felt where the need is greatest. This is peculiarly true of those things which are chiefly useful as tending to raise the character of human beings. The uncultivated cannot be competent judges of cultivation. Those who most need to be made wiser and better, usually desire it least, and if they desire it, would be incapable of finding the way to it by their own lights. It will continually happen, on the voluntary system, that, the end not being desired, the means will not be provided at all, or that, the persons requiring improvement having an imperfect or altogether erroneous conception of what they want, the supply called forth by the demand of the market will be anything but what is really required. Now any well-intentioned and tolerably civilized government may think without presumption that it does or ought to possess a degree of cultivation above the average of the community which it rules, and that it should therefore be capable of offering better education and better instruction to the people, than the greater number of them would spontaneously demand. Education, therefore, is one of those things which it is admissible in principle that a government should provide for the people. The case is one to which the reasons of the non-interference principle do not necessarily or universally extend.

VIII
PHILOSOPHY
AND RELIGION

Drugs Again:
The Nature of
Religious Experience

INTRODUCTION TO THE CONTEMPORARY DISPUTE

We began with drugs and we end with drugs. In Section I the debate between Timothy Leary and Jerome Lettvin led us into the ancient metaphysical dispute concerning the nature of appearance and reality. At the time, I remarked that the Lettvin-Leary dispute raised many other philosophical questions as well. In this final section we shall take up one of them, namely, the nature and significance of religious experience.

If it is true that there is no human society without some art, it is equally true that there is no human society without religion. Pantheism, monotheism, worship of the heavens, rivers and lakes, of the animals of the forest, of one's own ancestors—the forms of religious belief are endless. Those of us who are familiar with Judaism and Christianity may think of religion very much in terms of a set of tenets—a theological **doctrine** defining the nature of God and man's relation to Him. But looking at the subject of religion more broadly, we might as plausibly focus on certain sorts of **experiences** as the distinctive mark of religion. When we listen to the religious practitioners themselves, we find them speaking of a sense of transcendence, an awareness of, or communication with, something beyond the ordinary world of people and things. Frequently, we are presented with detailed descriptions of visions of this world beyond our senses, and in some cases—as with the American Plains Indians—a vision may serve as the defining experience for a man's entire adult life.

Some visions simply come upon us, as though we turn a corner on a path and suddenly behold a wondrous view. But most often, men have sought religious experiences by prayer, by meditation, by long fasting, **and by drugs.** Whatever else we may think of Dr. Leary's celebration of LSD, we must surely grant his claim that many cultures have used such substances to stimulate religious experiences.

In order to introduce the subject of drugs and religious experience, I have departed somewhat from our debate format in order to present you with the scholarly analysis of Professor Huston Smith of MIT. Smith, an expert on Eastern religions, has spent much time in Buddhist monasteries as well as in American universities. His examination of the religious significance of drug-induced visions is dispassionate and objective, but he is quite clearly convinced that the traditional scepticism of the scientific empiricist is too narrow to encompass the full range of human experience and truth. As you will see as you read the selections in this section, philosophers take very strong positions on both sides of this dispute.

HUSTON SMITH

Do Drugs Have
Religious Import?

Until six months ago, if I picked up my phone in the Cambridge area and dialed KISS-BIG, a voice would answer, "If-if." These were coincidences: KISS-BIG happened to be the letter equivalents of an arbitrarily assigned telephone number, and I.F.I.F. represented the initials of an organization with the improbable name of the International Federation for Internal Freedom. But the coincidences were apposite to the point of being poetic. "Kiss big" caught the euphoric, manic, life-embracing attitude that characterized this most publicized of the organizations formed to explore the newly synthesized consciousness changing substances; the organization itself was surely one of the "iffy-est" phenomena to appear on our social and intellectual scene in some time. It produced the first firings in Harvard's history, an ultimatum to get out of Mexico in five days, and "the miracle of Marsh Chapel," in which, during a two-and-one-half-hour Good Friday service, ten theological students and professors ingested psilocybin and were visited by what they generally reported to be the deepest religious experiences of their lives.

Despite the last of these phenomena and its numerous if less dramatic parallels, students of religion appear by and large to be dismissing the psychedelic drugs that have sprung to our attention in the '60s as having little religious relevance. The position taken in one of the most forward-looking volumes of theological essays to have appeared in recent years—*Soundings*, edited by A. R. Vidler[1]—accepts R. C. Zaehner's *Mysticism Sacred and Profane* as having "fully examined and refuted" the religious claims for mescalin which Aldous Huxley sketched in *The Doors of Perception*. This closing of the case strikes me as premature, for it looks as if the drugs have light to throw on the history of religion, the phenomenology of religion, the philosophy of religion, and the practice of the religious life itself.

1. Drugs and Religion
Viewed Historically

In his trial-and-error life explorations man almost everywhere has stumbled upon connections between vegetables (eaten or brewed) and actions (yogi

The emended version of a paper presented to The Woodrow Wilson Society, Princeton University, on May 16, 1964. "Do Drugs Have Religious Import?" by Huston Smith. *Journal of Philosophy*, LXI, No. 18 (October 1, 1964), 517–30. © The Journal of Philosophy, 1964. Reprinted by permission of The Journal of Philosophy.

[1] *Soundings: Essays concerning Christian Understandings*, A. R. Vidler, ed. (Cambridge: University Press, 1962). The statement cited appears on page 72, in H. A. Williams's essay on "Theology and Self-awareness."

breathing exercises, whirling-dervish dances, flagellations) that alter states of consciousness. From the psychopharmacological standpoint we now understand these states to be the products of changes in brain chemistry. From the sociological perspective we see that they tend to be connected in some way with religion. If we discount the wine used in Christian communion services, the instances closest to us in time and space are the peyote of The Native American [Indian] Church and Mexico's 2000-year-old "sacred mushrooms," the latter rendered in Aztec as "God's Flesh"—striking parallel to "the body of our Lord" in the Christian eucharist. Beyond these neighboring instances lie the *soma* of the Hindus, the *haoma* and hemp of the Zoroastrians, the Dionysus of the Greeks who "everywhere . . . taught men the culture of the vine and the mysteries of his worship and everywhere [was] accepted as a god,"[2] the *benzoin* of Southeast Asia, Zen's tea whose fifth cup purifies and whose sixth "calls to the realm of the immortals,"[3] the *pituri* of the Australian aborigines, and probably the mystic *kykeon* that was eaten and drunk at the climactic close of the sixth day of the Eleusinian mysteries.[4] There is no need to extend the list, as a reasonably complete account is available in Philippe de Félice's comprehensive study of the subject, *Poisons sacrés, ivresses divines*.

More interesting than the fact that consciousness-changing devices have been linked with religion is the possibility that they actually initiated many of the religious perspectives which, taking root in history, continued after their psychedelic origins were forgotten. Bergson saw the first movement of Hindus and Greeks toward "dynamic religion" as associated with the "divine rapture" found in intoxicating beverages;[5] more recently Robert Graves, Gordon Wasson, and Alan Watts have suggested that most religions arose from such chemically induced theophanies. Mary Barnard is the most explicit proponent of this thesis. "Which . . . was more likely to happen first," she asks,[6] "the spontaneously generated idea of an afterlife in which the disembodied soul, liberated from the restrictions of time and space, experiences eternal bliss, or the accidental discovery of hallucinogenic plants that give a sense of euphoria, dislocate the center of consciousness, and distort time and space, making them balloon outward in greatly expanded vistas?" Her own answer is that "the [latter] experience might have had . . . an almost explosive effect on the largely dormant minds of men, causing them to think of things they had never thought of before. This, if you like, is direct revelation." Her use of the subjunctive "might" renders this formulation of her answer equivocal, but she concludes her essay on a note that is completely unequivocal: "Looking at the

---

[2] Edith Hamilton, *Mythology* (New York: Mentor, 1953), p. 55.

[3] Quoted in Alan Watts, *The Spirit of Zen* (New York: Grove Press, 1958), p. 110.

[4] George Mylonas, *Eleusis and the Eleusinian Mysteries* (Princeton, N.J.: Princeton Univ. Press, 1961), p. 284.

[5] *Two Sources of Morality and Religion* (New York: Holt, 1935), pp. 206–12.

[6] "The God in the Flowerpot," *The American Scholar*, XXXII, No. 4 (Autumn 1963), 584, 586.

matter coldly, unintoxicated and unentranced, I am willing to prophesy that fifty theobotanists working for fifty years would make the current theories concerning the origins of much mythology and theology as out-of-date as pre-Copernican astronomy."

This is an important hypothesis—one which must surely engage the attention of historians of religion for some time to come. But as I am concerned here only to spot the points at which the drugs erupt onto the field of serious religious study, not to ride the geysers to whatever heights, I shall not pursue Miss Barnard's thesis. Having located what appears to be the crux of the historical question, namely the extent to which drugs not merely duplicate or simulate theologically sponsored experiences but generate or shape theologies themselves, I turn to phenomenology.

2. Drugs and Religion
Viewed Phenomenologically

Phenomenology attempts a careful description of human experience. The question the drugs pose for the phenomenology of religion, therefore, is whether the experiences they induce differ from religious experiences reached naturally, and if so how.

Even the Bible notes that chemically induced psychic states bear *some* resemblance to religious ones. Peter had to appeal to a circumstantial criterion —the early hour of the day—to defend those who were caught up in the Pentecostal experience against the charge that they were merely drunk: "These men are not drunk, as you suppose, since it is only the third hour of the day" (Acts 2:15); and Paul initiates the comparison when he admonishes the Ephesians not to "get drunk with wine . . . but [to] be filled with the spirit" (Ephesians 5:18). Are such comparisons, paralleled in the accounts of virtually every religion, superficial? How far can they be pushed?

Not all the way, students of religion have thus far insisted. With respect to the new drugs, Prof. R. C. Zaehner has drawn the line emphatically. "The importance of Huxley's *Doors of Perception*," he writes, "is that in it the author clearly makes the claim that what he experienced under the influence of mescalin is closely comparable to a genuine mystical experience. If he is right, . . . the conclusions . . . are alarming."[7] Zaehner thinks that Huxley is not right, but I fear that it is Zaehner who is mistaken.

There are, of course, innumerable drug experiences that have no religious feature; they can be sensual as readily as spiritual, trivial as readily as transforming, capricious as readily as sacramental. If there is one point about which every student of the drug agrees, it is that there is no such thing as the drug experience *per se*—no experience that the drugs, as it were, merely secrete.

[7] *Mysticism, Sacred and Profane* (New York: Oxford, 1961), p. 12.

Every experience is a mix of three ingredients: drug, set (the psychological make-up of the individual), and setting (the social and physical environment in which it is taken). But given the right set and setting, the drugs can induce religious experiences indistinguishable from experiences that occur spontaneously. Nor need set and setting be exceptional. The way the statistics are currently running, it looks as if from one-fourth to one-third of the general population will have religious experiences if they take the drugs under naturalistic conditions, meaning by this conditions in which the researcher supports the subject but does not try to influence the direction his experience will take. Among subjects who have strong religious inclinations to begin with, the proportion of those having religious experiences jumps to three-fourths. If they take the drugs in settings that are religious too, the ratio soars to nine in ten.

How do we know that the experiences these people have really are religious? We can begin with the fact that they are. The "one-fourth to one-third of the general population" figure is drawn from two sources. Ten months after they had had their experiences, 24 per cent of the 194 subjects in a study by the California psychiatrist Oscar Janiger characterized their experiences as having been religious.[8] Thirty-two per cent of the 74 subjects in Ditman and Hayman's study reported, looking back on their LSD experience, that it looked as if it had been "very much" or "quite a bit" a religious experience; 42 per cent checked as true the statement that they "were left with a greater awareness of God, or a higher power, or ultimate reality."[9] The statement that three-fourths of subjects having religious "sets" will have religious experiences comes from the reports of sixty-nine religious professionals who took the drugs while the Harvard project was in progress.[10]

In the absence of (a) a single definition of religious experience acceptable to psychologists of religion generally and (b) foolproof ways of ascertaining whether actual experiences exemplify any definition, I am not sure there is any better way of telling whether the experiences of the 333 men and women involved in the above studies were religious than by noting whether they seemed so to them. But if more rigorous methods are preferred, they exist; they have been utilized, and they confirm the conviction of the man in the street that drug experiences can indeed be religious. In his doctoral study at Harvard University, Walter Pahnke worked out a typology of religious experience (in this instance of the mystical variety) based on the classic cases of mystical experiences as summarized in Walter Stace's *Mysticism and Philosophy*. He then administered psilocybin to ten theology students and professors in the setting of a Good Friday service. The drug was given "double-blind," meaning that neither

---

[8] Quoted in William H. McGlothlin, "Long-lasting Effects of LSD on Certain Attitudes in Normals," printed for private distribution by the RAND Corporation, May 1962, p. 16.

[9] *Ibid.*, pp. 45, 46.

[10] Timothy Leary, "The Religious Experience: Its Production and Interpretation," *The Psychedelic Review*, I, No. 3 (1964), 325.

Dr. Pahnke nor his subjects knew which ten were getting psilocybin and which ten placebos to constitute a control group. Subsequently the reports the subjects wrote of their experiences were laid successively before three college-graduate housewives who, without being informed about the nature of the study, were asked to rate each statement as to the degree (strong, moderate, slight, or none) to which it exemplified each of the nine traits of mystical experience enumerated in the typology of mysticism worked out in advance. When the test of significance was applied to their statistics, it showed that "those subjects who received psilocybin experienced phenomena which were indistinguishable from, if not identical with . . . the categories defined by our typology of mysticism."[11]

With the thought that the reader might like to test his own powers of discernment on the question of being considered, I insert here a simple test I gave to a group of Princeton students following a recent discussion sponsored by the Woodrow Wilson Society:

> Below are accounts of two religious experiences. One occurred under the influence of drugs, one without their influence. Check the one you think *was* drug-induced.

I

> Suddenly I burst into a vast, new, indescribably wonderful universe. Although I am writing this over a year later, the thrill of the surprise and amazement, the awesomeness of the revelation, the engulfment in an overwhelming feeling-wave of gratitude and blessed wonderment, are as fresh, and the memory of the experience is as vivid, as if it had happened five minutes ago. And yet to concoct anything by way of description that would even hint at the magnitude, the sense of ultimate reality . . . this seems such an impossible task. The knowledge which has infused and affected every aspect of my life came instantaneously and with such complete force of certainty that it was impossible, then or since, to doubt its validity.

II

> All at once, without warning of any kind, I found myself wrapped in a flame-colored cloud. For an instant I thought of fire . . . the next, I knew that the fire was within myself. Directly afterward there came upon me a sense of exultation, of immense joyousness accompanied or immediately followed by an intellectual illumination impossible to describe. Among other things, I did not merely come to believe, but I saw that the universe is not composed of dead matter, but is, on the contrary, a living Presence; I became conscious in myself of eternal life. . . . I saw that all men are immortal: that the cosmic order is

[11] "Drugs and Mysticism: An Analysis of the Relationship between Psychedelic Drugs and the Mystical Consciousness," a thesis presented to the Committee on Higher Degrees in History and Philosophy of Religion, Harvard University, June 1963.

such that without any preadventure all things work together for the good of
each and all; that the foundation principle of the world . . . is what we call
love, and that the happiness of each and all is in the long run absolutely certain.

On the occasion referred to, twice as many students (46) answered incorrectly as answered correctly (23). I bury the correct answer in a footnote
to preserve the reader's opportunity to test himself.[12]

Why, in the face of this considerable evidence, does Zaehner hold that
drug experiences cannot be authentically religious? There appear to be three
reasons:

1. His own experience was "utterly trivial." This of course proves that not
all drug experiences are religious; it does not prove that no drug experiences are
religious.

2. He thinks the experiences of others that appear religious to them are
not truly so. Zaehner distinguishes three kinds of mysticism: nature mysticism,
in which the soul is united with the natural world; monistic mysticism, in
which the soul merges with an impersonal absolute; and theism, in which the
soul confronts the living, personal God. He concedes that drugs can induce the
first two species of mysticism, but not its supreme instance, the theistic. As
proof he analyzes Huxley's experience as recounted in *The Doors of Perception*
to show that it produced at best a blend of nature and monistic mysticism.
Even if we were to accept Zaehner's evaluation of the three forms of mysticism, Huxley's case, and indeed Zaehner's entire book, would prove only that
not every mystical experience induced by the drugs is theistic. Insofar as
Zaehner goes beyond this to imply that drugs do not and cannot induce theistic
mysticism, he not only goes beyond the evidence but proceeds in the face of it.
James Slotkin reports that the peyote Indians "see visions, which may be of
Christ Himself. Sometimes they hear the voice of the Great Spirit. Sometimes
they become aware of the presence of God and of those personal shortcomings
which must be corrected if they are to do His will."[13] And G. M. Carstairs,
reporting on the use of psychedelic *bhang* in India, quotes a Brahmin as saying,
"It gives good bhakti. . . . You get a very good bhakti with bhang," *bhakti*
being precisely Hinduism's theistic variant.[14]

3. There is a third reason why Zaehner might doubt that drugs can induce
genuinely mystical experiences. Zaehner is a Roman Catholic, and Roman
Catholic doctrine teaches that mystical rapture is a gift of grace and as such
can never be reduced to man's control. This may be true; certainly the empiri-

---

[12] The first account is quoted anonymously in "The Issue of the Consciousness-
expanding Drugs," *Main Currents in Modern Thought*, XX, No. 1 (September-October
1963), 10–11. The second experience was that of Dr. R. M. Bucke, the author of *Cosmic
Consciousness*, as quoted in William James, *The Varieties of Religious Experience* (New
York: Modern Library, 1902), pp. 390–91. The former experience occurred under the influence of drugs; the latter did not.

[13] James S. Slotkin, *Peyote Religion* (New York: Free Press of Glencoe, 1956).

[14] "Daru and Bhang," *Quarterly Journal of the Study of Alcohol*, XV (1954), 229.

cal evidence cited does not preclude the possibility of a genuine ontological or theological difference between natural and drug-induced religious experiences. At this point, however, we are considering phenomenology rather than ontology, description rather than interpretation, and on this level there is no difference. Descriptively, drug experiences cannot be distinguished from their natural religious counterpart. When the current philosophical authority on mysticism, W. T. Stace, was asked whether the drug experience is similar to the mystical experience, he answered, "It's not a matter of its being *similar* to mystical experience; it *is* mystical experience."

What we seem to be witnessing in Zaehner's *Mysticism Sacred and Profane* is a reenactment of the age-old pattern in the conflict between science and religion. Whenever a new controversy arises, religion's first impulse is to deny the disturbing evidence science has produced. Seen in perspective, Zaehner's refusal to admit that drugs can induce experiences descriptively indistinguishable from those which are spontaneously religious is the current counterpart of the seventeenth-century theologians' refusal to look through Galileo's telescope or, when they did, their persistence on dismissing what they saw as machinations of the devil. When the fact that drugs can trigger religious experiences becomes incontrovertible, discussion will move to the more difficult question of how this new fact is to be interpreted. The latter question leads beyond phenomenology into philosophy.

3. Drugs and Religion Viewed Philosophically

Why do people reject evidence? Because they find it threatening, we may suppose. Theologians are not the only professionals to utilize this mode of defense. In his *Personal Knowledge*,[15] Michael Polanyi recounts the way the medical profession ignored such palpable facts as the painless amputation of human limbs, performed before their own eyes in hundreds of successive cases, concluding that the subjects were imposters who were either deluding their physicians or colluding with them. One physician, Esdaile, carried out about 300 major operations painlessly under mesmeric trance in India, but neither in India nor in Great Britain could he get medical journals to print accounts of his work. Polanyi attributes this closed-mindedness to "lack of a conceptual framework in which their discoveries could be separated from specious and untenable admixtures."

The "untenable admixture" in the fact that psychotomimetic drugs can induce religious experience is its apparent implicate: that religious disclosures are no more veridical than psychotic ones. For religious skeptics, this conclusion is obviously not untenable at all; it fits in beautifully with their thesis that *all*

[15] Chicago: Univ. of Chicago Press, 1958.

religion is at heart an escape from reality. Psychotics avoid reality by retiring into dream worlds of make-believe; what better evidence that religious visionaries do the same than the fact that identical changes in brain chemistry produce both states of mind? Had not Marx already warned us that religion is the "opiate" of the people?—apparently he was more literally accurate than he supposed. Freud was likewise too mild. He "never doubted that religious phenomena are to be understood only on the model of the neurotic symptoms of the individual."[16] He should have said "psychotic symptoms."

So the religious skeptic is likely to reason. What about the religious believer? Convinced that religious experiences are not fundamentally delusory, can he admit that psychotomimetic drugs can occasion them? To do so he needs (to return to Polanyi's words) "a conceptual framework in which [the discoveries can] be separated from specious and untenable admixtures," the "untenable admixture" being in this case the conclusion that religious experiences are in general delusory.

One way to effect the separation would be to argue that, despite phenomenological similarities between natural and drug-induced religious experiences, they are separated by a crucial *ontological* difference. Such an argument would follow the pattern of theologians who argue for the "real presence" of Christ's body and blood in the bread and wine of the Eucharist despite their admission that chemical analysis, confined as it is to the level of "accidents" rather than "essences," would not disclose this presence. But this distinction will not appeal to many today, for it turns on an essence-accident metaphysics which is not widely accepted. Instead of fighting a rear-guard action by insisting that if drug and non-drug religious experiences cannot be distinguished empirically there must be some transempirical factor that distinguishes them and renders the drug experience profane, I wish to explore the possibility of accepting drug-induced experiences as religious without relinquishing confidence in the truth-claims of religious experience generally.

To begin with the weakest of all arguments, the argument from authority: William James did not discount *his* insights that occurred while his brain chemistry was altered. The paragraph in which he retrospectively evaluates his nitrous oxide experiences has become classic, but it is so pertinent to the present discussion that it merits quoting once again.

> One conclusion was forced upon my mind at that time, and my impression of its truth has even since remained unshaken. It is that our normal waking consciousness, rational consciousness as we call it; is but one special type of consciousness, whilst all about it, parted from it by the filmiest of screens, there lie potential forms of consciousness entirely different. We may go through life without suspecting their existence; but apply the requisite stimulus, and at a touch they are there in all their completeness, definite types of mentality which probably somewhere have their field of application and adaptation. No account of the universe in its totality can be final which leaves these other forms

---

[16] *Totem and Taboo* (New York: Modern Library, 1938).

of consciousness quite disregarded. How to regard them is the question—for they are so discontinuous with ordinary consciousness. Yet they may determine attitudes though they cannot furnish formulas, and open a region though they fail to give a map. At any rate, they forbid a premature closing of our accounts with reality. Looking back on my own experiences, they all converge toward a kind of insight to which I cannot help ascribing some metaphysical significance (*op. cit.*, pp. 378–79).

To this argument from authority, I add two arguments that try to provide something by ways of reasons. Drug experiences that assume a religious cast tend to have fearful and/or beatific features, and each of my hypotheses relates to one of these aspects of the experience.

Beginning with the ominous, "fear of the Lord," awe-ful features, Gordon Wasson, the New York banker-turned-mycologist, describes these as he encountered them in his psilocybin experience as follows: "Ecstacy! in common parlance . . . ecstacy is fun. . . . But ecstacy is not fun. Your very soul is seized and shaken until it tingles. After all, who will choose to feel undiluted awe? . . . The unknowing vulgar abuse the word; we must recapture its full and terrifying sense."[17] Emotionally the drug experience can be like having forty-foot waves crash over you for several hours while you cling desperately to a life-raft which may be swept from under you at any minute. It seems quite possible that such an ordeal, like any experience of a close call, could awaken rather fundamental sentiments respecting life and death and destiny and trigger the "no atheists in foxholes" effect. Similarly, as the subject emerges from the trauma and realizes that he is not going to be insane as he had feared, there may come over him an intensified appreciation like that frequently reported by patients recovering from critical illness. "It happened on the day when my bed was pushed out of doors to the open gallery of the hospital," reads one such report:

> I cannot now recall whether the revelation came suddenly or gradually; I only remember finding myself in the very midst of those wonderful moments, beholding life for the first time in all its young intoxication of loveliness, in its unspeakable joy, beauty, and importance. I cannot say exactly what the mysterious change was. I saw no new thing, but I saw all the usual things in a miraculous new light—in what I believe is their true light. I saw for the first time how wildly beautiful and joyous, beyond any words of mine to describe, is the whole of life. Every human being moving across that porch, every sparrow that flew, every branch tossing in the wind, was caught in and was a part of the whole mad ecstasy of loveliness, of joy, of importance, of intoxication of life.[18]

---

[17] "The Hallucinogenic Fungi of Mexico: An Inquiry into the Origins of the Religious Idea among Primitive Peoples," *Harvard Botanical Museum Leaflets*, XIX, No. 7 (1961).

[18] Margaret Prescott Montague, *Twenty Minutes of Reality* (St. Paul, Minn.: Macalester Park, 1947), pp. 15, 17.

If we do not discount religious intuitions because they are prompted by battle-fields and *physical* crises; if we regard the latter as "calling us to our senses" more often than they seduce us into delusions, need comparable intuitions be discounted simply because the crises that trigger them are of an inner, *psychic* variety?

Turning from the hellish to the heavenly aspects of the drug experience, *some* of the latter may be explainable by the hypothesis just stated; that is, they may be occasioned by the relief that attends the sense of escape from high danger. But this hypothesis cannot possibly account for *all* the beatific episodes, for the simple reason that the positive episodes often come first, or to persons who experience no negative episodes whatever. Dr. Sanford Unger of the National Institute of Mental Health reports that among his subjects "50 to 60% will not manifest any real disturbance worthy of discussion," yet "around 75% will have at least one episode in which exaltation, rapture, and joy are the key descriptions."[19] How are we to account for the drug's capacity to induce peak experiences, such as the following, which are *not* preceded by fear?

> A feeling of great peace and contentment seemed to flow through my entire body. All sound ceased and I seemed to be floating in a great, very very still void or hemisphere. It is impossible to describe the overpowering feeling of peace, contentment, and being a part of goodness itself that I felt. I could feel my body dissolving and actually becoming a part of the goodness and peace that was all around me. Words can't describe this. I feel an awe and wonder that such a feeling could have occurred to me.[20]

Consider the following line of argument. Like every other form of life, man's nature has become distinctive through specialization. Man has specialized in developing a cerebral cortex. The analytic powers of this instrument are a standing wonder, but the instrument seems less able to provide man with the sense that he is meaningfully related to his environment: to life, the world, and history in their wholeness. As Albert Camus describes the situation, "If I were . . . a cat among animals, this life would have a meaning, or rather this problem would not arise, for I should belong to this world. I would *be* this world to which I am now opposed by my whole consciousness."[21] Note that it is Camus' consciousness that opposes him to his world. The drugs do not knock this consciousness out, but while they leave it operative they also activate areas of the brain that normally lie below its threshold of awareness. One of the clearest objective signs that the drugs are taking effect is the dilation they produce in the pupils of the eyes, and one of the most predictable subjective signs is the

---

[19] "The Current Scientific Status of Psychedelic Drug Research," read at the Conference on Methods in Philosophy and the Sciences, New School for Social Research, May 3, 1964, and scheduled for publication in David Solomon, ed., *The Conscious Expanding Drug* (New York: Putnam, 1964).

[20] Quoted by Dr. Unger in the paper just mentioned.

[21] *The Myth of Sisyphus* (New York: Vintage, 1955), p. 38.

intensification of visual perception. Both of these responses are controlled by portions of the brain that lie deep, further to the rear than the mechanisms that govern consciousness. Meanwhile we know that the human organism is interlaced with its world in innumerable ways it normally cannot sense—through gravitational fields, body respiration, and the like: the list could be multiplied until man's skin began to seem more like a thoroughfare than a boundary. Perhaps the deeper regions of the brain which evolved earlier and are more like those of the lower animals—"If I were . . . a cat . . . I should belong to this world"—can sense this relatedness better than can the cerebral cortex which now dominates our awareness. If so, when the drugs rearrange the neurohumors that chemically transmit impulses across synapses between neurons, man's consciousness and his submerged, intuitive, ecological awareness might for a spell become interlaced. This is, of course, no more than a hypothesis, but how else are we to account for the extraordinary incidence under the drugs of that kind of insight the keynote of which James described as "invariably a reconciliation"? "It is as if the opposites of the world, whose contradictoriness and conflict make all our difficulties and troubles, were melted into one and the same genus, but *one of the species*, the nobler and better one, *is itself the genus, and so soaks up and absorbs its opposites into itself*" (*op. cit.*, p. 379).

4. The Drugs and Religion Viewed "Religiously"

Suppose that drugs can induce experiences indistinguishable from religious experiences and that we can respect their reports. Do they shed any light, not (as we now ask) on life, but on the nature of the religious life?

One thing they may do is throw religious experience itself into perspective by clarifying its relation to the religious life as a whole. Drugs appear able to induce religious experiences; it is less evident that they can produce religious lives. It follows that religion is more than religious experiences. This is hardly news, but it may be a useful reminder, especially to those who incline toward "the religion of religious experience"; which is to say toward lives bent on the acquisition of desired states of experience irrespective of their relation to life's other demands and components.

Despite the dangers of a faulty psychology, it remains useful to regard man as having a mind, a will, and feelings. One of the lessons of religious history is that, to be adequate, a faith must rouse and involve all three components of man's nature. Religions of experience have their comparable pitfalls, as evidenced by Taoism's struggle (not always successful) to keep from degenerating into quietism, and the vehemence with which Zen Buddhism has insisted that once students have attained *satori*, they must be driven out of it, back into the world. The case of Zen is especially pertinent here, for it pivots on an enlightenment experience—*satori*, or *kensho*—which some (but not all) Zennists say resembles LSD. Alike or different, the point is that Zen recognizes that unless the experience is joined to discipline, it will come to naught:

> Even the Buddha . . . had to sit. . . . Without *joriki*, the particular power developed through *zazen* [seated meditation], the vision of oneness attained in enlightenment . . . in time becomes clouded and eventually fades into a pleasant memory instead of remaining an omnipresent reality shaping our daily life. . . . To be able to live in accordance with what the Mind's eye has revealed through *satori* requires, like the purification of character and the development of personality, a ripening period of *zazen*.[22]

If the religion of religious experience is a snare and a delusion, it follows that no religion that fixes its faith primarily in substances that induce religious experiences can be expected to come to a good end. What promised to be a short cut will prove to be a short circuit; what began as a religion will end as a religion surrogate. Whether chemical substances can be helpful *adjuncts* to faith is another question. The peyote-using Native American Church seems to indicate that they can be; anthropologists give this church a good report, noting among other things that members resist alcohol and alcoholism better than do nonmembers.[23] The conclusion to which evidence currently points would seem to be that chemicals *can* aid the religious life, but only where set within a context of faith (meaning by this the conviction that what they disclose is true) and discipline (meaning diligent exercise of the will in the attempt to work out the implications of the disclosures for the living of life in the everyday, common-sense world).

Nowhere today in Western civilization are these two conditions jointly fulfilled. Churches lack faith in the sense just mentioned; hipsters lack discipline. This might lead us to forget about the drugs, were it not for one fact: the distinctive religious emotion and the emotion that drugs unquestionably can occasion—Otto's *mysterium tremendum, majestas, mysterium fascinans;* in a phrase, the phenomenon of religious awe—seems to be declining sharply. As Paul Tillich said in an address to the Hillel Society at Harvard several years ago:

> The question our century puts before us [is]: Is it possible to regain the lost dimension, the encounter with the Holy, the dimension which cuts through the world of subjectivity and objectivity and goes down to that which is not world but is the mystery of the Ground of Being?

Tillich may be right; this may be the religious question of our century. For if (as we have insisted) religion cannot be equated with religious experiences, neither can it long survive their absence.

---

[22] Philip Kapleau, *The Three Pillars of Zen: Teaching, Practice and Enlightenment.* Compiled and edited with translations, introductions, and notes. (New York, Harper & Row, 1966.)

[23] Slotkin, *op. cit.*

COMMENTARY ON THE CONTEMPORARY ISSUE

Philosophers frequently distinguish between statements **in** a language and statements **about** a language. For example, **Il pleut** is a statement **in** French (namely, "It is raining"), but "French is a romance language" is a statement **about** French. In an analogous manner, we can distinguish between religious statements and statements about religion. "Jesus died for our sins" is a religious statement, whereas "Christianity is a monotheistic faith" is a statement about religion.

Now, just as a linguist can talk about French without committing himself to the truth of particular statements in French, so a student of religion can talk about religions without committing himself to the truth of particular religious statements. He can develop a sociology of religion, a psychology of religion, a history of religion, a comparison of religions, even a phenomenology of religious experience—all without confronting the central religious question: Is it true? The trouble with accounts of drug-induced "religious" experiences is that we do not know whether to take them seriously as religious statements or to treat them as data for our own statements **about** religion. For example, if an LSD user tells us that he has looked upon God's face, are we to treat this as evidence for the existence of a transcendent being, or should we merely file the report under "God-visions, subcategory **faces**"?

Needless to say, our uncertainty concerning reports of religious experiences extends to **all** accounts of visions, ecstasies, and transports, not merely to those which are in some way drug-induced. Our first reading in this section is a classic description of a religious vision by the medieval catholic Saint Theresa of Avila. Her brief and rather low-key description of God's presentation of Himself to her can be compared with the several modern accounts of mystical visions which William James gives us later in the section.

There is no question whatsoever of the truth of these reports, considering them simply as descriptions of actual sensory experiences. We can find evidence for the occurrence of such experiences in every major language and culture in the history of man. Mongol shamans, American Plains Indian warriors, medieval saints, twentieth-century hippies—the list of those who have had visions is endless. But the mere piling-up of reports does not settle the crucial question: Do these experiences prove the existence of a God or spiritual realm transcending the world of everyday life?

Both David Hume and Sigmund Freud react with scepticism to the sorts of visions recounted by St. Theresa and William James. Hume's particular concern was the intense religiosity of Protestants and Catholics, for which he had a very strong distaste. Their "enthusiasm" and "superstition," as he called it, offended his cool, sceptically rational spirit. Freud goes much farther, offering a psychoanalytic explanation for **all** the varieties of religious belief. If he is correct, then the religious impulse is nothing more than a manifestation of the human proclivity for self-deluding wish fulfillment.

Paul Tillich, the twentieth-century Protestant theologian, cannot be assigned neatly to either camp. Although he is committed to Christianity, his reinterpretation of the nature and significance of faith leaves us unclear about the distinctively **religious** content of his views.

There is obviously a similarity between the present problem and the dilemma posed in Section III by reports of extrasensory perception. Some persons are sceptical of **all** religious claims, and tend therefore to treat every report of religious experience as no more than a subjective description of individual perceptions having no objective significance. Other persons believe in general that men can establish contact with a transcendent realm, power, or being. Hence, they try to distinguish between genuine and spurious religious experiences. Frequently, devout believers will scoff at religious claims for drug visions because they doubt that any pharmacologically induced episode can possibly have religious significance.

ST. THERESA OF AVILA

*We begin our exploration of the nature of religious experience with
an account of a series of visions of God by the great Carmelite nun
St. Theresa (1515–1582). This account, taken from St. Theresa's
autobiography, is addressed to her confessor. As such visions go,
these are not particularly striking or unusual. St. Theresa reports
that first the hands of the Lord, later His face, and finally His entire
form appeared to her. As you will see in the selection from William
James later in this section, mystical and religious visions can get a
good deal wilder than that.*

*What makes St. Theresa's account so interesting, for our pur-
poses, is the painful honesty with which she struggles to distinguish
genuine or veridical visions from mere hallucinations. Her concern is understandable when we recall that a false vision could very
well be a temptation of the devil, leading not to salvation but to
damnation. Her anxiety lest she be misled lends an air of tension to
St. Theresa's description of her experience that is lacking in "secular" accounts of hallucinatory visions.*

*These days, we all—religious and nonreligious alike—tend to
discount stories of visions as the mere products of emotional disturbance. Perhaps we should give some thought to the fact that in
terms of quantity of reports, sobriety and trustworthiness of witnesses, and corroboration of detail, there are very few phenomena
as well-verified by eyewitness testimony as visions of God!*

A Mystical Vision

I spent some days, though only a few, with that vision continually in
my mind, and it did me so much good that I remained in prayer unceasingly
and contrived that everything I did should be such as not to displease Him
Who, as I clearly perceived, was a witness of it. And, although I was given so
much advice that I sometimes became afraid, my fear was short-lived, for the
Lord reassured me. One day, when I was at prayer, the Lord was pleased to

Chapter 28, "A Vision of God." From *The Life of the Holy Mother Teresa of Jesus,* in
The Complete Works of St. Theresa, trans. and ed. by E. Allison Peers from the critical
edition of P. Silverio de Santa Teresa, C.D., published in three volumes by Sheed &
Ward, Inc., New York. Reprinted by permission of Sheed & Ward, Inc., and Sheed & Ward
Ltd.

reveal to me nothing but His hands, the beauty of which was so great as to be indescribable. This made me very fearful, as does every new experience that I have when the Lord is beginning to grant me some supernatural favour. A few days later I also saw that Divine face, which seemed to leave me completely absorbed. I could not understand why the Lord revealed Himself gradually like this since He was later to grant me the favour of seeing Him wholly, until at length I realized that His Majesty was leading me according to my natural weakness. May He be blessed for ever, for so much glory all at once would have been more than so base and wicked a person could bear: knowing this, the compassionate Lord prepared me for it by degrees.

Your Reverence may suppose that it would have needed no great effort to behold those hands and that beauteous face. But there is such beauty about glorified bodies that the glory which illumines them throws all who look upon such supernatural loveliness into confusion. I was so much afraid, then, that I was plunged into turmoil and confusion, though later I began to feel such certainty and security that my fear was soon lost.

One year, on Saint Paul's Day, when I was at Mass, I saw a complete representation of this most sacred Humanity, just as in a picture of His resurrection body, in very great beauty and majesty; this I described in detail to Your Reverence in writing, at your very insistent request. It distressed me terribly to have to do so, for it is impossible to write such a description without a disruption of one's very being, but I did the best I could and so there is no reason for me to repeat the attempt here. I will only say that, if there were nothing else in Heaven to delight the eyes but the extreme beauty of the glorified bodies there, that alone would be the greatest bliss. A most especial bliss, then, will it be to us when we see the Humanity of Jesus Christ; for, if it is so even on earth, where His Majesty reveals Himself according to what our wretchedness can bear, what will it be where the fruition of that joy is complete? Although this vision is imaginary, I never saw it, or any other vision, with the eyes of the body, but only with the eyes of the soul.

Those who know better than I say that the type of vision already described[1] is nearer perfection than this, while this in its turn is much more so than those which are seen with the eyes of the body. The last-named type, they say, is the lowest and the most open to delusions from the devil. At that time I was not aware of this, and wished that, as this favour was being granted me, it could have been of such a kind as was visible to the eyes of the body, and then my confessor would not tell me I was imagining it. And no sooner had the vision faded—the very moment, indeed, after it had gone—than I began to think the same thing myself—that I had imagined it—and was worried at having spoken about it to my confessor and wondered if I had been deceiving him. Here was another cause for distress, so I went to him and consulted him about it. He asked me if I had told him what the vision really looked like to

---

[1] I.e., the intellectual vision. By "this," of course, is meant the imaginary vision.

me or if I had meant to deceive him. I said I had told him the truth, for I felt sure I had not been lying or had had any such intention; I would not think one thing and say another for the whole world. This he well knew, and so he managed to calm me. It worried me so much to have to go to him about these things that I cannot imagine how the devil could ever have suggested to me that I must be inventing them and thus be torturing myself. But the Lord made such haste to grant me this favour and to make its reality plain that my doubt about its being fancy left me immediately and since then it has become quite clear to me how silly I was. For, if I were to spend years and years imagining how to invent anything so beautiful, I could not do it, and I do not even know how I should try, for, even in its whiteness and radiance alone, it exceeds all that we can imagine.

It is not a radiance which dazzles, but a soft whiteness and an infused radiance which, without wearying the eyes, causes them the greatest delight; nor are they wearied by the brightness which they see in seeing this Divine beauty. So different from any earthly light is the brightness and light now revealed to the eyes that, by comparison with it, the brightness of our sun seems quite dim and we should never want to open our eyes again for the purpose of seeing it. It is as if we were to look at a very clear stream, in a bed of crystal, reflecting the sun's rays, and then to see a very muddy stream, in an earthy bed and overshadowed by clouds. Not that the sun, or any other such light, enters into the vision: on the contrary, it is like a natural light and all other kinds of light seem artificial. It is a light which never gives place to night, and, being always light, is disturbed by nothing. It is of such a kind, indeed, that no one, however powerful his intellect, could, in the whole course of his life, imagine it as it is. And so quickly does God reveal it to us that, even if we needed to open our eyes in order to see it, there would not be time for us to do so. But it is all the same whether they are open or closed: if the Lord is pleased for us to see it, we shall do so even against our will. There is nothing powerful enough to divert our attention from it, and we can neither resist it nor attain to it by any diligence or care of our own. This I have conclusively proved by experience, as I shall relate.

I should like now to say something of the way in which the Lord reveals Himself through these visions. I do not mean that I shall describe how it is that He can introduce this strong light into the inward sense and give the understanding an image so clear that it seems like reality. That is a matter for learned men to explain. The Lord has not been pleased to grant me to understand how it is; and I am so ignorant, and my understanding is so dull that, although many attempts have been made to explain it to me, I have not yet succeeded in understanding how it can happen. There is no doubt about this: I have not a keen understanding, although Your Reverence may think I have; again and again I have proved that my mind has to be spoon-fed, as they say, if it is to retain anything. Occasionally my confessor used to be astounded at the depths of my ignorance, and it never became clear to me how God did this and how it was possible that He should; nor, in fact, did I want to know, so I never asked anyone about it, though, as I have said, I have for many years been in touch with men of sound learning. What I did ask them was whether certain things were sinful or no: as for the rest, all I needed was to remember that God did everything and then I realized that I had no reason to be afraid and every reason to praise Him. Difficulties like that only arouse devotion in me, and, the greater they are, the greater is the devotion.

I will describe, then, what I have discovered by experience. How the Lord effects it, Your Reverence will explain better than I and will expound everything obscure of which I do not know the explanation. At certain times it really seemed to me that it was an image I was seeing; but on many other occasions I thought it was no image, but Christ Himself, such was the brightness with which He was pleased to reveal Himself to me. Sometimes, because of its indistinctness, I would think the vision was an image, though it was likely no earthly painting, however perfect, and I have seen a great many good ones. It is ridiculous to think that the one thing is any more like the other than a living person is like his portrait: however well the portrait is done, it can never look completely natural: one sees, in fact, that it is a dead thing. But let us pass over that, apposite and literally true though it is.

I am not saying this as a comparison, for comparisons are never quite satisfactory: it is the actual truth. The difference is similar to that between something living and something painted, neither more so nor less. For if what I see is an image it is a living image—not a dead man but the living Christ. And He shows me that He is both Man and God—not as He was in the sepulchre, but as He was when He left it after rising from the dead. Sometimes He comes with such majesty that no one can doubt it is the Lord Himself; this is especially so after Communion, for we know that He is there, since the Faith tells us so. He reveals Himself so completely as the Lord of that inn, the soul, that it feels as though it were wholly dissolved and consumed in Christ. O my Jesus, if one could but describe the majesty with which Thou dost reveal Thyself! How completely art Thou Lord of the whole world, and of the heavens, and of a thousand other worlds, and of countless worlds and heavens that Thou hast created! And the majesty with which Thou dost reveal Thyself shows the soul that to be Lord of this is nothing for Thee.

Here it becomes evident, my Jesus, how trifling is the power of all the devils in comparison with Thine, and how he who is pleasing to Thee can trample upon all the hosts of hell. Here we see with what reason the devils trembled when Thou didst descend into Hades: well might they have longed for a thousand deeper hells in order to flee from such great Majesty! I see that Thou art pleased to reveal to the soul the greatness of Thy Majesty, together with the power of this most sacred Humanity in union with the Divinity. Here is a clear picture of what the Day of Judgment will be, when we shall behold the Majesty of this King and see the rigour of His judgment upon the wicked.

Here we find true humility, giving the soul power to behold its own wretchedness, of which it cannot be ignorant. Here is shame and genuine repentance for sin; for, though it sees God revealing His love to it, the soul can find no place to hide itself and thus is utterly confounded. I mean that, which the Lord is pleased to reveal to the soul so much of His greatness and majesty, the vision has such exceeding great power that I believe it would be impossible to endure, unless the Lord were pleased to help the soul in a most supernatural way by sending it into a rapture or an ecstasy, during the fruition of which the vision of that Divine Presence is lost. Though it is true that afterwards the vision is forgotten, the majesty and beauty of God are so deeply imprinted upon the soul that it is impossible to forget these—save when the Lord is pleased for the soul to suffer the great loneliness and aridity that I shall describe later; for then it seems even to forget God Himself. The soul is now a new creature: it is continuously absorbed in God; it seems to me that a new and living love of God is beginning to work within it to a very high degree; for, though the former type of vision which, as I said, reveals God without presenting any image of Him, is of a higher kind, yet, if the memory of it is to last, despite our weakness, and if the thoughts are to be well occupied, it is a great thing that so Divine a Presence should be presented to the imagination and should remain within it. These two kinds of vision almost invariably occur simultaneously, and, as they come in this way, the eyes of the soul see the excellence and the beauty and the glory of the most holy Humanity. And in the other way which has been described it is revealed to us how He is God, and that He is powerful, and can do all things, and rules all things, and fills all things with His love.

This vision is to be very highly esteemed, and, in my view, there is no peril in it, as its effects show that the devil has no power over it. Three or four times, I think, he has attempted to present the Lord Himself to me in this way, by making a false likeness of Him. He takes the form of flesh, but he cannot counterfeit the glory which the vision has when it comes from God. He makes these attempts in order to destroy the effects of the genuine vision that the soul has experienced; but the soul, of its own accord, resists them: it then becomes troubled, despondent and restless; loses the devotion and joy which it had before; and is unable to pray. At the beginning of my experiences, as I have said, this happened to me three or four times. It is so very different from a true vision that I think, even if a soul has experienced only the Prayer of Quiet, it will become aware of the difference from the effects which have been described in the chapter on locutions. The thing is very easy to recognize; and, unless a soul wants to be deceived, I do not think the devil will deceive it if it walks in humility and simplicity. Anyone, of course, who has had a genuine vision from God will recognize the devil's work almost at once; he will begin by giving the soul consolations and favours, but it will thrust them from it. And further, I think, the devil's consolations must be different from those of

God: there is no suggestion in them of pure and chaste love and it very soon becomes easy to see whence they come. So, in my view, where a soul has had experience, the devil will be unable to do it any harm.

Of all impossibilities, the most impossible is that these true visions should be the work of the imagination. There is no way in which this could be so: by the mere beauty and whiteness of a single one of the hands which we are shown the imagination is completely transcended. In any case, there is no other way in which it would be possible for us to see in a moment things of which we have no recollection, which we have never thought of, and which, even in a long period of time, we could not invent with our imagination, because, as I have already said, they far transcend what we can comprehend on earth. Whether we could possibly be in any way responsible for this will be clear from what I shall now say. If, in a vision, the representation proceeded from our own understanding, quite apart from the fact that it would not bring about the striking effects which are produced when a vision is of God, or, indeed, any effects at all, the position would be like that of a man who wants to put himself to sleep but stays awake because sleep has not come to him. He needs it—perhaps his brain is tired—and so is anxious for it; and he settles down to doze, and does all he can to go off to sleep, and sometimes thinks he is succeeding, but if it is not real sleep it will not restore him or refresh his brain—indeed, the brain sometimes grows wearier. Something like that will be the case here: instead of being restored and becoming strong, the soul will grow wearier and become tired and peevish. It is impossible for human tongue to exaggerate the riches which a vision from God brings to the soul: it even bestows health and refreshment on the body.

I used to put forward this argument, together with others, when they told me, as they often did, that I was being deceived by the devil and that it was all the work of my imagination. I also drew such comparisons as I could and as the Lord revealed to my understanding. But it was all to little purpose, because there were some very holy persons in the place, by comparison with whom I was a lost creature; and, as God was not leading these persons by that way, they were afraid and thought that what I saw was the result of my sins. They repeated to one another what I said, so that before long they all got to know about it, though I had spoken of it only to my confessor and to those with whom he had commanded me to discuss it.

I once said to the people who were talking to me in this way that if they were to tell me that a person whom I knew well and had just been speaking to was not herself at all, but that I was imagining her to be so, and that they knew this was the case, I should certainly believe them rather than my own eyes. But, I added, if that person left some jewels with me, which I was actually holding in my hand as pledges of her great love, and if, never having had any before, I were thus to find myself rich instead of poor, I could not possibly believe that this was delusion, even if I wanted to. And, I said, I could show them these jewels—for all who knew me were well aware how my soul had changed: my confessor himself testified to this, for the difference was very great in every respect, and no fancy, but such as all could clearly see. As I had previously been so wicked, I concluded, I could not believe that, if the devil were doing this to delude me and drag me down to hell, he would make use of means which so completely defeated their own ends by taking away my vices and making me virtuous and strong; for it was quite clear to me that these experiences had immediately made me a different person.

My confessor, who, as I have said, was a very holy Father of the Company of Jesus,[2] gave them—so I learned—the same reply. He was very discreet and a man of deep humility, and this deep humility brought great trials upon me; for, being a man of great prayer and learning, he did not trust his own opinion, and the Lord was not leading him by this path. Very great trials befell him on my account, and this in many ways. I knew they used to tell him that he must be on his guard against me, lest the devil should deceive him into believing anything I might say to him, and they gave him similar examples of what had happened with other people. All this worried me. I was afraid that there would be no one left to hear my confession, and that everyone would flee from me: I did nothing but weep.

By the providence of God this Father consented to persevere with me and hear me: so great a servant of God was he that for His sake he would have exposed himself to anything. So he told me that I must not offend God or depart from what he said to me, and if I were careful about that I need not be afraid that He would fail me. He always encouraged me and soothed me. And he always told me not to hide anything from him, in which I obeyed him. He would say that, if I did this, the devil—assuming it to be the devil—would not hurt me, and that in fact, out of the harm which he was trying to do my soul, the Lord would bring good. He did his utmost to lead my soul to perfection. And I was so fearful, I obeyed him in every way, though imperfectly. For the three years and more during which he was my confessor,[3] I gave him a great deal of trouble with these trials of mine, for during the grievous persecutions which I suffered and on the many occasions when the Lord allowed me to be harshly judged, often undeservedly, all kinds of tales about me were brought to him and he would be blamed on my account when he was in no way blameworthy.

Had he not been a man of such sanctity, and had not the Lord given him courage, he could not possibly have endured so much, for he had to deal with

[2] P. Baltasar Álvarez. As this Father was only twenty-five years of age when he became St. Teresa's director, it is not surprising that he was disinclined to trust his own opinion, the more so as his Rector, P. Dionisio Vázquez, was a man of a rigid and inflexible temperament. P. Luis de la Puente [who was under him at Medina and wrote his biography] tells us that he himself was very conscious of his deficiencies in this respect. Cf. La Puente: *Vida del Padre Baltasar Álvarez,* etc., Madrid, 1615, Chap. XIII.

[3] The period was actually of six years, but the author naturally dwells most upon the first three, which were the most difficult for her.

people who did not believe him but thought I was going to destruction and at the same time he had to soothe me and deliver me from the fears which were oppressing me, though these he sometimes only intensified. He had to reassure me; for, whenever I had a vision involving a new experience, God allowed me to be left in great fear. This all came from my having been, and my still being, such a sinner. He would comfort me most compassionately, and, if he had had more trust in himself, I should have had less to suffer, for God showed him the truth about everything and I believe the Sacrament itself gave him light.

Those of God's servants who were not convinced that all was well would often come and talk to me. Some of the things I said to them I expressed carelessly and they took them in the wrong sense. To one of them I was very much attached: he was a most holy man and my soul was infinitely in his debt and I was infinitely distressed at his misunderstanding me when he was so earnestly desirous that I should advance in holiness and that the Lord should give me light. Well, as I have said, I spoke without thinking what I was saying and my words seemed to these people lacking in humility. When they saw any faults in me, and they must have seen a great many, they condemned me outright. They would ask me certain questions, which I answered plainly, though carelessly; and they then thought I was trying to instruct them and considered myself a person of learning. All this reached the ears of my confessor (for they were certainly anxious to improve me), whereupon he began to find fault with me.

This state of things went on for a long time and I was troubled on many sides; but, thanks to the favours which the Lord granted me, I endured everything. I say this so that it may be realized what a great trial it is to have no one with experience of this spiritual road; if the Lord had not helped me so much, I do not know what would have become of me. I had troubles enough to deprive me of my reason, and I sometimes found myself in such a position that I could do nothing but lift up my eyes to the Lord. For though the opposition of good people to a weak and wicked woman like myself, and a timid one at that, seems nothing when described in this way, it was one of the worst trials that I have ever known in my life, and I have suffered some very severe ones. May the Lord grant me to have done His Majesty a little service here; for I am quite sure that those who condemned and arraigned me were doing Him service and that it was all for my great good.

HUME

Once again we encounter the Scottish sceptic David Hume. As you will have gathered from his discussion of miracles (in Section III), Hume was no friend of religion. Indeed, his friends were so concerned for his reputation that they prevailed upon him to withhold publication of his most important treatment of the subject, the Dialogues Concerning Natural Religion. It appeared only after his death.

The Dialogues made it clear that Hume saw little merit in any version of religious doctrine; but as a disciple of the calm rationality of the Roman stoics, he found the more intense forms of religious faith particularly distasteful. In this ironic essay, he castigates both the Puritans (whom he associates with "enthusiasm") and the Roman Catholics (whom he accuses of "superstition").

Hume's discussion raises, indirectly, a very thorny issue which has been largely ignored in contemporary America—namely, the inherent tolerance of religious faith. If a man truly believes that he has found the path to salvation and immortal life, he will surely place that belief above everything else in the world. His faith will be more important to him than friends, family, community, or nation. What is more, he will hardly be willing to compromise his faith merely to avoid conflict or unpleasantness in his social relationships. In short, a truly religious man must in a sense be intolerant and unyielding. To the man himself, such devotion will be the very mark of true belief, but to the rest of society it will appear as obstinacy and close-mindedness.

Americans have tried hard to combine a diversity of religious faiths in one plural society. Where but in America could one find a Council of Christians and Jews? Nevertheless, the suspicion remains that interfaith harmony can be achieved only by a watering down of the several faiths. Hume's dislike of religious orthodoxy really shows how unsympathetic he is to the religious temperament in general.

Of Superstition
and Enthusiasm

That the corruption of the best things produces the worst, is grown into a maxim, and is commonly proved, among other instances by the pernicious effects of *superstition* and *enthusiasm*, the corruptions of true religion.

These two species of false religion, though both pernicious, are yet of a different, and even of a contrary nature. The mind of man is subject to certain unaccountable terrors and apprehensions, proceeding either from the unhappy situation of private or public affairs, from ill health, from a gloomy and melancholy disposition, or from the concurrence of all these circumstances. In such a state of mind, infinite unknown evils are dreaded from unknown agents; and where real objects of terror are wanting, the soul, active to its own prejudice, and fostering its predominant inclination, finds imaginary ones, to whose power and malevolence it sets no limits. As these enemies are entirely invisible and unknown, the methods taken to appease them are equally unaccountable, and consist in ceremonies, observances, mortifications, sacrifices, presents, or in any practice, however absurd or frivolous, which either folly or knavery recommends to a blind and terrified credulity. Weakness, fear, melancholy, together with ignorance, are, therefore, the true sources of Superstition.

But the mind of man is also subject to an unaccountable elevation and presumption, arising from prosperous success, from luxuriant health, from strong spirits, or from a bold and confident disposition. In such a state of mind, the imagination swells with great, but confused conceptions, to which no sublunary beauties or enjoyments can correspond. Every thing mortal and perishable vanishes as unworthy of attention. And a full range is given to the fancy in the invisible regions or world of spirits, where the soul is at liberty to indulge itself in every imagination, which may best suit its present taste and disposition. Hence arise raptures, transports, and surprising flights of fancy; and confidence and presumption still encreasing, these raptures, being altogether unaccountable, and seeming quite beyond the reach of our ordinary faculties, are attributed to the immediate inspiration of that Divine Being, who is the object of devotion. In a little time, the inspired person comes to regard himself as a distinguished favourite of the Divinity; and when this frenzy once takes place, which is the summit of enthusiasm, every whimsy is consecrated: Human reason, and even morality are rejected as fallacious guides: And the fanatic madman delivers himself over, blindly, and without reserve, to the supposed illapses [transports] of the spirit, and to inspiration from above. Hope, pride, presumption, a warm imagination, together with ignorance, are, therefore, the true sources of Enthusiasm.

From *Essays Moral and Political*. Originally published in 1741.

These two species of false religion might afford occasion to many speculations; but I shall confine myself, at present to a few reflections concerning
their different influence on government and society.

My first reflection is, *That superstition is favourable to priestly power,*
and enthusiasm not less or rather more contrary to it than sound reason and
philosophy. As superstition is founded on fear, sorrow, and a depression of
spirits, it represents the man to himself in such despicable colours, that he
appears unworthy, in his own eyes, of approaching the divine presence, and
naturally has recourse to any other person, whose sanctity of life, or, perhaps,
impudence and cunning, have made him be supposed more favoured by the
Divinity. To him the superstitious entrust their devotions: To his care they
recommend their prayers, petitions, and sacrifices: And by his means, they
hope to render their addresses acceptable to their incensed Deity. Hence the
origin of Priests, who may justly be regarded as an invention of a timorous
and abject superstition, which, ever diffident of itself, dares not offer up its
own devotions, but ignorantly thinks to recommend itself to the Divinity, by
the mediation of his supposed friends and servants. As superstition is a considerable ingredient in almost all religions, even the most fanatical; there
being nothing but philosophy able entirely to conquer these unaccountable
terrors; hence it proceeds, that in almost every sect of religion there are priests
to be found: But the stronger mixture there is of superstition, the higher is the
authority of the priesthood.

On the other hand, it may be observed, that all enthusiasts have been
free from the yoke of ecclesiastics, and have expressed great independence in
their devotion; with a contempt of forms, ceremonies, and traditions. The
quakers are the most egregious, though, at the same time, the most innocent
enthusiasts that have yet been known; and are, perhaps, the only sect, that have
never admitted priests among them. The *independents*, of all the English sectaries, approach nearest to the *quakers* in fanaticism, and in their freedom from
priestly bondage. The *presbyterians* follow after, at an equal distance in both
particulars. In short, this observation is founded in experience; and will also appear to be founded in reason, if we consider, that, as enthusiasm arises from a
presumptuous pride and confidence, it thinks itself sufficiently qualified to
approach the Divinity, without any human mediator. Its rapturous devotions
are so fervent, that it even imagines itself *actually* to *approach* him by the way
of contemplation and inward converse; which makes it neglect all those outward ceremonies and observances, to which the assistance of the priests
appears so requisite in the eyes of their superstitious votaries. The fanatic con-
secrates himself, and bestows on his own person a sacred character, much superior to what forms and ceremonies institutions can confer on any other.

My *second* reflection with regard to these species of false religion is, *that*
religions, which partake of enthusiasm are, on their first rise, more furious and
violent than those which partake of superstition; but in a little time become
more gentle and moderate. The violence of this species of religion, when

excited by novelty, and animated by opposition, appears from numberless instances; of the *anabaptists* in Germany, the *camisars* in France, the *levellers* and other fanatics in England, and the *covenanters* in Scotland. Enthusiasm being founded on strong spirits, and a presumptuous boldness of character, it naturally begets the most extreme resolutions; especially after it rises to that height as to inspire the deluded fanatic with the opinion of divine illuminations, and with a contempt for the common rules of reason, morality, and prudence.

It is thus enthusiasm produces the most cruel disorders in human society; but its fury is like that of thunder and tempest, which exhaust themselves in a little time, and leave the air more calm and serene than before. When the first fire of enthusiasm is spent, men naturally, in all fanatical sects, sink into the greatest remissness and coolness in sacred matters; there being no body of men among them, endowed with sufficient authority, whose interest is concerned to support the religious spirit: No rites, no ceremonies, no holy observances, which may enter into the common train of life, and preserve the sacred principles from oblivion. Superstition, on the contrary, steals in gradually and insensibly; renders men tame and submissive; it is acceptable to the magistrate, and seems inoffensive to the people: Till at last the priest, having firmly established his authority, becomes the tyrant and disturber of human society, by his endless contentions, persecutions, and religious wars. How smoothly did the Romish church advance in her acquisition of power? But into what dismal convulsions did she throw all Europe, in order to maintain it? On the other hand, our sectaries, who were formerly such dangerous bigots, are now become very free reasoners; and the *quakers* seem to approach nearly the only regular body of *deists* in the universe, the *literati*, or the disciples of Confucius in China.[1]

My *third* observation on this head is, *that superstition is an enemy to civil liberty, and enthusiasm a friend to it.* As superstition groans under the dominion of priests, and enthusiasm is destructive of all ecclesiastical power, this sufficiently accounts for the present observation. Not to mention, that enthusiasm, being the infirmity of bold and ambitious tempers, is naturally accompanied with a spirit of liberty; as superstition, on the contrary, renders men tame and abject, and fits them for slavery. We learn from English history, that, during the civil wars, the *independents* and *deists,* though the most opposite in their religious principles; yet were united in their political ones, and were alike passionate for a common-wealth. And since the origin of *whig* and *tory,* the leaders of the *whigs* have either been *deists* or profest *latitudinarians* in their principles; that is, friends to toleration, and indifferent to any particular sect of *christians:* While the sectaries, who have all a strong tincture of enthusiasm, have always, without exception, concurred with that party, in defence of civil liberty. The resemblance in their superstitions long united the high-church *tories,* and the *Roman catholics,* in support of prerogative and

---

[1] The Chinese Literati have no priests or ecclesiastical establishment.

kingly power; though experience of the tolerating spirit of the *whigs* seems of late to have reconciled the *catholics* to that party.

The *molinists* and *jansenists* in France have a thousand unintelligible disputes, which are not worthy the reflection of a man of sense: But what principally distinguishes these two sects, and alone merits attention, is the different spirit of their religion. The *molinists* conducted by the *jesuits*, are great friends to superstition, rigid observers of external forms and ceremonies, and devoted to the authority of the priests, and to tradition. The *jansenists* are enthusiasts, and zealous promoters of the passionate devotion, and of the inward life; little influenced by authority; and, in a word, but half catholics. The consequences are exactly conformable to the foregoing reasoning. The *jesuits* are the tyrants of the people, and the slaves of the court: And the *jansenists* preserve alive the small sparks of the love of liberty, which are to be found in the French nation.

JAMES

William James was a man of the broadest imaginable interests and sympathies. In addition to his philosophical writings, which you have already sampled in Section III, James made major contributions to psychology and to the phenomenology of religious experience. He even taught medicine at Harvard for a while.

James believed strongly that philosophers should look at the real world before they theorized about it. Consequently, he began his investigation of religion by a wide-ranging study of actual reports of religious experience. He read the accounts of saints, mystics, sceptics, and even of the antireligious. After a while he began to observe a pattern to the accounts, and only then did he attempt to generalize. The result, his massive Varieties of Religious Experience, *is still one of the best introductions to the entire religious dimension of human life.*

The question which immediately occurs to us when we read descriptions of religious experience is: What does it all prove? No one doubts that men have visions, hear voices, feel a sense of oneness with the universe, or reach out for the infinite. What we want to know is whether these experiences are genuine revelations of a transcendent realm, or whether they are merely states of subjective consciousness with no further significance.

James himself hedges on this fundamental question. As you will see, he is prepared to formulate certain hypotheses—and even to put some measure of credence in them. But it is unlikely that his experimental, hesitant approach would satisfy either the sceptic or the true believer.

The Varieties of
Mystical Experience

The Reality
of the Unseen

Were one asked to characterize the life of religion in the broadest and most general terms possible, one might say that it consists of the belief that

Lectures 3 and 20. From *The Varieties of Religious Experience* by William James. From the Gifford Lectures on Natural Religion delivered at Edinburgh in 1901–2.

there is an unseen order, and that our supreme good lies in harmoniously adjusting ourselves thereto. This belief and this adjustment are the religious attitude in the soul. I wish during this hour to call your attention to some of the psychological peculiarities of such an attitude as this, of belief in an object which we cannot see. All our attitudes, moral, practical, or emotional, as well as religious, are due to the "objects" of our consciousness, the things which we believe to exist, whether really or ideally, along with ourselves. Such objects may be present to our senses, or they may be present only to our thought. In either case they elicit from us a *reaction;* and the reaction due to things of thought is notoriously in many cases as strong as that due to sensible presences. It may be even stronger. The memory of an insult may make us angrier than the insult did when we received it. We are frequently more ashamed of our blunders afterwards than we were at the moment of making them; and in general our whole higher prudential and moral life is based on the fact that material sensations actually present may have a weaker influence on our action than ideas of remoter facts.

The more concrete objects of most men's religion, the deities whom they worship, are known to them only in idea. It has been vouchsafed, for example, to very few Christian believers to have had a sensible vision of their Saviour; though enough appearances of this sort are on record, by way of miraculous exception, to merit our attention later. The whole force of the Christian religion, therefore, so far as belief in the divine personages determines the prevalent attitude of the believer, is in general exerted by the instrumentality of pure ideas, of which nothing in the individual's past experience directly serves as a model.

But in addition to these ideas of the more concrete religious objects, religion is full of abstract objects which prove to have an equal power. God's attributes as such, his holiness, his justice, his mercy, his absoluteness, his infinity, has omniscience, his tri-unity, the various mysteries of the redemptive process, the operation of the sacraments, etc., have proved fertile wells of inspiring meditation for Christian believers. We shall see later that the absence of definite sensible images is positively insisted on by the mystical authorities in all religions as the *sine qua non* of a successful orison, or contemplation of the higher divine truths. Such contemplations are expected (and abundantly verify the expectation, as we shall also see) to influence the believer's subsequent attitude very powerfully for good. . . .

It is as if there were in the human consciousness a *sense of reality, a feeling of objective presence, a perception* of what we may call *"something there,"* more deep and more general than any of the special and particular "senses" by which the current psychology supposes existent realities to be originally revealed. If this were so, we might suppose the senses to waken our attitudes and conduct as they so habitually do, by first exciting this sense of reality; but anything else, any idea, for example, that might similarly excite it, would have that same prerogative of appearing real which objects of sense normally possess. So far as religious conceptions were able to touch this reality-feeling, they would be believed in in spite of criticism, even though they might be so vague and remote as to be almost unimaginable, even though they might be such non-entities in point of *whatness*, as Kant makes the objects of his moral theology to be.

The most curious proofs of the existence of such an undifferentiated sense of reality as this are found in experiences of hallucination. It often happens that an hallucination is imperfectly developed: the person affected will feel a "presence" in the room, definitely localized, facing in one particular way, real in the most emphatic sense of the word, often coming suddenly, and as suddenly gone; and yet neither seen, heard, touched, nor cognized in any of the usual "sensible" ways. Let me give you an example of this, before I pass to the objects with whose presence religion is more peculiarly concerned.

An intimate friend of mine, one of the keenest intellects I know, has had several experiences of this sort. He writes as follows in response to my inquiries:—

> I have several times within the past few years felt the so-called "consciousness of a presence." The experiences which I have in mind are clearly distinguishable from another kind of experience which I have had very frequently, and which I fancy many persons would also call the "consciousness of a presence." But the difference for me between the two sets of experience is as great as the difference between feeling a slight warmth originating I know not where, and standing in the midst of a conflagration with all the ordinary senses alert.
>
> It was about September, 1884, when I had the first experience. On the previous night I had had, after getting into bed at my rooms in College, a vivid tactile hallucination of being grasped by the arm, which made me get up and search the room for an intruder; but the sense of presence properly so called came on the next night. After I had got into bed and blown out the candle, I lay awake awhile thinking on the previous night's experience, when suddenly I *felt* something come into the room and stay close to my bed. It remained only a minute or two. I did not recognize it by any ordinary sense, and yet there was a horribly unpleasant "sensation" connected with it. It stirred something more at the roots of my being than any ordinary perception. The feeling had something of the quality of a very large tearing vital pain spreading chiefly over the chest, but within the organism—and yet the feeling was not *pain* so much as *abhorrence*. At all events, something was present with me, and I knew its presence far more surely than I have ever known the presence of any fleshly living creature. I was conscious of its departure as of its coming: an almost instantaneously swift going through the door, and the "horrible sensation" disappeared.
>
> On the third night when I retired my mind was absorbed in some lectures which I was preparing, and I was still absorbed in these when I became aware of the actual presence (though not of the *coming*) of the thing that was there the night before, and of the "horrible sensation." I then mentally concentrated all my effort to charge this "thing," if it was evil, to depart, if it was *not* evil, to tell me who or what it was, and if it could not explain itself, to go, and that

I would compel it to go. It went as on the previous night, and my body quickly recovered its normal state.

On two other occasions in my life I have had precisely the same "horrible sensation." Once it lasted a full quarter of an hour. In all three instances the certainty that there in outward space there stood *something* was indescribably *stronger* than the ordinary certainty of companionship when we are in the close presence of ordinary living people. The something seemed close to me, and intensely more real than any ordinary perception. Although I felt it to be like unto myself, so to speak, or finite, small, and distressful, as it were, I didn't recognize it as any individual being or person.

Of course such an experience as this does not connect itself with the religious sphere. Yet it may upon occasion do so; and the same correspondent informs me that at more than one other conjuncture he had the sense of presence developed with equal intensity and abruptness, only then it was filled with a quality of joy.

> There was not a mere consciousness of something there, but fused in the central happiness of it, a startling awareness of some ineffable good. Not vague either, not like the emotional effect of some poem, or scene, or blossom, or music, but the sure knowledge of the close presence of a sort of mighty person, and after it went, the memory persisted as the one perception of reality. Everything else might be a dream, but not that.

My friend, as it oddly happens, does not interpret these latter experiences theistically, as signifying the presence of God. But it would clearly not have been unnatural to interpret them as a revelation of the deity's existence. When we reach the subject of mysticism, we shall have much more to say upon this head. . . .

We may now lay it down as certain that in the distinctively religious sphere of experience, many persons (how many we cannot tell) possess the objects of their belief, not in the form of mere conceptions which their intellect accepts as true, but rather in the form of quasi-sensible realities directly apprehended. As his sense of the real presence of these objects fluctuates, so the believer alternates between warmth and coldness in his faith. Other examples will bring this home to one better than abstract description, so I proceed immediately to cite some. . . .

Here is [an] . . . experience from a manuscript communication by a clergyman,—I take it from Starbuck's manuscript collection:—

> I remember the night, and almost the very spot on the hilltop, where my soul opened out, as it were, into the Infinite, and there was a rushing together of the two worlds, the inner and the outer. It was deep calling unto deep,—the deep that my own struggle had opened up within being answered by the unfathomable deep without, reaching beyond the stars. I stood alone with Him who had made me, and all the beauty of the world, and love, and sorrow, and

even temptation. I did not seek Him, but felt the perfect unison of my spirit with His. The ordinary sense of things around me faded. For the moment nothing but an ineffable joy and exaltation remained. It is impossible fully to describe the experience. It was like the effect of some great orchestra when all the separate notes have melted into one swelling harmony that leaves the listener conscious of nothing save that his soul is being wafted upwards, and almost bursting with its own emotion. The perfect stillness of the night was thrilled by a more solemn silence. The darkness held a presence that was all the more felt because it was not seen. I could not any more have doubted that *He* was there than that I was. Indeed, I felt myself to be, if possible, the less real of the two.

My highest faith in God and truest idea of him were then born in me. I have stood upon the Mount of Vision since, and felt the Eternal round about me. But never since has there come quite the same stirring of the heart. Then, if ever, I believe, I stood face to face with God, and was born anew of his spirit. There was, as I recall it, no sudden change of thought or of belief, except that my early crude conception had, as it were, burst into flower. There was no destruction of the old, but a rapid, wonderful unfolding. Since that time no discussion that I have heard of the proofs of God's existence has been able to shake my faith. Having once felt the presence of God's spirit, I have never lost it again for long. My most assuring evidence of his existence is deeply rooted in that hour of vision, in the memory of that supreme experience, and in the conviction, gained from reading and reflection, that something the same has come to all who have found God. I am aware that it may justly be called mystical. I am not enough acquainted with philosophy to defend it from that or any other charge. I feel that in writing of it I have overlaid it with words rather than put it clearly to your thought. But, such as it is, I have described it as carefully as I now am able to do. . . .

Such is the human ontological imagination, and such is the convincingness of what it brings to birth. Unpicturable beings are realized, and realized with an intensity almost like that of an hallucination. They determine our vital attitude as decisively as the vital attitude of lovers is determined by the habitual sense, by which each is haunted, of the other being in the world. A lover has notoriously this sense of the continuous being of his idol, even when his attention is addressed to other matters and he no longer represents her features. He cannot forget her; she uninterruptedly affects him through and through.

I spoke of the convincingness of these feelings of reality, and I must dwell a moment longer on that point. They are as convincing to those who have them as any direct sensible experiences can be, and they are, as a rule, much more convincing than results established by mere logic ever are. One may indeed be entirely without them; probably more than one of you here present is without them in any marked degree; but if you do have them, and have them at all strongly, the probability is that you cannot help regarding them as genuine perceptions of truth, as revelations of a kind of reality which no adverse argument, however unanswerable by you in words, can expel from your belief. The opinion opposed to mysticism in philosophy is sometimes spoken of as *rationalism*. Rationalism insists that all our beliefs ought ultimately to find for themselves articulate grounds. Such grounds, for rationalism, must consist of four things: (1) definitely statable abstract principles; (2) definite facts of sensation; (3) definite hypotheses based on such facts; and (4) definite inferences logically drawn. Vague impressions of something indefinable have no place in the rationalistic system, which on its positive side is surely a splendid intellectual tendency, for not only are all our philosophies fruits of it, but physical science (amongst other good things) is its result.

Nevertheless, if we look on man's whole mental life as it exists, on the life of men that lies in them apart from their learning and science, and that they inwardly and privately follow, we have to confess that the part of it of which rationalism can give an account is relatively superficial. It is the part that has the *prestige* undoubtedly, for it has the loquacity, it can challenge you for proofs, and chop logic, and put you down with words. But it will fail to convince or convert you all the same, if your dumb intuitions are opposed to its conclusions. If you have intuitions at all, they come from a deeper level of your nature than the loquacious level which rationalism inhabits. Your whole subconscious life, your impulses, your faiths, your needs, your divinations, have prepared the premises, of which your consciousness now feels the weight of the result; and something in you absolutely *knows* that that result must be truer than any logic-chopping rationalistic talk, however clever, that may contradict it. This inferiority of the rationalistic level in founding belief is just as manifest when rationalism argues for religion as when it argues against it. That vast literature of proofs of God's existence drawn from the order of nature, which a century ago seemed so overwhelmingly convincing, to-day does little more than gather dust in libraries, for the simple reason that our generation has ceased to believe in the kind of God it argued for. Whatever sort of a being God may be, we *know* to-day that he is nevermore that mere external inventor of "contrivances" intended to make manifest his "glory" in which our great-grandfathers took such satisfaction, though just how we know this we cannot possibly make clear by words either to others or to ourselves. I defy any of you here fully to account for your persuasion that if a God exist he must be a more cosmic and tragic personage than that Being.

The truth is that in the metaphysical and religious sphere, articulate reasons are cogent for us only when our inarticulate feelings of reality have already been impressed in favor of the same conclusion. Then, indeed, our intuitions and our reason work together, and great world-ruling systems, like that of the Buddhist or of the Catholic philosophy, may grow up. Our impulsive belief is here always what sets up the original body of truth, and our articulately verbalized philosophy is but its showy translation into formulas. The unreasoned and immediate assurance is the deep thing in us, the reasoned argument is but a surface exhibition. Instinct leads, intelligence does but follow. If a person feels the presence of a living God after the fashion shown by my quotations, your critical arguments, be they never so superior, will vainly set themselves to change his faith.

Please observe, however, that I do not yet say that it is *better* that the subconscious and non-rational should thus hold primacy in the religious realm. I confine myself to simply pointing out that they do so hold it as a matter of fact. . . .

Conclusions

. . . Summing up in the broadest possible way the characteristics of the religious life, as we have found them, it includes the following beliefs:—

1. That the visible world is part of a more spiritual universe from which it draws its chief significance;

2. That union or harmonious relation with that higher universe is our true end;

3. That prayer or inner communion with the spirit thereof—be that spirit "God" or "law"—is a process wherein work is really done, and spiritual energy flows in and produces effects, psychological or material, within the phenomenal world.

Religion includes also the following psychological characteristics:—

4. A new zest which adds itself like a gift to life, and takes the form either of lyrical enchantment or of appeal to earnestness and heroism.

5. An assurance of safety and a temper of peace, and, in relation to others, a preponderance of loving affections. . . .

. . . Ought it to be assumed that in all men the mixture of religion with other elements should be identical? Ought it, indeed, to be assumed that the lives of all men should show identical religious elements? . . .

To these questions I answer "No" emphatically. And my reason is that I do not see how it is possible that creatures in such different positions and with such different powers as human individuals are, should have exactly the same functions and the same duties. No two of us have identical difficulties, nor should we be expected to work out identical solutions. Each, from his peculiar angle of observation, takes in a certain sphere of fact and trouble, which each must deal with in a unique manner. One of us must soften himself, another must harden himself; one must yield a point, another must stand firm,—in order the better to defend the position assigned him. If an Emerson were forced to be a Wesley, or a Moody forced to be a Whitman, the total human consciousness of the divine would suffer. The divine can mean no single quality, it must mean a group of qualities, by being champions of which in alternation, different men may all find worthy missions. Each attitude being a syllable in human nature's total message, it takes the whole of us to spell the meaning out completely. So a "god of battles" must be allowed to be the god for one kind of person, a god of peace and heaven and home, the god for another. We must frankly recognize the fact that we live in partial systems, and that parts are not interchangeable in the spiritual life. If we are peevish and jealous, destruction of the self must be an element of our religion; why need it be one if we are good and sympathetic from the outset? If we are sick souls, we require a religion of deliverance; but why think so much of deliverance, if we are healthy-minded? Unquestionably, some men have the completer experience and the higher vocation, here just as in the social world; but for each man to stay in his own experience, whate'er it be, and for others to tolerate him there, is surely best.

But, you may now ask, would not this one-sidedness be cured if we should all espouse the science of religions as our own religion? In answering this question I must open again the general relations of the theoretic to the active life.

Knowledge about a thing is not the thing itself. You remember what Al-Ghazzali told us in the Lecture on Mysticism,—that to understand the causes of drunkenness, as a physician understands them, is not to be drunk. A science might come to understand everything about the causes and elements of religion, and might even decide which elements were qualified, by their general harmony with other branches of knowledge, to be considered true; and yet the best man at this science might be the man who found it hardest to be personally devout. *Tout savoir c'est tout pardonner.* . . .

For this reason, the science of religions may not be an equivalent for living religion; and if we turn to the inner difficulties of such a science, we see that a point comes when she must drop the purely theoretic attitude, and either let her knots remain uncut, or have them cut by active faith. To see this, suppose that we have our science of religions constituted as a matter of fact. Suppose that she has assimilated all the necessary historical material and distilled out of it as its essence the same conclusions which I myself a few moments ago pronounced. Suppose that she agrees that religion, wherever it is an active thing, involves a belief in ideal presences, and a belief that in our prayerful communion with them, work is done, and something real comes to pass. She has now to exert her critical activity, and to decide how far, in the light of other sciences and in that of general philosophy, such beliefs can be considered *true*.

Dogmatically to decide this is an impossible task. Not only are the other sciences and the philosophy still far from being completed, but in their present state we find them full of conflicts. The sciences of nature know nothing of spiritual presences, and on the whole hold no practical commerce whatever with the idealistic conceptions towards which general philosophy inclines. The scientist, so-called, is, during his scientific hours at least, so materialistic that one may well say that on the whole the influence of science goes against the notion that religion should be recognized at all. And this antipathy to religion finds an echo within the very science of religions itself. The cultivator of this science has to become acquainted with so many groveling and horrible superstitions that a presumption easily arises in his mind that any belief that is religious probably is false. In the "prayerful communion" of savages with such mumbo-jumbos of deities as they acknowledge, it is hard for us to see what genuine spiritual work—even though it were work relative only to their dark savage obligations—can possibly be done.

The consequence is that the conclusions of the science of religions are as likely to be adverse as they are to be favorable to the claim that the essence of religion is true. There is a notion in the air about us that religion is probably only an anachronism, a case of "survival," an atavistic relapse into a mode of thought which humanity in its more enlightened examples has outgrown; and this notion our religious anthropologists at present do little to counteract.

This view is so widespread at the present day that I must consider it with some explicitness before I pass to my own conclusions. Let me call it the "Survival theory," for brevity's sake.

The pivot round which the religious life, as we have traced it, revolves, is the interest of the individual in his private personal destiny. . . . Science, on the other hand, has ended by utterly repudiating the personal point of view. . . .

. . . The God whom science recognizes must be a God of universal laws exclusively, a God who does a wholesale, not a retail business. He cannot accommodate his processes to the convenience of individuals. The bubbles on the foam which coats a stormy sea are floating episodes, made and unmade by the forces of the wind and water. Our private selves are like those bubbles,—epiphenomena, as Clifford, I believe, ingeniously called them; their destinies weigh nothing and determine nothing in the world's irremediable currents of events. . . .

In spite of the appeal which this impersonality of the scientific attitude makes to a certain magnanimity of temper, I believe it to be shallow, and I can now state my reason in comparatively few words. That reason is that, so long as we deal with the cosmic and the general, we deal only with the symbols of reality, but *as soon as we deal with private and personal phenomena as such, we deal with realities in the completest sense of the term.* I think I can easily make clear what I mean by these words.

The world of our experience consists at all times of two parts, an objective and a subjective part, of which the former may be incalculably more extensive than the latter, and yet the latter can never be omitted or suppressed. The objective part is the sum total of whatsoever at any given time we may be thinking of, the subjective part is the inner "state" in which the thinking comes to pass. What we think of may be enormous,—the cosmic times and spaces, for example,—whereas the inner state may be the most fugitive and paltry activity of mind. Yet the cosmic objects, so far as the experience yields them, are but ideal pictures of something whose existence we do not inwardly possess but only point at outwardly, while the inner state is our very experience itself; its reality and that of our experience are one. A conscious field *plus* its object as felt or thought of *plus* an attitude towards the object *plus* the sense of a self to whom the attitude belongs—such a concrete bit of personal experience may be a small bit, but it is a solid bit as long as it lasts; not hollow, not a mere abstract element of experience, such as the "object" is when taken all alone. It is a *full* fact, even though it be an insignificant fact; it is of the *kind* to which all realities whatsoever must belong; the motor currents of the world run through the like of it; it is on the line connecting real events with real events. That unsharable feeling which each one of us has of the pinch of his individual destiny as he privately feels it rolling out on fortune's wheel may be disparaged for its egotism, may be sneered at as unscientific, but it is the one thing that fills up the measure of our concrete actuality, and any would-be existent that should lack such a feeling, or its analogue, would be a piece of reality only half made up.

If this be true, it is absurd for science to say that the egotistic elements of experience should be suppressed. The axis of reality runs solely through the egotistic places,—they are strung upon it like so many beads. To describe the world with all the various feelings of the individual pinch of destiny, all the various spiritual attitudes, left out from the description—they being as describable as anything else—would be something like offering a printed bill of fare as the equivalent for a solid meal. Religion makes no such blunder. The individual's religion may be egotistic, and those private realities which it keeps in touch with may be narrow enough; but at any rate it always remains infinitely less hollow and abstract, as far as it goes, than a science which prides itself on taking no account of anything private at all.

A bill of fare with one real raisin on it instead of the word "raisin," with one real egg instead of the word "egg," might be an inadequate meal, but it would at least be a commencement of reality. The contention of the survival-theory that we ought to stick to non-personal elements exclusively seems like saying that we ought to be satisfied forever with reading the naked bill of fare. I think, therefore, that however particular questions connected with our individual destinies may be answered, it is only by acknowledging them as genuine questions, and living in the sphere of thought which they open up, that we become profound. But to live thus is to be religious; so I unhesitatingly repudiate the survival-theory of religion, as being founded on an egregious mistake. It does not follow, because our ancestors made so many errors of fact and mixed them with their religion, that we should therefore leave off being religious at all. By being religious we establish ourselves in possession of ultimate reality at the only points at which reality is given us to guard. Our responsible concern is with our private destiny, after all.

You see now why I have been so individualistic throughout these lectures, and why I have seemed so bent on rehabilitating the element of feeling in religion and subordinating its intellectual part. Individuality is founded in feeling;

and the recesses of feeling, the darker, blinder strata of character, are the only places in the world in which we catch real fact in the making, and directly perceive how events happen, and how work is actually done. Compared with this world of living individualized feelings, the world of generalized objects which the intellect contemplates is without solidity or life. As in stereoscopic or kinetoscopic pictures seen outside the instrument, the third dimension, the movement, the vital element, are not there. We get a beautiful picture of an express train supposed to be moving, but where in the picture, as I have heard a friend say, is the energy or the fifty miles an hour?

Let us agree, then, that Religion, occupying herself with personal destinies and keeping thus in contact with the only absolute realities which we know, must necessarily play an eternal part in human history. The next thing to decide is what she reveals about those destinies, or whether indeed she reveals anything distinct enough to be considered a general message to mankind. We have done as you see, with our preliminaries, and our final summing up can now begin. . . .

First, is there, under all the discrepancies of the creeds, a common nucleus to which they bear their testimony unanimously?

And second, ought we to consider the testimony true?

I will take up the first question first, and answer it immediately in the affirmative. The warring gods and formulas of the various religions do indeed cancel each other, but there is a certain uniform deliverance in which religions all appear to meet. It consists of two parts:—

1. An uneasiness; and
2. Its solution.

1. The uneasiness, reduced to its simplest terms, is a sense that there is *something wrong about us* as we naturally stand.

2. The solution is a sense that *we are saved from the wrongness* by making proper connection with the higher powers.

In those more developed minds which alone we are studying, the wrongness takes a moral character, and the salvation takes a mystical tinge. I think we shall keep well within the limits of what is common to all such minds if we formulate the essence of their religious experiences in terms like these:—

The individual, so far as he suffers from his wrongness and criticises it, is to that extent consciously beyond it, and in at least possible touch with something higher, if anything higher exist. Along with the wrong part there is thus a better part of him, even though it may be but a most helpless germ. With which part he should identify his real being is by no means obvious at this stage; but when stage 2 (the stage of solution or salvation) arrives, the man identifies his real being with the germinal higher part of himself; and does so in the following way. *He becomes conscious that this higher part is con-terminous and continuous with a* MORE *of the same quality, which is operative in the universe outside of him, and which he can keep in working touch with, and in a fashion get on board of and save himself when all his lower being has gone to pieces in the wreck.*

It seems to me that all the phenomena are accurately describable in these very simple general terms. They allow for the divided self and the struggle; they involve the change of personal centre and the surrender of the lower self; they express the appearance of exteriority of the helping power and yet account for our sense of union with it; and they fully justify our feelings of security and joy. . . .

So far, however, as this analysis goes, the experiences are only psychological phenomena. They possess, it is true, enormous biological worth. Spiritual strength really increases in the subject when he has them, a new life opens for him, and they seem to him a place of conflux where the forces of two universes meet; and yet this may be nothing but his subjective way of feeling things, a mood of his own fancy, in spite of the effects produced. I now turn to my second question: What is the objective "truth" of their content?

The part of the content concerning which the question of truth most pertinently arises is that "MORE of the same quality" with which our own higher self appears in the experience to come into harmonious working relation. Is such a "more" merely our own notion, or does it really exist? If so, in what shape does it exist? Does it act, as well as exist? And in what form should we conceive of that "union" with it of which religious geniuses are so convinced?

It is in answering these questions that the various theologies perform their theoretic work, and that their divergencies most come to light. They all agree that the "more" really exists; though some of them hold it to exist in the shape of a personal god or gods, while others are satisfied to conceive it as a stream of ideal tendency embedded in the eternal structure of the world. They all agree, moreover, that it acts as well as exists, and that something really is effected for the better when you throw your life into its hands. It is when they treat of the experience of "union" with it that their speculative differences appear most clearly. Over this point pantheism and theism, nature and second birth, works and grace and karma, immortality and reincarnation, rationalism and mysticism, carry on inveterate disputes.

At the end of my lecture on Philosophy I held out the notion that an impartial science of religions might sift out from the midst of their discrepancies a common body of doctrine which she might also formulate in terms to which physical science need not object. This, I said, she might adopt as her own reconciling hypothesis, and recommend it for general belief. I also said that in my last lecture I should have to try my own hand at framing such an hypothesis.

The time has now come for this attempt. Who says "hypothesis" renounces the ambition to be coercive in his arguments? The most I can do is, accordingly, to offer something that may fit the facts so easily that your scientific logic will find no plausible pretext for vetoing your impulse to welcome it as true.

The "more," as we called it, and the meaning of our "union" with it, form the nucleus of our inquiry. Into what definite description can these words be translated, and for what definite facts do they stand? It would never do for us to place ourselves offhand at the position of a particular theology, the Christian theology, for example, and proceed immediately to define the "more" as Jehovah, and the "union" as his imputation to us of the righteousness of Christ. That would be unfair to other religions, and, from our present standpoint at least, would be an over-belief.

We must begin by using less particularized terms; and, since one of the duties of the science of religions is to keep religion in connection with the rest of science, we shall do well to seek first of all a way of describing the "more," which psychologists may also recognize as real. The *subconscious self* is nowadays a well-accredited psychological entity; and I believe that in it we have exactly the mediating term required. Apart from all religious considerations, there is actually and literally more life in our total soul than we are at any time aware of. . . . Much of the content of this larger background against which our conscious being stands out in relief is insignificant. Imperfect memories, silly jingles, inhibitive timidities, . . . enter into it for a large part. But in it many of the performances of genius seem also to have their origin; and in our study of conversion, of mystical experiences, and of prayer, we have seen how striking a part invasions from this region play in the religious life.

Let me then propose, as an hypothesis, that whatever it may be on its *farther* side, the "more" with which in religious experience we feel ourselves connected is on its *hither* side the subconscious continuation of our conscious life. Starting thus with a recognized psychological fact as our basis, we seem to preserve a contact with "science" which the ordinary theologian lacks. At the same time the theologian's contention that the religious man is moved by an external power is vindicated, for it is one of the peculiarities of invasions from the subconscious region to take on objective appearances, and to suggest to the Subject an external control. In the religious life the control is felt as "higher"; but since on our hypothesis it is primarily the higher faculties of our own hidden mind which are controlling, the sense of union with the power beyond us is a sense of something, not merely apparently, but literally true.

This doorway into the subject seems to me the best one for a science of religions, for it mediates between a number of different points of view. Yet it is only a doorway, and difficulties present themselves as soon as we step through it, and ask how far our transmarginal consciousness carries us if we follow it on its remoter side. Here the over-beliefs begin: here mysticism and the conversion-rapture and Vedantism and transcendental idealism bring in their monistic interpretations and tell us that the finite self rejoins the absolute self, for it was always one with God and identical with the soul of the world. Here the prophets of all the different religions come with their visions, voices, raptures, and other openings, supposed by each to authenticate his own peculiar faith.

Those of us who are not personally favored with such specific revelations must stand outside of them altogether and, for the present at least, decide that, since they corroborate incompatible theological doctrines, they neutralize one another and leave no fixed result. . . .

Disregarding the over-beliefs, and confining ourselves to what is common and generic, we have in *the fact that the conscious person is continuous with a wider self through which saving experiences come*, a positive content of religious experience which, it seems to me, *is literally and objectively true as far as it goes*. If I now proceed to state my own hypothesis about the farther limits of this extension of our personality, I shall be offering my own over-belief— though I know it will appear a sorry under-belief to some of you—for which I can only bespeak the same indulgence which in a converse case I should accord to yours.

The further limits of our being plunge, it seems to me, into an altogether other dimension of existence for the sensible and merely "understandable" world. Name it the mystical region, or the supernatural region, whichever you choose. So far as our ideal impulses originate in this region (and most of them do originate in it, for we find them possessing us in a way for which we cannot articulately account), we belong to it in a more intimate sense than that in which we belong to the visible world, for we belong in the most intimate sense wherever our ideals belong. Yet the unseen region in question is not merely ideal, for it produces effects in this world. When we commune with it, work is actually done upon our finite personality, for we are turned into new men, and consequences in the way of conduct follow in the natural world upon our regenerative change. But that which produces effects within another reality must be termed a reality itself, so I feel as if we had no philosophic excuse for calling the unseen or mystical world unreal.

God is the natural appellation, for us Christians at least, for the supreme reality, so I will call this higher part of the universe by the name of God. We and God have business with each other; and in opening ourselves to his influence our deepest destiny is fulfilled. The universe, at those parts of it which our personal being constitutes, takes a turn genuinely for the worse or for the better in proportion as each one of us fulfills or evades God's demands. As far as this goes I probably have you with me, for I only translate into schematic language what I may call the instinctive belief of mankind: God is real since he produces real effects.

The real effects in question, so far as I have as yet admitted them, are exerted on the personal centres of energy of the various subjects, but the spontaneous faith of most of the subjects is that they embrace a wider sphere than this. Most religious men believe (or "know," if they be mystical) that not only they themselves, but the whole universe of beings to whom the God is present, are secure in his parental hands. There is a sense, a dimension, they are sure, in which we are *all* saved, in spite of the gates of hell and all adverse terrestrial appearances. God's existence is the guarantee of an ideal order that shall be permanently preserved. This world may indeed, as science assures us, some day burn up or freeze; but if it is part of his order, the old ideals are sure to be brought elsewhere to fruition, so that where God is, tragedy is only provisional and partial, and shipwreck and dissolution are not the absolutely final things. Only when this farther step of faith concerning God is taken, and remote objective consequences are predicted, does religion, as it seems to me, get wholly free from the first immediate subjective experience, and bring a *real hypothesis* into play. A good hypothesis in science must have other properties than those of the phenomenon it is immediately invoked to explain, otherwise it is not prolific enough. God, meaning only what enters into the religious man's experience of union, falls short of being an hypothesis of this more useful order. He needs to enter into wider cosmic relations in order to justify the subject's absolute confidence and peace.

That the God with whom, starting from the hither side of our own extra-marginal self, we come at its remoter margin into commerce should be the absolute world-ruler, is of course a very considerable over-belief. Over-belief as it is, though, it is an article of almost every one's religion. Most of us pretend in some way to prop it upon our philosophy, but the philosophy itself is really propped upon this faith. What is this but to say that Religion, in her fullest exercise of function, is not a mere illumination of facts already elsewhere given, not a mere passion, like love, which views things in a rosier light. It is indeed that, as we have seen abundantly. But it is something more, namely, a postulator of new *facts* as well. The world interpreted religiously is not the materialistic world over again, with an altered expression: it must have, over and above the altered expression, *a natural constitution* different at some point from that which a materialistic world would have. It must be such that different events can be expected in it, different conduct must be required.

This thoroughly "pragmatic" view of religion has usually been taken as a matter of course by common men. They have interpolated divine miracles into the field of nature, they have built a heaven out beyond the grave. It is only transcendentalist metaphysicians who think that, without adding any concrete details to Nature, or subtracting any, but by simply calling it the expression of absolute spirit, you make it more divine just as it stands. I believe the pragmatic way of taking religion to be the deeper way. It gives it body as well as soul, it makes it claim, as everything real must claim, some characteristic realm of fact as its very own. What the more characteristically divine facts are, apart from the actual inflow of energy in the faith-state and the prayer-state, I know not. But the over-belief on which I am ready to make my personal venture is that they exist. The whole drift of my education goes to persuade me that the world of our present consciousness is only one out of many worlds of consciousness that exist, and that those other worlds must contain experiences which have a meaning for our life also; and that although in the main their experiences and those of this world keep discrete, yet the two become continuous at certain points, and higher energies filter in. By being faithful in my poor measure to this over-belief, I seem to myself to keep more sane and true. I *can*, of course, put myself into the sectarian scientist's attitude, and imagine vividly that the world of sensations and of scientific laws and objects may be all. But whenever I do this, I hear that inward monitor of which W. K. Clifford once wrote, whispering the word "bosh!" Humbug is humbug, even though it bear the scientific name, and the total expression of human experience, as I view it objectively, invincibly urges me beyond the narrow "scientific" bounds. Assuredly, the real world is of a different temperament,—more intricately built than physical science allows. So my objective and my subjective conscience both hold me to the over-belief which I express. Who knows whether the faithfulness of individuals here below to their own poor over-beliefs may not actually help God in turn to be more effectively faithful to his own greater tasks?

FREUD

After the devotion of St. Theresa, the ironic scepticism of Hume, and the experimental eclecticism of James, Sigmund Freud's straightforward attack on religion hits us with the force of a bucket of cold water. Freud (1856–1939), the founder of the psychoanalytic school of psychology, minces no words—religion is an illusion, a fantasy, a mere wish-fulfillment daydream. It has no place in the life of a healthy and rational man; the sooner we put religion behind us, the better off we shall be.

Freud was the first student of human nature to develop a full-scale scientific theory of the irrational components of personality. Because of his emphasis upon the unconscious sources of motivation, he is frequently taken to be an apologist for the irrational. Actually, the truth is precisely opposite. In his insistence on the necessity of reality-orientation and his faith in the possibility of overcoming the irrational self-destructiveness of the neurotic personality, Freud aligns himself with the eighteenth-century apostles of the Enlightenment.

Like the Enlightenment sceptics, Freud sees religion as mere superstition. He goes beyond them only in his psychoanalytic explanation of the appeal which religion seems to have for so many men and women. The final paragraph of this selection is a moving statement of Freud's fundamental faith in the power of reason to overcome man's darker nature.

Religion Is
an Illusion

. . . What . . . is the psychological significance of religious ideas and under what heading are we to classify them? . . . Religious ideas are teachings and assertions about facts and conditions of external (or internal) reality which tell one something one has not discovered for oneself and which lay claim to one's belief. . . .

There are, of course, many such teachings about the most various things

From *The Future of an Illusion* by Sigmund Freud. Permission of Liveright, Publishers, New York, and Hogarth Press, London. Copyright 1961 by James Strachey.

in the world. . . . Let us take geography. We are told that the town of Constance lies on the Bodensee. . . . I happen to have been there and can confirm the fact. . . .

All teachings like these . . . demand belief in their contents, but not without producing grounds for their claim. They are put forward as the epitomized result of a longer process of thought based on observation and certainly also on inferences. . . .

Let us try to apply the same test to the teachings of religion. When we ask on what their claim to be believed is founded, we are met with three answers, which harmonize remarkably badly with one another. Firstly, these teachings deserve to be believed because they were already believed by our primal ancestors; secondly, we possess proofs which have been handed down to us from those same primaeval times; and thirdly, it is forbidden to raise the question of their authentication at all. . . .

This third point is bound to rouse our strongest suspicions. After all, a prohibition like this can only be for one reason—that society is very well aware of the insecurity of the claim it makes on behalf of its religious doctrines. . . .

. . . In past times religious ideas, in spite of their incontrovertible lack of authentication, have exercised the strongest possible influence on mankind. . . . We must ask where the inner force of those doctrines lies and to what it is that they owe their efficacy, independent as it is of recognition by reason.

I think we have prepared the way sufficiently for an answer to both these questions. It will be found if we turn our attention to the psychical origin of religious ideas. These, which are given out as teachings, are not precipitates of experience or end-results of thinking: they are illusions, fulfillments of the oldest, strongest and most urgent wishes of mankind. . . .

When I say that these things are all illusions, I must define the meaning of the word. An illusion is not the same thing as an error; nor is it necessarily an error. . . . What is characteristic of illusions is that they are derived from human wishes. In this respect they come near to psychiatric delusions. . . . We call a belief an illusion when a wish-fulfilment is a prominent factor in its motivation, and in doing so we disregard its relations to reality, just as the illusion itself sets no store by verification. . . .

Religious doctrines . . . are illusions and insusceptible of proof. No one can be compelled to think them true, to believe in them. Some of them are so improbable, so incompatible with everything we have laboriously discovered about the reality of the world, that we may compare them—if we pay proper regard to the psychological differences—to delusions. . . .

[But, someone may object,] "You permit yourself contradictions which are hard to reconcile with one another. . . . On the one hand you admit that men cannot be guided through their intelligence, they are ruled by their passions and their instinctual demands. But on the other hand you propose to replace the affective basis of their obedience to civilization by a rational one. Let who can understand this. To me it seems that it must be either one thing or the other.". . .

. . . Since men are so little accessible to reasonable arguments and are so entirely governed by their instinctual wishes, why should one set out to deprive them of an instinctual satisfaction and replace it by reasonable arguments? It is true that men are like this; but have you asked yourself whether they *must* be like this, whether their innermost nature necessitates it? . . . I think it would be a very long time before a child who was not influenced began to trouble himself about God and things in another world. . . . We introduce him to the doctrines of religion at an age when he is neither interested in them nor capable of grasping their import. . . . By the time the child's intellect awakens, the doctrines of religion have already become unassailable. . . . When a man has once brought himself to accept uncritically all the absurdities that religious doctrines put before him and even to overlook the contradictions between them, we need not be greatly surprised at the weakness of his intellect. But we have no other means of controlling our instinctual nature but our intelligence. How can we expect people who are under the dominance of prohibitions of thought to attain the psychological idea, the primacy of the intelligence? . . .

Thus I must contradict you when you . . . argue that men are completely unable to do without the consolation of the religious illusion, that without it they could not bear the troubles of life and the cruelties of reality. That is true, certainly, of the men into whom you have instilled the sweet—or bitter-sweet—poison from childhood onwards. But what of the other men, who have been sensibly brought up? Perhaps those who do not suffer from the neurosis will need no intoxicant to deaden it. They will, it is true, find themselves in a difficult situation. They will have to admit to themselves the full extent of their helplessness and their insignificance in the machinery of the universe; they can no longer be the centre of creation, no longer the object of tender care on the part of a beneficent Providence. They will be in the same position as a child who has left the parental house where he was so warm and comfortable. But surely infantilism is destined to be surmounted. Men cannot remain children forever; they must in the end go out into "hostile life." We may call this "*education to reality*.". . .

TILLICH

From the time of Plato to the end of the eighteenth century, systematic theology flourished as a branch of metaphysics in Western philosophy. It was widely believed that men could have knowledge of God and His creation in very much the same manner that one could have knowledge of the stars and planets or of man himself. Periodically, sceptics voiced doubts about the possibility of rational knowledge of God, but it was only in the late eighteenth and early nineteenth centuries that the sceptical attack succeeded. The arguments of Hume and Kant, together with the dramatic advances in the natural sciences, fatally undermined the claims of the traditional theology. A crisis occurred in Christian thought, and philosophical reflections on religion took a new direction.

By and large, traditional theology had treated the doctrines of Christianity literally: There was an infinite, divine Being, creator of the universe, who became Flesh in order to save man from his sins. The rituals and sacraments were taken at face value, although philosophical subtlety was exercised in their interpretation. The principal effect of the sceptical re-evaluation of Christianity was to cast doubt on this literal construal of the faith. Theologians had to find some new way of understanding God, creation, incarnation, salvation, and faith itself.

The first great reinterpreter of Christianity was the Danish existentialist Sören Kierkegaard, whom you have already encountered. Kierkegaard shifted his attention from the objective reference of religious doctrines (God, heaven, etc.) to the subjective, inward experience of religious doubt, anguish, and faith. For Kierkegaard, "truth is subjectivity"; the religious experience became the center of theological concern, not a mere peripheral concomitant.

The contemporary thinker who stands most directly in the tradition of Christian thought initiated by Kierkegaard is the German Protestant philosopher Paul Tillich (1886–1965). In a number of books, both scholarly and popular in their orientation, Tillich sought to discover a new meaning in the Christian message, a meaning which transcended the parochial limits of any particular sect and which was invulnerable to the attacks of scepticism and science. For Tillich, faith is a risk, an adventure, a gamble fraught with danger; it is not a comfortable credo on which one can lean with security.

At the beginning of this section, I drew a distinction between religious statements and statements about religion. In the present selection, Tillich goes a long way toward breaking down that distinction. He makes no attempt to separate expressions of faith from *descriptions of faith. Indeed, in other writings he has made it clear that he believes such a distinction to be a holdover from an earlier and invalid conception of religion.*

Faith as Ultimate Concern

What Faith Is

FAITH AS ULTIMATE CONCERN

Faith is the state of being ultimately concerned: the dynamics of faith are the dynamics of man's ultimate concern. Man, like every living being, is concerned about many things, above all about those which condition his very existence, such as food and shelter. But man, in contrast to other living beings, has spiritual concerns—cognitive, aesthetic, social, political. Some of them are urgent, often extremely urgent, and each of them as well as the vital concerns can claim ultimacy for a human life or the life of a social group. If it claims ultimacy it demands the total surrender of him who accepts this claim, and it promises total fulfillment even if all other claims have to be subjected to it or rejected in its name. If a national group makes the life and growth of the nation its ultimate concern, it demands that all other concerns, economic well-being, health and life, family, aesthetic and cognitive truth, justice and humanity, be sacrificed. The extreme nationalisms of our century are laboratories for the study of what ultimate concern means in all aspects of human existence, including the smallest concern of one's daily life. Everything is centered in the only god, the nation—a god who certainly proves to be a demon, but who shows clearly the unconditional character of an ultimate concern.

But it is not only the unconditional demand made by that which is one's ultimate concern, it is also the promise of ultimate fulfillment which is accepted in the act of faith. The content of this promise is not necessarily defined. It can be expressed in indefinite symbols or in concrete symbols which cannot be taken literally, like the "greatness" of one's nation in which one participates even if one has died for it, or the conquest of mankind by the "saving race," etc. In each of these cases it is "ultimate fulfillment" that is promised, and it is exclusion from such fulfillment which is threatened if the unconditional demand is not obeyed.

An example—and more than an example—is the faith manifest in the religion of the Old Testament. It also has the character of ultimate concern in demand, threat and promise. The content of this concern is not the nation—although Jewish nationalism has sometimes tried to distort it into that—but the content is the God of justice, who, because he represents justice for everybody and every nation, is called the universal God, the God of the universe. He is the ultimate concern of every pious Jew, and therefore in his name the great commandment is given: "You shall love the Lord your God with all your heart, and with all your soul, and with all your might" (Deut 6:5). This is what ultimate concern means and from these words the term "ultimate concern" is derived. They state unambiguously the character of genuine faith, the demand of total surrender to the subject of ultimate concern. The Old Testament is full of commands which make the nature of this surrender concrete, and it is full of promises and threats in relation to it. Here also are the promises of symbolic indefiniteness, although they center around fulfillment of the national and individual life, and the threat is the exclusion from such fulfillment through national extinction and individual catastrophe. Faith, for the men of the Old Testament, is the state of being ultimately and unconditionally concerned about Jahweh and about what he represents in demand, threat and promise. . . .

Faith is the state of being ultimately concerned. The content matters infinitely for the life of the believer, but it does not matter for the formal definition of faith. And this is the first step we have to make in order to understand the dynamics of faith.

FAITH AS A CENTERED ACT

Faith as ultimate concern is an act of the total personality. It happens in the center of the personal life and includes all its elements. Faith is the most centered act of the human mind. It is not a movement of a special section or a special function of man's total being. They all are united in the act of faith. But faith is not the sum total of their impacts. It transcends every special impact as well as the totality of them and it has itself a decisive impact on each of them.

Since faith is an act of the personality as a whole, it participates in the dynamics of personal life. These dynamics have been described in many ways, especially in the recent developments of analytic psychology. Thinking in polarities, their tensions and their possible conflicts, is a common characteristic of most of them. This makes the psychology of personality highly dynamic and requires a dynamic theory of faith as the most personal of all personal acts. The first and decisive polarity in analytic psychology is that between the so-called unconscious and the conscious. Faith as an act of the total personality is not imaginable without the participation of the unconscious elements in the personality structure. They are always present and decide largely about the content of faith. But, on the other hand, faith is a conscious act and the unconscious elements participate in the creation of faith only if they are taken into the personal center which transcends each of them. If this does not happen, if unconscious forces determine the mental status without a centered act, faith does not occur, and compulsions take its place. For faith is a matter of freedom. Freedom is nothing more than the possibility of centered personal acts. The frequent discussion in which faith and freedom are contrasted could be helped by the insight that faith is a free, namely, centered act of the personality. In this respect freedom and faith are identical.

Also important for the understanding of faith is the polarity between what Freud and his school call ego and superego. The concept of the superego is quite ambiguous. On the one hand, it is the basis of all cultural life because it restricts the uninhibited actualization of the always-driving libido; on the other hand, it cuts off man's vital forces, and produces disgust about the whole system of cultural restrictions, and brings about a neurotic state of mind. From this point of view, the symbols of faith are considered to be expressions of the superego or, more concretely, to be an expression of the father image which gives content to the superego. Responsible for this inadequate theory of the superego is Freud's naturalistic negation of norms and principles. If the superego is not established through valid principles, it becomes a suppressive tyrant. But real faith, even if it uses the father image for its expressions, transforms this image into a principle of truth and justice to be defended even against the "father." Faith and culture can be affirmed only if the superego represents the norms and principles of reality.

This leads to the question of how faith as a personal, centered act is related to the rational structure of man's personality which is manifest in his meaningful language, in his ability to know the true and to do the good, in his sense of beauty and justice. All this, and not only his possibility to analyze, to calculate and to argue, makes him a rational being. But in spite of this larger concept of reason we must deny that man's essential nature is identical with the rational character of his mind. Man is able to decide for or against reason, he is able to create beyond reason or to destroy below reason. This power is the power of his self, the center of self-relatedness in which all elements of his being are united. Faith is not an act of any of his rational functions, as it is not an act of the unconscious, but it is an act in which both the rational and the nonrational elements of his being are transcended.

Faith as the embracing and centered act of the personality is "ecstatic." It transcends both the drives of the nonrational unconscious and the structures of the rational conscious. It transcends them, but it does not destroy them. The ecstatic character of faith does not exclude its rational character although it is not identical with it, and it includes nonrational strivings without being identical with them. In the ecstasy of faith there is an awareness of truth and of ethical value; there are also past loves and hates, conflicts and reunions, individual and collective influences. "Ecstasy" means "standing outside of oneself"—without ceasing to be oneself—with all the elements which are united in the personal center. . . .

THE SOURCE OF FAITH

We have described the act of faith and its relation to the dynamics of personality. Faith is a total and centered act of the personal self, the act of unconditional, infinite and ultimate concern. The question now arises: what is the source of this all-embracing and all-transcending concern? The word "concern" points to two sides of a relationship, the relation between the one who is concerned and his concern. In both respects we have to imagine man's situation in itself and in his world. The reality of man's ultimate concern reveals something about his being, namely, that he is able to transcend the flux of relative and transitory experiences of his ordinary life. Man's experiences, feelings, thoughts are conditioned and finite. They not only come and go, but their content is of finite and conditional concern—unless they are elevated to unconditional validity. But this presupposes the general possibility of doing so; it presupposes the element of infinity in man. Man is able to understand in an immediate personal and central act the meaning of the ultimate, the unconditional, the absolute, the infinite. This alone makes faith a human potentiality.

Human potentialities are powers that drive toward actualization. Man is driven toward faith by his awareness of the infinite to which he belongs, but which he does not own like a possession. This is in abstract terms what concretely appears as the "restlessness of the heart" within the flux of life.

The unconditional concern which is faith is the concern about the unconditional. The infinite passion, as faith has been described, is the passion for the infinite. Or, to use our first term, the ultimate concern is concern about what is experienced as ultimate. In this way we have turned from the subjective meaning of faith as a centered act of the personality to its objective meaning, to what is meant in the act of faith. It would not help at this point of our analysis to call that which is meant in the act of faith "God" or "a god." For at this step we ask: What in the idea of God constitutes divinity? The answer is: It is the element of the unconditional and of ultimacy. This carries the quality of divinity. If this is seen, one can understand why almost every thing "in heaven and on earth" has received ultimacy in the history of human religion. But we also can understand that a critical principle was and is at work in man's religious consciousness, namely, that which is really ultimate over against what claims to be ultimate but is only preliminary, transitory, finite.

The term "ultimate concern" unites the subjective and the objective side of the act of faith—the *fides qua creditur* (the faith through which one believes) and the *fides quae creditur* (the faith which is believed). The first is the classical term for the centered act of the personality, the ultimate concern. The second is the classical term for that toward which this act is directed, the ultimate itself, expressed in symbols of the divine. This distinction is very important, but not ultimately so, for the one side cannot be without the other. There is no faith without a content toward which it is directed. There is always something meant in the act of faith. And there is no way of having the content of faith except in the act of faith. All speaking about divine matters which is not done in the state of ultimate concern is meaningless. Because that which is meant in the act of faith cannot be approached in any other way than through an act of faith.

In terms like ultimate, unconditional, infinite, absolute, the difference between subjectivity and objectivity is overcome. The ultimate of the act of faith and the ultimate that is meant in the act of faith are one and the same. This is symbolically expressed by the mystics when they say that their knowledge of God is the knowledge God has of himself; and it is expressed by Paul when he says (I Cor. 13) that he will know as he is known, namely, by God. God never can be object without being at the same time subject. Even a successful prayer is, according to Paul (Rom. 8), not possible without God as Spirit praying within us. The same experience expressed in abstract language is the disappearance of the ordinary subject-object scheme in the experience of the ultimate, the unconditional. In the act of faith that which is the source of this act is present beyond the cleavage of subject and object. It is present as both and beyond both.

This character of faith gives an additional criterion for distinguishing true and false ultimacy. The finite which claims infinity without having it (as, e.g., a nation or success) is not able to transcend the subject-object scheme. It remains an object which the believer looks at as a subject. He can approach it with ordinary knowledge and subject it to ordinary handling. There are, of course, many degrees in the endless realm of false ultimacies. The nation is nearer to true ultimacy than is success. Nationalistic ecstasy can produce a state in which the subject is almost swallowed by the object. But after a period the subject emerges again, disappointed radically and totally, and by looking at the nation in a skeptical and calculating way does injustice even to its justified claims. The more idolatrous a faith the less it is able to overcome the cleavage between subject and object. For that is the difference between true and idolatrous faith. In true faith the ultimate concern is a concern about the truly ultimate; while in idolatrous faith preliminary, finite realities are elevated to the rank of ultimacy. The inescapable consequence of idolatrous faith is "existential disappointment," a disappointment which penetrates into the very existence of man! This is the dynamics of idolatrous faith: that it is faith, and as such, the centered act of a personality; that the centering point is something which is more or less on the periphery; and that, therefore, the act of faith leads to a loss of the center and to a disruption of the personality. The ecstatic character of even an idolatrous faith can hide this consequence only for a certain time. But finally it breaks into the open. . . .

FAITH AND DOUBT

We now return to a fuller description of faith as an act of the human personality, as its centered and total act. An act of faith is an act of a finite being who is grasped by and turned to the infinite. It is a finite act with all the limitations of a finite act, and it is an act in which the infinite participates beyond the limitations of a finite act. Faith is certain in so far as it is an experience of the holy. But faith is uncertain in so far as the infinite to which it is related is received by a finite being. This element of uncertainty in faith cannot be removed, it must be accepted. And the element in faith which accepts this is courage. Faith includes an element of immediate awareness which gives certainty and an element of uncertainty. To accept this is courage. In the courageous standing of uncertainty, faith shows most visibly its dynamic character.

If we try to describe the relation of faith and courage, we must use a larger concept of courage than that which is ordinarily used.[1] Courage as an element of faith is the daring self-affirmation of one's own being in spite of the powers of "nonbeing" which are the heritage of everything finite. Where there is daring and courage there is the possibility of failure. And in every act of faith this possibility is present. The risk must be taken. Whoever makes his nation his ultimate concern needs courage in order to maintain this concern. Only certain is the ultimacy as ultimacy, the infinite passion as infinite passion. This is a reality given to the self with his own nature. It is as immediate and as much beyond doubt as the self is to the self. It *is* the self in its self-transcending quality. But there is not certainty of this kind about the content of our ultimate concern, be it nation, success, a god, or the God of the Bible: They all are contents without immediate awareness. Their acceptance as matters of ultimate concern is a risk and therefore an act of courage. There is a risk if what was considered as a matter of ultimate concern proves to be a matter of preliminary and transitory concern—as, for example, the nation. The risk to faith in one's ultimate concern is indeed the greatest risk man can run. For if it proves to be a failure, the meaning of one's life breaks down; one surrenders oneself, including truth and justice, to something which is not worth it. One has given away one's personal center without having a chance to regain it. . . . Ultimate concern is ultimate risk and ultimate courage. It is not risk and needs no courage with respect to ultimacy itself. But it is risk and demands courage if it affirms a concrete concern. And every faith has a concrete element in itself. It is concerned about something or somebody. But this something or this somebody may prove to be not ultimate at all. Then faith is a failure in its concrete expression, although it is not a failure in the experience of the unconditional itself. A god disappears; divinity remains. Faith risks the vanishing of the concrete god in whom it believes. It may well be that with the vanishing of

[1] Cf. Paul Tillich, *The Courage to Be.* Yale University Press.

the god the believer breaks down without being able to re-establish his centered self by a new content of his ultimate concern. This risk cannot be taken away from any act of faith. There is only one point which is a matter not of risk but of immediate certainty and herein lies the greatness and the pain of being human; namely, one's standing between one's finitude and one's potential infinity.

All this is sharply expressed in the relation of faith and doubt. If faith is understood as belief that something is true, doubt is incompatible with the act of faith. If faith is understood as being ultimately concerned, doubt is a necessary element in it. It is a consequence of the risk of faith.

The doubt which is implicit in faith is not a doubt about facts or conclusions. It is not the same doubt which is the lifeblood of scientific research. Even the most orthodox theologian does not deny the right of methodological doubt in matters of empirical inquiry or logical deduction. A scientist who would say that a scientific theory is beyond doubt would at that moment cease to be scientific. He may believe that the theory can be trusted for all practical purposes. Without such belief no technical application of a theory would be possible. One could attribute to this kind of belief pragmatic certainty sufficient for action. Doubt in this case points to the preliminary character of the underlying theory.

There is another kind of doubt, which we could call skeptical in contrast to the scientific doubt which we could call methodological. The skeptical doubt is an attitude toward all the beliefs of man, from sense experiences to religious creeds. It is more an attitude than an assertion. For as an assertion it would conflict with itself. Even the assertion that there is no possible truth for man would be judged by the skeptical principle and could not stand as an assertion. Genuine skeptical doubt does not use the form of an assertion. It is an attitude of actually rejecting any certainty. Therefore, it can not be refuted logically. It does not transform its attitude into a proposition. Such an attitude necessarily leads either to despair or cynicism, or to both alternately. And often, if this alternative becomes intolerable, it leads to indifference and the attempt to develop an attitude of complete unconcern. But since man is that being who is essentially concerned about his being, such an escape finally breaks down. This is the dynamics of skeptical doubt. It has an awakening and liberating function, but it also can prevent the development of a centered personality. For personality is not possible without faith. The despair about truth by the skeptic shows that truth is still his infinite passion. The cynical superiority over every concrete truth shows that truth is still taken seriously and that the impact of the question of an ultimate concern is strongly felt. The skeptic, so long as he is a serious skeptic, is not without faith, even though it has no concrete content.

The doubt which is implicit in every act of faith is neither the methodological nor the skeptical doubt. It is the doubt which accompanies every risk. It is not the permanent doubt of the scientist, and it is not the transitory doubt of the skeptic, but it is the doubt of him who is ultimately concerned about a concrete content. One could call it the existential doubt, in contrast to the methodological and the skeptical doubt. It does not question whether a special proposition is true or false. It does not reject every concrete truth, but it is aware of the element of insecurity in every existential truth. At the same time, the doubt which is implied in faith accepts this insecurity and takes it into itself in an act of courage. Faith includes courage. Therefore, it can include the doubt about itself. Certainly faith and courage are not identical. Faith has other elements besides courage and courage has other functions beyond affirming faith. Nevertheless, an act in which courage accepts risk belongs to the dynamics of faith.

This dynamic concept of faith seems to give no place to that restful affirmative confidence which we find in the documents of all great religions, including Christianity. But this is not the case. The dynamic concept of faith is the result of a conceptual analysis, both of the subjective and of the objective side of faith. It is by no means the description of an always actualized state of mind. An analysis of structure is not the description of a state of things. The confusion of these two is a source of many misunderstandings and errors in all realms of life. An example, taken from the current discussion of anxiety, is typical of this confusion. The description of anxiety as the awareness of one's finitude is sometimes criticized as untrue from the point of view of the ordinary state of mind. Anxiety, one says, appears under special conditions but is not an ever-present implication of man's finitude. Certainly anxiety as an acute experience appears under definite conditions. But the underlying structure of finite life is the universal condition which makes the appearance of anxiety under special conditions possible. In the same way doubt is not a permanent experience within the act of faith. But it is always present as an element in the structure of faith. This is the difference between faith and immediate evidence either of perceptual or of logical character. There is no faith without an intrinsic "in spite of" and the courageous affirmation of oneself in the state of ultimate concern. This intrinsic element of doubt breaks into the open under special individual and social conditions. If doubt appears, it should not be considered as the negation of faith, but as an element which was always and will always be present in the act of faith. Existential doubt and faith are poles of the same reality, the state of ultimate concern.

The insight into this structure of faith and doubt is of tremendous practical importance. Many Christians, as well as members of other religious groups, feel anxiety, guilt and despair about what they call "loss of faith." But serious doubt is confirmation of faith. It indicates the seriousness of the concern, its unconditional character. This also refers to those who as future or present-ministers of a church experience is not only scientific doubt about doctrinal statements—this is as necessary and perpetual as theology is a perpetual need—but also existential doubt about the message of their church, e.g., that Jesus can be called the Christ. The criterion according to which they should judge themselves is the seriousness and ultimacy of their concern about the content of both their faith and their doubt. . . .

The Life of Faith

FAITH AND COURAGE

Everything said about faith in the previous chapters is derived from the experience of actual faith, of faith as a living reality, or in a metaphoric abbreviation, of the life of faith. This experience is the subject of our last chapter. The "dynamics of faith" are present not only in the inner tensions and conflicts of the content of faith, but also present in the life of faith, and of course the one is dependent on the other.

Where there is faith there is tension between participation and separation, between the faithful one and his ultimate concern. We have used the metaphor "being grasped" for describing the state of ultimate concern. And being grasped implies that he who is grasped and that by which he is grasped are, so to speak, at the same place. Without some participation in the object of one's ultimate concern, it is not possible to be concerned about it. In this sense every act of faith presupposes participation in that toward which it is directed. Without a preceeding experience of the ultimate no faith in the ultimate can exist. The mystical type of faith has emphasized this point most strongly. Here lies its truth which no theology of "mere faith" can destroy. Without the manifestation of God in man the question of God and faith in God are not possible. There is no faith without participation!

But faith would cease to be faith without separation—the opposite element. He who has faith is separated from the object of his faith. Otherwise he would possess it. It would be a matter of immediate certainty and not of faith. The "in-spite-of element" of faith would be lacking. But the human situation, its finitude and estrangement, prevents man's participation in the ultimate without both the separation and the promise of faith. Here the limit of mysticism becomes visible: it neglects the human predicament and the separation of man from the ultimate. There is no faith without separation.

Out of the element of participation follows the certainty of faith; out of the element of separation follows the doubt in faith. And each is essential for the nature of faith. Sometimes certainty conquers doubt, but it cannot eliminate doubt. The conquered of today may become the conqueror of tomorrow. Sometimes doubt conquers faith, but it still contains faith. Otherwise it would be indifference. Neither faith nor doubt can be eliminated, though each of them can be reduced to a minimum, in the life of faith. Since the life of faith is the life in the state of ultimate concern and no human being can exist completely without such a concern, we can say: Neither faith nor doubt can be eliminated from man as man.

Faith and doubt have been contrasted in such a way that the quiet certainty of faith has been praised as the complete removal of doubt. There is, indeed, a serenity of the life in faith beyond the disturbing struggles between faith and doubt. To attain such a state is a natural and justified desire of every human being. But even if it is attained—as in people who are called saints or in others who are described as firm in their faith—the element of doubt, though conquered, is not lacking. In the saints it appears, according to holy legend, as a temptation which increases in power with the increase of saintliness. In those who rest on their unshakable faith, pharisaism and fanaticism are the unmistakable symptoms of doubt which has been repressed. Doubt is overcome not by repression but by courage. Courage does not deny that there is doubt, but it takes the doubt into itself as an expression of its own finitude and affirms the content of an ultimate concern. Courage does not need the safety of an unquestionable conviction. It includes the risk without which no creative life is possible. For example, if the content of someone's ultimate concern is Jesus as the Christ, such faith is not a matter of doubtless certainty, it is a matter of daring courage with the risk to fail. Even if the confession that Jesus is the Christ is expressed in a strong and positive way, the fact that it is a confession implies courage and risk.

All this is said of living faith, of faith as actual concern, and not of faith as a traditional attitude without tensions, without doubt and without courage. Faith in this sense, which is the attitude of many members of the churches as well as of society at large, is far removed from the dynamic character of faith as described in this book. One could say that such conventional faith is the dead remnant of former experiences of ultimate concern. It is dead but it can become alive. For even nondynamic faith lives in symbols. In these symbols the power of original faith is still embodied. Therefore, one should not underestimate the importance of faith as a traditional attitude. It is not actual, not living faith; it is potential faith which can become actual. This is especially relevant for education. It is not meaningless to communicate to children or immature adults objective symbols of faith and with them expressions of the living faith of former generations. The danger of this method, of course, is that the faith, mediated in education, will remain a traditional attitude and never break through to a state of living faith. However, if this causes people to become hesitant about communicating any of the given symbols and to wait until independent questions about the meaning of life have arisen, it can lead to a powerful life of faith, but it also can lead to emptiness, to cynicism, and, in reaction to it, to idolatrous forms of ultimate concern.

Living faith includes the doubt about itself, the courage to take this doubt into itself, and the risk of courage. There is an element of immediate certainty in every faith, which is not subject to doubt, courage and risk—the unconditional concern itself. It is experienced in passion, anxiety, despair, ecstasy. But it is never experienced in isolation from a concrete content. It is experienced in, with and through the concrete content, and only the analytic mind can isolate it theoretically. Such theoretical isolation is the basis of this whole book; it is the way to the definition of faith as ultimate concern. But the life of faith itself does not include such analytic work. Therefore, the doubt about the concrete content of one's ultimate concern is directed against faith in its totality, and faith as a total act must affirm itself through courage.

The use of the term "courage" in this context (fully explained in my book *The Courage to Be*) needs some interpretation, especially in its relation to faith. In a short formulation one could say that courage is that element in faith which is related to the risk of faith. One cannot replace faith by courage, but neither can one describe faith without courage. In mystical literature the "vision of God" is described as the stage which transcends the state of faith either after the earthly life or in rare moments within it. In the complete reunion with the divine ground of being, the element of distance is overcome and with it uncertainty, doubt, courage and risk. The finite is taken into the infinite; it is not extinguished, but it is not separated either. This is not the ordinary human situation. To the state of separated finitude belong faith and the courage to risk. The risk of faith is the concrete content of one's ultimate concern. But it may not be the truly ultimate about which one is concerned. Religiously speaking, there may be an idolatrous element in one's faith. It may be one's own wishful thinking which determines the content; it may be the interest of one's social group which holds us in an absolute tradition; it may be a piece of reality which is not sufficient to express man's ultimate concern, as in old and new polytheism; it may be an attempt to use the ultimate for one's own purposes, as in magic practices and prayers in all religions. It may be the confusion of the bearer of the ultimate with the ultimate itself. This is done in all types of faith and has been, from the first gospel stories on, the permanent danger of Christianity. A protest against such a confusion is found in the Fourth Gospel, which has Jesus say: "He who believes in me does not believe in me but in him who has sent me." But the classical dogma, the liturgies and the devotional life are not kept free from it. Nevertheless, the Christian can have the courage to affirm his faith in Jesus as the Christ. He is aware of the possibility and even the inevitability of idolatrous deviations, but also of the fact that in the picture of the Christ itself the criterion against its idolatrous abuse is given—the cross.

Out of this criterion comes the message which is the very heart of Christianity and makes possible the courage to affirm faith in the Christ, namely, that in spite of all forces of separation between God and man this is overcome from the side of God. One of these forces of separation is a doubt which tries to prevent the courage to affirm one's faith. In this situation faith still can be affirmed if the certainty is given that even the failure of the risk of faith cannot separate the concern of one's daring faith from the ultimate. This is only the absolute certainty of faith which corresponds with the only absolute content of faith, namely, that in relation to the ultimate we are always receiving and never giving. We are never able to bridge the infinite distance between the infinite and the finite from the side of the finite. This alone makes the courage of faith possible. The risk of failure, of error and of idolatrous distortion can be taken, because the failure cannot separate us from what is our ultimate concern.

FAITH AND THE INTEGRATION OF THE PERSONALITY

The last consideration is decisive for the relation of faith to the problems of man's life as a personality. If faith is the state of being ultimately concerned, all preliminary concerns are subject to it. The ultimate concern gives depth, direction and unity to all other concerns and, with them, to the whole personality. A personal life which has these qualities is integrated, and the power of a personality's integration is his faith. It must be repeated at this point that such an assertion would be absurd if faith were what it is in its distorted meaning, the belief in things without evidence. Yet the assertion is not absurd, but evident, if faith is ultimate concern.

Ultimate concern is related to all sides of reality and to all sides of the human personality. The ultimate is one object beside others, and the ground of all others. As the ultimate is the ground of everything that is, so ultimate concern is the integrating center of the personal life. Being without it is being without a center. Such a state, however, can only be approached but never fully reached, because a human being deprived completely of a center would cease to be a human being. For this reason one cannot admit that there is any man without an ultimate concern or without faith.

The center unites all elements of man's personal life, the bodily, the unconscious, the conscious, the spiritual ones. In the act of faith every nerve of man's body, every striving of man's soul, every function of man's spirit participates. But body, soul, spirit, are not three parts of man. They are dimensions of man's being, always within each other; for man is a unity and not composed of parts. Faith, therefore, is not a matter of the mind in isolation, or of the soul in contrast to mind and body, or of the body (in the sense of animal faith), but is the centered movement of the whole personality toward something of ultimate meaning and significance.

Ultimate concern is passionate concern; it is a matter of infinite passion. Passion is not real without a bodily basis, even if it is the most spiritual passion. In every act of genuine faith the body participates, because genuine faith is a passionate act. The way in which it participates is manifold. The body can participate both in vital ecstasy and in asceticism leading to spiritual ecstasy. But whether in vital fulfillment or vital restriction, the body participates in the life of faith. The same is true of the unconscious strivings, the so-called instincts of man's psyche. They determine the choice of symbols and types of faith. Therefore, every community of faith tries to shape the unconscious strivings of its members, especially of the new generations. If the faith of somebody expresses itself in symbols which are adequate to his unconscious strivings, these strivings cease to be chaotic. They do not need repression, because they have received "sublimation" and are united with the conscious activities of the person. Faith also directs man's conscious life by giving it a central object of "con-centration." The disrupting trends of man's consciousness are one of the great problems of all personal life. If a uniting center is absent, the infinite variety of the encountered world, as well as of the inner movements of the human mind, is able to produce or complete disintegration of the personality. There can be no other uniting center than the ultimate concern of the mind. There are various ways in which faith unites man's mental life and gives it a dominating center. It can be the way of discipline which regulates the daily life; it can be the way of meditation and contemplation; it can be the way of concentration on the ordinary work, or on a special aim or on another human being. In each case, faith is presupposed; none of it could be done without faith. Man's spiritual function, artistic creation, scientific knowledge, ethical formation and political organization are consciously or unconsciously expressions of an ultimate concern which gives passion and creative *eros* to them, making them inexhaustible in depth and united in aim.

We have shown how faith determines and unites all elements of the personal life, how and why it is its integrating power. In doing so we have painted a picture of what faith can do. But we have not brought into this picture the forces of disintegration and disease which prevent faith from creating a fully integrated personal life, even in those who represent the power of faith most conspicuously, the saints, the great mystics, the prophetic personalities. Man is integrated only fragmentarily and has elements of disintegration or disease in all dimensions of his being.

One can only say that the integrating power of faith has healing power. This statement, however, needs comment in view of linguistic and actual distortions of the relation of faith and healing. Linguistically (and materially) one must distinguish the integrating power of faith from what has been called "faith healing." Faith healing, as the term is actually used, is the attempt to heal others or oneself by mental concentration on the healing power in others or in oneself. There is such healing power in nature and man, and it can be strengthened by mental acts. In a nondepreciating sense one could speak of the use of magic power; and certainly there is healing magic in human relationships as well as in the relation to oneself. It is a daily experience and sometimes one that is astonishing in its intensity and success. But one should not use the word "faith" for it, and one should not confuse it with the integrating power of an ultimate concern.

The integrating power of faith in a concrete situation is dependent on the subjective and objective factors. The subjective factor is the degree to which a person is open for the power of faith, and how strong and passionate is his ultimate concern. Such openness is what religion calls "grace." It is given and cannot be produced intentionally. The objective factor is the degree to which a faith has conquered its idolatrous elements and is directed toward the really ultimate. Idolatrous faith has a definite dynamic: it can be extremely passionate and exercise a preliminary integrating power. It can heal and unite the personality, including its soul and body. The gods of polytheism have shown healing power, not only in a magic way but also in terms of genuine reintegration. The objects of modern secular idolatry, such as nation and success, have shown healing power, not only by the magic fascination of a leader, a slogan or a promise but also by the fulfillment of otherwise unfulfilled strivings for a meaningful life. But the basis of the integration is too narrow. Idolatrous faith breaks down sooner or later and the disease is worse than before. The one limited element which has been elevated to ultimacy is attacked by other limited elements. The mind is split, even if each of these elements represents a high value. The fulfillment of the unconscious drives does not last; they are repressed or explode chaotically. The concentration of the mind vanishes because the object of concentration has lost its convincing character. Spiritual creativity shows an increasingly shallow and empty character, because no infinite meaning gives depth to it. The passion of faith is transformed into the suffering of unconquered doubt and despair, and in many cases into an escape to neurosis and psychosis. Idolatrous faith has more disintegrating power and indifference, just because it is faith and produces a transitory integration. This is the extreme danger of misguided, idolatrous faith, and the reason why the prophetic Spirit is above all the Spirit which fights against the idolatrous distortion of faith.

The healing power of faith raises the question of its relation to other agencies of healing. We have already referred to an element of magic influence from mind to mind without referring to the medical art, its scientific presuppositions and its technical methods. There is an overlapping of all agencies of healing and none of them should claim exclusive validity. Nevertheless, it is possible conceptually to limit each of them to a special function. Perhaps one can say that the healing power of faith is related to the whole personality, independent of any special disease of body or mind, and effective positively or negatively in every moment of one's life. It precedes, accompanies and follows all other activities of healing. But it does not suffice alone in the development of the personality. In finitude and estrangement man is not a whole, but is disrupted into different elements. Each of these elements can disintegrate independently of the other elements. Parts of the body can become sick, without producing mental disease; and the mind can become sick without visible body failures. In some forms of mental sickness, especially neurosis, and in almost all forms of bodily disease the spiritual life can remain completely healthy and even gain in strength. Therefore, medical art must be used wherever such separated elements of the whole of the personality are disintegrating for external or internal reasons. This is true of mental as well as of bodily medicine. And there is no conflict between them and the healing power of the state of ultimate concern. It is also clear that medical activities, including mental healing, cannot produce a reintegration of the personality as a whole. Only faith can do this. The tension between the two agencies of health would disappear if both sides knew their special functions and their special limits. Then they would not be worried about the third agency, the healing by magic concentration on the powers of healing. They would accept its help while revealing at the same time its great limitations.

There are as many types of integrated personalities as there are types of faith. There is also the type of integration which unites many characteristics of the different types of personal integration. It was this kind of personality which was created by early Christianity, and missed again and again in the history of the Church. Its character cannot be described from the point of view of faith alone; it leads to the questions of faith and love, and of faith and action.

AFTERWORD

The dispute in this section brings us to the limits of philosophy as a discipline. Despite the extraordinary breadth of their points of view, philosophers agree almost unanimously that reasoned argument is the proper path to truth. Even those philosophers who exalt instinct or feeling and deride man's rational faculties, nevertheless present their antirational views in the form of arguments.

But there comes a point at which conceptual analysis, empirical observation, and deductive reasoning simply fail to overcome fundamental disagreements. Nowhere is this breakdown more striking than in the debate over the religious significance of visions and hallucinations. Those who have taken the drugs and experienced revelation need no further proof of their religious convictions. Those who have **not** had visions—or who have, but do not interpret them religiously—insist that a drug trip is no evidence whatsoever for the existence of a transcendent realm.

At this point, the philosopher will attempt to mediate the disagreement. He will analyze the language in which the believer expresses his faith; he will criticize the canons of evidence which the sceptic has used in his rejection of the religious testimony. The concepts of "God," "existence," and "religion" will be clarified and defined. But in the end, this philosophical activity will probably fail. What can one say to a man who insists that he has seen God! When religious convictions are under debate, the very ground rules of logic are called into question. One great theologian of the Christian faith, Tertullian, even said, "I believe **because** it is absurd!"

If you will think back to the debate between Timothy Leary and Jerome Lettvin with which this book opened, I think you will see that they were set apart from one another by just this sort of difference in fundamental orientation. To sceptical rationalists like David Hume and Sigmund Freud, no experience could prove the reality of a realm beyond the world of everyday life. By their principles of evidence and inference, drug-induced experiences could only reveal some new fact **within** the world. For St. Theresa and Paul Tillich, on the other hand, the reality of the religious dimension is not an open question. Their concern is not **whether** there is a God, but how we stand in relation to Him. William James stands poised between the two camps, uncertain which way to commit himself. His epistemological doctrine of pragmatism aligns him with the empiricism of David Hume. His medical training inclines him to approach the phenomenon of religious experience with the same clinical detachment exhibited by Freud. But there is in him something that pulls him toward the mysticism of St. Theresa.

Since this book is a good deal more personal than most introductory philosophical texts, perhaps I ought to conclude by saying that I am wholeheartedly committed to the rational approach to questions of religion, as well as to questions of science, morality, and politics. In this dispute, my heart belongs to Hume and Freud, rather than to St. Theresa and Tillich. I hope that through your experience with this book, you have come closer to defining your own point of view.